Easter Island is an island west of Chile. It is famous for more than 600 stone statues. These statues were carved on Easter Island hundreds of years ago. Some of these stone statues are as tall as 40 feet.

Harcourt SOCIAL Studies

World Regions

Harcourt

SCHOOL PUBLISHERS

www.harcourtschool.com

HARCOURT SOCIAL Studies

World Regions

General Editor

Dr. Michael J. Berson
Associate Professor
Social Science Education
University of South Florida
Tampa, Florida

Contributing Author

Dr. Robert Bednarz
Professor
Department of Geography
Texas A&M University
College Station, Texas

Series Consultants

Dr. Robert Bednarz
Professor
Department of Geography
Texas A&M University
College Station, Texas

Dr. Barbara Caffee
Coordinator, K–12 Social Studies
Carrollton–Farmers Branch
  Independent School District
Carrollton, Texas

Dr. Asa Grant Hilliard III
Fuller E. Callaway Professor
  of Urban Education
Georgia State University
Atlanta, Georgia

Dr. Thomas M. McGowan
Chairperson and Professor
Center for Curriculum and Instruction
University of Nebraska
Lincoln, Nebraska

Dr. John J. Patrick
Professor of Education
Indiana University
Bloomington, Indiana

Dr. Cinthia Salinas
Assistant Professor
Department of Curriculum and Instruction
University of Texas at Austin
Austin, Texas

Dr. Philip VanFossen
Associate Professor,
  Social Studies Education,
  and Associate Director,
  Purdue Center for Economic Education
Purdue University
West Lafayette, Indiana

Dr. Hallie Kay Yopp
Professor
Department of Elementary, Bilingual, and
  Reading Education
California State University, Fullerton
Fullerton, California

Content Reviewers

Dr. Phillip Bacon
Professor Emeritus
Geography and Anthropology
University of Houston
Houston, Texas

Shabbir Mansuri
Founding Director
Susan L. Douglass
Affiliated Scholar
Council on Islamic Education
Fountain Valley, California

Dr. Nancy J. Obermeyer
Associate Professor of Geography
Department of Geography, Geology and
  Anthropology
Indiana State University
Terre Haute, Indiana

United States and Canada

Dr. Brock Brown
Associate Professor
Department of Geography
Southwest Texas State University
San Marcos, Texas

Dr. Chris Merrett
Associate Professor
Department of Geography
Illinois Institute for Rural Affairs
Western Illinois University
Macomb, Illinois

Richard Nichols
President
Richard Nichols and Associates
Fairview, New Mexico

Middle America and South America

Dr. Jorge Brea
Associate Professor
Department of Geography
Central Michigan University
Mt. Pleasant, Michigan

Rebecca Kosary
Instructor of History
Department of History and Geography
Texas Lutheran University
Seguin, Texas

Dr. David J. Robinson
Dellplain Professor of Latin American
  Geography
Department of Geography
Syracuse University
Syracuse, New York

Dr. Robert B. South
Professor and Department Head
Department of Geography
University of Cincinnati
Cincinnati, Ohio

Dr. John J. Winberry
Professor of Geography and
  Associate Dean of the Graduate
  School
Department of Geography
University of South Carolina
Columbia, South Carolina

Europe

Dr. Gregory Ioffe
Professor of Geography
Department of Geography
Radford University
Radford, Virginia

Dr. Jerzy Jemiolo
Associate Professor
Department of Geography
Ball State University
Muncie, Indiana

Dr. Linda McCarthy
Department of Geography
University of Wisconsin–Milwaukee
Milwaukee, Wisconsin

Southwest Asia and North Africa

Dr. Diana K. Davis
Assistant Professor
Department of Geography
University of Texas at Austin
Austin, Texas

Dr. Jeffrey A. Gritzner
Professor of Geography
Department of Geography
The University of Montana
Missoula, Montana

Dr. Thomas R. Paradise
Professor
Department of Geosciences and the
  King Fahd Center for Middle East and
  Islamic Studies
University of Arkansas
Fayetteville, Arkansas

Dr. Dona J. Stewart
Assistant Professor
Department of Anthropology and Geography
Georgia State University
Associate Director
Center for Middle East Peace, Culture and
  Development
Atlanta, Georgia

Africa South of the Sahara

Dr. Bakama Bernard BakamaNume
Associate Professor
Department of Geography
College of Arts and Sciences
Prairie View A&M University
Prairie View, Texas

Dr. Ezekiel Kalipeni
Associate Professor of Geography
Department of Geography
University of Illinois
Urbana, Illinois

Asia

Dr. Christine Drake
Professor of Geography
Department of Political Science and
  Geography
Old Dominion University
Norfolk, Virginia

Dr. Jayati Ghosh
Assistant Professor
Department of Geography and Geology
University of Wisconsin-Whitewater
Whitewater, Wisconsin

Dr. Pradyumna Karan
Professor
Department of Geography
University of Kentucky
Lexington, Kentucky

Dr. Nanda Shrestha
Professor
School of Business and Industry
Florida A&M University
Tallahassee, Florida

The Pacific Realm

Dr. Andrew Klein
Assistant Professor of Geography
Department of Geography
Texas A&M University
College Station, Texas

Classroom Reviewers

Carol Egbo
Social Studies Consultant
Waterford Schools
Waterford, Michigan

Sue Hendricks
Reading Specialist
Paradise Professional Development Center
Las Vegas, Nevada

Robert Kostka
Social Studies Coordinator
Bridgewater–Raynham School District
Bridgewater, Massachusetts

Juanell Palmore
Teacher
Lovett Ledger Intermediate School
Copperas Cove, Texas

Caroline Rice
Higher Ability Learner Specialist
Bellevue Public Schools
Bellevue, Nebraska

Dr. Holly Sharpe
Curriculum Coordinator, Retired
Plano Independent School District
Plano, Texas

Chuck Smith
Director of School Studies Pre-K–12
Rochester City School District
Rochester, New York

Eileen Stahulak
Elementary/Primary Social Science
  Curriculum Lead
Medill Professional Development Center
Chicago, Illinois

Doug Wilson
Teacher
Cesar Chavez Learning Center
Dallas, Texas

Laurie Zachry
Teacher
Ousley Junior High School
Arlington, Texas

Maps
researched and prepared by

Readers
written and designed by

WITHDRAWN

Take a Field Trip
video tour segments provided by

Acknowledgments appear in the back of
this book.

Printed in the United States of America

ISBN-13: 978-0-15-356683-7

ISBN-10: 0-15-356683-3

3 4 5 6 7 8 9 10 048 10 09 08

Contents

· UNIT ·
1

A View of the World

· UNIT ·

2

The United States and Canada

· UNIT ·

3

Middle America and South America

· UNIT ·

4

Europe

· UNIT ·

5

Southwest Asia and North Africa

· UNIT ·

6

Africa South of the Sahara

· UNIT ·

8

The Pacific Realm

Reference

Features You Can Use

Skills

Citizenship

Music and Literature

Primary Sources

Biography

Geography

Time Lines

Reading Your Textbook

Getting Started

Your textbook is divided into eight units.

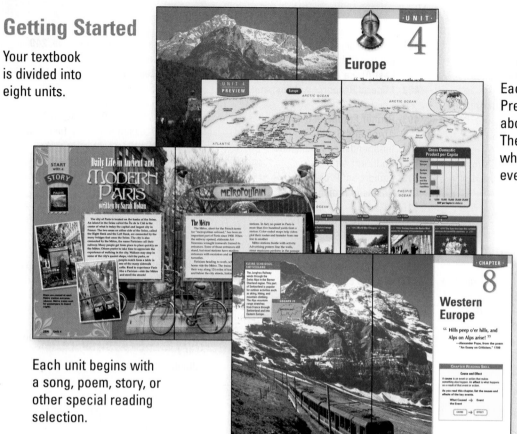

Each unit has a Unit Preview that gives facts about important events. The Preview also shows where and when those events took place.

Each unit begins with a song, poem, story, or other special reading selection.

Each unit is divided into chapters, and each chapter is divided into lessons.

The Parts of a Lesson

This statement gives you the lesson's main idea. It tells you what to look for as you read.

This statement tells you why it is important to read the lesson.

These are the new vocabulary terms you will learn in the lesson.

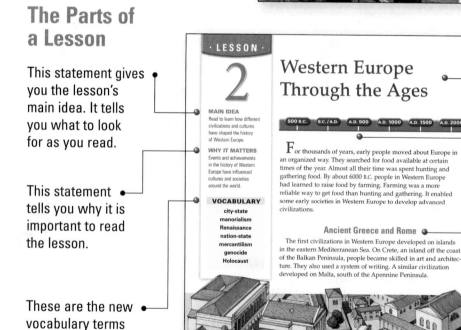

Lesson title

Some lessons include time lines to help you understand when events happened.

Each new vocabulary term is highlighted in yellow and defined.

Each lesson is divided into several short sections.

Each lesson, like each chapter and each unit, ends with a review. There may be a Summary Time Line that shows the order of the events covered in the lesson. Questions and a performance activity help you check your understanding of the lesson.

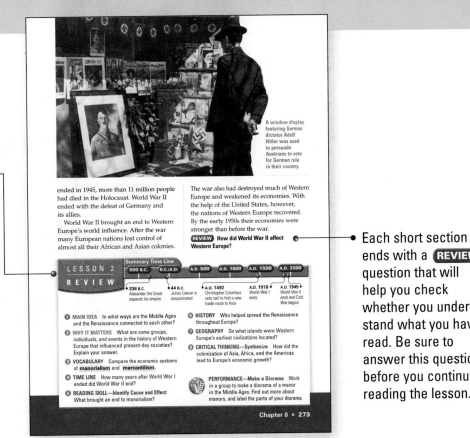

Each short section ends with a REVIEW question that will help you check whether you understand what you have read. Be sure to answer this question before you continue reading the lesson.

Skills

Your textbook has lessons that will help you build your reading, citizenship, chart and graph, and map and globe skills.

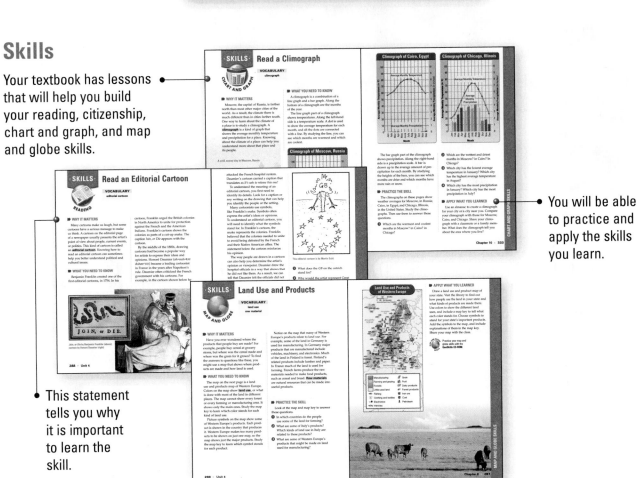

You will be able to practice and apply the skills you learn.

This statement tells you why it is important to learn the skill.

Special Features

The feature called
Examine Primary
Sources shows
you ways to learn
about different kinds
of objects and
documents.

The Visit feature lets
you "visit" many
interesting places.

Atlas

The Atlas provides maps
and a list of geography
terms with illustrations.

For Your Reference

At the back of your textbook, you will find
the reference tools listed below.

- Almanac
- Biographical Dictionary
- Gazetteer
- Glossary
- Index

You can use these tools to look up words
and to find information about people,
places, and other topics.

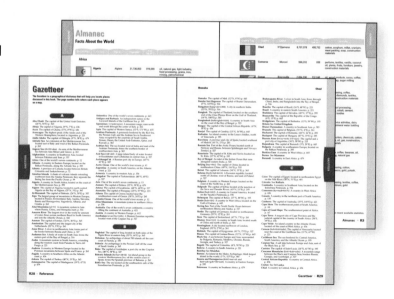

Atlas

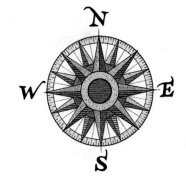

A1

·SKILLS·

MAP AND GLOBE

Read a Map

▶ WHY IT MATTERS

Maps provide a visual way to learn about a place and to see where it is in relation to other places. Knowing how to read and understand maps is an important skill for learning social studies.

▶ WHAT YOU NEED TO KNOW

A map is a drawing of some or all of Earth on a flat surface. Mapmakers often include certain features to help people understand and use maps more easily.

- A **map title** tells the subject of the map. The title may also help you identify what kind of map it is.

  - Political maps show cities, states, and countries.

  - Physical maps show kinds of land and bodies of water.

  - Historical maps show parts of the world as they were in the past.

- A **map key**, or legend, explains the symbols used on a map. Symbols may be colors, patterns, lines, or other special marks.

To help people find places on a map, mapmakers sometimes include lines that cross each other to form a pattern of squares. This pattern of squares is called a **grid system**. Look at the map of Venezuela below. Around the grid system are letters and numbers. The rows, which run left and

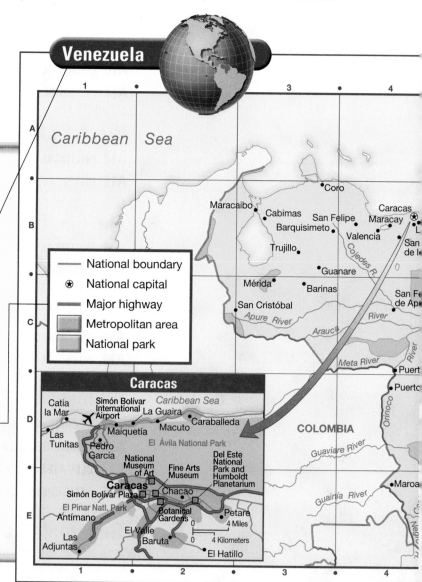

right, have letters. The columns, which run up and down, have numbers. Each square on the map can be identified by its letter and number. For example, the top row of squares in the map includes square A1, square A2, square A3, and so on.

Mapmakers sometimes also include smaller maps called **inset maps** within larger maps. Inset maps usually show in greater detail an area on the main map. Look at the map of Venezuela below. The inset map of Caracas allows you to see the Caracas area more clearly.

▶ PRACTICE THE SKILL

Use the map of Venezuela to answer these questions.

1. What cities are located in square C6?
2. In what direction would you travel if you went from Valencia to Canaima?
3. Find the map key. What symbol is used to show a national capital?
4. About how many miles is it from Maturín to Ciudad Bolívar?
5. Las Tunitas and Petare can be found on the Caracas inset map. What is the distance between these two places?

▶ APPLY WHAT YOU LEARNED

Imagine that you must explain the parts of a map to a younger student. Look in the Atlas maps that follow in this book. Select a country that looks interesting to you. Draw a map of that country. Add all the necessary map parts. Then add a brief explanation of each map part.

- A **locator** is a small map or picture of a globe that shows where the place on the main map is located.

- A **compass rose**, or direction marker, shows directions.

  - The **cardinal directions**, or main directions, are north, south, east, and west.

  - The **intermediate directions**, or directions between the cardinal directions, are northeast, northwest, southeast, and southwest.

- A **map scale** compares a distance on the map to a distance in the real world. It can be used to find the real distance between places on a map.

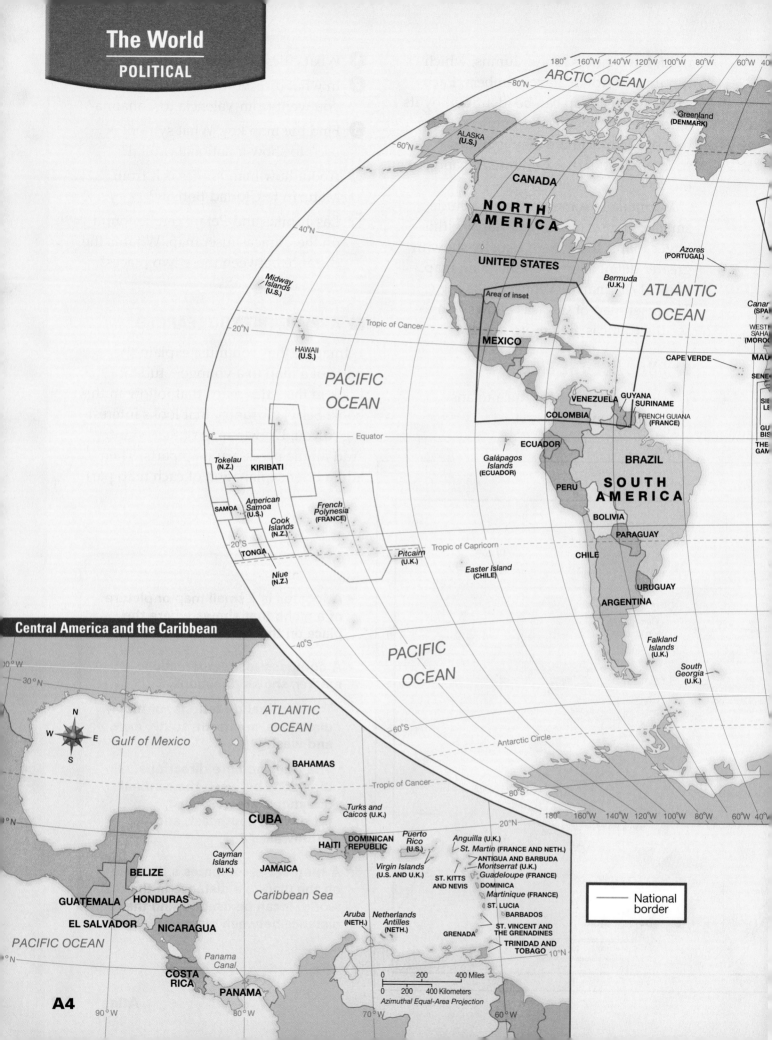

The World
POLITICAL

ARCTIC OCEAN

Greenland (DENMARK)

ALASKA (U.S.)

CANADA

NORTH AMERICA

UNITED STATES

Azores (PORTUGAL)

Bermuda (U.K.)

ATLANTIC OCEAN

Canar (SPA)

Midway Islands (U.S.)

Tropic of Cancer

Area of inset

MEXICO

WEST SAHA (MOROC)

HAWAII (U.S.)

PACIFIC OCEAN

MAU

SENE

CAPE VERDE

VENEZUELA GUYANA SURINAME

SIE LE

COLOMBIA

FRENCH GUIANA (FRANCE)

GU BIS

ECUADOR

THE GAM

Equator

Galápagos Islands (ECUADOR)

BRAZIL

Tokelau (N.Z.)

KIRIBATI

PERU

SOUTH AMERICA

American Samoa (U.S.)

SAMOA

Cook Islands (N.Z.)

French Polynesia (FRANCE)

BOLIVIA

PARAGUAY

TONGA

Tropic of Capricorn

Pitcairn (U.K.)

CHILE

Niue (N.Z.)

Easter Island (CHILE)

URUGUAY

ARGENTINA

PACIFIC OCEAN

Falkland Islands (U.K.)

South Georgia (U.K.)

Antarctic Circle

Central America and the Caribbean

ATLANTIC OCEAN

Gulf of Mexico

Tropic of Cancer

BAHAMAS

CUBA

Turks and Caicos (U.K.)

Cayman Islands (U.K.)

HAITI

DOMINICAN REPUBLIC

Puerto Rico (U.S.)

Anguilla (U.K.)

St. Martin (FRANCE AND NETH.)

ANTIGUA AND BARBUDA

BELIZE

JAMAICA

Virgin Islands (U.S. AND U.K.)

Montserrat (U.K.)

Guadeloupe (FRANCE)

GUATEMALA

HONDURAS

Caribbean Sea

ST. KITTS AND NEVIS

DOMINICA

Martinique (FRANCE)

EL SALVADOR

NICARAGUA

ST. LUCIA

BARBADOS

PACIFIC OCEAN

Aruba (NETH.)

Netherlands Antilles (NETH.)

GRENADA

ST. VINCENT AND THE GRENADINES

TRINIDAD AND TOBAGO

Panama Canal

COSTA RICA

0   200   400 Miles

0   200   400 Kilometers

Azimuthal Equal-Area Projection

PANAMA

	National border

A4

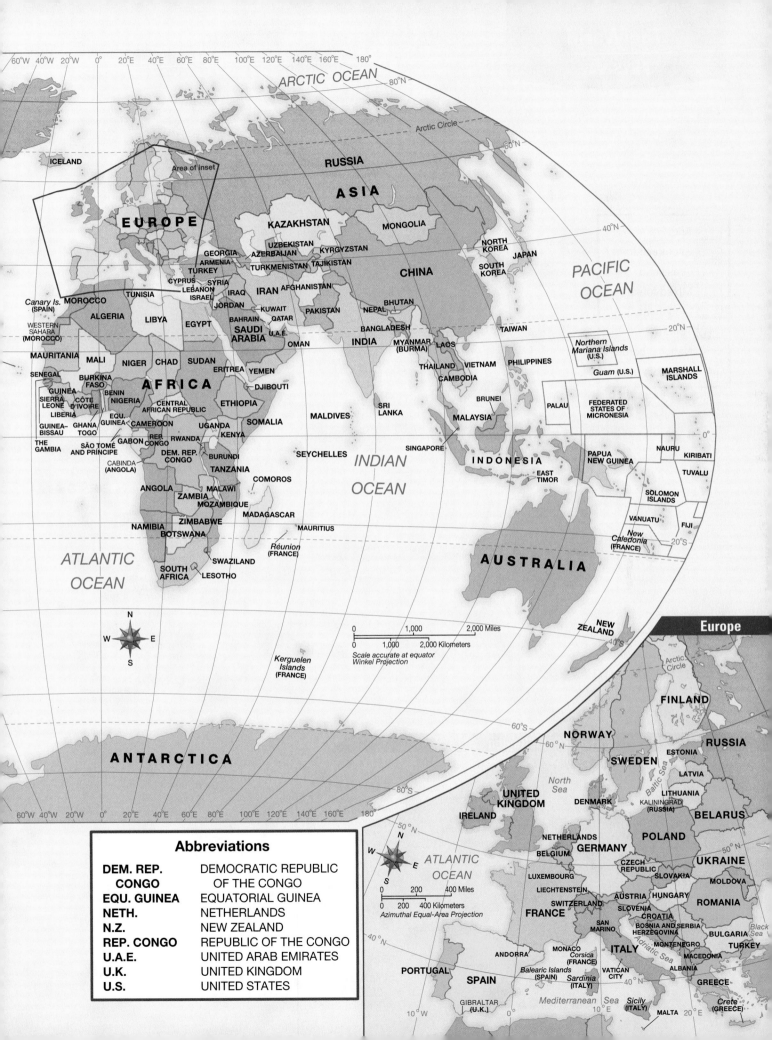

60°W 40°W 20°W 0° 20°E 40°E 60°E 80°E 100°E 120°E 140°E 160°E 180°

ARCTIC OCEAN

80°N

Arctic Circle

60°N

ICELAND

RUSSIA

ASIA

EUROPE

Area of inset

KAZAKHSTAN

MONGOLIA

40°N

UZBEKISTAN

GEORGIA
ARMENIA
AZERBAIJAN KYRGYZSTAN
TURKEY
CYPRUS SYRIA TURKMENISTAN TAJIKISTAN
LEBANON
ISRAEL IRAQ IRAN AFGHANISTAN
JORDAN
KUWAIT
PAKISTAN

NORTH
KOREA JAPAN
SOUTH
KOREA

PACIFIC
OCEAN

CHINA

Canary Is.
(SPAIN) MOROCCO
TUNISIA

NEPAL BHUTAN

BAHRAIN
WESTERN ALGERIA LIBYA EGYPT SAUDI QATAR
SAHARA ARABIA U.A.E.
(MOROCCO) OMAN

BANGLADESH
INDIA MYANMAR LAOS
(BURMA)

TAIWAN

20°N

Northern
Mariana Islands
(U.S.)

MAURITANIA MALI NIGER CHAD SUDAN ERITREA YEMEN

THAILAND VIETNAM PHILIPPINES

Guam (U.S.)

MARSHALL
ISLANDS

SENEGAL
BURKINA
GUINEA FASO
SIERRA CÔTE BENIN
LEONE D'IVOIRE NIGERIA
LIBERIA
GUINEA- GHANA EQU.
BISSAU TOGO GUINEA CAMEROON
THE
GAMBIA SÃO TOMÉ GABON REP.
AND PRÍNCIPE CONGO
CABINDA
(ANGOLA)

AFRICA

CENTRAL
AFRICAN REPUBLIC

DJIBOUTI

CAMBODIA

BRUNEI

PALAU

FEDERATED
STATES OF
MICRONESIA

0°

ETHIOPIA
SOMALIA
UGANDA
KENYA
RWANDA
DEM. REP. BURUNDI
CONGO
TANZANIA

MALDIVES

SRI
LANKA

MALAYSIA

SINGAPORE

SEYCHELLES

INDONESIA

INDIAN

PAPUA
NEW GUINEA

EAST
TIMOR

NAURU KIRIBATI

TUVALU

SOLOMON
ISLANDS

ANGOLA MALAWI COMOROS
ZAMBIA
MOZAMBIQUE
ZIMBABWE MADAGASCAR
NAMIBIA
BOTSWANA MAURITIUS
SOUTH SWAZILAND
AFRICA LESOTHO

OCEAN

VANUATU

New
Caledonia
(FRANCE)

FIJI

20°S

N
W E
S

ATLANTIC
OCEAN

Réunion
(FRANCE)

AUSTRALIA

0 1,000 2,000 Miles

0 1,000 2,000 Kilometers
Scale accurate at equator
Winkel Projection

NEW
ZEALAND

40°S

Kerguelen
Islands
(FRANCE)

N.Z.

60°S

ANTARCTICA

80°S

60°W 40°W 20°W 0° 20°E 40°E 60°E 80°E 100°E 120°E 140°E 160°E 180°

Abbreviations

DEM. REP. CONGO	DEMOCRATIC REPUBLIC OF THE CONGO
EQU. GUINEA	EQUATORIAL GUINEA
NETH.	NETHERLANDS
N.Z.	NEW ZEALAND
REP. CONGO	REPUBLIC OF THE CONGO
U.A.E.	UNITED ARAB EMIRATES
U.K.	UNITED KINGDOM
U.S.	UNITED STATES

Europe

Arctic Circle

FINLAND

NORWAY
SWEDEN RUSSIA
ESTONIA
60°N
LATVIA
North
UNITED Sea DENMARK LITHUANIA
KINGDOM KALININGRAD
(RUSSIA)
IRELAND BELARUS
NETHERLANDS POLAND
50°N BELGIUM GERMANY
50°N
LUXEMBOURG CZECH UKRAINE
REPUBLIC
SLOVAKIA
LIECHTENSTEIN AUSTRIA HUNGARY MOLDOVA
SWITZERLAND ROMANIA
N SLOVENIA
W E FRANCE CROATIA
S SAN BOSNIA AND SERBIA Black
MARINO HERZEGOVINA Sea
ATLANTIC MONTENEGRO
OCEAN BULGARIA
ANDORRA MONACO ITALY MACEDONIA
Corsica TURKEY
(FRANCE) VATICAN ALBANIA
0 200 400 Miles CITY
Balearic Islands 40°N GREECE
0 200 400 Kilometers PORTUGAL (SPAIN) Sardinia
Azimuthal Equal-Area Projection SPAIN (ITALY)
GIBRALTAR Mediterranean Sea Sicily Crete
(U.K.) (ITALY) MALTA (GREECE)
10°W 0° 10°E 20°E

The World
PHYSICAL

Legend:
- Arid
- Evergreen forest
- Grassland
- Mixed forest
- Mountains
- Tundra
- — National border
- ▲ Mountain peak

ARCTIC OCEAN

80°N

Beaufort Sea

Denali (Mt. McKinley) 20,320 ft. (6,194 m) ▲

Queen Elizabeth Islands

Great Bear Lake

Baffin Island

60°N

Bering Sea

Yukon R.

Mt. Logan 19,550 ft. (5,959 m) ▲

Mackenzie R.

Great Slave Lake

Hudson Bay

Aleutian Islands

Gulf of Alaska

ROCKY MOUNTAINS

NORTH AMERICA

Vancouver Island

Columbia R.

GREAT PLAINS

Missouri R.

Great Lakes

Newfoundland

40°N

Mt. Whitney 14,495 ft. (4,418 m) ▲

Colorado R.

Mississippi R.

Ohio R.

APPALACHIAN MTS.

Bermuda

ATLANTIC OCEAN

20°N

Hawaiian Islands

Tropic of Cancer

Gulf of California

Rio Grande

Gulf of Mexico

Bahamas

Cuba

Hispaniola

PACIFIC OCEAN

Yucatán Peninsula

West Indies

Pico de Orizaba 18,855 ft. (5,747 m) ▲

Caribbean Sea

Equator

Galápagos Islands

Orinoco River

Guiana Highlands

Polynesia

AMAZON BASIN

Amazon R.

SOUTH AMERICA

ANDES MOUNTAINS

Brazilian Highlands

20°S

Tropic of Capricorn

Atacama Desert

Gran Chaco

Paraná River

Mt. Aconcagua 22,834 ft. (6,960 m) ▲

Pampas

40°S

PACIFIC OCEAN

Patagonia

Falkland Islands

Strait of Magellan

Cape Horn

Tierra del Fuego

60°S

Antarctic Circle

Ross Sea

Antarctic Peninsula

180° 160°W 140°W 120°W 100°W 80°W

Northern Polar Region

ASIA

EUROPE

Sea of Okhotsk

Novaya Zemlya

Severnaya Zemlya

Barents Sea

Baltic Sea

Kamchatka Peninsula

New Siberian Is.

ARCTIC OCEAN

North Pole

Norwegian Sea

North Sea

0 400 800 Miles
0 400 800 Kilometers
Azimuthal Equidistant Projection

Wrangel Island

Svalbard

British Isles

Bering Sea

Bering Strait

Greenland Sea

Iceland

BROOKS RANGE

Beaufort Sea

North Magnetic Pole

Queen Elizabeth Islands

Greenland

ATLANTIC OCEAN

PACIFIC OCEAN

NORTH AMERICA

Baffin Bay

Arctic Circle

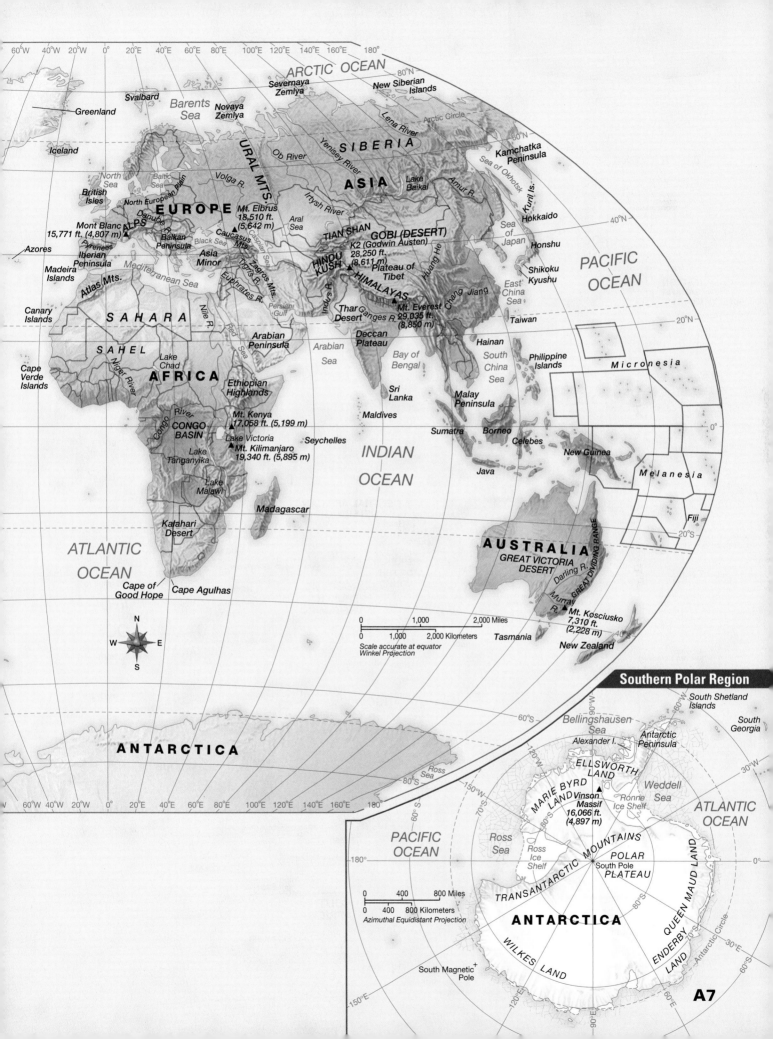

ARCTIC OCEAN

60°W 40°W 20°W 0° 20°E 40°E 60°E 80°E 100°E 120°E 140°E 160°E 180°

Greenland

Svalbard
Severnaya
Zemlya
New Siberian
Islands
80°N
Barents
Sea
Novaya
Zemlya
Arctic Circle
Iceland
60°N
Lena River
SIBERIA
Kamchatka
Peninsula
North
Sea
Baltic Sea
Ob River
Yenisey River
ASIA
Sea of Okhotsk
British
Isles
North European Plain
EUROPE
Mt. Elbrus
18,510 ft.
(5,642 m)
Volga R.
Irtysh River
Lake
Baikal
Amur R.
Kuril Is.
40°N
Mont Blanc
15,771 ft. (4,807 m)
ALPS
Danube R.
Caucasus
Mts.
Aral
Sea
TIAN SHAN
GOBI (DESERT)
Hokkaido
Sea
of
Japan
Honshu
Azores
Pyrenees
Balkan
Peninsula
Black Sea
K2 (Godwin Austen)
28,250 ft.
(8,611 m)
Huang He
Shikoku
Kyushu
PACIFIC
OCEAN
Iberian
Peninsula
Asia
Minor
Caspian Sea
Zagros Mts.
HINDU
KUSH
Plateau of
Tibet
Madeira
Islands
Atlas Mts.
Mediterranean Sea
Tigris R.
Euphrates R.
HIMALAYAS
Mt. Everest
29,035 ft.
(8,850 m)
Chang Jiang
East
China
Sea
Canary
Islands
SAHARA
Nile R.
Persian
Gulf
Thar
Desert
Ganges R.
Taiwan
20°N
SAHEL
Red Sea
Arabian
Peninsula
Deccan
Plateau
Hainan
Cape Verde
Islands
Niger River
Lake
Chad
AFRICA
Arabian
Sea
Bay of
Bengal
South
China
Sea
Philippine
Islands
Micronesia
Ethiopian
Highlands
Mt. Kenya
17,058 ft. (5,199 m)
Sri
Lanka
Malay
Peninsula
Congo River
CONGO
BASIN
Lake Victoria
Mt. Kilimanjaro
19,340 ft. (5,895 m)
Maldives
Seychelles
Sumatra
Borneo
Celebes
New Guinea
Melanesia
Lake
Tanganyika
INDIAN
Java
Lake
Malawi
OCEAN
Fiji
Madagascar
20°S
Kalahari
Desert
AUSTRALIA
GREAT VICTORIA
DESERT
Darling R.
GREAT DIVIDING RANGE
ATLANTIC
OCEAN
Cape of
Good Hope
Cape Agulhas
Murray R.
Mt. Kosciusko
7,310 ft.
(2,228 m)

N
W E
S

0   1,000   2,000 Miles
0   1,000   2,000 Kilometers
Scale accurate at equator
Winkel Projection

Tasmania
New Zealand
40°S

ANTARCTICA

Ross
Sea
80°S

60°W 40°W 20°W 0° 20°E 40°E 60°E 80°E 100°E 120°E 140°E 160°E 180°

Southern Polar Region

South Shetland
Islands
60°S
Bellingshausen
Sea
Alexander I.
Antarctic
Peninsula
South
Georgia
ELLSWORTH
LAND
Weddell
Sea
MARIE
BYRD
LAND
Vinson
Massif
16,066 ft.
(4,897 m)
Ronne
Ice Shelf
ATLANTIC
OCEAN
30°W
PACIFIC
OCEAN
Ross
Sea
Ross
Ice
Shelf
TRANSANTARCTIC MOUNTAINS
South Pole
POLAR
PLATEAU
QUEEN MAUD LAND
0°
180°
ANTARCTICA
WILKES LAND
ENDERBY
LAND
Arctic Circle
30°E
South Magnetic
Pole
60°E
90°E

0   400   800 Miles
0   400   800 Kilometers
Azimuthal Equidistant Projection

A7

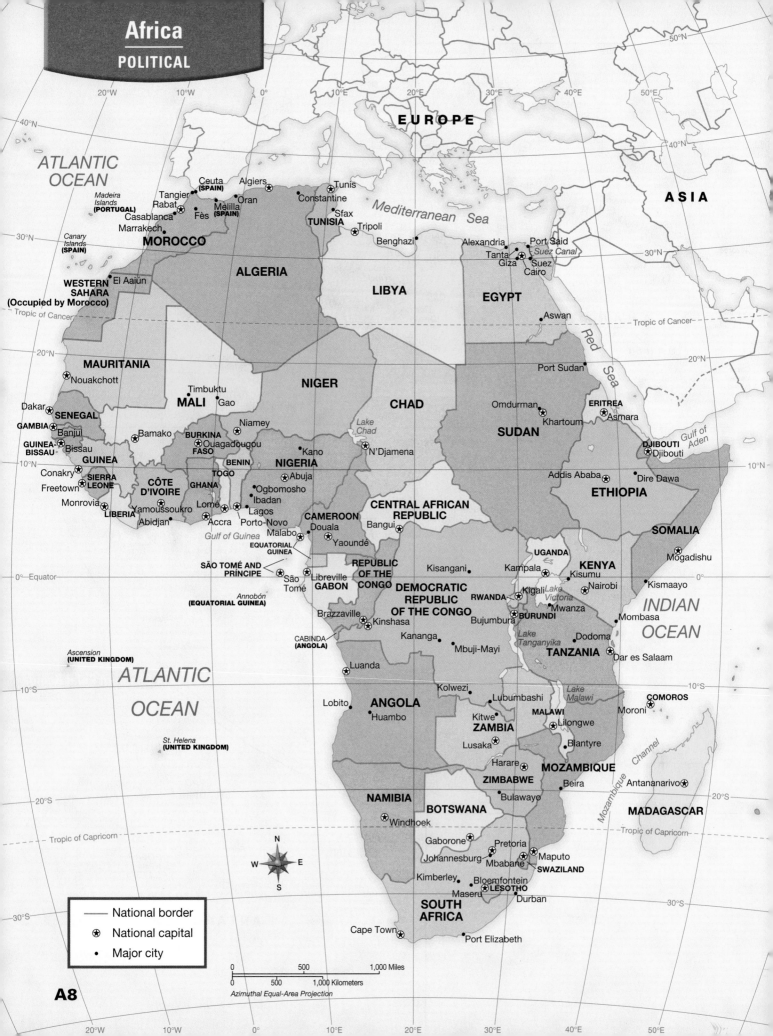

Africa
POLITICAL

EUROPE

ASIA

ATLANTIC OCEAN

Mediterranean Sea

MOROCCO
Ceuta (SPAIN)
Tangier
Rabat
Casablanca
Marrakech
Melilla (SPAIN)
Fès
Algiers
Oran
Tunis
Constantine
Sfax
TUNISIA
Tripoli
Benghazi

Madeira Islands (PORTUGAL)

Canary Islands (SPAIN)

WESTERN SAHARA (Occupied by Morocco)
El Aaiún

ALGERIA

LIBYA

EGYPT
Alexandria
Tanta
Giza
Cairo
Port Said
Suez Canal
Suez

Aswan

Tropic of Cancer

Red Sea

MAURITANIA
Nouakchott

MALI
Timbuktu
Gao

NIGER

CHAD
N'Djamena
Lake Chad

Port Sudan

SUDAN
Omdurman
Khartoum

ERITREA
Asmara

DJIBOUTI
Djibouti

Gulf of Aden

Dakar
SENEGAL
GAMBIA
Banjul
GUINEA-BISSAU
Bissau
GUINEA
Conakry
Freetown
SIERRA LEONE
Monrovia
LIBERIA

Bamako

BURKINA FASO
Ouagadougou
Niamey
Kano
NIGERIA
Abuja
Ogbomosho
Ibadan
Lagos
Porto-Novo
BENIN
TOGO
Lomé
GHANA
Accra
Abidjan
Yamoussoukro
CÔTE D'IVOIRE

Malabo
EQUATORIAL GUINEA

CAMEROON
Douala
Yaoundé

CENTRAL AFRICAN REPUBLIC
Bangui

Addis Ababa
Dire Dawa
ETHIOPIA

SOMALIA
Mogadishu

Gulf of Guinea

SÃO TOMÉ AND PRÍNCIPE
São Tomé

Annobón (EQUATORIAL GUINEA)

GABON
Libreville

REPUBLIC OF THE CONGO
Brazzaville

DEMOCRATIC REPUBLIC OF THE CONGO
Kinshasa
Kisangani
Kananga
Mbuji-Mayi

UGANDA
Kampala
RWANDA
Kigali
BURUNDI
Bujumbura

Lake Victoria
Mwanza

KENYA
Kisumu
Nairobi
Mombasa

Kismaayo

INDIAN OCEAN

Equator

Ascension (UNITED KINGDOM)

ATLANTIC OCEAN

Luanda
Lobito
Huambo
ANGOLA

Kolwezi
Lubumbashi
Kitwe
ZAMBIA
Lusaka

CABINDA (ANGOLA)

TANZANIA
Dodoma
Dar es Salaam

Lake Tanganyika

Lake Malawi

MALAWI
Lilongwe
Blantyre

COMOROS
Moroni

St. Helena (UNITED KINGDOM)

Harare
ZIMBABWE
Bulawayo

MOZAMBIQUE
Beira

Antananarivo
MADAGASCAR

Mozambique Channel

NAMIBIA
Windhoek

BOTSWANA
Gaborone

Tropic of Capricorn

Johannesburg
Pretoria
Mbabane
Maputo
SWAZILAND

Kimberley
Bloemfontein
LESOTHO
Maseru
Durban

SOUTH AFRICA

Cape Town
Port Elizabeth

N
W   E
S

Legend
— National border
⊛ National capital
• Major city

0   500   1,000 Miles
0   500   1,000 Kilometers
Azimuthal Equal-Area Projection

A8

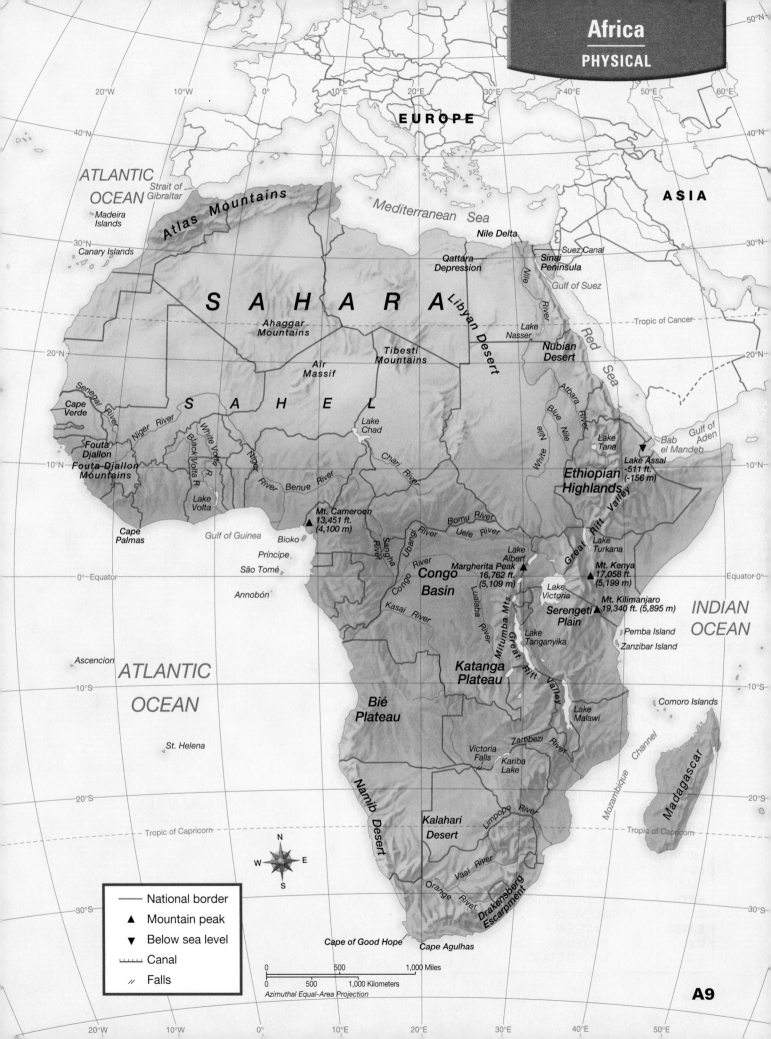

Africa
PHYSICAL

EUROPE

ASIA

ATLANTIC OCEAN

Strait of Gibraltar

Madeira Islands

Canary Islands

Mediterranean Sea

Nile Delta

Suez Canal

Qattara Depression

Sinai Peninsula

Gulf of Suez

Atlas Mountains

S A H A R A

Libyan Desert

Tropic of Cancer

Ahaggar Mountains

Tibesti Mountains

Aïr Massif

Nile River

Lake Nasser

Nubian Desert

Red Sea

S A H E L

Senegal River

Cape Verde

Niger River

White Volta R.

Black Volta R.

Lake Chad

Chari River

Atbara River

Blue Nile

Lake Tana

Bab el Mandeb

Gulf of Aden

Fouta Djallon

Fouta Djallon Mountains

Niger River

Benue River

White Nile

Lake Assal -511 ft. (-156 m)

Lake Volta

Ethiopian Highlands

Cape Palmas

Gulf of Guinea

Bioko

Mt. Cameroon 13,451 ft. (4,100 m)

Sangha River

Ubangi River

Bomu River

Uele River

Great Rift Valley

Lake Turkana

Príncipe

São Tomé

Congo River

Lake Albert

Margherita Peak 16,762 ft. (5,109 m)

Mt. Kenya 17,058 ft. (5,199 m)

Equator

Annobón

Congo Basin

Kasai River

Lualaba River

Lake Victoria

Mt. Kilimanjaro 19,340 ft. (5,895 m)

INDIAN OCEAN

Equator

Ascencion

Mitumba Mts.

Serengeti Plain

Pemba Island

Zanzibar Island

Lake Tanganyika

Great Rift Valley

ATLANTIC OCEAN

Katanga Plateau

Lake Malawi

Comoro Islands

St. Helena

Bié Plateau

Victoria Falls

Zambezi River

Kariba Lake

Mozambique Channel

Madagascar

Namib Desert

Limpopo River

Tropic of Capricorn

Kalahari Desert

Tropic of Capricorn

N
W   E
S

Vaal River

Orange River

Drakensberg Escarpment

Cape of Good Hope

Cape Agulhas

——	National border
▲	Mountain peak
▼	Below sea level
⊢⊢⊢⊢	Canal
∥	Falls

0   500   1,000 Miles

0   500   1,000 Kilometers

Azimuthal Equal-Area Projection

A9

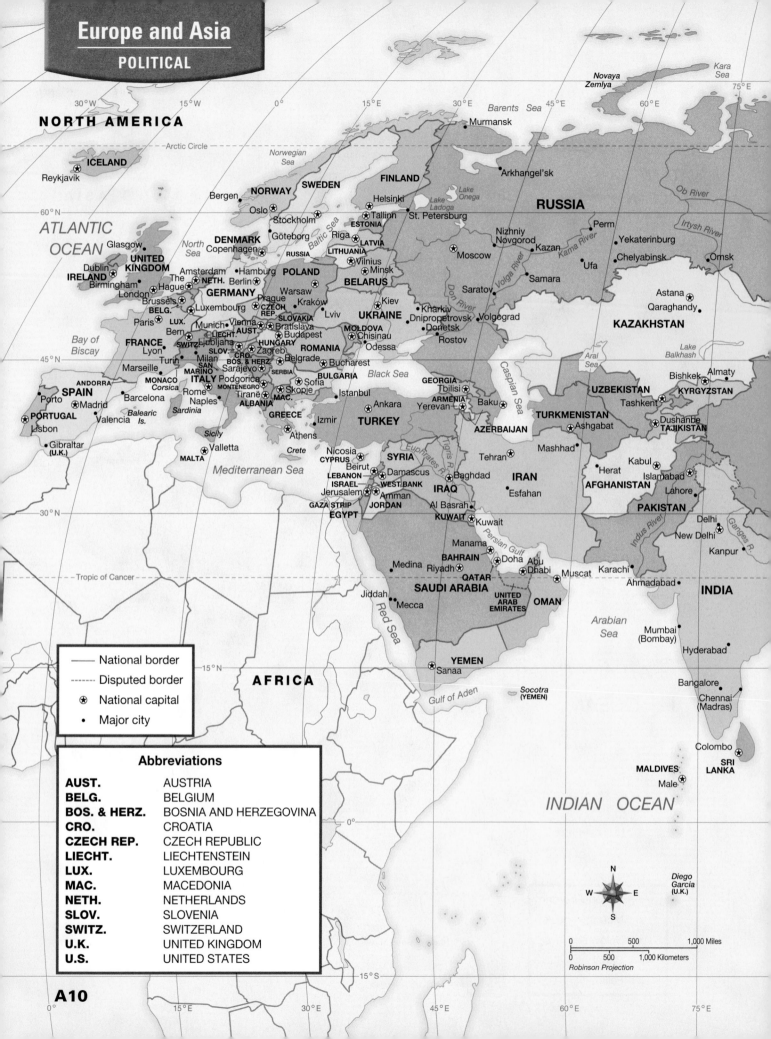

Europe and Asia
POLITICAL

NORTH AMERICA

ICELAND
Reykjavik

ATLANTIC OCEAN

Arctic Circle

Novaya Zemlya
Kara Sea
75°E

30°W · 15°W · 0° · 15°E · 30°E · Barents Sea · 45°E · 60°E

Murmansk

Norwegian Sea

Bergen
NORWAY · SWEDEN · FINLAND
Oslo · Stockholm · Helsinki · Arkhangel'sk
Göteborg · Lake Onega · RUSSIA
60°N

Ob River
Irtysh River

DENMARK · Tallinn · St. Petersburg · Perm
Copenhagen · ESTONIA · Nizhniy Novgorod · Yekaterinburg
North Sea · Riga · LATVIA · Moscow · Kazan · Chelyabinsk
Glasgow · RUSSIA · LITHUANIA · Kama River · Ufa · Omsk
UNITED KINGDOM · Vilnius · Minsk · Samara
Dublin · Amsterdam · Hamburg · POLAND · BELARUS · Saratov · Astana
IRELAND · The · NETH. · Berlin · Warsaw · Kiev · Volga River · Qaraghandy
Birmingham · Hague · GERMANY · Kraków · Kharkiv · Don River
London · Brussels · Prague · Lviv · UKRAINE · Dnipropetrovsk · Volgograd · KAZAKHSTAN
Paris · BELG. · CZECH REP. · SLOVAKIA · Donetsk · Lake Balkhash
LUX. · Luxembourg · Vienna · MOLDOVA · Rostov · Aral Sea
FRANCE · Munich · AUST. · Bratislava · Chisinau · Bishkek · Almaty
Bern · LIECHT. · Budapest · Odessa · UZBEKISTAN · KYRGYZSTAN
SWITZ. · Ljubljana · HUNGARY · ROMANIA · Tashkent
Turin · SLOV. · Zagreb · Belgrade · Bucharest · Caspian Sea · Dushanbe
Milan · CRO. · BOS. & HERZ. · SERBIA · BULGARIA · Black Sea · GEORGIA · Ashgabat · TAJIKISTAN
Marseille · SAN MARINO · Sarajevo · Sofia · Tbilisi · TURKMENISTAN
ANDORRA · MONACO · Podgorica · Skopje · Istanbul · ARMENIA · Baku · Mashhad · Kabul
SPAIN · Corsica · ITALY · MONTENEGRO · MAC. · Ankara · Yerevan · AZERBAIJAN · Herat · Islamabad
Barcelona · Rome · Tiranë · GREECE · Izmir · TURKEY · Tehran · AFGHANISTAN · Lahore
Madrid · Naples · ALBANIA · Athens · IRAN · PAKISTAN
PORTUGAL · Balearic Is. · Sardinia · Sicily · Crete · Nicosia · SYRIA · Esfahan · Karachi
Lisbon · Valencia · CYPRUS · Beirut · Damascus · Baghdad · Delhi
Gibraltar (U.K.) · Valletta · Mediterranean Sea · LEBANON · WEST BANK · IRAQ · New Delhi
MALTA · ISRAEL · Amman · Kuwait · Ganges R. · Kanpur
Jerusalem · JORDAN · Al Basrah · Persian Gulf
GAZA STRIP · KUWAIT · Kuwait · Indus River
EGYPT · Manama · BAHRAIN · Doha · Abu Dhabi · Muscat · Karachi · Ahmadabad · INDIA
Tropic of Cancer · Medina · Riyadh · QATAR · UNITED ARAB EMIRATES · OMAN · Arabian Sea · Mumbai (Bombay) · Hyderabad
Jiddah · Mecca · SAUDI ARABIA · Red Sea · Bangalore · Chennai (Madras)
15°N · AFRICA · YEMEN · Sanaa · Socotra (YEMEN) · Colombo · SRI LANKA
Gulf of Aden · MALDIVES · Male
INDIAN OCEAN

Bay of Biscay
45°N
30°N

Lake Ladoga

Euphrates R. · Tigris R.

Legend
— National border
--- Disputed border
⊛ National capital
• Major city

Abbreviations

AUST.	AUSTRIA
BELG.	BELGIUM
BOS. & HERZ.	BOSNIA AND HERZEGOVINA
CRO.	CROATIA
CZECH REP.	CZECH REPUBLIC
LIECHT.	LIECHTENSTEIN
LUX.	LUXEMBOURG
MAC.	MACEDONIA
NETH.	NETHERLANDS
SLOV.	SLOVENIA
SWITZ.	SWITZERLAND
U.K.	UNITED KINGDOM
U.S.	UNITED STATES

N · W · E · S
Diego Garcia (U.K.)

0 · 500 · 1,000 Miles
0 · 500 · 1,000 Kilometers
Robinson Projection

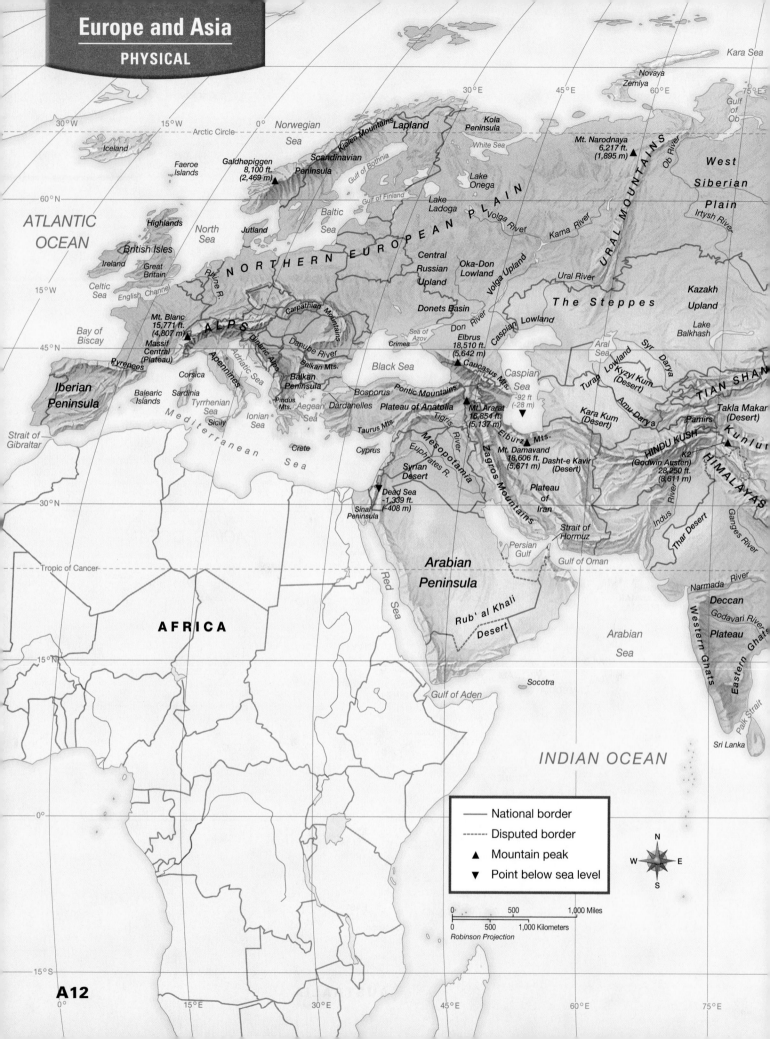

Europe and Asia
PHYSICAL

ATLANTIC OCEAN

Kara Sea

Novaya Zemlya

Gulf of Ob

Arctic Circle

Iceland

Faeroe Islands

Norwegian Sea

Kjølen Mountains

Lapland

Kola Peninsula

White Sea

Mt. Narodnaya 6,217 ft. (1,895 m)

URAL MOUNTAINS

Ob River

West Siberian Plain

Galdhøpiggen 8,100 ft. (2,469 m)

Scandinavian Peninsula

Gulf of Bothnia

Lake Onega

Irtysh River

Highlands

North Sea

Jutland

Baltic Sea

Gulf of Finland

Lake Ladoga

Volga River

NORTHERN EUROPEAN PLAIN

Central Russian Upland

Oka-Don Lowland

Kama River

Kazakh Upland

British Isles

Ireland

Great Britain

Celtic Sea

English Channel

Rhine R.

Ural River

The Steppes

Lake Balkhash

Mt. Blanc 15,771 ft. (4,807 m)

Carpathian Mountains

Donets Basin

Don River

Volga Upland

ALPS

Massif Central (Plateau)

Pyrenees

Bay of Biscay

Dinaric Alps

Danube River

Balkan Mts.

Sea of Azov

Crimea

Elbrus 18,510 ft. (5,642 m)

Caucasus Mts.

Caspian Lowland

Caspian Sea -92 ft. (-28 m)

Aral Sea

Turan Lowland

Syr Darya

Kyzyl Kum (Desert)

TIAN SHAN

Iberian Peninsula

Corsica

Balearic Islands

Sardinia

Apennines

Adriatic Sea

Balkan Peninsula

Pindus Mts.

Tyrrhenian Sea

Sicily

Ionian Sea

Aegean Sea

Bosporus

Dardanelles

Black Sea

Pontic Mountains

Plateau of Anatolia

Mt. Ararat 16,854 ft. (5,137 m)

Elburz Mts.

Mt. Damavand 18,606 ft. (5,671 m)

Kara Kum (Desert)

Amu Darya

Takla Makan (Desert)

Pamirs

HINDU KUSH

Kunlun

Strait of Gibraltar

Mediterranean Sea

Crete

Cyprus

Taurus Mts.

Tigris River

Euphrates R.

Mesopotamia

Syrian Desert

Zagros Mountains

Dasht-e Kavir (Desert)

Plateau of Iran

K2 (Godwin Austen) 28,250 ft. (8,611 m)

HIMALAYAS

Dead Sea -1,339 ft. (-408 m)

Sinai Peninsula

Strait of Hormuz

Gulf of Oman

Indus River

Thar Desert

Ganges River

Tropic of Cancer

Red Sea

Arabian Peninsula

Persian Gulf

Narmada River

Godavari River

Deccan Plateau

AFRICA

Rub' al Khali Desert

Arabian Sea

Western Ghats

Eastern Ghats

Gulf of Aden

Socotra

Palk Strait

Sri Lanka

INDIAN OCEAN

	National border
- - -	Disputed border
▲	Mountain peak
▼	Point below sea level

N
W E
S

0   500   1,000 Miles
0   500   1,000 Kilometers
Robinson Projection

ARCTIC OCEAN

Taymyr Peninsula

Laptev Sea

New Siberian Islands

East Siberian Sea

Wrangel Island

Chukchi Sea

Bering Strait

75°N

90°E 105°E 120°E 135°E 150°E 165°E 180° 165°W

North Siberian Lowland

Central Siberian Plateau

Kolyma Lowland

Arctic Circle

Chukchi Peninsula

S I B E R I A

Yenisey River

Ob River

Angara River

Lena River

Verkhoyansk Range

Kolyma R.

Kolyma Mountains

Korya Range

60°N

Bering Sea

Stanovoy Range

Dzhugdzhur Range

Central Range

Kamchatka Peninsula

Sayan Mountains

Yenisey R.

Lake Baikal

Yablonovy Range

Sea of Okhotsk

Altai Mountains

Junggar Basin

Plateau of Mongolia

Greater Khingan Range

Amur River

Sikhote Alin Range

Sakhalin

Kuril Islands

45°N

Turpan Depression -505 ft. (-154 m)

Gobi (Desert)

Manchurian Plain

Hokkaido

Tarim Basin

Qilian Shan

Shan

North China

Korean Peninsula

Sea of Japan

Honshu

Mt. Fuji 12,388 ft. (3,776 m)

NORTH PACIFIC OCEAN

Plateau of Tibet

Huang He

China Plain

Yellow Sea

Kyushu

Shikoku

Mt. Everest 29,028 ft. (8,848 m)

Kanchenjunga 28,208 ft. (8,598 m)

Sichuan Basin

Chang Jiang

East China Sea

30°N

Ganges R.

Irrawaddy River

Mekong R.

Ryukyu Islands

Tropic of Cancer

Bay of Bengal

Khorat Plateau

Indochina Peninsula

Taiwan

Philippine Sea

Gulf of Tonkin

Hainan

South China Sea

Luzon

15°N

Andaman Islands

Philippine Islands

Andaman Sea

Gulf of Thailand

Palawan

Sulu Sea

Nicobar Islands

Malay Peninsula

Mindanao

Strait of Malacca

Celebes Sea

Sumatra

Greater Sunda Islands

Halmahera

0° Equator

Borneo

Celebes

Moluccas

SOUTH PACIFIC OCEAN

Rantekombola 11,335 ft. (3,455 m)

Ceram

Java Sea

Banda Sea

New Guinea

Java

Bali

Sumbawa

Flores

Timor

Lombok

Sumba

Timor Sea

Arafura Sea

Lesser Sunda Islands

15°S

90°E 105°E 120°E 135°E 150°E 165°E

A13

AUSTRALIA

Western Hemisphere
POLITICAL

ARCTIC OCEAN

Beaufort Sea

Viscount Melville Sound

Baffin Bay

Greenland
(DENMARK)

Bering Strait

Arctic Circle

ALASKA
(U.S.)
Fairbanks
Anchorage
Yukon River

Mackenzie River

Great Bear Lake

Yellowknife
Great Slave Lake

Whitehorse
Liard River

Foxe Basin

Hudson Strait

Davis Strait

60°N

Juneau
Gulf of Alaska

Peace River

Athabasca R.
Lake Athabasca

CANADA

Hudson Bay

James Bay

Labrador Sea

Bering Sea

Edmonton
Calgary
Saskatoon
Saskatchewan R.
Lake Winnipeg

Regina
Winnipeg
Thunder Bay
Great Lakes
St. Lawrence River

St. John's

Vancouver
Seattle
Puget Sound
Portland
Columbia R.
Boise
Snake R.

UNITED STATES

Ottawa
Quebec
Montreal
St. John
Halifax
Gulf of St. Lawrence

Toronto
Detroit
Albany
Boston
Cleveland
New York City

Reno
Great Salt Lake
Salt Lake City
Denver
Colorado R.
Missouri R.
Chicago
Indianapolis
Philadelphia
Washington, D.C.
Richmond
Norfolk

San Francisco
Las Vegas
Mississippi R.
St. Louis
Memphis
Atlanta
Raleigh
Charleston

Los Angeles
San Diego
Phoenix
Tucson
El Paso
Rio Grande
Dallas
Houston
New Orleans
Savannah
Jacksonville

ATLANTIC OCEAN

30°N

Hermosillo
Gulf of California
Chihuahua
San Antonio
Tampa
Orlando

MEXICO
Durango
Monterrey
Gulf of Mexico
Miami
BAHAMAS
Nassau

Tropic of Cancer

León
Tampico
Havana
CUBA
HAITI
Port-au-Prince
Santo Domingo

Honolulu
HAWAII
(U.S.)

Guadalajara
Mexico City
Veracruz
Puebla
BELIZE
JAMAICA
Puerto Rico (U.S.)
DOMINICAN REPUBLIC

PACIFIC OCEAN

Acapulco
GUATEMALA
Belmopan
Kingston

Guatemala City
HONDURAS
San Salvador
Tegucigalpa
EL SALVADOR
Managua
San José
Caribbean Sea

NICARAGUA
COSTA RICA
Panama City
Maracaibo
Caracas
GUYANA
SURINAME
Paramaribo

PANAMA
Medellín
Cali
Bogotá
VENEZUELA
Georgetown
Cayenne
FRENCH GUIANA (FRANCE)

Equator

COLOMBIA
Quito
Rio Negro
Amazon R.

Galápagos
Islands
(ECUADOR)

Guayaquil
Manaus
Belém
Fortaleza

ECUADOR
Iquitos

Trujillo
PERÚ
Tapajós River
Xingu R.
Tocantins R.
Recife

Lima
Cuzco
BRAZIL

French Polynesia
(FRANCE)

Lake Titicaca
La Paz
Brasília
Salvador
São Francisco R.

Papeete
Arequipa
BOLIVIA
Sucre
Goiânia
Belo Horizonte

Antofagasta
Campo Grande
Rio de Janeiro

Tropic of Capricorn

PARAGUAY
Salta
Asunción
São Paulo
Curitiba

San Miguel de Tucumán
Paraná R.

CHILE
Córdoba
Pôrto Alegre

Valparaíso
Rosario
URUGUAY

30°S

Santiago
Buenos Aires
La Plata
Montevideo
Rio de la Plata

Concepción
Mar del Plata

Valdivia
Bahía Blanca

ARGENTINA

Map Scale

0   1,000   2,000 Miles

0   1,000   2,000 Kilometers

Miller Cylindrical Projection

Legend

— National border
⊛ National capital
• City

A14

Falkland Islands
(U.K.)

South Georgia
(U.K.)

Punta Arenas

150°W   120°W   90°W   60°W   30°W

Western Hemisphere
PHYSICAL

ARCTIC OCEAN

North Magnetic Pole +
Queen Elizabeth Islands

Ellesmere Island

Melville Island

Viscount Melville Sound

Devon Island

Baffin Bay

Greenland

Bering Strait
Point Barrow

Beaufort Sea

Banks Island

Victoria Island

Baffin Island

Davis Strait

Arctic Circle

Brooks Range

Yukon River

Mt. McKinley
20,320 ft.
(6,194 m)

Alaska Range

Mackenzie Mts.

Mackenzie River

Great Bear Lake

Great Slave Lake

Foxe Basin

Hudson Strait

60°N

Cape Farewell

Yukon Plateau

Mt. Logan
19,550 ft.
(5,959 m)

Liard R.

Peace River

Athabasca R.

Lake Athabasca

Hudson Bay

James Bay

Labrador Sea

Kodiak Island

Gulf of Alaska

Alaska Peninsula
Bering Sea
Aleutian Islands

Queen Charlotte Islands

Coast Mountains

Saskatchewan River

Lake Winnipeg

CANADIAN

GREAT

SHIELD

Labrador

Newfoundland

Gulf of St. Lawrence

Vancouver Island
Puget Sound

Cascade Range

ROCKY

NORTH AMERICA

Black Hills

Missouri R.

Great Lakes

Mississippi

St. Lawrence R.

Nova Scotia
Bay of Fundy

Snake R.

Coast Ranges

MOUNTAINS

Platte

Ohio R.

APPALACHIAN MTS.

Cape Cod
Long Island

Sierra Nevada

Great Salt Lake
GREAT BASIN

PLAINS

INTERIOR PLAINS

Ozark Plateau

Cape Hatteras

ATLANTIC OCEAN

Mt. Whitney
14,495 ft. (4,418 m)

Colorado R.

Arkansas

Death Valley
(lowest point in N.A.)
-282 ft. (-86 m)

Rio Grande

COASTAL PLAIN

30°N

Hawaiian Islands

Sonoran Desert

Sierra Madre Occidental

Gulf of California

Baja California

Gulf of Mexico

Bahamas

Tropic of Cancer

PACIFIC OCEAN

Pico de Orizaba
18,855 ft.
(5,747 m)

Sierra Madre Oriental

Yucatán Peninsula

Greater Antilles

Cuba

Hispaniola
Puerto Rico

Lesser Antilles

Caribbean Sea

Lake Maracaibo

Line Islands

Lake Nicaragua

Isthmus of Panama

Llanos

Orinoco R.

Guiana Highlands

Equator

Galápagos Islands

Chimborazo
20,702 ft.
(6,310 m)

Rio Negro

Amazon R.

Cape São Roque

Marquesas Islands

ANDES

AMAZON BASIN

Tapajós River

Xingu River

Tocantins

São Francisco River

Brazilian

Cook Islands

Tuamotu Archipelago

Society Islands

Huascarán
22,205 ft.
(6,768 m)

Lake Titicaca

Mato Grosso Plateau

Paraguay R.

Highlands

SOUTH AMERICA

Tropic of Capricorn

Altiplano

Atacama Desert

Gran Chaco

Paraná R.

Iguazú Falls

30°S

0   1,000   2,000 Miles
0   1,000   2,000 Kilometers
Miller Cylindrical Projection

Mt. Aconcagua
22,834 ft.
(6,960 m)

MOUNTAINS

Uruguay R.

Pampas

Rio de la Plata

▲ Mountain peak
▼ Point below sea level
— National border
≈ Waterfall

N
W   E
S

Patagonia

Valdés Peninsula
(lowest point in S.A.)
-131 ft. (-40 m)

Falkland Islands

South Georgia

Strait of Magellan

Cape Horn

Tierra del Fuego

60°W

30°W

150°W

120°W

90°W

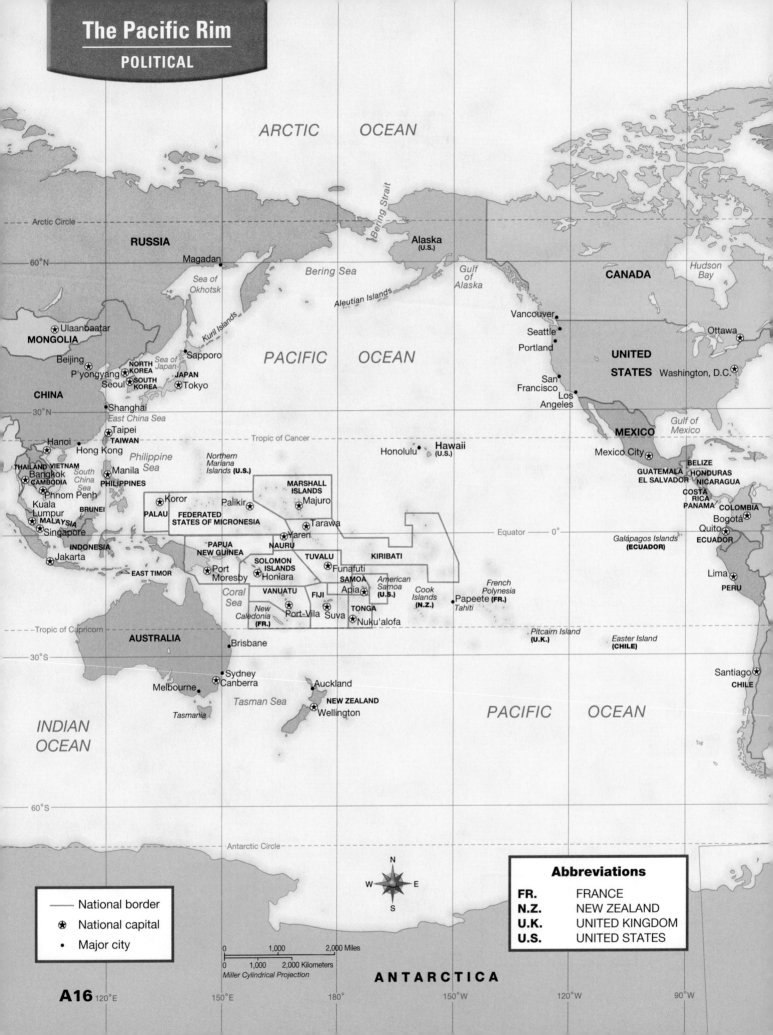

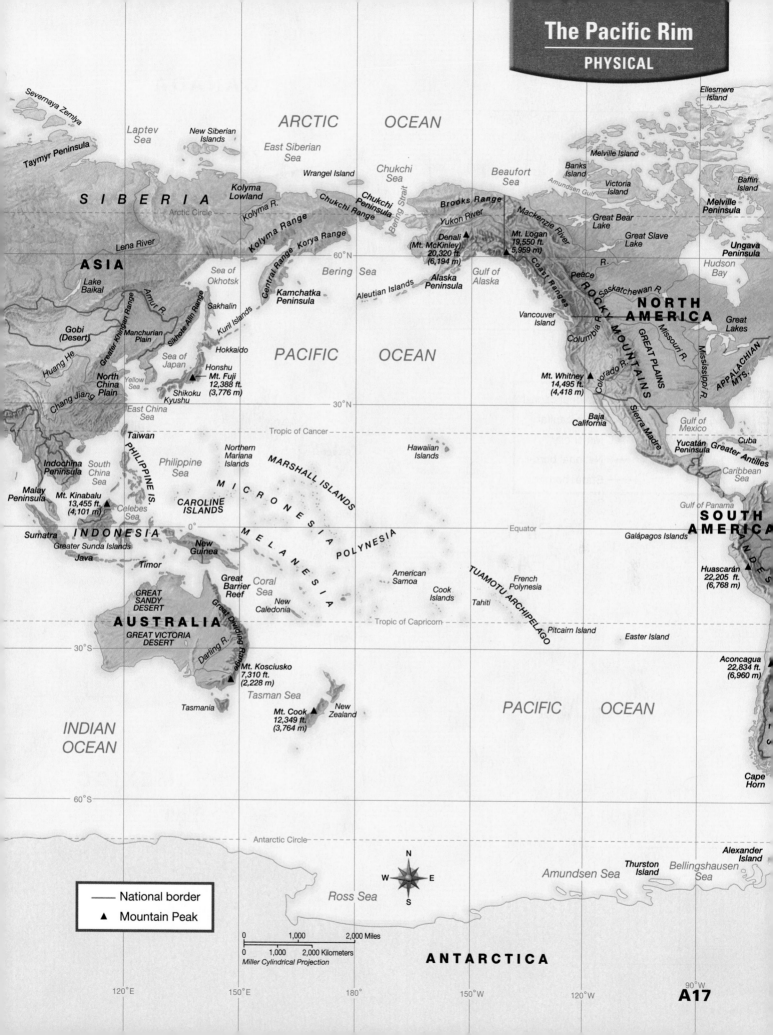

Severnaya Zemlya

ARCTIC OCEAN

Laptev Sea

New Siberian Islands

Taymyr Peninsula

East Siberian Sea

Wrangel Island

Chukchi Sea

Ellesmere Island

Melville Island

Banks Island

Beaufort Sea

Amundsen Gulf

Victoria Island

Melville Peninsula

Baffin Island

SIBERIA

Kolyma Lowland

Arctic Circle

Kolyma R.

Chukchi Peninsula

Chukchi Range

Bering Strait

Brooks Range

Yukon River

Mackenzie River

Great Bear Lake

Great Slave Lake

Ungava Peninsula

Lena River

Kolyma Range

Korya Range

Denali (Mt. McKinley) 20,320 ft. (6,194 m) ▲

Mt. Logan 19,550 ft. 5,959 m ▲

Peace R.

Hudson Bay

ASIA

60°N

Coast Ranges

ROCKY MOUNTAINS

NORTH AMERICA

Lake Baikal

Sea of Okhotsk

Bering Sea

Kamchatka Peninsula

Aleutian Islands

Alaska Peninsula

Gulf of Alaska

Saskatchewan R.

Amur R.

Sakhalin

Greater Khingan Range

Manchurian Plain

Sikhote Alin Range

Kuril Islands

Vancouver Island

Columbia R.

Missouri R.

Great Lakes

Gobi (Desert)

Huang He

Hokkaido

PACIFIC OCEAN

Colorado R.

GREAT PLAINS

APPALACHIAN MTS.

Sea of Japan

Honshu ▲ Mt. Fuji 12,388 ft. (3,776 m)

30°N

Mt. Whitney 14,495 ft. (4,418 m) ▲

Sierra Madre

Mississippi R.

North China Plain

Yellow Sea

Chang jiang

Shikoku
Kyushu

East China Sea

Tropic of Cancer

Baja California

Gulf of Mexico

Yucatán Peninsula

Greater Antilles

Cuba

Taiwan

Northern Mariana Islands

Hawaiian Islands

Caribbean Sea

Indochina Peninsula

South China Sea

PHILIPPINE IS.

Philippine Sea

MARSHALL ISLANDS

MICRONESIA

Malay Peninsula

Mt. Kinabalu 13,455 ft. (4,101 m) ▲

CAROLINE ISLANDS

Celebes Sea

Gulf of Panama

SOUTH AMERICA

Sumatra

INDONESIA

0°

MELANESIA

POLYNESIA

Equator

Galápagos Islands

ANDES

Greater Sunda Islands

New Guinea

Java

Timor

American Samoa

Cook Islands

TUAMOTU ARCHIPELAGO

French Polynesia

Huascarán 22,205 ft. (6,768 m) ▲

Great Barrier Reef

Coral Sea

New Caledonia

Tahiti

GREAT SANDY DESERT

AUSTRALIA

GREAT VICTORIA DESERT

Great Dividing Range

Tropic of Capricorn

Pitcairn Island

Easter Island

30°S

Darling R.

Mt. Kosciusko 7,310 ft. (2,228 m) ▲

Aconcagua 22,834 ft. (6,960 m) ▲

Tasmania

Tasman Sea

Mt. Cook 12,349 ft. (3,764 m) ▲

New Zealand

PACIFIC OCEAN

INDIAN OCEAN

Cape Horn

60°S

Antarctic Circle

Alexander Island

Thurston Island

Bellingshausen Sea

Amundsen Sea

Ross Sea

N
W   E
S

0   1,000   2,000 Miles

0   1,000   2,000 Kilometers

Miller Cylindrical Projection

ANTARCTICA

120°E   150°E   180°   150°W   120°W   90°W

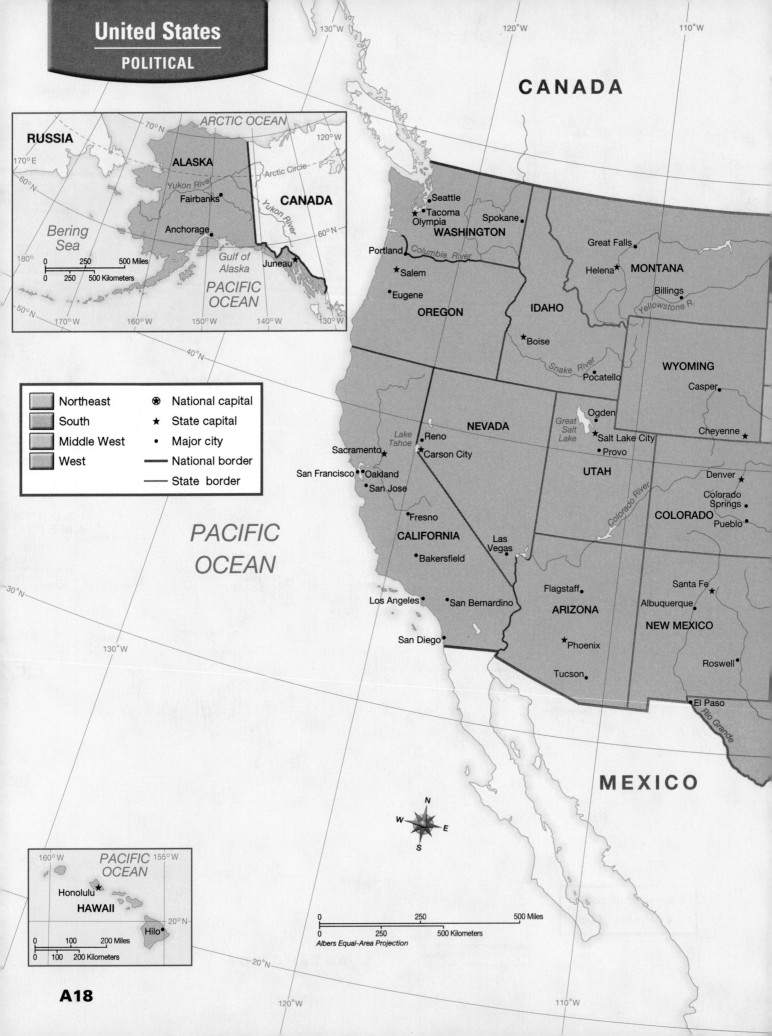

United States
POLITICAL

CANADA

RUSSIA
ARCTIC OCEAN
70° N
170° E
120° W
ALASKA
Arctic Circle
60° N
Yukon River
Fairbanks
CANADA
Bering Sea
180°
Anchorage
Yukon River
60° N
Gulf of Alaska
Juneau
50° N
PACIFIC OCEAN
170° W   160° W   150° W   140° W   130° W

40° N

Legend	
Northeast	⊛ National capital
South	★ State capital
Middle West	• Major city
West	National border
	State border

PACIFIC OCEAN

Seattle
★ Tacoma
Olympia
Spokane
WASHINGTON
Portland   Columbia River
★ Salem
Eugene
OREGON
IDAHO
★ Boise

Great Falls
Helena ★   MONTANA
Billings
Yellowstone R.

Snake River
Pocatello

WYOMING
Casper

NEVADA
Lake Tahoe • Reno
Sacramento ★   Carson City
San Francisco • Oakland
San Jose
Fresno
CALIFORNIA
Bakersfield
Las Vegas

Great Salt Lake
Ogden
★ Salt Lake City
• Provo
UTAH

Colorado River

Cheyenne ★

Denver
Colorado Springs
Pueblo
COLORADO

Los Angeles
San Bernardino
Flagstaff
ARIZONA
Phoenix
San Diego
Tucson

Santa Fe ★
Albuquerque
NEW MEXICO
Roswell
El Paso
Rio Grande

30° N

130° W

MEXICO

N
W   E
S

160° W   PACIFIC OCEAN   155° W
Honolulu ★
HAWAII
Hilo
20° N
0   100   200 Miles
0   100   200 Kilometers

0   250   500 Miles
0   250   500 Kilometers
Albers Equal-Area Projection

120° W   110° W

20° N

A18

0   250   500 Miles (Alaska inset)
0   250   500 Kilometers

A19

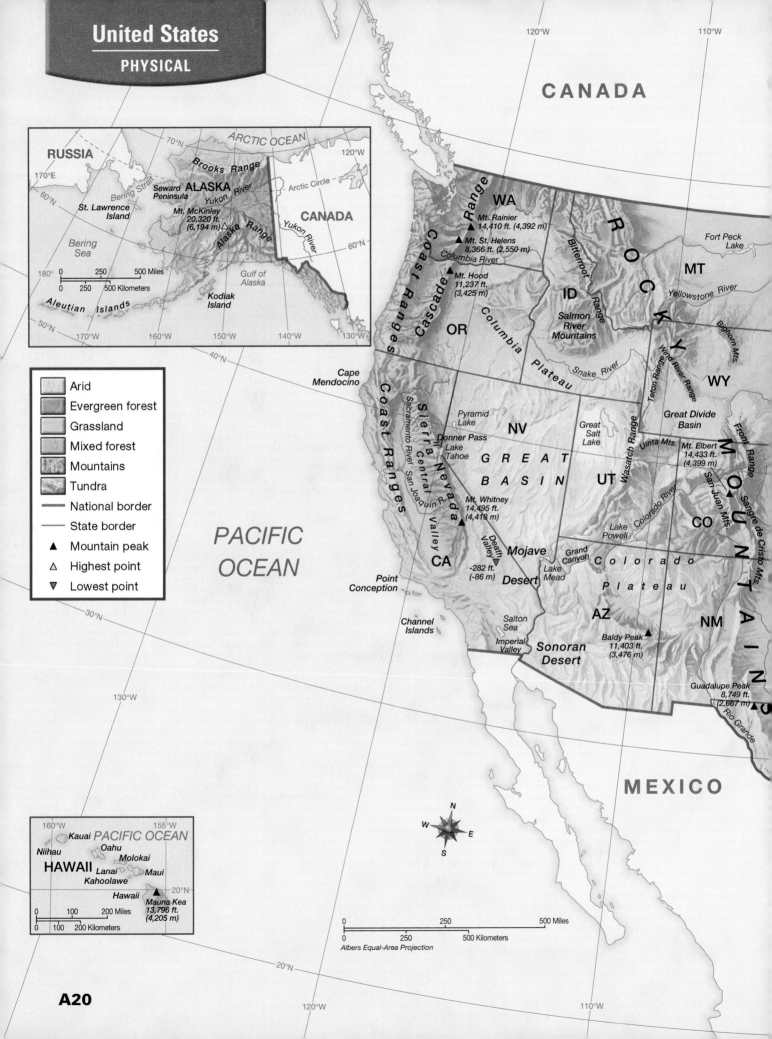

United States
PHYSICAL

CANADA

RUSSIA

ARCTIC OCEAN

Brooks Range

Seward
Peninsula **ALASKA** Yukon River

Bering Strait

St. Lawrence
Island

Mt. McKinley
20,320 ft.
(6,194 m) △ Alaska Range

Arctic Circle

CANADA

Yukon River

Bering
Sea

Gulf of
Alaska

Kodiak
Island

Aleutian Islands

0   250   500 Miles
0   250   500 Kilometers

CANADA

WA

Mt. Rainier
14,410 ft. (4,392 m)

Coast Range

Mt. St. Helens
8,366 ft. (2,550 m)

Columbia River

Cascade Range

Mt. Hood
11,237 ft.
(3,425 m)

OR

Columbia Plateau

Bitterroot Range

ID

Salmon
River
Mountains

Snake River

ROCKY

Fort Peck
Lake

MT

Yellowstone River

Bighorn Mts.

Teton Range

Wind River Range

WY

Great Divide
Basin

Front Range

Mt. Elbert
14,433 ft.
(4,399 m)

MOUNTAINS

Cape
Mendocino

Coast Ranges

Sierra Nevada

Sacramento River

Central Valley

San Joaquin R.

Pyramid
Lake

Donner Pass
Lake
Tahoe

NV

GREAT
BASIN

Great
Salt
Lake

Wasatch Range

Uinta Mts.

UT

Colorado River

Lake
Powell

San Juan Mts.

Sangre de Cristo Mts.

CO

Mt. Whitney
14,495 ft.
(4,418 m)

CA

Death
Valley
-282 ft.
(-86 m)

Mojave
Desert

Grand
Canyon

Lake
Mead

Colorado
Plateau

**PACIFIC
OCEAN**

Point
Conception

Channel
Islands

Salton
Sea

Imperial
Valley

Sonoran
Desert

AZ

Baldy Peak
11,403 ft.
(3,476 m)

NM

Guadalupe Peak
8,749 ft.
(2,667 m)

Rio Grande

Legend

	Arid
	Evergreen forest
	Grassland
	Mixed forest
	Mountains
	Tundra
▬	National border
▬	State border
▲	Mountain peak
△	Highest point
▽	Lowest point

MEXICO

160°W   PACIFIC OCEAN   155°W

Kauai

Niihau   Oahu
Molokai
HAWAII   Lanai   Maui
Kahoolawe

Hawaii   20°N
Mauna Kea
13,796 ft.
(4,205 m)

0   100   200 Miles
0   100   200 Kilometers

N
W   E
S

0   250   500 Miles
0   250   500 Kilometers
Albers Equal-Area Projection

Oceans and Rivers of the World

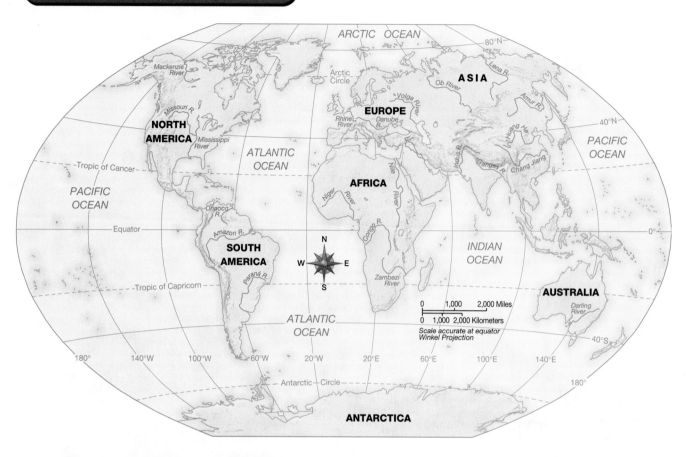

Mountain Ranges of the World

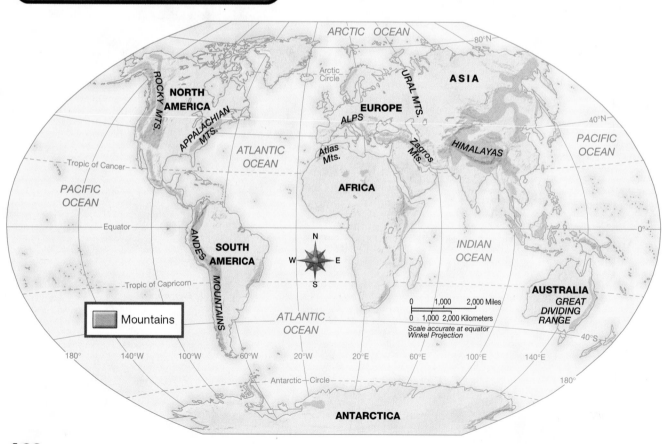

Plains of the World

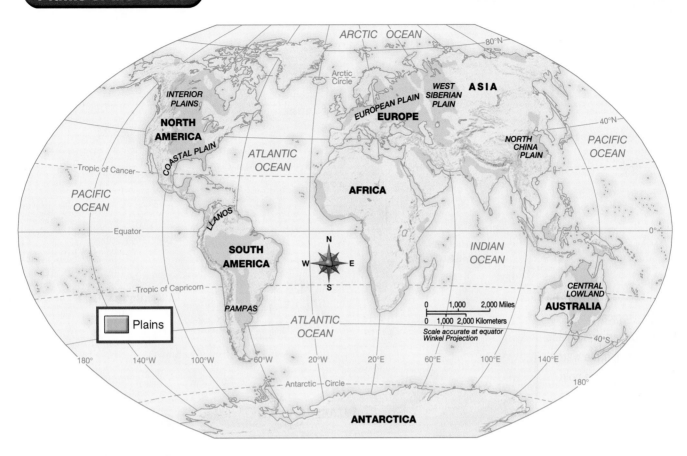

Deserts of the World

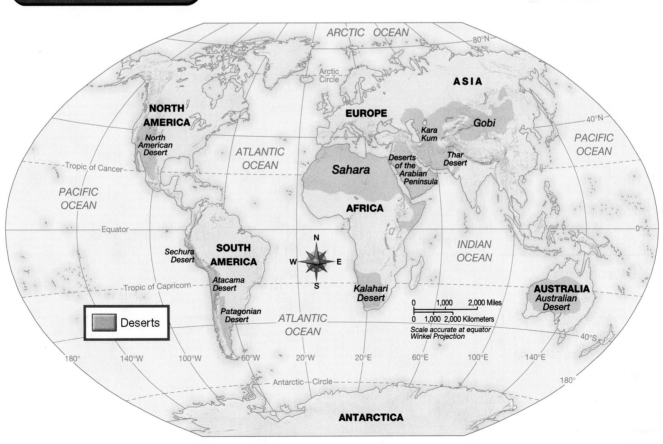

Climates of the World

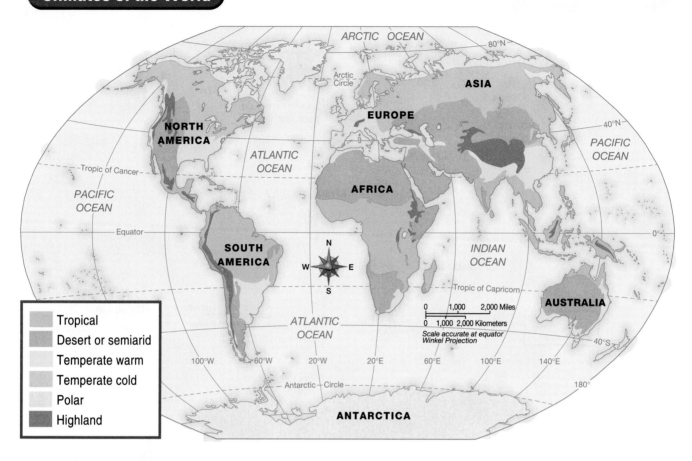

Legend:
- Tropical
- Desert or semiarid
- Temperate warm
- Temperate cold
- Polar
- Highland

ARCTIC OCEAN
ASIA
EUROPE
NORTH AMERICA
AFRICA
ATLANTIC OCEAN
PACIFIC OCEAN
SOUTH AMERICA
INDIAN OCEAN
AUSTRALIA
ANTARCTICA
PACIFIC OCEAN
ATLANTIC OCEAN

Arctic Circle
Tropic of Cancer
Equator
Tropic of Capricorn
Antarctic Circle

80°N
40°N
0°
40°S
100°W 60°W 20°W 20°E 60°E 100°E 140°E 180°

0 1,000 2,000 Miles
0 1,000 2,000 Kilometers
Scale accurate at equator
Winkel Projection

World Land Use

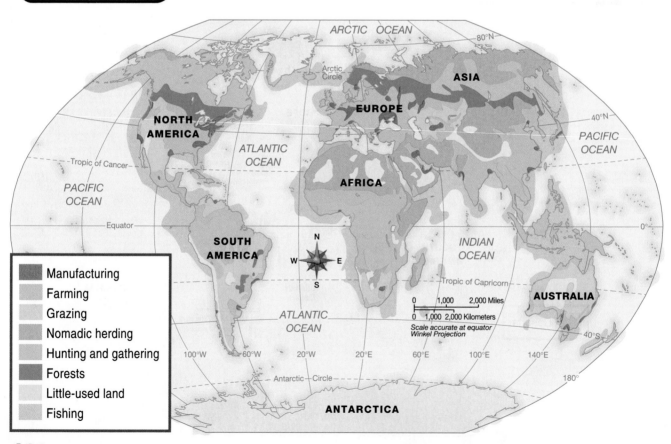

Legend:
- Manufacturing
- Farming
- Grazing
- Nomadic herding
- Hunting and gathering
- Forests
- Little-used land
- Fishing

ARCTIC OCEAN
ASIA
EUROPE
NORTH AMERICA
AFRICA
ATLANTIC OCEAN
PACIFIC OCEAN
SOUTH AMERICA
INDIAN OCEAN
AUSTRALIA
ANTARCTICA
PACIFIC OCEAN
ATLANTIC OCEAN

Arctic Circle
Tropic of Cancer
Equator
Tropic of Capricorn
Antarctic Circle

80°N
40°N
0°
40°S
100°W 60°W 20°W 20°E 60°E 100°E 140°E 180°

0 1,000 2,000 Miles
0 1,000 2,000 Kilometers
Scale accurate at equator
Winkel Projection

World Religions

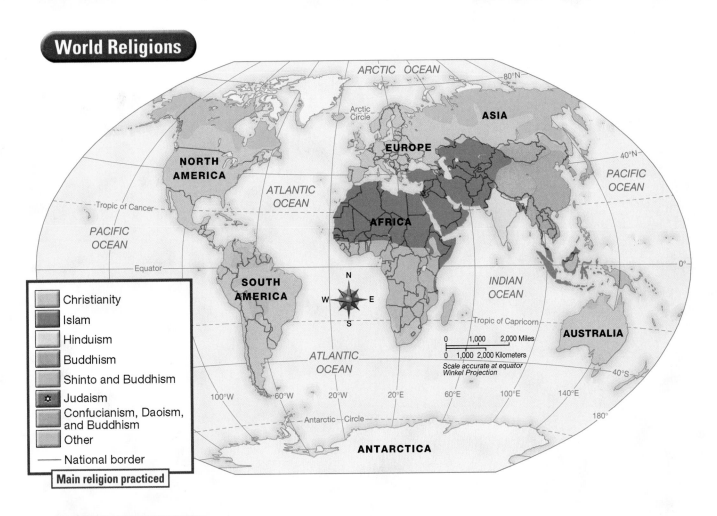

Main religion practiced

- Christianity
- Islam
- Hinduism
- Buddhism
- Shinto and Buddhism
- Judaism
- Confucianism, Daoism, and Buddhism
- Other
- National border

ARCTIC OCEAN
80°N
Arctic Circle
ASIA
EUROPE
NORTH AMERICA
ATLANTIC OCEAN
40°N
PACIFIC OCEAN
Tropic of Cancer
PACIFIC OCEAN
AFRICA
SOUTH AMERICA
INDIAN OCEAN
Equator
0°
N
W E
S
Tropic of Capricorn
AUSTRALIA
ATLANTIC OCEAN
40°S
0 1,000 2,000 Miles
0 1,000 2,000 Kilometers
Scale accurate at equator
Winkel Projection
100°W 60°W 20°W 20°E 60°E 100°E 140°E 180°
Antarctic Circle
ANTARCTICA

World Languages

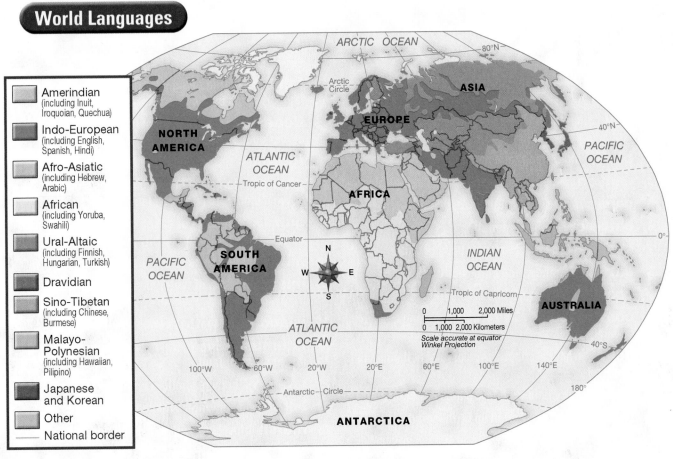

- Amerindian (including Inuit, Iroquoian, Quechua)
- Indo-European (including English, Spanish, Hindi)
- Afro-Asiatic (including Hebrew, Arabic)
- African (including Yoruba, Swahili)
- Ural-Altaic (including Finnish, Hungarian, Turkish)
- Dravidian
- Sino-Tibetan (including Chinese, Burmese)
- Malayo-Polynesian (including Hawaiian, Pilipino)
- Japanese and Korean
- Other
- National border

ARCTIC OCEAN
80°N
Arctic Circle
ASIA
EUROPE
NORTH AMERICA
ATLANTIC OCEAN
40°N
PACIFIC OCEAN
Tropic of Cancer
AFRICA
Equator
PACIFIC OCEAN
SOUTH AMERICA
INDIAN OCEAN
N
W E
S
Tropic of Capricorn
AUSTRALIA
ATLANTIC OCEAN
40°S
0 1,000 2,000 Miles
0 1,000 2,000 Kilometers
Scale accurate at equator
Winkel Projection
100°W 60°W 20°W 20°E 60°E 100°E 140°E 180°
Antarctic Circle
ANTARCTICA

Geography Terms

1. **basin** bowl-shaped area of land surrounded by higher land
2. **bay** an inlet of the sea or some other body of water, usually smaller than a gulf
3. **bluff** high, steep face of rock or earth
4. **canyon** deep, narrow valley with steep sides
5. **cape** point of land that extends into water
6. **cataract** large waterfall
7. **channel** deepest part of a body of water
8. **cliff** high, steep face of rock or earth
9. **coast** land along a sea or ocean
10. **coastal plain** area of flat land along a sea or ocean
11. **delta** triangle-shaped area of land at the mouth of a river
12. **desert** dry land with few plants
13. **dune** hill of sand piled up by the wind

14. **fall line** area along which rivers form waterfalls or rapids as the rivers drop to lower land
15. **floodplain** flat land that is near the edges of a river and is formed by silt deposited by floods
16. **foothills** hilly area at the base of a mountain
17. **glacier** large ice mass that moves slowly down a mountain or across land
18. **gulf** part of a sea or ocean extending into the land, usually larger than a bay
19. **hill** land that rises above the land around it
20. **inlet** any area of water extending into the land from a larger body of water
21. **island** land that has water on all sides
22. **isthmus** narrow strip of land connecting two larger areas of land
23. **lagoon** body of shallow water
24. **lake** body of water with land on all sides
25. **marsh** lowland with moist soil and tall grasses

A26

#	Term	Definition
26	**mesa**	flat-topped mountain with steep sides
27	**mountain**	highest kind of land
28	**mountain pass**	gap between mountains
29	**mountain range**	row of mountains
30	**mouth of river**	place where a river empties into another body of water
31	**oasis**	area of water and fertile land in a desert
32	**ocean**	body of salt water larger than a sea
33	**peak**	top of a mountain
34	**peninsula**	land that is almost completely surrounded by water
35	**plain**	area of flat or gently rolling low land
36	**plateau**	area of high, mostly flat land
37	**reef**	ridge of sand, rock, or coral that lies at or near the surface of a sea or ocean
38	**river**	large stream of water that flows across the land
39	**riverbank**	land along a river
40	**savanna**	area of grassland and scattered trees
41	**sea**	body of salt water smaller than an ocean
42	**sea level**	the level of the surface of an ocean or a sea
43	**slope**	side of a hill or mountain
44	**source of river**	place where a river begins
45	**strait**	narrow channel of water connecting two larger bodies of water
46	**swamp**	area of low, wet land with trees
47	**timberline**	line on a mountain above which it is too cold for trees to grow
48	**tributary**	stream or river that flows into a larger stream or river
49	**valley**	low land between hills or mountains
50	**volcano**	opening in the earth, often raised, through which lava, rock, ashes, and gases are forced out
51	**waterfall**	steep drop from a high place to a lower place in a stream or river

Introduction

> **"A [person's] feet should be planted in his country, but his eyes should survey the world."**
>
> —George Santayana, *The Life of Reason*, 1906

Learning About the World

Despite differences in appearance, language, or ways of life, the people of the world share basic needs for food, clothing, and shelter. As you read this book, you will find out about people in other countries. You will learn about their history and how they live today. You will also learn how they and you are alike and different. Knowing about people around the world will help you better understand world events of the past, present, and future.

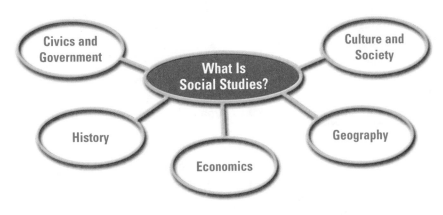

Civics and Government

Culture and Society

What Is Social Studies?

History

Economics

Geography

Why Geography Matters

VOCABULARY

geography	physical feature	modify	effect
relative location	human feature	adapt	analyze
absolute location	region	cause	

By studying **geography**, you can find answers to questions about Earth and the people who live on it. Geographers, the people who study geography, try to understand relationships between people and places on Earth and between different places.

Themes of Geography

Geographers think about the following topics when they study a place. These five topics are so important that people call them the five themes of geography. Most of the maps in this book focus on one of the five themes. Keeping the five themes in mind will help you think like a geographer.

Location

Everything on Earth has its own location, or where it can be found. The **relative location** of a place tells where it is in relation to other places. The **absolute location**, or exact location, of a place is its "global address," where it is on the whole Earth.

Human-Environment Interactions

Humans and their surroundings affect each other. People **modify**, or change, their surroundings by building cities, for example. Surroundings can affect people, causing them to **adapt**, or change to fit, the way they act, such as wearing warm clothing in cold places.

Place

Every location on Earth has a place identity made up of unique features. Landforms, bodies of water, climate, and plant and animal life are some of the **physical features** of a place. Buildings, roads, and people are some of a place's **human features**.

Movement

People, products, and ideas move from place to place by transportation and communication. Geography helps you understand how people came to live where they do. It also helps you understand the causes and effects of movement. A **cause** is an action that makes something else happen. An **effect** is what happens as a result of that action.

Regions

Areas on Earth that differ from each other because of their features are called **regions**. Such features can be physical, human, economic, cultural, or political.

GEOGRAPHY THEME

Essential Elements of Geography

Geographers also use six other topics to understand Earth and its people. These topics are called the six essential elements of geography. You will find special features in this book that focus on the essential elements.

GEOGRAPHY ESSENTIAL ELEMENTS

• GEOGRAPHY •

The World in Spatial Terms
Geographers organize spatial, or location, information about people and places by creating maps. They also use maps to **analyze**, or examine, information.

Human Systems
Geographers study population and human activities, including settlement, trade, and interaction. They also organize these human systems into patterns.

Places and Regions
Geographers identify regions to group together places with similar physical and human features.

Environment and Society
Geographers study ways that physical surroundings and people affect each other.

Physical Systems
Geographers study physical parts of Earth, such as landforms and climate, and organize them into patterns.

The Uses of Geography
Knowing how to think like a geographer and how to use the tools of geography will help you understand the present and plan for the future. For example, citizens might study the features of a neighborhood region to decide how it should be used.

REVIEW In what two ways do geographers study Earth and its people?

Why History Matters

VOCABULARY

history   oral history   historical empathy

chronology   perspective

Many things contribute to the way people live, and one of the most important is **history**, or what happened in the past. History affects all people. Some beliefs and customs, or ways of doing things, have been passed down from generation to generation. In this book you will read about people from the past and the present. You will see how their ways of life have stayed the same or changed over time.

Relating Events in Time

In history, time is the main subject of concern. The time order in which events in history take place is called **chronology** (kruh•NAH•luh•jee). Historians, the people who study history, analyze the chronology of events to find links between the past and the present.

Finding Evidence

Historians look for evidence, or clues, about the past in the objects and records that people have left behind. Historians analyze buildings, works of art, photographs, and everyday tools, not just books and papers. They also listen to or read the stories that people tell about the past. A story told aloud by a person who did not write down what happened or who did not have a written language is an **oral history**. By examining the many kinds of historical evidence, historians can often explain why events happened as they did.

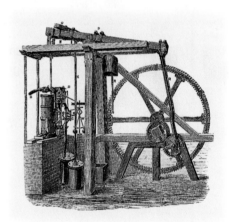

Historians can study these illustrations created in the 1800s to understand the beginnings of industry in Britain.

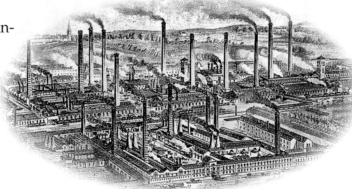

Identifying Perspective

By reading the words and studying the objects of people in the past, historians begin to understand **perspectives**, or different points of view. A person's perspective often depends on whether that person is old or young, a man or a woman, rich or poor. Perspective is also shaped by what a person believes. Your understanding of the world will grow as you study the many points of view of people around the world. You will see that all people, even those from other places and other times, may have different perspectives but still are a lot like you.

Understanding Frames of Reference

Historians have a frame of reference, their own perspective, as they study the past. They see the past from the present. Because of this, they need to be careful not to judge the actions of people in the past based on the way people act today. In the same way, as you read this book, you must be careful not to judge people in the past and in other places based on your beliefs and point of view. **Historical empathy** is the ability to understand people of the past in their own frame of reference.

Drawing Conclusions

To understand an event in the past, historians need to analyze its causes and effects. When you analyze something, you break it into its parts and look closely at how those parts connect with one another. Once you have analyzed an event, you can summarize it or draw a conclusion about how or why it happened.

REVIEW What do you learn when you study history?

People around the world may have different perspectives, or points of view.

Compare Primary and Secondary Sources

⮞ WHY IT MATTERS

People who study history learn about the past from many sources. These sources provide evidence of what actually happened.

⮞ WHAT YOU NEED TO KNOW

A **primary source** gives the actual words of people who were there when an event took place, or it can be a picture or object made during that time. The people's words may be found in letters, diaries, or records of interviews. Their drawings or photographs may show the people, places, or events that they saw.

Sometimes the only way to learn about the past is from a secondary source. A **secondary source** gives information written at a later time by someone who was not there to see what happened. Your social studies book is mostly a secondary source. Encyclopedias and other print and online references are also mostly secondary sources.

Each kind of source can be helpful in gathering information. A primary source can make you feel that you were there when an event happened. A secondary source may give more facts about an event, such as names and dates.

There can also be problems with each kind of source. A primary source might give just one person's view of what happened. The writer of a secondary source might not understand what really happened, since he or she was not there at the time. In both kinds of sources, the writer might state his or her own opinion as a fact.

Both kinds of sources on page 7 tell about events in 1930. Indian leader Mohandas Gandhi led hundreds of followers on

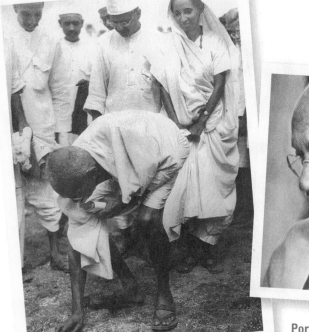

Portrait of Mohandas Gandhi (above) and at the Salt March (left)

a 200-mile (320-km) march to the sea, where they made salt from seawater. They were protesting a British colonial law that made it a crime to possess salt that was not bought from the government. Below is a letter from Gandhi to the British governor, Lord Irwin, concerning what was called the Salt March. Compare the letter with the newspaper article on the same subject.

▶ PRACTICE THE SKILL

Answer these questions about the sources.

1 Which is a primary source, and which is a secondary source? Explain how you know.

2 What kind of information does each source provide?

3 What are the advantages and disadvantages in using each source to understand the events of the Salt March?

▶ APPLY WHAT YOU LEARNED

Using this social studies book, you will have many opportunities to examine a variety of primary and secondary sources. Look through the book, and identify one example of a primary source and one example of a secondary source. Explain to a classmate what makes these sources primary or secondary.

Source A

Letter to Lord Irwin

Dear Friend,

Before embarking on Civil Disobedience and taking the risk I have dreaded to take all these years, I would fain [like to] approach you and find a way out.

. . . the whole revenue system has to be so revised as to make the peasant's good its primary concern. . . . the British system seems to be designed to crush the very life out of him [the peasant]. Even the salt he must use to live is so taxed . . .

. . . If the [Indian] people join me as I expect they will, the sufferings they will undergo . . . will be enough to melt the stoniest hearts.

I respectfully invite you to pave the way for immediate removal of those evils, and thus open a way for a real conference between equals.

. . . But if you cannot see your way to deal with these evils and if my letter makes no appeal to your heart, on the eleventh day of this month I shall proceed with such co-workers of the Ashram as I can take, to disregard the provisions of the Salt Laws . . .

Your Sincere Friend,
M.K. Gandhi

Source B

Thursday, March 13, 1930

For a fortnight Gandhi's march is intended to be a demonstration. Then, when he expects to be at the sea, he will begin to produce salt from brine, and so infringe the Government monopoly, defying the Government to arrest and punish him. At the same time his supporters everywhere have been incited by him to refuse to pay local taxes.

There were sympathetic demonstrations yesterday in various parts of India, but apparently little excitement, and no reported incident of serious disorder. Gandhi, of course, represents a section of India only. His campaign has no support in the National Assembly.

Why Culture and Society Matter

Children and mothers in Bolivia

VOCABULARY
culture   heritage
society

As you study world regions, you will compare and contrast how people live. You will explore people's languages and religious beliefs. These ways of acting, speaking, and believing make up a **culture**. Each human group, or **society**, has a culture that is unique, or different from others, in some way. The people in a society also share a heritage. Their **heritage** is the wealth of ideas that have been passed down through their history.

In this book you will study cultures and societies in seven regions of the world.
• The United States and Canada
• Middle America and South America
• Europe
• Southwest Asia and North Africa
• Africa South of the Sahara
• Asia
• The Pacific Realm

REVIEW What do you learn when you study culture and society?

Regions of the World

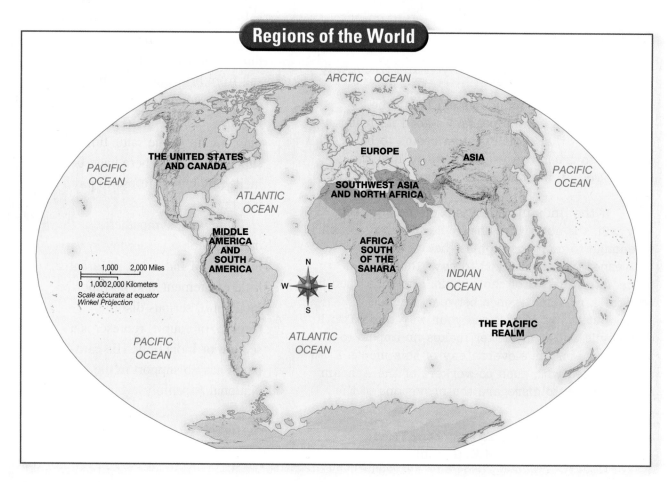

Why Civics and Government Matter

VOCABULARY

government   civic participation

To keep order and resolve conflicts in a society, people need a government. A **government** is a system of leaders and laws that helps people live safely together in their community, state, or country. You will discover as you read this book that there are many different kinds of governments in the world. You will find out about the people and events that shaped governments in the past and how government works today. You will also learn about civics, or the rights and responsibilities of citizens. You will see how citizens' rights and responsibilities vary from one kind of government to the next. In addition, you will learn about civic participation. **Civic participation** means being concerned with and involved in issues related to your community, state, or country, or the entire world.

REVIEW What do you learn when you study government and civic participation?

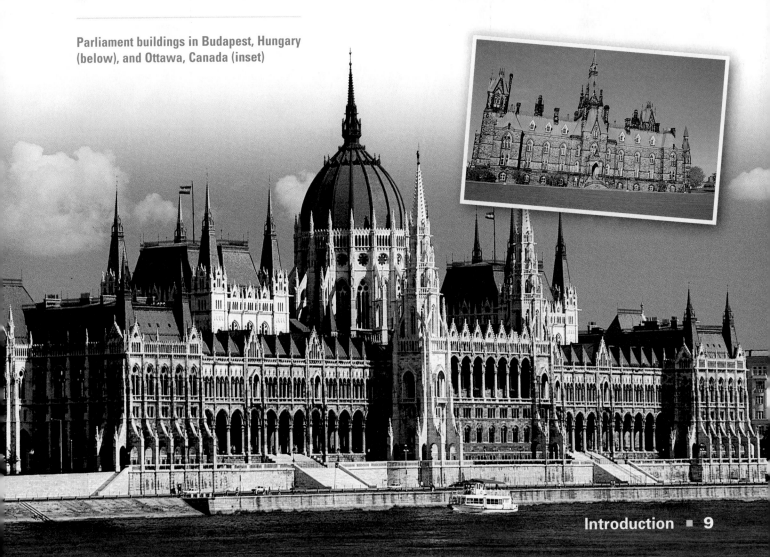

Parliament buildings in Budapest, Hungary (below), and Ottawa, Canada (inset)

Why Economics Matters

VOCABULARY

economy

economics

To support its people, a society must have an **economy**, or a system of using resources to meet needs. The people must be able to make, buy, sell, and trade goods and services to get what they need and want. In this book you will compare and contrast different economic systems—from the simple ones of the past to the more complex ones of today. **Economics** is the study of the way that goods and wealth are produced, distributed, and used in the world. You will learn how economic systems came to be, how they changed over time, and how they work in today's world.

REVIEW What do you learn when you study economics?

In Chile raising nectarines for sale (below left) is part of the country's economy. Pictured below is money from around the world—Japan (top), Canada (middle), and Madagascar (bottom).

A View of the World

Celestial globe with clockwork,
sixteenth-century Austria

Earth from the Moon, 1969

A View of the World

> **66** . . . we all live under this same sky,
> whether New York or Dhaka, we
> see the same sun and the same moon. **99**
>
> —Zia Hyder, from "Under This Sky," 1992

Preview the Content

Use the chapter and lesson titles to fill in the first two columns of a K-W-L chart. In the first two columns, write what you know and want to learn about the world's geography and people. After reading, note in the third column what you learned.

Preview the Vocabulary

Compound Words   Compound words are made up of two or more words. Use the meanings of smaller words to write meanings for the compound words. Record your responses in a chart, and use the Glossary to check your answers.

SMALLER WORD		SMALLER WORD		COMPOUND WORD	MEANING
flood	+	plain	=	**floodplain**	_____
land	+	form	=	**landform**	_____

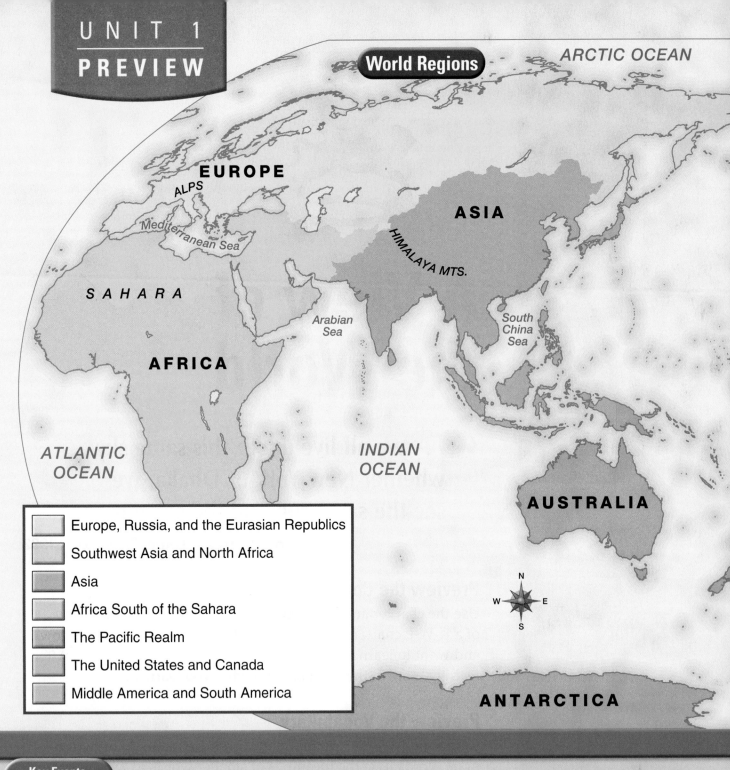

World Regions

ARCTIC OCEAN

EUROPE

ALPS

Mediterranean Sea

ASIA

HIMALAYA MTS.

SAHARA

Arabian Sea

South China Sea

AFRICA

ATLANTIC OCEAN

INDIAN OCEAN

AUSTRALIA

Europe, Russia, and the Eurasian Republics

Southwest Asia and North Africa

Asia

Africa South of the Sahara

The Pacific Realm

The United States and Canada

Middle America and South America

N
W E
S

ANTARCTICA

Key Events

Landforms (p. 20) and Bodies of Water (p. 26)

Climates and Vegetation p. 34

Natural Resources p. 40

12

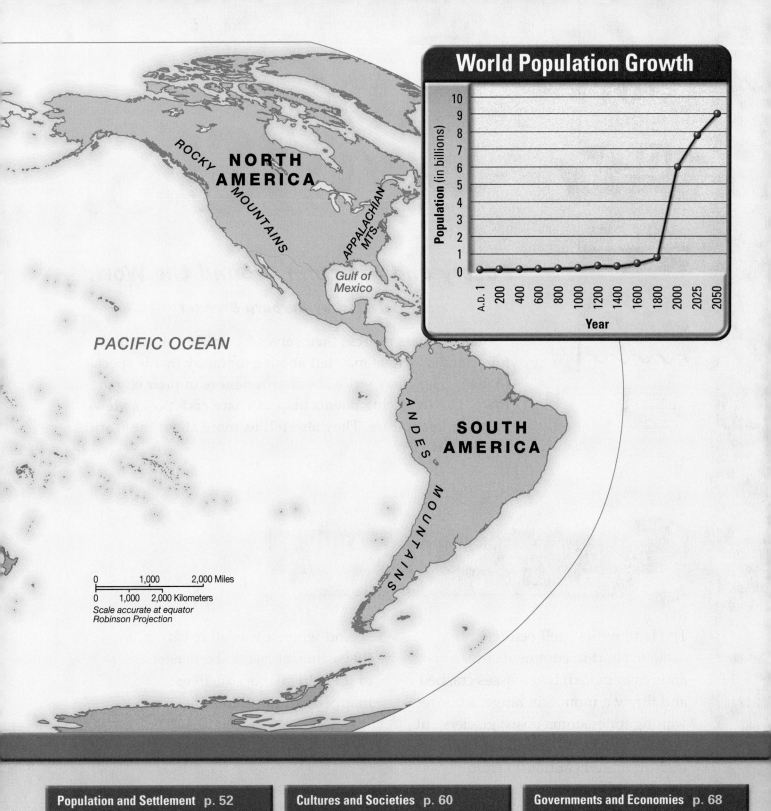

World Population Growth

Population (in billions)

10
9
8
7
6
5
4
3
2
1
0

A.D. 1 200 400 600 800 1000 1200 1400 1600 1800 2000 2025 2050

Year

NORTH
AMERICA

ROCKY MOUNTAINS

APPALACHIAN MTS.

Gulf of
Mexico

PACIFIC OCEAN

SOUTH
AMERICA

ANDES MOUNTAINS

0   1,000   2,000 Miles

0   1,000   2,000 Kilometers

Scale accurate at equator
Robinson Projection

Population and Settlement p. 52

Cultures and Societies p. 60

Governments and Economies p. 68

VOICES:

Poetry and Art from Around the World

selected by Barbara Brenner

Many writers express themselves by writing about their homelands. Writers may tell about geography that is special to them. They may write about experiences in their city or town. The following poems help us share each poet's view of his or her culture. They also tell us more about the world in which we live.

GEOGRAPHY 2

by Sheenagh Pugh · United Kingdom

The land wrote itself before any
came to chart it: continents broke
and reassembled; two masses crashed
and threw a mountain range, a border
waiting for customs posts; glaciers cut
narrow valleys, close and separate,
each shuttered cautiously from
   its neighbour.
A coast curved itself into a haven
for shipping; a hill kept watch
on the landscape till the fort was built.
A river spread rich gentle living
over these fields; elsewhere, the want
of water made the contours stand out
like starved bones.

And when it was all ready
they came, at last, to be masters
of it all; to take up the lives
mapped out for them.

Landscape in Wales, homeland of the poet

MOVED

by Uvavnuk (Iglulik Inuit woman) · Canada

The great sea stirs me.
The great sea sets me adrift,
it sways me like the weed
on a river-stone.

The sky's height stirs me.
The strong wind blows through
    my mind.
It carries me with it,
so I shake with joy.

**This sun ray mask was made
by Native Canadians in 1875.**

MAWU OF THE WATERS

by Abena P. A. Busia · Ghana

With mountains as my footstool
    and stars in my curls
I reach down to reap the waters with
    my fingers
and look!, I cup lakes in my palms.
I fling oceans around me like a shawl
and am transformed
into a waterfall.
Springs flow through me
and spill rivers at my feet
as fresh streams surge to make seas.

Victoria Falls in Zimbabwe

NATURE

by H. D. Carberry · Jamaica

We have neither Summer nor Winter
Neither Autumn nor Spring.
We have instead the days
When the gold sun shines on the lush green canefields—
Magnificently.
The days when the rain beats like bullets on the roofs
And there is no sound but the swish of water in the gullies
And trees struggling in the high Jamaica winds.
Also there are the days when leaves fade from off
    guango trees
And the reaped canefields lie bare and fallow to the sun.
But best of all there are the days when the mango and the
    logwood blossom
When the bushes are full of the sound of bees and the scent
    of honey,
When the tall grass sways and shivers to the slightest breath
    of air,
When the buttercups have paved the earth with yellow stars
And beauty comes suddenly and the rains have gone.

This painting by J. H. Wilner is called *Rich Harvest*.

LANDFALL

Traditional (Aboriginal) · Australia

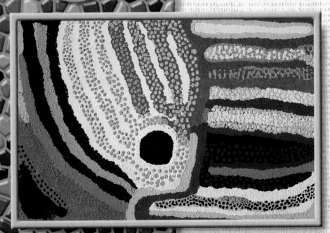

I arrive where an unknown earth is under
    my feet,
I arrive where a new sky is above me,
I arrive at this land
A resting place for me.
O spirit of the earth! The stranger humbly
    offers his
heart as food for thee.

**This dot painting by Aboriginal artist Lucy Yukenbarri
shows the landscape of Australia's Great Sand Desert.**

HOME

by Thuong Chieu · Vietnam

This painting is a Vietnamese artist's vision of home.

No color or complexion distinguishes the Way,
Still its message flares up everywhere:
Of the thousands of worlds,
numerous as grains of sand,
Which is not home?

Analyze the Literature

1 Which poem was your favorite? Why? What feeling did the writer give you about his or her country?

2 What is unique about the place where you live? Write a poem that shares how you feel about it.

READ A BOOK

START THE UNIT PROJECT

Make Maps and Models Make a map and a model with a group of classmates. As you read this unit, take notes about the lands and bodies of water on Earth. These notes will help you decide what to show on your map and what kind of land to feature in your model.

USE TECHNOLOGY

Visit The Learning Site at **www.harcourtschool.com/ socialstudies** for additional activities, primary sources, and other resources to use in this unit.

ULURU (AYERS ROCK), AUSTRALIA

Uluru, also called Ayers Rock, is located in the Northern Territory of Australia. It is more than 2 miles (3.2 km) long, about 1.5 miles (2.4 km) wide, and 1,100 feet (335 m) high. Because Uluru is made of a special kind of sandstone, it changes color with the angle of the sun's rays. At sunset, Uluru becomes brilliant red.

LOCATE IT

AUSTRALIA

Uluru
(Ayers Rock)

The World's Geography

 Landscapes have a language of their own, . . . from the mighty peaks to the smallest of the tiny flowers . . .

—Alexandra David-Neel, from
My Journey to Lhasa, 1927

CHAPTER READING SKILL

Main Idea and Supporting Details

The **main idea** is the most important thought of a chapter, lesson, or paragraph. **Supporting details** are the facts, reasons, and examples that provide information to support main ideas.

As you read each lesson, think about the main idea and the details supporting it.

Most Important Idea	←	Facts, Examples, and Reasons

MAIN IDEA	←	DETAILS

MAIN IDEA
Read to find out how Earth's landforms were shaped and reshaped over time.

WHY IT MATTERS
Earth's landforms continue to change, affecting all people on Earth.

VOCABULARY

landform
plate tectonics
continental drift
fault
magma
lava
weathering
erosion
deposition
floodplain
delta

Earth's Landforms

Although the surface of planet Earth is largely water, it is the wrinkled, broken, warped, and worn shapes of land that make studying Earth so interesting. These shapes of land are called **landforms**. A landform may be as large as the tallest mountain or as small as a mound in your backyard. Earth's major landforms—its plains, mountains, and hills—came to be through forces of nature.

How Landforms Came to Be

One idea about how Earth's landforms and continents came to be is the plate tectonics (tek•TAH•niks) theory. According to **plate tectonics**, Earth's surface is made up of several large, slow-moving slabs, or plates. The continents and ocean floors form the tops of these plates, which move and carry the continents and ocean floors with them.

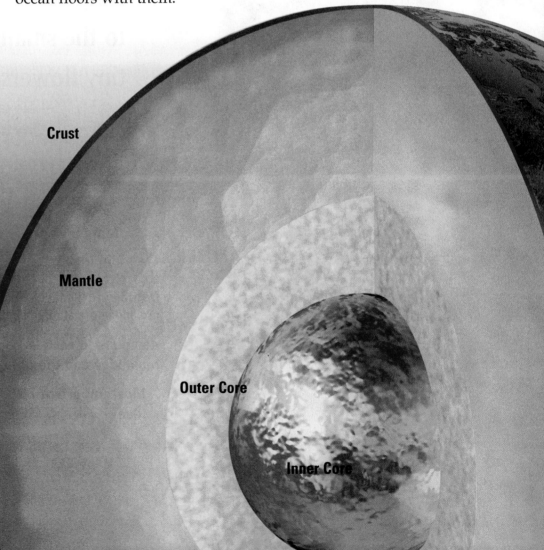

Crust

Mantle

Outer Core

Inner Core

FAST FACT Earth is not perfectly round. The distance through the planet from the North Pole to the South Pole is 7,900 miles (12,714 km). The distance through Earth at the equator is 7,926 miles (12,756 km).

Scientists believe that long ago all of Earth's landmasses formed one huge supercontinent, known as Pangaea (pan•JEE•uh). They say that forces within Earth caused Pangaea to break up into continental plates and drift apart. This movement is called **continental drift**. The forces that cause it are the result of Earth's structure.

Earth is made up of layers similar to those of an apple. The outer layer, at the surface like an apple's skin, is the crust. Earth's crust is between 10 and 25 miles (16 and 40 km) thick. Beneath the crust, and extending some 1,800 miles (2,900 km) below Earth's surface, is the mantle. The mantle is thought by scientists to be composed of hot, rocklike materials.

At Earth's center is a metal core. The core is very hot, with temperatures as hot as 5,000°F (2,760°C). The inner core is solid. Surrounding the solid inner core is a molten, or melted, outer core.

Extreme heat from the core causes the mantle to create pressure on the crust, forcing the crust in some places to rise. As the crust rises, it pushes large blocks of rock upward, forming mountains and plateaus. The portion of the Rocky Mountains extending from Montana into New Mexico in the United States formed this way.

Earth's History

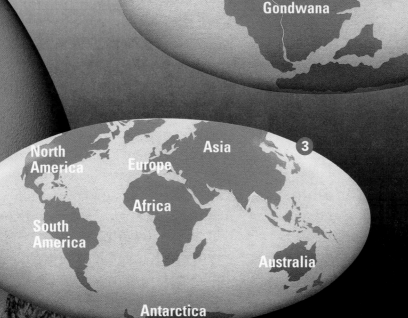

Analyze Diagrams

Scientists believe that the seven continents were once joined.
1. 200 million years ago
2. 120 million years ago
3. Present
? Which of the present-day continents was at one time joined to the east side of South America?

Measuring Earthquakes

A seismograph (SYZ•muh•graf) is a machine that can locate an earthquake and record its motion. When Earth is still, the seismograph's needle does not move. As the ground begins to move during an earthquake, the seismograph's needle moves as well. The needle draws a line that zigzags across a strip of paper. Scientists use the data from a seismograph to rate the amount of energy released by an earthquake. They do this with a set of guidelines called the Richter scale. The higher the number an earthquake receives, the more powerful it is. The most powerful earthquake ever recorded measured 8.5 on the Richter scale. It occurred on May 22, 1960, in the country of Chile in South America.

The results of an earthquake in India

The forces within Earth cause the tectonic plates on the surface to move in many ways. When the plates push together, their edges may crumble and fold, creating mountains. Most of the highest mountains in the world, including the Himalayas (hih•muh•LAY•uhz), were formed as a result of this folding action.

Mountains are also formed when two plates collide and one moves up over the other. The Cascade Mountains in the western United States were formed in this way.

The same forces that formed mountains and other landforms on Earth are still at work today. You may not feel them, but Earth's plates are constantly shifting and settling.

At times, the movement of the plates shakes Earth's surface, causing an earthquake. Earthquakes are common and most destructive in areas along faults. A **fault** is a break in Earth's crust where movement occurs. An earthquake occurs when the movement is sudden. Most faults cannot be seen, but some, like the San Andreas

Fault in the western United States, are visible above the ground.

The San Andreas Fault runs through much of California. The fault lies along an area where two of Earth's plates meet and move past each other. The shifting of these two plates in 1906 caused a terrible earthquake in San Francisco. The San Andreas Fault shifted then as much as 21 feet (6.4 m).

REVIEW How do moving tectonic plates create landforms such as mountains?

Volcanoes Add Land

Sometimes when two of Earth's plates push against each other, the edge of one plate slides beneath the other. As rock in the upper plate is pushed up, rock in the lower plate is pushed down into Earth's mantle. Heat within the mantle causes rock in the lower plate to melt. This molten rock is called **magma**.

When rock melts, it produces gases. The gases mix with the magma, and the gas-filled magma gradually rises through cracks in the crust onto Earth's surface. **Lava** is the name for magma that has escaped onto the surface. Sometimes lava escapes slowly. At other times it erupts with a tremendous explosion.

Openings through which lava flows are commonly called volcanoes. Volcanoes have many shapes and sizes. Some are cone-shaped, while others are wide and flat. The size and shape of a volcano depend on the kind of lava that comes out.

Lava that flows easily can spread over great distances. This kind of lava flow forms a shield volcano. Mauna Loa (MOW•nuh LOH•uh) in Hawaii is a good example of a shield volcano.

Thicker lava may erupt more violently, throwing rock and ash high into the air. When the rock and ash land near the opening on the surface, they form a steep-sided, cinder-cone mountain. Paricutín (puh•ree•kuh•TEEN) in western Mexico is a cinder-cone volcano. It began to form in 1943, when a crack opened in a farm field. When the eruptions ended in 1952, the cone was 1,345 feet (410 m) high.

Scientists also classify volcanoes by how often they erupt. Active volcanoes have erupted since people have been keeping records. Dormant volcanoes have become inactive, but not long enough for people to know if they will erupt again. Extinct volcanoes have no record of activity and probably will not erupt again.

REVIEW How are volcanoes formed?

Shaping Earth's Surface

There are several ways in which Earth's surface can change. One of these is by weathering. **Weathering** is the process of breaking up rocks into smaller pieces called sediment. All agents, or causes, of weathering involve some kind of motion.

Water is an agent of weathering. Moving water tumbles rocks against each other, breaking them into pieces. In this way, moving streams and rivers weather away land and produce canyons.

Mount Ruapehu is New Zealand's most active volcano.

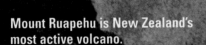

Crater Lake in Oregon is a dormant volcano.

Hawaii's Kilauea volcano

Ocean waves weather away sea cliffs, turning them into beach sand or causing them to fall into the sea.

Moving ice in the form of glaciers can also change landforms. Glaciers are thick sheets of ice formed in areas where more snow falls than melts. As glaciers move, they grind the land below them. Because of a glacier's huge size, it weathers away anything under it.

Wind is another agent of weathering. Strong, steady wind carrying sand can grind hard desert rock. In the western United States, wind has helped to shape some landforms. Rainbow Bridge in Utah looks like a sweeping arch. Other landforms shaped by water, ice, and wind look like tall columns or flat tables.

After weathering has broken rocks into sediment, erosion and deposition move the sediment to new places. **Erosion** is the process of moving sediment. **Deposition** is the process of dropping, or depositing, sediment in a new location.

Erosion and deposition enlarge landforms and produce new ones. Rivers, for example, pick up sediment as they move downstream. When rivers flood, they deposit the sediment in flat areas along their banks. These deposits add to the **floodplain**, the land next to the river. A river also deposits sediment at its mouth, forming a triangle-shaped piece of land called a **delta**.

REVIEW What physical processes shape landforms?

Shipton's Arch in western China shows how erosion can shape the land.

LOCATE IT

CHINA

Shipton's Arch

People Change the Land

In addition to forces in nature, human activities also change Earth. Rivers form floodplains and deltas, but people make those landforms farming areas. The rich soil makes floodplains and deltas excellent for farming. People also have chosen to build cities near floodplains and deltas.

Other people have chosen to build farms and cities on landforms that seemed impossible to use. In Asia some people raise rice on mountain slopes. They do this by cutting into the slopes, forming flat fields along them. This prevents erosion and keeps water on the fields.

People also reshape waterways and create new ones. They build dams to control the flow of rivers and produce electricity. In doing so, they create lakes to store water. These lakes sometimes cover what were once fields or valleys.

People drain water from wetlands to create dry land for cities and farms. They also direct water into dry places. This makes it possible for people in places such as the western United States to live and work in the middle of deserts.

REVIEW **What are some ways in which people change the physical environment?**

LOCATE IT

Ḥā'il

SAUDI ARABIA

For centuries, farmers in Ḥā'il, Saudi Arabia, have moved water to grow crops in dry places.

LESSON 1 REVIEW

1. **MAIN IDEA** How has activity within Earth changed the landforms on its surface?

2. **WHY IT MATTERS** How does the shifting of Earth's plates affect people's lives? Give one example.

3. **VOCABULARY** What is the difference between **magma** and **lava**?

4. **READING SKILL—Main Idea and Supporting Details** How are landforms created? How are they changed?

5. **GEOGRAPHY** What is one difference between the inner core and the outer core of Earth?

6. **GEOGRAPHY** What was Pangaea?

7. **GEOGRAPHY** What causes earthquakes?

8. **CRITICAL THINKING—Apply** How would a large storm with heavy rains and high winds off the coast of Florida affect that state's beaches?

 PERFORMANCE—Make a Scrapbook Page Use the library and the Internet to find an example of people changing a place on Earth. Then make a scrapbook page using the information you have found. Write a paragraph that tells what the place was like at first. Then write another paragraph describing the land after people changed it. Add your page to a class scrapbook titled People Change the World.

Earth's Bodies of Water

Water covers more than 70 percent of Earth's surface. It fills rivers, lakes, and oceans. It is in the ground and in the air we breathe. Without water, there would be no life. People, plants, and animals all must have water to survive.

Streams and Rivers

Streams are bodies of water that flow over land in a channel. Most streams begin on high ground, among hills or mountains. The source, or beginning, of a stream may be a melting snowfield or glacier, or it might be an overflowing lake. Streams flow from high ground to low ground. At the end of a stream is its mouth, where it empties into another body of water.

Some streams are as small as shallow, little brooks. Others are broad and deep. These are rivers, the largest and most important streams. Most rivers form by many smaller streams coming together. These smaller streams are called **tributaries** of the river. As more tributaries empty into a river, it grows larger. Together a river and its tributaries make up a **river system**.

Each continent, except Antarctica, has major rivers and river systems. Africa's most important river is the Nile. Asia's is the Chang Jiang (CHANG JYAHNG), also called the Yangtze (YANG•SEE). Australia's most important river is the Murray, and Europe's is the Danube. In North America it is the Mississippi River. In South America, it is the Amazon.

The Amazon River (right) begins as a small stream created by melting snow and ice (inset).

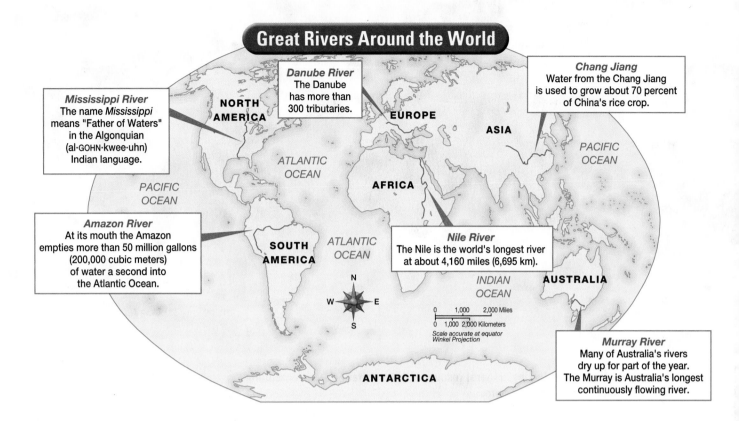

Great Rivers Around the World

Mississippi River
The name *Mississippi* means "Father of Waters" in the Algonquian (al·GOHN·kwee·uhn) Indian language.

Danube River
The Danube has more than 300 tributaries.

Chang Jiang
Water from the Chang Jiang is used to grow about 70 percent of China's rice crop.

Amazon River
At its mouth the Amazon empties more than 50 million gallons (200,000 cubic meters) of water a second into the Atlantic Ocean.

Nile River
The Nile is the world's longest river at about 4,160 miles (6,695 km).

Murray River
Many of Australia's rivers dry up for part of the year. The Murray is Australia's longest continuously flowing river.

NORTH AMERICA
EUROPE
ASIA
AFRICA
SOUTH AMERICA
AUSTRALIA
ANTARCTICA
ATLANTIC OCEAN
PACIFIC OCEAN
PACIFIC OCEAN
ATLANTIC OCEAN
INDIAN OCEAN

N S E W

0   1,000   2,000 Miles
0 1,000 2,000 Kilometers
Scale accurate at equator
Winkel Projection

GEOGRAPHY THEME

Location The rivers of the world vary in length and size of drainage basin.

❓ What is the major river on each continent?

The Nile is Earth's longest river. It flows about 4,160 miles (6,695 km) from its source in Central Africa to its mouth at the Mediterranean Sea. A huge amount of water flows down the Amazon, making it the largest river system. The Amazon River carries more water than the Mississippi, the Nile, and the Chang Jiang combined.

River systems drain, or carry water away from, the land around them. Land drained by a river system is called a **drainage basin**. Long rivers can have large drainage basins. The Amazon River, for example, has a drainage basin of about 2.7 million square miles (7 million sq km).

Many of the world's first settlements and civilizations developed along rivers because rivers are important sources of water for human life. They provide water for drinking, cleaning, and other uses.

Today many of the world's largest cities are located along rivers for the same reason.

Some rivers are also valuable energy sources. The fast-moving water at waterfalls and other steep places along a river may power machines to generate electricity. Rivers are also useful for transportation and trade. They were often the first "highways" used by explorers, traders, and pioneers as they entered new lands.

REVIEW Why did many of the world's first settlements form along rivers?

Lakes

Lakes are bodies of water surrounded by land. The word *lake* comes from a Greek word meaning "hole." Most lakes formed when water filled a hole or opening in Earth's surface.

The Caspian Sea provides fishing, mineral resources, transportation, and recreation. Here a man collects salt from its shore.

Lakes exist on every continent, except Antarctica. The greatest number are in places once covered by glaciers, such as North America and northern Europe. During the last Ice Age, glaciers gouged huge holes and basins in Earth's surface and deposited water in the holes as the glaciers melted.

Lakes also form where rainwater collects in huge holes made in other ways. Crater Lake in the western United States formed in the crater, or hole, of an extinct volcano. Lake Baikal (by•KAHL) in Russia is the deepest lake on Earth, measuring 5,315 feet (1,620 m) deep. It formed in a huge crack in Earth's crust. East Africa also has several large lakes that formed in this way, including Lakes Victoria, Tanganyika, and Malawi. The **rift**, a long and deep crack that formed these lakes, stretches through what is called the Great Rift Valley.

North America has more lakes by far than any other continent. The largest of these are the Great Lakes, on the border between Canada and the United States.

One-fifth of all the fresh water on Earth's surface is found in the Great Lakes.

Some large bodies of water that are called seas are actually lakes. These include the Dead Sea, the Sea of Galilee, and the Caspian Sea, all in Southwest Asia. Unlike other lakes, which contain fresh water, these are called seas because they contain salt water, like the ocean.

The Dead Sea, between Israel and Jordan, lies about 1,310 feet (400 m) below sea level. It is one of the lowest-lying lakes on Earth. The highest lake on Earth is Lake Titicaca (tee•tee•KAH•kah) in South America. It is at 12,507 feet (3,812 m) above sea level.

Not all lakes are made by nature, however. Some are made when people build dams to control river flooding or to generate electricity. A lake that forms behind a human-made dam is called a **reservoir** (REH•zuh•vwar). Many reservoirs are known as lakes.

REVIEW How did Ice Age glaciers form lakes in North America and Europe?

Earth's Ocean

Earth's ocean is the great body of water that covers much of the planet. Continents and other landmasses divide Earth's ocean into four parts. In order of size, they are the Pacific Ocean, the Atlantic Ocean, the Indian Ocean, and the Arctic Ocean.

The Pacific Ocean is much bigger than the others. It covers about 70 million square miles (181 million sq km) compared to the 36 million square miles (93 million sq km) covered by the Atlantic Ocean, the second-largest ocean. The Pacific covers nearly one-third of Earth's surface and is big enough to hold all seven continents. Where the Pacific is at its widest, it stretches more than 15,000 miles (24,000 km) from Panama to Malaysia. The Pacific is also the deepest ocean, with an average depth of about 12,900 feet (3,900 m).

The land beneath the ocean has varied features. It consists of mountain ranges, broad plains and basins, and long, deep valleys. The mid-ocean ridges make up the single largest feature. The ridges consist of a chain of mountains that runs about 37,000 miles (60,000 km) through the Pacific, Indian, and Atlantic Oceans. Most of the mountains are about 5,000 feet (1,500 m) tall. Some of the tallest peaks rise above the surface of the water to form islands, such as Iceland in the Atlantic Ocean.

The deepest ocean valley, or **trench**, ever explored is in the western Pacific near the island of Guam. Called the Mariana Trench, it sinks down almost 7 miles (11 km) below the ocean's surface.

The Water Cycle

Analyze Diagrams Earth's water moves continuously from oceans, to the air, to the land, and back to the oceans again.

1. Sun's heat causes water to evaporate, forming water vapor.
2. Water vapor cools, forming clouds.
3. Water falls back to Earth as rain, snow, and other forms of precipitation.

❖ How does water get back to the oceans?

Robert Ballard   1942–

Character Trait: Inventiveness

Oceanographer Robert Ballard explores the deepest parts of Earth's oceans and shares his discoveries with people around the world. Ballard helped create new tools so he could study the deepest parts of the oceans. Some places that Ballard wanted to see were too small for people wearing diving equipment to fit into. To solve this problem, Ballard helped create a remote-controlled submarine that could travel through small openings and take pictures of what was inside. Ballard's most famous discovery was the wreck of the sunken ship *Titanic*.

Deep and vast, the waters of Earth's oceans move constantly. **Currents**, or giant streams of ocean water, course through the oceans like giant rivers. Ocean currents are set in motion by the wind. In general, they move in clockwise patterns in the Northern Hemisphere and in counterclockwise patterns in the Southern Hemisphere.

Ocean currents tend to carry cold water from near the North and South Poles toward the equator. Warm water near the equator moves toward the poles. These ocean currents have a strong influence on the temperatures of land areas. They also influence ocean transportation, since it is easier and faster for ships to sail with the ocean currents rather than against them.

Wind also causes ocean waves, the up-and-down action of the oceans. Ocean waves can be small ripples or giant waves of more than 100 feet (30 m) caused by earthquakes and severe storms. Some people call giant waves **tidal waves**, though ocean tides do not cause them.

Tides are still another way that oceans move. The pull of the moon and sun causes ocean **tides**, the regular, rhythmic rise and fall of the ocean waters. Every day, the ocean water slowly rises and falls along the shoreline. This movement, together with waves, often pushes sand and rock onto or away from beaches, constantly changing their size and shape. The Bay of Fundy in Canada has tides that rise and fall more than 80 feet (24 m) at certain times of the year. Over time these extreme tides have carved enormous rock towers out of cliffs that line the bay.

Each part of Earth's ocean includes many kinds of smaller bodies of water, called seas, straits, gulfs, and bays. These smaller bodies of water lie along the ocean edges. For example, the Gulf of Mexico, the Davis Strait, and the Bay of Biscay are all actually part of the Atlantic Ocean. In the same way, the Mediterranean Sea, which lies between Europe and Africa, is part of the Atlantic Ocean. The word *sea* also refers to the ocean in general.

REVIEW How do ocean currents affect people?

The Water We Drink

Earth's ocean covers more than 140 million square miles (363 million sq km) and contains about 97 percent of all the water on Earth. The total water supply is huge.

With all of this water, it may be hard to imagine shortages. Yet more than 99 percent of the total water supply is unsafe for people to drink. This includes ocean water, which is too salty to drink.

Much of Earth's fresh water is out of reach. Frozen glaciers and ice caps contain about 70 percent of Earth's fresh water. Some fresh water floats around as water vapor in the air, and some exists as dampness in the soil. Only about 6 percent of Earth's fresh water is in lakes and rivers.

Fortunately, Earth's **water cycle** continuously replaces the supply of fresh water. As rain falls on the land, it soaks into the soil and collects underground.

Groundwater is water that is stored within Earth. When heavy rains occur, the soil cannot soak up all the water. Water that the soil does not soak up is called surface water. Surface water flows across the land in sheets and channels and collects in rivers, streams, and other bodies of water. Most of the water that humans use every day, about 80 percent of it, comes from surface water in freshwater rivers and lakes.

REVIEW How is the supply of fresh water continuously replaced?

Analyze Graphs The circle graph shows Earth's available fresh water in percents.

❓ Where is most of Earth's fresh water found?

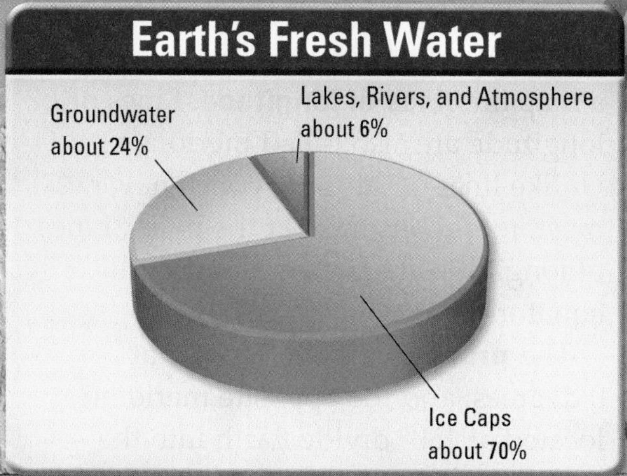

Earth's Fresh Water

Groundwater about 24%

Lakes, Rivers, and Atmosphere about 6%

Ice Caps about 70%

LESSON 2
REVIEW

1. **MAIN IDEA** What are three kinds of bodies of water, and how is each kind formed?

2. **WHY IT MATTERS** What are some of the ways in which water is important to our survival?

3. **VOCABULARY** Use the term **current** to describe transportation on the ocean.

4. **READING SKILL—Main Idea and Supporting Details** How do the waters of the ocean help support life on Earth?

5. **TECHNOLOGY** How is a reservoir made?

6. **CRITICAL THINKING—Analyze** What do you think would happen if the ice caps and glaciers were to melt?

PERFORMANCE—Draw a Map Find out more about a body of water or a waterway in or near your community, and draw a map of it. If it is a river, label its source, mouth, and tributaries. If it is a lake, tell whether it is natural or made by people.

Use Latitude and Longitude

VOCABULARY

line of latitude
equator
line of longitude
prime meridian

▶ WHY IT MATTERS

When you study geography, it is important to know exactly where places in the world are located. To show location, mapmakers draw lines of latitude and longitude as a grid on maps and globes. These lines, of course, do not exist on Earth. However, they make it possible for people to describe exact locations on Earth.

▶ WHAT YOU NEED TO KNOW

On a map the lines that run east and west are called **lines of latitude**. They are parallel, or always the same distance from each other.

Because they are parallel, lines of latitude never meet. Lines of latitude are measured in degrees north or south of the equator, which is labeled 0 degrees. The **equator** is an imaginary line that circles the Earth halfway between the North Pole and the South Pole. It divides the Earth into the Northern Hemisphere and the Southern Hemisphere.

Lines of latitude north of the equator are marked *N* for *north latitude*. For example, *30°N* refers to the line of

latitude in the Northern Hemisphere 30 degrees north of the equator. Lines of latitude south of the equator are marked *S* for *south latitude*.

The lines that run north and south on a map are **lines of longitude**. Lines of longitude are also called meridians. Unlike lines of latitude, which never meet, meridians meet at the poles. Lines of longitude are farthest apart at the equator.

The **prime meridian**, located at 0 degrees, and the opposite meridian located at 180° divide Earth into the Eastern Hemisphere and the Western Hemisphere. The prime meridian runs north and south through Greenwich, a city in Britain.

Lines of longitude west of the prime meridian, in the Western Hemisphere, are marked *W* for *west longitude*. Lines of longitude east of the prime meridian, in the Eastern Hemisphere, are marked *E* for *east longitude*. The 180° meridian is the dividing point for the Eastern Hemisphere and Western Hemisphere. This meridian runs north and south opposite to the prime meridian and through the Pacific Ocean.

Earth's Bodies of Water

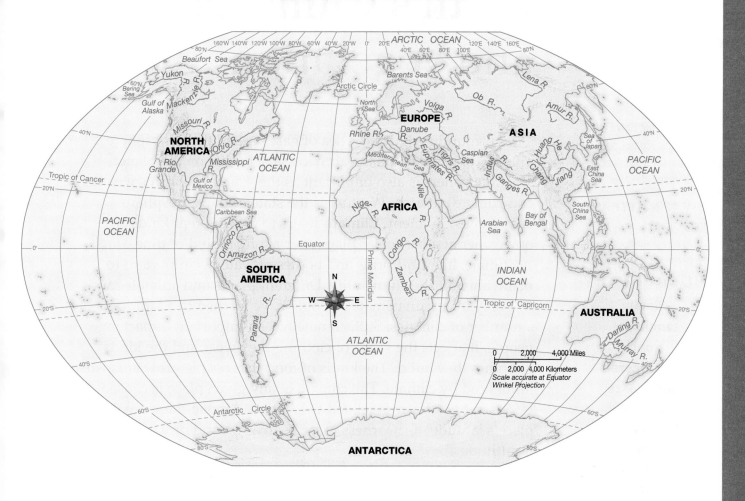

▶ PRACTICE THE SKILL

The map above shows the locations of Earth's major rivers and bodies of water. Lines of longitude and latitude form a grid on the map. Study this grid and answer the following questions:

1 In which ocean do the lines 20°S and 80°E cross?

2 Which rivers on the map are closest to the equator?

3 The prime meridian runs north and south through which ocean?

4 The Caspian Sea can be found between which two lines of longitude?

▶ APPLY WHAT YOU LEARNED

Use the map above to think of five more questions about latitude and longitude. Write your five questions on a sheet of paper. When you are finished, trade papers with a classmate and answer each other's questions.

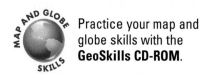

Practice your map and globe skills with the **GeoSkills CD-ROM**.

Earth's Climates and Vegetation

MAIN IDEA
Read to find out how Earth, the sun, the oceans, and wind interact to produce Earth's varied climates.

WHY IT MATTERS
Climate affects animals, plants, and people.

VOCABULARY

climate
temperate
tropic
sea breeze
land breeze
altitude
rain shadow
vegetation
rain forest
arid

Surrounding Earth is a sea of gases called the atmosphere. This sea of gases holds the air necessary for life on the planet. The atmosphere is also important as the source of Earth's weather and climate patterns. Weather is the state of the atmosphere at any given moment. **Climate** refers to the different kinds of weather at a particular place over a long period of time.

Climate, like landforms and bodies of water, is important to plant, animal, and human life. Different plants and animals can live only in certain climates. People have learned to adapt to a number of climates. Still, climate has an important impact on people. It affects the kinds of clothing they wear and the kinds of homes they build. The kinds of food that people grow are also influenced by climate. The climate of any given place is caused by a number of factors related to location. Among these are the place's latitude, its nearness to large areas of land or water, and its altitude above sea level.

The Effect of Latitude

How far north or south of the equator a place is located—its latitude—is important in determining climate. Because the surface of the planet is curved, the sun's rays hit Earth at different angles. Near the equator the sun's rays hit Earth's surface more vertically, or directly, than at other latitudes. These vertical rays concentrate a lot of heat into a small area. This makes climates near the equator hot or warm. Areas near the poles never receive vertical rays. As a result, the climate there is cold all year.

Areas in the middle latitudes receive vertical rays only part of the year, which creates the seasons. For this reason the areas at the middle latitudes are called temperate. In **temperate** places the overall climate is neither very hot nor very cold, although temperatures can be very hot or very cold at times, depending on the season.

FAST FACT — Groundhog Day is a tradition in the United States for predicting the arrival of spring. Similar traditions in Europe involve bears, badgers, and other animals.

The Change of Seasons

March 20 or 21
Spring in the Northern Hemisphere

December 21 or 22
Winter in the Northern Hemisphere

June 21 or 22
Summer in the Northern Hemisphere

September 22 or 23
Autumn in the Northern Hemisphere

Analyze Diagrams   **As Earth moves around the sun, the seasons change.**

❖ **When does winter begin in the Northern Hemisphere?**

Seasons occur because Earth is tilted on its axis 23.5 degrees in relation to Earth's path around the sun. This tilt exposes the Northern and Southern Hemispheres to the more vertical rays of the sun at different times of the year. When the Northern Hemisphere is tilted toward the sun, it is summer there. At the same time, it is winter in the Southern Hemisphere. When the Southern Hemisphere is tilted toward the sun, it is summer there and winter in the Northern Hemisphere.

Around June 22 the vertical rays of the sun hit Earth at 23.5° north latitude. This is the farthest north that vertical rays ever reach. This latitude is called the Tropic of Cancer. By December 22 the sun's rays are vertical at 23.5° south latitude, along the Tropic of Capricorn. The word **tropic** refers to the area on Earth at or near the equator.

REVIEW   **How does latitude affect climate on Earth?**

The Effect of Land and Water

Another important effect on climate is the heating and cooling differences between land and water. Land heats more quickly than bodies of water. It also cools more quickly. Water takes longer to warm up, but it stays warm longer. As a result, places in the middle of a large continent are likely to be much colder than places along the coast.

Ocean currents also affect the temperatures of some land areas. One example is the North Atlantic Drift. This current brings warm temperatures to Western Europe as it flows across the Atlantic Ocean from the Gulf of Mexico. Without the effect of this ocean current, Western Europe would have a much colder climate.

The differences in the heating and cooling of land and water also cause winds. During daylight hours, air over land is heated more quickly than air over water. Cooler air from the water blows in and pushes the warmer air up. The result is known as a **sea breeze**.

At night, the land cools more quickly than the water. Warmer air over the water is pushed up by the cooler air blowing out from the land. This is a **land breeze**.

REVIEW How do land and water affect climate?

Analyze Diagrams **Prevailing winds result from the general circulation of air around Earth.**

❖ **Which winds blow across North America from west to east?**

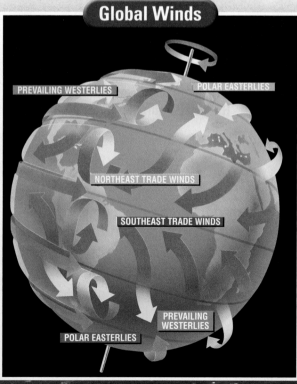

Global Winds

PREVAILING WESTERLIES
POLAR EASTERLIES
NORTHEAST TRADE WINDS
SOUTHEAST TRADE WINDS
PREVAILING WESTERLIES
POLAR EASTERLIES

The Effect of Altitude

A third major effect on climate is the elevation, or **altitude**, of landforms above sea level. Going up a mountain is something like moving from the equator to one of the poles. The air temperature gets cooler the higher you go. For every 1,000 feet (305 m) of altitude, the temperature drops almost 3°F (1.7°C).

Because of the effects of altitude, it is possible to find a place with a cold climate in a larger region with a warm climate. Tanzania in East Africa mostly has a warm climate. However, snow and ice all year long cover the top of Mount Kilimanjaro (kih•luh•muhn•JAHR•oh). The climate at the top is highland.

Altitude has another effect on climate, in addition to temperature change. As air moves up one side of a mountain, it cools. As a result, clouds form and precipitation falls. This side of the mountain, where the air is moving up, receives a lot of rain or snow. The other side, however, receives little. As the air moves down the other side of the mountain, it warms up. It then absorbs moisture from the surrounding land. This drier side of the mountain is often said to be in the **rain shadow**.

REVIEW How does altitude affect climate?

Sailboat racing near Hawaii

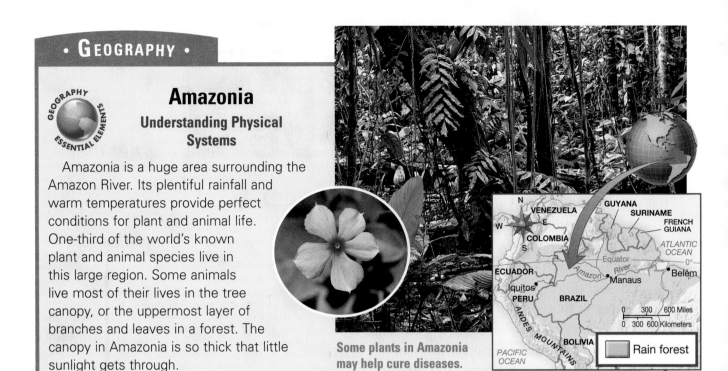

Amazonia
Understanding Physical Systems

Amazonia is a huge area surrounding the Amazon River. Its plentiful rainfall and warm temperatures provide perfect conditions for plant and animal life. One-third of the world's known plant and animal species live in this large region. Some animals live most of their lives in the tree canopy, or the uppermost layer of branches and leaves in a forest. The canopy in Amazonia is so thick that little sunlight gets through.

Some plants in Amazonia may help cure diseases.

Climate and Vegetation

Although no two places on Earth have exactly the same climate, our planet can be divided into six major climate regions— tropical, desert, temperate warm, temperate cold, polar, and highland. Each region has its own climate patterns and its own kinds of plant life, or **vegetation**.

Most of Earth's tropical climates are along or near the equator, as far north as the Tropic of Cancer and as far south as the Tropic of Capricorn. Tropical climates are generally warm all year round and have a lot of precipitation.

Rain forests with thick vegetation and tall trees exist in many areas of the tropical climate region. The largest rain forests are in the areas surrounding the Amazon River in South America and the Congo River in Central Africa, and on the islands of Indonesia and Malaysia in Southeast Asia. In these places the average yearly temperature is close to 80°F (27°C). Rainfall may reach as much as 100 inches (256 cm) a year.

Desert climates are found in areas where there is little precipitation for the whole year. These places are considered **arid**, or dry. An area that receives 10 inches (25 cm) or less of precipitation in a year is considered a desert. Deserts can be either hot or cold, but all deserts are dry.

To survive in a desert climate, vegetation has adapted to the arid surroundings. Some plants have leaves and stems that store much water. Others have long root systems that reach water over a large area. Most desert plants grow far apart from each other so they do not compete for the same water supply.

The major difference between tropical and desert climates is precipitation. In temperate warm and temperate cold climates, the major difference is temperature.

Temperate climates are generally found in the temperate zones, away from the equator and the North and South Poles. A temperate warm climate is influenced chiefly by water, and a temperate cold climate is affected by land.

Areas with a temperate cold climate are mostly inland. In this kind of climate, big changes in temperature take place from summer to winter, and there are about the same amounts of precipitation all year. Temperate cold climates support a variety of trees that grow in thick forests.

Temperate warm climates are found along coastal areas near oceans and seas. Two kinds of temperate warm climates are marine and Mediterranean. The word *marine* refers to the sea. Marine climates are warm and generally damp or wet. Mediterranean climates are named for the sea between Africa and Europe. Around the Mediterranean Sea many areas of land are warm and mostly dry. Other areas of Mediterranean climate are found in California, part of Chile in South America, southern Australia, and Southern Africa.

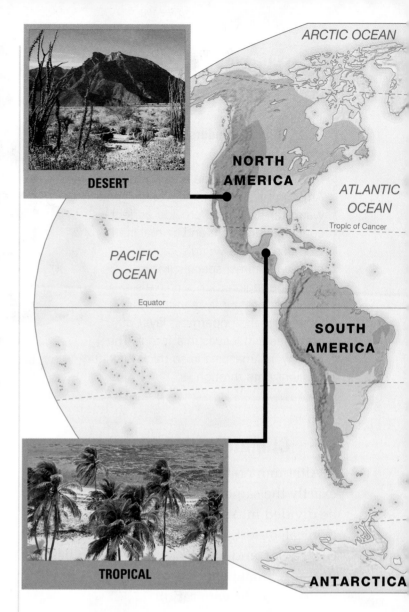

DESERT

TROPICAL

ARCTIC OCEAN

NORTH AMERICA

ATLANTIC OCEAN

Tropic of Cancer

PACIFIC OCEAN

Equator

SOUTH AMERICA

ANTARCTICA

North and south of the temperate zones are regions with a polar climate. The name *polar* comes from their location near the North and South Poles. A polar climate is the opposite of a tropical climate. A tropical climate has no winters. A polar climate has no summers. In some parts of a polar climate, mosses and some grasses grow. In other parts, there is no vegetation at all.

Places in hilly or mountainous regions have a highland climate. This kind of climate cannot be defined exactly. Temperature, precipitation, and vegetation may all vary depending on altitude, the main winds, and the rain shadow.

REVIEW **What is the relationship between climate and vegetation?**

Climate Regions

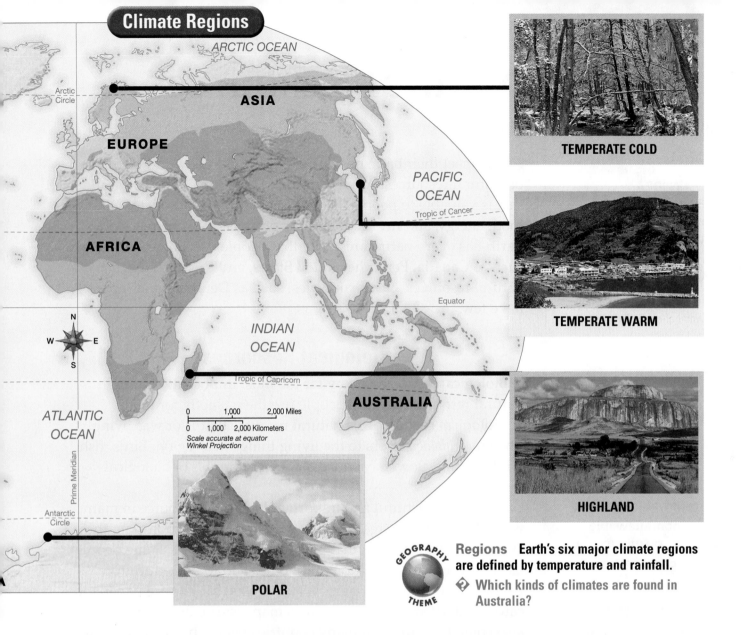

ARCTIC OCEAN

ASIA

EUROPE

AFRICA

PACIFIC OCEAN

Arctic Circle

Tropic of Cancer

Equator

INDIAN OCEAN

ATLANTIC OCEAN

Tropic of Capricorn

AUSTRALIA

0   1,000   2,000 Miles
0   1,000   2,000 Kilometers
Scale accurate at equator
Winkel Projection

Antarctic Circle

Prime Meridian

N W E S

TEMPERATE COLD

TEMPERATE WARM

HIGHLAND

POLAR

GEOGRAPHY THEME

Regions Earth's six major climate regions are defined by temperature and rainfall.

◈ Which kinds of climates are found in Australia?

LESSON 3 REVIEW

1 **MAIN IDEA** How do Earth and the sun work together to affect climate?

2 **WHY IT MATTERS** How can climate information help people adapt to their physical surroundings?

3 **VOCABULARY** What is the difference between a **sea breeze** and a **land breeze**?

4 **READING SKILL—Main Idea and Supporting Details** What are the general characteristics of the six major climate regions?

5 **GEOGRAPHY** How do the heating and cooling differences between land and water affect us?

6 **GEOGRAPHY** Why is it generally warmer near the equator than it is near Earth's poles?

7 **CRITICAL THINKING—Synthesize** When it is summer in the United States, it is winter in Australia. Why is this so? Use what you know about Earth's revolution and the tilt of Earth's axis to explain.

PERFORMANCE—Make a Brochure Describe your climate region in a travel brochure. List the kinds of weather, temperatures, precipitation, and vegetation common to your region. In your brochure, describe the advantages and disadvantages of living in your region. Draw pictures to illustrate your brochure.

4

MAIN IDEA
Read to learn about Earth's natural resources and why they are important to people.

WHY IT MATTERS
The use and management of natural resources around the world affect both countries and individuals.

VOCABULARY

natural resource
biological resource
fertile soil
mineral
fossil fuel
renewable resource
nonrenewable resource
conservation
scarce
recycling

As people cut down trees for their use (below), new trees are planted for future use (inset).

Natural Resources

To meet their basic needs, people around the world depend on natural resources. A **natural resource** is something in nature that is valuable to people. People use natural resources to make food, energy, and raw materials for products. No one place on Earth has every natural resource that people use. Some countries, such as Canada, Peru, the United States, and Russia, have many natural resources. Other countries, such as Denmark and Japan, have few.

Biological Resources

Biological resources are by far the most important kind of natural resources because people use them chiefly for food. A **biological resource** is a natural resource that is or was living. The word *biology* refers to the living things in a region. Birds, fish, wild animals, flowers, and trees are all examples of biological resources.

Trees are a plentiful and important biological resource in many ways. People value trees because they absorb pollution from the air and produce oxygen that people need to breathe. Some people use the wood from trees to build homes and to make furniture. People make wood into pulp, which is used to produce paper and cardboard. Products as different as maple syrup and paint thinner also come from trees. In many countries people burn wood from trees to heat their homes and cook their food.

Just as people depend on biological resources, biological resources depend on other natural resources. Most plants

Land Use and Resources Around the World

Legend:
- Ⓑ Bauxite
- 🪨 Coal
- Copper
- Diamonds
- Emeralds
- Ⓖ Gold
- Iron
- Ⓛ Lead
- Natural Gas
- Oil
- Ⓟ Platinum
- Ⓢ Silver
- Ⓣ Tin
- Zn Zinc

- Manufacturing
- Farming
- Grazing
- Forests
- Little-used land
- Fishing
- Nomadic herding
- Hunting and gathering

Scale accurate at equator
Winkel Projection

Human-Environment Interactions The natural resources of an area can affect the way people use the land.

❖ What mineral resources are mined in Africa?

and animals cannot live without air, sunshine, and water. Living things also depend on soil as a direct or indirect source of food. Plants use the sun's energy to make food, and they obtain nourishing substances from the soil through their roots. People and animals then get nourishment by eating the plants.

Soil is a plentiful resource that covers much of Earth's land surface. In places with **fertile soil**, or soil that is good for growing crops, people generally do not worry about having enough food to eat. Where soil is not fertile, a lack of food can make people's lives difficult. Places that cannot produce enough food often need to get it from somewhere else.

REVIEW How do people use biological resources?

Mineral and Fuel Resources

Minerals are another important kind of natural resource. A **mineral** is a natural resource found in rocks, the solid material from which Earth is made. There are more than 3,000 kinds of minerals, but only about 100 are common and used by people. People use minerals to make products. For example, people use graphite to make pencils. Other products made from minerals include cement for building, fertilizers for farming, and chemicals for manufacturing.

Many people use the term *mineral* for any substance taken from Earth and used by people. These minerals include fossil fuels, such as coal, natural gas, and petroleum. A **fossil fuel** is a natural resource used to provide heat and other energy.

The gold (left) was taken from a deep underground mine in Canada.

People use fossil fuels to cook food, heat buildings, and power machines.

Like most minerals, fossil fuels were formed long ago deep within Earth. Fossil fuels, however, are not made of rocks. They were formed from prehistoric plant and animal remains that were buried and under pressure for a long time.

People gather fossil fuels by mining or drilling in Earth's crust. Miners and oil workers in such countries as Norway, Saudi Arabia, the United States, and Venezuela bring fossil fuels to the surface. These fossil fuels are made into products that people use. Some families in India, for example, use coal or natural gas to heat their homes and cook their food. Drivers in Germany and in other places around the world use the gasoline and motor oil made from petroleum to run their automobiles. In addition to using fossil fuels for energy, people use them to produce paint, aspirin, carpets, and just about everything made of plastic.

REVIEW How do people use mineral and fossil fuel resources?

Renewable and Nonrenewable Resources

All natural resources can be described as either renewable or nonrenewable. A **renewable resource** can be made again by nature or by people in a practical amount of time. A **nonrenewable resource** is one that takes too long to replace or cannot be replaced at all.

Fresh water is an important natural resource that is automatically renewed in nature by the water cycle. Another renewable resource that people depend on is soil. Earth's natural processes always create more soil. Weathering by wind, ice, and rain breaks rock into smaller pieces that become part of new soil. When trees, leaves, plants, and animals die, they too contribute to renewing soil by adding nourishing substances and by helping soil hold moisture.

Nature replaces renewable natural resources. However, often they are not replaced as fast as people use them. If the people living in a place use fresh water faster than the water cycle replaces it, water might become limited, or **scarce**, there. People also might cut down thousands of trees in a forest. It would take years for new trees to grow back. If people do not plant seedlings, other vegetation might replace the trees.

To prevent renewable natural resources from becoming limited or used up completely, people can take certain actions. For example, people can conserve them, or keep them from being lost or wasted. Examples of **conservation** include planting new trees to replace the ones cut down or using less water to allow the water cycle to recover.

Conservation is particularly important for nonrenewable resources such as fossil fuels. Although they were produced naturally, the process took thousands of years. As a result, Earth contains a limited supply of fossil fuels.

To save even more natural resources, many people and communities around the world recycle. **Recycling** is a process designed to recover and reuse materials instead of throwing them away. The most common materials for recycling include aluminum and steel cans, glass and plastic containers, and paper, particularly newspaper. Other recycling programs collect petroleum products, including used motor oil and automobile tires.

Recycled wastes provide materials for a variety of products.

In Germany special bins are used for collecting materials to recycle.

Manufacturers use aluminum and steel from recycled cans to make new cans and other metal products. Recycled paper is used not only in making paper and cardboard but also in manufacturing building materials, such as insulation and plasterboard. Manufacturers grind up old glass and use it to make new glass containers or materials used in making roads and highways. Some plastic containers are melted and molded into new plastic products. Recycled motor oil is used as industrial fuel oil. Recycled tires are made into shoes and playground surfaces.

REVIEW **Why is it important to use natural resources wisely?**

Many businesses and industries recycle office waste, such as paper and cardboard.

Using Old Resources in New Ways

In addition to conservation and recycling, some people look for new ways to meet the demand for resources. One way is to make better use of previously underused resources, especially for providing energy. The sun, the wind, and the oceans are among those resources.

Solar, or sun, power can provide heat for people's use. In a solar-powered house, the sun might heat water stored inside panels on the roof. Once warmed, that water may heat the house or provide hot water for bathing and cleaning. On a large scale, many solar panels concentrate heat to turn water into steam. This steam then turns machinery that generates electricity. This is a clean way to produce energy because little pollution is created.

The wind is another source of clean energy. People have used the power of wind for centuries. In the Netherlands, people would grind grain and pump water by using energy from windmills. Today places around the world gather wind power. Air flowing over the blades of a special engine called a turbine causes the blades to turn and produce electricity. However, wind energy can be unreliable and is not available everywhere.

There is a similar problem of availability in using ocean tides as an energy resource. Tidal energy, as it is called, comes from the energy of water as it flows from high tide to low tide. Energy is captured in a dam built across a bay. As the ocean tide rises, the bay fills with water and the dam is closed to hold in the water. At low tide, the stored water is released through a turbine in order to generate electricity. The chief disadvantage of tidal energy is that dams can be built in only a few places.

REVIEW How are the sun, the wind, and the tides being used as energy resources?

Why Natural Resources Matter

How valuable a resource is usually depends on how much there is and how many people want it. Because of this, natural resources have value. Some natural resources, such as water, are so valuable that people cannot live without them. The value of mineral resources such as gold and silver, which are scarce and in demand, is usually great.

Having plentiful natural resources can give a group of people independence. If a group has the resources it needs, then it does not have to trade with other groups. However, one group of people rarely has all of the natural resources it needs. A natural resource that is scarce in one part of the world might be abundant in another. Through trade with each other, groups can meet their needs.

Wind turbines such as these in California produce electricity for use in homes and businesses.

LOCATE IT

Alameda County

CALIFORNIA

How people use and manage natural resources affects everyone around the world. People might cut down forests in one country to create a field for growing crops. A rare type of plant that grew only in that forest could then die and become extinct. Any benefits that people might have gotten from that plant, such as life-saving medicine, would be lost forever.

REVIEW How do groups that lack natural resources meet their needs?

Electric cars (inset) and solar-powered satellites show how technology can help people make better use of resources.

LESSON 4
REVIEW

1. **MAIN IDEA** What are three kinds of natural resources that people use?

2. **WHY IT MATTERS** What natural resources do you depend on most? Explain.

3. **VOCABULARY** What are **fossil fuels** and how are they produced?

4. **READING SKILL—Main Idea and Supporting Details** Why do people value natural resources?

5. **GEOGRAPHY** How are renewable resources such as trees and fertile soil replaced?

6. **TECHNOLOGY** How can underused resources create clean energy?

7. **CRITICAL THINKING—Hypothesize** Imagine that one group of people controlled all of a nonrenewable resource, such as oil. How might this control affect the lives of all the other people on Earth?

PERFORMANCE—Make a Prediction Picture yourself as a scientist. Write a speech in which you make predictions about the future use of resources. Include information about the importance of conservation, recycling, and the possible use of alternative forms of energy.

·SKILLS· Solve a Problem

CITIZENSHIP

▶ WHY IT MATTERS

Today people have to face the fact that some natural resources may someday be gone. The limited supply of nonrenewable resources is a problem that affects the whole world. For example, much of the energy that people use to provide electricity and to operate motor vehicles comes from fossil fuels such as coal and petroleum. Because they are nonrenewable, these fossil fuels will someday run out. In recent years people have found new ways to produce energy from renewable sources such as rivers, the sun, and the wind. Like any problem, the problem of finding other sources of energy is easier to tackle if it is broken down into steps.

▶ WHAT YOU NEED TO KNOW

Listed below are some steps you can follow to solve problems, large or small.

Step 1 Identify the problem. Get a clear idea of the problem. You may want to state the problem as a question.

Step 2 Think of possible solutions. Come up with at least two solutions that might work.

Step 3 Look at the facts of the situation, and compare how each solution would work. After taking a close look at the situation, you can usually rule out the solutions that are not the best choices.

Step 4 Plan a way to carry out the solution. Come up with a plan to put the solution into action.

Step 5 Evaluate the solution, and think about how well it solves the problem. It is important to try out any solution to make sure it actually does the job of solving the problem.

A solar panel uses the sun's rays to make electricity.

Facts About Rajasthan

LAND AND CLIMATE

More than half desert.

Temperatures range from 68°F to 108°F.

Between 250 and 300 sunny days per year.

RIVERS AND WATER

Only one major river flows year-round.

Water is scarce in much of the region.

WINDS

Hot winds and dust storms sometimes occur in desert areas.

From April to October, seasonal winds blow and bring rainfall to the non-desert parts of Rajasthan.

Windmills harness the power of the wind.

➡ PRACTICE THE SKILL

The state of Rajasthan in northwestern India is looking for a way to harness a clean, renewable resource (such as water, wind, or sun) to reduce its dependence on fossil fuels. Use what you have learned in the lesson and the information contained in the table to find the best solution to Rajasthan's search for a clean, renewable source of energy.

1 What problem does Rajasthan have? What are some possible solutions?

2 What are the facts about Rajasthan? How might each solution work? How would you carry out the solution you think is best?

3 Why do you think your solution is the best way to solve Rajasthan's problem?

➡ APPLY WHAT YOU LEARNED

Think of a resource-related problem in your community or state. Use the problem-solving steps to come up with a solution. Write an e-mail to a friend and describe the problem. Discuss the advantages and disadvantages of possible solutions, and explain why you think the solution you chose is the best.

Dams capture the energy of flowing rivers.

Review and Test Preparation

Complete this graphic organizer to show that you understand how to identify the main idea and supporting details for each lesson of Chapter 1. A copy of this graphic organizer appears on page 14 of the Activity Book.

Main Ideas About the World's Geography

MAIN IDEA → DETAILS

Lesson 1 Main Idea: Earth's landforms have been shaped and reshaped over time.

Detail: _____

Detail: _____

Detail: _____

Lesson 2 Main Idea: Earth's bodies of water support life on the planet.

Detail: _____

Detail: _____

Detail: _____

The World's Geography

Lesson 3 Main Idea: The Earth, the sun, the oceans, and the wind interact to produce Earth's varied climates.

Detail: _____

Detail: _____

Detail: _____

Lesson 4 Main Idea: Earth's natural resources are important to people.

Detail: _____

Detail: _____

Detail: _____

THINK & WRITE

Write a Speech   Think about some items your family uses every day. Can some of these items be recycled or reused in other ways? Write a speech describing how an item that you would normally throw away can be reused. Deliver this speech to your family or classmates.

Write a Tall Tale   A tall tale is a story that explains how something happened in a way that is impossible. Create a tall tale that explains how mountains are formed. When you are finished, write a paragraph that describes how mountains are actually formed.

USE VOCABULARY

Identify the term that correctly matches each definition.

fault (p. 22)
trench (p. 29)
temperate (p. 34)
altitude (p. 36)
mineral (p. 41)

1 a deep ocean valley

2 a natural resource found in rocks

3 a break in Earth's crust where movement occurs

4 the elevation of landforms above sea level

5 a climate that is neither very hot nor very cold

RECALL FACTS

Answer these questions.

6 How are volcanoes formed?

7 Why were many of the world's first settlements developed along rivers?

8 What is the world's largest ocean? How many square miles does it cover?

Write the letter of the best choice.

9 **TEST PREP** People adapt to different kinds of climates by doing all of the following *except*—
A wearing different kinds of clothing.
B building different kinds of homes.
C growing different kinds of foods.
D living on a boat.

10 **TEST PREP** All of Earth's tropical climates are found—
F near the poles.
G in South America.
H between the Tropic of Cancer and the Tropic of Capricorn.
J in the oceans.

11 **TEST PREP** All of the following are renewable resources *except*—
A fresh water.
B fossil fuels.
C trees.
D fertile soil.

12 **TEST PREP** The sun, the wind, and the ocean tides produce energy that is—
F clean.
G very reliable.
H nonrenewable.
J available everywhere.

THINK CRITICALLY

13 Which climate do you think is the best climate to live in? Why?

14 What do you think would happen if there were no renewable resources on Earth?

APPLY SKILLS

Use Latitude and Longitude

15 Use the map on page 33 to find which continents the equator passes through and which continents the prime meridian passes through.

Solve a Problem

16 Read a recent print or online article to find out about a problem that exists in your community or somewhere else in the world. Use the problem-solving steps on page 46 to come up with possible solutions to this problem.

LONGSHENG, CHINA

People often have to adapt to or modify the environment in which they live. Long ago, Chinese farmers carved "steps" into the mountain slopes of Guangxi Province to create needed farmland. Today, farmers still use this method for growing crops.

LOCATE IT

CHINA

Longsheng

2

Patterns of Life

"The most incomprehensible thing about the world is that it is comprehensible."
—Albert Einstein, from an article in the *New York Times*, April 1955

CHAPTER READING SKILL

Generalize

To **generalize** means to make a broad statement based on information that includes many details. This broad statement can then be applied to other situations. Words such as *many, some, most,* and *usually* often signal generalizations.

As you read this chapter, use facts and details from each lesson to generalize.

FACTS + DETAILS GENERALIZATION

MAIN IDEA
Read to find out the reasons people moved to and settled in certain regions.

WHY IT MATTERS
Geography has often influenced patterns of populations in regions.

VOCABULARY

population distribution
environment
irrigation
desertification
drought
migration
urbanization
metropolitan area
demographer

Population and Settlement

The world's population includes all the human beings everywhere on Earth. However, for many reasons, the human population is spread, or distributed, very unevenly over Earth's surface. The **population distribution** is the way the population is spread out over the land. Some areas are heavily populated while others have few people or none. Taken as a whole, the world has four centers of population with the greatest numbers of people. These are East Asia, South Asia, Europe, and eastern North America. Each has its own settlement pattern. Of all the continents, only Antarctica has no permanent human population.

People, Climate, and Vegetation

Have you ever wondered why there are no cities or towns in Antarctica? Several reasons are the harsh climate, the rugged land, and the lack of fertile soil, all of which make it difficult for anyone to live there. People, in general, have difficulty living in extreme **environments**, or surroundings. The environment and the ability of people to live in it have influenced human settlement patterns.

FAST FACT Antarctica was first sighted by European explorers in 1820. In 1959 twelve countries signed a treaty to use the continent for research.

On February 11, 2001, Liv Arnesen and Ann Bancroft became the first women to cross the continent of Antarctica.

No place on Earth has a completely perfect environment for human beings. People must adapt to every region in which they live. The most obvious example of people adapting to an environment is the clothing they wear. People living in polar and highland climates need heavy sweaters and coats, while people in tropical and hot desert climates can wear lightweight clothing all year round.

People also adapt by building different kinds of homes. In Greenland, for example, many homes have few windows and doors, to keep out cold winds. In contrast, homes on the tropical island of Samoa in the Pacific Ocean have many openings. This allows cool sea breezes to blow through the homes.

People also adapt to their environment by shaping it to fit their needs. Today many people in cold climates, such as Greenland, live comfortably by using heaters. Life in tropical and hot desert climates is made more comfortable because of air conditioning.

Because of modern methods of heating and cooling, people have been able to settle in places once considered too extreme. The desert is a good example. Once viewed as only a dry, rocky, and sandy place, some desert land now supports growing cities and sprawling farms. The western United States cities of Los Angeles, Phoenix, and Las Vegas are among the fastest-growing cities in the country. Desert cities are also common in the Southwest Asian country of Saudi Arabia.

To create cities or farms in the desert, people have developed systems of irrigation. **Irrigation** is the use of connected ditches, canals, or pipes to move water to dry areas.

However, using desert land is a growing challenge because desert regions are

LOCATE IT

IRELAND

Dingle

The temperate climate of Ireland helps keep its countryside green.

expanding. This expansion occurs because of the continual loss of fertile soil, farming land, and forests on the outskirts of deserts. The loss occurs chiefly from destroying plant life by overgrazing, overfarming, or cutting down trees and not replanting. The change of fertile land into desert land is called **desertification**.

In the 1930s, farmers in parts of the Middle West had farmed the land too much. In addition, **drought**, or long periods of dry weather, in much of the region caused fertile soil to blow away. The region came to be called the Dust Bowl. As a result, many people who had made their living by farming in the region had to move to other places.

REVIEW How do people adapt to climate?

People have adapted their clothing to Bermuda's warm climate.

People, Land, and Water

The physical features of land and water also affect population distribution. Landforms and bodies of water limit the number of people who can live in a place. For example, it is easier for people to live on flat land near water than on the tops of mountains.

The greatest numbers of people in East Asia are in the country of China. China has more people than any other country in the world. Most live along the three major river valleys of eastern China—the Chang Jiang, Huang He (HWAHNG HUH), and the Xi Jiang (YEE JYAHNG). Concentrations of people in East Asia are also found on the eastern coast of China, the Korea Peninsula, and the islands of Japan.

India is the center for population in South Asia. India is the second-most populous country in the world. There, the largest numbers of people are found in the Ganges River valley in northern India. There is also a large concentration of people in South Asia at the mouth of the Ganges in the country of Bangladesh.

The third-largest concentration of people on Earth is in Europe. One of Europe's largest clusters of people is in central and southern England. Another cluster stretches along the Great European Plain. It begins on the southern coast of the North Sea, in the countries of the Netherlands and Belgium, and extends along the Rhine River between France and Germany. This same cluster extends farther east through Central Europe as far as the Dnieper (NEE•per) River in Ukraine. Northern Italy and southern France also contain large concentrations of people.

LOCATE IT

Venice

ITALY

In Venice, Italy, canals replace streets.

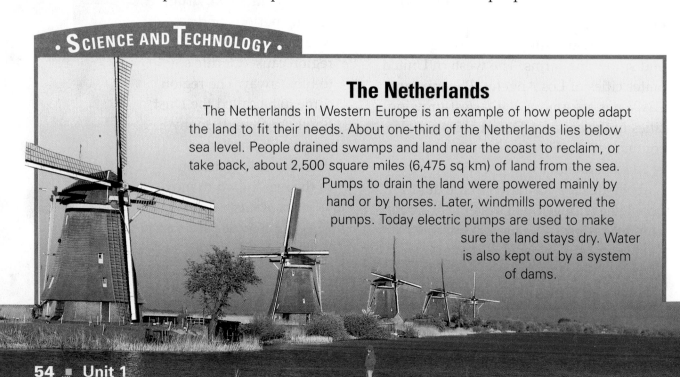

• SCIENCE AND TECHNOLOGY •

The Netherlands

The Netherlands in Western Europe is an example of how people adapt the land to fit their needs. About one-third of the Netherlands lies below sea level. People drained swamps and land near the coast to reclaim, or take back, about 2,500 square miles (6,475 sq km) of land from the sea. Pumps to drain the land were powered mainly by hand or by horses. Later, windmills powered the pumps. Today electric pumps are used to make sure the land stays dry. Water is also kept out by a system of dams.

World Population

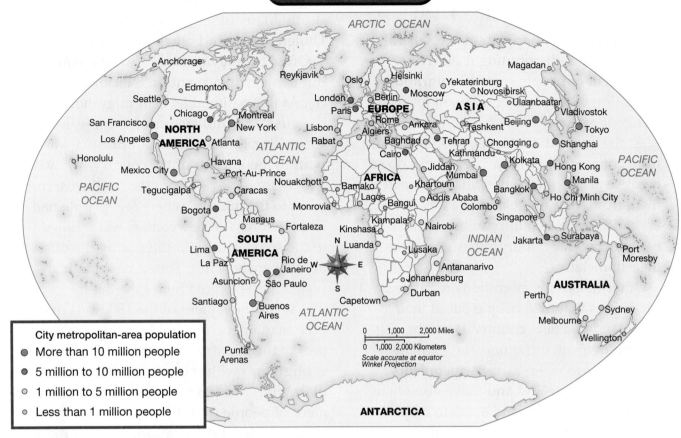

City metropolitan-area population
- ● More than 10 million people
- ● 5 million to 10 million people
- ○ 1 million to 5 million people
- · Less than 1 million people

Location The world's four largest centers of population are in East Asia, South Asia, Europe, and eastern North America.

❖ **What is similar about their locations?**

The largest concentration of people in North America is in the northeastern part of the United States and in southeastern Canada. A desert climate and rugged mountains are two factors that have limited population and settlement in the western part of the continent.

Of the remaining continents, Africa supports the largest population. One large cluster of people in Africa is in the Nile River valley. Other clusters are found around the large lakes of East Africa and along the northern, southern, and western coasts.

South America as a whole is lightly populated compared to many other areas of the world. Its population distribution has a pattern that follows the edge of the continent. The largest numbers of people in South America are along the southeastern coast, on the Atlantic Ocean.

A similar pattern of population distribution occurs in Australia, where the population is concentrated along the eastern and southern coasts, with few people in the middle.

REVIEW What geographic features make places easy for people to live in?

Not far from Ho Chi Minh City, Vietnam, a farmer tosses rice to clean it.

People on the Move

Earth's human population is constantly moving and redistributing itself. This movement of people is called **migration**. Migration takes place at different levels for different reasons.

At the international level, people migrate from country to country. They might do so because of conditions that attract, or *pull*, them from their homeland to a new place. Perhaps the new country offers them better economic opportunities than does their homeland.

Other causes for migration are unpleasant conditions that *push* people out of their homeland to a new country. Drought, unemployment, or famine—an extreme shortage of food—may cause people to leave their homeland and move elsewhere. During the 1800s Ireland's potato crop failed for several years in a row. Because of this, food in Ireland became scarce and large numbers of Irish people starved to death. Many others moved to Britain, the United States, and other countries.

Often people move not to a new country but to a new place within their own country. At this national level of migration, the push and pull factors also apply. In the 1950s Brazil's new capital of Brasília was built in the interior of the country. Many people then moved from the southeastern coast to the interior, where few people had lived before. The newcomers were pulled to the sparsely settled interior by the offer of inexpensive land. The same thing happened in the United States during the westward movement of the 1800s. At that time many people moved from the eastern part of the country to the West.

Migration within countries also takes place from rural to urban areas. The movement of people from the countryside to the cities is called **urbanization**. All over the world, people have been moving to cities.

Analyze Tables The world's largest metropolitan areas have populations of more than 10 million.

How many more people live in Tokyo than in New York City?

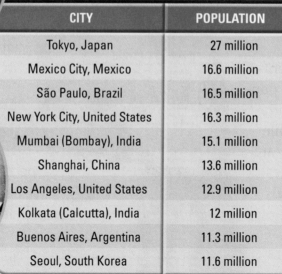

World's Largest Metropolitan Areas	
CITY	POPULATION
Tokyo, Japan	27 million
Mexico City, Mexico	16.6 million
São Paulo, Brazil	16.5 million
New York City, United States	16.3 million
Mumbai (Bombay), India	15.1 million
Shanghai, China	13.6 million
Los Angeles, United States	12.9 million
Kolkata (Calcutta), India	12 million
Buenos Aires, Argentina	11.3 million
Seoul, South Korea	11.6 million

Villagers carry firewood across the Kali Gandaki River in Nepal.

LOCATE IT

NEPAL

Tatopani

Some move because of the difficulty they have in making a living by farming. Others are attracted to city life by the economic opportunities of better jobs and more income for their families.

As a result of urbanization, the largest concentrations of people are now in the world's **metropolitan areas**—the big cities and the sprawling suburbs that surround them. Tokyo in Japan already has more than 20 million people living there. **Demographers**, or population geographers, predict that Mexico City in Mexico, São Paulo in Brazil, New York City in the United States, and Mumbai in India will become just as large.

This increase in population is due partly to migration. Also, more people are born every day, and advances in health care and nutrition have meant that people are living longer. Demographers estimate that the world's population is more than 6 billion today and will grow to more than 8 billion by the year 2020. However, many factors that can affect future trends in world population growth need to be considered.

REVIEW What are some push and pull factors that cause migration?

LESSON 1 REVIEW

1. **MAIN IDEA** What are four reasons people have moved to and settled certain regions?

2. **WHY IT MATTERS** How do climate and landforms affect population in your community?

3. **VOCABULARY** Explain how **migration** and **urbanization** are related.

4. **READING SKILL—Generalize** Why have cities grown in size over the years?

5. **GEOGRAPHY** Why do most desert areas not have large populations?

6. **TECHNOLOGY** How is irrigation used to bring water to dry areas?

7. **TECHNOLOGY** What are some ways people adapt to the climates in which they live?

8. **CRITICAL THINKING—Analyze** From what you know about climate and landforms, which would have a larger population, a northern city in the mountains or a southern city along the coast? Explain your answer.

 PERFORMANCE—Create a Poster Make a poster that tells about your region. In this poster, explain why people would like living where you do. Include pictures or illustrations and a list of your region's benefits.

Read a Population Map

VOCABULARY

thematic map
population density

WHY IT MATTERS

Sometimes geographers use thematic maps to show different kinds of information. **Thematic maps** focus on one geographic theme, or subject. One kind of thematic map used by geographers is a population map. Knowing how to read a population map will make it easier for you to find out which parts of the world are most crowded and which parts are least crowded.

WHAT YOU NEED TO KNOW

You may live in a large city, a small town, or in an area with few people. Each kind of place has a different population density. **Population density** is the number of people who live in an area of a certain size. The size is usually 1 square mile or 1 square kilometer. You can find population density by dividing the number of people living on a given amount of land by the area of that land. For example, if 2,000 people live on 10 square miles (26 sq km) of land, the population density is 200 people per square mile.

Look at the map key on the map on these pages. It tells you which colors on the map stand for different population densities. On the map key, red stands for the most crowded areas—more than 250 people per square mile. Light tan stands for one of the least crowded areas—2 or fewer people per square mile.

Notice that the world's population is not spread out evenly. Where people live close together, population is *dense*. Where people live far apart, population is *sparse*.

World Population

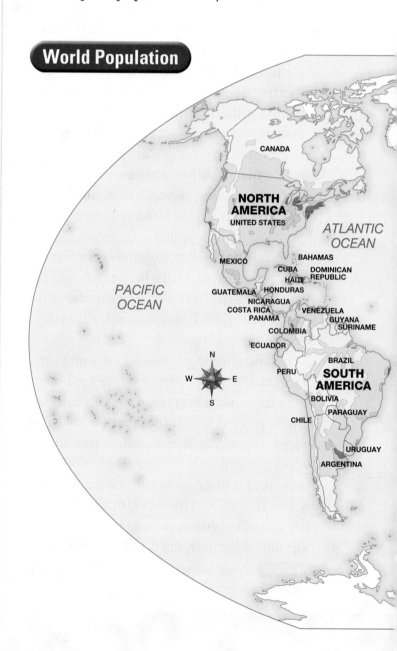

CANADA

NORTH AMERICA
UNITED STATES

ATLANTIC OCEAN

PACIFIC OCEAN

BAHAMAS
MEXICO
CUBA   DOMINICAN REPUBLIC
HAITI
GUATEMALA   HONDURAS
NICARAGUA
COSTA RICA   VENEZUELA
PANAMA   GUYANA
SURINAME
COLOMBIA
ECUADOR

BRAZIL
PERU   SOUTH AMERICA
BOLIVIA
PARAGUAY
CHILE

URUGUAY
ARGENTINA

PRACTICE THE SKILL

Study the map and the map key to answer these questions.

1 Which continent on the map has the lowest population density?

2 Which continent on the map has the highest population density?

3 Find the country of India on the map. Is India's overall population density higher or lower than Canada's?

APPLY WHAT YOU LEARNED

Refer to the Atlas at the front of this book on pages A4–A21. Using the population map below, find on each continent one city that lies in a densely populated area. Make a list of these cities and share it with the class.

Practice your map and globe skills with the **GeoSkills CD-ROM**.

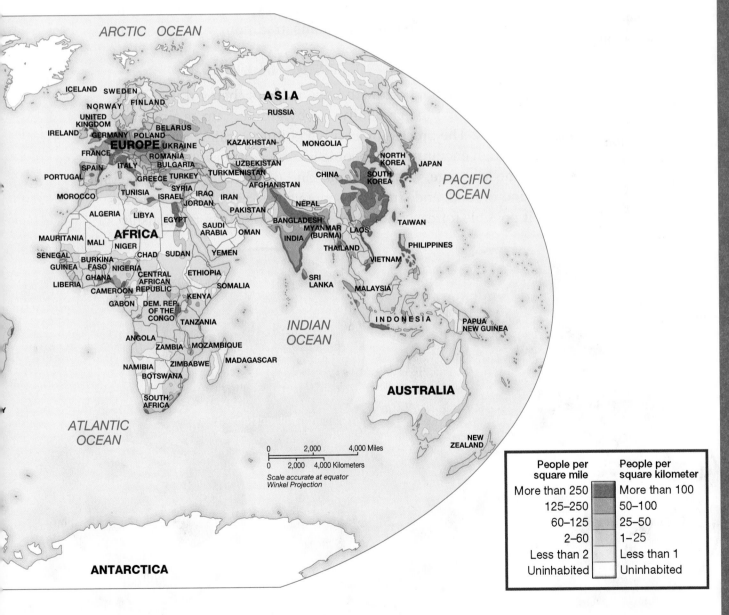

People per square mile		People per square kilometer
More than 250		More than 100
125–250		50–100
60–125		25–50
2–60		1–25
Less than 2		Less than 1
Uninhabited		Uninhabited

Scale accurate at equator
Winkel Projection

Cultures and Societies

MAIN IDEA
Read to find out what makes every culture in the world unique.

WHY IT MATTERS
Today more and more communities have people of many different cultures.

VOCABULARY

human society
enculturation
culture trait
cultural borrowing
cultural diffusion
technology
assimilation
acculturation
ethnic group
cultural diversity

Imagine sailing around the world. At the different ports where you stop, people greet you in different ways. Some shake your hand. Some give you a hug. Others bow to show respect for you as their guest. You meet people whose ways of doing things, like greeting you, are their own and different from yours. The word *culture* is used to describe these customs, as well as the ideas, skills, arts, and tools that are different in each of the world's many human societies. A **human society** is an organized group of people identified by its customs, traditions, and way of life.

Characteristics of Culture

People are not born with knowledge of their culture. They learn it by living in a family and by growing up as a member of a society. The process of learning culture is called **enculturation**. Through enculturation, people in a society learn to speak the same language, wear the same kind of clothing, prepare the same kind of food, and share the same values. Enculturation makes it possible for each person in a society to have a relationship, or

Earth is home to people of many different cultures.

Masai

Polynesian

Mongolian

Sami

Peruvian

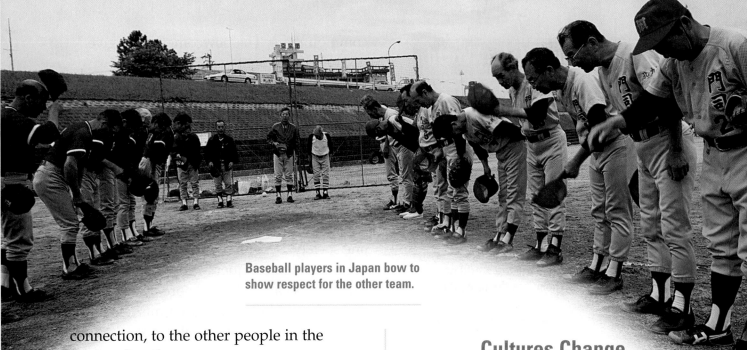
Baseball players in Japan bow to show respect for the other team.

connection, to the other people in the same cultural group.

A society's culture is made up of **culture traits**, or characteristics. These can be either material or nonmaterial.

Material culture traits include objects such as clothes, buildings, artworks, and machines. Differences in material culture can be seen easily when visiting places with different cultures or when viewing pictures of those places.

Nonmaterial culture traits include practices and beliefs such as customs, ceremonies, spoken language, and religion. Forms of greeting, such as shaking hands, hugging, or bowing, are examples of nonmaterial culture traits.

Nonmaterial culture traits can be expressed through material culture. The kinds of paintings or literature made by the people of a cultural group might show that group's ideas of beauty.

A group of related culture traits make up a cultural pattern. Cultural patterns may include both material and nonmaterial traits. For example, language patterns include both written language, which is a material culture trait, and spoken language, which is nonmaterial.

REVIEW What are some traits that define the culture of a society?

Cultures Change

Some countries include many cultural groups with very different cultures. Other countries have only one culture. In Japan, for example, most of the culture traits are shared by most of the people. Japan has a single culture because its people have a very long history of cultural unity. In addition, the island nation of Japan has an ethnic population made up of nearly 100 percent Japanese.

No society, however, is so isolated that it never has contact in some way with others. When societies interact, they sometimes take culture traits from one another and use them as their own. As a result of this **cultural borrowing**, only about 10 percent of a society's culture traits are its very own, found just in that society. About 90 percent are borrowed.

Cultural borrowing can be seen easily in clothing, music, and sports. The game of baseball, for example, began in the United States but has been borrowed by many societies in the world. In each society the rules of the game remain the same. Each society, however, adds customs that make the game its own.

REVIEW How does cultural borrowing affect cultures in the world?

Major Religions of the World

RELIGION	NUMBER OF PEOPLE
✝ Christianity	2 billion
☪ Islam	1.3 billion
🕉 Hinduism	900 million
☸ Buddhism	360 million
✡ Judaism	14 million

Analyze Tables People around the world practice many different religions. These are the largest major religions in the world.

❖ **Which major religion has the most followers?**

Cultures Spread

When one society borrows a culture trait from another society, this spread of culture is called **cultural diffusion**. Throughout history many factors have contributed to cultural diffusion.

Today one of these factors is communication technology. **Technology** is the knowledge and skills that put science to use in everyday life. People with television and the Internet, even in remote parts of the world, can now see and read about other people and more easily borrow culture traits.

Migration is another factor. When people of one culture move to another country, they may find that another culture is more common there. The newcomers may give up their traditional ways and become part of the main culture. As a result of this **assimilation**, the culture traits of the newcomers become similar to those of the people in their new country.

When two societies have contact with one another for a long time, the exchange of culture traits is called **acculturation**. Acculturation has often taken place when one society has gone beyond its country's boundaries to conquer or occupy other societies. As a result, the more powerful society may force its culture traits on the less powerful one. This took place when people from Western Europe settled in North America, beginning in the 1500s. Western cultures—those of England, Spain, Portugal, and France—came to dominate

People in China, as elsewhere, get information about the world from newspapers (far right) as well as the Internet.

Technology helps spread culture and ideas to many places. Here, people in rural Turkey watch the news to learn about world events.

the many societies of Native Americans in North America.

The more powerful group in the process of acculturation may also be affected, however. The more powerful group may adopt some culture traits of the less powerful group. Corn growing, for example, was begun thousands of years ago by Native Americans in what is now Mexico. After contact with western cultures, corn growing spread throughout the world.

The diffusion of western cultures continued throughout the 1900s. Because of this, English, Spanish, Portuguese, and French are languages now spoken in many places outside the original countries. English became the chief language of countries such as the United States, Australia, and New Zealand. It is also one of the main languages of Canada and South Africa. Spanish became the chief language throughout most countries of South America. Portuguese became the main language of Angola, Brazil, and Mozambique.

French, like English, is an important language in Canada. It is also spoken in Vietnam and in Algeria, Morocco, Chad, Côte d'Ivoire (KOHT dee•VWAR), and other countries in Africa.

Religion is another culture trait that has spread throughout the world. Christianity started in Southwest Asia during the time that the Roman Empire stretched into the region. It soon spread to Europe. As western culture spread throughout the world from the 1500s to the 1900s, so did Christianity. Islam, too, began in Southwest Asia. As a result of cultural diffusion, Islam today is the chief religion not only in Southwest Asia but also in Bangladesh, Pakistan, Malaysia, Indonesia, and the countries of North Africa. Buddhism, which developed in India, has also become an international religion. It is now a major religion of many people in South Asia and East Asia, including Japan and Korea.

REVIEW What factors contribute to cultural diffusion?

National Cultures

As a result of migration and cultural diffusion, some countries include a wide variety of ethnic groups. An **ethnic group** is a group of people who have the same culture and share a way of life. Having different ethnic groups within the same country is known as **cultural diversity**. *Diversity* means "the condition of being different or varied."

Although some people within a country may be divided into ethnic groups, they are united through their shared national culture. Like societies, a national culture has its own culture traits, both material and nonmaterial.

A flag, for example, is a material trait that identifies a country. The symbols or colors on a country's flag often express beliefs that are important to the citizens of the country. The cross, a symbol of Christianity, is displayed on flags of many Christian countries. The crescent and star in the flags of many Muslim countries are symbols of peace and life. These are important beliefs in the religion of Islam. The Shield of David, popularly known as the Star of David, is an ancient symbol of Judaism and appears on the flag of Israel. Stars on a country's flag often stand for unity. The number of stars may show how many states or different groups of people were united to form the country.

The number of stars on the United States flag shows that the country is made up of 50 states. The people of the United States share their unity and their loyalty to the country when they say the Pledge of Allegiance.

> **I pledge allegiance to the Flag of the United States of America, and to the Republic for which it stands, one Nation under God, indivisible, with liberty and justice for all.**

People in a country also share their unity when they sing their national anthem, or official patriotic song. The words of some anthems express the beliefs on which the country was founded. The people of Gambia in West Africa share their national beliefs when they sing their anthem together.

> **We strive and work and pray,
> That all may live in unity,
> Freedom and peace each day.
> Let justice guide our actions
> Towards the common good,
> And join our diverse peoples
> To prove man's brotherhood.**

People from other countries become United States citizens at this ceremony on New York City's Ellis Island.

Another way people remember their country's history or heritage is by celebrating national holidays. A country's heritage includes the ways of life, customs, and beliefs that have come from the past and continue today. National holidays are important traits of a national culture. One of the most important holidays in any country is the day it became a country. India's national day is August 15. In Greece it is March 25. In the United States, of course, it is July 4.

Countries also celebrate national holidays to remember other important historical events. Many countries have holidays that honor their founders and leaders.

National flags, anthems, and holidays remind citizens of their country's heritage. A country's culture traits and heritage are learned through the process of enculturation. They are passed on to newcomers in the country through the process of assimilation.

REVIEW How does a national culture help unite people in a country?

• HERITAGE •

New Year Celebrations

For many of the world's cultures, the new year traditionally has been a celebration of a new beginning, or starting over. Early societies marked the new year as a time to celebrate the harvest. However, the harvesting of crops usually occurred in fall or spring. About 2,000 years ago the Romans made January 1 the official date for the new year on their calendar. Today many countries use the Gregorian calendar, which is based on the Roman calendar, and celebrate New Year's Day on January 1. Other cultures celebrate the new year at times that have religious or cultural meaning. The Jewish calendar begins the year in the fall with Rosh Hashanah, which means "beginning of the year" in Hebrew. In Chinese culture the new year begins in late January or early February.

LESSON 2
REVIEW

1. **MAIN IDEA** What makes every culture of the world special in its own way?

2. **WHY IT MATTERS** What are some of the different cultures that can be found in your community?

3. **VOCABULARY** Describe how **ethnic groups** add to a society's **cultural diversity**.

4. **READING SKILL—Generalize** Why do people adopt ideas from other cultures?

5. **TECHNOLOGY** What kinds of technologies help spread cultural ideas today?

6. **CULTURE** How does religion affect culture?

7. **CRITICAL THINKING—Apply** Why do cultures borrow from each other?

PERFORMANCE—Conduct an Interview Talk with a person from a culture other than your own. Find out about that person's customs. In the interview, ask questions about cultural traits, such as art, celebrations, dance, dress, food, holidays, music, and religious practices. Then write a one-paragraph report describing that person's culture.

·SKILLS·

CHART AND GRAPH

Read Parallel Time Lines

VOCABULARY	
parallel time line	A.D.
	B.C.E.
B.C.	C.E.

➡ WHY IT MATTERS

Just as maps help you understand *where* something happened, time lines help you understand *when* something happened. Time lines show events in sequence.

Some time lines are simple to read and understand. Others, such as parallel time lines, are more difficult. A **parallel time line** is really several time lines in one. Parallel time lines are useful because you can compare when related events occurred in different places.

One of the most important advancements of any culture is the development of writing. The parallel time line on page 67 allows you to compare when different cultures made important advances in written communication.

➡ WHAT YOU NEED TO KNOW

When looking at a parallel time line, you will notice that the time line covers a certain time period. That time period is then subdivided into smaller time spans. The time line on page 67 covers the period of 4000 B.C to A.D. 1000 and is divided into time spans of 1,000 years. A parallel time line also has a title that tells you what is being compared.

Depending on the time period covered, the time line may use the abbreviations B.C. and A.D. The abbreviation **B.C.** stands for "before Christ." **A.D.** stands for *anno Domini*, a Latin phrase meaning "in the year of the Lord." This abbreviation tells how many years have passed since the birth of Jesus Christ.

A daily newspaper speeds through a printing press.

A boy learns to read and write in China.

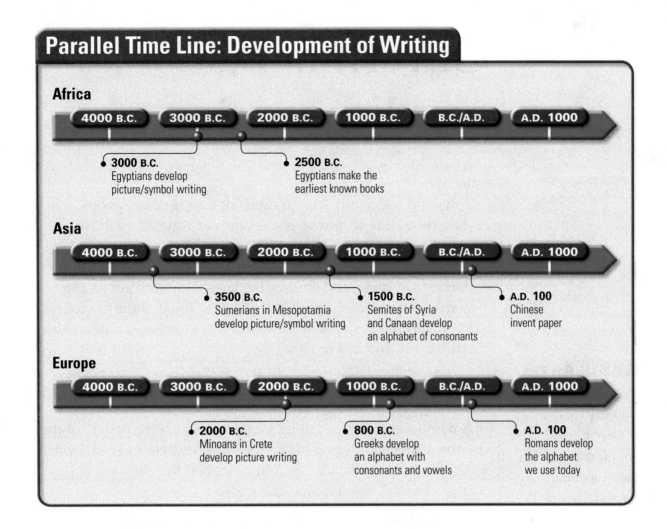

Parallel Time Line: Development of Writing

Africa

4000 B.C. | 3000 B.C. | 2000 B.C. | 1000 B.C. | B.C./A.D. | A.D. 1000

3000 B.C.
Egyptians develop picture/symbol writing

2500 B.C.
Egyptians make the earliest known books

Asia

4000 B.C. | 3000 B.C. | 2000 B.C. | 1000 B.C. | B.C./A.D. | A.D. 1000

3500 B.C.
Sumerians in Mesopotamia develop picture/symbol writing

1500 B.C.
Semites of Syria and Canaan develop an alphabet of consonants

A.D. 100
Chinese invent paper

Europe

4000 B.C. | 3000 B.C. | 2000 B.C. | 1000 B.C. | B.C./A.D. | A.D. 1000

2000 B.C.
Minoans in Crete develop picture writing

800 B.C.
Greeks develop an alphabet with consonants and vowels

A.D. 100
Romans develop the alphabet we use today

It is important to remember that with B.C. dates, the greater the number, the longer ago an event happened. For example, an event that happened in 3500 B.C. took place 500 years *before* an event that occurred in 3000 B.C.

Some time lines are labeled B.C.E. and C.E. rather than B.C. and A.D. The abbreviation **B.C.E.** stands for "before the Common Era," and **C.E.** stands for "Common Era." The abbreviations B.C.E. and C.E. refer to the same years as B.C. and A.D.

No one knows exactly when some events of long ago happened. Therefore, some dates on time lines are approximate, or not exact. Approximate dates are often shown after the Latin term *circa* or after *c.*, its abbreviation. The term *circa* means "about."

▶ **PRACTICE THE SKILL**

Study the parallel time line. Then use it to answer these questions.

1. Where did writing first develop?

2. When and where were the earliest books made?

3. What else happened at about the same time the Romans developed the alphabet we use today?

▶ **APPLY WHAT YOU LEARNED**

Use the parallel time line to come up with three more questions. Write a three-question quiz. Write the answers on a separate sheet of paper. Exchange quizzes with a classmate. Then use your answer sheet to check your classmate's answers.

CHART AND GRAPH SKILLS

Governments and Economies

MAIN IDEA
Read to find out how governments and economies affect countries around the world.

WHY IT MATTERS
More and more, the actions of any one country affect other countries around the world.

VOCABULARY

democracy
majority rule
right
monarchy
dictatorship
oligarchy
industry
developed country
developing country
GDP
subsistence farming
free enterprise

Imagine a society with hundreds of thousands of people and no rules. Life would be chaos without ways to establish order, ensure safety, and manage conflict. That is why societies form governments. Governments organize societies. They run countries and make and enforce the laws. Different governing systems do these things in different ways. Today there are four main governing systems in the world—democracies, monarchies, dictatorships, and oligarchies.

Democracy

A **democracy** is a governing system in which the people of the country take part. During his Gettysburg Address in 1863, United States President Abraham Lincoln described the democratic government of the United States, calling it

❝of the people, by the people, for the people.❞

By this, Lincoln meant a government created by citizens and run by citizens for the good of citizens.

South Korean leader Kim Dae-Jung (right) greets the leader of North Korea, Kim Jong-Il (left), on July 13, 2000.

Citizens in democratic countries consider voting to be one of their most important rights. Voting gives them a voice in their government. Citizens can vote, however, only when they meet certain requirements. In the United States and Canada, for example, citizens must be 18 or older to vote.

In the 1800s and 1900s, many democratic countries extended the right to vote to people who previously did not have it. In 1870 the United States extended the right to vote to all adult male citizens and prohibited any state from denying a citizen the right to vote because of race.

In 1893 New Zealand became the first country to grant women full voting rights. Australia gave women the right to vote in national elections in 1902. Women in the United States gained full voting rights in 1920.

Analyze the Value

1 Why is voting an important individual right?

2 **Make It Relevant** Select one country that interests you. Find out the requirements for voting in that country. Compare these voting requirements with those of the United States. Write a paragraph that explains your findings.

Citizens in a democracy vote and are free to choose their government leaders. For a democracy to work well, people need to participate and to stay informed.

The ancient Greeks in the city of Athens formed the first democracy in the world. This early system was a direct democracy, also called a pure democracy. That means that all citizens who had the right to vote could play a direct role in making every decision. Citizens in present-day democracies instead choose a small number of people to represent them in the government. These elected leaders make laws and decisions for all the citizens.

In a democracy, decisions need to be approved by a majority, or most of a group, before the decisions can take effect. This idea is called **majority rule**. It is used to elect leaders to make laws. Majority rule is based on the idea that the judgment of many is better than the judgment of a few.

Democracy, however, is more than a governing system. It is a way of life in which an important idea is that all citizens are equal. As equals, all citizens in a democracy have certain **rights**, or freedoms. These rights include the basic freedoms of speech, the press, assembly, and religious worship. Freedom of the press is the right to publish opinions and facts, and freedom of assembly is the right to meet with other people. In a democracy these rights can never be taken away, even by a majority.

Today more than 140 countries in the world have some form of democracy. These include the United States, Argentina, Australia, Canada, Egypt, Germany, India, Italy, Israel, Mexico, and Venezuela.

REVIEW How would you describe democracy?

Other Governing Systems

Most early governments were not democracies. Often one person ruled, rather than many people. A governing system in which one person rules is a **monarchy**. The word *monarchy* means "rule by one." In this system a monarch— a king or a queen—can make the decisions for all the people. The position of monarch is usually inherited, which means it is passed down within one family.

Growing cotton is a primary industry.

Making cotton into blue jeans is a secondary industry.

In some monarchies, the rulers have complete control, or absolute authority. In others, laws limit their authority. At one time, the monarch of England had authority to rule however he or she chose. Then in the year 1215, the ruler at that time, King John, signed the Magna Carta.

The Magna Carta not only listed the rights of England's upper class, but also limited the power of the monarchy. Today England still has a monarchy, but the monarch's authority is limited. In addition, England has a democracy with elected leaders who run the country.

Though there are few absolute monarchies in the world today, there are still leaders who rule in this way. A governing system in which one person claims complete control is a **dictatorship**. The difference between a monarchy and a dictatorship is that dictators do not inherit their authority. Instead, they take control, often in a sudden and violent way.

One of the first dictatorships was in ancient Rome. At first, Roman dictators served only briefly during emergencies. Later, they refused to give up their control. Dictators, like monarchs, often rule until their deaths or until they are overthrown.

In the governing system called an **oligarchy**, a group of people who are not elected by the citizens controls the country. In the ancient Greek city of Sparta the rulers were a group of landowners. In present-day China the group is made up of members of the Chinese Communist party. The people in this group share the same ideas about government and work together to spread their ideas.

REVIEW What are the four main governing systems in the world?

Economies Around the World

Just as governments can be classified into different kinds, the economies of the world can also be classified, based on industries. An **industry** is all the businesses that make one kind of product or provide one kind of service. The four main kinds of industries

TERTIARY

Selling cotton blue jeans is a tertiary industry.

QUATERNARY

Preparing advertisements is a quaternary industry.

in the world are described as primary, secondary, tertiary, and quaternary.

A *primary industry* provides natural resources. Primary industries include farming, fishing, logging, and mining. A primary industry brings natural resources to market. Usually the natural resources are the raw materials that a secondary industry uses to make goods.

A *secondary industry* turns a natural resource into a finished product. Clothing factories, for example, use raw wool or cotton to make clothing that people can buy. Secondary industries also include refineries that turn petroleum into gasoline, and mills that turn iron ore into steel.

A *tertiary industry* sells and transports to market the natural resources of primary industries and the finished products of secondary industries. Stores and trucking companies are examples of businesses in a tertiary industry. However, tertiary industries provide not only goods but also services. Banking, education, and health care are examples of service industries.

A *quaternary industry* is one that involves research, information gathering, or business management. Scientists, accountants, architects, lawyers, and engineers are people who work in quaternary industries. Because these people provide services, however, they are also considered a part of tertiary industries.

The kinds of industries in a country can often determine whether the country is developed or developing. Countries that have well-established economies, generally with all four kinds of industries, are called **developed countries**. Countries whose economies are still being built are called **developing countries**. They generally have fewer kinds of industries.

Because developed countries have more kinds of industries, they produce more goods and services than developing ones do. One measure of the total value of goods and services a country produces is its **GDP**, or gross domestic product. The GDP of developed countries is higher than the GDP of developing ones.

Developed countries with a high GDP include the United States, whose GDP is more than 9 trillion dollars. By comparison, the Caribbean country of Dominica, which is developing, has a GDP of just about 225 million dollars.

Another measure of a country's economy is its *standard of living,* or how well its people live. The standard of living can be indicated by the average person's income and *purchasing power,* or spending. It can also be indicated by how much income is left after spending for basic needs.

REVIEW How are economies around the world measured?

Economic Systems

Each country has an economic system, or a way to make decisions about how to use its resources. There are three main kinds of economic systems in the world today—traditional economies, command economies, and market economies.

A *traditional economy* shows little change. Over the years, people do the same kinds of work as people did in earlier times.

Economic decisions are based on custom or habit. Most people in a traditional economy practice **subsistence farming**, raising only enough food for themselves and their families. Because of this, they are not able to buy better tools to improve their way of farming. They must work as they always have. Traditional economies are found in many developing countries in Africa, Asia, and South America.

In a *command economy* the government or some central authority makes most of the economic decisions. It controls both farms and factories. People and businesses in a command economy are not free to make their own decisions. The government determines what and how much will be produced. The government also decides how much the workers will earn and how much the goods and services will cost. This system often leads to less than enough or too much of different products. The island country of Cuba in the Caribbean has one of the few remaining command economies in the world.

In a *market economy* the people own and control businesses. They make their

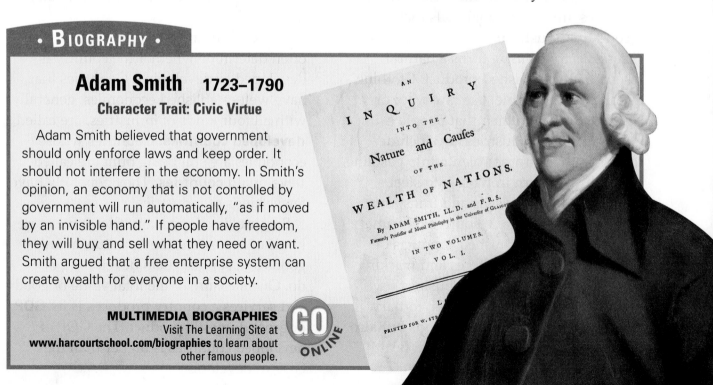

• BIOGRAPHY •

Adam Smith 1723–1790
Character Trait: Civic Virtue

Adam Smith believed that government should only enforce laws and keep order. It should not interfere in the economy. In Smith's opinion, an economy that is not controlled by government will run automatically, "as if moved by an invisible hand." If people have freedom, they will buy and sell what they need or want. Smith argued that a free enterprise system can create wealth for everyone in a society.

MULTIMEDIA BIOGRAPHIES
Visit The Learning Site at
www.harcourtschool.com/biographies to learn about other famous people.

GO ONLINE

AN
INQUIRY
INTO THE
Nature and Caufes
OF THE
WEALTH OF NATIONS.
By ADAM SMITH, LL.D. and F.R.S.
Formerly Profeffor of Moral Philofophy in the Univerfity of Glafgow
IN TWO VOLUMES.
VOL. I.

Around the world, countries that have free enterprise can provide their citizens with many choices.

own choices about which goods and services they will buy or produce. They decide how they will spend their money and what kind of work they will do. This freedom of individuals and businesses in a market economy is often called **free enterprise**.

Market economies follow the principle of supply and demand. When someone buys goods or services, the buyer is showing a *demand* for that product. If there is a demand and buyers are willing to pay a certain price, the producer will increase the *supply*, or the amount of the goods or services for sale. The producer will increase the supply to make a greater profit by selling more goods or services.

Many countries in the world with democratic governments, including the United States, have market economies. Some, however, have a combination of a market economy and a command economy. Canada's government has control over many parts of the country's economy. It controls some major industries, such as broadcasting and health care. Most other industries are free of government control.

REVIEW What are the three main kinds of economic systems?

LESSON 3
REVIEW

1. **MAIN IDEA** How do democracies and market economies affect how people live?

2. **WHY IT MATTERS** How would your life be different if the government chose which products you could buy?

3. **VOCABULARY** Define each of the following: **democracy**, **monarchy**, **oligarchy**, and **dictatorship**.

4. **READING SKILL—Generalize** What is the difference between the economy of a developed country and the economy of a developing country?

5. **ECONOMICS** How are primary and secondary industries different from each other?

6. **ECONOMICS** What are the four kinds of industries? Give an example for each.

7. **CIVICS AND GOVERNMENT** What kind of economy is usually found in democratic countries?

8. **CRITICAL THINKING—Evaluate** What are some benefits of free enterprise that are not found in a command economy?

PERFORMANCE—Make a Table
Use an almanac to find information about the governments and economies of five countries on the same continent. Make a table that lists the following for each country: name, form of government, GDP, and main industries. Then tell whether you think each country is developing or developed.

World Currencies

Currency is the money that is used in a country. Throughout the world today, currency comes chiefly in two forms—coins and paper money. Around the seventh century B.C., the ancient Lydian people of Turkey became the first people to use coined money issued by a government. The Chinese were the first to use paper money, beginning about the eleventh century A.D. World currency today can tell you much about a country and its people.

FROM THE SMITHSONIAN INSTITUTION NATIONAL NUMISMATIC COLLECTION

Currency exchange
in France

The motto of the country

The country or bank
that issued the currency

The date
when the
currency
was issued

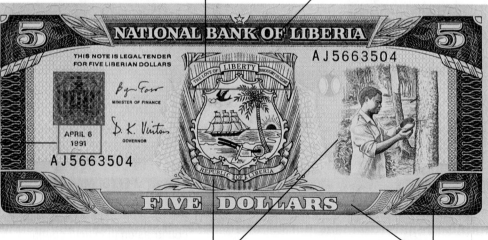

A picture, portrait, or
symbol for the country

The value
of the currency

Analyze the Primary Source

❶ What kind of information appears on the currency below?

❷ What makes each kind of currency unique?

❸ What generalizations can you make about all currency?

A.

B.

C.

D.

ACTIVITY

Design and Draw   Design a coin or paper money that might be used in your school. Draw both the front and back of your currency. Explain the meaning of any special pictures or symbols.

RESEARCH

 GO ONLINE

Visit The Learning Site at **www.harcourtschool.com/primarysources** to research other world currencies.

MAIN IDEA
Read to find out how Earth can be divided into different kinds of regions.

WHY IT MATTERS
Knowing the types of regions makes it easier to compare and contrast areas.

VOCABULARY

border
empire
colony
subregion
cultural region

FAST FACT Mapmakers use computers to draw maps. Computers can scan aerial photographs, base maps, or actual physical surfaces and then use the data to print a map. Space exploration has also contributed many new tools for mapmaking.

Looking at Regions

Think about the way you picture the world. Some people think of satellite images of swirling blues, whites, and browns. Others think of a world globe on a table. Solid blue oceans and brightly colored continents come to mind. Another way to look at the world—and to study it—is by its human regions. These include the world's political, cultural, and economic divisions.

Political Regions

The word *political* refers to government. A political region is an area of land where the people are ruled under one government. An area of land in which people live together under the same government can also be called a country or a nation. The world has almost 200 nations.

The world's largest nation in area is Russia. It covers more than 6.5 million square miles (17 million sq km). Each of the next four largest nations—Canada, China, the United States, and Brazil— covers more than 3 million square miles (7.8 million sq km). By contrast, the five smallest nations in the world each cover less than 25 square miles (65 sq km). Most metropolitan areas are larger! These small countries include Monaco (MAH•nuh•koh), Nauru (nah•OO•roo), San Marino, Tuvalu (too•VAH•loo), and Vatican City. Vatican City, located in the middle of Rome, has an area of only one-sixth of one square mile (0.4 sq km).

Each nation usually has clearly defined borders. A **border**, as seen on a map, is a line that divides one nation from another. On the land, most borders are invisible lines, such as the long border between the United States and Canada. In some places, however, borders follow physical features. Part of the border between the United States and Mexico follows the river known in the United States as the Rio Grande.

Throughout history the political map of the world has changed as some nations gained land and others lost it. Nations' borders change when new nations are created and when old nations break up.

A mapmaker at work

Analyze Primary Sources

This world map by Juan Vespucci shows what he knew about the world in 1526. Vespucci's map is one example of how maps were different long ago.

1 **North America**

2 **South America**

3 **Europe**

4 **Africa**

5 **Asia**

❖ Why do you think Vespucci's map does not look complete?

During ancient times powerful civilizations in Africa, Asia, Europe, North America, and South America built great empires. An **empire** consists of vast lands that come under the control of one ruler. By conquering new lands, each empire grew in size and expanded its borders. During later periods of history, many empires rose and fell. Borders changed again and again.

From the 1500s to the 1900s, many European nations established colonies in Africa, Asia, Australia, North America, and South America. A **colony** is an area of land ruled by a government in another land. The borders that were established for colonies by the ruling countries usually remained unchanged after the colonies began to rule themselves.

In the 1900s the most important border changes resulted from major wars. After World War I the defeated nations lost land or were broken up and reduced to smaller nations. After World War II several nations gained or lost land. In addition, many new nations were established. In Africa more than 45 new nations were created beginning in the 1950s. In the 1990s a major change in the world map also occurred when the Soviet Union broke up into 15 separate nations.

Not only nations but also areas within nations can be political regions. Mexico, for example, is made up of 33 states. The people in each state follow state laws as well as national laws. In the United States smaller divisions, or **subregions**, are also called states. States can be divided into even smaller political subregions. In the United States, these include cities, townships, and counties, which are referred to as parishes in Louisiana.

Only a sign marks the border between the countries of Argentina and Chile.

A CLOSER LOOK

Patterns of Growth

Populations of cities often grow outward from an urban center. This creates many subregions with no clearly defined borders. This diagram shows the pattern of outward growth for a typical city.

1 Urban

2 Suburban

3 Rural

❖ Which subregion lies farthest from the urban center?

Even smaller political subregions include neighborhoods and school districts.

Nations can also be grouped together to form larger political regions. These political regions, however, have no single government. They are grouped together for other political reasons. For example, the Organization of African Unity, or OAU, is made up of nations from Africa. The OAU works to promote unity among African people. It also helps member nations stricken by natural disasters. A similar organization is made up of nations from North America and South America. It is called the Organization of American States, or OAS.

REVIEW What makes a region a political region?

Cultural Regions

Geographers sometimes divide the world into regions based on culture traits. These kinds of regions are called **cultural regions**.

Like political regions, cultural regions can be shown on maps. On a map showing cultural regions, areas where different languages are spoken might be shown in different colors. Areas where different religions are followed might be marked with different symbols. The regions shown, however, do not have definite borders.

Cultural regions, like political regions, can change over time. This is because people are constantly moving and culture traits are being spread. Cultural regions can also vary in size. They can be as small as a neighborhood or as large as a country or a group of nations.

The world can be divided into large cultural regions. Each is made up of more than one country. Each has one or more culture traits that help unify it as a cultural region. At the same time, those traits set it apart from other cultural regions.

The United States and Canada are often grouped together as a cultural region called Anglo-America. The term *Anglo* comes from *Anglo-Saxon*, which refers to a people who settled England in about 500 B.C. The United States and Canada have English as a common language and Christianity as a major religion.

Middle America and South America are together called Latin America. Today most people in the region speak Spanish, Portuguese, or French, each of which developed from Latin. A second unifying culture trait in Latin America is the Roman Catholic faith, which is a kind of Christianity.

Although Europe is a culturally diverse region, most of the varied languages spoken there are actually from the same language family. Language is also what unifies the African nations south of the Sahara into one cultural region. The various peoples south of the Sahara speak various languages belonging to the Bantu language family.

The major culture trait that links the nations of Southwest Asia and North Africa is the religion of Islam. The Jewish nation of Israel is the important exception.

People from different cultural regions can still share common interests.

Another unifying factor in the region is the Arabic language, although other languages are also spoken there.

Asia is so large that it is made up of three different cultural regions. They are East Asia, South Asia, and Southeast Asia.

The countries of East Asia can trace their common culture to China. The cultures of both Japan and Korea borrowed from China many culture traits, such as religion and the written forms of their languages. The countries of South Asia were once British colonies. This region has two major religions, however—Hinduism and Islam. Southeast Asia is a mixture of influences from East Asia and South Asia.

Like Asia, countries in the Pacific are divided into two different cultural regions. Australia and New Zealand make up one region. They are similar to the United States and Canada in language and religion. The Pacific Islands, which make up the other region, have great cultural diversity. They are grouped together not because of a common culture but because they are all islands in the Pacific Ocean.

REVIEW What makes a region a cultural region?

Economic Regions

Economists generally divide the world into two groups, developing nations and developed nations. Within each group, however, there are economic regions

· GEOGRAPHY ·

The Pampas
Understanding Places and Regions

The name Pampas (PAHM•puhs) comes from a Native American word meaning "flat surface." The Pampas cover about 295,000 square miles (764,000 sq km) of grassy plain in Argentina. The main economic activity is cattle herding. The Pampas also yield abundant crops. More than two-thirds of Argentina's people live and work on the Pampas.

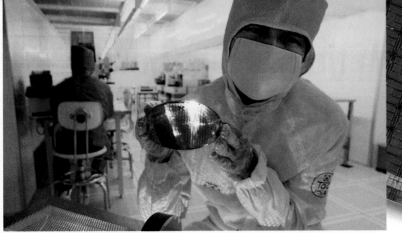
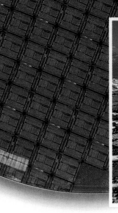

Silicon Valley (inset) is defined as the area in and around San Jose, California. It is a center for the computer industry in the United States.

based on the kinds of economic activities found in them.

Some maps of economic regions show levels of economic activity, such as primary, secondary, tertiary, and quaternary industries. Others show economic activity in more detail. A map of primary industries, for example, may show farming, fishing, logging, or mining.

Silicon Valley is the name given to an economic region in California in the United States. It is called Silicon Valley because its major economic activity is the production

of computer chips, which are usually made from the element silicon. The economic activity there gives the people a common bond and makes the region different from other regions.

Like political and cultural regions, economic regions are different sizes. They also can change greatly over time, as the resources needed for economic activities change. These include people, machines, and natural resources.

REVIEW What makes a region an economic region?

LESSON 4
REVIEW

① **MAIN IDEA** Why do geographers divide Earth into regions?

② **WHY IT MATTERS** What are some features that make different regions unique?

③ **VOCABULARY** Describe an **empire**, using the term **colony**.

④ **READING SKILL—Generalize** Where can cultural regions be found?

⑤ **GEOGRAPHY** Which kind of region usually has clearly defined borders?

⑥ **GEOGRAPHY** What do cultural regions have in common?

⑦ **ECONOMICS** Why is Silicon Valley in California considered a region?

⑧ **CRITICAL THINKING—Apply** Describe the different political, cultural, and economic regions in which you live.

PERFORMANCE—Make a Map First, create an imaginary country. Then, draw a map of this country. On this map, draw borders for political, economic, cultural, and physical regions, and make the borders of each region a different color. On the map, label each kind of region with a title of your choosing. In a map key, show which colors stand for which kind of region. On a separate sheet of paper, write a paragraph describing the features of each region. Tell why the region fits its specific category.

· SKILLS · CITIZENSHIP

Identify National Symbols

VOCABULARY
heraldry

▶ WHY IT MATTERS

Since the formation of the first countries, flags have been used as symbols of national identity. A flag stands for a nation's land, its people, and its government. It also expresses ideas or qualities valued by the people of a nation. Knowing the kinds of things flags represent can help you better understand today's nations and their history and culture.

▶ WHAT YOU NEED TO KNOW

The designs on many flags were used in **heraldry**, or the system of colors, patterns, and picture symbols that knights used during the Middle Ages in Europe.

Most national flags today use one or more of seven colors: black, blue, green, orange, red, white, and yellow. These colors were used in heraldry to stand for different qualities. For example, blue stands for loyalty, red for courage, and white for freedom. To Arab nations, the colors black, green, red, and white symbolize Arab unity. The Arab nations use these colors in their national flags to indicate their unity as an ethnic group.

Patterns on many present-day national flags are similar to those used in heraldry. Some knights in the Middle Ages used a stripe of white or yellow to separate two colors. The flag of Mexico, for example, has a white stripe between stripes of green and red.

The picture symbols used on some flags have a religious meaning. Some flags have a cross, a symbol for Christianity. On other flags the star and crescent, a symbol of Islam, appears. The flag of Israel has the Star of David, a Jewish symbol.

On some flags, stars stand for unity. The number of stars in a flag is sometimes equal to the number of states or provinces united to form a country.

ALGERIA

ARGENTINA

BHUTAN

CANADA

UNITED KINGDOM

UNITED STATES

ISRAEL

KAZAKHSTAN

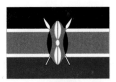

KENYA

SUDAN

FRANCE

INDIA

KUWAIT

MEXICO

ST. LUCIA

PAKISTAN

Picture symbols sometimes show an important event in a nation's history. The Mexican flag shows an eagle perching on a cactus and holding a snake in its mouth. This represents the history of the Aztec Empire in Mexico.

Picture symbols can even tell you something about a nation's physical features. The flag of St. Lucia has two triangles that represent the island nation's two volcanic peaks, the Pitons. The triangles are set against a blue background that represents the sea.

▶ PRACTICE THE SKILL

Study the national flags above. Use what you learned about flags and their meanings to answer these questions.

1 Which two nations have flags with a religious symbol of Islam?

2 Which nations are Arab nations?

3 Why do you think the color white is included in the United States flag?

▶ APPLY WHAT YOU LEARNED

Choose a flag from this page or from the Almanac on pages R2–R21 of this book. Research its importance as a national symbol. Then make a bookmark by drawing the flag on a strip of paper or cardboard. Include on the bookmark at least three facts about the flag's importance to the nation's history and culture.

Review and Test Preparation

USE YOUR READING SKILLS

Complete this graphic organizer to show that you understand how to use facts and details to make a generalization. A copy of this graphic organizer appears on page 25 of the Activity Book.

Patterns of Settlement and Culture

FACTS + DETAILS → GENERALIZATION

People settle where the climate is mild and the soil is fertile. People also settle in cities to find work. Bodies of water are often near these places.

_____
_____
_____
_____
_____
_____
_____
_____

Differences in language, customs, and religion often separate cultures. Contact between cultures, however, spreads cultural ideas. Through technology, cultures can more easily communicate with each other.

_____
_____
_____
_____
_____
_____
_____
_____

THINK & WRITE

Write an Advertisement   Think about the patterns of settlement and population you learned about in this chapter. Use this information to write an advertisement for a place where people might want to live.

Write a Description   Identify a cultural region in your city or state. Write a short paragraph describing the region and the culture of the people who live there. Mention the cultural traits that unite this region.

USE VOCABULARY

Use the terms on the right to complete the sentences.

drought (p. 53)

metropolitan area (p. 57)

cultural borrowing (p. 61)

ethnic group (p. 64)

free enterprise (p. 73)

heraldry (p. 82)

1 Tokyo, Japan, has a large _____, with more than 20 million people.

2 Businesses that have the freedom to decide what goods to produce and how to spend their money operate in a _____ system.

3 During the Middle Ages in Europe, knights used _____, or a system of colors, patterns, and picture symbols.

4 Because of _____, only about 10 percent of a society's cultural traits were originally to be found in that society.

5 In the 1930s, farmers in the Middle West experienced a _____, or long period of dry weather.

6 The Garifuna of Belize are an _____ who have the same culture and share a way of life.

RECALL FACTS

Answer these questions.

7 What are some of the factors that affect population distribution?

8 What technology have people used to create cities and farms in the desert?

9 How has technology improved communication and affected cultures around the world?

Write the letter of the best choice.

10 **TEST PREP** The physical feature that forms part of the border between the United States and Mexico is—
A the Grand Canyon.
B the Rio Grande.
C the Great Lakes.
D the Rocky Mountains.

11 **TEST PREP** A ruler who inherits control of a government is a—
F dictator.
G president.
H monarch.
J senator.

THINK CRITICALLY

12 Why do you think it is important for a nation to have cultural diversity?

13 What might be some benefits to citizens of limiting the authority of a ruler?

14 Compare a market economy with a traditional economy. Which economic system do you think provides a better standard of living?

APPLY SKILLS

Read a Population Map

15 Use the map on pages 58–59 to identify three countries that have a high population density.

Read Parallel Time Lines

16 Look at the parallel time line on page 67 to determine which group developed writing first.

Identify National Symbols

17 Use this book's Almanac, pages R2–R21, to find ten countries that have stars on their flags.

VISIT

THE UNITED NATIONS

GET READY

The United Nations has its headquarters in New York City, but the land and the buildings it occupies are considered international territory. The United Nations is an international governmental organization that was founded in 1945. Over time, many nations around the world have become members. The United Nations still operates with its original set of goals. These are to bring the world's nations together to work for peace, justice, and the well-being of all people.

When you visit the United Nations, a tour guide will show you the rooms where representatives from different countries meet. You will notice that the architecture and art that you see throughout are a reflection of the organization's many nations and many cultures.

LOCATE IT

UNITED STATES

New York City

WHAT TO SEE

The General Assembly Hall is the largest room in the United Nations. It is where all of the member nations can meet to discuss issues.

Each member nation's flag flies in front of the United Nations headquarters.

Former First Lady Nancy Reagan presented this mosaic as a gift from the United States.

Tour guides at the United Nations come from all over the world. Many speak several languages.

Kofi Annan, Secretary-General of the United Nations, rings the Peace Bell, a gift from Japan. Children from 60 countries collected the coins from which it was made.

TAKE A FIELD TRIP

A VIRTUAL TOUR
Visit The Learning Site at **www.harcourtschool.com/tours** to find virtual tours of world organizations.

A VIDEO TOUR
Check your media center or classroom library for a videotape tour of the United Nations headquarters.

1 Review and Test Preparation

VISUAL SUMMARY

Write a Description Look closely at each picture, and read the captions to help you review Unit 1. Then write a description of each picture, and tell how it relates to the social studies ideas presented in this unit.

USE VOCABULARY

For each group of terms, write a sentence or two that explains how the terms are related.

1 **conservation** (p. 43), **recycling** (p. 43)

2 **migration** (p. 56), **urbanization** (p. 56)

3 **democracy** (p. 68), **majority rule** (p. 69)

4 **empire** (p. 77), **colony** (p. 77)

RECALL FACTS

Answer these questions.

5 What are some factors that lead to desertification?

6 What are the two kinds of cultural traits?

7 What are some ways to measure a country's economy?

Write the letter of the best choice.

8 **TEST PREP** The continent that has no permanent population of humans is—
A Australia.
B Antarctica.
C Asia.
D South America.

9 **TEST PREP** Each of the following is one of the four main governing systems *except*—
F democracy.
G monarchy.
H oligarchy.
J majority rule.

10 **TEST PREP** The world's largest nation in area is—
A Russia.
B Monaco.
C China.
D Canada.

11 **TEST PREP** Geographers determine how to divide cultural regions by—
F population distribution.
G population density.
H cultural traits.
J heraldry.

Visual Summary

Landforms (p. 20) and Bodies of Water (p. 26)

Climates and Vegetation p. 34

Natural Resources p. 40

12 Do you think that a national culture is important in a culturally diverse society? Explain.

13 How do citizens' rights allow people to participate in a democracy?

14 Can a secondary industry exist without a primary industry? Explain.

APPLY SKILLS

Read a Population Map
Use the population map of India on this page to answer these questions.

15 Which cities on the map have a population density of between 500 and 1,000 people per square mile?

16 What is the population density of India's capital?

17 What is the population density near India's border with Myanmar?

18 Which city along India's west coast is the most densely populated?

19 The population density of Kanpur is more than 1,000 people per square mile. How many people per square kilometer is this?

20 What is the population density of much of the land in central India?

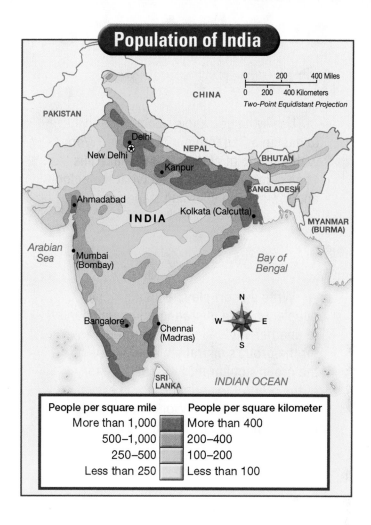

Population of India

People per square mile	People per square kilometer
More than 1,000	More than 400
500–1,000	200–400
250–500	100–200
Less than 250	Less than 100

Population and Settlement p. 52

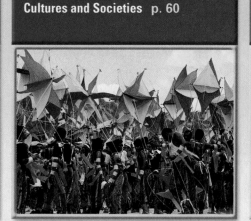

Cultures and Societies p. 60

Governments and Economies p. 68

Unit Activities

Visit The Learning Site at www.harcourtschool.com/socialstudies/activities for additional activities.

Make a Classroom Flag

Use what you know about heraldry to design a flag for your classroom. Work with a group of classmates to make this flag. Then display it, and explain what the colors and symbols on your flag stand for.

Write a Play

Write a short play about a group of people who are migrating from one country to another. Include in your script the reason for the group's migration, a summary of the group's cultural traits, and the story of the group's experiences upon arrival in their new country. Work with a group to perform your play for the class.

VISIT YOUR LIBRARY

■ **Around the World in 80 Pages: An Adventurous Picture Atlas of the World** by Antony Mason. Copper Beech Books.

■ **Mapping the World** by Sylvia A. Johnson. Atheneum.

■ **This Same Sky: A Collection of Poems from Around the World** selected by Naomi Shihab Nye. Four Winds Press.

COMPLETE THE UNIT PROJECT

Make Maps and Models Work with a group of classmates to complete the unit project. First, decide which area to show on your map. Then, work together to draw your map and label the landforms, bodies of water, and cities that appear on it. Next, choose one landform or body of water on your map, and make a model of it. As a group, present your map and model to the class.

The United States and Canada

Kwakiutl sun mask,
Northwest coast of North America

Atlin Lake, the source of the Yukon River in Canada

2

The **United States** and **Canada**

“ I am the blue horse that runs in
the plain
I am the fish that rolls, shining,
in the water ”

—N. Scott Momaday, from "The Delight
Song of Tsoai-Talee," 1975

Preview the Content

Use the lesson titles to develop a web for each chapter.
Write words and phrases to identify each chapter's main topics.

Preview the Vocabulary

Suffixes   Suffixes are word parts added to the end of words. Use
the meaning of the suffix and the root word to figure out the
meaning of each Vocabulary Word below. Record your responses
in a chart, and use the Glossary to confirm each meaning.

SUFFIX	ROOT WORD	VOCABULARY WORD	MEANING
-ity	minor	**minority**	
-ism	national	**nationalism**	
-ist	separate	**separatist**	

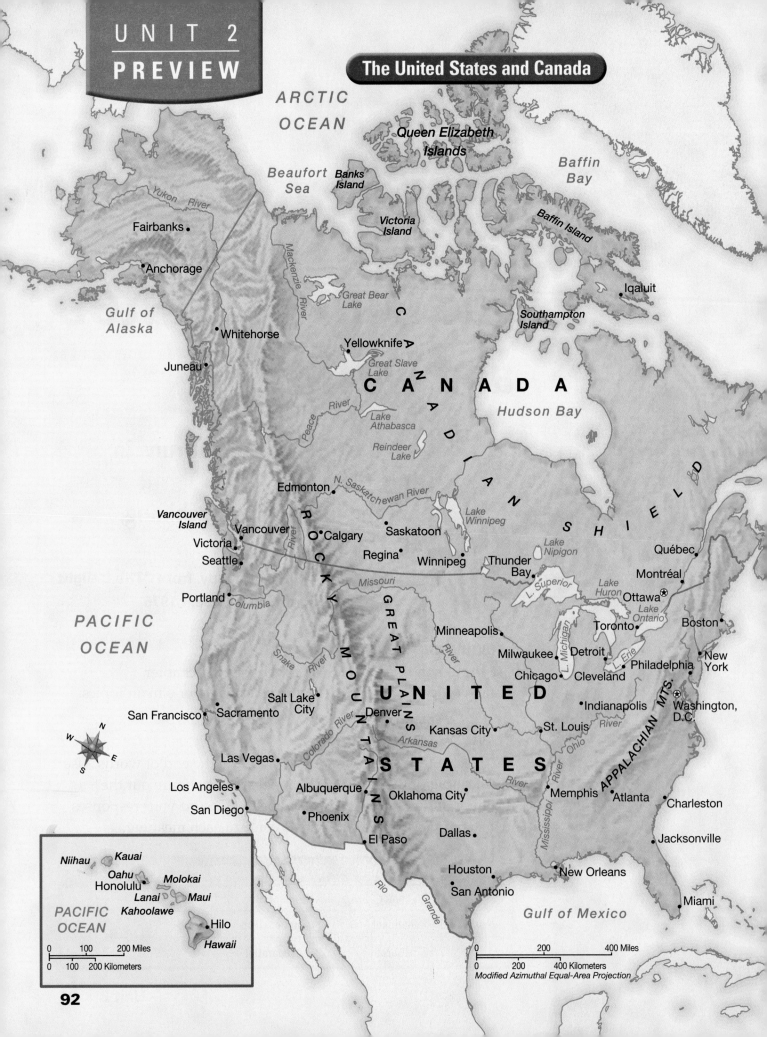

The United States and Canada

ARCTIC
OCEAN

Queen Elizabeth
Islands

Beaufort
Sea

Banks
Island

Baffin
Bay

Baffin Island

Victoria
Island

Yukon River

Fairbanks

Anchorage

Gulf of
Alaska

Mackenzie River

Great Bear
Lake

Iqaluit

Whitehorse

Southampton
Island

Yellowknife

Juneau

Great Slave
Lake

C A N A D A

Hudson Bay

Peace River

Lake
Athabasca

Reindeer
Lake

C A N A D I A N   S H I E L D

Edmonton

N. Saskatchewan River

Vancouver
Island

Vancouver

R O C K Y   River

Calgary

Saskatoon

Lake
Winnipeg

Québec

Victoria

Regina

Winnipeg

Thunder
Bay

Lake
Nipigon

Montréal

Seattle

Missouri

L. Superior

Lake
Huron

Ottawa

Portland

Columbia

Lake
Ontario

Boston

PACIFIC
OCEAN

Minneapolis

L. Michigan

Toronto

Snake   River

Milwaukee

Detroit

L. Erie

Philadelphia

New
York

Chicago

Cleveland

M
O
U
N
T
A
I
N
S

G R E A T   P L A I N S

U N I T E D

Indianapolis

Washington,
D.C.

Salt Lake
City

Denver

River

Colorado River

St. Louis

APPALACHIAN   MTS.

San Francisco

Sacramento

Kansas City

Arkansas

Ohio
River

Las Vegas

S T A T E S

Memphis

Atlanta

Charleston

Los Angeles

Albuquerque

Oklahoma City

Mississippi   River

San Diego

Phoenix

Dallas

Jacksonville

El Paso

Houston

New Orleans

Rio   Grande

San Antonio

Miami

Gulf of Mexico

N
W   E
S

Niihau
Kauai
Oahu
Honolulu
Molokai
Lanai   Maui
Kahoolawe

PACIFIC
OCEAN

Hilo

Hawaii

0   100   200 Miles
0 100 200 Kilometers

0   200   400 Miles
0   200   400 Kilometers
Modified Azimuthal Equal-Area Projection

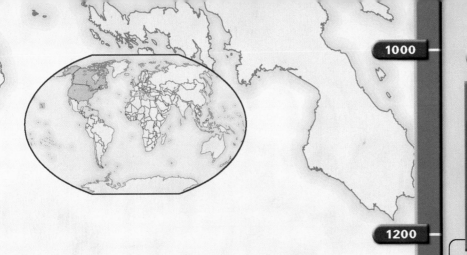

Populations of the United States and Canada

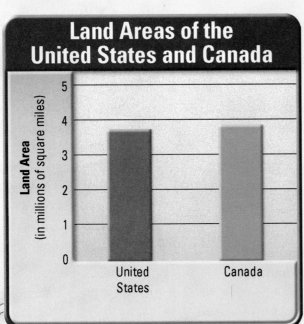

People (in millions)

300
250
200
150
100
50
0

United States   Canada

Island of Newfoundland

St. John's

ATLANTIC OCEAN

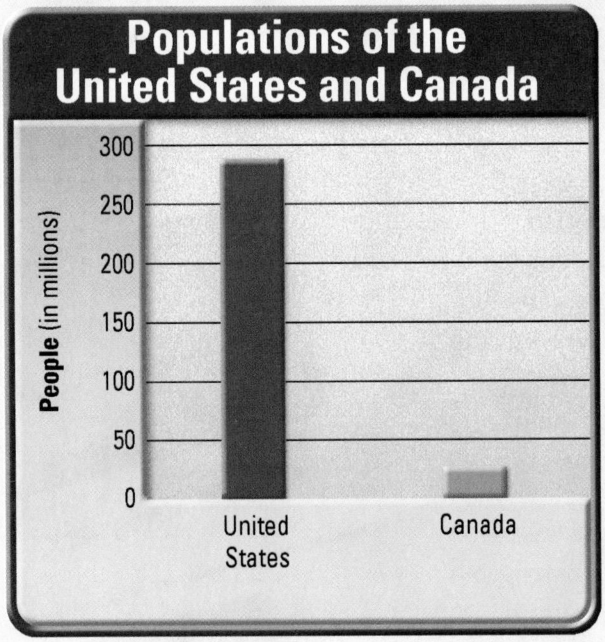

Land Areas of the United States and Canada

Land Area (in millions of square miles)

5
4
3
2
1
0

United States   Canada

1000

1200

1400

1600

1800

2000

Key Events

1400 Native Americans live throughout North America p. 106

1565 Europeans build settlements in North America p. 107

1775 The American Revolution begins p. 108

1964 Canada adopts a new flag p. 147

2000 United States has a growing and diverse population p. 114

VANCOUVER

written by Vivien Bowers

Traveling to a new city can be full of wonderful experiences. New places, sounds, smells, and people inspire travelers to record thoughts and feelings in travelogues or journals. Guy is a 12-year-old boy having an adventure with his family as they travel across Canada. Read to find out about Guy's visit to one of Canada's biggest cities, Vancouver, British Columbia.

I now have a scraped elbow and a sore. . . . Well, let's just say I'm sore all over. Maybe in-line skating isn't my thing. But how could I expect that a huge wave would splash me on the Stanley Park sea wall path just as I got up speed? My whole family was on skates, but next thing I knew I was the only one sprawled in a puddle. Mom says people always get wet in Vancouver because it rains so much, but it takes real talent to get drenched on a sunny day.

The sea wall path goes all around the edge of Stanley Park, right beside the ocean. When I wasn't falling into puddles, I counted seventeen freighters anchored in the bay, alongside sailboats and sailboards. Later, at the port, we watched huge orange cranes unloading containers of stuff from freighters from Japan and Taiwan.

We skated up to some totem poles. Mom said they were built by the Squamish people, Native Canadians who lived here before anyone else.

Totem poles in Stanley Park.

In-line skating through Stanley Park.

Vancouver's Chinatown.

Vancouver skyline

A gondola ride through mountains near Vancouver.

We traded our skates for shoes and walked through Vancouver's Chinatown. There were golden dragons on the streetlights, and the roofs on the telephone booths were shaped like the roofs on Chinese pagodas. The signs were written in Chinese characters. Mom says there are thousands of characters in the Chinese alphabet.

For lunch, we ate warm buns that we bought from a Chinese bakery. They were stuffed with barbecued pork, curried beef, and (surprise!) hot dogs. Yum!

We finished the day with a gondola ride to the top of one of the mountains near Vancouver. People ski there in the winter. From the top, we could look down on the whole city. It looked like the imaginary city maps I get to design in one of my favorite computer games. We watched the sun set and the lights of the city turn on. I sat there for a long time, wondering how I could create that same effect with computer graphics.

Analyze the Literature

1 Does the selection make you want to visit Vancouver? Why or why not?

2 Write a travelogue about your city or town. Describe places, people, or foods that would interest visitors.

READ A BOOK

START THE UNIT PROJECT

Form a Democratic Government
Form a democratic government with your classmates. As you read this unit, take notes about the governments of the United States and Canada. Your notes will help you as you work to form a democratic government in your classroom.

USE TECHNOLOGY

Visit The Learning Site at **www.harcourtschool.com/ socialstudies** for additional activities, primary sources, and other resources to use in this unit.

STATUE OF LIBERTY, THE UNITED STATES

A gift from the people of France in 1884, the Statue of Liberty stands on Liberty Island at the entrance to New York Harbor. It was the first thing that many newcomers saw as they entered the United States. For many, the statue has become a symbol of the freedoms and opportunities found in the United States.

LOCATE IT

NEW YORK

New York City

The United States

" Give me your tired,
your poor,
Your huddled masses
yearning to breathe
free . . . "

—Emma Lazarus, from "The New Colossus:
Inscription for the Statue of Liberty, 1883"

CHAPTER READING SKILL

Summarize

To **summarize**, restate the most important ideas, or key points, in your own words.

As you read this chapter, think about the key points of each lesson. Then summarize each lesson.

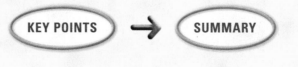

KEY POINTS → SUMMARY

From Sea to Shining Sea

Majestic! That one word describes best the geography of the United States. It describes not only this grand country's diverse landforms and waterways but also its enormous size. The United States covers an area of more than 3.6 million square miles (9.3 million sq km), making it the fourth-largest country in the world. Forty-eight of its 50 states lie on the North American continent between the Atlantic Ocean and the Pacific Ocean. These 48 states are called **contiguous** (kuhn•TIH•gyuh•wuhs) because they touch one another. Only the states of Alaska, in the far north, and Hawaii, a group of islands in the Pacific Ocean, do not touch any other state.

To study such a large and diverse country, geographers often group the states of the United States into regions. The major regions of the United States are the Northeast, the South, the Middle West, and the West.

The Northeast

Compared to other regions, the Northeast is the smallest in size but large in population. About one-fifth—nearly 60 million people of the country's more than 281 million people—live in the Northeast. Most of them live in cities.

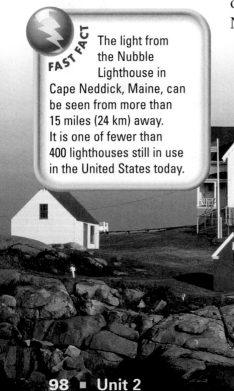

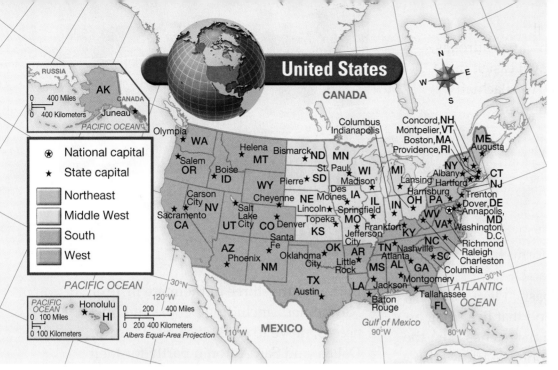

United States

CANADA

RUSSIA
AK
CANADA
0 400 Miles
0 400 Kilometers
Juneau
PACIFIC OCEAN

⊛ National capital
★ State capital
Northeast
Middle West
South
West

PACIFIC OCEAN

PACIFIC OCEAN
Honolulu
HI
0 100 Miles
0 100 Kilometers

0 200 400 Miles
0 200 400 Kilometers
Albers Equal-Area Projection

MEXICO

Olympia
WA
Salem
OR
Helena
MT
Boise
ID
WY
Cheyenne
Carson City
NV
Sacramento
CA
Salt Lake City
UT
CO
Denver
Santa Fe
AZ
Phoenix
NM

Bismarck
ND
Pierre
SD
NE
Lincoln
Topeka
KS
OK
Oklahoma City

Columbus
Indianapolis
MN
St. Paul
WI
Madison
Des Moines
IA
Springfield
IL
MO
Jefferson City
AR
Little Rock
TX
Austin

Concord, NH
Montpelier, VT
Boston, MA
Providence, RI
MI
Lansing
NY
Albany
Hartford
Harrisburg
OH
PA
IN
Frankfort
KY
TN
Nashville
MS
AL
GA
Jackson
Montgomery
LA
Baton Rouge
Tallahassee
FL

ME
Augusta
CT
NJ
Trenton
Dover, DE
Annapolis, MD
WV
VA
Washington, D.C.
Richmond
NC
Raleigh
SC
Charleston
Columbia

ATLANTIC OCEAN

Gulf of Mexico

GEOGRAPHY THEME

Regions
Some geographers group the 50 states into four major regions. These are called the Northeast, the Middle West, the South, and the West.

❓ Which region includes Alaska and Hawaii?

Many of the largest cities are found along the Atlantic coast, where natural harbors encouraged settlement. Many of the towns, such as New York, Philadelphia, and Boston, were built on these harbors and grew into huge metropolitan areas.

Because of their locations the metropolitan areas in the Northeast became important centers of manufacturing and trade—and sources for jobs. As a result, the Northeast has the largest population density of any region. Population density tells how many people live in an area of a certain size, usually one square mile or one square kilometer.

Inland, beyond the coastal cities, the Northeast is a region of broad valleys and rolling hills. To the west are the Appalachian (a•puh•LAY•chee•uhn) Mountains, a hilly land of rounded peaks and dense forests. For many of the early settlers, the Appalachians formed a natural barrier to westward settlement.

Philadelphia, Pennsylvania (above), is one of the oldest cities in the Northeast.

Even today, when highways, railroads, and airplanes make travel easier, more people live east of the Appalachian Mountains than west of them.

REVIEW **Why does the Northeast region have such a high population density?**

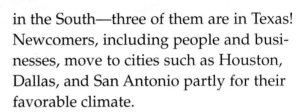

The Blue Ridge Mountains (above) and the architecture of Charleston, South Carolina (left)

The South

The two major landforms in the South are the Appalachian Mountains and the Coastal Plain. A **coastal plain** is low land that lies along an ocean. The Coastal Plain stretches from the Northeast, where it is only a narrow strip of land, south along the Atlantic Ocean, where it gets wider toward the Florida Peninsula. The Coastal Plain then stretches west along the Gulf of Mexico into Texas.

The South contains some of the country's largest swamps. A **swamp** is a wet, spongy area of shallow water where trees and bushes grow. Swamps attract many kinds of birds and other wildlife. One of the largest and most unusual swamps in the United States covers about 4,000 square miles (about 10,000 sq km) at the tip of southern Florida. This area is called the **everglades**, or "river of grass," from which Everglades National Park gets its name.

Like the Northeast, the South has a large population that continues to grow. Some of the country's largest cities are

in the South—three of them are in Texas! Newcomers, including people and businesses, move to cities such as Houston, Dallas, and San Antonio partly for their favorable climate.

Warm temperatures, long summers, and frequent rainfall have made the South an important agricultural region, too. Farms along the Coastal Plain grow a variety of cash crops, including peanuts, cotton, and citrus fruit. Farmers in the South also raise

· GEOGRAPHY ·

GEOGRAPHY ESSENTIAL ELEMENTS

Dallas
Understanding Places and Regions

Dallas began in the 1840s as a small village along the Trinity River in eastern Texas. It stayed small until the 1870s, when the railroad made Dallas grow. In the 1920s and 1930s, the demand for cotton grew and the discovery of oil near Dallas caused an economic boom. Today Dallas is an important banking and industrial center and home to 1.2 million people.

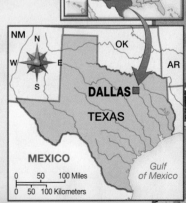

Chicago
ILLINOIS

Chicago, Illinois, lies on the banks of Lake Michigan. It is the largest city in the Middle West region of the United States.

and sell hogs, chickens, and herds of beef and dairy cattle.

A warm climate and sandy beaches help the South attract visitors from all over the world. Beaches stretch hundreds of miles along the coastline from Virginia to Texas.

Although the climate of the South offers a pleasant way of life and attracts many visitors, it can be dangerous. During the months from June through November, hurricanes often strike the southern coast of the United States. A **hurricane** is a huge storm with heavy rains and high winds of greater than 74 miles (119 km) per hour. Hurricanes are powerful enough to destroy property and endanger the lives of people.

REVIEW What factors allow the South to grow in population?

The Middle West

A huge area of flat plains dominates the landscape of the Middle West region of the United States. The Interior Plains, as these plains are known, consist of two parts. They are the Central Plains and the Great Plains. The fertile soil of the Interior Plains region makes it the farming center, or

"heartland," of the United States. Enough food, especially wheat, is produced in this region to meet the needs of the United States as well as many other countries.

The Central Plains begin in Ohio and end just west of the Mississippi River. Where the Central Plains end, the Great Plains begin. The Great Plains include some of the most remote areas of the United States, where few people live. Extreme hot and cold temperatures and long dry seasons can make the Great Plains a difficult place to live. Sprawling ranches and scattered farms cover much of this treeless grassland.

As in the South, dangerous storms sometimes threaten people, animals, crops, and property in the Middle West. These storms are called tornadoes. A **tornado** is a funnel-shaped, spinning windstorm. Powerful tornado winds can reach more than 200 miles (about 320 km) per hour.

Much of the Middle West region lies within the drainage basin of the great Mississippi River system.

Corn is an important crop grown on the plains of the Middle West.

The Pacific Coast Highway runs along California's rocky coastline.

The system includes hundreds of rivers and streams that flow into the Mississippi River. The Mississippi and its tributaries are sources of water for cities and farms. They are also water highways for travel and trade in the interior of the United States. From its source at Lake Itasca in Minnesota to its mouth at the Gulf of Mexico, the Mississippi is 2,348 miles (3,787 km) long.

The Great Lakes are another important waterway in the Middle West. The Great Lakes were formed thousands of years ago by moving glaciers as they slid across North America. When the glaciers melted, they formed five of the largest freshwater lakes in the world. The five Great Lakes—Superior, Michigan, Huron, Erie, and Ontario—are used for travel and trade and as a source of water. Many of the Middle West's largest cities, such as Chicago, Detroit, and Cleveland, lie along the shores of the Great Lakes.

REVIEW Which part of the Middle West is the country's agricultural center?

The West

Mountains are the most prominent landform in the West. The largest of these are the Rocky Mountains. They stretch more than 3,000 miles (4,838 km) north from Mexico into Canada and into Alaska. The Rocky Mountains are newer than the Appalachian Mountains in the eastern United States. The Rockies have not been worn down as much by wind and water. Unlike the Appalachians with their rounded tops, the Rockies have many high, jagged peaks. The highest peak in the Rocky Mountains is Mount Elbert in Colorado. It rises to 14,433 feet (4,399 m) above sea level.

Running along the ridge of the highest peaks in the Rocky Mountains is an imaginary line called the **Continental Divide**. As the name suggests, the Continental Divide divides the North American continent into two parts. East of the divide, streams and rivers flow eastward. They drain into the Mississippi River system and into other rivers that flow into the Gulf of Mexico. Rivers west of the Continental Divide flow west toward the Pacific Ocean.

In addition to mountains, the West is made up of large plateaus and deep canyons carved by the region's fast-moving rivers. One of the largest canyons is Arizona's Grand Canyon. It is among the world's most famous landforms. Carved out by the Colorado River, the Grand Canyon is as much as a mile (1.6 km) deep. Yet the bottom of the canyon is not the lowest point in the United States. The lowest is Death Valley in California.

One place in Death Valley lies 282 feet (86 m) below sea level, making it also the lowest point in all of the Western Hemisphere. Death Valley is part of a large area of desert in the southwestern United States. Between the desert and the Pacific Ocean are more mountains, many of them formed by volcanoes. Movements in Earth's crust that formed these mountains also cause the West's frequent earthquakes.

The West is a region with large areas of forests that cover the lower slopes of the Rockies as well as the mountains along the Pacific coast. The mild, rainy climate in this part of the West is perfect for growing some of the world's biggest trees. Some of the giant sequoias (sih•KWOY•uhz) and redwoods grow higher than 300 feet (91 m) and as large as 40 feet (12 m) across.

The West contains Alaska and Hawaii, the two states that are not contiguous with the rest of the United States. Their unusual geography also makes them among the least populated states.

Hawaii's population is limited mostly by the state's small size. Yet physically Hawaii is still growing. This is so because the Hawaiian Islands are really the tops of volcanoes that rise from the floor of the Pacific Ocean. Two of these volcanoes are still active. Every time they erupt, they add new land to Hawaii.

With an average of about one person living in each square mile (2.6 sq km), Alaska has the lowest population density of any state. Despite its large size and many miles of coastline, its cold climate and rugged landscape make it a difficult place to live.

REVIEW **Why does Alaska have the lowest population density of any state?**

The snow-capped Kenai Mountains tower above the fishing village of Homer, Alaska.

LESSON 1
REVIEW

❶ **MAIN IDEA** What are the four major regions in the United States?

❷ **WHY IT MATTERS** Where do most of the people live in the United States?

❸ **VOCABULARY** Use the term **contiguous** in a sentence about the United States.

❹ **READING SKILL—Summarize** How have the Appalachian Mountains affected settlement in the Northeast?

❺ **GEOGRAPHY** Which river system drains much of the Middle West?

❻ **GEOGRAPHY** Which kinds of storms often threaten the Middle West and the South?

❼ **CRITICAL THINKING—Hypothesize** How might the United States be different if there were more natural harbors in the South and West?

 PERFORMANCE—Make a Map On a blank sheet of paper, draw an outline map of the United States. Fill it in with labels identifying the major areas of mountains, plains, and deserts.

Read a Relief and Elevation Map

➡ WHY IT MATTERS

Different kinds of maps provide different information. To find the heights of physical features in a region, you would look at an elevation map. **Elevation** is the height of the land in relation to sea level. To get a picture of the physical features of a region, you might look at a relief map. **Relief** is the differences in height in an area of land.

➡ WHAT YOU NEED TO KNOW

On an elevation map (Map B), the land is measured from sea level. The elevation of land at sea level is 0 feet (0 m). Find sea

level on Drawing A. The lines that circle the hill are contour lines. A **contour line** connects all points of equal elevation. On Drawing A, the 100-foot (30-m) contour line connects all points that are 100 feet above sea level.

On a relief map (Map A), relief is often shown by shading. Heavy shading shows high relief, or sharp rises and drops in the land. Low relief, where the land rises or falls gently, is lightly shaded. No shading shows land that is mainly flat.

Like the shading on a relief map, the red and green lines on Drawings A and B show how sharply the land rises or falls. Drawing B shows the hill from above.

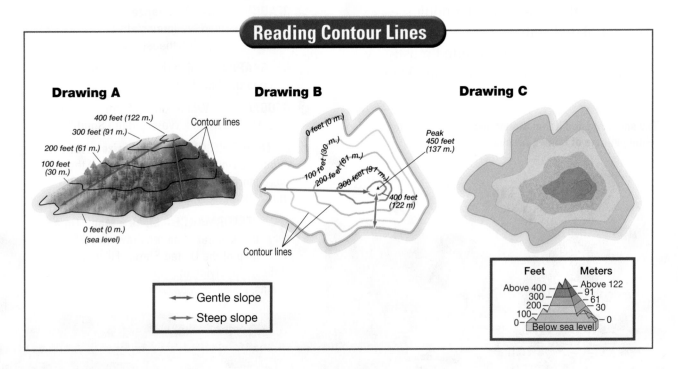

Reading Contour Lines

Drawing A

400 feet (122 m.)
300 feet (91 m.)
200 feet (61 m.)
100 feet (30 m.)
Contour lines
0 feet (0 m.) (sea level)

⟷ Gentle slope
⟷ Steep slope

Drawing B

0 feet (0 m.)
100 feet (30 m.)
200 feet (61 m.)
300 feet (91 m.)
400 feet (122 m)
Peak 450 feet (137 m.)
Contour lines

Drawing C

Feet   Meters
Above 400 — Above 122
300 — 91
200 — 61
100 — 30
0 — 0
Below sea level

Map A: Relief Map of Texas

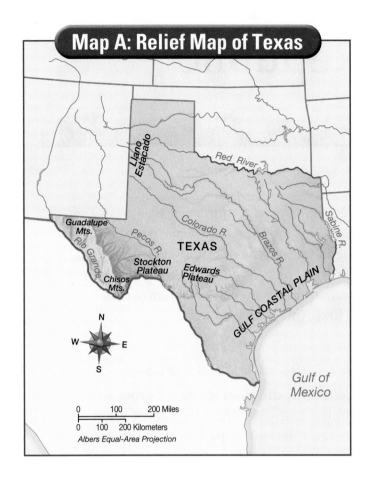

Map B: Elevation Map of Texas

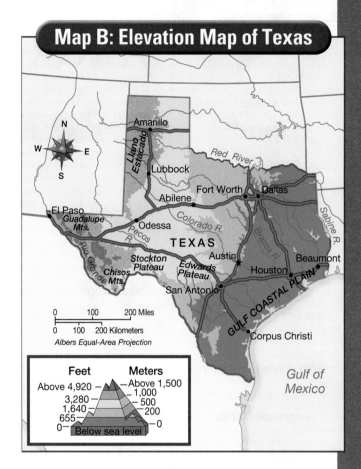

On the steeper side of the hill, the contour lines are closer together. On the gently sloping side, they are farther apart.

In Drawing C the color between contour lines shows elevation. The land shown in green is between sea level and 100 feet. Drawing C, however, does not show exact elevations. Instead, the key shows the range of elevations each color stands for. Map B also uses color to show ranges of elevation.

▶ PRACTICE THE SKILL

Use the maps above to answer the following questions.

1 Which city is at a higher elevation—Amarillo, Texas, or Houston, Texas? Explain your answer.

2 What part of Texas has the greatest range of elevations?

3 Look at Map A. Which area has the highest relief?

▶ APPLY WHAT YOU LEARNED

Plan a trip by car between two cities in Texas. Try to find the most direct route using the roads shown on Map B. Write a paragraph describing the different elevations you would cross on your journey. Compare your paragraph with that of a classmate.

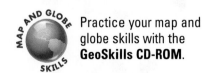

Practice your map and globe skills with the **GeoSkills CD-ROM**.

MAP AND GLOBE SKILLS

A New Republic

| 1400 | 1600 | 1800 | 2000 |

MAIN IDEA
Read to find out how the United States grew from a group of colonies to an independent, self-governing nation.

WHY IT MATTERS
The issues that helped found a new nation are still important.

VOCABULARY

indigenous
representation
revolution
declaration
independence
constitution
republic
amendment

Long before the United States was a country, it was a land of many different people. These **indigenous** (in•DIH•juh•nuhs) people, or people native to the land, may have numbered more than a million before the first Europeans arrived. The Europeans called the indigenous people *Indians*. Today they are also known as Native Americans, or the first Americans.

Native Americans and Europeans

By about A.D. 1400, hundreds of different tribes, or groups of Native Americans, lived in the many different regions of what is now the United States. Each tribe developed its own way of life. Farming, however, was an activity shared by many Native Americans living in every region. Besides farming, those in the forests of the Northeast and the South hunted deer and other animals. Native Americans in the Middle West relied on hunting bison, or buffalo. They used all parts of the buffalo to meet almost all their needs for food, clothing, and shelter. Some native people in the West, those living along the Pacific coast, fished and hunted whales.

This reenactment shows how a feast at Plymouth Colony may have looked.

In 1492 the first Europeans arrived. Led by Christopher Columbus, an Italian hired by Spain, the Europeans sailed across the Atlantic Ocean and landed on the island of San Salvador, not far from the North American coast. The goal of Columbus and his sailors was to find a new trade route to Asia. Instead, they opened the Americas to settlement.

Not long after Columbus arrived, European settlers set up colonies in the lands they claimed as their own. Some colonists, or people who lived in the colonies, had come to the Americas hoping to get rich. Others wanted religious freedom, which they did not have in their homelands.

The Spanish were the first Europeans to reach the present-day United States. As a result, Spain claimed much of the land in the South and the West. The French arrived next, and France claimed what is now Canada and, later, much of the Middle West region. A few people also came to North America from the Netherlands and Sweden. The English—or British, as they came to be called—claimed the land along the Atlantic coast. By the 1700s England had set up 13 separate colonies.

REVIEW What countries claimed the most land in what is now the United States?

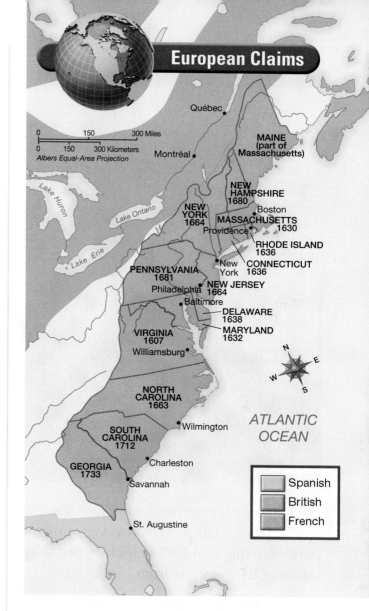

European Claims

150 300 Miles
150 300 Kilometers
Albers Equal-Area Projection

Québec

MAINE
(part of Massachusetts)

NEW HAMPSHIRE 1680

NEW YORK 1664

MASSACHUSETTS 1630

Boston

Providence

RHODE ISLAND 1636

CONNECTICUT 1636

PENNSYLVANIA 1681

New York

Philadelphia

NEW JERSEY 1664

Baltimore

DELAWARE 1638

VIRGINIA 1607

MARYLAND 1632

Williamsburg

NORTH CAROLINA 1663

SOUTH CAROLINA 1712

Wilmington

ATLANTIC OCEAN

GEORGIA 1733

Charleston

Savannah

St. Augustine

Lake Huron

Lake Ontario

Lake Erie

Montréal

Spanish
British
French

GEOGRAPHY THEME

Regions Three European nations controlled most of eastern North America in the 1700s.

❷ Which country controlled Virginia?

Rebellion and Independence

Problems soon arose between the British government and the colonists. In 1763 the British had just helped the colonists fight a war against the French over who would control the land between the Appalachian Mountains and the Mississippi River. British victory in this war, which was called the French and Indian War, gave the British almost complete control of the eastern part of North America. Now the British government wanted the colonists to pay for the cost of the war. The British government began to tax the colonists on goods sent from Britain and sold in the colonies.

The new taxes made the colonists angry because they were taxed without being asked by the British government. The colonists had no **representation**, or no one to speak for them, in the British government. Many colonists believed that "taxation without representation" was unfair and did not respect their rights as British citizens.

Thomas Jefferson   1743–1826
Character Trait: Civic Virtue

The Second Continental Congress appointed a committee to write a declaration announcing the colonies' independence from Britain. John Adams nominated Thomas Jefferson to write the declaration. Jefferson was aware that listing the colonists' grievances and announcing their independence was only part of his task. He knew that he had the chance—and the duty—to express the ideals that would guide the newly independent country. With that in mind, Jefferson began to write the Declaration of Independence.

MULTIMEDIA BIOGRAPHIES
Visit The Learning Site at
www.harcourtschool.com/biographies
to learn about other famous people.

GO ONLINE

Some colonists spoke out because the idea of freedom, or liberty, was very important to them. In 1775 Patrick Henry, a leader of the colonists from Virginia, said,

> **❝I know not what course others may take; but as for me, give me liberty or give me death!❞**

The British government, however, continued to make more laws for the colonists without asking them. Every new law seemed to take away more and more of the colonists' individual rights, or freedoms.

In September 1774, representatives from the American colonies met in Philadelphia. The meeting came to be known as the First Continental Congress. There, the Americans decided to challenge British rule. They voted not to obey any more laws that took away their rights as British citizens.

Then, on April 19, 1775, fighting broke out at Lexington and Concord, in Massachusetts, between British troops and American Patriots. *Patriots* was the name given to the colonists who opposed British rule and believed in fighting for their freedom. The American Revolution had begun. A **revolution** is a sudden and complete change in government or in people's lives.

In May 1775 the Second Continental Congress met and decided to form an army. The Congress chose George Washington to lead the Americans in a war against the British. The next year, on July 4, 1776, the Congress approved a **declaration**, or official statement, of American independence from the British government. **Independence** is the freedom to rule oneself. That day, July 4, would become the first national holiday of the future United States of America—Independence Day.

The war against the British lasted until 1781, when the British army finally gave up. On September 3, 1783, British and American leaders signed the Treaty of Paris, bringing an end to the war.

The 13 American colonies had become an independent country made up of 13 states. At the same time, it became a symbol for freedom, opportunity, and change for many people around the world.

REVIEW When did the United States of America officially become an independent country?

Forming a More Perfect Union

Under the Articles of Confederation, the new country's first **constitution**, or written plan of government, the 13 states held most of the authority. Congress, the group of representatives elected from each state to run the country, had little authority. The citizens wanted it that way. They worried that a strong central government might rule unfairly like the British and take away the rights that they had won in the American Revolution. They soon realized, however, that their new government needed to be improved.

In May 1787 Congress called for a Constitutional Convention to recommend changes in the first constitution. Instead, the convention created a whole new plan of government. It was called the Constitution of the United States of America. The Constitution gave some authority to the states and some authority to the central government. Other authority was to be shared. The Constitution also outlined the duties of three branches of government— the executive, the legislative, and the judicial. Each branch would have its own areas of authority, with no one branch having greater authority than the others.

The Constitution made the United States a republic. In a **republic**, citizens vote for officials who represent them in governing.

DEMOCRATIC VALUES
Individual Rights

The Bill of Rights limits the power of government by promising certain individual rights. These rights prevent government from having too much control. For example, the First Amendment, or the first part of the Bill of Rights, protects each citizen's right to free speech. It also prevents the government from forcing citizens to practice any certain religion.

Analyze the Value

❶ Why is the Bill of Rights important to United States citizens?

❷ **Make It Relevant** Read a copy of the Bill of Rights. Write a paragraph that explains its impact on your life.

This painting by Thomas P. Rossiter is called *The Signing of the Constitution.*

The most important authority in a republic rests with the citizens, not with government leaders.

Although the United States Constitution was approved in 1788, changes, or **amendments**, were made to it in 1791. The first ten amendments to the Constitution are called the Bill of Rights. The Bill of Rights guarantees the freedoms of all citizens in the United States. Today the Constitution remains the most important document in governing the United States and its people.

REVIEW How did the Constitution change the government of the United States in 1788?

Growth and Growing Pains

With its new government in place, the United States soon grew in size and population. In 1803 the United States purchased the Louisiana Territory from France, doubling the size of the country. In the years that followed, more lands were gained through purchase, treaty, and war. By 1853 the United States controlled all of the land

CHARLESTON
MERCURY
EXTRA:

Passed unanimously at 1.15 o'clock, P .M., December 20th, 1860.

AN ORDINANCE

To dissolve the Union between the State of South Carolina and other States united with her under the compact entitled "The Constitution of the United States of America."

We, the People of the State of South Carolina, in Convention assembled, do declare and ordain, and it is hereby declared and ordained,

That the Ordinance adopted by us in Convention, on the twenty-third day of May, in the year of our Lord one thousand seven hundred and eighty-eight, whereby the Constitution of the United States of America was ratified, and also, all Acts and parts of Acts of the General Assembly of this State, ratifying amendments of the said Constitution, are hereby repealed; and that the union now subsisting between South Carolina and other States, under the name of "The United States of America," is hereby dissolved.

THE
UNION
IS
DISSOLVED!

South Carolina was the first state to withdraw from the United States during Civil War times.

that would become the 48 contiguous United States. By 1900 the United States also obtained Alaska and Hawaii.

The country's population grew as the United States developed its economy. At first a country of farms, it became a nation of factories by the late 1800s.

Economic growth soon attracted waves of people from other countries looking for jobs and better ways of life. By 1920 more people in the United States were living in cities than living on farms.

As it grew, the United States faced many challenges. The first great challenge came in the 1800s with the American Civil War, when the United States was almost divided in two. The war was fought between the northern and southern regions of the country over the rights of states to make their own laws. Many of these laws had to do with slavery. The Civil War started

John Shobart painted this scene of goods and people moving westward on the Mississippi River system in the 1800s.

MARTHA

in 1861 and lasted four years. The North finally won the war, and the United States remained united.

In the 1900s the United States took part in two world wars. More than 100,000 Americans died fighting in World War I, and more than 400,000 died in World War II. Between the wars there was a period of hard times called the Great Depression. Many people were without work in the United States and all over the world. After World War II, better times followed. The United States led the way in space exploration and landed the first astronauts on the moon in 1969. All this time the United States was becoming more powerful among the nations of the world.

Today the United States is a world leader. Once 13 colonies fighting for freedom, the United States has become a model of freedom throughout the world.

REVIEW What challenges did the United States face as it grew?

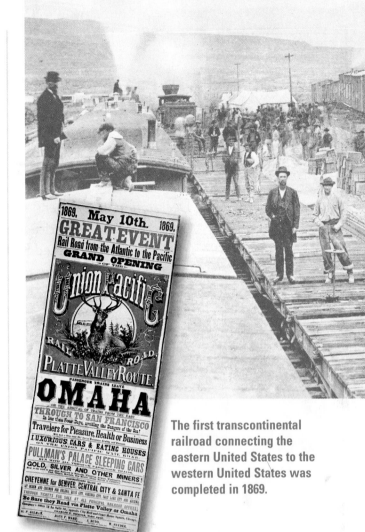

The first transcontinental railroad connecting the eastern United States to the western United States was completed in 1869.

LESSON 2 REVIEW

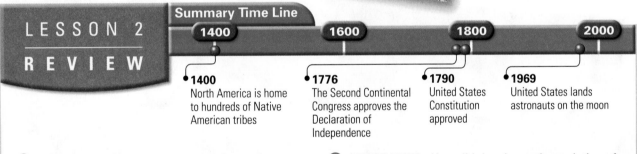

Summary Time Line

1400 — 1600 — 1800 — 2000

1400
North America is home to hundreds of Native American tribes

1776
The Second Continental Congress approves the Declaration of Independence

1790
United States Constitution approved

1969
United States lands astronauts on the moon

1. **MAIN IDEA** How did the United States become an independent country?

2. **WHY IT MATTERS** What are two issues that concern United States citizens today just as they concerned American colonists long ago?

3. **VOCABULARY** Use the words **constitution**, **republic**, and **amendment** to describe the United States government.

4. **TIME LINE** Could the Constitution have been mentioned in the Declaration of Independence? Why or why not?

5. **READING SKILL—Summarize** Why did Americans after the Revolution not want a strong central government?

6. **GEOGRAPHY** How did the size and population of the United States change after 1800?

7. **CRITICAL THINKING—Hypothesize** What might have happened if the North had not won the American Civil War?

PERFORMANCE—Create an Advertisement
Imagine that you are living in one of the 13 colonies in 1776. You have become convinced that it is necessary for the American colonies to break away from British control. Create an advertisement to persuade others to support the colonies in their revolt against British rule. Provide logical reasons. Include at least one illustration in your advertisement. Share your advertisement with your class.

Primary Sources

Charters of Freedom

The Declaration of Independence and the Constitution of the United States of America are two of the most important documents in United States history. They are often called the nation's Charters of Freedom. One declared the United States a free nation. The other provided the new nation's plan of government and, after being amended, guaranteed the rights of its citizens.

FROM THE UNITED STATES GOVERNMENT NATIONAL ARCHIVES AND RECORDS ADMINISTRATION

This inkstand was used by the signers of the Declaration and the Constitution.

IN CONGRESS. JULY 4. 1776.

The unanimous Declaration of the thirteen united States of America.

Thomas Jefferson
Author of the
Declaration

Declaration of Independence

When in the Course of human events it becomes necessary for one people to dissolve the political bands which have connected them with another, and to assume among the powers of the earth, the separate and equal station to which the Laws of Nature and of Nature's God entitle them, a decent respect to the opinions of mankind requires that they should declare the causes which impel them to the separation.

Constitution

We the people of the United States, in order to form a more perfect Union, establish justice, insure domestic tranquillity, provide for the common defense, promote the general welfare, and secure the blessings of liberty to ourselves and our posterity, do ordain and establish this Constitution for the United States of America.

James Madison
Father of the
Constitution

Analyze the Primary Source

1. **What do these documents tell you about the time during which they were created?**

2. **If these documents were created today, how might they look different?**

ACTIVITY

Write a Report Use print or electronic reference tools to gather more information about these two documents. Prepare a short report about how each document was created and what its purpose was.

RESEARCH

Visit The Learning Site at **www.harcourtschool.com/ primarysources** to research other documents.

The Charters of Freedom can be seen at the National Archives in Washington, D.C.

MAIN IDEA
Read to find out how the United States is a united nation made up of many different groups who bring unique cultural influences.

WHY IT MATTERS
Despite differences among people living in the United States, the people are all Americans.

VOCABULARY
immigrant
discrimination
literacy
pluralistic
western

Immigrants from Europe in the 1900s entered the United States by way of Ellis Island.

One People, Many Cultures

From its beginning the United States of America has been a country of immigrants. An **immigrant** (IH•mih•gruhnt) is a person who comes to live in a country after leaving his or her homeland. Even early Native Americans may have come to North America by way of Asia. Imagine walking along a busy street in any city in the United States. The faces you see represent the rich mix of histories, traditions, and ideas in American society today.

A Mosaic of People

The people of the United States form one of the more diverse populations in the world. Some people have described it as a mosaic. The term *mosaic* suggests that the population of the United States does not blend into a single culture. Instead, the culture of each group contributes a part of its own ideas and practices to the whole American culture.

The largest group of Americans consists of people whose ancestors were European immigrants. During the country's early history, most of the immigrants came from Britain and from other countries in Western Europe.

In the years between 1860 and 1920, during a time of industrial growth, about 30 million new immigrants from Western and Eastern Europe came to work in American factories. Presently, people of European culture account for three-fourths of the total population, or about 210 million people.

Hispanic Americans make up the fastest growing group of American people. A little more than 1 in 8 Americans, or about 35 million, are of Hispanic, or Spanish-speaking, culture. More than three-fourths of them live in the South and the West. California and Texas have the largest Hispanic populations, but the state with the highest percentage of Hispanics is New Mexico. More than 4 of every 10 people in New Mexico are Hispanic.

About 35 million Americans, or about 1 in 8, are of African culture. The first Africans arrived as slaves in the early 1600s to work on Southern plantations. After the American Civil War, when slavery was ended, some moved to the West. Others moved to the Northeast and the Middle West during World War I to work in factories. This movement of African Americans is called the "Great Migration." It is often compared to the great migration of Europeans between 1860 and 1920.

The Asian population of the United States began arriving in the 1850s. The Chinese came first, during the California gold rush. Japanese and Filipino people came in the late 1800s and settled mainly in the West, along the Pacific coast and in Hawaii. Today people of Asian culture make up about 3.5 percent of the total population, or more than 10 million people.

The Native American population of the United States makes up less than 1 percent of the total population, or 2.5 million.

European Americans celebrate their heritage with a street festival in New York City's Little Italy (below) and with a St. Patrick's Day parade in Chicago.

Welcome To Little Italy
MULBERRY STREET MALL

Dr. Martin Luther King, Jr., a leader for equal rights, delivered his famous "I Have a Dream" speech at the Lincoln Memorial in Washington, D.C. Dr. King won the Nobel Peace Prize in 1964.

Native American people live mostly in the Interior Plains. Oklahoma, which was known as Indian Territory in the 1800s, has the greatest density of indigenous people.

REVIEW What major groups make up the United States population?

A Changing Population

Of the more than 281 million people in the United States today, slightly more are female than male. While their populations are nearly equal, men and women have not always been treated equally in the United States. For many years women faced discrimination. **Discrimination** is unfair treatment of certain people or groups, such as women.

Many years ago, women in the United States could not own property, hold certain jobs, or even vote. Women gained the right to vote in 1920 by way of the Nineteenth Amendment to the United States Constitution. By the 1970s other new laws required men and women to be treated equally. Today women in the United States hold important positions in almost every job and profession.

Just as there are more females than males in the United States, there are also more older people than younger people. The average age of an American today is about 35 years, the oldest it has been in the country's history. This is mainly the result of people living longer today.

Because the population is aging, it is estimated that by the year 2020 nearly 1 out of 5 Americans will be over the age of 65. As the population grows older, people are

Susan B. Anthony is remembered for helping women gain the right to vote.

choosing to work beyond the traditional retirement age of 65. As the number of older Americans increases, they will have more voting power in the future.

Native American storyteller figure made by Mary Trujillo

While the American population is older than it has ever been, it is also better educated. The literacy rate of Americans, about 97 percent, is higher than it has ever been. **Literacy** means the ability to read and write. In addition, more Americans, including older Americans, are attending college.

REVIEW How has discrimination against women in the United States changed over time?

Expressions of Culture

American society can also be described as **pluralistic**. That is, the people share common cultural elements while also maintaining many of the traditional ways

of their ancestors. Cultural differences among Americans can be seen in the ways people worship, the kinds of music they play, the languages they speak, and the food they eat.

Religion is an important part of culture for many groups. Religious beliefs affect the way people think about themselves and others. Most Americans, about 84 percent, are Christians, including Baptists, Methodists, Presbyterians, Lutherans, Quakers, Episcopalians, and Roman Catholics. Not all Americans are Christians, however. There are Muslims, Jews, Buddhists, Hindus, and other religious groups in the United States, too. As more people have moved to the United States from other places in the world, the number of people who practice some of these religions has grown.

This mural in Los Angeles shows the influence of California's early Spanish settlers.

Jazz singer Billie Holiday (above) records a new song in 1939. Today jazz is recorded and listened to in the United States and around the world.

Music in the United States is also as varied as its people, and various kinds of music can be heard throughout the country. However, western music is the most popular. **Western** refers to the heritage of people of European descent. There are two chief kinds of western music, classical and popular. Classical music includes symphonies, operas, and ballets. Popular music includes country music, folk music, and rock music. Jazz music is sometimes called the first original American art form. It developed in the South in the early 1900s and drew its inspiration from African American religious songs and work songs.

The United States does not have an official language, but English has always been the country's chief language. The immigrants from Britain, who included the country's founders, spoke English. Today Spanish is the second most common language in the United States. In some places, public documents and signs are written in both English and Spanish. Other languages are also spoken in the areas where recent immigrants live.

Americans eat a wide variety of foods. Some regions and people of the United States have distinctive food specialties. The South is known for chicken and grits, made of coarsely ground corn. Among people of German descent, dishes include sauerkraut and pork. Southern Louisiana has a reputation for dishes of fish with spices. In Hawaii, rice and fresh fruits, such as bananas and papayas, are basic parts of the diet.

REVIEW What does it mean to have a pluralistic society?

Young dancers practice ballet. Ballet is a classical form of dance that uses set movements.

Americans Join Together

Americans unite to celebrate holidays. Like its people, the national holidays of the United States have many origins. Some, such as Thanksgiving Day, Memorial Day, and Independence Day, cause Americans to remember important events in their nation's history. Others, such as Dr. Martin Luther King, Jr., Day and Presidents' Day, honor national leaders past and present.

Sad times also bring Americans together. On September 11, 2001, the United States suffered from a horrible act of terrorism, or the deliberate use of violence to promote a cause. Terrorists hijacked, or illegally took control of, four airplanes. They crashed two planes into the twin towers of the World Trade Center in New York City. Another plane hit the Pentagon near Washington, D.C. The fourth plane crashed into a field in Pennsylvania. Thousands of Americans died on that tragic day.

Ordinary citizens became heroes as they rushed to help in whatever way they could. At the same time the United States government declared a war on terrorism and vowed to prevent future attacks. These actions helped ensure that the country, and the world, would remain safe and free.

REVIEW Why did the United States declare a war on terrorism?

LESSON 3
REVIEW

1 **MAIN IDEA** How has human migration influenced the character of the United States?

2 **WHY IT MATTERS** What do all people living in the United States have in common?

3 **VOCABULARY** What is **discrimination**?

4 **READING SKILL—Summarize** What is jazz? Why is it important to the history of the creative arts in the United States?

5 **CULTURE** How is the United States like a mosaic?

6 **GEOGRAPHY** Where do three-fourths of Hispanic Americans live?

7 **CULTURE** What are some of the main religious groups found in the United States?

8 **CRITICAL THINKING—Synthesize** Review a list of United States holidays. Pick at least two examples. What do those holidays tell you about Americans?

PERFORMANCE—Draw a Picture Choose a holiday that is important to you or your family. Draw a picture or diagram that shows how you celebrate. Label and describe special symbols, decorations, foods, or activities associated with the holiday.

Twin beams of light shine in memory of the twin towers of the World Trade Center.

·SKILLS·

Determine Point of View

VOCABULARY
point of view

▶ WHY IT MATTERS

In a nation of many cultures, people have many different points of view. A person's **point of view** is the set of beliefs he or she holds. A point of view may be shaped by such traits as a person's age, gender, culture, religion, race, and nationality.

Changes in points of view have often brought about social changes. Today most Americans share the point of view that discrimination against groups of people is wrong. However, this was not always the point of view held by the majority of Americans.

Until the 1950s and 1960s, laws in the South allowed discrimination against African Americans. For example, there were laws that made it illegal for African Americans to eat at the same restaurants and attend the same schools as whites.

These African American students from North Carolina express their point of view at a sit-in in 1960.

Studying points of view and how they can change is the key to understanding how people and ideas shape history.

▶ WHAT YOU NEED TO KNOW

The 1950s and 1960s were a time of social change and clashing points of view. For years African Americans had been discriminated against and denied basic rights. Many called for change. One leader of this call for change, known as the Civil Rights movement, was Dr. Martin Luther King, Jr. In 1963 he gave a speech in Washington, D.C. Here is an excerpt from this speech:

"I have a dream that one day this nation will rise up and live out the true meaning of its creed: 'We hold these truths to be self-evident; that all men are created equal.' . . . This is our hope. . . . With this faith we will be able to transform the jangling discords of our nation into the beautiful symphony of brotherhood . . . we will be able to speed up that day when all of God's children, black men and white men, Jews and Gentiles, Protestants and Catholics, will be able to join hands and sing in the words of the old Negro spiritual: 'Free at last! Free at last! Thank God Almighty, we are free at last!'"

To determine points of view, you can use the following steps.

Step 1 Identify the person. In an article, look for the writer's name at the beginning or the end of the article.

Sometimes there may also be biographical information about the writer that will help you better understand the writer's reasons for his or her statements.

Step 2 Think about the situation in which statements were made. When reading about the past, look for clues of what life was like then. When reading about the present day, look for references to people or issues in the news. How might the situation have influenced a person's point of view?

Step 3 Look for words that help you find a person's point of view. Statements giving points of view may contain phrases such as *I think, I believe, I hope, in my opinion.*

▶ PRACTICE THE SKILL

Refer to Dr. King's speech to answer these questions.

1 Do you think King believed that discrimination could be ended? Explain your answer.

2 How would you describe King's mood when he gave the speech?

3 Which of King's sentences best summarizes his point of view? Why?

▶ APPLY WHAT YOU LEARNED

Look at the Letters to the Editor section in a newspaper or magazine (print or online versions). Find a letter about an issue familiar to you. Clip out or print the letter. Determine the writer's point of view by using the steps described in "What You Need to Know." Highlight any words or phrases in the letter that signal point of view, and then write a summary of the issue and the writer's point of view.

Dr. Martin Luther King, Jr., addresses the crowd during the March on Washington in 1963.

Demonstrators protest discrimination during the March on Washington.

MAIN IDEA
Read to find out how freedom is part of both the government and the economy in the United States.

WHY IT MATTERS
All citizens in the United States need to know how their government and economy work.

VOCABULARY

constitutional democracy

representative democracy

federal government

Cabinet

political party

common good

market price

deficit

Let Freedom Ring

When people in the world talk about the United States government and economy, one word often comes to mind—*freedom*. That is because the United States government and economic system protect the freedom of the country's citizens and businesses. Citizens are free to choose their government leaders, their work, and the products they buy. Businesses are free to set prices for the goods and services they choose to make and sell. These freedoms have made the United States one of the strongest nations in the world.

American Democracy

The United States has a form of government known as a constitutional democracy. In a **constitutional democracy**, the goals of the government and the ways it will work to achieve them are laid out in a constitution, or a written plan of governing. Today most countries in the world have constitutions. Yet not all countries with constitutions are democracies. Democracy is a governing system in which the people of a country take part.

The United States government is also a **representative democracy** because its citizens elect people to make laws and decisions for them. These laws and decisions are made at three levels of government—local, state, and national. Each level has its own duties and areas of authority. Local governments, for example, make laws and decisions for cities and towns, counties, and school districts. Each state government, which meets at its own state capital, makes laws and decisions for all the people living in that state. State governments control government matters involving education, state roads, and state parks. The national government, which meets in Washington, D.C., controls government matters related to the military, money, and relations with other countries.

The national government is also called the **federal government**. It is divided into three branches—the executive, the legislative, and the judicial branches. The President, Vice President, and a group of appointed advisers who make up the **Cabinet** lead the executive branch of government. The legislative branch is made up of elected officials from each state who form two houses of Congress—the

People in Des Plaines, Illinois, celebrate Independence Day.

Senate and the House of Representatives. The judicial branch is made up of the United States Supreme Court and the federal court system. Its judges are appointed by the President and approved by the Senate. To balance authority among the three branches, a system of checks and balances lets each branch of government have some control over the other branches.

Americans elect many of their leaders and representatives under a system of political parties. A **political party** is a group of people involved in government who try to get others to agree with their ideas. The nation's two largest parties are the Democratic party and the Republican party. Each party has its own candidates who represent the party's ideas and ways of thinking. Each voter supports the party that best matches his or her beliefs.

REVIEW How is the United States government an example of a constitutional democracy?

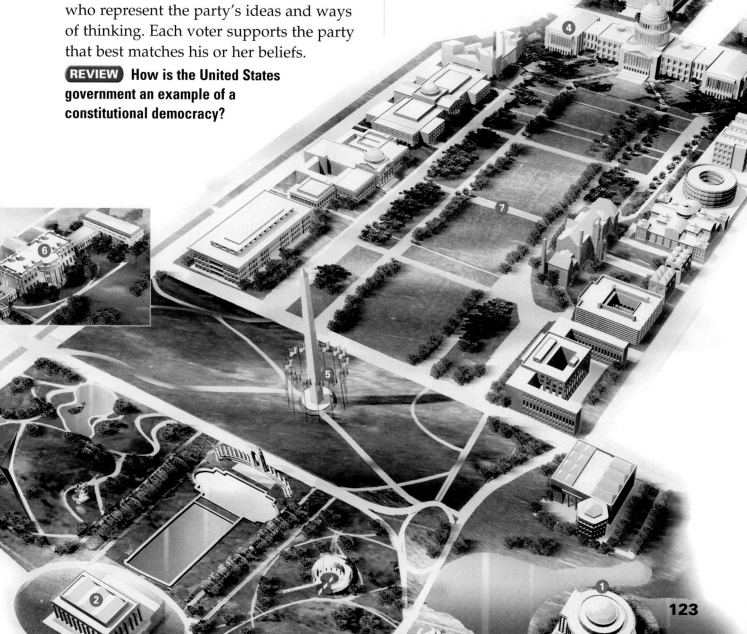

A CLOSER LOOK
Washington, D.C.

Washington, D.C., the United States capital, has many beautiful monuments, museums, and government buildings.
1. Jefferson Memorial
2. Lincoln Memorial
3. Supreme Court Building
4. United States Capitol
5. Washington Monument
6. White House
7. The National Mall with the museums of the Smithsonian Institution on both sides

In which building does Congress meet?

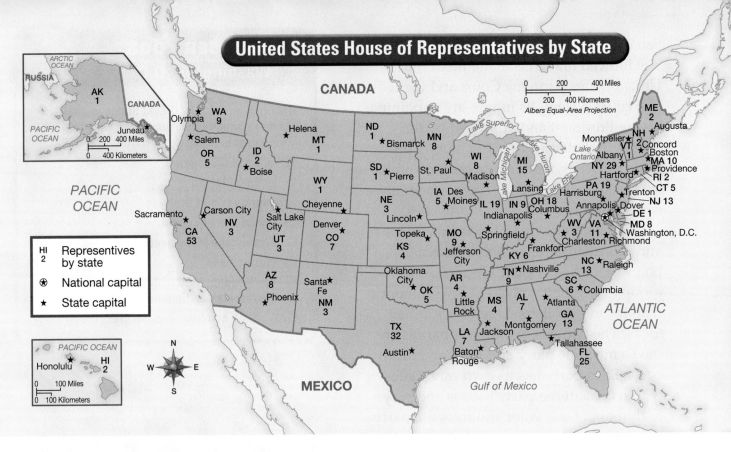

United States House of Representatives by State

RUSSIA

AK 1

CANADA

Juneau ★

PACIFIC OCEAN

0 200 400 Miles
0   400 Kilometers

PACIFIC OCEAN

CANADA

★ Olympia WA 9

★ Salem OR 5

★ Helena MT 1

★ Boise ID 2

Cheyenne ★ WY 1

★ Sacramento CA 53

Carson City ★ NV 3

Salt Lake City ★ UT 3

Denver ★ CO 7

★ Phoenix AZ 8

Santa Fe ★ NM 3

ND 1 ★ Bismarck

SD 1 ★ Pierre

St. Paul MN 8

WI 8 Madison ★

NE 3 Lincoln ★

Des Moines IA 5

Topeka ★ KS 4

Oklahoma City ★ OK 5

TX 32 Austin ★

Lansing ★ MI 15

IL 19 IN 9 Columbus OH 18
Indianapolis ★ Springfield ★

MO 9 Jefferson City ★

AR 4 Little Rock ★

MS 4 Jackson ★

LA 7 Baton Rouge ★

AL 7 Montgomery ★

GA 13 Atlanta ★

Lake Superior

Lake Michigan Lake Huron Lake Erie Lake Ontario

ME 2 Augusta ★

Montpelier ★ NH 2 Concord ★ Boston ★

VT Albany ★ NY 29

Hartford ★ MA 10 Providence ★ RI 2

PA 19 Harrisburg ★ Trenton ★ CT 5 NJ 13

Annapolis ★ Dover ★ DE 1

WV 3 VA 11 MD 8 Washington, D.C.

Charleston ★ Richmond ★

KY 6 Frankfort ★

TN 9 ★ Nashville

NC 13 ★ Raleigh

SC 6 ★ Columbia

Tallahassee ★ FL 25

ATLANTIC OCEAN

MEXICO Gulf of Mexico

0 200 400 Miles
0 200 400 Kilometers
Albers Equal-Area Projection

Legend

HI 2 Representives by state

⊛ National capital

★ State capital

PACIFIC OCEAN

Honolulu ★ HI 2

0 100 Miles
0 100 Kilometers

N W E S

Regions The number of representatives each state can elect to the United States Congress is based on the population of that state.

◆ Which state has the most representatives?

Rights and Responsibilities

The United States government gives and guarantees many rights for all American citizens. These rights are protected under the Constitution and the Bill of Rights. Some of these rights include freedom of speech and the right to fair treatment and a fair trial.

Along with these rights, American citizens also have responsibilities. Each citizen in the United States has both personal and civic responsibilities. A personal responsibility is an action that a person takes to improve his or her life. Someone who studies or works hard, who eats healthful foods, and who exercises regularly shows personal responsibility.

A civic responsibility is an action that a person takes for the **common good**, or to help all citizens as a group. Someone who obeys laws, pays taxes, votes, and helps out in the community shows civic responsibility. Civic responsibility may also include public service, or taking part in government. Citizens take part in government by sharing ideas about issues involving the common good, by running for public office, and by helping other people who seek to serve in local, state, or national government.

Vote! I Did.

REVIEW How do American citizens show civic responsibility?

An Economic Superpower

The economy of the United States is the largest and strongest of any economy in the world. It has the world's largest gross domestic product, or GDP, at about $10 trillion. That is more than two times the GDP of Japan, which is second-largest at $4.6 trillion.

Several factors need to work together to make a country's economy successful. Such factors include a country's people, its natural resources, and its economic system.

The United States economy benefits from its people's hard work and their ingenuity, or ability to discover and invent. Americans use their ingenuity to develop new technologies and to put them to work in the economy. Americans make up just 5 percent of the world's population but produce at least 25 percent of all the world's goods and services.

The United States has a plentiful supply of natural resources ranging from fertile soil to fuels. Its agricultural resources provide the United States with a food surplus. Its fuel resources help the country produce the energy needed to power schools, homes, and factories.

The kind of economy the United States has is known as a market economy. In a market economy, people make their own choices about which goods and services they buy. They decide how they spend their money and what kind of work they do. Businesses in a market economy are free to create goods and services of their choice, and to sell them at **market prices**, or what people are willing to pay. The freedom of individuals and businesses in a market economy is called free enterprise.

Technology, such as the robotic arm, helps modern assembly lines move quickly.

· SCIENCE AND TECHNOLOGY ·

Henry Ford's Assembly Line

In the early 1900s Henry Ford designed one of the best-known automobiles in history—the Model T. He wanted to produce the Model T in large numbers but at a low price. To do this, Ford created the world's first moving assembly line for automobiles.

Many tasks are required to build an automobile. In Ford's system each automobile being built moved from worker to worker until the automobile was complete. Each worker was responsible for just one task. This made it easier for workers to learn their jobs and to become experts at doing them.

Ford's inventiveness allowed the price of the Model T to drop from $950 in 1909 to $290 by 1926. Ford's company produced half of the world's automobiles at that time.

The Chicago Board of Trade (above) and the New York Stock Exchange are centers for economic activity in the United States.

As a result of a strong economy in the United States, the American people enjoy a high standard of living. One measure of a country's standard of living is based on the goals that the country's people set for themselves as consumers. That is, when the people have enough material things for comfort and happiness, they have achieved a high standard of living.

REVIEW What factors help make an economy successful?

A Dynamic Economy

The United States economy benefits from producing goods and services for American consumers. It also benefits from trading goods and services with other countries around the world. The United States trades most with its closest neighbors, Canada and Mexico. About 11 percent of the nation's trade is with Canada, and 11 percent is with Mexico. The United States also trades this same amount with Japan.

International trade has made a strong United States economy even stronger.

Analyze Graphs This graph compares the value of goods bought by the United States to the value of goods sold.

◈ How much more does the country buy than sell?

United States International Trade

Amount of Trade (in billions of dollars)

$1,400
$1,200
$1,000
$800
$600
$400
$200

United States Imports   United States Exports

However, international trade has its problems. One problem is that the United States has an unfavorable balance of trade. That is, it imports more than it exports. When a country buys more goods and services from other countries than it sells to them, it creates a trade **deficit**, or shortage.

Even with a trade deficit, the United States has enough wealth to help other countries. The United States government gives and loans money to other countries through federal programs and membership in international organizations, such as the World Bank. A country in need can use this money to make its economy grow, to rebuild after a disaster, or to improve its education or trade.

Over the years, the United States economy has changed continually. During the 1800s the country's economy changed from one based on agriculture to one based on manufacturing. During the 1900s the United States economy moved from one based on producing goods to one based on providing services. Today an American is more likely to work at a job that involves doing something for people rather than producing a product to sell to them. Tourism and health care are examples of service industries.

Goods traded between the United States and other countries are sometimes transported in large container ships.

With economic changes come changes for workers. As businesses use more technology, so do their workers. The key to future success for the United States economy is continuing education for everyone.

REVIEW Which countries are the top trading partners of the United States?

LESSON 4
REVIEW

1. **MAIN IDEA** In what way is freedom an important part of the government and economic system of the United States?

2. **WHY IT MATTERS** What are two rights guaranteed by the United States Constitution and the Bill of Rights?

3. **VOCABULARY** What is meant by the term **common good**?

4. **READING SKILL—Summarize** What causes a trade deficit?

5. **CIVICS AND GOVERNMENT** What makes the United States a representative democracy?

6. **CIVICS AND GOVERNMENT** What is the importance of voluntary civic participation in the United States?

7. **ECONOMICS** What are the benefits of free enterprise?

8. **CRITICAL THINKING—Evaluate** United States law says that a citizen must be 18 years old to vote. Do you agree or disagree with this law? Would you choose a different age if you could? If so, what age would you choose? Why?

PERFORMANCE—Deliver a Speech Imagine that you are going to run for a local political office. Prepare a short speech that describes why people should vote for you. In the speech, be sure to include a community problem and your solution.

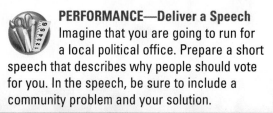

Make Economic Choices

VOCABULARY

scarcity
trade-off
opportunity cost

► WHY IT MATTERS

The United States is a wealthy nation. It has a plentiful supply of natural resources and a skilled workforce. Both of these factors contribute greatly to the nation's strong economy. This wealth, however, does not mean that every American consumer can buy all the goods and services he or she wants.

Sometimes the resources used to produce goods and services are limited, which limits the amount of goods and services available. This condition of limited resources and products is known as **scarcity**. Because of scarcity, some goods can be very expensive. Consumers must make economic choices based on the cost and availability of goods they want or need.

Learning how to make wise economic choices can help you make the best use of your money.

► WHAT YOU NEED TO KNOW

When you make an economic choice, you decide to buy one thing instead of another. When you do this, you are making a **trade-off**—you give up one thing in order to get another.

When you make an economic choice, what you decide to give up is known as an **opportunity cost**. For example, suppose you have just finished playing softball. You are hungry and thirsty, but you have only enough money to buy either something to drink or a slice of pizza. If you decide to buy the pizza, you give up the opportunity of satisfying your thirst.

These shoppers make economic choices.

These girls choose which sweater to buy.

Making economic choices can be difficult, so you'll want to think carefully before you make them. Using the following steps can help you.

Step 1 **Get a clear idea of the choice you need to make by determining the trade-off.**

Step 2 **Determine the opportunity cost of deciding in favor of each of the choices.**

Step 3 **Decide which choice has an opportunity cost that you can most easily accept, and then make your decision.**

➡ PRACTICE THE SKILL

Suppose a school has set some money aside. School officials are trying to decide whether to use the money to buy new computers or more books for the library.

1 What is the trade-off?

2 Suppose the school officials decide to use the money to buy more books. What is the opportunity cost of this economic choice?

3 Suppose you were in charge of choosing whether your school should buy new computers or more books. What choice would you make? Explain.

➡ APPLY WHAT YOU LEARNED

Write a journal entry titled "The Best Economic Choice I Ever Made." What trade-off did you have to make? What was the opportunity cost of your decision? Why do you feel you made the right choice?

Review and Test Preparation

Summary Time Line

1400 ──────────── **1500**

1400
North America is home
to hundreds of Native
American tribes

USE YOUR READING SKILLS

Complete this graphic organizer to show that you understand
how to summarize key points about the United States. A copy of
this graphic organizer appears on page 35 of the Activity Book.

Summarize Key Points About the United States

KEY POINTS
↓
SUMMARY

LESSON 1: KEY POINTS	LESSON 2: KEY POINTS

↓

LESSON 1: SUMMARY	LESSON 2: SUMMARY

LESSON 3: KEY POINTS	LESSON 4: KEY POINTS

↓

LESSON 3: SUMMARY	LESSON 4: SUMMARY

THINK & WRITE

Write a Speech   Write a speech that
you, as a Native American chief, will
give to the first Europeans who have
come to the Americas. Explain how
you feel about their arrival and what
compromises you think are necessary
for both groups to live in peace.

Write a Persuasive Letter   Think about
how checks and balances limit the
power of the United States government.
Write a letter to a dictator in another
country who has complete control.
Explain why you would or would not
support this dictator's government.

1600	1700	1800	1900	2000

1607
The first permanent British settlement is built at Jamestown, Virginia

1776
The Second Continental Congress approves the Declaration of Independence

1783
The Treaty of Paris ends the American Revolution

1865
The Union army wins the Civil War, ending slavery in the United States

1959
Alaska and Hawaii become the forty-ninth and fiftieth states

USE THE TIME LINE

Use the chapter summary time line to answer these questions.

1 How many years were there between the Civil War and the American Revolution?

2 In what year did Alaska and Hawaii become states?

USE VOCABULARY

Use each term in a sentence that explains both what the term means and how that meaning relates to the United States.

3 contiguous (p. 98)

4 revolution (p. 108)

5 republic (p. 109)

6 immigrant (p. 114)

7 constitutional democracy (p. 122)

RECALL FACTS

Answer these questions.

8 Which region of the United States is most likely to be hit by a hurricane?

9 What activity did most Native American tribes share?

10 In what ways has discrimination in the United States decreased over the years?

Write the letter of the best choice.

11 **TEST PREP** American society can be described as a mosaic because the people—
A like many of the same things.
B all practice the same religion.
C blend into a single culture.
D have different customs that contribute to American culture as a whole.

12 **TEST PREP** The United States national government in Washington, D.C., directly controls all of the following *except*—
F the military.
G education.
H international relations.
J money.

THINK CRITICALLY

13 How might your life be different right now if the American Revolution had failed?

14 Imagine that it is the late 1800s and that you are an immigrant arriving in the United States. What country did you come from? Why did you decide to come to the United States?

APPLY SKILLS

Read a Relief and Elevation Map

15 Use the elevation map on page 105 to compare the elevations of Houston, Texas, and Odessa, Texas. Which place has the higher elevation?

Determine Point of View

16 Reread the excerpt from Dr. Martin Luther King, Jr.'s speech on page 120. What words does he use that help you determine his point of view?

Make Economic Choices

17 Think of a time when you had to make the choice to buy one thing rather than another. Explain what the opportunity cost of your decision was.

BANFF NATIONAL PARK, CANADA

Founded in 1885, Banff National Park is located in Alberta, Canada. Jagged mountain peaks frame the park's spectacular scenery. Melting ice from active glaciers, such as Crowfoot glacier, feed Banff's many lakes and streams.

LOCATE IT

Banff National Park

CANADA

Canada

" O Canada! Where pines
and maples grow.
Great prairies spread and
lordly rivers flow. "

—from the National Anthem of
Canada, 1908

CHAPTER READING SKILL

Draw Conclusions

A conclusion is a statement that is true, based on information. To **draw a conclusion**, use evidence from what you read and what you already know about the subject.

As you read this chapter, use what you read and what you already know to draw conclusions about places and ideas.

WHAT YOU READ + WHAT YOU KNOW → CONCLUSION

MAIN IDEA
Learn how unusual geography and extreme weather affect life and business in Canada.

WHY IT MATTERS
Geography and climate affect where people live and how they live.

VOCABULARY
prairie
tundra
fjord
province
territory
export
import
protectionism
free trade
economic indicator

Land and People

Canada is an enormous country, covering a land area of more than 3.8 million square miles (10 million sq km). It is the world's second-largest country in size, but more than 30 other countries have more people. Most of the 32 million people in Canada live within 100 miles (161 km) of its southern border with the contiguous United States. Much of northern Canada is so cold that few people choose to live there.

The Physical Regions of Canada

In almost every part of Canada, the landscape is spectacular. The country has rugged mountains, dense forests, rolling hills, beautiful frozen lands, and much more. At least 1 million rivers and lakes lie within Canada. Hudson Bay, a huge arm of the Atlantic Ocean, is located in the northeast. The Mackenzie River, Canada's longest river, is in the northwest.

This rich and varied land can be divided into seven physical regions. The largest is the Canadian Shield, a huge, rocky region. The Shield curves around Hudson Bay like a giant horseshoe. It covers about 1.8 million square miles (about 4.6 million sq km), or almost half the country's land area. During the last Ice Age, glaciers covered the Canadian Shield. When the ice masses melted, they left behind a wilderness of rocks, lakes, and swamps,

A view of the Rocky Mountains across Moraine Lake in Banff National Park

FAST FACT Banff National Park began as an area of only 10 square miles (26 sq km). Today Banff covers an area of more than 2,500 square miles (6,475 sq km).

Appalachian Region
St. Lawrence Lowlands
Canadian Shield
Hudson Bay Lowlands
Interior Plains
Western Mountains
Arctic Islands

RUSSIA
ARCTIC OCEAN
ALASKA (U.S.)
Greenland (DENMARK)
Baffin Bay
YUKON TERRITORY
NUNAVUT
NORTHWEST TERRITORIES
Labrador Sea
Hudson Bay
BRITISH COLUMBIA
ALBERTA
MANITOBA
NEWFOUNDLAND and LABRADOR
QUEBEC
PRINCE EDWARD ISLAND
ATLANTIC OCEAN
PACIFIC OCEAN
ONTARIO
SASKATCHEWAN
NOVA SCOTIA
NEW BRUNSWICK
UNITED STATES

0   600   1,200 Miles
0   600   1,200 Kilometers
Albers Equal-Area Projection

Regions
Geographers divide Canada into seven physical regions. These regions reflect the varied landscapes of Canada.

? What different physical regions can be found in Manitoba?

with very little soil. Because of the lack of soil, few people live in this region. Instead, most Canadians live in the lowlands to the south. One Canadian author wrote

66the Shield and the wilderness bear down upon us, a crushing weight, squeezing us like toothpaste along the borders of your country [the United States].99

Southeast of the Canadian Shield is the St. Lawrence Lowlands region. This is Canada's smallest region, but it has more industries and more people than any other region. This lowland area features the country's best farmland and a major waterway—the St. Lawrence Seaway.

East of the Shield and the St. Lawrence Lowlands is the Appalachian region. This region of fertile valleys and low mountains is rich in forests, mineral resources, and fish. Sandy beaches line its coast. Along the coast several underwater mountains rise above sea level to form large islands. One of these is Prince Edward Island.

West of the Shield is the Interior Plains region. The southern part of the Interior Plains is dotted with prairies and farms.

A **prairie** is a large area of flat land covered by grasses and wildflowers but few trees. Wheat and other crops grow well in the fertile soil there. In contrast, the northern part of the Interior Plains has poor soil and is too cold for farming. Forests cover the land in the north.

The Western Mountains region lies west of the Interior Plains and extends to the Pacific Ocean. In addition to its high mountains, this region is known for its forests, mineral resources, rivers, and wildlife.

Stretching across the southern shore of Hudson Bay is the Hudson Bay Lowlands region. For the most part, this region is made up of swamps.

In Canada's far north is the Arctic Islands region. It is too cold here for trees to grow. The land is mainly **tundra**, a large, flat plain of frozen ground. This region is made up of 12 large islands and hundreds of small ones. The islands have many glaciers, tall mountains, and deep fjords (fee•AWRDZ). A **fjord** is a narrow inlet of the sea between steep cliffs.

REVIEW Why does the St. Lawrence Lowlands region have more people and more industries than other regions?

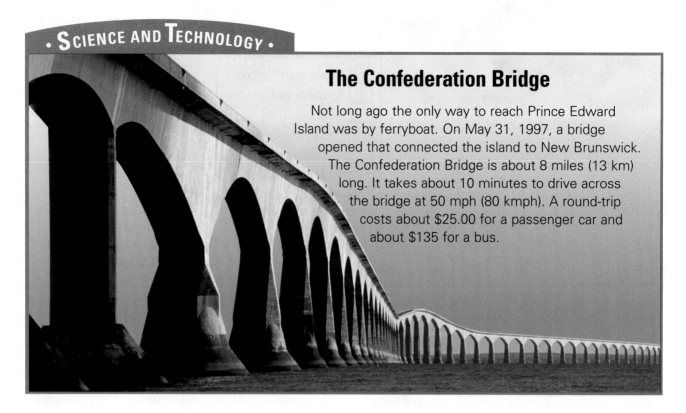

The Confederation Bridge

Not long ago the only way to reach Prince Edward Island was by ferryboat. On May 31, 1997, a bridge opened that connected the island to New Brunswick. The Confederation Bridge is about 8 miles (13 km) long. It takes about 10 minutes to drive across the bridge at 50 mph (80 kmph). A round-trip costs about $25.00 for a passenger car and about $135 for a bus.

Canada's Economic Regions

In addition to its physical regions, Canada can be divided into five economic regions. These regions are groups of the nation's political subregions—ten provinces and three territories. The **provinces** rule themselves much like the states in the United States. The **territories** are large divisions of Canada that do not have the same rights of self-government as the provinces.

Along the Atlantic coast are Canada's Atlantic, or Maritime, Provinces—Nova Scotia, Prince Edward Island, New Brunswick, and Newfoundland and Labrador. They are called the Atlantic Provinces because they have at least one border on the Atlantic Ocean or one of its gulfs or seas. They are also known as the Maritime Provinces. The word *maritime* means "having to do with the sea."

Fishing has been the central economic activity of the Atlantic Provinces since the time of European settlement. The Grand Banks, off the coast of Newfoundland, has long been one of the best fishing areas in the world. The fishing industry today, however, employs only about 3 percent of the region's workers. Most jobs are in manufacturing, farming, mining, shipping, and tourism.

The fishing village of Rose Blanche lies along the coast of Newfoundland.

Ottawa

CANADA

In the winter the people of Ottawa can skate from place to place on the frozen Rideau Canal.

The provinces of Ontario and Quebec form two separate cultural regions. Ontario is English Canadian, and Quebec is French Canadian. Together, however, they form a single economic region that is the "heartland" of Canada. Most of the country's manufactured goods are made in Ontario and Quebec. Their factories produce a range of consumer goods and products from other industries, including iron and steel.

Much of the economic success of the region is due to its location near major waterways. Four of the five Great Lakes—Superior, Huron, Erie, and Ontario—form part of Ontario's and Canada's southern border. Only Lake Michigan lies entirely outside Canada.

The St. Lawrence River provides Ontario and Quebec with a direct water route between the Great Lakes and the Atlantic Ocean. At one time, parts of the 800-mile (1,287-km) river were not deep enough or wide enough for large ships to use. In 1954 the governments of Canada and the United States took action to change this. Together they began work on the St. Lawrence Seaway. This system of canals and locks bypasses the shallow and narrow parts of the river. The seaway now makes it possible for large ships to travel from the Atlantic Ocean inland to ports on the western shore of Lake Superior.

Montreal, Quebec's economic center, is located on an island in the St. Lawrence River about 40 miles (64 km) north of Canada's border with the United States. Its location makes the city a major trading port for ships traveling through the St. Lawrence Seaway. Ontario's economic center is an area called the Golden Horseshoe. It lies on the western shore of Lake Ontario and has access to the Great Lakes. The area includes Toronto, which is Ontario's major city.

Most of Canada's people live in Ontario and Quebec. The region includes the nation's two largest metropolitan areas. Toronto, Ontario, has more than 4 million people. Montreal, Quebec, has more than 3 million.

Toronto is one of the most culturally diverse cities in North America. Four out of ten people are English Canadian. The rest come from many places around the world.

Toronto's citizens today trace their cultural homelands to such places as Greece, Italy, Germany, China, and various Caribbean islands.

Montreal's population is becoming more diverse, but it remains a center for French Canadian culture. French is spoken by almost all of Montreal's citizens. In fact, you would have to go to Paris, France, to find a city with more people who speak French.

The region made up of Ontario and Quebec also includes two other important cities. Quebec City is Canada's oldest. Ottawa is Canada's capital city.

West of Ontario and Quebec lie the Prairie Provinces of Alberta, Manitoba, and Saskatchewan (suh•SKA•chuh•wuhn). They make up about 20 percent of the nation's land area and 80 percent of Canada's farmland. Known as Canada's "breadbasket," the southern part of the region has many wheat farms and cattle ranches. Lakes and forests cover its northern part.

In the past the major economic activity of the Prairie Provinces was farming, because of the fertile soil. Today what is under the soil is also important. The Prairie Provinces supply most of Canada's fossil fuels, including coal, oil, and natural gas.

The largest cities in the Prairie Provinces are Edmonton and Calgary in Alberta and Winnipeg in Manitoba. Each metropolitan area has less than 1 million people.

The Rocky Mountains form the border between the Prairie Provinces and British Columbia. British Columbia is Canada's westernmost province and its third-largest in area and population. In addition to being a province, it is one of Canada's economic regions. The forest industry makes up much of the economic activity. Evergreen forests cover much of the land, and many of the people work at cutting down trees, processing lumber, and manufacturing paper.

POINTS OF VIEW
Great Bear Rainforest

The Great Bear Rainforest is an ancient temperate rain forest in British Columbia. It is home to 1,000-year-old trees and rare all-white Spirit bears. The Great Bear Rainforest was once threatened by logging. On April 4, 2001, parts of this rain forest became protected. The following quotations tell the story of how people worked together to protect this land.

IAN MCALLISTER, activist, Rainforest Conservation Society

66 These ancient temperate rainforests are more endangered than the Amazon because they cover historically such a small part of the globe. 99

ROBERT F. KENNEDY, JR., environmental attorney

66 There's a way to log many of these rainforests without destroying them. 99

GUUJAW, president of the Haida Nation

66 It involves compromise from all parties. 99

Analyze the Viewpoints
1 What view about the Great Bear Rainforest does each person hold?
2 **Make It Relevant** Find out if there are areas in your community that people want to use in different ways. Identify the different viewpoints on the issue.

The many rivers and lakes in British Columbia make fishing, recreation, and the production of hydroelectric power other important economic activities. *Hydroelectric* refers to electricity that is produced by moving water.

Vancouver is British Columbia's largest city. It is also Canada's third-largest metropolitan area with almost 2 million people. Vancouver has Canada's busiest port, which links Canada to trading partners chiefly in the United States and Asia. In addition, many people from Asia have immigrated to Vancouver. This has made Vancouver a city with a culturally diverse population, like Toronto's.

Besides the provinces, Canada has three territories—the Yukon Territory, the Northwest Territories, and Nunavut (NOO•nuh•voot). These territories form an economic region in a huge area of northern Canada. Together they cover about 40 percent of Canada's land area, but very few people live there, and there are no large cities. As a result, there is little major economic activity other than mining. Most of the people meet their basic needs by hunting and fishing.

REVIEW What are the main economic activities in the Prairie Provinces?

Canada's Economy

Canada is a developed nation with a high GDP, or gross domestic product. The GDP is about $722 billion, making Canada one of the wealthiest nations in the world. Much of Canada's wealth comes from its wide range of natural resources. The Canadian Shield is rich in minerals, such as copper, gold, iron, nickel, and uranium. Fossil fuels, including coal, oil, and natural gas, are found in the Interior Plains. Fisheries bring in huge catches of fish on the Atlantic and Pacific coasts. Throughout much of southern Canada, farmers produce large and varied harvests. In much of the rest of Canada, which is not suited to farming, trees grow very well.

Canada's primary industries, those that gather natural resources, are varied. However, its secondary industries are not. Canada has basically two kinds of manufacturing. One involves processing natural resources, such as turning trees into lumber, pulp, and paper products. The other involves making finished products for use by Canadians. Factories in Quebec and Ontario produce more than three-fourths of Canada's manufactured goods.

Glaciers helped shape the Richardson Mountains in the Yukon Territory. The Air Force Glacier (inset) is in Nunavut.

LOCATE IT

Richardson Mountains

CANADA

Industry

Agriculture

Services

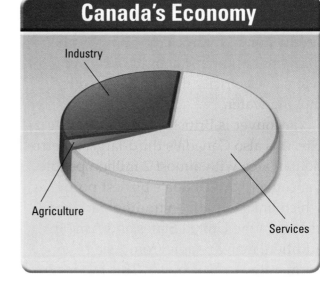
Canada's Economy

Industry

Agriculture

Services

Analyze Graphs The photographs above represent the different industries of Canada's economy that are shown on the circle graph.

◆ Which part of Canada's economy is the largest?

Today the largest part of Canada's GDP comes from tertiary, or service, industries such as finance, tourism, trade, and recreation. These industries employ about three-fourths of Canadian workers.

Canada's economy is based on free enterprise, in which businesses are privately owned. However, Canada also has parts of a command economy. Its government owns or controls certain businesses and industries, including the nation's health care system. The Canadian government provides medical care for each citizen.

Canada ranks among the world's leading nations in international trade. Its **exports**, or goods sold to other countries, total hundreds of billions of dollars each year. About two-thirds of Canada's international trade, both exports and imports, are with the United States. **Imports** are goods bought from other countries.

In the past some Canadians believed that Canada should trade within the country instead of trading with other countries.

Because of this feeling, Canadians at that time followed a trade policy of **protectionism**. That is, the Canadian government protected Canadian businesses by passing special laws. These laws taxed imports. The taxes made the imports cost more in Canada. As a result, people bought less of them, and the number of imports coming into Canada decreased.

Protectionism helped some Canadian businesses because Canadians bought more products made in their own country. However, it hurt Canadians by limiting the products that were available.

Today the Canadian government follows a policy of **free trade**, or trade without limits or protections. In 1994 Canada joined the United States and Mexico in the North American Free Trade Agreement, or NAFTA. This agreement opened Canada to more trade with countries other than the United States.

REVIEW How has Canada's trade policy changed?

Canada's Standard of Living

As a result of the nation's strong economy, Canadians enjoy a high standard of living. It is similar to that in the United States. A country's standard of living is an **economic indicator**, or measure of how well its people live. The standard of living can be measured in different ways.

One way is to gather two important pieces of information—a country's GDP and its total population. When you divide the GDP by the total population, you get the country's *per capita GDP*, or GDP per person. This is the average income of a country's citizens. Canada's per capita GDP is about $23,300 a year. In the United States it is about $33,900.

Two other ways to measure a country's standard of living are the literacy rate and life expectancy. Canada's literacy rate, or the percentage of people who can read and write, is about 96 percent. That compares with about 97 percent in the United States. Life expectancy in Canada is about 79 years compared with 77 years in the United

States. *Life expectancy* is a measure of the average number of years that people may expect to live. Life expectancy varies from country to country because of differences in public health and other living conditions.

REVIEW What are three important measures of a country's standard of living?

LESSON 1 REVIEW

1. **MAIN IDEA** How have people adapted to the geography and climate of Canada?

2. **WHY IT MATTERS** How do climate and geography affect how you and your family live?

3. **VOCABULARY** On a map of Canada, locate a **fjord**, a **province**, and a **territory**.

4. **READING SKILL—Draw Conclusions** Why do so many people in Canada live near the border with the United States?

5. **GEOGRAPHY** What geographic factor helps explain why few people live in the Hudson Bay Lowlands region? in the Canadian Shield region?

6. **GEOGRAPHY** How does the St. Lawrence Seaway help the economy of Canada?

7. **ECONOMY** Which industries in Canada are tertiary industries?

8. **CRITICAL THINKING—Hypothesize** How might Canada be different if it had a warmer climate?

PERFORMANCE—Create a Brochure Imagine that you work in the department of tourism for a Canadian province or territory. Design a brochure that will get businesses and people to move to your province or territory and tourists to visit. What does your province or territory have to offer? You may need to do additional research to gather more information.

2

MAIN IDEA
Read to find out how Canada grew from a vast wilderness to the independent country it is today.

WHY IT MATTERS
The early settlement of Canada helped give the country its interesting mix of cultures.

VOCABULARY
descendant
Loyalist
dominion
nationalism

Through the Centuries

| 1000 | 1200 | 1400 | 1600 | 1800 | 2000 |

Canada's history is a series of stories. They trace the development of the land from a wilderness to a wealthy, culturally diverse nation. The story of Canada begins thousands of years ago with the earliest people.

Canada's Early People

Most experts believe that the earliest people came from Asia in two separate migrations, or movements. The first may have taken place at least 25,000 years ago, when people crossed a land bridge that once connected Asia and North America. Over thousands of years these people and their **descendants**, or children's children, are thought to have spread out all over North America and South America. Those who came to live in what is now Canada became known as Native Canadians, or Canada's First Nations.

The second migration of people may have taken place about 5,000 years ago. These people settled Canada's most northern regions. Their descendants came to be known as the Inuit (IH•nu•wuht). Today descendants of the Inuit still live in the Arctic Islands region. Many speak their ancient language and follow traditional Inuit culture.

Although the Inuit remained a single-culture society, the other Native Canadians formed hundreds of different cultures. Each had its own way of life. Groups of them, however, shared common environments and common natural resources.

Some Native Canadians settled in the thick forests of the Appalachian region, the St. Lawrence Lowlands, and the southern Canadian Shield. These people included the Algonkins (al•GAHN•kinz), Hurons, Iroquois, Ojibwas (oh•JIB•wayz), and Ottawas. They spoke different languages and followed different customs. Yet they shared a common natural resource—trees. The people used wood and tree bark to make shelters and light boats

American artist George Catlin painted this picture of Wun-nes-tou, a leader of the Blackfoot tribe.

These three Native Canadian artifacts (left to right) are a ceremonial mask from the Bella Coola tribe, an Inuit comb, and an Inuit-carved figure.

called canoes. Traveling in the canoes on the region's many rivers and lakes, they interacted with one another through trade.

Unlike the eastern regions of Canada, the Interior Plains had few trees. Instead of a forest, there was a vast prairie. The people living on the prairie, such as the Assiniboines (uh•SIH•nuh•boynz) and Blackfeet, developed different cultures, but they all came to depend on the same natural resource. To meet many of their basic needs, the people of the Interior Plains hunted the huge herds of bison, or buffalo, that fed on the grasses and wildflowers of the prairie. The people used the meat of the bison for food. They used its skin for food and shelter and other parts of the animal to make tools and weapons.

Native Canadians living in what is now western Canada relied on the ocean and the region's thick forests for their natural resources. People such as the Haidas (HY•duhz) and Nootkas (NOOT•kuhz) used cedar trees to build their shelters. The

trees also provided wood for building large dugouts. Dugouts are boats made from large, hollowed-out logs. In their dugouts they hunted whales, sea otters, and other ocean animals.

Native Canadians also settled the vast northern Canadian Shield, where the Chipewyans (chip•uh•WY•anz), Crees, and other groups lived a harsh life. In land too cold to farm, they relied on hunting small animals.

Farther north, in the Arctic Islands region, lived the Inuit. Because there were no trees with which to build shelters, the people lived in tents made of animal skins or in houses made of earth. When traveling in search of animals to hunt, they built houses out of snow as temporary shelters. Like the Native Canadians living in the Canadian Shield, the Inuit found ways to use every part of the scarce natural resources they had. They made tools, weapons, and artworks from the animals' bones, antlers, horns, and teeth.

REVIEW How did different groups of Native Canadians adapt to the conditions of their environment?

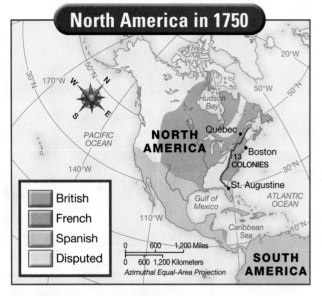

North America in 1750

British
French
Spanish
Disputed

0   600   1,200 Miles
0   600 1,200 Kilometers
Azimuthal Equal-Area Projection

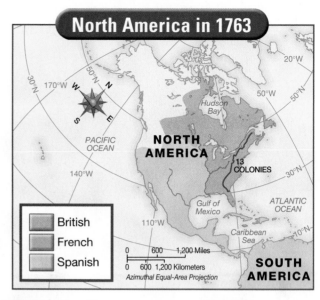

North America in 1763

British
French
Spanish

0   600   1,200 Miles
0   600 1,200 Kilometers
Azimuthal Equal-Area Projection

GEOGRAPHY THEME

Regions These maps show the North America lands claimed by Europeans in 1750 and how the claims had changed by 1763.

❖ Which country controlled what is now Canada in 1763?

The French and the British

The first Europeans to arrive in what is now Canada were Vikings. Long ago Vikings lived in what are today the countries of Norway, Sweden, and Denmark. In about A.D. 1000 they crossed the Atlantic Ocean and landed in what is today Newfoundland. The Vikings stayed briefly and did not establish a permanent, or long-lasting, settlement.

Nearly 500 years passed before other Europeans arrived. In the late 1400s and early 1500s, explorers sailing for England and France came. These two European countries would prove to be important in Canada's history. In 1497 an Italian explorer named Giovanni Caboto claimed for England what is now Newfoundland. In 1535 the French explorer Jacques Cartier (kar•TYAY) sailed inland on the St. Lawrence River. In claiming the northern land for France, he used the Iroquois word *kanata*, meaning "group of huts," to describe it. It became *Canada*.

Jacques Cartier, exploring the St. Lawrence River in 1535

Analyze Primary Sources

This 1758 engraving shows the British siege of Quebec during the French and Indian War. A siege is a long-lasting attack. The siege ended with the British taking control of the city.

1. Quebec was a walled city.
2. The British fired on Quebec from ships in the St. Lawrence River.
3. Quebec was the capital of New France.

❖ Why do you think the British wanted to capture Quebec?

QUEBEC, *The Capital of* NEW-FRANCE, *a Bishoprick, and Seat of the Soverain Court.*

Unlike the English, the French sent people to live in the land they claimed, which they called New France. In 1608 Samuel de Champlain started the first permanent French settlement in what is now Canada. It was located along the St. Lawrence River and was named Quebec.

The French ruled New France for more than 150 years. Then in 1754 a war began between the French and the English, who were also called the British by this time. The war was called the French and Indian War. It started in North America, and the fighting soon spread to Europe. In 1763 the French and the British ended the war and signed a peace treaty. The treaty gave the British control of New France, which they renamed Quebec. The British ruled Quebec as a colony.

Far more French people than British lived in Britain's new colony. Britain already was having trouble with its 13 American colonies in what is now the United States. To avoid still more trouble in North America, the British passed a law called the Quebec Act. It gave the French people in the British colony the right to keep their own laws, their own language, and their Roman Catholic religion.

While the Quebec Act pleased many in Canada, it angered the American colonists in the 13 British colonies to the south. They thought the law gave the French more freedom than they had. In time, the angry feelings between the colonists in the 13 American colonies and the British led to the American Revolution.

In 1776 the 13 American colonies rebelled against British rule. The British government watched to see if the people in Quebec would join the revolution. They never did. Most French people felt Britain showed in the Quebec Act that it would govern them fairly.

REVIEW How did the French and Indian War and the Quebec Act change Canada's history?

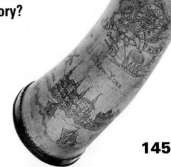

A gunpowder horn used in the French and Indian War

145

Canada Day

Canada's national holiday, Canada Day, is celebrated on July 1. Canada Day celebrations are similar to the United States celebrations of the Fourth of July. Festivities include fireworks, parades, and the singing of "O Canada," the country's national anthem.

Canada Day honors July 1, 1867, the day that a British act of Parliament created the Dominion of Canada. Until 1982 the holiday was called Dominion Day. When Canada became independent, it changed the holiday's name to Canada Day.

Becoming a Nation

From 1780 to 1850 Canada grew both in population and size. During this time more English-speaking people began moving there. Some came from Britain. Others came from the American colonies. These **Loyalists**, as they were called, had remained loyal to the British during the American Revolution. Many Loyalists settled in Quebec. Others settled in a part called Nova Scotia, or what the British called Acadia. Soon, the Loyalists in Nova Scotia demanded a colony of their own. In 1784 the British gave half of Nova Scotia to the Loyalists. This half became known as New Brunswick.

Loyalists in Quebec soon wanted their own colony, too. So, in 1791 the British divided Quebec into two colonies, Upper Canada and Lower Canada, each with its own government. English-speaking Canadians made up the majority in Upper Canada, which later became known as Ontario. French-speaking Canadians made up the majority in Lower Canada, which later became known as Quebec.

By the mid-1800s many Canadians worried that the United States might expand into Canada. To strengthen their separate Canadian colonies, the British on July 1, 1867, approved a law setting up a single Canadian government. This government was made up of the former colonies, which were now called provinces. By the British North America Act of 1867, as the law was called, Canada became the Dominion of Canada. A **dominion** is a self-governing nation. The new Dominion of Canada, however, was not totally independent. The British continued to rule over foreign matters. The British monarch also continued to act as head of state.

As Canada grew, more provinces were added to the dominion. In 1869 Canada purchased from the Hudson's Bay Company a vast region it had called Rupert's Land. From it the provinces of Manitoba, Alberta, and Saskatchewan were later formed. In 1871 British Columbia was formed and joined the dominion. Prince Edward Island joined in 1873. Newfoundland became Canada's tenth province in 1949.

Two young Canadians celebrate Canada Day with face paintings of a national symbol.

As their country grew, Canadians felt a growing sense of nationalism. **Nationalism** is a devotion or loyalty to one's own nation, or country. The people began to think of themselves as Canadians. Nationalism also helped unite the British and the French cultures that in time formed what became Canadian society.

In 1964 the Canadian government chose a new national flag, which first flew on February 15, 1965. It was an important event for Canadian nationalism. The country had long used British national symbols on its flag. The new flag now showed Canada's unique identity. Finally, in 1982, Canada's independence was complete. Canada received total authority over all of its own govern-

Canadian students play hockey outside their school in British Columbia.

Canadians use both English and French.

ment matters when the British government approved the Constitution Act. The Constitution Act also included a new bill of rights called the Charter of Rights and Freedoms.

REVIEW Why did Canadians choose a new national flag in 1964?

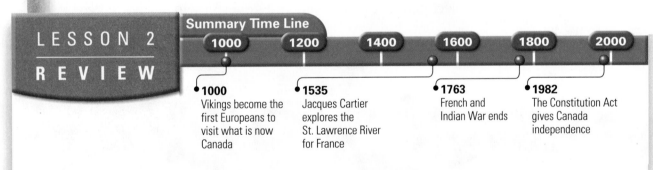

LESSON 2 REVIEW

Summary Time Line

1000 — 1200 — 1400 — 1600 — 1800 — 2000

1000 Vikings become the first Europeans to visit what is now Canada

1535 Jacques Cartier explores the St. Lawrence River for France

1763 French and Indian War ends

1982 The Constitution Act gives Canada independence

1 **MAIN IDEA** What major events contributed to changing Canada from a wilderness to an independent nation?

2 **WHY IT MATTERS** How is Canada's cultural diversity a reflection of its history?

3 **VOCABULARY** Write a paragraph that explains how Canada was united into one country. Use the words **nationalism** and **dominion**.

4 **TIME LINE** In what year did Canada gain full independence?

5 **READING SKILL—Draw Conclusions** How do you think the arrival of Europeans changed the lives of Native Canadians?

6 **CULTURE** In what ways did British and French culture influence Canadian culture?

7 **CIVICS AND GOVERNMENT** How did nationalism affect Canadians?

8 **CRITICAL THINKING—Analyze** How did the American Revolution affect Canadian history?

PERFORMANCE—Make a Time Line Create a time line that includes at least ten events, people, or government acts that are important in Canada's history. Use additional resources for research, if needed. Share your time line with a partner or in a classroom display.

MAIN IDEA
Learn how Canada's system
of government works.

WHY IT MATTERS
Canada's long relationship
with Britain is reflected in
its government structure.

VOCABULARY

commonwealth
free election
minority
parliamentary
democracy
prime minister
federal system
separatist
referendum

Canada's Government

Canada is an independent nation. However, it remains connected to Britain as a member of the Commonwealth of Nations, a group of independent nations that in the past have been ruled by the British government. **Commonwealth** is a term sometimes used for one nation, for a group of nations, or for a state. Canada started developing its independence from Britain when it became a dominion in 1867. That is when it formed its own government, modeled on the British government.

Democracy in Canada

The kind of governing system formed in Canada was a democracy. In a democracy the citizens of a nation take an active role. They elect people to represent and govern them.

FAST FACT The Canadian Parliament buildings in Ottawa, Ontario, include chambers of the House of Commons and the Senate. The central tower, called Peace Tower, houses a set of 53 bells.

The Canadian House of Commons meets in Ottawa. Most of the important bills that are introduced in Canada's Parliament start in the House of Commons.

Canada's democracy shares three important traits of all democracies. These traits are free elections, majority rule, and a guarantee of individual rights.

A **free election** is one in which any citizen can vote as long as he or she meets the requirements. These may vary from one nation to the next. Usually they depend on age and proof of citizenship. In a free election, voters choose the leaders of the government according to majority rule. That is, the wishes of the majority, or most of the voters, determine who is elected.

Citizens in a democracy, such as Canada, are guaranteed certain personal rights and freedoms. The guarantee includes the rights of people with minority views. A **minority** is a small part of a group.

Political parties are also an important part of Canada's democracy. Each party consists of a group of people involved in government who try to get others to agree with their ideas. The parties compete with one another to elect their own members to government offices and to influence the actions of the government. Canada has many important political parties, compared with just two major ones in the United States.

REVIEW What are four traits of Canada's democracy?

A Parliamentary Democracy

Canada's government is similar to Britain's parliamentary democracy. In a **parliamentary democracy** the people elect members of the legislature, called the parliament. The members of the parliament then choose the chief executive of the government. This system is different from the representative democracy in the United States. In the United States, the people elect both the members of the legislature and the chief executive of the country. In the United States, leadership of the legislative branch and the executive branch of government is kept separate. In Canada the same person, called a **prime minister**, leads both the executive and legislative branches.

In Canada, Parliament has two houses, the Senate and the House of Commons. The House of Commons is the more important of the two because it has most of the lawmaking authority. Citizens vote directly for its members. They serve five-year terms, unless an election is called earlier.

Canadian Prime Minister Jean Chrétien (middle), United States President George W. Bush (right), and Mexican President Vicente Fox Quesada (left) in April 2001

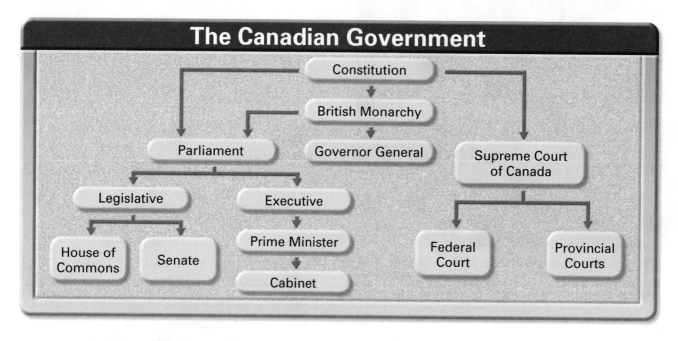

The Canadian Government

Constitution

British Monarchy

Parliament

Governor General

Supreme Court of Canada

Legislative

Executive

House of Commons

Senate

Prime Minister

Cabinet

Federal Court

Provincial Courts

Analyze Diagrams This diagram shows the structure of Canada's government.

❖ Which two branches of government make up Parliament?

Each province elects a certain number of members, based on population. Canada's Senate is mostly an advisory body. It studies important issues, such as poverty and health care, and suggests new laws.

Because Canada is a member of the Commonwealth of Nations, the British monarch plays a role in its government. The king or queen is officially the head of Canada's government. In practice, however, the monarch has no authority at all.

The prime minister is the head of the executive branch, directing the government's day-to-day business. The prime minister is usually the head of the political party with the most members in the House of Commons.

The prime minister chooses other members of the House of Commons to form a Cabinet. This group of officials, called ministers, advises the nation's chief executive. The Cabinet ministers almost always belong to the same political party as the prime minister. Each Cabinet minister is in charge of a separate department of government, such as agriculture or transportation.

The judicial branch of Canada's government consists of a national court system. The highest court is the Supreme Court of Canada. It has a chief justice and eight associate judges. They interpret laws and hear final appeals of court cases. The prime minister and the Cabinet choose people to be judges for the Supreme Court.

REVIEW How are the duties of Canada's prime minister different from those of the United States President?

A Constitutional Government

Canada, like the United States, has a constitution, or a plan of government. The constitution sets up the government's organization and rules. Unlike that of the United States, Canada's constitution is partly written and partly unwritten.

The unwritten part includes the customs and practices that have become part of Canada's government over time. One such practice is the prime minister's selection of a Cabinet that runs government departments.

Prince Charles of Britain greets children in Ottawa. Although Canada is an independent nation, its ties to Britain remain strong.

The written parts of the constitution come from the two documents that created Canada's government. These are the British North America Act of 1867 and the Constitution Act of 1982, including the Charter of Rights and Freedoms.

The British North America Act established a federal system for Canada. A **federal system** divides authority between the national government and the provincial (pruh•VINT•shuhl) governments.

In Canada's federal system, the authority of the national government and that of the provinces and territories are separate but not equal. The national government is clearly in control, because Canada's founding leaders wanted a strong central government. The British North America Act limited the authority of the provincial governments. They share little authority with the national government.

The chief role of Canada's national government is to solve national problems and to settle disputes among the provinces and the territories. The national government handles issues that affect Canada as a whole nation.

• HERITAGE •

The Speaker's Parade

The Canadian Speaker's Parade is a custom borrowed from British government to mark the opening session of Parliament. Attendants wearing neck scarves, black robes, and tri-cornered hats lead the speaker of the House of Commons in parade to his or her seat in the House chamber. The sergeant-of-arms, or the House's head officer, leads the parade carrying a golden mace. The mace, which has a crown on one end, is the traditional symbol of the monarch's authority. Once at his or her seat, the speaker calls the Parliament to order, and the members begin their work.

Unlike the United States national government, Canada's national government can disallow, or reject, laws passed by the provincial governments. This, too, reflects the founders' desire for a strong central government.

REVIEW How does Canada's federal system limit the authority of the provinces?

Provincial Authority

The ten provinces in Canada, just like the 50 states in the United States, have governing bodies, or assemblies, that make their own laws. The three territories also have assemblies but with a limited amount of authority. The national government directs most of their matters.

The voters of each province elect the members of their own provincial assembly. The leader of the provincial assembly and the head of the provincial government are the same person, a premier (prih•MIR).

The Royal Canadian Mounted Police is Canada's national police force.

Just as a prime minister heads both the legislative and executive branches of the national government, a premier heads both branches in the provincial government. Each territory also has a premier. In addition, the national government appoints a commissioner to serve as the honorary head of each territorial government.

The provincial governments chiefly control matters of education, property ownership, and citizens' rights. Some provinces, however, are demanding more authority. In Quebec, for example, an important matter is the preservation of French culture. Some people in Quebec have gone so far as to suggest that their province become an independent nation. These people are called **separatists**.

These separatist protesters in Montreal want the province of Quebec to become an independent nation.

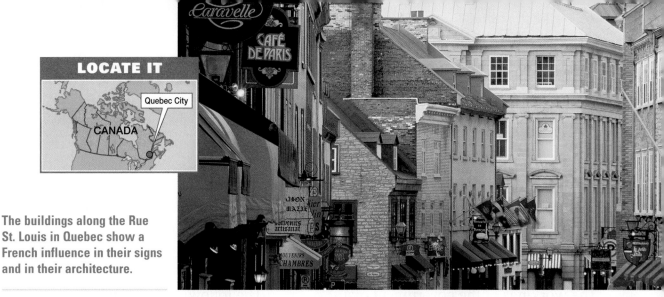

Quebec City

CANADA

The buildings along the Rue St. Louis in Quebec show a French influence in their signs and in their architecture.

To address some of Quebec's concerns, the Canadian government passed the Official Languages Act in 1969. This law makes Canada a two-language country. It says that both French and English are to be accepted everywhere in Canada.

For some separatists in Quebec, the national government has not gone far enough. In recent years the people of Quebec twice voted on the issue of separation. Each time, they took part in a special election called a referendum (reh•fuh•REN•duhm). A **referendum** is an election in which the voters decide whether to accept or to reject a suggested law or change in government rules. Both times, the voters decided against separation.

Quebec is not the only place in Canada where there has been talk by separatists. Some western provinces, especially Alberta, want greater control of their own natural resources, including scarce fossil fuels. Separatist leaders have complained that the national government has tried to satisfy Quebec without thinking of the other provinces. Until the issue of separation is settled, Canadian unity remains an important concern.

REVIEW Who are the people who want their provinces to become independent nations?

LESSON 3 REVIEW

1 **MAIN IDEA** In what ways is Canada's government similar to the government in the United States?

2 **WHY IT MATTERS** In what ways is Canada's government similar to the government in Great Britain?

3 **VOCABULARY** Use the terms **prime minister** and **parliamentary democracy** in a paragraph that describes Canada's government.

4 **READING SKILL—Draw Conclusions** Why do Canadian citizens honor the monarch of Britain?

5 **CIVICS AND GOVERNMENT** Why is Canada's government considered to be a limited government?

6 **CULTURE** What unites and what separates Canada's English-speaking people and French-speaking people?

7 **CRITICAL THINKING—Analyze** How is the role of the Canadian prime minister the same as that of the President of the United States? How are the two positions different?

 PERFORMANCE—Write a Persuasive Letter Imagine that you live in the province of Quebec. Do you think Quebec should separate or stay a part of Canada? Write a letter to convince others to share your views.

·SKILLS·
CHART AND GRAPH

Follow a Flow Chart

▶ WHY IT MATTERS

The workings of the government of a large country such as Canada are complex. Sometimes it is easier to understand complex processes if they are shown visually. One way to understand a process better is to look at a flow chart.

A **flow chart** can be thought of as a map that shows a process rather than a location. A flow chart breaks down the steps involved in a process. It shows the sequence, or order, and the relationship of each step.

Flow charts help people visualize how a process works. People use flow charts to help them understand a new process or make improvements to an old process.

▶ WHAT YOU NEED TO KNOW

The following tips can help you follow a flow chart.

- **Read the title.** The title of a flow chart tells what process is being explained.
- **Identify the steps.** Brief descriptions of steps or tasks in a process usually appear in boxes or ovals.
- **Follow the arrows.** Arrows between steps show how the steps are linked. Most flow charts "flow" from left to right or from top to bottom.
- **Be alert for "if-then" situations.** A step may be followed by more than one possible next step. This is indicated by two (or more) arrows leading to the possible next steps.

Royal Assent ceremony at the Canadian Parliament building in Ottawa, Canada

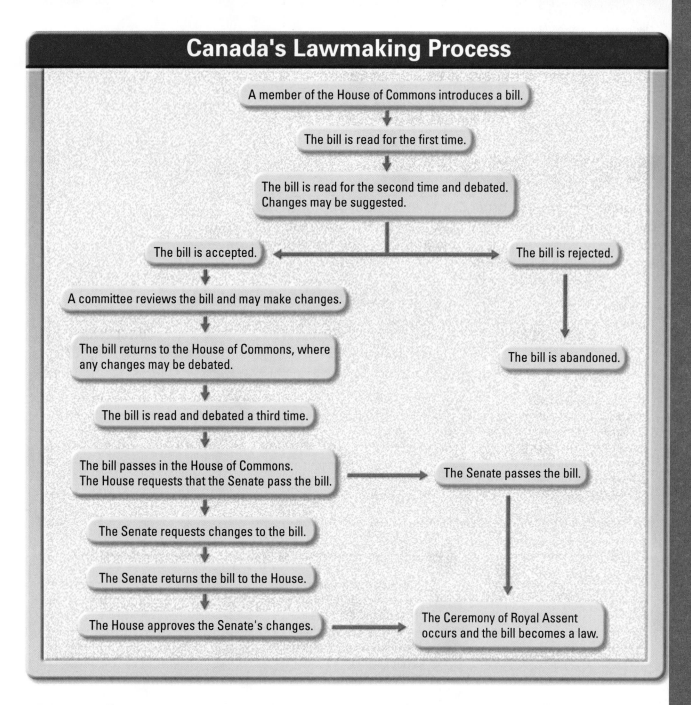

Canada's Lawmaking Process

A member of the House of Commons introduces a bill.

The bill is read for the first time.

The bill is read for the second time and debated. Changes may be suggested.

The bill is accepted.

The bill is rejected.

A committee reviews the bill and may make changes.

The bill is abandoned.

The bill returns to the House of Commons, where any changes may be debated.

The bill is read and debated a third time.

The bill passes in the House of Commons. The House requests that the Senate pass the bill.

The Senate passes the bill.

The Senate requests changes to the bill.

The Senate returns the bill to the House.

The House approves the Senate's changes.

The Ceremony of Royal Assent occurs and the bill becomes a law.

➡ PRACTICE THE SKILL

The flow chart above shows the path a bill takes before being passed into law by Canada's Parliament. Use the flow chart to answer these questions.

➊ What is the first step in the process?

➋ Once the bill has been accepted, what happens next?

➌ What must happen before the Royal Assent ceremony can take place?

➡ APPLY WHAT YOU LEARNED

Think of a process with which you are familiar. Make a flow chart that shows the steps in that process. Trade flow charts with a partner, and see if each of you would be able to work through the process using your partner's flow chart. Share feedback about the strengths and weaknesses of both charts.

4 Review and Test Preparation

Summary Time Line

1000   1200

1000
Vikings become the first
Europeans to visit Canada

USE YOUR READING SKILLS

Complete this graphic organizer to show that you understand
how to draw conclusions by combining what you read with what
you already know. A copy of this graphic organizer appears on
page 43 of the Activity Book.

Draw Conclusions About Canada

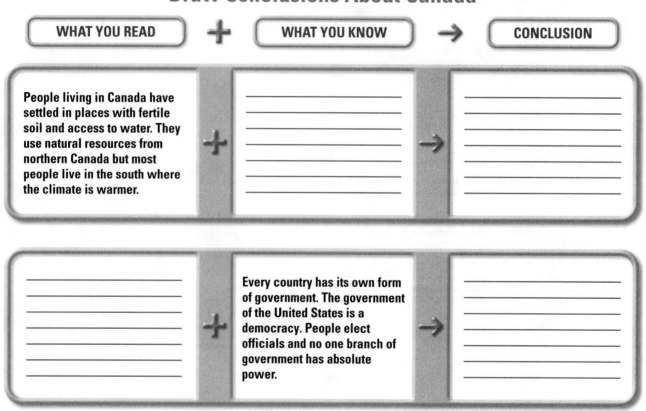

WHAT YOU READ **+** **WHAT YOU KNOW** → **CONCLUSION**

People living in Canada have
settled in places with fertile
soil and access to water. They
use natural resources from
northern Canada but most
people live in the south where
the climate is warmer.

Every country has its own form
of government. The government
of the United States is a
democracy. People elect
officials and no one branch of
government has absolute
power.

THINK & WRITE

Write a Speech to Parliament
Imagine that you are a Canadian
member of Parliament representing
the people of Quebec. Many people
in Quebec want you to pass strict
laws to limit the use of the English
language. Write an address to the
Canadian Parliament, stating your
position on the issue of separatism.

Write a Short Story Many experts
believe that early people crossed a
land bridge from Asia to the Americas.
These people had to endure many
changes. The first settlers had to learn
to adapt to their new land. Write a short
story about one group of early Native
Canadians, describing how they
adapted to their new land.

1497
Giovanni Caboto
explores Canada
for Britain

1608
Quebec founded by
French explorer Samuel
de Champlain

1763
French and Indian War
ends; Britain controls
much of North America

1867
The British North
America Act creates
the Dominion of Canada

1982
The Constitution
Act gives Canada
independence

USE THE TIME LINE

Use the chapter summary time line to answer these questions.

1 Which European explorer arrived in Canada first?

2 In what year did Canada gain independence?

USE VOCABULARY

For each pair of terms, write a sentence or two to explain how the terms are different.

3 **territory** (p. 136), **province** (p. 136)

4 **export** (p. 140), **import** (p. 140)

5 **protectionism** (p. 140), **free trade** (p. 140)

6 **commonwealth** (p. 148), **federal system** (p. 151)

7 **Loyalist** (p. 146), **separatist** (p. 152)

RECALL FACTS

Answer these questions.

8 What landforms are found in Canada's Arctic Islands region?

9 Why do the territories of northern Canada have few farms or businesses?

10 How did Native Canadians use the buffalo?

Write the letter of the best choice.

11 **TEST PREP** The Quebec Act of 1774 did all of the following *except*—
  A allow the French in Quebec to speak their native language.
  B anger the American colonists.
  C allow the French in Quebec to practice Roman Catholicism.
  D allow the French in Quebec to rule themselves.

12 **TEST PREP** The Canadian prime minister is—
  F directly elected by the Canadian people.
  G the leader of the majority party in the Canadian Senate.
  H the leader of the majority party in the Canadian House of Commons.
  J appointed by the British monarch.

13 **TEST PREP** Canada's national government does all of the following *except*—
  A settle disputes among provinces and territories.
  B reject some laws passed by provincial governments.
  C control matters of education.
  D handle the issues that affect Canada as a nation.

THINK CRITICALLY

14 Aside from the uses they have for people, why do you think Canadian wildlife and forests are important?

15 How might history be different if the American colonists had convinced the Canadians to rebel against the British during the American Revolution?

APPLY SKILLS

Follow a Flow Chart

16 Use the flow chart on page 155 to determine two possible next steps for a bill that passes the House of Commons and goes to the Senate.

17 Create a flow chart showing your daily morning routine before school. In your flow chart, include some unexpected happenings, such as oversleeping or missing your ride to school.

VISIT

Calgary, Alberta

GET READY

WHAT TO SEE

Calgary, Alberta's largest city, lies in the rolling foothills of the Canadian Rocky Mountains. Surrounded by beautiful, sweeping wheat fields, Calgary is a center for distribution of wheat and cattle. Calgary was established in 1875, when the North-West Mounted Police—now the Royal Canadian Mounted Police—set up a fort there. The city began to grow in 1883, when the railroad arrived. Although Calgary is now a modern city, a visit there can reveal its colorful past.

The restored Fort Calgary is designed to let visitors see what daily life was like in Calgary's past.

LOCATE IT

CANADA

Calgary

In 1988 Calgary hosted the winter Olympic Games. One Olympic site, Canada Olympic Park, features two ski jumps, a luge track, and a bobsled run.

A celebration of the ranching industry, the Calgary Exhibition and Stampede features a chuck wagon race, and also livestock shows, rodeo events, and carnival rides.

TAKE A FIELD TRIP

GO ONLINE

A VIRTUAL TOUR
Visit The Learning Site at
www.harcourtschool.com/tours
to take virtual tours of other cities around the world.

CNN Turner Le@rning

A VIDEO TOUR
Check your media center or classroom library for a videotape tour of Calgary, Alberta.

2 Review and Test Preparation

Write a Paragraph Study the pictures and captions on page 161 to help you review Unit 2. Then choose one of the events shown. Write a paragraph that describes what happened and how that event affected the United States or Canada.

VISUAL SUMMARY

USE VOCABULARY

Use one of the terms in the box to complete each sentence.

immigrant (p. 114)

literacy (p. 117)

pluralistic (p. 117)

constitutional democracy (p. 122)

referendum (p. 153)

1 The people of Quebec held a _____ on whether to separate from Canada.

2 The United States is a _____ because its goals are written in a plan for governing.

3 Because of their strong educational systems, the United States and Canada have high rates of _____.

RECALL FACTS

Answer these questions.

4 What is the fastest-growing group of people in the United States?

5 How did the Constitution Act change Canada in 1982?

6 What kind of responsibility does someone who obeys the laws, helps the community, and votes in elections demonstrate?

Write the letter of the best choice.

7 **TEST PREP** The United States and Canada have a federal system of government because—
   A power is shared by the national government and the states or provinces.
   B a monarch acts as an honorary leader.
   C the states or provinces hold all of the power.
   D citizens elect people to represent them in the government.

8 **TEST PREP** To which holiday in the United States is Canada Day similar?
   F Presidents' Day
   G Memorial Day
   H Thanksgiving
   J Independence Day

THINK CRITICALLY

9 How is the phrase "no taxation without representation" related to the underlying causes of the American Revolution?

10 How might discrimination hurt the way people live? Explain.

11 Why is the system of checks and balances important to the governments of the United States and Canada?

12 How does American inventiveness help make the economy of the United States strong?

APPLY SKILLS

Read an Elevation Map
Use the elevation map on this page to answer the following questions.

13 Which mountain range has a higher elevation, the Rocky Mountains or the Appalachian Mountains? Explain.

14 Where is the lowest point in the United States? the highest point?

15 What is the elevation of Canada's capital, Ottawa?

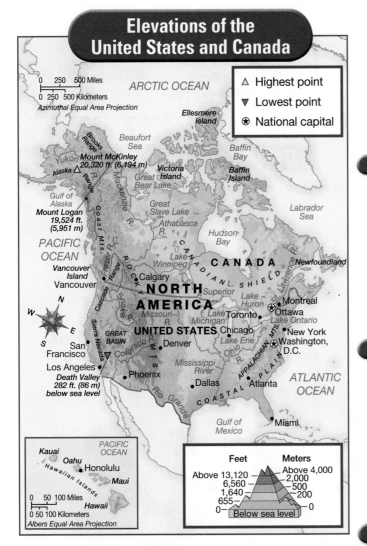

Elevations of the United States and Canada

0 250 500 Miles
0 250 500 Kilometers
Azimuthal Equal Area Projection

ARCTIC OCEAN

△ Highest point
▽ Lowest point
✱ National capital

Ellesmere Island

Brooks Range
Beaufort Sea

Yukon R.
Mount McKinley 20,320 ft. (6,194 m) △
Alaska

Baffin Bay
Baffin Island

Victoria Island
Great Bear Lake
Mackenzie R.

Gulf of Alaska
Mount Logan 19,524 ft. (5,951 m)

Great Slave Lake
Athabasca R.

Labrador Sea

PACIFIC OCEAN

Hudson Bay

Lake Winnipeg

CANADA

Newfoundland

Vancouver Island
Vancouver

Calgary

Coast Mts.

Fraser R.

Cascade Range

Snake R.

ROCKY

NORTH AMERICA

CANADIAN SHIELD

Superior

Lake Huron

St. Lawrence R.

Montreal
✱ Ottawa
Lake Ontario

Toronto

New York

San Francisco
Los Angeles
Death Valley 282 ft. (86 m) below sea level ▽

Sierra Nevada

GREAT BASIN

Colorado R.

MTS.

UNITED STATES
Denver

Missouri R.

Lake Michigan

Chicago

Lake Erie

Ohio R.

✱ Washington, D.C.

APPALACHIAN MTS.

Phoenix

Dallas

Mississippi River

Atlanta

COASTAL PLAIN

ATLANTIC OCEAN

Rio Grande

Gulf of Mexico

Miami

Kauai
Oahu
Honolulu
Maui
Hawaiian Islands
Hawaii

PACIFIC OCEAN

0 50 100 Miles
0 50 100 Kilometers
Albers Equal Area Projection

Feet	Meters
Above 13,120	Above 4,000
6,560	2,000
1,640	500
655	200
0	0
Below sea level	

Visual Summary

1400 Native Americans live throughout North America p. 106

1565 Europeans build settlements in North America p. 107

1775 The American Revolution begins p. 108

1964 Canada adopts a new flag p. 147

2000 United States has a growing and diverse population p. 114

1000

1200

1400

1600

1800

2000

161

Unit Activities

Visit The Learning Site at
www.harcourtschool.com/
socialstudies/activities
for additional activities.

Create a Flow Chart

Work in a group to make two large flow charts. On the first flow chart, show the events that led to independence in the United States. On the second flow chart, show the events that led to Canadian independence. Illustrate your flow charts with pictures or drawings. Use the flow charts as you take turns comparing the events that led to independence in Canada and the United States.

Honor Your Hero

Choose someone you admire from history in the United States or Canada to be the subject of a poster. First, research the person's life, and write a short biography to include on your poster. Then, find or draw pictures to illustrate your poster, and give your poster a title. Around the pictures, add words or phrases that tell what made the person a hero. Use your poster to introduce your hero to the class.

VISIT YOUR LIBRARY

- **The Big Rivers: The Missouri, the Mississippi, and the Ohio** by Bruce Hiscock. Atheneum.

- **The Kids Book of Canada** by Barbara Greenwood. Kids Can Press.

- **Legends of Landforms: Native American Lore and the Geology of the Land** by Carole Garbuny Vogel. Millbrook Press.

COMPLETE THE UNIT PROJECT

Form a Democratic Government Work with a group of classmates to complete the unit project—a model democratic government. First, decide whether to use the United States or Canada as a model. Then, decide which students want to belong to which branch of the government—executive, legislative, or judicial. Work together to discover how checks and balances function in a democratic government. Propose a new classroom rule, and use the three branches of government to make the proposed rule into a classroom law.

Middle America
and South America

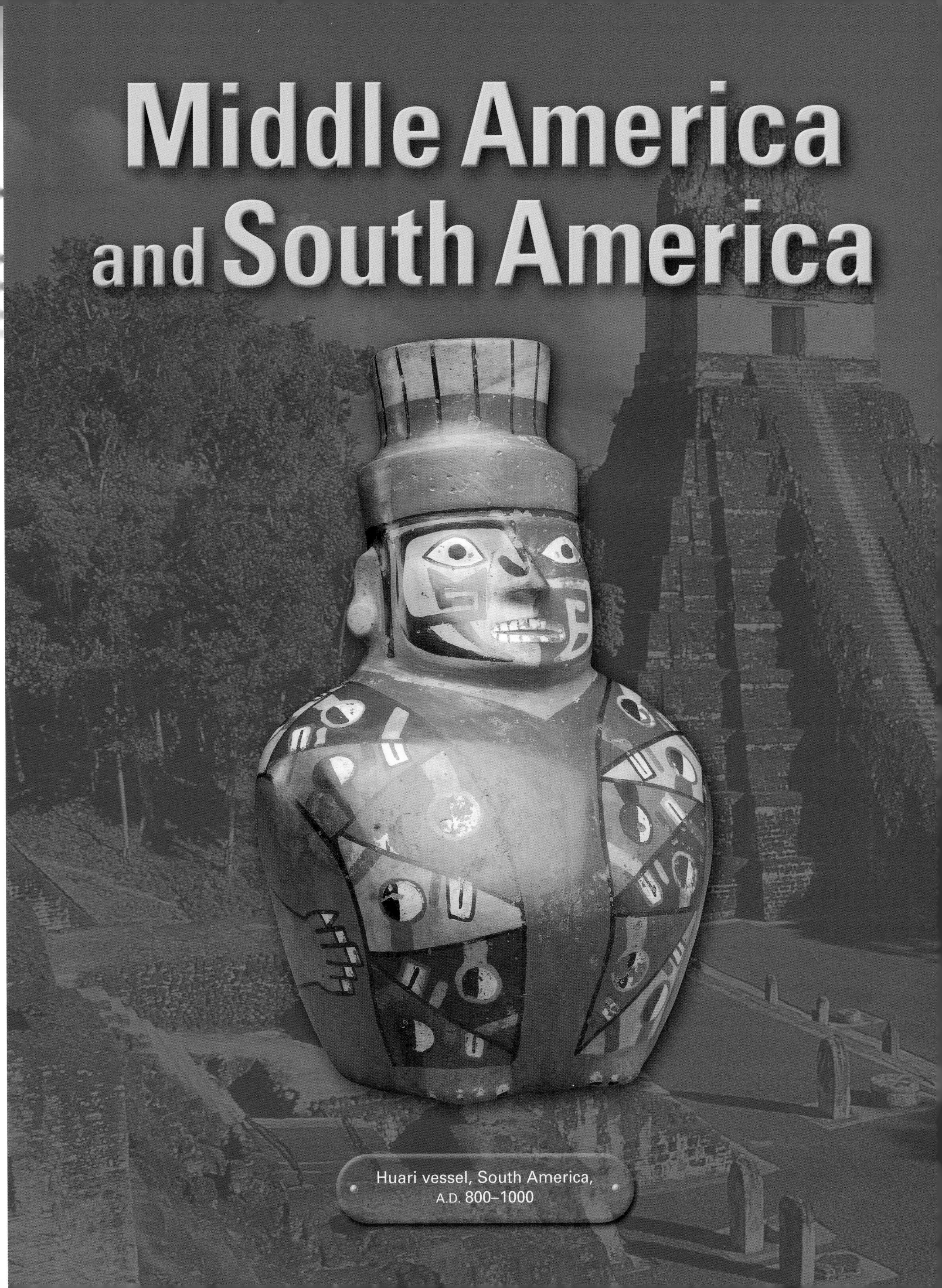

Mayan ruins at Tikal National Park, Guatemala

3

Middle America and South America

" . . . a land of natural dreamscapes . . . mysterious presences and absences. "

—Miguel Angel Asturias, from *The Mirror of Lida Sal: Tales Based on Mayan Myths and Guatemalan Legends,* 1997

Preview the Content

Read the Main Idea statement for each lesson. Work with a partner to identify what you think the focus of each lesson will be.

Preview the Vocabulary

Words from Other Languages   Foreign words often become part of the English language. Read each of the words below. Then look up each word in the dictionary. Find its meaning and the language it comes from. Copy the chart below to record your findings.

| adobe | fiesta | junta | mulatto |
| cordillera | guerrilla | mestizo | sierra |

VOCABULARY WORD	ORIGIN	MEANING

ATLANTIC
OCEAN

Gulf of Mexico

•Monterrey

Nassau
⊛ **BAHAMAS**

MEXICO

Havana
⊛

CUBA

Guadalajara •

Mérida •

PUERTO RICO (U.S.)
VIRGIN ISLANDS (U.S./U.K.)
ST. MARTIN (Fr./Neth.)

Mexico ⊛
City

**DOMINICAN
REPUBLIC**

ST. KITTS AND NEVIS
ANTIGUA AND BARBUDA

JAMAICA

HAITI

BELIZE

Guatemala
City

Belmopan

Kingston

Port-
au-Prince

Santo
Domingo

DOMINICA
MARTINIQUE (Fr./Neth.)

HONDURAS

Caribbean Sea

**ST. VINCENT AND
THE GRENADINES**

ST. LUCIA

GUATEMALA

⊛

•Tegucigalpa

BARBADOS

San Salvador •

ARUBA
(Neth.)

GRENADA

EL SALVADOR

NICARAGUA

TRINIDAD AND TOBAGO

Managua

Panama
City

Maracaibo •

Port-of-Spain

COSTA RICA

San José

Caracas •

Georgetown

PANAMA

VENEZUELA

•

Paramaribo

Medellín •

GUYANA

• Cayenne

Bogotá

Orinoco

SURINAME

**FRENCH
GUIANA
(Fr.)**

Cali •

COLOMBIA

Quito ⊛

A   M   A   Z   O   N

Belém •

ECUADOR

Guayaquil •

Amazon

Manaus •

River

B   A   S   I   N

Fortaleza •

Madeira

Xingu

Trujillo •

Río

BRAZIL

Recife •

PERU

B   R   A   Z   I   L   I   A   N

Salvador •

Lima ⊛

Rio Tocantins

Lake
Titicaca

Rio

PACIFIC OCEAN

La Paz
⊛

BOLIVIA

Brasília ⊛

⊛Sucre

H   I   G   H   L   A   N   D   S

•Belo Horizonte

Antofagasta •

PARAGUAY

São Paulo •

Rio de Janeiro

Asunción ⊛

Paraná

CHILE

Pôrto Alegre •

Río

Valparaiso •

•Córdoba

URUGUAY

Santiago ⊛

Rosario •

Concepción •

Buenos Aires ⊛

Montevideo •

A   N   D   E   S   M   O   U   N   T   A   I   N   S

ARGENTINA

ATLANTIC

OCEAN

N
W ⊛ E
S

0   500   1,000 Miles
0   500   1,000 Kilometers
Azimuthal Equal-Area Projection

164

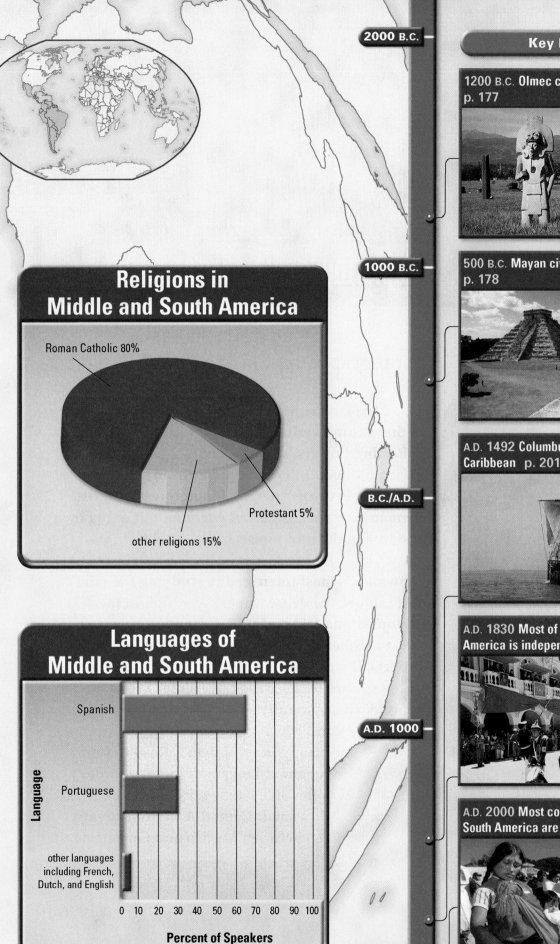

Religions in Middle and South America

Roman Catholic 80%

Protestant 5%

other religions 15%

Languages of Middle and South America

Language

Spanish

Portuguese

other languages including French, Dutch, and English

0 10 20 30 40 50 60 70 80 90 100

Percent of Speakers

2000 B.C.

1000 B.C.

B.C./A.D.

A.D. 1000

A.D. 2000

Key Events

1200 B.C. **Olmec civilization begins** p. 177

500 B.C. **Mayan civilization begins** p. 178

A.D. 1492 **Columbus lands in the Caribbean** p. 201

A.D. 1830 **Most of Middle and South America is independent** p. 208

A.D. 2000 **Most countries of Middle and South America are republics** p. 209

START with a STORY

The Most Beautiful Roof in the World

in the World

Exploring the Rain Forest Canopy

written by Kathryn Lasky
photographs by Christopher G. Knight

Dr. Meg Lowman has always been interested in the natural world. As a young girl, she started collecting flowers, seashells, butterflies, and rocks. That childhood interest took her from state science fairs to an exciting career as a rain forest scientist. Lowman now spends half of every month living in and studying the rain forests of the world.

Lowman is most interested in studying the rain forest canopy, the dense upper layer high in the treetops of the rain forest. The canopy supports a great number of species of plants, animals, and insects. It was once too difficult to get close to these species because they live so far above the ground. Today scientists like Lowman use new technologies and expert climbing ability to explore the canopy in great detail. Read to find out about Lowman's journey through the Blue Creek rain forest of Belize, a small Central American country between Mexico and Guatemala.

Deep in Belize, in Central America, there is a place called Blue Creek. Almost every month nearly 40 inches (102 centimeters) of rain falls. Blue Creek is considered one of the most humid places on the entire planet. In this shadowed world, pierced occasionally by slivers of sunlight, are more varieties of living things than perhaps any other place on earth. Within a 16-foot (five-meter) square there can be upward of two hundred different species of plants.

And there are animals, too. Bats swoop through the canopy. Vipers coil among buttress roots, waiting in ambush. A rare and mysterious tree salamander slinks into the petals of an orchid. Poison dart frog tadpoles swim high above the forest floor in the tanks of bromeliads.

The rain forest is a timeless, uncharted world, where mysteries abound and new or rare species appear like undiscovered islands. Within the tangled vines under the rotting bark of fallen trees, caught in the slime and mold of decaying vegetation and fungi , life teems with ceaseless energy. When a tree falls, the stump rots, bark loosens, and new creatures move in and take over the altered habitats . It is the very diversity of the rain forest that allows life to thrive everywhere, to spring back with a rush of opportunistic species to fill the gaps.

Meg Lowman believes that science is the machinery that runs the earth. She explains, "I think that science is really the way things work, and that's exciting. It is important to understand the bigger picture of our planet and where we live, how it functions, what we do with it, and how that will have impact . . . ."

fungi any of a major group of flowerless plants that lack chlorophyll and live on dead or organic matter

habitat the part of an environment in which a plant or animal naturally lives or grows

diversity the condition of being different

opportunistic taking advantage of opportunities regardless of what might happen

Viewed from an airplane, the top of the rain forest at Blue Creek looks like a field of gigantic broccoli. The bright green florets are actually the <u>emergent growth</u> of the very tallest trees. The crowns of these trees extend above the canopy in the layer known as the pavilion. The pavilion is to the canopy as a roof is to a ceiling. From the emergent growth to the floor of the rain forest is a drop of 150 feet (46 meters) or more. Meg wants to go to the canopy, a layer below the emergent one. At Blue Creek a canopy walkway designed by specialists in rain forest platform construction has been built.

Meg is up at first light. It is drizzling, but she will not wear rain gear. It is too hot. She has beans and rice for breakfast because this is all that is available. For her boys she has brought along Cheez Whiz and crackers because they are tired of beans and rice. Unless the Mayan people who live in the nearby village come into the forest with chickens or melons, the menu does not vary. She kisses the boys good-bye and leaves them with her brother, Ed, who helped build the walkway. She puts on a hard hat and climbs into her safety harness. The harness has two six-foot lengths of rope attached. At the end of the ropes are Jumars, or ascenders. Jumars are used in technical rock climbing. The metal U-shaped device has a hinged and grooved gate that allows the rope to slide up as one climbs but locks instantly with downward motion. To descend, the

emergent growth a tree that rises out of the surrounding forest.

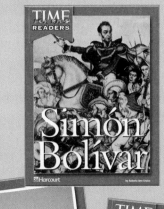

climber must manually push the gate open to allow the rope to slide through.

"Bye, Mom," James waves as he watches his mother begin her climb at the base of the *Ormosia*, or cabbage bark tree.

"Remember, it's our turn next," calls Edward as he watches his mom climb higher.

The boys have accompanied their mother to rain forests all over the world. Now, for the first time, Meg feels they are old enough to go with her into the canopy. She has ordered special child-size harnesses for them. They are excited, but first their mother has work to do—traps to set for insects, leaves to tag, drawings to make, flowers to count. It will be many hours before they can join her. In the meantime, they can swim in the creek and explore a secret cave that their uncle promises to take them to.

Analyze the Literature

1 What sort of skills would you need to be a scientist who studies the rain forest, as Meg Lowman does?

2 Go outside and take a picture or draw a sketch of a plant or insect you find there. See if you can identify it by using resources at your local library. Write a short description of what you found and its role in the environment in which you live.

READ A BOOK

START THE UNIT PROJECT

Make Postcards As you read this unit, gather information about the geography and cultures of Middle America and South America. Use this information to help you create postcards that describe the cultural landscape of Middle America and South America.

USE TECHNOLOGY

Visit The Learning Site at **www.harcourtschool.com/ socialstudies** for additional activities, primary sources, and other resources to use in this unit.

CHICHÉN ITZÁ, MEXICO

Located on Mexico's Yucatán Peninsula, the city of Chichén Itzá was built by the Maya in around A.D. 600. The pyramid called El Castillo rises out of the main square of the ancient city. Many people visit Chichén Itzá during the spring and fall to see the sun cast a serpent-shaped shadow on the stairway of El Castillo. The serpent was a symbol of Kukulcán, an important Mayan god.

LOCATE IT

Chichén Itzá

MEXICO

5

Mexico

❝ **Mexico has always been a country of architects, from pre-Columbian times to the present.** ❞

—Octavio Paz, from
*The Labyrinth
of Solitude*, 1950

CHAPTER READING SKILL

Compare and Contrast

When you **compare** and **contrast** people, places, events, or ideas, you analyze how they are alike and how they are different.

As you read this chapter, look for similarities and differences among people, places, events, and ideas. Record them in a Venn diagram.

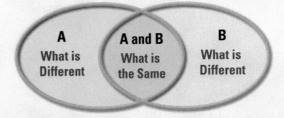

A	A and B	B
What is Different	What is the Same	What is Different

MAIN IDEA
Read to find out about the rugged landscape and contrasting climates of Mexico.

WHY IT MATTERS
People can find a way to live in almost any climate and environment.

VOCABULARY

isthmus
peninsula
plateau
sierra
tierra caliente
frost
tierra templada
tierra fría

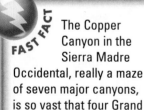

FAST FACT The Copper Canyon in the Sierra Madre Occidental, really a maze of seven major canyons, is so vast that four Grand Canyons could fit inside it.

A Rugged Land

In 1528 the Spanish explorer Hernando Cortés (kawr•TEZ) returned to Spain after a long journey through what is now Mexico. The Spanish king, Charles V, asked Cortés to describe the land where he had been. Cortés took a piece of paper. He crumpled it in his hand. "There, Your Highness, is Mexico," was said to be his reply. His action described Mexico as a rugged land of sharp physical differences.

Mexico's Landforms

On a map the Mexican mainland appears something like a triangle in shape. The broad base of the triangle is in the north, where Mexico shares a 2,000-mile (3,220-km) border with the United States. The Río Bravo del Norte, known in the United States as the Rio Grande, flows along a large portion of the border.

To the south the land narrows. It is narrowest at the Isthmus of Tehuantepec (tuh•WAHN•tuh•pek). An **isthmus** is a narrow strip of land that connects two larger land areas. At this point only about 140 miles (225 km) separates the Pacific Ocean and the Gulf of Mexico. South of the isthmus the land widens slightly as Mexico stretches toward its border with Belize and Guatemala.

West of the Mexican mainland is a narrow strip of land known as Baja (BAH•hah) California, or Lower California. It is a long **peninsula**, or piece of land that is mostly surrounded by water. It extends south from its northern border with the state of California in the United States. The Gulf of California separates Baja California from the mainland of Mexico except near the border

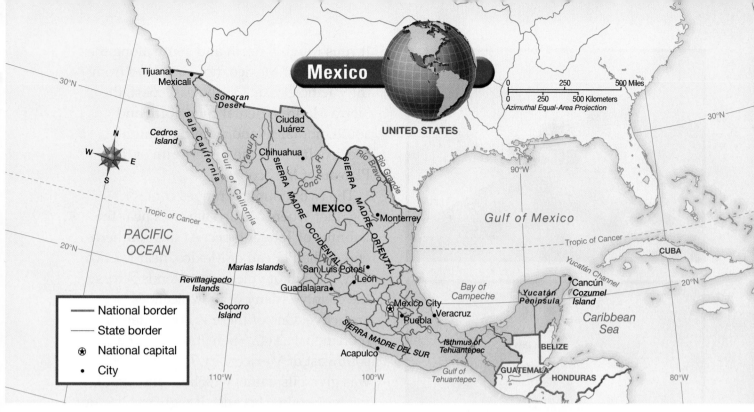

Mexico

UNITED STATES

0 250 500 Miles
0 250 500 Kilometers
Azimuthal Equal-Area Projection

Tijuana
Mexicali
Sonoran Desert
Ciudad Juárez
Cedros Island
Chihuahua
Baja California
Gulf of California
SIERRA MADRE OCCIDENTAL
SIERRA MADRE ORIENTAL
Conchos R.
Yaqui R.
Rio Grande
Rio Bravo
MEXICO
Monterrey
San Luis Potosí
León
Guadalajara
Marías Islands
Revillagigedo Islands
Socorro Island
Mexico City
Puebla
Veracruz
Acapulco
SIERRA MADRE DEL SUR
Isthmus of Tehuantepec
Gulf of Tehuantepec
Bay of Campeche
Yucatán Peninsula
Yucatán Channel
Cancún
Cozumel Island
BELIZE
GUATEMALA
HONDURAS
CUBA
Gulf of Mexico
Caribbean Sea
PACIFIC OCEAN
Tropic of Cancer

30°N
20°N
110°W
100°W
90°W
80°W

N W E S

— National border
— State border
⊛ National capital
• City

GEOGRAPHY THEME

Regions   **Mexico is made up of 31 states.**

❖ **Which countries border Mexico?**

with the United States. The Plateau of Mexico is Mexico's largest physical feature. A **plateau** is a raised plain that covers a large area. Most of the Mexican people live on the plateau of Mexico, where two of the largest cities, Mexico City and Guadalajara (gwah•dah•lah•HAH•rah), are located.

This relatively flat land is wedged between two large mountain ranges in a V shape. They are both called the Sierra Madre (SYAIR•ah MAH•dray), or "Mother Range." One is the Sierra Madre

Occidental, and the other is the Sierra Madre Oriental. A **sierra** is a rugged chain of mountains. In Spanish, *occidental* means "western," and *oriental* means "eastern." These are the mountains that make Mexico look like Cortés's crumpled paper.

The Sierra Madre Occidental forms the western rim of the Plateau of Mexico.

This Mexican family (right) lives in the rugged mountains of the Sierra Madre.

Chapter 5 ■ 173

It runs roughly north and south along the west coast of Mexico, not far inland from the Pacific Ocean. On the east coast, the Sierra Madre Oriental runs north and south, not far inland from the Gulf of Mexico. It forms the eastern rim of the Plateau of Mexico.

The two mountain ranges come together where Mexico narrows near the Isthmus of Tehuantepec. At this southern end of the Plateau of Mexico, near Mexico City, a chain of volcanoes extends across the country. Many of the volcanoes are active. One of these is Popocatépetl (poh•poh•kah•TAY•peh•tuhl), located southeast of Mexico City. Popocatépetl was given its name, which means "smoking mountain," because it regularly lets out puffs of smoke. For hundreds of years people lived on the slopes of the volcano and farmed its fertile soil. Then in 1996 lava poured out, forcing many people to move.

Most volcanoes form because of the movement of Earth's tectonic plates. The same movement also causes earthquakes, especially in southern Mexico. Because of earthquakes, the ancient Aztec people called Mexico "land of the shaking earth."

REVIEW **What causes volcanoes and earthquakes in Mexico?**

Popocatépetl is one of the many active volcanoes in Mexico. This series of photos shows Popocatépetl erupting.

FAST FACT

Volcanic activity produces many hot springs in central Mexico. In spite of the unpleasant sulfur smell, the springs are popular places for swimming. The warm, soothing water is considered good for such ailments as arthritis.

LOCATE IT

Popocatépetl Volcano

MEXICO

LOCATE IT

MEXICO

Cabo San Lucas

Cabo San Lucas (left) and areas along the Gulf of Mexico (above) are parts of Mexico's "hot land."

Climate and Vegetation

Mexico's climate varies greatly from the deserts in the northern Sonoran Desert to the southern rain forests of the Yucatán (yoo•kah•TAHN) Peninsula. People in Mexico, however, use three terms to describe the climate zones in which they live. Each is linked to a different elevation, or altitude.

The first of these climate zones is the **tierra caliente**, or "hot land." In general, the *tierra caliente* includes elevations that extend from sea level to 3,000 feet (914 m). This zone has hot summers and mild winters with no frost. **Frost** is a covering of tiny ice crystals that form on a surface when dew or water freezes.

Higher in elevation is the climate zone called **tierra templada**, or "temperate land." The *tierra templada* includes elevations between 3,000 and 6,000 feet (914 and 1,829 m). Average temperatures in the *tierra templada* are between 80°F and 50°F (27°C and 10°C). Most of Mexico's farms are in this zone, and most of its people live there.

Higher still is the **tierra fría**, or "cold land." The *tierra fría* includes elevations rising above 6,000 feet (1,829 m). "Cold land"

is a little misleading, however. Although temperatures in the *tierra fría* do not get very hot, they also do not get very cold, because they lie in the tropics. Frost is infrequent in much of the zone below 8,000 feet (2,400 m). The highest mountain peaks in the *tierra fría* are colder and are covered with snow all year round.

Elevation in the tropics affects not only temperature but also rainfall. In general, winds blowing off the Gulf of Mexico and the Pacific Ocean drop most of their moisture as rain on the low-lying coastal areas. The eastern and western Sierra Madre chains create a rain shadow. They stop the rain from reaching much of the central Plateau of Mexico. This results in desert or near-desert conditions in northern Mexico. Farther south, some sea breezes break through the mountain passes to bring rain to the plateau.

Rainfall in central Mexico varies in amount, but when it comes is predictable. There is a definite rainy season as well as a dry season. In Mexico City the dry season is fall and winter. The rainy season is spring and summer. In southern areas of Mexico and on the Yucatán Peninsula, the rainy season begins earlier and lasts longer. Most rain falls in the summer, usually as short daily downpours in the afternoon.

Chapter 5 ■ **175**

Mexico City

Understanding Human Systems

Mexico City sits on land that used to hold a lake. The capital is located in the southern part of the Plateau of Mexico. Mountains rise around much of the city. About one-fourth of all Mexicans live in and around Mexico City. As many as 16 million people call Mexico City home.

As a result of so much rain, tropical rain forests are found in this part of Mexico. Forests cover about one-fifth of Mexico. In addition to the rain forests in the south, hardwood forests cover the northwestern central mountains. Hardwoods, such as mahogany and walnut, are valuable in making furniture. Large pine forests throughout the rest of Mexico supply trees for Mexico's paper industry.

REVIEW In what climate zone do most of Mexico's people live?

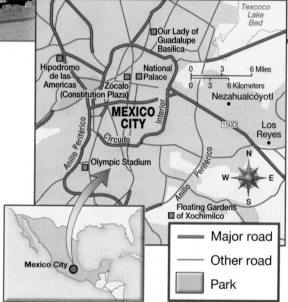

LESSON 1 REVIEW

1 MAIN IDEA What are some of Mexico's physical features?

2 WHY IT MATTERS Why do most people in Mexico live on the Plateau of Mexico?

3 VOCABULARY Use the word **sierra** in a sentence about Mexico's mountains.

4 READING SKILL—Compare and Contrast How does the climate near Mexico City differ from the climate in northern Mexico?

5 GEOGRAPHY How has plate tectonics affected the land of Mexico?

6 HISTORY Why did the Aztecs call Mexico "land of the shaking earth"?

7 CRITICAL THINKING—Apply Why are people willing to live near volcanoes? How do they affect people in both positive and negative ways? Give examples that relate to Mexico.

PERFORMANCE—Write a Poem The Aztecs described the land of Mexico in creative ways. Write a poem about a region in Mexico, using descriptive language.

Creating a Mexican Culture

| 2000 B.C. | 1000 B.C. | B.C./A.D. | A.D. 1000 | A.D. 2000 |

MAIN IDEA
Find out how Mexican culture developed from native and Spanish cultures.

WHY IT MATTERS
Knowing about the sources of Mexican culture is important to understanding Mexican society today.

VOCABULARY
civilization
innovation
reclaim
missionary
fiesta
mestizo

The land that is now Mexico, as well as some of the land in Central America, was home to three early civilizations. The term **civilization** is similar in meaning to *culture*, but it refers mostly to a culture that has a complex economic, governing, and social system. A civilization is also more advanced in technology than other cultures of its time.

The Olmecs

The earliest civilization of Mexico was that of the Olmecs (AHL•meks). The Olmec people first settled along the coast of the Gulf of Mexico in what are now the Mexican states of Veracruz and Tabasco. By the early 1200s B.C., the Olmecs were living along coastal rivers in villages of small houses made of reeds and straw. The people fished in the rivers and farmed land made fertile by river flooding.

Like other farming societies, the Olmecs came to depend on seasonal flooding to water their crops and make the soil rich. The Olmecs, like many early people in other parts of the world, developed a counting system and a calendar to keep track of the flood season. The Olmecs also used a form of picture writing to keep a record of important events.

Statues like the ones below were used in the Olmec religion. The grass-covered ruins (left) show the plan of Olmec settlements.

An Olmec mask covered
in turquoise

The Olmecs are probably best known today for their carvings and artworks. Many of these objects, both large and small, were made for religious purposes. Like the people of other early civilizations, the Olmecs based their religion on the forces of nature that affected the growing of crops. The Olmecs worshiped many different gods, but the most important was a god in the form of a jaguar that they believed brought rain.

Some Olmec villages became centers of religion. Over time, these centers grew to the size of cities. In the middle of each Olmec city were great temples made of huge stones. Olmec artists decorated the temples with carved stone faces, some more than 9 feet (2.7 m) tall and weighing 36,000 pounds (16,330 kg). Each face may have been carved to look like an Olmec ruler or priest.

Many experts believe that the Olmec builders had moved some of the giant stones more than 50 miles (80 km), and no one knows exactly how they did it. Their technology did not include the wheel.

Olmec **innovations**, or new ways of doing things, spread to other societies as the Olmecs interacted with them through trade. These other societies borrowed the Olmecs' religious ideas, their art and architecture, and their technology. Later cultures, such as those of the Maya and the Aztecs, also used and added to Olmec innovations. For this reason, the Olmec civilization is often called the "mother civilization" of the Americas.

REVIEW How did Olmec culture traits spread to other cultures?

The Maya

About the same time that the Olmecs were building religious centers in Mexico, the Maya had a simple farming culture in the rain forests of what are now Belize, Guatemala, Honduras, and southern Mexico. By about 500 B.C., however, Mayan civilization began to take shape. Borrowing many Olmec culture traits, the Maya cleared the forest to farm more land and to build cities. They built more than 100 cities.

The largest Mayan city was Tikal, with as many as 100,000 people. It was located on the Yucatán Peninsula in what is now Guatemala. In the center of Tikal stood six large temples. Each was made of huge blocks of limestone and was shaped like a pyramid, with four sloping sides that came together at the top. A jaguar is carved on top of Tikal's largest temple. It is a religious symbol borrowed from the Olmecs.

The Maya also borrowed other Olmec innovations and improved them. The Maya created a 365-day calendar to keep track of planting, harvesting, and seasonal flooding. To record their crops, they developed a number system, including a symbol for zero—an important idea in mathematics. They also used picture writing.

Scientists who study early civilizations know that the Mayan civilization lasted for more than 600 years. After A.D. 900, however, some of the Mayan cities were left empty and were **reclaimed**, or taken back, by the surrounding rain forests. The culture of the Maya, like that of the Olmecs, would contribute to the cultures of later civilizations in Mexico.

REVIEW How was the Olmec civilization important to the Maya?

Mexico Long Ago

MEXICO

Valley of Mexico
Lake Texcoco
•Teotihuacán
Tenochtitlán
Gulf of Mexico
Mayapán•
Chichén Itzá•
Yucatán Peninsula
Balsas River
La Venta•
San Lorenzo•
Usumacinta River
Grijalva River
Caribbean Sea

N
W E
S

PACIFIC OCEAN

0   150   300 Miles
0   150   300 Kilometers
Azimuthal Equal-Area Projection

	Olmec settlements, 1200 B.C.–400 B.C.
	Maya settlements, 500 B.C.–A.D. 1450
	Aztec Empire, A.D. 1325–A.D. 1519

GEOGRAPHY THEME

Regions This map shows the areas that the Olmec, Mayan, and Aztec civilizations occupied.

❷ Which civilization covered the largest area?

The Aztecs

The Aztec civilization developed in the A.D. 1200s, when its people settled in the Valley of Mexico. In many ways the Aztec civilization was like the Mayan.

The Aztecs had an accurate calendar and used mathematics to help them grow their crops. They developed a system of writing, as the Maya had done, and constructed many well-organized cities with large buildings.

Tenochtitlán (tay•nohch•teet•LAHN) was the largest of the Aztec cities. By the 1400s it had more than 300,000 people. It was not only the center of Aztec civilization but also the capital city of a huge empire that included 200,000 square miles (518,000 sq km). The Aztec Empire covered much of what is now central and southern Mexico.

The Aztec Empire may have had as many as 5 million people. These included Aztecs as well as the many peoples that the Aztecs had conquered to build their empire. Often the diverse cultures of the Aztec Empire came into contact with one another at the market in Tenochtitlán. More than 60,000 people came to this market every day to exchange goods. At the same time, they exchanged ideas, adding new ways to Aztec culture.

Mayan ruins near a village in Chiapas, Mexico

Some contributions of Aztec culture can be found in present-day Mexico. The Aztecs have thousands of descendants living in Mexico today. Some of them speak a form of Nahuatl (NAH•wah•tuhl), the spoken language of the Aztecs. Many names of places in Mexico, as well as the name *Mexico* itself, come from Nahuatl.

Aztec influence can also be seen in today's traditional Mexican foods. The main food of the Aztecs was a thin cornmeal pancake called a *tlaxcalli*. The Spanish later called it a *tortilla*. The Aztecs used these pancakes to scoop up other foods or to wrap bits of meat and vegetables to form tacos.

REVIEW What Aztec cultural contributions are found in present-day Mexico?

The Spanish

Between 1519 and 1521, Spanish explorers led by Hernando Cortés conquered the Aztec Empire and claimed the land for Spain. As a result, the Spanish began forming colonies. One of these colonies was called New Spain. Its capital was Mexico City, which was built on the ruins of Tenochtitlán. New Spain eventually

A mural showing Mexican history

included all of present-day Mexico, most of Central America, and much of the present southwestern United States.

Mexico remained a Spanish colony for almost 300 years. During that time many people moved to Mexico from Spain, bringing Spanish culture with them. As a result, almost all Mexicans today speak Spanish. Some native languages, such as Mayan, Nahuatl, and Zapotec, are still spoken in Mexico. However, Spanish is the official language.

A further result of the culture brought to Mexico from Spain is that most Mexicans today follow the Roman Catholic religion. Beginning in the early 1500s, Roman Catholic **missionaries**, or religious teachers, taught their religion to millions of native peoples. Today about 97 percent of the people of Mexico are Catholics.

The Spanish colonial government recognized the Roman Catholic Church as the official religion. The government did not allow other religions. The Church in Mexico became wealthy and powerful as a result.

Because of the importance of religion over the years, religious holidays are among the most important holidays celebrated by the Mexican people.

A CLOSER LOOK
Tenochtitlán

In the 1400s Tenochtitlán was one of the largest cities in the world. It was built on islands in a lake.

❶ The Aztecs worshiped their gods at the main temple.

❷ Stalls in the market offered food, jewelry, clothing, and the services of doctors.

❸ The people used canals, as well as streets, for transportation.

❹ Farmers made floating gardens, called *chinampas*, out of reeds.

❖ Why do you think farmers made floating gardens?

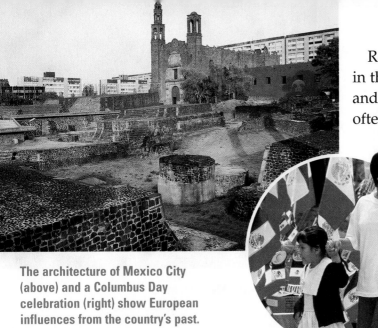

The architecture of Mexico City (above) and a Columbus Day celebration (right) show European influences from the country's past.

Religious influences can also be seen in the buildings of most Mexican cities and towns. Catholic churches there are often large. Some have the ornate, highly decorated architecture of the Spanish colonial period. Other churches show the influence of different styles and cultures.

During colonial times many colonists married native people already living in what is now Mexico. The children of these marriages were called **mestizos** (meh•STEE•zohs).

Today most people in Mexico are mestizos, and being mestizo is often a matter of national pride. This shows the link between the nation's long native past and the Spanish colonial period.

REVIEW What traits of Spanish culture are seen in present-day Mexico?

Every Mexican city and town holds a yearly **fiesta**, or festival, to honor the Catholic saint believed to be the place's protector. Guadalupe Day is Mexico's most important religious holiday. It honors the mother of Jesus Christ and is celebrated on December 12.

LESSON 2 REVIEW

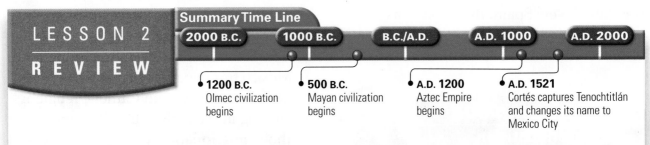

Summary Time Line

| 2000 B.C. | 1000 B.C. | B.C./A.D. | A.D. 1000 | A.D. 2000 |

1200 B.C. Olmec civilization begins

500 B.C. Mayan civilization begins

A.D. 1200 Aztec Empire begins

A.D. 1521 Cortés captures Tenochtitlán and changes its name to Mexico City

① **MAIN IDEA** What are Mexico's main cultural heritages?

② **WHY IT MATTERS** Why do you think it is important to know the history of Mexico's people?

③ **VOCABULARY** Use the words **civilization** and **innovation** to describe the Maya.

④ **TIME LINE** Which was the earliest civilization of Mexico—the Mayan, the Aztec, or the Olmec?

⑤ **READING SKILL—Compare and Contrast** In this lesson you have read about how the Olmecs, Maya, Aztecs, and Spanish built civilizations in Mexico. How were the civilizations alike? How were they different?

⑥ **HISTORY** Why are the Olmecs called the "mother civilization" of the Americas?

⑦ **TECHNOLOGY** What Mayan innovation is still important in mathematics today?

⑧ **HISTORY** Why is Hernando Cortés important in Mexico's history?

⑨ **CRITICAL THINKING—Hypothesize** What do you think might have happened if Cortés had not conquered the Aztecs?

PERFORMANCE—Make a Mural Mexican artist Diego Rivera painted murals that showed what life in Aztec cities may have been like. What do you think life was like? Work with a group to make a mural of Aztec city life.

Yesterday and Today

Mexico remained a Spanish colony until September 15, 1810, when the Mexican people first rebelled against Spanish rule. In a speech known as the Cry of Dolores, Miguel Hidalgo (ee•DAHL•goh), a Catholic priest, urged the Mexican people to rebel so that Mexicans could govern Mexico themselves. For the next 11 years, the Mexican people continued the struggle. They finally won independence in 1821. The Mexican people celebrate their independence as a nation each year on September 16.

Building a Nation

From 1821 to 1877 two emperors, several dictators, and many presidents and chief executives governed Mexico. None, however, was able to solve the two major problems left over from the long years of Spanish rule—democratic rights and land ownership.

During this time, too, Mexico had serious problems with the United States. Many settlers from the United States as well as from Mexico had gone to live in the Mexican province of Texas, north of the Río Bravo. In 1836 the Texans declared their independence from Mexico. In 1845 the United States government voted to **annex** Texas, or add it to the nation. Then, after defeat in a war with the United States, between 1846 and 1848, Mexico agreed to give up all claims to Texas. The Treaty of Guadalupe Hidalgo ended the war. Under the treaty, Mexico sold to the United States the area made up of the present states of California, Nevada, Utah, most of Arizona and New Mexico, and parts of Wyoming and Colorado.

MAIN IDEA
Read to find out about how Mexico's government and economy developed.

WHY IT MATTERS
Mexico's political and economic activities affect its neighbor, the United States.

VOCABULARY

annex

finances

presidential democracy

maquiladora

The National Palace in Mexico City is located on the site where an Aztec palace once stood.

LOCATE IT

Mexico City

MEXICO

Benito Juárez 1806–1872

Character Trait: Justice

Benito Juárez, a Zapotec Indian from the state of Oaxaca, became a political leader whose sense of justice kept him fighting for the rights of all Mexicans. After serving in the national congress and as governor of the state of Oaxaca, he became president of Mexico in 1858. During his term in office, Juárez led opposition to a French invasion, keeping Mexico independent.

MULTIMEDIA BIOGRAPHIES
Visit The Learning Site at
www.harcourtschool.com/biographies
to learn about other famous people.

During the late 1800s and early 1900s, Mexico experienced many problems. Under President Benito Juárez (HWAH•rays), reforms were tried. He ended special privileges for the Catholic Church and the army. He also wanted free elections and education. The government did not have enough money to do all this. Much of the money Mexico received for the land it lost to the United States had gone to pay for the war. Juárez's effort to reform Mexico ended when he died in 1872.

In 1876 Porfirio Díaz (pawr•FEER•ee•oh DEE•ahz) took control of the government and named himself president. He wanted to reform the nation's **finances**, or money matters. Díaz's 30-year rule brought growth and order to Mexico but at a cost. Foreign investors and wealthy landowners did well in Mexico during this time. Yet many poor farmers lost their land.

In 1910 a landowner named Francisco Madero called for an end to Díaz's rule. He believed that Mexico should become the kind of democracy that Juárez had wanted. Soon a revolution broke out. After seven years the leaders of the revolution took control of Mexico. In 1917 the Mexican Revolution came to an end with the writing of a new constitution. The Constitution of 1917 provided land reform by returning land to the poor farmers. It also established a **presidential democracy**, in which an elected president is the chief decision maker.

FAST FACT At the center of the Mexican flag is an image from an Aztec legend. The legend tells how the Aztecs came to settle in the Valley of Mexico. It was there the early Aztecs saw an eagle perched on a cactus, devouring a serpent.

Beginning in 1929 one political party controlled Mexico's government. It was the Institutional Revolutionary Party, or PRI. Only its candidates won the presidency. Members of the PRI held the office of president for 71 years, until Vicente Fox Quesada of the National Action Party, or PAN, was elected in 2000.

Although Mexico is a republic with three branches of government, Mexico's president plays a greater role than do presidents in other republics. The president of Mexico not only heads the executive branch but also has great influence over the legislative and judicial branches. The president establishes government policies, proposes new laws, and controls the nation's finances. The president also appoints judges and a Cabinet, which runs all government operations. The Constitution of 1917, however, limited presidential rule to one six-year term.

While the PRI controlled the office of president, other political parties controlled the less powerful General Congress, the national legislature of Mexico. This consists of the Senate and the Chamber of Deputies. The Senate has 64 members. The Chamber of Deputies has 500 members. Three hundred of the deputies are elected from the nation's electoral districts. The remaining 200 are representatives-at-large. This means they do not represent a particular district or group of people.

REVIEW How is Mexico's democracy different from other democracies?

A Zapotec Indian weaves at a city market in Oaxaca.

Mexico's Economy

For much of its history, Mexico's economy was based on primary industries—chiefly farming and mining. Beginning in the 1940s the government started to promote the development of manufacturing. Mexico now produces many of the finished products its people buy and use.

Many of Mexico's new factories were built along its border with the United States. The factories are mostly assembly plants known as **maquiladoras** (mah•kee•lah•DOH•rahs), where workers put together products from parts imported into Mexico. The finished products are then exported, mainly to the United States. The *maquiladoras* add to Mexico's economy.

In this modern building (left) stock traders (right) work in Mexico City's stock exchange.

Tourists who visit Mexico's many historic and cultural sites also bring money into the country.

Although there are many *maquiladoras*, Mexico City remains Mexico's main manufacturing center. The city and its suburbs produce about half the nation's consumer goods. Monterrey and Guadalajara are also important manufacturing areas.

In the 1970s Mexico became a major oil exporter. Much of its oil is sold to the

The cultural center in Tijuana offers information about Mexican culture to the city's many tourists.

LOCATE IT

Tijuana

MEXICO

United States. Income from oil, which the government controls, served to help diversify Mexico's economy. As a result, the government built new factories and started new businesses that offer services.

Services provide more than half of Mexico's jobs. Hospitals, hotels, police and fire protection, restaurants, schools, and stores are included in the service industry. Banking, communication, trade, and transportation are also included.

Today the GDP, or gross domestic product, of Mexico is about $865 billion, which is larger than that of Canada. However, Mexico's per capita GDP, which is one measure of a country's standard of living, is only $8,500. That compares with $23,300 for Canada. Life expectancy in Mexico, 71 years, is also lower than that in Canada, 79 years.

REVIEW What natural resource does Mexico export?

Mexico Today

The nation of Mexico has one of the fastest-growing populations in the world. In 1970 Mexico had 51 million people. Just ten years later there were 70 million. Today there are about 100 million people in Mexico. More than half are under 25 years of age.

Seven of every ten Mexicans live in cities and towns with populations of at least 2,500. The largest cities are Mexico City, Guadalajara, and Monterrey. Mexico City, the nation's capital, is known as the Federal District. Separate from Mexico's 31 states, the Federal District is similar to the District of Columbia in the United States.

Mexico's largest cities have grown quickly. Many people have moved to these urban areas from Mexico's rural areas to find jobs. This large migration to the cities has caused serious social and environmental problems. Houses in some cities lack electricity and running water. The large number of automobiles causes traffic jams and adds to air pollution.

Many of the people who have moved to the cities of Mexico do not have regular jobs. Others do not earn enough to support their families. Because of these conditions, some Mexicans have tried to leave the country to find work elsewhere. Many go to the United States. At times this situation has strained relations between Mexico and the United States.

Although there are problems, Mexico continues to make progress as a nation. Many miles of new roads have been built, as well as new seaports for trade. Educational opportunities for the people have also been expanded.

REVIEW Where do most people live in Mexico?

Traffic jams are part of daily life on Mexico City's crowded streets and highways.

LESSON 3
REVIEW

1. **MAIN IDEA** What are some ways Mexico's government and economy have changed over the years?

2. **WHY IT MATTERS** How does Mexico's economy affect the United States?

3. **VOCABULARY** Explain the meaning of **maquiladora**.

4. **READING SKILL—Compare and Contrast** Both the United States and Mexico are democracies. How are they alike? How are they different?

5. **GEOGRAPHY** What states of the United States were once part of Mexico?

6. **HISTORY** In what ways did Benito Juárez try to reform Mexico?

7. **CRITICAL THINKING—Analyze** Why do you think the early years of one-party rule under the PRI party brought peace and economic growth to Mexico? Why do you think Mexicans grew dissatisfied with such rule?

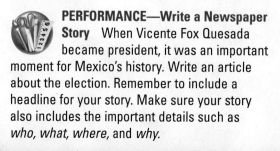

PERFORMANCE—Write a Newspaper Story When Vicente Fox Quesada became president, it was an important moment for Mexico's history. Write an article about the election. Remember to include a headline for your story. Make sure your story also includes the important details such as *who, what, where,* and *why.*

·SKILLS· READING

Identify Cause and Effect

▶ WHY IT MATTERS

When you read about history, you will notice that events are often linked. To find links between different events, you need to understand cause and effect. A cause is something that makes something else happen. What happens is an effect.

For example, when Benito Juárez became president of Mexico, the new government was able to pass the Reform Laws. The cause was the election of Juárez, and the effect was the passage of the Reform Laws. The two events were linked. If Mexico's dictator, Santa Anna, had remained in power, the laws would not have passed.

Learning about cause and effect is important not only for understanding history and current events but also for making personal decisions. It can help you think about the consequences before you make decisions.

▶ WHAT YOU NEED TO KNOW

The following tips can help you identify cause-and-effect relationships when you read.

- A cause-and-effect relationship can be simple: one cause leads to one effect.

- Some cause-and-effect relationships are more complex: one cause may lead to two or more separate effects, or two or more separate causes may lead to one effect.

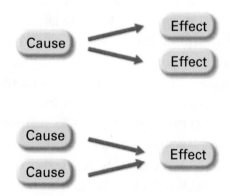

- In some cases a single cause may lead to a chain of linked effects. Each effect is the cause of another effect.

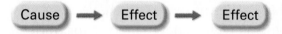

Portrait of Benito Juárez

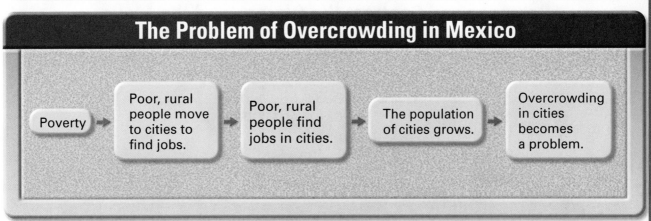

Mexico's Economy During the 1970s

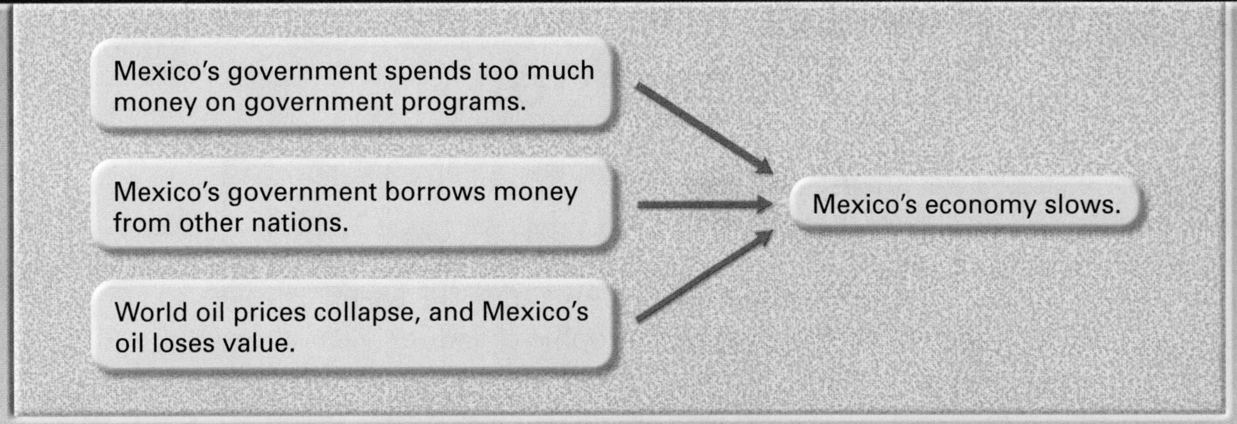

Mexico's government spends too much money on government programs.

Mexico's government borrows money from other nations.

World oil prices collapse, and Mexico's oil loses value.

Mexico's economy slows.

The Problem of Overcrowding in Mexico

Poverty → Poor, rural people move to cities to find jobs. → Poor, rural people find jobs in cities. → The population of cities grows. → Overcrowding in cities becomes a problem.

• When you read, look for words that signal cause-and-effect relationships, such as *because, as a result, since, consequently, for this reason, in response.* Words, such as *also* and *in addition,* often are used to signal relationships in which there are multiple causes or multiple effects.

▶ PRACTICE THE SKILL

Above are two diagrams that show cause-and-effect relationships. Use the diagrams to answer these questions.

❶ Which diagram shows a single cause that led to a chain of effects?

❷ What effect did spending too much money on government programs have?

❸ Which of the following is both a cause and an effect? The population of cities grows. OR Mexico's government borrows money from other nations.

▶ APPLY WHAT YOU LEARNED

Read the passage below. Then use the information to make your own cause-and-effect diagram.

The early years of one-party rule brought peace and economic growth to Mexico. Under the PRI, the government took possession of oil and mineral rights and all railways. It also broke up large haciendas and increased services to the Mexican people. Business and industry flourished once again. Many Mexicans earned more money.

· CHAPTER ·

5 Review and Test Preparation

Summary Time Line
2000 B.C.
1000 B.C.
1200 B.C.
Olmec civilization begins

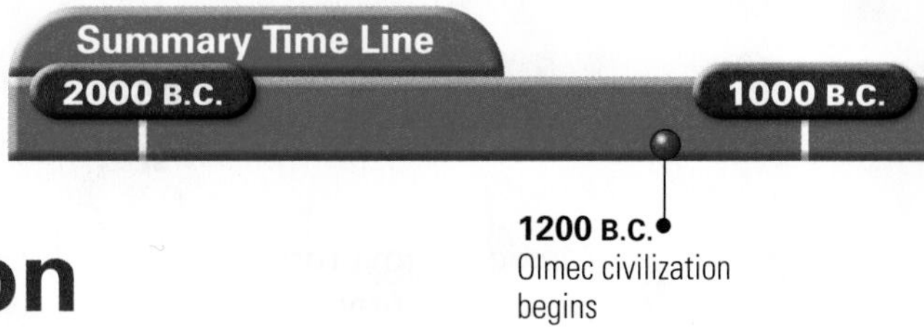

Use Your Reading Skills

Complete this graphic organizer to show that you understand how to compare and contrast different groups and cultures, such as the Olmecs and the Maya. A copy of this graphic organizer appears on page 51 of the Activity Book.

Compare and Contrast the Olmecs and the Maya

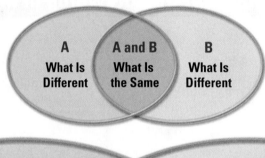

A
What Is Different
A and B
What Is the Same
B
What Is Different

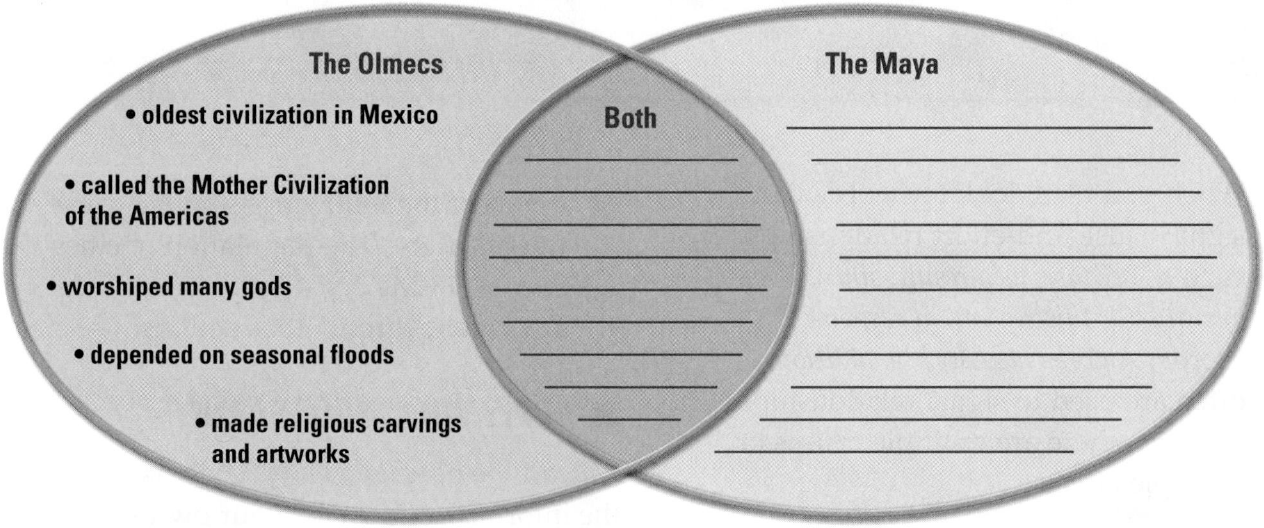

The Olmecs
• oldest civilization in Mexico
• called the Mother Civilization of the Americas
• worshiped many gods
• depended on seasonal floods
• made religious carvings and artworks
Both
The Maya

Think & Write

Write a Newspaper Story Think about some of the innovations of the Olmecs, Maya, and Aztecs. Write a newspaper headline about one of these innovations. Then write a newspaper story describing the innovation and why it is important.

Write a Travelogue Suppose you are a Spanish explorer who recently visited the Aztec Empire for the first time. Write a travelogue about the people and cultures that you encountered. Include descriptions of Tenochtitlán and the landforms that surround it.

500 B.C.
Mayan civilization begins

A.D. 900
Mayan civilization begins to decline

A.D. 1200
Aztec Empire begins

A.D. 1519
Spanish arrive in Mexico

A.D. 1521
Cortés captures Tenochtitlán and changes its name to Mexico City

A.D. 2000
Seventy percent of Mexicans live in urban areas

USE THE TIME LINE

Use the chapter summary time line to answer these questions.

1 In what year did Cortés capture Tenochtitlán, the Aztec capital?

2 How many years passed between the beginning of the Mayan civilization and its decline?

USE VOCABULARY

Identify the term that correctly matches each definition.

isthmus (p. 172)

tierra templada (p. 175)

missionary (p. 181)

fiesta (p. 182)

presidential democracy (p. 184)

3 a festival in Mexico, such as one to honor a saint

4 a narrow strip of land that connects two larger land areas

5 Mexico's government, in which the head of state is the main decision maker

6 land in Mexico at middle elevations with average temperatures between 80°F and 50°F (27°C and 10°C)

7 a religious teacher

RECALL FACTS

Answer these questions.

8 What are Mexico's two main mountain ranges?

9 Where did the Olmec people first settle?

10 What kind of government does Mexico have today? How is it organized?

Write the letter of the best choice.

11 **TEST PREP** The Olmecs, Maya, and Aztecs used each of the following innovations, *except*—
A picture writing.
B a calendar.
C the wheel.
D a counting system.

12 **TEST PREP** All of the following have been Mexican leaders *except*—
F Guadalupe Hildago.
G Porfirio Díaz.
H Benito Juárez.
J Vicente Fox Quesada.

13 **TEST PREP** The political party that controlled the Mexican presidency for 71 years was the—
A National Action Party (PAN).
B National Democratic Party.
C Institutional Revolutionary Party (PRI).
D Chamber of Deputies.

THINK CRITICALLY

14 Why do you think most of Mexico's farms and people are in a *tierra templada* climate?

15 What are some characteristics of Mexican society today that reflect the influence of historical events or groups?

APPLY SKILLS

Identify Cause and Effect

16 Identify a recent event or problem in your community. Make a cause-and-effect diagram to show the causes that created the event or problem.

READING SKILLS

TERRE DE HAUT, GUADELOUPE, FRENCH WEST INDIES

Found in a small string of islands called Les Saintes, Terre de Haut is part of the French possession Guadeloupe. Like other Caribbean islands, Terre de Haut enjoys warm temperatures and pleasant weather. The island's beautiful beaches and climate make it popular with tourists from around the world.

LOCATE IT

ATLANTIC OCEAN

FRENCH WEST INDIES

Terre de Haut

Caribbean Sea

6

Central America and the Caribbean

"Out of many, One people."
—from Jamaica's national motto

CHAPTER READING SKILL

Sequence

The order in which events, processes, or ideas happen is called **sequence.** Sequence tells what happens first, next, and last.

As you read this chapter, tell what events, processes, or ideas happened and in what order they happened.

FIRST → NEXT → LAST

Mountains, Volcanoes, Islands, and Hurricanes

Middle America is a region of the world made up of Mexico and two smaller subregions—Central America and the Caribbean. Central America is a narrow bridge of land south of Mexico that includes seven countries—Belize (buh•LEEZ), Costa Rica, El Salvador, Guatemala (gwah•tuh•MAH•luh), Honduras, Nicaragua, and Panama. The Caribbean consists of a chain, or **archipelago** (ar•kuh•PEH•luh•goh), of many islands in the Caribbean Sea, an arm of the Atlantic Ocean.

Central America

Although Central America is made up of seven countries, it is smaller in size than the state of Texas. It covers about 202,000 square miles (523,000 sq km). The Pacific Ocean lies to the west, and the Caribbean Sea lies to the east. The landscape of Central America has a clear pattern. There are two areas of lowlands with rugged mountains in between.

The island city of Flores, Guatemala, in Lake Petén Itzá

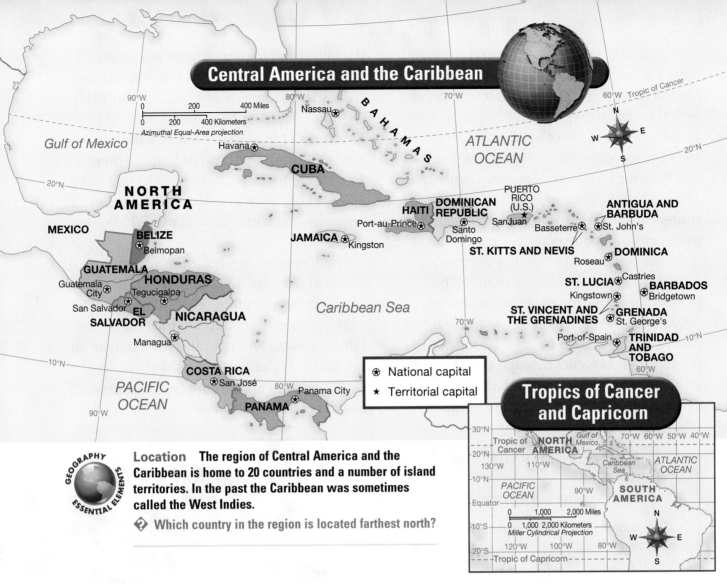

Central America and the Caribbean

90°W · 80°W · 70°W · 60°W Tropic of Cancer

0 · 200 · 400 Miles
0 · 200 · 400 Kilometers
Azimuthal Equal-Area projection

Gulf of Mexico

Nassau ⊛

B A H A M A S

ATLANTIC OCEAN

20°N

Havana ⊛

CUBA

NORTH AMERICA

20°N

MEXICO

BELIZE
Belmopan ⊛

GUATEMALA
Guatemala City ⊛
San Salvador ⊛
EL SALVADOR

HONDURAS
Tegucigalpa ⊛

NICARAGUA

Managua ⊛

JAMAICA ⊛ Kingston

HAITI
Port-au-Prince ⊛

DOMINICAN REPUBLIC ⊛
Santo Domingo

PUERTO RICO (U.S.)
San Juan ★

ANTIGUA AND BARBUDA
Basseterre ⊛ ⊛ St. John's

ST. KITTS AND NEVIS
Roseau ⊛ DOMINICA

ST. LUCIA ⊛ Castries
Kingstown ⊛
ST. VINCENT AND THE GRENADINES ⊛ GRENADA
St. George's

BARBADOS
⊛ Bridgetown

Caribbean Sea

70°W

Port-of-Spain ⊛ TRINIDAD AND TOBAGO

10°N

60°W

COSTA RICA
⊛ San José

80°W Panama City

PACIFIC OCEAN

90°W

PANAMA

Panama City ⊛

10°N

⊛ National capital
★ Territorial capital

Tropics of Cancer and Capricorn

30°N
Tropic of Cancer NORTH AMERICA Gulf of Mexico 70°W 60°W 50°W 40°W
20°N
130°W 110°W Caribbean Sea ATLANTIC OCEAN
10°N
PACIFIC OCEAN 90°W SOUTH AMERICA
Equator
0 · 1,000 · 2,000 Miles
10°S
0 · 1,000 · 2,000 Kilometers
Miller Cylindrical Projection
20°S
120°W 100°W 80°W
Tropic of Capricorn

GEOGRAPHY ESSENTIAL ELEMENTS

Location The region of Central America and the Caribbean is home to 20 countries and a number of island territories. In the past the Caribbean was sometimes called the West Indies.

❓ Which country in the region is located farthest north?

The chain of mountains that runs through much of Central America is part of a global geographic zone called the Ring of Fire. The **Ring of Fire** is a circle of volcanoes around the Pacific Ocean. The movement of Earth's tectonic plates in this zone causes frequent volcanic eruptions, as well as earthquakes. As a result, eruptions and earthquakes are a constant danger in Central America. In Nicaragua alone there is a line of about 40 active volcanoes along the western coast.

Volcanic eruptions in Central America often damage crops and buildings. However, the ash from the eruptions helps keep the soil fertile. Because much of this fertile soil is along the sides of the mountains,

most people in Central America live in the highlands. There they earn a living on tiny farms. The mountain areas of Central America are also where many plantations, or large farms, are located. Central America's highland plantations produce much of the world's coffee crop.

On both sides of the central mountains are the two other important physical features in Central America—the narrow Pacific Lowland to the west and the wider Atlantic Lowland to the east. The few important rivers in Central America flow from the mountains toward the Atlantic side, where lowland plantations produce much of the world's banana crop. Bananas and other farm products are shipped on the rivers to ports on the Atlantic and then go to world markets.

The coastal lowlands of Central America have a tropical climate with plenty of rain. On the Atlantic side the rainfall is as much as 100 to 250 inches (254 to 635 cm) in a single year. Because of all the rain, tropical rain forests cover much of both the Pacific and Atlantic Lowlands. Grasses, shrubs, and **coniferous** (kuh•NIH•fuh•ruhs) trees, or cone-bearing evergreens, are more common in the mountain areas.

At the southernmost end of Central America is the Isthmus of Panama. The isthmus at its narrowest point measures only about 30 miles (48 km) wide. Near this point the Panama Canal, a human-made waterway, cuts through the isthmus and links the Atlantic and Pacific Oceans. The Panama Canal is important because it enables ships to greatly shorten their voyage from one ocean to the other. Before the Panama Canal was completed in 1914, a ship going from New York City to San Francisco in the United States had to travel around the southern tip of South America. The whole trip was more than 13,000 miles (20,900 km). By way of the Panama Canal, however, the trip is only about 5,200 miles (8,370 km).

The United States built the Panama Canal at a cost of $380 million. Thousands of workers from all over the world took ten years to complete it. Today the country of Panama owns and operates the canal as an important waterway in world trade.

REVIEW What are the three important physical features of Central America?

• SCIENCE AND TECHNOLOGY •

The Panama Canal

The Panama Canal has been called the twentieth century's greatest engineering marvel. So that ships can cross the land, the canal raises them above sea level and then lowers them by means of a series of locks. A lock is an enclosure in which the water level can be changed. When a ship enters a lock, a large gate is closed behind the ship. Water then flows into or out of the lock to raise or lower the ship to the next level. When this is completed, the gate in front of the ship is opened and the ship moves on.

It takes 8 to 10 hours for a ship to travel through all the locks of the Panama Canal. Ship owners pay thousands of dollars in tolls, which are based on the size of the ship. However, using the canal is less expensive, as well as faster, than sailing all the way around South America.

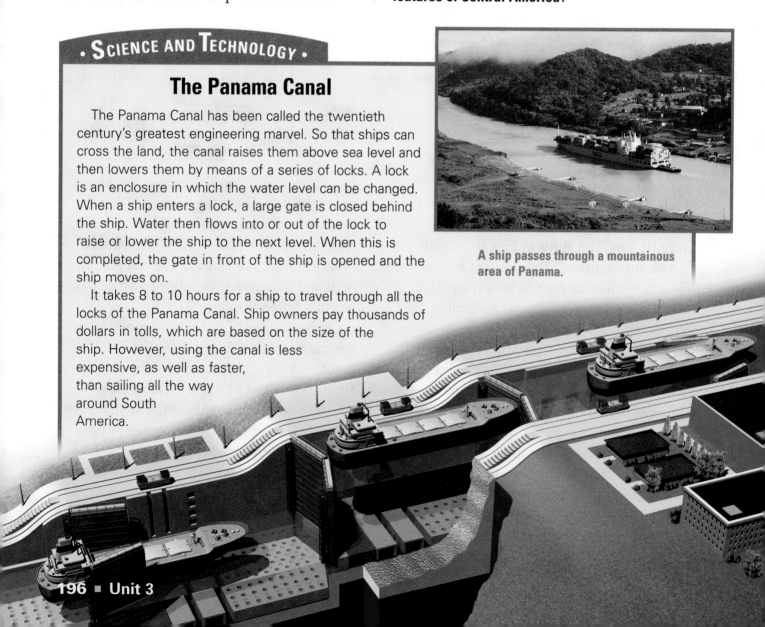

A ship passes through a mountainous area of Panama.

"Taxi" drivers wait for passengers along the Malecon, Havana's famous seaside drive.

The Greater Antilles

The islands of the Caribbean divide the Caribbean Sea from the rest of the Atlantic Ocean. They stretch almost 2,000 miles (3,200 km) from near Florida to the northern coast of Venezuela. Three groups of islands make up the Caribbean. These are the Bahamas (buh•HAH•muhz), the Greater Antilles (an•TIH•leez), and the Lesser Antilles. *Greater* and *lesser* in these names refer to the sizes of the islands.

The islands of the Greater Antilles include the four large islands of Cuba, Hispaniola (ees•pah•NYOH•lah), Jamaica, and Puerto Rico. They have many kinds of terrain. However, the differences from one place to another are not as great as on a large land area such as Mexico. Parts of these islands are rugged and steep. In general, they each have highlands in the middle that slope down to the sea.

Because of the islands' location and the direction of the prevailing, or most frequent, winds, the northeast side of the islands gets the most rain. An example of this is on the island of Jamaica, the third-largest island in the Greater Antilles. It has a chain of mountains in the northeast, running east and west. On the northeast coast, rainfall reaches 200 inches (508 cm) a year. Southwest of the mountains, it averages only about 30 inches (76 cm) a year.

Cuba is by far the largest of the four islands in the Greater Antilles. It is about the size of the state of Tennessee, and it is located only 90 miles (145 km) south of Florida. The country of Cuba consists of this large island and more than 1,600 smaller ones. The main island has a varied landscape, with mountains and hills covering about one-fourth of it. The rest is chiefly rolling plains and wide, fertile valleys. In areas of plentiful rainfall, rain forests and shrubs are the natural vegetation. Coniferous forests cover the mountain areas.

Second in size in the Greater Antilles is the island of Hispaniola, with an area of about 29,500 square miles (76,400 sq km). The Republic of Haiti occupies the western third of Hispaniola, and the Dominican Republic covers the eastern two-thirds of the island. The smallest island in the Greater Antilles is Puerto Rico. At 3,515 square miles (9,100 sq km), it is near in size to the state of Delaware.

REVIEW What are the four largest islands of the Greater Antilles?

The constant trade winds that blow across Aruba bend these divi-divi trees toward the southeast.

The Lesser Antilles

The islands of the Lesser Antilles are southeast of Puerto Rico. They are divided into two groups, the Leeward Islands and the Windward Islands. The northeast trade winds are the reason for dividing them. The **trade winds** are winds that consistently blow from the northeast toward the equator.

During the time when sailing ships were used to carry goods, the northern islands of the Lesser Antilles—from the Virgin Islands to Dominica (dah•muh•NEE•kuh)— were called the Leeward Islands. They were named *Leeward* because they are in the lee of, or sheltered from, the trade winds. The southern islands, from Martinique (mar•tuhn•EEK) to Grenada (gruh•NAY•duh) were called the Windward Islands because they face toward the northeast trade winds. These names were used by the countries with colonies in the Lesser Antilles and are still used today.

The northeast trade winds help give the Lesser Antilles a generally mild climate all year. However, the winds also put the islands in the path of hurricanes in the summer months. These huge storms begin with winds blowing westward off the coast of Africa. They grow in strength over warm ocean waters within ten degrees north or south of the equator.

Moving to the west, hurricanes build in intensity. As they near the Caribbean, their winds blow at more than 74 miles (117 km) per hour. If hurricanes move over land areas, they can cause great damage from high winds and flooding. Sometimes many people are killed. There is a danger of hurricanes every year in the Lesser Antilles, though the storms do not always follow the same path. There is a regular climate pattern, however, of high winds and heavy rain in the late summer.

Most of the year the climate of the Lesser Antilles is warm and sunny. Because of the climate, the beautiful beaches, and the tropical scenery, the islands of the Lesser Antilles attract large numbers of tourists.

REVIEW Why are the Lesser Antilles divided into two groups?

The Bahamas

The Bahamas are the northernmost group of islands in the Caribbean. They extend more than 500 miles (800 km), from about 50 miles (80 km) off the eastern coast of Florida to the northeastern tip of Cuba.

The Bahamas are made up of about 700 islands and 2,400 cays (KAYZ), most of which have no people. A **cay** is a small, low-lying island made of sand, limestone, or coral. **Coral** is a hard, stony substance that is made up of the skeletons of many tiny sea animals.

Of the 700 islands in the Bahamas, people live on only about 20. Four out of every five Bahamians live on just two islands—Grand Bahama and New Providence.

Because the Bahamas are mainly long, narrow strips of limestone and coral, they have only small pockets of fertile soil. As a result, there is little farming. There are, however, forests of hardwood trees that provide an important resource for trade.

REVIEW How are the Bahamas different from the rest of the islands of the Caribbean?

LOCATE IT Along the coast of New Providence near Nassau

BAHAMAS

Nassau, New Providence

LESSON 1 REVIEW

1 **MAIN IDEA** How are the geography of Central America and the geography of Caribbean islands similar?

2 **WHY IT MATTERS** How do land and climate in this region affect the lives of the people who live there?

3 **VOCABULARY** What is an **archipelago**? Use the term in a sentence about the countries in the Caribbean.

4 **READING SKILL—Sequence** Put the island groups of the Caribbean in order from north to south.

5 **GEOGRAPHY** What are the seven countries of Central America?

6 **HISTORY** When was the Panama Canal completed?

7 **CRITICAL THINKING—Hypothesize** How would life in Central America be different if parts of the region did not lie along the Ring of Fire?

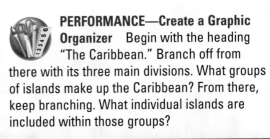

PERFORMANCE—Create a Graphic Organizer Begin with the heading "The Caribbean." Branch off from there with its three main divisions. What groups of islands make up the Caribbean? From there, keep branching. What individual islands are included within those groups?

Influences of the Past

| 500 B.C. | B.C./A.D. | A.D. 500 | A.D. 1000 | A.D. 1500 | A.D. 2000 |

MAIN IDEA
Read to find out how the past has influenced the development of cultures in Central America and the Caribbean.

WHY IT MATTERS
Many societies today are a blend of cultures from both past and present.

VOCABULARY
mulatto
commercial farming
abolish
indentured servant
Columbian exchange
legacy

In the Caribbean over the years, the need for workers has led to today's diverse population. Many people in the Caribbean are descendants of Africans who were brought to the islands as slaves. Others today are **mulattoes** (muh•LAH•tohs), people of both African and European descent. In Central America, too, the past has influenced the present. Ancient native civilizations and colonial Spanish rule have had important effects on present-day life.

In the Caribbean

At about the time that the Aztecs controlled much of Mexico, in the A.D. 1300s and 1400s, three different native groups lived in the Caribbean. They were the Arawaks (AR•uh•wahks), the Caribs (KAR•ibz), and the Ciboneys (see•buh•NAYZ).

The Ciboneys are thought to have been the first group in the islands. They were followed by the Arawaks sometime between 200 B.C. and A.D. 100. The Arawaks settled mostly in the Greater Antilles. About A.D. 1300 the Caribs moved into the Caribbean from South America. The Caribs took over Arawak lands in the Lesser Antilles and adopted many of the Arawak culture traits. It is the mix of cultures that some people in the Caribbean today identify as their heritage.

In 1492 Christopher Columbus, an Italian explorer sailing for Spain, landed in the Bahamas. Within ten years the Spanish had built their first settlement in the Caribbean on Hispaniola. Soon the search for gold and other riches attracted more people, who started colonies on Cuba, Jamaica, and Puerto Rico.

Spanish colonists dug mines and set up plantations for commercial farming. **Commercial farming** is the growing of crops to be sold for profit. The Spanish grew mainly sugarcane and sold the sugar made from it to traders in Europe. This "sweet gold" made many plantation owners rich.

To get workers for the plantations, owners forced many of the Arawaks into slavery. Slavery was not new to many cultures in the Americas, but the harsh working conditions of the plantations were. When Arawaks began dying, the owners looked for other workers. First, they enslaved Arawaks and Caribs from the Lesser Antilles. Later, they brought Africans to work on the plantations as slaves.

In the 1700s and 1800s, European colonists built sugarcane plantations (below) throughout the Caribbean. An old sugar mill (right) still stands as a reminder of the past.

By the early 1600s colonists from Denmark, England, France, and the Netherlands were starting settlements in the Caribbean. These were mostly in the Lesser Antilles. The Spanish considered those islands too small and too far from the center of the Spanish Caribbean empire in the Greater Antilles.

In the late 1600s the English and the French took advantage of a weakening government in Spain to expand their holdings. In 1670 Spain gave up Jamaica to England. In 1697 the French took control of the western third of the island of Hispaniola. The French called the new colony St. Domingue (SEN daw•MENG). It occupied the area of the present-day country of Haiti.

The English and the French colonists, like the Spanish, realized that sugarcane could bring in more money than any other kind of crop. They also realized that to make their large commercial farms successful, they needed many workers. So, like the Spanish, the English and the

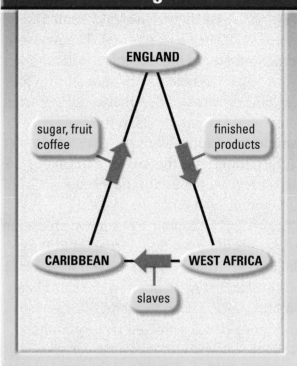

The Triangle Trade

ENGLAND

sugar, fruit coffee

finished products

CARIBBEAN ← WEST AFRICA

slaves

Analyze Graphs Some English traders followed a triangle-shaped route between England, West Africa, and the English colonies in the Caribbean.

❓ What was traded at each point?

French turned to the African slave trade for workers.

As sugar production in the Caribbean grew in the 1700s, so did the number of Africans in the Caribbean population. In 1775, for example, one-fourth of the Cuban population was made up of Africans. By 1827 four out of ten Cubans were of African descent. Because of the slave trade, a large part of the Caribbean population today can trace its heritage to Africa.

In the 1800s sugar production grew so much that the supply was greater than the demand. Sugar prices

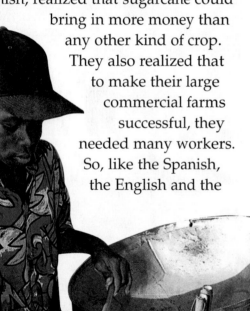

This boy is playing steel drums, musical instruments made from oil drums used for shipping. He plays calypso music, which is based on African work songs.

fell, and some plantations closed. Others cut back their operations and needed fewer workers. These conditions led some islands in the Caribbean to **abolish**, or end, slavery.

With slavery abolished, there was a need for farmworkers. Some owners did not want to hire former slaves because they did not want to pay wages to people who once had to work without pay. Instead, many owners hired indentured servants. An **indentured servant** is a person who agrees to work for another person without pay for a certain amount of time in exchange for travel expenses. In the late 1800s and early 1900s, indentured servants arrived from China and India. Workers also came from Japan, Ireland, Germany, Portugal, Spain, and countries in West Africa.

REVIEW What past influence has given the Caribbean a diversity of people?

• HERITAGE •

Mayan Weaving

Weaving is one way that the Maya of Guatemala preserve their past. Almost every community has its own colorful style of clothing. Patterns on the clothing include symbols from nature. Brilliant dyes for the clothing are created from plants, insects, and the bark of trees. Blue, for example, comes from the indigo plant, which grows wild in parts of Central America. Many of the styles have remained unchanged for centuries.

In Central America

Like the Caribbean, Central America was home to many native groups for thousands of years before Europeans arrived. One of the most important of these groups was the Maya. The people of the Mayan civilization built more than 100 cities in what are today the countries of Belize, El Salvador, Guatemala, and Honduras. Some of these cities had populations of more than 100,000.

By about A.D. 900 the Mayan civilization was in decline. Some of its once-great cities were abandoned. No one knows the reasons for certain. Today, however, many descendants of the Maya live in the mountain areas of Central America. Most of these people are in Guatemala, where more than half the population is descended from native peoples. Many of the descendants wear traditional Mayan clothing, speak Mayan languages, and live in communities that follow Mayan ways of life.

When the Spanish arrived in Central America in the 1500s, their influence was quickly felt. Spanish missionaries set up schools and converted many of the native people to the Roman Catholic religion. As a result, most people in Central America today are Roman Catholic and speak Spanish. Only in Belize is the official language English rather than Spanish. Belize, unlike the other six Central American countries, was once an English colony.

Spanish colonists also set up the first plantations in Central America to grow products for the home country. These large commercial farms made huge profits for the plantation owners and the Spanish government. However, most of the people in Central America lived by subsistence farming. They grew only enough to feed their families.

Plantations remained important in Central America, even after slavery was abolished and many of the countries in the region gained their independence. Coffee production began in the middle of the 1800s. Banana production became important in the late 1800s. Since the 1940s, cotton has become an important plantation crop. As in the past, however, many of the people today do not benefit from the sale of plantation crops. They have remained chiefly subsistence farmers.

Much of Central America today is a blend of influences. Mestizos make up much of the populations of El Salvador, Honduras, and Nicaragua. Many of the people of Belize and Panama are of African descent. The ancestors of most present-day Costa Ricans came from Europe.

This blend of people and cultures is the result of a larger movement of people, animals, plants, and ideas between the Eastern and Western Hemispheres. This movement is known today as the **Columbian exchange**. Many believe it started in 1492 with the arrival of Christopher Columbus in the Americas and continued with the arrival of Europeans and Africans.

The most important exchange that took place involved people. However, the exchange of food is also a lasting legacy of the Columbian exchange. A **legacy** is anything handed down from an ancestor. New foods from Asia, Africa, and Europe were combined with native foods to change the way Central Americans eat.

When the Spanish arrived, they brought a variety of foods to Central America and other parts of the Western Hemisphere. Among the foods from Europe were cabbage, cauliflower, lettuce, melons, onions, and radishes. The Spanish also brought bananas, rice, and yams. Bananas are Asian in origin and were first sent to the Americas from the Canary Islands. Rice is also native to Asia but was widespread in the Mediterranean by the 1400s. Yams were sent from Africa.

The most important contributions of the Americas to this worldwide exchange of food are potatoes and maize, which is a

During an Easter celebration in Guatemala, Christians carry a float (far left) representing Jesus Christ. The ground they walk on is covered with designs made of rose petals and colored sawdust (left).

Damaging storms (left) put food supplies at risk. A Red Cross worker (above) helps residents of Nicaragua after Hurricane Mitch.

form of corn. Other crops of American origin include beans, cassava, peanuts, pumpkins, squash, sweet potatoes, and tomatoes. Cassava is used to make tapioca pudding. Today cassava is an important food source in Africa and Asia, as well as in Central and South America. In addition to food, the Columbian exchange involved livestock, including cattle, pigs, and horses. Most important for Central America was the arrival of pigs. Today pigs are an important source of food for all of the people in the region.

REVIEW How did the Columbian exchange affect the people, culture, and food of Central America?

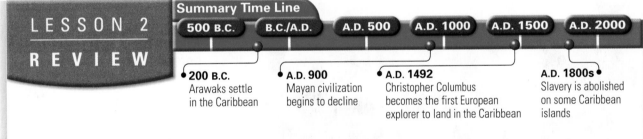

LESSON 2 REVIEW

Summary Time Line

500 B.C.   B.C./A.D.   A.D. 500   A.D. 1000   A.D. 1500   A.D. 2000

200 B.C.
Arawaks settle in the Caribbean

A.D. 900
Mayan civilization begins to decline

A.D. 1492
Christopher Columbus becomes the first European explorer to land in the Caribbean

A.D. 1800s
Slavery is abolished on some Caribbean islands

1 **MAIN IDEA** What groups had an influence on cultures in present-day Central America and the Caribbean?

2 **WHY IT MATTERS** What are some ways that the people of Central America and the Caribbean have blended different cultural influences?

3 **VOCABULARY** How is an **indentured servant** different from a slave?

4 **TIME LINE** Did Spanish explorers arrive before or after the decline of the Mayan civilization?

5 **READING SKILL—Sequence** In what order did native peoples arrive in the Caribbean?

6 **HISTORY** When did Europeans, other than the Spanish, begin colonies in the region?

7 **ECONOMICS** Why was sugarcane important to the economies of the Caribbean?

8 **CRITICAL THINKING—Hypothesize** How might the cultures of Central America and the Caribbean be different if African slaves had not been brought to the region?

PERFORMANCE—Make a Scrapbook
Make a scrapbook showing the different cultures of Central America and the Caribbean. First, use your library and the Internet to learn more about both regions. Then, include descriptions of dance, art, poetry, literature, and music in each region. You can illustrate your scrapbook with drawings or pictures from magazines and newspapers.

PRIMARY SOURCES

Art of the Americas

Each culture in the world celebrates its traditions and innovations through its art. During the colonial times in Middle America and South America, artists often imitated European styles. In about the 1900s artists in the region developed styles that were distinct to the Americas. The artwork shown here is a small sample of the diversity of art styles of Latin America.

FROM THE SMITHSONIAN INSTITUTION
MUSEUM OF AMERICAN ART, ARTE LATINO COLLECTION

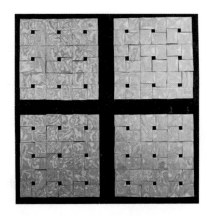

The Caban Family (Puerto Rico)
The Three Magi, about 1875–1900
painted wood with metal and string

Unknown artist (Puerto Rico)
Joaquín José Goyena y O'Daly,
before 1834
watercolor on ivory

María Castagliola (Cuba)
A Matter of Trust, 1994
paper on fiberglass with
cotton thread

Analyze the Primary Source

1 Identify each artwork as a painting or a sculpture.

2 What materials were used to make each artwork?

3 What does each artwork show?

Patrociño Barela (New Mexico)
Man in the Time of Solomon, about
1935–43
carved juniper wood

Jesse Treviño (Mexico)
My Brothers, 1976
acrylic paint

ACTIVITY

Collect and Compile Make a book showing art from around the world. Identify examples of art that go beyond regional boundaries and have themes common in every world region.

RESEARCH

Visit The Learning Site at
www.harcourtschool.com/primarysources
to research other artwork.

Luis Alfonso
Jiménez, Jr.
(Mexico)
Vaquero, cast
1990
acrylic
urethane,
fiberglass,
and steel

MAIN IDEA

Read to find out how governments in different parts of Central America and the Caribbean are limited and unlimited.

WHY IT MATTERS

The governments of Central America and the Caribbean reflect the history of each region.

VOCABULARY

limited government
unlimited government
federation
states' rights
guerrilla
civil war
petition
communism
self-government
dependency

Leaders of Central America and Mexico meet.

Contrasts in Governing

The nations of Central America and the Caribbean have a history of different governing traditions. These traditions include some governments that are limited and some that are not. In a **limited government** everyone, including government leaders, must obey the laws. Constitutions, statements of citizens' rights, or other laws define the limits. In an **unlimited government** a ruler alone has control, and there are no limits on the ruler's authority.

Central America's Political Past

The Central American countries of Costa Rica, El Salvador, Guatemala, Honduras, and Nicaragua became independent from Spain in 1821. At the time, Belize remained under British control, and Panama became part of Colombia.

Also in 1821 Mexico won its independence and united for a time with the five independent Central American countries. After only two years they separated, and the Central American countries formed a **federation**, or union, among themselves. They called it the United Provinces of Central America.

It was not long, however, before disagreements began to divide the federation. Some of the countries wanted a strong central government. Others favored **states' rights**, or the idea that the individual countries, or states, have greater authority than the central government.

The federation's constitution, which provided for states' rights, was completed in 1824. The constitution also provided for the abolition of slavery. In addition, it put an end to the special privileges of wealthy landowners. Disagreements over these issues eventually brought an end to the United Provinces of Central America. By the late 1830s each of the countries had become an independent republic, in which the citizens voted for officials who represented them.

To win back the privileges they had lost, wealthy landowners often supported dictators. These were leaders who ruled with no limits to their authority.

Dictators often took control of the government in sudden and violent ways. They used the same ways to keep their control. To fight the authority of the dictators, some people formed guerrilla groups. A **guerrilla** is a member of a small group of soldiers who are not part of the regular army. The goal of these guerrillas was to overthrow the dictatorships.

Civil wars and other conflicts were common in Central America. A **civil war** is a war between people of the same country. In Nicaragua, for example, conflicts over the control of government continued through the 1800s and into the 1900s.

In recent times there have been steps toward reducing the conflict. In 1987 Óscar Arias Sánchez, then president of Costa Rica, won the Nobel Peace Prize for his leadership in creating a Central American peace plan. Along with the presidents of El Salvador, Guatemala, Honduras, and Nicaragua, he signed a peace agreement for the region. It ordered an end to the fighting by rival groups.

REVIEW Why did the United Provinces of Central America break up?

Democracy in Central America

Today the seven Central American countries are all democracies. The people in each country elect the head of the government and a legislature to make the country's laws.

Belize, which became independent from Britain in 1981, is a parliamentary democracy. As in the government of Canada, a prime minister with the help of a Cabinet carries out the operations of the Belize government. A legislature, of which the prime minister is also a part, makes the laws. Because of its colonial ties with Britain, Belize is part of the Commonwealth of Nations. The British monarch is the official head of the government but has little say in governing.

Costa Rica, El Salvador, Guatemala, Honduras, Nicaragua, and Panama are all republics, as is the United States. (Panama became independent from Colombia in 1903.) Each of these countries has three separate branches of government. A president serves as head of the government, and a legislature makes the laws. There is a judicial branch that decides if laws are fair.

Peace in their country gives these Guatemalan schoolchildren a safe place to learn.

President Óscar Arias Sánchez of Costa Rica won the Nobel Peace Prize in 1987.

Costa Rica was among the first of the Central American countries to embrace democracy. It has the important traits of all democracies. These traits are free elections, majority rule, the participation of political parties, and a guarantee of individual rights. Costa Rica's constitution guarantees rights that the government cannot take away. These rights include freedom of speech, equality before the law, and the rights to own property, to assemble, and to **petition**, or formally ask for government action.

REVIEW How is Belize's government different from the others in the region?

Independence Day Parade in Costa Rica

Governing the Caribbean

Haiti, once a French colony, became the first republic in the Caribbean after winning its independence in 1804. Haiti controlled all of Hispaniola until 1844, when the Dominican Republic declared its own independence.

By the late 1800s many European nations were losing interest in their Caribbean colonies. At that time, however, the United States began playing a more active role in the region. In 1898 a revolution in Cuba drew the United States into a war with Spain. After the United States won the Spanish-American War, Cuba became independent and Puerto Rico became a United States colony. In 1917 the United States purchased from Denmark what are now the United States Virgin Islands.

CITIZENSHIP

DEMOCRATIC VALUES
Popular Sovereignty

In 1948 disagreements over the results of its presidential election threatened Costa Rica's long democratic tradition. In that year, the people elected Otilio Ulate president. The current government, however, refused to recognize Ulate as the winner because he won by only a few votes over a candidate of the current government's political party. After 40 days of civil war, a wealthy landowner, José Figueres, and his supporters won victory. Although Ulate was a candidate of a different political party, Figueres turned over control of the government to the new president.

Analyze the Value

❶ Why was it important for democracy in Costa Rica that Figueres gave control of the government to Ulate?

❷ **Make It Relevant** Research the election processes in two different countries other than the United States.

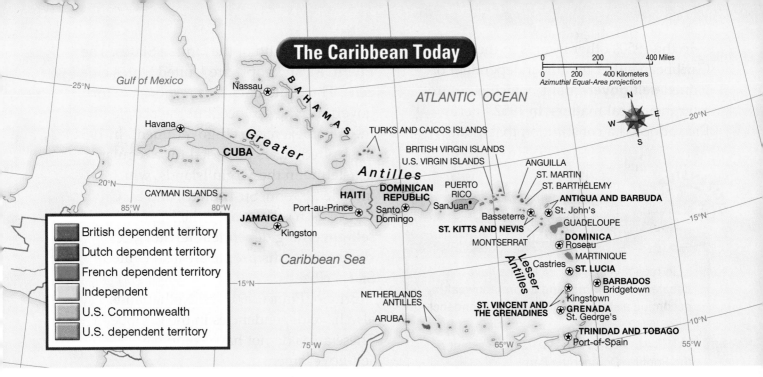

The Caribbean Today

Regions The United States and Europe influence the region.

◈ Which island is a United States commonwealth?

Dictators controlled Cuba, Haiti, and the Dominican Republic during much of the early 1900s. Then in 1959 guerrilla leader Fidel Castro and his supporters overthrew Cuba's dictator. Castro had said his goals were to bring equal rights to all Cubans and to solve many of Cuba's economic problems. To reach these goals, Castro introduced communism to Cuba. **Communism** is a system in which all property and all means of production belong to the people as a group.

Dictators continued to rule the Dominican Republic and Haiti into the second half of the twentieth century. From time to time, however, attempts have been made in both countries to set up a democracy with free elections. As in Cuba, social and economic problems have plagued both Haiti and the Dominican Republic. Their people are among the poorest in the Western Hemisphere. Haiti's per capita GDP is only $1,340, and life expectancy is 49 years. Their problems are difficult ones to solve.

Fidel Castro ruled Cuba from the capital city of Havana.

In the 1950s other islands in the Caribbean either became independent or gained **self-government**, which is control over their local matters. In 1952 Puerto Rico adopted a constitution that made it a commonwealth of the United States. The Puerto Rican people are United States citizens. The United States is responsible for governing Puerto Rico, but the people of the island exercise self-government. In 1954 the United States provided for a regular legislature in the Virgin Islands, which include St. John, St. Thomas, and St. Croix (SAYNT KROY). That made the islands a self-governing dependent territory, or **dependency**. Its people are also United States citizens.

Britain, France, and the Netherlands also have dependencies in the Caribbean. These areas do not have complete self-government.

Anguilla (an·GWIH·luh), the British Virgin Islands, the Cayman Islands, and Montserrat (mahn·suh·RAT) are dependencies of Britain. The people living in them are British citizens. Each dependency has a governor appointed by the British Parliament, and the governor holds all authority.

POINTS OF VIEW
Puerto Rican Statehood

In recent years, Puerto Ricans have debated about remaining a commonwealth, becoming a state, or declaring independence.

ANIBAL ACEVEDO-VILA, president of the Popular Democratic Party

66 It allows us to be Puerto Ricans while still being U.S. citizens . . . If you choose statehood, you will put in danger your culture, your identity . . . If you choose independence, you will lose your U.S. citizenship. 99

REPRESENTATIVE CARLOS ROMERO-BARCELO, Puerto Rico's delegate to the United States Congress

66 It is now time . . . to take action to bring to these 3.8 million U.S. citizens political, economic, and social equality. 99

AN ANONYMOUS PUERTO RICAN CITIZEN

66 Puerto Rico is a different nation with a different culture . . . so that means that it can be independent, it should be independent. 99

Analyze the Viewpoints

1 What views about statehood does each person hold?

2 **Make It Relevant** Learn more about Puerto Rico's history as a commonwealth of the United States. Then write a paragraph arguing for or against statehood. Use examples to support your argument.

Built in 1747, this government building in St. Croix shows a Dutch influence in its design.

Britain also has strong ties with many of the islands that were once British colonies. Like Belize in Central America, these islands have parliamentary democracies modeled after the British government. They are also members of the British Commonwealth. They include Antigua and Barbuda, the Bahamas, Barbados, Grenada, Jamaica, St. Kitts and Nevis, St. Lucia, St. Vincent and the Grenadines, and Trinidad and Tobago.

Martinique, Guadeloupe, and half of the island of St. Martin are dependencies of France. Each has a leader called a prefect, chosen by the government in France. The people, who are considered French citizens, elect members to a local legislature. Each dependency also sends representatives to the French national legislature.

The Netherlands has a similar relationship with its Caribbean island dependencies—Aruba, half of St. Martin, and the Netherlands Antilles. On these islands, the Netherlands controls defense

LOCATE IT

FRENCH WEST INDIES

Case-Pilote

MARTINIQUE

French signs in Martinique

and relations with other countries. Locally elected officials tend to the islands' other governing needs.

REVIEW What are examples of limited and unlimited government in the Caribbean?

LESSON 3 REVIEW

1 MAIN IDEA What are the characteristics of limited and unlimited governments?

2 WHY IT MATTERS How do the governments of some Central American and Caribbean countries reflect their history as European colonies?

3 VOCABULARY What is a **guerrilla**? Use the term in a sentence that shows you understand its meaning.

4 READING SKILL—Sequence What events occurred as the countries of Central America went from colonies to independent republics?

5 GOVERNMENT How are the rights of United States citizens in Puerto Rico similar to the rights of citizens living in a state? How are they different?

6 GOVERNMENT Which Caribbean islands have ties to France?

7 CRITICAL THINKING—Evaluate What are some advantages of Puerto Rico remaining a commonwealth? What are some disadvantages? Do you think Puerto Rico should become a state? Why or why not?

PERFORMANCE—Write a Constitution On a sheet of paper, write a constitution for a new country. As you write your constitution, decide how your country's government will be organized. Will there be a president or a prime minister? a parliament or a congress? What rights will the citizens have? When you are finished, share your constitution with the class.

·SKILLS·
CITIZENSHIP

Make a Thoughtful Decision

▶ WHY IT MATTERS

Every action has a consequence, or result. Some consequences are short-term—they last only a short time. Other consequences are long-term—they last a long time. An action can also have positive or negative consequences—or sometimes both. Although you cannot always predict all the consequences, thinking about possible consequences before taking action is essential to making a thoughtful decision.

One important decision with long-term consequences was the building of the Panama Canal. For years people had suggested that a canal cut through the narrowest part of Central America would shorten the voyage from New York to California by thousands of miles. Slicing a canal through tons of solid land, however, was not a decision to be taken lightly.

▶ WHAT YOU NEED TO KNOW

The following set of steps can be used to make a thoughtful decision. Many people use these steps to make decisions in their personal and professional lives.

Step 1 Identify your goal.

Step 2 List the actions that you could take to reach your goal. Identify actions that you think would have positive consequences and those that would have negative consequences.

A steam shovel helps dig the Panama Canal (below left). This postcard (right) shows how ships pass through San Francisco on their way to the Panama Canal.

Step 3 Decide which actions to take.

Step 4 Take the actions that seem to have the most positive consequences and the fewest negative consequences.

Step 5 Evaluate whether your decision helped you reach your goal, and determine if there were unexpected negative consequences.

▶ **PRACTICE THE SKILL**

Read the paragraphs below about how the United States decided on a site for the canal through Central America. Then answer the questions in the next column.

In 1899 a committee began researching the best location for a canal route through Central America. They narrowed the choices down to two: Nicaragua or Panama. A canal in Nicaragua would be closer to the United States, but the canal would have to be four times longer than one built across Panama. Nicaragua also had a number of active volcanoes that could cause earthquakes. In Panama, on the other hand, builders could take advantage of work already begun by the French. French engineers had started building a canal in Panama but later abandoned the project.

The committee decided that Panama would be the better choice and began building in 1904. From the beginning, there were many problems that builders had to overcome. Thousands of workers died from deadly diseases spread by mosquitoes and rats. In some places the rocky landscape made the digging more difficult than expected. In addition, the hot, humid climate of Panama made working conditions uncomfortable. In 1914, however, workers completed the Panama Canal, at a cost of $380 million.

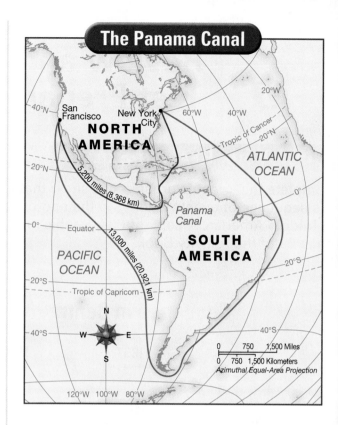

The Panama Canal

❶ What was the goal of the canal project?

❷ What might one possible negative consequence of building the canal in Nicaragua have been?

❸ What did the United States view as a possible positive consequence of building the canal in Nicaragua?

❹ What was one negative consequence of building in Panama that became clear after building began?

❺ Do you think the United States made the right decision in choosing Panama as the site for the canal? Explain.

▶ **APPLY WHAT YOU LEARNED**

Write an illustrated short story about a situation in which a character did NOT make a thoughtful decision. Describe or draw the negative consequences of the character's actions. Have another character explain how a more thoughtful decision could have been made.

CITIZENSHIP SKILLS

Review and Test Preparation

USE YOUR READING SKILLS

Complete this graphic organizer to show that you understand the sequence of events leading to the end of Spanish control in Middle America. A copy of this graphic organizer appears on page 59 of the Activity Book.

Sequence in Central America and the Caribbean

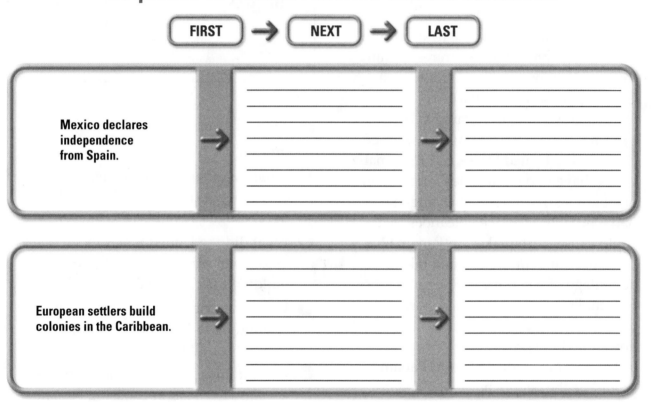

FIRST → NEXT → LAST

Mexico declares independence from Spain.

European settlers build colonies in the Caribbean.

THINK & WRITE

Write a Journal Entry   Suppose that you are a worker building the Panama Canal. Write a journal entry that describes the working conditions and hardships you and other workers face daily.

Write "Who Am I?" Questions   Choose a person introduced in the chapter. First, write a list of "Who Am I?" questions that describe the person you chose. Then, exchange lists with a classmate, and try to guess the person described.

A.D. 900
Mayan civilization begins to decline

A.D. 1300
Caribs move into the Caribbean from South America

A.D. 1492
Christopher Columbus becomes the first European explorer to land in the Caribbean

A.D. 1700s
Sugarcane becomes the most important crop in the Caribbean

A.D. 1800s
Slavery is abolished on some Caribbean islands

USE THE TIME LINE

Use the chapter summary time line to answer these questions.

1 How many years after the Caribs arrived in the Caribbean did Columbus land there?

2 When was slavery abolished on some Caribbean islands?

USE VOCABULARY

Use the terms on the right to complete the sentences.

> coniferous (p. 196)
>
> cays (p. 199)
>
> mulatto (p. 200)
>
> Columbian exchange (p. 204)

3 The movement of people, animals, plants, and ideas between the Eastern and Western Hemisphere is known as the _____.

4 Many of the islands that make up the Bahamas are _____, or small islands made of coral or sand.

5 Grasses, shrubs, and _____ trees, or cone-bearing evergreens, are common in the mountainous areas of Central America.

6 A _____ is a person with both European and African heritage.

RECALL FACTS

Answer these questions.

7 How are islands formed by coral?

8 What was the main industry in the Caribbean after European colonization?

Write the letter of the best choice.

9 **TEST PREP** All of the following are subregions of the Caribbean *except*—
  A the Lesser Antilles.
  B Central America.
  C the Greater Antilles.
  D the Bahamas.

10 **TEST PREP** The countries that formed the United Provinces of Central America were—
  F El Salvador, Guatemala, Honduras, Nicaragua, and Costa Rica.
  G El Salvador, Belize, Costa Rica, Nicaragua, and Guatemala.
  H Nicaragua, Panama, Costa Rica, Honduras, and Nicaragua.
  J El Salvador, Panama, Belize, Guatemala, and Honduras.

THINK CRITICALLY

11 What effect do you think the Columbian exchange had on cultures in Central America, Europe, and around the world?

12 In 1949 the constitution of Costa Rica outlawed the military. Do you think that was a good idea? Explain.

APPLY SKILLS

Make a Thoughtful Decision

13 Think about a decision that you might need to make in the future. Use the steps on pages 214–215 to analyze this decision. First, make a list of the possible actions and evaluate them. Then, decide which action to take.

RIO DE JANEIRO, BRAZIL

The city of Rio de Janeiro grew from a Portuguese fort built in 1565. The name *Rio de Janeiro* means "River of January" in the Portuguese language. The city lies on Guanabara Bay, a part of the Atlantic Ocean. Jutting out into the bay, Sugarloaf Mountain rises to a height of 1,325 feet (404 m).

LOCATE IT

BRAZIL

Rio de Janeiro

South America

"I've never beheld such a paradise. The people are enchanting . . . all dwell in a peace that passes describing."

—Stefan Zweig, from a letter to his wife, Friderike, August 26, 1936

CHAPTER READING SKILL

Make Inferences

To understand what you read, you sometimes need to make inferences. An **inference** is an educated guess based on details from your reading and from your own knowledge and experience.

As you read this chapter, combine the details with your own knowledge and experiences to make inferences.

DETAILS + KNOWLEDGE → INFERENCES

MAIN IDEA
Read to find out how South America's high mountains and nearby oceans affect the continent's climate and vegetation as well as its people's way of life.

WHY IT MATTERS
Water from melting snow in South America's mountains and rainfall east of the Andes provide important moisture to the continent's farms, rain forests, and grasslands.

VOCABULARY

cordillera
escarpment
El Niño
humidity
transportation
corridor
estuary
sharecropping
factors of production

A Vast Land

South America lies south of the Isthmus of Panama. As the fourth-largest continent, South America makes up about one-eighth of Earth's land area. Its landscape is vast and its climate is varied. The world's largest mountain range stretches the length of South America. In the middle of the continent lies the world's largest tropical rain forest. South America is also a place of spectacular waterfalls, huge lakes, and rolling grasslands that spread out as far as the eye can see.

Land Regions

The land of South America looks very much like that of North America. Both continents have high, rugged mountains in the west and rounded, less rugged mountains in the east. In the middle is a large central plain. This is drained by five huge river systems, one of which is the Amazon River system, the largest in the world.

The Andes Mountains form Earth's largest mountain range. They stretch through western South America for more than 4,500 miles (7,200 km) from Venezuela in the north to the tip of the continent in the south. The Andes Mountains are actually made up of several ranges, also known as cordilleras (kawr•duhl•YAIR•uhs). A **cordillera** is a system of parallel mountain ranges.

Many of the peaks in the Andes rise over 20,000 feet (6,100 m). Only the Himalayas in Asia have more mountains that are higher. Aconcagua (ah•kohn•KAH•gwah), in Argentina, is the highest peak in the Andes and the highest in the Western Hemisphere. It rises almost 23,000 feet (7,000 m). Aconcagua is also an extinct volcano. Like the Rocky Mountains in North America, the

Llamas provide food, wool, and a way of transporting heavy loads for people living in the Andes.

Andes Mountains were formed as a result of tremendous forces deep inside Earth. These forces continue to cause eruptions and earthquakes.

Compared to the Andes Mountains, the eastern mountains of South America are much lower and much older. The eastern mountains consist of two separate mountain regions—the Brazilian Highlands and the Guiana Highlands.

The Brazilian Highlands begin on the eastern "bulge" of the continent, south of the Amazon. These highlands include rounded hills and flat plateaus, the largest of which is the Mato Grosso Plateau. The highest mountains in this region are no more than 9,500 feet (2,900 m) high. The eastern edge of the Brazilian Highlands drops sharply to the Atlantic Ocean. This area is called the Great Escarpment. An **escarpment** is a steep slope between a higher surface and a lower one.

The Guiana Highlands are north of the Amazon. They are only 3,000 to 5,000 feet (900 to 1,500 m) high. The Guiana Highlands consist mainly of open grasslands with scattered trees.

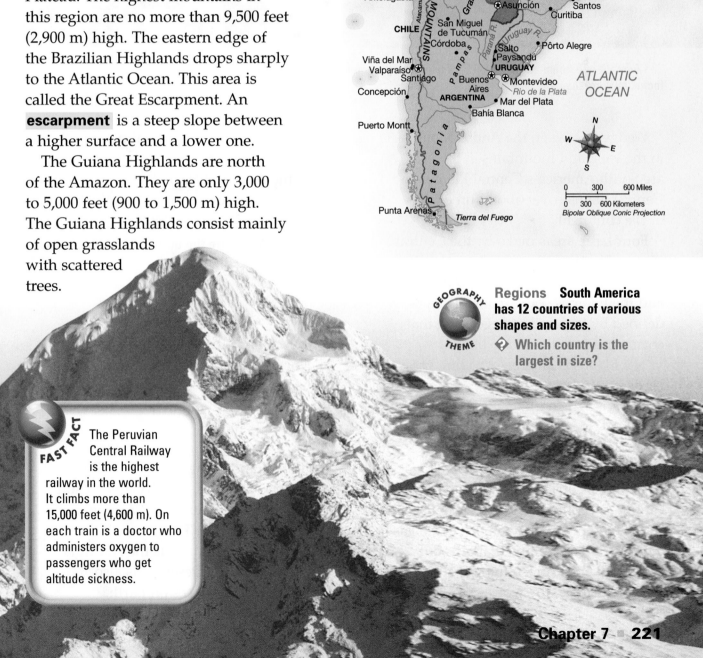

South America

Caribbean Sea
Barranquilla · Maracaibo · Caracas · Cumaná
Cartagena · Valencia
Medellín · Orinoco · Ciudad Guayana · Georgetown
Bogotá · **VENEZUELA** · **GUYANA** · Paramaribo · Cayenne
Cali · Guiana · **SURINAME** · **FRENCH GUIANA** (FRANCE)
Quito · **COLOMBIA** · Highland
ECUADOR · Rio Negro
Guayaquil · A M A Z O N · River · Belém
Iquitos · Amazon · Manaus
Trujillo · B A S I N · Xingu R. · Fortaleza
· Tapajos R. · Natal
PERU · **BRAZIL** · São Francisco R. · Recife
Lima · Cuzco · Mato Grosso · Tocantins R.
BOLIVIA · Plateau · Brazilian · Salvador
Arequipa · Santa · Goiânia · Brasília · Highlands
PACIFIC · Arica · La Paz · Cruz · Campo · Belo Horizonte
OCEAN · Iquique · Sucre · Paraguay R. · Grande
Antofagasta · Gran Chaco · Campos · São Paulo · Rio de Janeiro
· **PARAGUAY** · Santos
San Miguel · Asunción · Curitiba
CHILE · de Tucumán · Paraná R. · Uruguay R. · Pôrto Alegre
Córdoba · Salto
Viña del Mar · Pampas · Paysandú
Valparaíso · **URUGUAY**
Santiago · Buenos · Montevideo · **ATLANTIC**
Concepción · Aires · Rio de la Plata · **OCEAN**
ARGENTINA · Mar del Plata
Bahía Blanca

Puerto Montt

Patagonia

N
W · E
S

0   300   600 Miles
0   300   600 Kilometers
Bipolar Oblique Conic Projection

Punta Arenas · Tierra del Fuego

GEOGRAPHY THEME
Regions **South America has 12 countries of various shapes and sizes.**

Which country is the largest in size?

FAST FACT The Peruvian Central Railway is the highest railway in the world. It climbs more than 15,000 feet (4,600 m). On each train is a doctor who administers oxygen to passengers who get altitude sickness.

Chapter 7   221

A woolly monkey

A bromeliad

Scarlet macaws

A poison dart frog

A squash bug

The Amazon rain forest has more kinds of living things than any other place on Earth, including more than one million kinds of insects.

Wedged between the Andes Mountains in the west and mountains in the east are South America's Central Plains. The Central Plains cover about three-fifths of the continent.

Four large areas make up the Central Plains. These are the Llanos (YAH·nohs), the Selva, the Gran Chaco (CHAH·koh), and the Pampas (PAHM·pahs). Each is defined by the kind of vegetation that covers much of it.

The Llanos is an area of rolling grasslands in southern Colombia and Venezuela. The Selva, which means "jungle" or "rain forest" in Spanish, covers the Amazon Basin in Bolivia, Brazil, and Peru. The Gran Chaco consists of scrub forest, or small trees and shrubs. It runs through north-central Argentina, western Paraguay, and southern Bolivia. The Pampas is the vast grassland in Argentina that fans out around Buenos Aires. In the native language Quéchua, the word *pampa* means

"level land." Like the coastal plain of the United States, the Pampas stretches inland from the Atlantic Ocean. Its landforms and climate, however, are more like the Interior Plains of the United States.

REVIEW What are the three main land regions of South America?

A Range of Climates

South America's climates are as varied as its landforms. The climate areas range from dry deserts to wet tropical rain forests and from hot lowlands to frigid mountain peaks.

The driest parts are in southern Argentina and along the coast of Peru and northern Chile. The dry area in southern Argentina is known as Patagonia (pa·tuh·GOH·nyuh). The dry area along the western coast is the Atacama (ah·tah·KAH·mah) Desert. It is also one of the driest places on Earth.

The climate in Patagonia is dry as a result of a rain shadow. Moisture in the southwest winds is blocked by the Andes. As a result, Patagonia gets only about 8 inches (20 cm) of rain in a year. The Atacama Desert is dry for another reason. The cold ocean current that flows northward along the coast from Antarctica adds to the dry conditions.

This cold ocean current, known as the Peru Current, cools the air that blows across it. Since cold air cannot hold much moisture, little rain falls. Every few years, however, the Peru Current weakens. When this happens, warm ocean water flows southward along the coast from the equator. The result is often sudden, heavy rain that causes flooding in the region. This weather event is called **El Niño**, the Spanish word for "child," because it usually occurs around Christmas. The name *El Niño* refers to the Christ child.

Aside from Patagonia and the Atacama Desert, South America receives regular, ample rainfall. Four areas receive a great deal of rain, more than 80 inches (200 cm) in a year. These areas are the Amazon Basin; coastal French Guiana, Guyana, and Suriname; southwestern Chile; and the coasts of Colombia and Ecuador. The wettest place in South America is Quibdó (keeb•DOH), Colombia. It receives more than 350 inches (890 cm) of rain a year.

The hottest weather in South America is in the middle of the continent. In Argentina's Gran Chaco lowland, temperatures in the summer may reach 110°F (43°C). (In the Southern Hemisphere, summer begins in December and winter starts in June.) Amazon temperatures rarely get as high as those in the Gran Chaco. They range mostly from 70° to 90°F (21° to 32°C). It feels hotter because of the humidity. **Humidity** is the amount of moisture, or water, in the air.

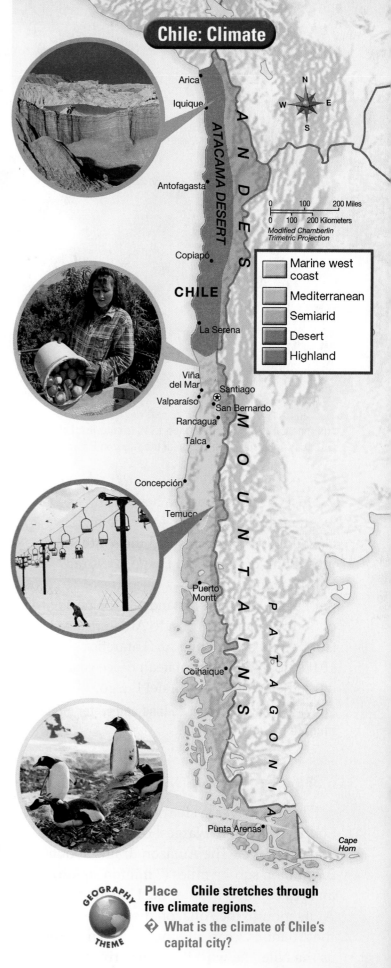

Chile: Climate

0   100   200 Miles
0   100   200 Kilometers
Modified Chamberlin Trimetric Projection

Marine west coast
Mediterranean
Semiarid
Desert
Highland

Place Chile stretches through five climate regions.

❖ What is the climate of Chile's capital city?

Manaus

Mouth of the Amazon

Belém

Iquitos

Nauta

Pacific Ocean

The Amazon River has more than 1,000 tributaries. Lake Titicaca (right) lies at the edge of the Amazon Basin.

Most of South America has warm weather during the year. Only the high elevations of the Andes and the southern-most point of Tierra del Fuego (TYER·rah del FWAY·goh) are always cold. Tierra del Fuego, a chain of islands, is the part of South America closest to Antarctica. Cold air masses rolling off Antarctica's 10,000-foot (3,000-m) plateau of ice easily cross the ocean to Tierra del Fuego.

REVIEW In what ways do land and water affect climate in South America?

The Waters of South America

Five huge river systems drain most of South America, the largest of which is the Amazon River. The Amazon drains about 2.7 million square miles (7 million sq km), an area equal to most of the United States. At its mouth, the Amazon discharges into the Atlantic Ocean 50 times as much water as the Nile, the world's longest river.

With a length of nearly 4,000 miles (6,437 km), the Amazon is the longest river in South America. It begins high in the Andes Mountains of Peru as a small stream called the Apurímac (ah·poo·REE·mahk) River. As the Apurímac flows to the east, it empties into the Ucayali (oo·kah·YAH·lee) River, and the Ucayali then joins the Marañón (mah·rah·NYOHN) River. Here, near Iquitos (ee·KEE·tohs), Peru, the main channel of the Amazon River is formed.

From Iquitos to the Atlantic Ocean, a distance of 2,300 miles (3,700 km), the Amazon provides a transportation corridor from the interior to the coast. A **transportation corridor** is a route on which people and goods move from one place to another. Belém, on the northeast Atlantic coast, and Manaus, 1,000 miles (1,600 km) upstream from the mouth of the Amazon, are important trade ports on this corridor. Finished goods and raw materials pass through these ports.

In addition to the Amazon, four other river systems are important to South America. These are the river systems of the Magdalena River, the Orinoco (ohr•ee•NOH•koh) River, the São Francisco River, and the Río de la Plata.

The Magdalena River and its tributary, the Cauca River, flow between cordilleras in Colombia and empty into the Caribbean Sea. The Orinoco River drains the Llanos of central Venezuela and the Guiana Highlands. The São Francisco River drains the Brazilian Highlands to the east.

The Río de la Plata is actually an estuary, not a river. An **estuary** is the wide mouth of a river where the ocean flows in and seawater and fresh water mix. The Río de la Plata is the body of water into which the Paraná (pah•rah•NAH) and Uruguay Rivers flow. These rivers drain the Brazilian Highlands and the Gran Chaco to the south.

In addition to its large rivers, South America has several large lakes. It does not have as many lakes as North America, however, because South America did not have as many glaciers. Two of South America's largest and most important lakes are Lake Titicaca (tee•tee•KAH•kah) and Lake Maracaibo (mah•rah•KY•boh).

Lake Titicaca is a freshwater lake on a high plateau in the Andes on the border between Bolivia and Peru. It is the highest navigable lake on Earth at more than 12,500 feet (3,810 m) above sea level. Crops that normally could not grow at such a high elevation grow near Lake Titicaca because its waters warm the air.

• GEOGRAPHY •

Angel Falls
Understanding Physical Systems

In 1935, while exploring the rain forests of Venezuela, American adventurer James C. Angel discovered a spectacular waterfall. Later, the waterfall was named in honor of Angel. Today, Venezuela's Angel Falls is recognized as the world's highest waterfall.

Lake Maracaibo in Venezuela is South America's largest lake. It covers more than 5,200 square miles (13,500 sq km), making it larger in size than the state of Connecticut. Lake Maracaibo is large enough for large oceangoing ships to cross it. A short channel connects the lake with the Caribbean Sea and the Gulf of Venezuela. Smaller ships use the channel to supply the numerous oil wells that operate in the lake and along its shores.

REVIEW What main transportation corridor links the interior of South America with the Atlantic coast?

Rich in Resources

South America is a land rich in fertile soil, raw materials used in manufacturing, and fossil fuels. Many countries in South America, however, use only a small part of their resources to benefit their economies.

About four-fifths of South America's land could be used for farming. Yet, only about one-third is used that way. Most is used as pastureland or is unused. Nevertheless, South America has some of the largest farms in the world. In countries such as Argentina and Brazil, there are farms larger than most of the states in the United States. These large commercial farms produce export products that include bananas, beef, coffee, and grains.

Sharecroppers and low-paid laborers do most of the work on these commercial farms. Under the system of **sharecropping**, a landowner gives a worker shelter, tools, and seed. The worker then farms the land. At harvesttime the landowner takes part of the crop, plus enough to cover the cost of the worker's rent and supplies. What is left is the worker's share.

Argentina, Brazil, and Chile are the leading manufacturing countries in South America. They produce almost all of the continent's airplanes, automobiles, and computers. In most of the other countries, manufacturing is limited to consumer goods.

The raw materials used in much of the manufacturing come from South America, where there are huge amounts of copper, iron ore, tin, and other minerals. It also has large deposits of fossil fuels, including coal and oil. They are, however, unevenly distributed. Many are in remote places.

Argentina, Chile, Uruguay, and Venezuela have the most-developed economies with a variety of successful industries. To have successful industries, a country must have all three of the

Rain forest

Removal of trees

Result of not replanting

Replanting trees in the Amazon rain forest (below) helps the forest recover from damage caused by humans.

Regions South America's resources are unevenly distributed.

❖ Which resources are found in Uruguay?

Natural Resources of South America

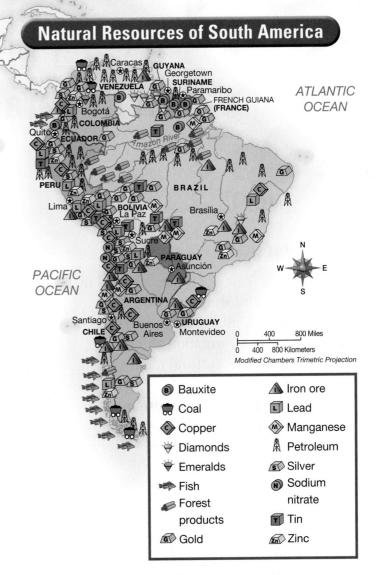

ATLANTIC OCEAN

PACIFIC OCEAN

Caracas
GUYANA
Georgetown
SURINAME
VENEZUELA
Paramaribo
FRENCH GUIANA
(FRANCE)
Bogotá
COLOMBIA
Quito
ECUADOR
Amazon River
PERU
BRAZIL
Lima
BOLIVIA
La Paz
Brasília
Sucre
PARAGUAY
Asunción
ARGENTINA
Santiago
Buenos
Aires
URUGUAY
CHILE
Montevideo

0   400   800 Miles
0   400   800 Kilometers
Modified Chambers Trimetric Projection

Symbol	Resource	Symbol	Resource
Ⓑ	Bauxite	⚠	Iron ore
⛏	Coal	Ⓛ	Lead
Ⓒ	Copper	Ⓜ	Manganese
♦	Diamonds	⚲	Petroleum
▽	Emeralds	Ⓢ	Silver
🐟	Fish	Ⓝ	Sodium nitrate
✎	Forest products	Ⓣ	Tin
Ⓖ	Gold	Ⓩ	Zinc

necessary resources to produce goods and services. These productive resources, or **factors of production**, are natural, human, and capital resources. Natural resources are the raw materials. Human resources are the workers. Capital resources are the money, buildings, and machines needed to run a business.

The other countries of South America have developing economies. They rely on a small number of primary industries in farming and mining. As a result, the people in these countries have a relatively low standard of living. Average per capita GDP in these countries is slightly more than $4,000, compared with about $10,000 in Argentina, Chile, Uruguay, and Venezuela.

REVIEW How do the factors of production influence economies?

LESSON 1 REVIEW

1 MAIN IDEA Which mountain system has the greatest effect on life in South America?

2 WHY IT MATTERS Why are most farms found east of the Andes?

3 VOCABULARY Use the term **transportation corridor** in a sentence describing South America's waterways.

4 READING SKILL—Make Inferences What can you infer about the climate of South America?

5 GEOGRAPHY Why is Patagonia's climate cold while Chile's is mild?

6 GEOGRAPHY How is Lake Maracaibo useful for transportation and for helping Venezuela's economy?

7 ECONOMICS What makes the economies of some South American countries more successful than others?

8 CRITICAL THINKING—Evaluate What effect does Lake Titicaca have on the lands surrounding it?

PERFORMANCE—Research and Draw On a piece of paper, draw the South American continent. Choose a river or a lake that you are interested in and add it to your sketch. Under the picture, list the facts you learned about the river or lake that you chose. You might include its length or size, its source, where it ends, and how it affects the people living near it.

Read a Map of Cultural Regions

➡ WHY IT MATTERS

Like other kinds of maps, cultural maps can give you information about a region of the world. Cultural maps use symbols or colors to give information about ways of life. For example, cultural maps can show where people speak certain languages or follow certain religions. These maps can help you understand more about the culture of the people in different regions.

➡ WHAT YOU NEED TO KNOW

The map on page 229 is a cultural map showing the languages that people speak in South America today. The colors on the map key stand for the languages spoken in the regions shown on the map. The map key also divides the languages spoken in South America into two groups—official languages and indigenous languages.

Indigenous, or native, languages are spoken mainly by South America's Indian groups. These groups were living in South America for hundreds of years

before European explorers arrived on the continent.

When European settlers built colonies in South America, they brought their languages with them. After years of colonial rule, many South Americans spoke European languages, such as Spanish, Portuguese, Dutch, French, and English. Except for French Guiana, all of South America is made up of independent countries today. However, European languages are still the official languages of most countries.

➡ PRACTICE THE SKILL

Study the cultural map and map key to answer these questions.

❶ In which country do many people speak Portuguese?

❷ What languages do people speak in Argentina? Which of these languages is spoken most widely?

❸ Which country on the map has no indigenous languages?

❹ Which indigenous languages are spoken in Peru?

➡ APPLY WHAT YOU LEARNED

Draw a cultural map that shows the religions practiced by the people of South America. Use an encyclopedia, atlas, or almanac to gather information about the religions. You may use colors or symbols to show where people practice the different religions. Have a classmate use your map to make some generalizations.

Peruvians in traditional dress

MAP AND GLOBE SKILLS

Practice your map and globe skills with the **GeoSkills CD-ROM**.

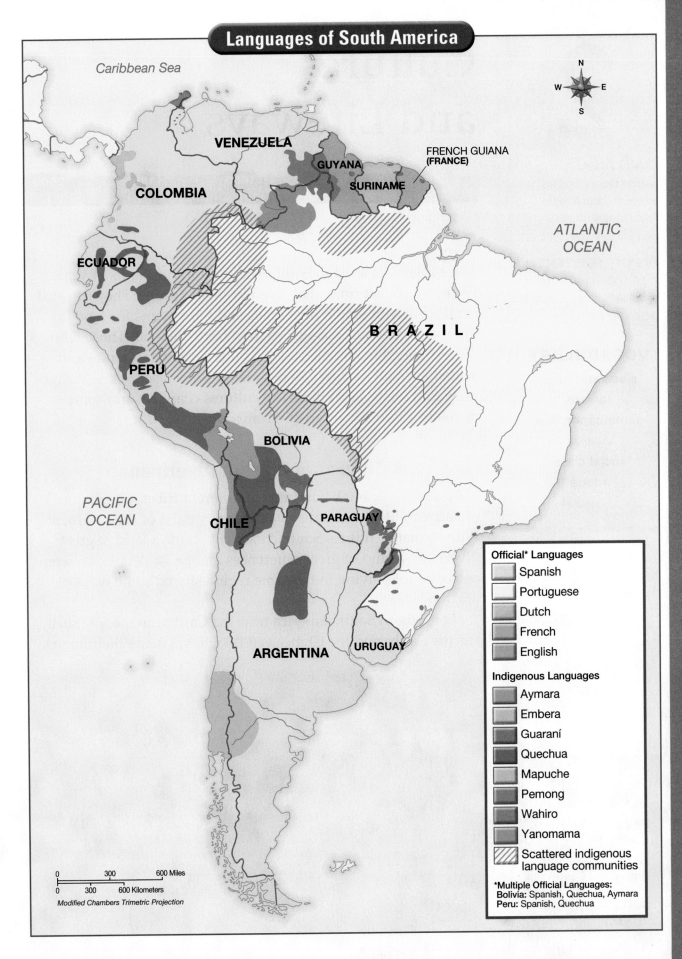

Languages of South America

Caribbean Sea

VENEZUELA

GUYANA

SURINAME

FRENCH GUIANA
(FRANCE)

COLOMBIA

ATLANTIC
OCEAN

ECUADOR

B R A Z I L

PERU

PACIFIC
OCEAN

BOLIVIA

CHILE

PARAGUAY

ARGENTINA

URUGUAY

Official* Languages
- Spanish
- Portuguese
- Dutch
- French
- English

Indigenous Languages
- Aymara
- Embera
- Guaraní
- Quechua
- Mapuche
- Pemong
- Wahiro
- Yanomama
- Scattered indigenous language communities

*Multiple Official Languages:
Bolivia: Spanish, Quechua, Aymara
Peru: Spanish, Quechua

0   300   600 Miles
0   300   600 Kilometers
Modified Chambers Trimetric Projection

Cultures and Lifeways

| 1200 | 1400 | 1600 | 1800 | 2000 |

People have lived in South America for thousands of years. For much of that time, they lived in small groups. They traveled continuously in search of animals and wild plants for food. In time, some of these people began to farm the land. Those who did, remained in one place. They built permanent homes and settled in small villages. As populations increased, some villages grew into towns and cities. The cultures changed, and some developed into advanced civilizations.

The Earliest South Americans

By about A.D. 1400, hundreds of different tribes, or groups, of native South Americans lived in many parts of the continent. With so many cultures South America became a land of great diversity—a land of great differences among its people. Different native peoples living in the same region shared some ways of life, however.

In northern South America near the Caribbean, people such as the Caribs and the Chibchas (CHIB•chahz) made their homes.

Ancient ruins in present-day Bolivia

LOCATE IT

Tiahuanaco

BOLIVIA

1
Slice and freeze

2
Protect from the sun

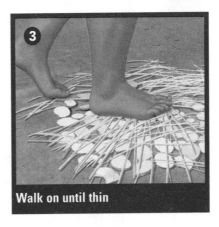
3
Walk on until thin

Analyze Diagrams **Early people in the Andes made a kind of potato chip. The process they used is shown above.**

◆ Why do you think these people made potato chips?

This region included much of present-day Colombia and Venezuela. Many of the people there lived in thatched homes made of straw and palm leaves. Farming provided most of their food, but much also came from the sea and the rivers.

Among the tribes living in the tropical rain forests were the Tupí-Guaraní (too•PEE•gwahr•uh•NEE). Many of these people still live there today. In fact, the Guaraní language is still widely spoken in Paraguay and is one of the nation's two official languages. The other is Spanish.

The Tupí-Guaranís were chiefly farmers. Because the soil in the rain forest is not naturally fertile, these early people used a method of farming called **slash and burn** to prepare the soil for planting. First, the farmers cleared the trees and brush from the land. Next, they burned the trees and mixed the ashes with the soil to fertilize it. Later, they planted many different kinds of crops, such as cassava, maize, and beans, together in the fields. After several years, however, the worn-out soil no longer

produced healthy crops. The farmers and their villages then had to move to new fields and begin again.

The people of southern South America, including the Tehuelches (tuh•WEL•cheez), depended on hunting. They roamed the vast Pampas in search of rheas, large birds similar to the ostrich. The Tehuelches lived in caves or simple shelters made of wood.

Early Peoples of South America

VENEZUELA
GUYANA
SURINAME
FRENCH GUIANA
(FRANCE)
COLOMBIA
ECUADOR
PERU
MOCHE
CHAVÍNS
PARACAS HUARIS
INCAS BOLIVIA
NAZCAS Lake Titicaca
UROS TIAHUANACOS
AYMARAS
BRAZIL
CHILE
PARAGUAY
TUPÍ-GUARANÍ
ATLANTIC
OCEAN
PACIFIC
OCEAN
URUGUAY
ARGENTINA
N
W E
S
PATAGONIA
Tierra
ONAS del Fuego

Present-day border
PERU Present-day country

0   500   1,000 Miles
0   500   1,000 Kilometers
Modified Chamberlin Trimetric Projection

GEOGRAPHY THEME

Regions **This map shows the early peoples who lived throughout South America.**

◆ Which present-day country had the most groups?

The most advanced native cultures in South America were found in the highlands of the Andes Mountains and in nearby coastal areas. This large region today includes southwestern Colombia, central Ecuador, coastal Peru, most of Chile, and parts of western Bolivia and Argentina.

The Chavíns in Peru's north-central highlands developed the first known civilization in South America. They were followed by the Mochicas (moh•CHEE•kuhz), also in northern Peru. Each had an advanced civilization and a large trading network that included other cultures.

By the 1400s more native people lived in the Andes than in any other region of South America. However, many people at that time had come under the control of one group, the Incas. The name *Inca* was originally the title given to the ruler. The name was later given to all the people the ruler governed.

REVIEW What were some of the tribes that lived in South America?

Like people around the world today, early people in South America wore jewelry. These Peruvian ear ornaments were made sometime before A.D. 500.

The Incas

The Incas in South America built their empire in much the same way as the Aztecs did in Mexico. They conquered one group of people after another. By the 1400s the Inca emperor ruled more than 9 million diverse people in an area that covered almost half a million square miles (about 1.3 million sq km). The Incas called this area the Four Quarters of the World.

To hold this diverse empire together, the Incas made the peoples they conquered follow the Inca way of life. The Incas believed that the many peoples of the empire would be less likely to rebel if everyone had the same beliefs and spoke the same language.

The Incas also brought unity to their empire by overcoming trade and travel barriers. They connected all parts of the empire with roads.

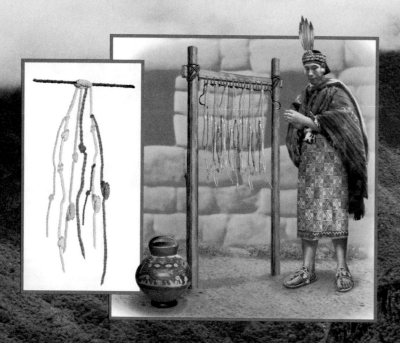

Inca runners carried messages by using *quipu* (left). Information was recorded in a series of knots tied in multicolored strings.

The Incas built roads that were wide and made of stone. Where roads could not go across deep mountain gorges, they built bridges made of rope. Runners passed messages to other runners along these roads and bridges.

Inca roads led to the capital city of Cuzco (KOOS•koh) and other cities. The buildings in these cities were made of stones cut so carefully that they fit together perfectly. This way of building can be seen in the ruins of the Inca city of Machu Picchu (mah•choo PEE•choo) in present-day Peru.

The Incas found ways to adapt conquered land to their needs. For example, they made sloping land more suitable for farming. They began by building **terraces**, giant staircases cut into hillsides. Then, using irrigation and fertilizer, the Incas raised beans, maize, squash, and as many as 200 different kinds of potatoes on these terraces.

Most of the food grown on these terraces went to government warehouses, or buildings where goods are stored. It was used to feed the Inca armies and was given to anyone who needed it. In return for this food, the Inca rulers expected the people to work for them on their many building projects.

Today the Andes region has the largest native population in South America. More than 20 million people speak Quéchua (KEH•chuh•wuh), which is the Inca language. Quéchua is one of Peru's two official languages. The other is Spanish.

REVIEW What transportation barriers did the Incas overcome to unite their empire?

Machu Picchu

LOCATE IT

PERU

Machu Picchu

Analyze Primary Sources

This sixteenth-century illustration shows the first meeting between Incas and Spaniards, in November 1532. One goal of the Spaniards was to spread Christianity.

1 Inca ruler
2 Spanish priest
3 Spanish soldier

❖ Who do you think drew this illustration? Explain your answer.

A Blend of People

In 1492 Christopher Columbus landed in the Caribbean and claimed all of North America and South America for Spain. Portugal disagreed with Spain's claim and in 1493 asked Pope Alexander VI to settle the dispute. The Pope decided on a north-south **demarcation line**—a line that marks a boundary—to divide the world, as he knew it, between Spain and Portugal.

Portugal got all lands east of the line, and Spain got all lands west of the line.

A year later, in 1494, Portugal and Spain signed the Treaty of Tordesillas (tawr•day•SEEL•yahs). This treaty moved the demarcation line farther west. Because of the new line, Portuguese explorer Pedro Cabral (kah•BRAHL) could claim Brazil for Portugal when his fleet accidentally sailed there in 1500.

By the 1530s the Portuguese had set up colonies in Brazil at Recife (ruh•SEE•fee) and Salvador in the northeast and at São Vicente in southern Brazil. These colonies were based on the commercial farming of mainly sugarcane and cotton for export to Europe. As the Spanish did in their colonies, the Portuguese enslaved first native workers and then Africans.

As a result of the Portuguese influence, Brazil today has three main ethnic groups—Europeans, Africans, and people of mixed ancestry. These mixed groups include *caboclos*, who are descendants of both European and native ancestors, as well as *mulattoes*, who are descendants of both Africans and Europeans.

According to the Brazilian government, Europeans make up about 55 percent of the nation's population. They include Portuguese, German, Italian, Spanish, and Polish people. People of mixed ancestry make up 38 percent. People of African ancestry make up 6 percent. People of Japanese, Arab, and native ancestry together make up 1 percent.

Because of Brazil's longtime colonial ties with Portugal, most of Brazil's people today speak Portuguese and worship as Roman Catholics. Native groups such as the Tupí-Guaranís, however, still use traditional languages and follow traditional beliefs.

Except in Brazil, the Spanish have had a greater influence in South America than the

Portuguese. This influence began in the 1520s, when the Spanish adventurer Francisco Pizarro (pee•SAR•oh) arrived. Pizarro had heard stories of a native people whose empire was far richer and more powerful than that of the Aztecs in Mexico. These people, he learned, were the Incas.

About 1527 Pizarro and his followers landed near the Inca city of Tumbes on Peru's northern coast. They became the first Europeans to set foot in Peru. The riches they saw in Tumbes convinced them that the stories about the Incas were true. Between 1531 and 1533, Pizarro and his followers traveled throughout the Andes, conquering the native peoples and taking their riches. By 1533 Pizarro had taken control of the Inca capital at Cuzco. In doing so, he expanded Spain's empire and ended the Incas'.

In 1535 Pizarro founded the city of Lima (LEE•mah), the first city built by Europeans in South America. During the 1600s and 1700s, Lima served as the capital for the Spanish government in South America. It ruled thousands of colonists who had come from Spain to set up plantations and mines.

To head its colonial government, the king of Spain appointed a **viceroy**, or governor. The viceroy's duty was to enforce Spanish laws and customs. As a result, the native peoples who had been conquered had to become Catholics and take Spanish names.

The Spanish also set up a strict system of **social classes**, or groups in society with different levels of importance. The upper, or more important, social class was made up of Europeans—government officials, priests, landowners, and mine operators. These people held both wealth and power in colonial society. They controlled a huge lower class made up of native peoples. As the number of mestizos grew, most of them also became part of the lower class.

This class system lasted for nearly 300 years. Today many South American countries also have a middle class made up mostly of business workers and professional people, such as doctors, lawyers, and teachers. The great majority of South Americans still belong to the lower class. These include mestizos and native peoples.

Modern office and apartment buildings line wide boulevards in downtown Buenos Aires.

LOCATE IT

ARGENTINA

Buenos Aires

The small upper class in most South American countries is still almost entirely people with European ancestry.

REVIEW What traits of European culture are seen in present-day South America?

Ways of Life

The people of South America share traditions that come from their common heritage. However, there are great differences in the ways of life throughout the continent. These differences can be seen by comparing urban and rural areas.

Today more than 70 percent of the people in South America live in urban areas. Three South American cities and their suburbs are among the largest metropolitan areas in the world. They are São Paulo, Brazil, with 17.9 million people; Buenos Aires, Argentina, with 13.2 million; and Rio de Janeiro, Brazil, with 10.6 million.

The large cities are the centers of their countries' government, economic, and social lives. Like cities everywhere in the world, they offer a variety of activities for learning and for recreation. Soccer, which

the South Americans call *fútbol*, is the most popular sport. The countries' national soccer teams play against teams from other countries in huge stadiums. Millions watch each game on television.

Large cities in South America look and sound like most large cities in other parts of the world. Skyscrapers rise in the business districts. Apartment buildings and shops line the streets and avenues. Cars and trucks clog highways during rush hour, as trains and subways also carry people to and from work. Radio stations play everything from traditional music to the latest hit tunes from South America, the United States, and Europe.

Almost every city and town in South America holds an annual festival. As in Mexico and other places of Spanish heritage, this festival, or *fiesta*, honors the Catholic saint believed to be the place's protector. The fiesta includes dancing and special meals.

Like most large cities, South America's cities face problems such as overcrowding and poverty. Rio de Janeiro is one of the world's most densely populated cities.

Soccer fans in South America

It has an average of about 13,400 people per square mile (5,200 per sq km).

Many large cities have huge slums crowded with very poor people. Such areas, called *favelas* (fah•VEH•lahs) in Brazil, have grown as millions of people migrate to urban areas to find jobs. In some cities, such as Rio de Janeiro, up to 30 percent of the population live in these slum areas. Most slums lack running water, electricity, and sewers.

Although a great many people in South American cities are poor, a growing number enjoy a good standard of living. This can be seen in the growing middle class in the large cities. Most middle-class families live in houses or apartments. Large numbers of these middle-class people work in banks, factories, hotels, office buildings, and stores. Some provide government services, such as fire and police protection. Others own their own businesses.

Life in urban areas contrasts sharply with life in rural areas, where little has changed over the centuries. Most people in rural areas feed their families by subsistence farming or by earning some money on commercial farms. These large farms, owned by wealthy landowners or private companies, are often called *haciendas* (ah•see•EN•dahs) in Spanish-speaking countries. They are called *fazendas* (fah•ZEN•dahs) in Portuguese-speaking Brazil.

Most rural homes have one or two rooms. In the desert areas, these small houses are made of **adobe**, sun-dried bricks of clay mixed with straw. Where trees are plentiful, wooden houses are common. In the rain forest, most homes have walls built of twigs or bamboo poles and a roof of grass or palm leaves. Most rural houses in South America lack electricity and running water.

REVIEW How is the standard of living the same and different in urban and rural areas?

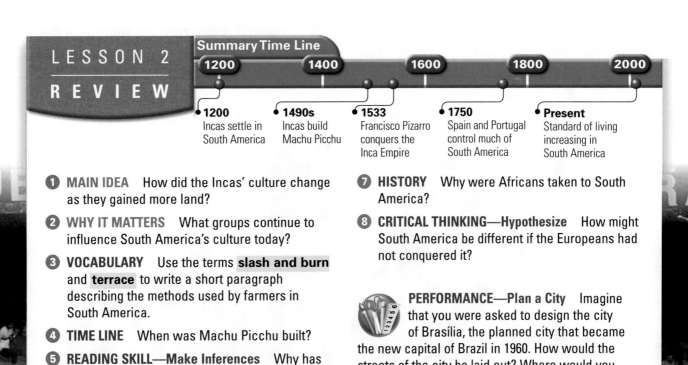

LESSON 2 REVIEW

Summary Time Line

1200 — 1400 — 1600 — 1800 — 2000

- **1200** Incas settle in South America
- **1490s** Incas build Machu Picchu
- **1533** Francisco Pizarro conquers the Inca Empire
- **1750** Spain and Portugal control much of South America
- **Present** Standard of living increasing in South America

1. **MAIN IDEA** How did the Incas' culture change as they gained more land?

2. **WHY IT MATTERS** What groups continue to influence South America's culture today?

3. **VOCABULARY** Use the terms **slash and burn** and **terrace** to write a short paragraph describing the methods used by farmers in South America.

4. **TIME LINE** When was Machu Picchu built?

5. **READING SKILL—Make Inferences** Why has it been easier for native South Americans in the countryside to preserve their way of life than for those who live in cities?

6. **HISTORY** How did the Incas overcome physical and cultural barriers to unite their empire?

7. **HISTORY** Why were Africans taken to South America?

8. **CRITICAL THINKING—Hypothesize** How might South America be different if the Europeans had not conquered it?

PERFORMANCE—Plan a City Imagine that you were asked to design the city of Brasília, the planned city that became the new capital of Brazil in 1960. How would the streets of the city be laid out? Where would you put houses, businesses, schools, and government buildings? Would you include theaters, museums, stadiums, playgrounds, and parks? Sketch your design for the city on a sheet of paper, and share your ideas with your class.

·SKILLS·

CHART AND GRAPH

Read a Double-Bar Graph

VOCABULARY

statistics
double-bar graph
x-axis
y-axis

VOCABULARY

statistics
double-bar graph
x-axis
y-axis

➡ WHY IT MATTERS

Graphs make it easy to compare statistics. **Statistics** are facts shown with numbers. A **double-bar graph** makes it easy to compare two sets of statistics. If you compare statistics shown on double-bar graphs, you can easily see differences or identify trends.

Governments often use double-bar graphs to display statistics about people. Sometimes double-bar graphs are used to compare males and females, births and deaths, or urban and rural populations.

Some cities in South America are centuries old. Until the 1900s, however, most South Americans worked as farmers and lived in rural areas. During the second half of the 1900s, farmers began moving to cities in search of jobs. The double-bar graphs on page 239 compare urban and rural populations as they were in 1970 and in 2000.

➡ WHAT YOU NEED TO KNOW

The following steps can help you read and compare double-bar graphs.

Step 1 **Identify the statistics being displayed in the graph by reading the labels on the horizontal x-axis and the vertical y-axis. In Graphs A and B, countries are shown on the x-axis and population percentages are shown on the y-axis.**

Plaza de Armas, Cuzco, Peru

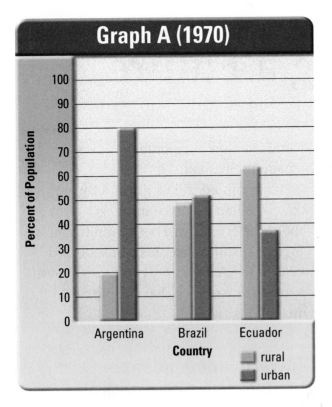

Graph A (1970)

Percent of Population

Country

- rural
- urban

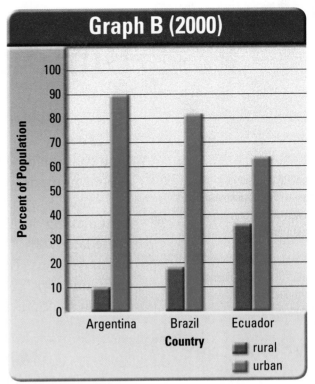

Graph B (2000)

Percent of Population

Country

- rural
- urban

Step 2 **Identify the purpose of the different bars by looking at the legend. The legend in Graph A, for example, tells you that the orange bars show the percentage of people living in rural areas, and that the red bars show the percentage living in urban areas, or cities.**

Step 3 **Read a double-bar graph by running your finger up to the top of each bar and then left to a number. If the top of the bar is between two numbers, the exact percentage is between those two.**

▶ PRACTICE THE SKILL

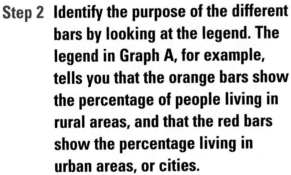

Study the two double-bar graphs above. Then answer these questions.

1 Look at Graph A. In 1970, which country had more people living in rural areas than in urban areas?

2 Look at Graph B. In 2000, which two countries had more than 80 percent of their populations living in urban areas?

3 Now compare Graphs A and B. Did the percentage of people living in the rural areas of Brazil rise or fall between 1970 and 2000? By how much?

4 How did Ecuador's population change between 1970 and 2000?

▶ APPLY WHAT YOU LEARNED

Make a double-bar graph of your test scores in social studies and in two other subjects. Begin by listing the subjects on the x-axis. Along the y-axis, list a range of your possible test scores by tens from 0 to 100 percent. Find your two most recent tests in each of the subjects and graph the scores. Use one color for the most recent test and another color for the second most recent. Make a legend that explains the colors. Study your completed graph. Do your test scores indicate which subject is your strongest? Can you tell in which subjects you are making improvement? On which subjects do you need to spend more time?

MAIN IDEA
Read to find out how the desire for independence led to democracy and growth in South America.

WHY IT MATTERS
Some South Americans continue to work toward freedom.

VOCABULARY
junta
aristocracy
landlocked
diversify
invest
mutual defense
free trade zone

Building a Future

Government, trade, and religion in colonial South America were controlled by laws made in Spain and in Portugal. Officials in South America who were appointed in Europe strictly enforced these laws. Most of the colonists had no voice in the government or in making decisions about the economy. That began to change in the late 1700s, however, as a result of events in Europe and North America. The success of the American Revolution showed many unhappy colonists in South America that people could fight for their freedom and win.

Moves Toward Independence

Two of the best-known freedom fighters in Spanish South America were Simón Bolívar (see•MOHN boh•LEE•var) and José de San Martín (hoh•SAY day san mar•TEEN). Bolívar helped win independence for much of northern South America. San Martín fought for the freedom of southern South America.

South Americans began their move toward independence in 1806. That is when an unsuccessful revolt against the Spanish took place in Venezuela. In 1813 Simón Bolívar began a new effort, which led to ten years of fighting throughout much of northern South America. Finally, in 1824, Simón Bolívar and his followers won an important victory at Ayacucho, Peru. The victory ensured independence for Bolivia, Colombia, Ecuador, Peru, and Venezuela.

The map (left) shows the Americas in 1631. Spanish ships (below) defended their nation's colonies.

One South American said of Simón Bolívar, who has often been called the George Washington of South America,

> **Neither Washington nor Bolívar was destined to have children of his own, so that we Americans might call ourselves their children.**

In southern South America, also, fighting led to freedom. In 1811 Paraguayans overthrew the Spanish viceroy and declared their independence. In 1816 José de San Martín and his followers freed Argentina from Spanish rule. In 1818 San Martín and the Chilean leader Bernardo O'Higgins won independence for Chile. Later, San Martín and his army joined with Bolívar in fighting to win Peru's independence.

Meanwhile in Brazil, independence from Portugal was won peacefully. Prince Pedro, the son of the king of Portugal, had ruled the huge colony. He listened to the Brazilians' demand for freedom and granted independence in 1822.

After achieving independence, the new nations set up republics. The people, who as colonists had had no voice in government, could now elect their leaders. However, the new leaders had little experience in governing because the Spanish and Portuguese had been in control. Soon violent struggles over authority broke out throughout the continent. In a number of countries, dictators and their **juntas** (HUN•tahs), or governing councils, seized control. They were supported by the armies that had helped win independence.

In other countries the aristocracy, made up of wealthy landowners, gained control. An **aristocracy** is a class of people who have a high position in society because their families have great wealth or titles.

Struggles over national boundaries also began between the new countries. In 1825 a

This 1820 painting shows citizens of Argentina passing near troops.

war broke out between Argentina and Brazil about an area between them. A treaty ending the war three years later established the area as the independent nation of Uruguay.

More wars continued throughout the 1800s and 1900s. In the War of the Pacific in the late 1800s, Chile fought Bolivia and Peru over a mineral-rich area along the Pacific Ocean. Chile won the war and took over the area. This left Bolivia **landlocked**, or without access to the ocean.

REVIEW What struggles did South Americans face as they formed countries?

South America Today

Since colonial times most South American countries have depended on the export of farm or mining products.

Peru's President Alejandro Toledo

In some nations these exports consisted of only one product. In Colombia it was coffee. It was copper in Chile, petroleum in Venezuela, and tin in Bolivia. Each nation had economic problems if the market price of its exports dropped.

Since the middle of the 1900s, however, many countries in South America have spent large amounts of money to **diversify** their economies, or develop more types of businesses. Much of this money has come from loans and aid from other nations. It has also come from businesses wanting to invest in South America. To **invest** is to spend or loan money in order to make more money in return.

Diversifying was a way for South American countries to become less dependent on farm and mining exports. It was also a way to become less dependent on manufactured imports from Europe and North America.

To improve their economies further, many South American countries began working together. The countries formed trade organizations, such as the Latin American Integration Association, or LAIA. These groups have encouraged South American countries to trade with each other before trading with the rest of the world. The economic groups have also encouraged greater political cooperation.

Since the 1800s, leaders such as Simón Bolívar had encouraged cooperation among the South American countries. He believed the republics needed to work together to solve their common problems. He often spoke of a union that he called the United States of South America.

For many years disputes between countries kept South America from being united. Then in 1947 nearly all the countries of South America, Middle America, and North America signed a treaty providing **mutual defense**, or military defense of each other. A year later, in

LOCATE IT

ARGENTINA

Buenos Aires

A view of the city and port of Buenos Aires, Argentina

Launch pad and control center at French Guiana's space center

1948, they formed the Organization of American States, or OAS. Its purpose was to promote cooperation and the peaceful settlement of disputes. Today these countries are working to create a **free trade zone**, a region without rules or taxes that limit trade. They hope to make more economic improvements and to encourage the spread of democracy throughout the Western Hemisphere.

REVIEW What happens when a country relies on one product for export?

LESSON 3 REVIEW

1. **MAIN IDEA** When did many of the countries in South America gain independence?

2. **WHY IT MATTERS** Why do you think some South Americans continue to fight for freedom today?

3. **VOCABULARY** Explain the difference between a **junta** and an **aristocracy**.

4. **READING SKILL—Make Inferences** Why do South American countries import more than they export?

5. **HISTORY** What revolutions inspired South American independence?

6. **ECONOMY** What is one of South America's strongest trade associations?

7. **CRITICAL THINKING—Analyze** How can South American countries work together to build stronger economies?

PERFORMANCE—Draw a Portrait
Choose a revolutionary leader from South America. First, learn more about this leader at your library and on the Internet. Then, use what you learned to draw a portrait of the leader. Write a caption for your portrait. Include in your caption qualities that made this leader important.

• CHAPTER •

7 Review and Test Preparation

Summary Time Line

1200	1400
1200 Incas settle in South America	

Use Your Reading Skills

Complete this graphic organizer to show that you understand how to make inferences about South America by using the details from what you read and your own knowledge. A copy of this graphic organizer appears on page 69 of the Activity Book.

Influences in South America

DETAILS + KNOWLEDGE → INFERENCE

DETAILS		KNOWLEDGE		INFERENCE
The Incas settled in Peru and began conquering other civilizations. Spanish explorers who came to South America eventually conquered the Incas. Over the centuries many groups moved to South America, including Asians and Africans.	+	______	→	______

DETAILS		KNOWLEDGE		INFERENCE
______	+	Few people live in mountainous and desert areas. Rivers are important for agriculture and transportation. Natural resources are valuable. People usually live in places where the temperatures are mild and cool.	→	______

Think & Write

Write an Advertisement Early people in the Andes made freeze-dried potatoes, called chuño. Write an advertisement for chuño potato chips. In your advertisement, describe how they are made and how they taste. After you finish writing, illustrate your advertisement with pictures of chuño potato chips.

Write a "Packing for a Journey" List Reread the lesson about South America's geography. With this in mind, write a list of items you might pack if you were planning to explore the South American continent. Next to the name of each item, write a sentence explaining why you would pack that item.

1600	1800	2000

1490s
Incas build
Machu Picchu

1494
Treaty of Tordesillas
divides control of South
America between Spain
and Portugal

1500
Portuguese explorers
arrive in Brazil

1533
Francisco Pizarro
conquers the Inca
Empire

1750
Spain and Portugal
control much of
South America

Present
French Guiana is the only
South American country
that is not independent

USE THE TIME LINE

Use the chapter summary time line to answer these questions.

1 In what year did Spain and Portugal sign the Treaty of Tordesillas?

2 Which South American country is still not independent today?

USE VOCABULARY

Use each term in a sentence that explains both the meaning of the term and how that meaning relates to South America.

cordillera (p. 220)

estuary (p. 225)

adobe (p. 237)

junta (p. 241)

aristocracy (p. 241)

RECALL FACTS

Answer these questions.

3 Why do few people live in Patagonia?

4 What is South America's largest river system?

5 Where did the Caribs settle?

Write the letter of the best choice.

6 TEST PREP Spanish is one of Peru's official languages. The other is—
 A Guaraní.
 B Quéchua.
 C Portuguese.
 D English.

7 TEST PREP The revolutionary leader who dreamed of a United States of South America was—
 F San Martín.
 G King Philip II.
 H George W. Bush.
 J Simón Bolívar.

THINK CRITICALLY

8 Do you think Inca society benefited from making parts of conquered cultures their own? Explain.

9 How do you think Spain's giving up colonies to the rule of juntas affected independence in South America?

APPLY SKILLS

Read a Map of Cultural Regions

10 Use the map on page 229 to identify which European languages are spoken in South America. For each language, list the countries where it is spoken.

Read a Double-Bar Graph

11 Study the double-bar graphs on page 239. Use the information presented by these graphs to write a paragraph about the populations of Argentina, Brazil, and Ecuador. Where do most people in these countries live? How has this changed over time?

VISIT

The Atacama Desert

GET READY

The Atacama Desert in northern Chile is one of the driest regions on Earth. In spite of its dryness and small population, people enjoy visiting this desert for its dramatic beauty. In the Atacama Desert, you can see sand dunes that tower over the desert floor. You can hike an area, called the Valley of the Moon, that resembles the moon's surface. This area has twisted and curved rock formations that jut out of the earth. Visitors to the Atacama Desert leave with a deep appreciation and understanding of a desert environment.

WHAT TO SEE

The Atacama Desert is rich in minerals. Here a geologist searches for mineral deposits.

LOCATE IT

CHILE

Atacama Desert

Visitors can see unusual rock formations in the Valley of the Moon.

This is a geyser (GY•zer) called El Tatio. A geyser is a source of underground hot water that releases steam into the air.

Near the town of San Pedro de Atacama, a girl takes care of her sheep.

Hikers find that the enormous sand dunes are a good place to enjoy the desert scenery.

TAKE A FIELD TRIP

A VIRTUAL TOUR
Visit The Learning Site at **www.harcourtschool.com/tours** to take virtual tours of other parks and scenic areas.

A VIDEO TOUR
Check your media center or classroom library for a videotape tour of the Atacama Desert.

3 Review and Test Preparation

VISUAL SUMMARY

Write a Diary Entry On the visual summary time line on page 249, find the date Christopher Columbus landed in the Caribbean. Suppose that you are an explorer traveling with Columbus. Write a diary entry describing the day Columbus landed in the Caribbean.

USE VOCABULARY

Identify the term that correctly matches each definition.

peninsula (p. 172)   **mestizo** (p. 182)

dependency (p. 212)   **cordillera** (p. 220)

1. a territory that is controlled by a country but is not part of it

2. a piece of land that is mostly surrounded by water

3. a person with both Spanish and native ancestors

4. a system of parallel mountain ranges

RECALL FACTS

Answer these questions.

5. Why do Mexicans celebrate Guadalupe Day?

6. Why did Oscar Arias Sánchez win the Nobel Peace Prize?

7. What causes a rain shadow?

8. What ethnic groups are found in Brazil?

Write the letter of the best choice.

9. **TEST PREP**   During each summer, the people of the Caribbean and Central America are on the lookout for fierce storms called—
   A rain shadows.
   B droughts.
   C trade winds.
   D hurricanes.

10. **TEST PREP**   To farm the steep slopes of the Andes, Inca engineers built—
    F cordilleras.
    G terraces.
    H quipus.
    J Machu Picchu.

THINK CRITICALLY

11. Why do you think people take the risk to farm on the slopes of volcanoes?

12. How did the cultures of Europe and Africa influence basic features of Caribbean society?

13. Do you think the blend of people had an influence on the culture of South America? Explain.

Read a Map of Cultural Regions

Use the cultural map on this page to answer these questions.

14 In which country is English the official language? Why do you think this is so?

15 Where do people still speak the Mayan language?

16 What is the official language of Mexico and most countries of Central America? Why do you think this is so?

17 In which countries do some people speak Miskito?

18 What native languages are spoken in Mexico?

19 What two languages are spoken in Mexico and across the border in Guatemala?

Languages of Mexico and Central America

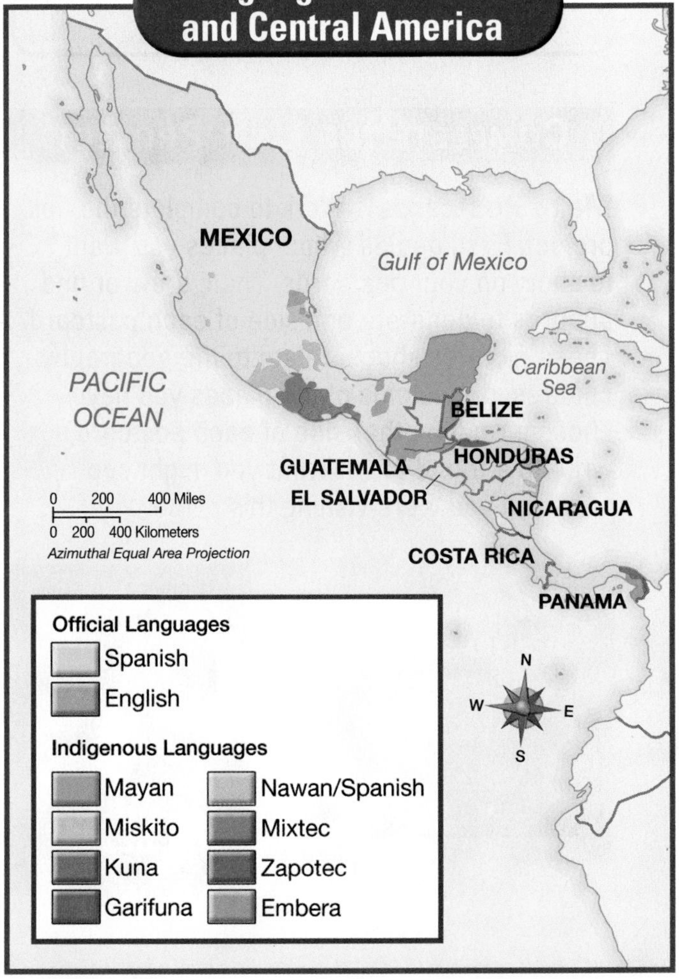

MEXICO

Gulf of Mexico

PACIFIC OCEAN

Caribbean Sea

BELIZE

GUATEMALA
EL SALVADOR

HONDURAS

NICARAGUA

COSTA RICA

PANAMA

0   200   400 Miles
0   200   400 Kilometers
Azimuthal Equal Area Projection

N
W   E
S

Official Languages
- Spanish
- English

Indigenous Languages
- Mayan
- Miskito
- Kuna
- Garifuna
- Nawan/Spanish
- Mixtec
- Zapotec
- Embera

2000 B.C.

1000 B.C.

B.C./A.D.

A.D. 1000

A.D. 2000

Visual Summary

1200 B.C. Olmec civilization begins p. 177

500 B.C. Mayan civilization begins p. 178

A.D. 1492 Columbus lands in the Caribbean p. 201

A.D. 1830 Most of Middle and South America is independent p. 208

A.D. 2000 Most countries of Middle and South America are republics p. 209

Unit Activities

Visit The Learning Site at www.harcourtschool.com/socialstudies/activities for additional activities.

Make a Quipu

Work in a group to create a quipu that tells a story or records an event. First, decide what each color of the cords will represent. Then, decide how each knot will be tied and what each knot will represent. Use your finished quipu to tell the story or describe the event to the class.

Make a Class Magazine

Work with your classmates to make a magazine about Middle America and South America. First, review Unit 3 to find interesting topics for stories in your magazine. Next, write at least one story on each region of Middle America and South America and illustrate each story. Then, make a cover for your magazine, and attach it to your stories.

VISIT YOUR LIBRARY

■ *Made in Mexico* by Peter Laufer and Susan L. Roth. National Geographic Society.

■ *The Tree Is Older Than You Are: A Bilingual Gathering of Poems and Stories from Mexico with Paintings by Mexican Artists* selected by Naomi Shihab Nye. Simon & Shuster.

■ *Salsa Stories* by Lulu Delacre. Scholastic.

COMPLETE THE UNIT PROJECT

Make Postcards Work to complete the unit project. First, decide which places you want to show on your postcards. Then, draw or find pictures to decorate one side of each postcard. These pictures should relate to the geography, cultures, or customs of the places you have chosen. On the other side of each postcard, write to a friend about what you might see or hear if you were visiting this place.

Europe

Knight's helmet, Italy,
sixteenth century

Castle Werfen, Austria

Europe

❝ **The splendor falls on castle walls
And snowy summits old in story.** ❞

—Alfred, Lord Tennyson,
from "The Splendor Falls
on Castle Walls," 1850

Preview the Content

Read the titles of the chapters and lessons. Use them to make an outline of the unit. Write down some questions about Europe.

Preview the Vocabulary

Related Words   Related words are words that have a relationship, such as sharing a root word and having similar meanings. Use the words listed below to form word pyramids. Each pyramid should contain one of the words listed below and words that are related to it. Then use the original words in sentences that show their meanings. Use the Glossary to confirm the meanings.

| collective | inflation | privatize |
| displace | institution | totalitarian |

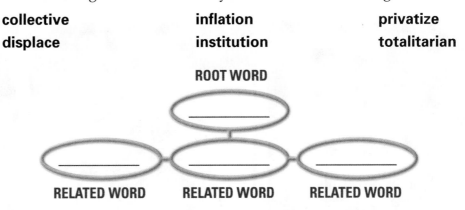

ROOT WORD

RELATED WORD   RELATED WORD   RELATED WORD

Russia, and the Eurasian Republics

ARCTIC OCEAN

GREENLAND
(DENMARK)

Kara Sea

Barents Sea

Norwegian Sea

ICELAND
Reykjavik

SWEDEN
FINLAND
NORWAY
Oslo
Helsinki
Tallinn
St. Petersburg

RUSSIA
Nizhniy Novgorod
Yekaterinburg
Chelyabinsk
Omsk

North Sea
Stockholm
ESTONIA
Riga

UNITED KINGDOM
DENMARK
Copenhagen
LITHUANIA
RUSSIA
LATVIA
Vilnius
Moscow
Samara
Astana

NETHERLANDS
Dublin
Amsterdam
Berlin
Minsk
POLAND
BELARUS
Volgograd
KAZAKHSTAN

IRELAND
London
Brussels
GERMANY
Warsaw
Kiev
Lake Balkhash

BELGIUM
Prague
CZECH REP.
SLOVAKIA
UKRAINE
Aral Sea

Paris
LUX.
LIECHT.
Vienna
Bratislava
MOLDOVA
Almaty

SWITZERLAND
Bern
AUSTRIA
Budapest
Chisinau
Bishkek
UZBEKISTAN
Tashkent
KYRGYZSTA

FRANCE
SLOVENIA
Ljubljana
HUNGARY
Odesa

MONACO
CROATIA
Zagreb
Belgrade
ROMANIA
CAUCASUS MTS.
Dushanbe

SAN MARINO
Sarajevo
Bucharest
GEORGIA
Caspian Sea
TAJIKISTAN

ANDORRA
Rome
BOSNIA & HERZ.
SERBIA
BULGARIA
Black Sea
Tbilisi
Baku
Ashgabat
TURKMENISTAN

PORTUGAL
Madrid
Barcelona
ITALY
Sofia
MACEDONIA
ARMENIA
Yerevan

Lisbon
SPAIN
VATICAN CITY
ALBANIA
Tiranë
Skopje
MONTENEGRO
GREECE
AZERBAIJAN

Valletta
MALTA
Athens

Mediterranean Sea

URAL MOUNTAINS
Ob' River
Volga River

ATLANTIC OCEAN

INDIAN OCEAN

0   500   1,000 Miles
0   500   1,000 Kilometers
Robinson Projection

Key Events

| 1000 B.C. | 500 B.C. | B.C./A.D. | A.D. 500 |

800 B.C. Earliest Greek city-states form p. 269

336 B.C. Alexander the Great expands his empire, p. 269

A.D. 400s Slavs settle in Eastern Europe and what is now Russia p. 334

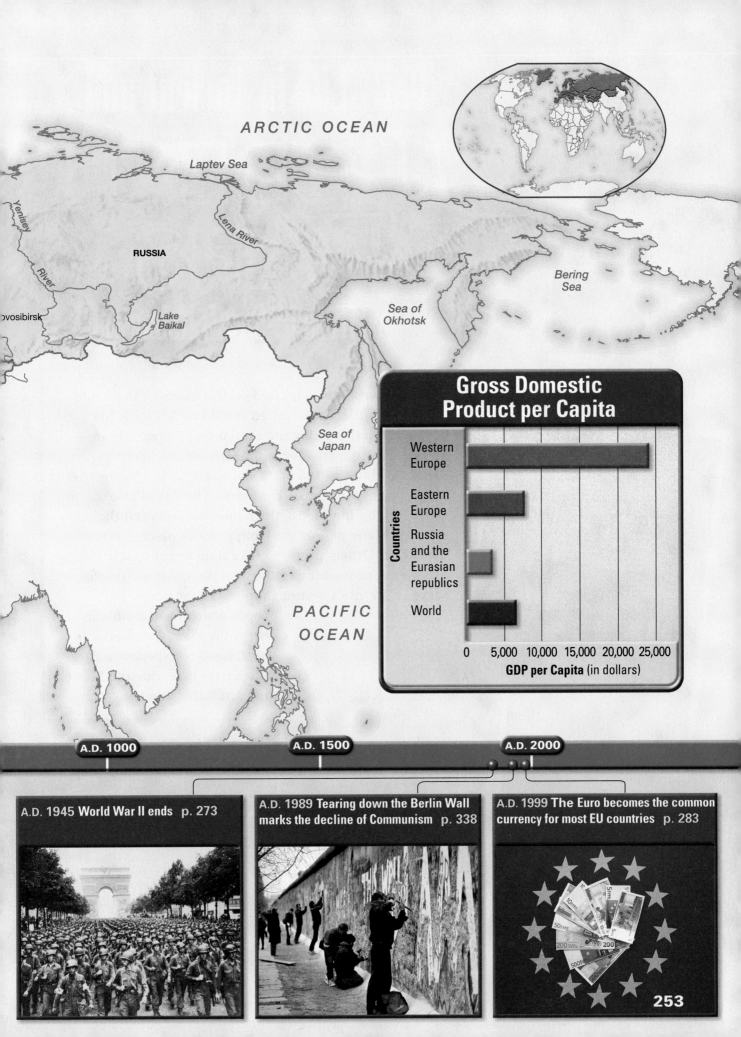

ARCTIC OCEAN

Laptev Sea

Yenisey River

RUSSIA

Lena River

ovosibirsk

Lake Baikal

Sea of Okhotsk

Bering Sea

Sea of Japan

PACIFIC OCEAN

Gross Domestic Product per Capita

Countries

- Western Europe
- Eastern Europe
- Russia and the Eurasian republics
- World

GDP per Capita (in dollars)

0   5,000   10,000   15,000   20,000   25,000

A.D. 1000

A.D. 1500

A.D. 2000

A.D. 1945 **World War II ends** p. 273

A.D. 1989 **Tearing down the Berlin Wall marks the decline of Communism** p. 338

A.D. 1999 **The Euro becomes the common currency for most EU countries** p. 283

253

START with a

STORY

Cities through Time
Daily Life in
Ancient and Modern
PARIS

by Sarah Hoban
illustrations by Bob Moulder

Daily Life in Ancient and
MODERN
PARIS

written by Sarah Hoban

The city of Paris is located on the banks of the Seine. An island in the Seine called the Île de la Cité is the center of what is today the capital and largest city in France. The two areas on either side of the Seine, called the Right Bank and the Left Bank, are connected by the many bridges that cross the Seine. The city is also connected by the Métro, the name Parisians call their subway. Many people get from place to place quickly on the Métro. Others prefer to take time to appreciate the experience of walking in the city. Walkers may stop in some of the city's quaint shops, visit the parks, or people-watch from a table in one of the many sidewalk cafés. Read to experience Paris like a Parisian—ride the Métro and stroll the streets!

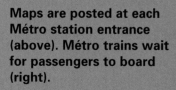

Maps are posted at each Métro station entrance (above). Métro trains wait for passengers to board (right).

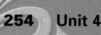

The Métro

The Métro, short for the French terms for "metropolitan railroad," has been an important part of Paris since 1900. When the subway opened, elaborate Art Nouveau wrought ironwork framed its entrances. Some of those entrances still stand, but most stations have modern entrances with escalators and automatic turnstiles.

Parisians heading to work, school, or home ride the Métro. The trains wind their way along 124 miles of track above and below the city streets, linking 368 stations. In fact, no point in Paris is more than five hundred yards from a station. Color-coded maps help riders plot their routes and transfer from one line to another.

Métro stations bustle with activity. Advertising posters line the walls, street musicians perform in the passage between tracks, and announcements occasionally blare from loudspeakers. The names of some of the stops are spelled out in intricate mosaic lettering, and other stops feature displays reflecting their location.

Entrance to Métro station

A City for Walking

The Métro helps Parisians get where they need to go quickly and allows them to travel long distances. But the best way to see Paris is on foot. For active, noisy street life, the wide boulevards offer crowded sidewalks and big stores selling everything from compact discs to stylish shoes. Take a break at one of the sidewalk cafés and order a sandwich, a soda, or a pastry. Chairs right on the sidewalks guarantee a view of the passing crowds.

Street vendors sell handicrafts and wind-up birds. Drummers and guitar players keep a steady beat for passersby. Paris has many quiet back streets, where you'll see the beautiful old apartment buildings, cozy restaurants, and little shops. Tiny, ancient streets only a few feet wide remind Parisians of how the city looked in the Middle Ages.

Paris also has many parks for walkers, from small neighborhood squares to

A woman and a child enjoy a *baguette,* or loaf of french bread (left). Young people meet at a sidewalk cafe (below). A Parisian feeds a bird (below left).

larger, more elegant spaces. Strollers amble through the little neighborhood parks, while children clamber over jungle gyms. Parents push strollers, grandparents feed birds from park benches, and schoolchildren sail boats in fountains. People play basketball at the lovely Jardin du Luxembourg or sketch the statues of the Jardin des Tuileries.

The Bois de Boulogne is a big woods at the edge of town, where people can go to the horse races, visit an amusement park, or simply stroll down a tree-lined path.

Produce markets line the streets (above)

Analyze the Literature

❶ What are the advantages of walking in Paris? What are the advantages of taking the Métro? What might you miss if you toured the city by car?

❷ Think about the city or town in which you live. Make a list of things you suggest visitors see and do there. If possible, design a walking, bus, or subway tour that maps out the best way to see the sites.

READ A BOOK

START THE UNIT PROJECT

Plan a Festival As you read this unit, collect information about the different cultures found in Europe. Start to research the ways people in Europe celebrate. Use the information you gather to work with your classmates to plan a European festival.

USE TECHNOLOGY

Visit The Learning Site at **www.harcourtschool.com/ socialstudies** for additional activities, primary sources, and other resources to use in this unit.

KLEINE SCHEIDEGG, SWITZERLAND

The Jungfrau Railway winds through the Swiss Alps in the Berner Oberland region. This part of Switzerland is popular for outdoor activities such as skiing, hiking, and mountain climbing. The Alps mountain range stretches from France through Switzerland and into Eastern Europe.

LOCATE IT

SWITZERLAND

Kleine Scheidegg

Western Europe

" Hills peep o'er hills, and Alps on Alps arise! "
—Alexander Pope, from the poem
"An Essay on Criticism," 1709

CHAPTER READING SKILL

Cause and Effect

A **cause** is an event or action that makes something else happen. An **effect** is what happens as a result of that event or action.

As you read this chapter, list the causes and effects of the key events.

What Caused → Event
the Event

CAUSE → EFFECT

MAIN IDEA
Read to learn about Western Europe's many landforms and land regions.

WHY IT MATTERS
Life in Western Europe varies greatly depending on geographic location.

VOCABULARY

Eurasia
bog
polder
loch
firth

The village of Oia on Santorini Island lies on the Aegean Sea, an arm of the Mediterranean.

Islands, Peninsulas, and Mountains

Western Europe is about one-third the size of the United States, yet more than 380 million people live in its 24 countries. On a map Western Europe looks like a giant peninsula extending from Asia into the surrounding oceans and seas. Since no body of water separates Europe and Asia completely, some geographers consider them to be one continent, which they call **Eurasia**.

Most countries in Western Europe are on peninsulas or islands. Rivers connect the inland countries to the ocean or to seas. This access to water has made it possible for the people of Western Europe to more easily exchange resources, ideas, and culture traits. The central mountains, however, have acted as barriers.

A Range of Climates

Much of northwestern Europe has a mild climate because of the North Atlantic Drift. The North Atlantic Drift is a continuation of the Gulf Stream. This ocean current carries warm water to Western Europe from the Gulf of Mexico across the Atlantic Ocean. The winds blowing over the water create mild temperatures from Britain to Norway.

Climate in the southern part of Western Europe is affected by the warm waters of the Mediterranean Sea and by the dry air that blows from Africa. These conditions result in hot, dry summers and mild winters from Spain to Greece.

In the central part of Western Europe, the continental landmass affects climate the most. At times strong winds build up over Germany and France, blocking the flow of warm air from the west and south. When this happens, temperatures drop in those countries.

In addition to the continental landmass, elevation also influences climate in the central part of Western Europe. The climate in the mountains is generally cooler and wetter than that of the surrounding lowlands. In some places, such as Austria and Switzerland, snow covers the mountain peaks all year long.

REVIEW What water and land areas influence climate in Western Europe?

Western Europe

Regions This map shows the 24 countries of Western Europe.

❓ Which countries share a border with Switzerland?

FAST FACT Chamonix, France (below right), lies at the base of Mont Blanc. Reaching a height of 15,771 feet (4,807 m), Mont Blanc is the highest peak in the Alps. It also has an 8-mile (13-km) tunnel, one of the world's longest. The tunnel connects France and Italy.

Western Europe's Islands

Thousands of islands lie off the Atlantic coast of Western Europe and in the Mediterranean Sea. Among these are Iceland, Malta, and the British Isles, which are by far the largest and most important. The British Isles lie northwest of the European mainland. The English Channel separates them from the continent. The two largest islands of the British Isles are Great Britain, which is often called Britain, and Ireland.

Two independent nations make up the British Isles. They are Ireland and the United Kingdom of Great Britain and Northern Ireland, often shortened to United Kingdom. The United Kingdom is made up of England, Scotland, Wales, and Northern Ireland.

Ireland is often called the Republic of Ireland to distinguish it from Northern Ireland. The island of Ireland lies west of Britain and is separated from it by the Irish Sea and the North Channel. Most of central Ireland is lowland with rolling hills and bogs. A **bog** is an area of marsh or swamp. Ireland's highest point is 3,414 feet (1,041 m) high, in the mountains in southern Ireland. The major river in Ireland is the River Shannon, the longest in the British Isles.

England is in the southeastern part of the island of Britain. It is separated from Scotland on the north by the Cheviot Hills and from Wales on the west by the Cambrian Mountains. A chain of low mountains extends through the center of England. The highest point in the chain is only 3,210 feet (978 m) high. To the east of the mountains is a wide lowland plain. It is actually part of the Great European Plain, which stretches to the east across the European mainland into Russia.

The Thames (TEMZ) is the largest river in Britain. It flows eastward across England. London, the capital of the United Kingdom, is located on the Thames. Over the years this once-small river settlement has grown into the United Kingdom's largest and most important city.

REVIEW What body of water lies between the British Isles and the European mainland?

Completed in 1894, Tower Bridge in London spans the Thames River.

LOCATE IT

UNITED KINGDOM

London

Thames R.

Mountains dominate the landscape of Italy.

Western Europe's Peninsulas

Three large land areas jut out from the southern part of Western Europe into the Mediterranean Sea. These land areas are the Iberian, Apennine, and Balkan Peninsulas. Mountain ranges, many with peaks higher than 10,000 feet (3,000 m), separate these peninsulas from the mainland. Arms of the Mediterranean Sea separate the peninsulas from one another.

The countries of Spain and Portugal share the Iberian Peninsula. The peninsula is isolated from the rest of Europe by the Pyrenees (PIR•uh•neez), mountains between Spain and France. High in the Pyrenees is the tiny country of Andorra (an•DAWR•uh). It is one of several very small countries in Western Europe.

Italy takes up nearly all of the boot-shaped Apennine Peninsula. It is a mountainous land dominated by the Apennines, mountains that run the entire length of Italy. In the north, the Alps cut off the Apennine Peninsula from the mainland. The Alps, with some peaks higher than 15,000 feet (4,600 m), isolate northern Italy from France, Switzerland, and Austria.

Nestled within Italy are the tiny countries of San Marino and Vatican City. Much of San Marino stands on Mount Titano in the Apennines. This country covers only 24 square miles (61 sq km). Vatican City is also small, no larger than an average city park. It lies within the city limits of Rome, the capital of Italy.

Greece is at the southern tip of the Balkan Peninsula, the third of the southern peninsulas of Western Europe. The Balkan Mountains cover most of the peninsula. These mountains isolate Greece from the countries of Central Europe that are farther north on the Balkan Peninsula.

• SCIENCE AND TECHNOLOGY •

The Eiffel Tower

When the French engineer Alexandre-Gustave Eiffel (a•layks•AHN•druh goos•TAHV EYE•fuhl) built the Eiffel Tower in Paris, France, in 1889, nothing like it had ever been built before. At the time, the 984-foot (300 m) tower was the largest human-made structure in the world. Eiffel built the tower out of steel and iron. The successful completion of the tower proved that iron and steel could be used to build tall and sturdy structures. This new way of building led to changes in architecture. Today the Eiffel Tower is one of the most popular tourist destinations in all of Western Europe.

The Rhine River flows from the Alps to the North Sea.

Scandinavia (skan•duh•NAY•vee•uh) is another of Western Europe's large peninsulas. It curves around the Baltic Sea in the far northern part of Western Europe. Norway and Sweden occupy the Scandinavian Peninsula. Denmark, which is part of the region of Scandinavia, is on a smaller peninsula called Jutland.

REVIEW What are the five main peninsulas in Western Europe?

Western Europe's Mainland

The mainland of Western Europe has three major land regions. They are, from north to south, the Great European Plain, the Central Uplands, and the Alpine Mountain System.

The Great European Plain stretches from northern France across Belgium, the Netherlands, and northern Germany to Central Europe and Russia. This plain consists of flat, rolling land with some low hills. It has Western Europe's best farmland. It is also one of the region's most densely populated areas. To create more land for living and working, countries such as Belgium and the Netherlands have drained water from their coastal areas. These areas of land reclaimed from the sea are called **polders**.

The Central Uplands extend from Portugal through southern France to central Germany. This region is made up of low mountains and plateaus with elevations from about 1,000 to 6,000 feet (300 to 1,800 m). Some parts of the Central Uplands have forests. Most of the land, however, is rocky, and most of the soil is not fertile enough for farming. Some good farmland, however, is found in the river valleys. One of Western Europe's most important waterways, the Rhine (RYN) River, crosses the Central Uplands. The Rhine flows along the borders of Switzerland, Liechtenstein, Austria, France, and Germany.

The Alpine Mountain System covers much of the southern part of Western

LOCATE IT

Brenner Pass

AUSTRIA

FAST FACT
Invaders used this pass in the Alps, now called Brenner Pass, to reach Italy during ancient times. After World War II the pass became the border between Austria and Italy.

These Icelanders (above) are swimming in one of the country's many hot springs. Geysers (right) are also common features in Iceland.

Europe. It is made up of several mountain chains—the Sierra Nevada in Spain, the Pyrenees, and the Alps. The Alps cover part of southern France and northern Italy, most of Switzerland, and part of southern Germany and Austria. The Alps have some of the highest mountains in Europe. With their snow-capped peaks and scenic valleys, they are among Western Europe's most spectacular physical features.

Other parts of Western Europe are well known for their physical features. Finland, for example, is known for its more than 60,000 lakes. Scotland is known for its long,

deep, narrow lakes called **lochs** and its funnel-shaped bays called **firths**. Glaciers that carved out the lochs and firths in Scotland also cut the steep-walled fjords of coastal Norway. Another recognized feature is the Rock of Gibraltar at the entrance to the Mediterranean Sea.

REVIEW What are the three major land regions on the mainland of Western Europe?

LESSON 1 REVIEW

1 MAIN IDEA What are the main landforms and land regions of Western Europe?

2 WHY IT MATTERS How does geography affect where people live in Western Europe?

3 VOCABULARY Write a paragraph about the British Isles using the words **loch** and **bog**.

4 READING SKILL—Identify Cause and Effect What caused people in Belgium and the Netherlands to create polders?

5 GEOGRAPHY What two countries are separated by the Pyrenees mountains?

6 ECONOMICS Where is Western Europe's best farmland?

7 CRITICAL THINKING—Hypothesize How would Western Europe be different if it was not warmed by the North Atlantic Drift?

 PERFORMANCE ACTIVITY—Make a Fact Sheet Using an almanac, create a fact sheet about five countries in Western Europe. Include the name of each country, its climate, its population, and its major landforms.

·SKILLS·

Land Use and Products

VOCABULARY

land use
raw material

MAP AND GLOBE

▶ WHY IT MATTERS

Have you ever wondered where the products that people buy are made? For example, people buy cereal at grocery stores, but where was the cereal made and where was the grain for it grown? To find the answers to questions like these, you might use a map that shows where products are made and how land is used.

▶ WHAT YOU NEED TO KNOW

The map on the next page is a land use and products map of Western Europe. Colors on the map show **land use**, or what is done with most of the land in different places. The map cannot show every forest or every farming or manufacturing area. It shows only the main ones. Study the map key to learn which color stands for each kind of land use.

Picture symbols on the map show some of Western Europe's products. Each product is shown in the country that produces it. Western Europe makes too many products to be shown on just one map, so the map shows just the major products. Study the map key to learn which symbol stands for each product.

Notice on the map that many of Western Europe's products relate to land use. For example, some of the land in Germany is used for manufacturing. In Germany major products that are manufactured include vehicles, machinery, and electronics. Much of the land in Finland is forest. Finland's related products include lumber and paper. In France much of the land is used for farming. French farms produce the raw materials needed to make food products, such as cereal and bread. **Raw materials** are natural resources that can be made into useful products.

▶ PRACTICE THE SKILL

Look at the map and map key to answer these questions.

1 In which countries do the people use some of the land for farming?

2 What are some of Italy's products? Which kinds of land use in Italy are related to these products?

3 What are some of Western Europe's products that might be made on land used for manufacturing?

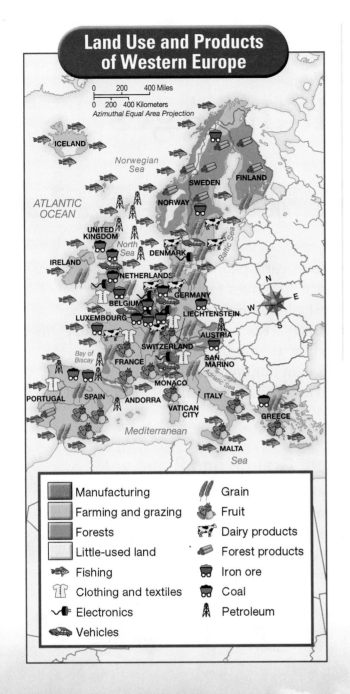

Land Use and Products of Western Europe

0   200   400 Miles

0   200   400 Kilometers
Azimuthal Equal Area Projection

ICELAND

Norwegian Sea

ATLANTIC OCEAN

SWEDEN

FINLAND

NORWAY

UNITED KINGDOM

North Sea

Baltic Sea

IRELAND

DENMARK

NETHERLANDS

BELGIUM

GERMANY

LIECHTENSTEIN

LUXEMBOURG

AUSTRIA

SWITZERLAND

Bay of Biscay

FRANCE

SAN MARINO

Adriatic Sea

MONACO

PORTUGAL

SPAIN

ANDORRA

VATICAN CITY

ITALY

GREECE

Aegean Sea

Mediterranean Sea

MALTA

N
W — E
S

Map Key

■ Manufacturing	Grain
■ Farming and grazing	Fruit
■ Forests	Dairy products
□ Little-used land	Forest products
Fishing	Iron ore
Clothing and textiles	Coal
Electronics	Petroleum
Vehicles	

▶ APPLY WHAT YOU LEARNED

Draw a land use and product map of your state. Visit the library to find out how people use the land in your state and what kinds of products are made there. Use colors to show the different land uses, and include a map key to tell what each color stands for. Choose symbols to stand for your state's important products. Add the symbols to the map, and include explanations of them in the map key. Share your map with the class.

MAP AND GLOBE SKILLS

Practice your map and globe skills with the **GeoSkills CD-ROM**.

MAP AND GLOBE SKILLS

2

VOCABULARY

city-state
manorialism
Renaissance
nation-state
mercantilism
genocide
Holocaust

Western Europe Through the Ages

500 B.C.	B.C. / A.D.	A.D. 500	A.D. 1000	A.D. 1500	A.D. 2000

For thousands of years, early people moved about Europe in an organized way. They searched for food available at certain times of the year. Almost all their time was spent hunting and gathering food. By about 6000 B.C. people in Western Europe had learned to raise food by farming. Farming was a more reliable way to get food than hunting and gathering. It enabled some early societies in Western Europe to develop advanced civilizations.

Ancient Greece and Rome

The first civilizations in Western Europe developed on islands in the eastern Mediterranean Sea. On Crete, an island off the coast of the Balkan Peninsula, people became skilled in art and architecture. They also used a system of writing. A similar civilization developed on Malta, south of the Apennine Peninsula.

Sailors from Crete and Malta spread their civilizations as they traded with other people in the Mediterranean. By about 800 B.C. people living in what is now Greece had developed a way of life borrowed from the people of Crete. The Greek civilization advanced during the 400s and 300s B.C. with the rise of Athens, Sparta, and other Greek city-states. A **city-state** is a city, plus its surrounding farms and villages, with its own leaders and government.

In Athens, unlike other Greek city-states, citizens took part in government decisions. This idea of civic, or citizen, participation in government grew into the first system of democracy.

In 338 B.C. the Greek city-states came under the control of Macedonia, a kingdom north of Greece. A Macedonian leader, Alexander the Great, went on to build a huge empire, the first great empire that began in Europe. It covered parts of Europe

A Greek vase that shows workers

but mostly Southwest Asia. Because Alexander respected Greek culture, he spread, or diffused, it across his empire.

The Roman Empire was the next important ancient civilization in Western Europe. Its capital city was Rome, in what is now Italy. The Romans built an empire extending from the Iberian Peninsula into Southwest Asia and along the coast of North Africa. Later they added much of the rest of Europe, including Britain.

The Romans united their empire with a vast system of well-constructed roads. They also united it through culture. Latin, the Roman language, was the official language of government and trade. Latin later became the basis for many of the languages now spoken in Europe.

REVIEW What were major contributions of ancient Greece and Rome?

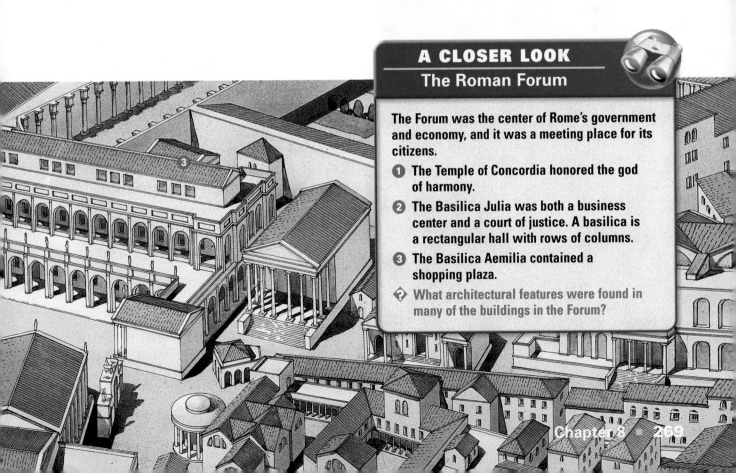

A CLOSER LOOK
The Roman Forum

The Forum was the center of Rome's government and economy, and it was a meeting place for its citizens.

1. The Temple of Concordia honored the god of harmony.
2. The Basilica Julia was both a business center and a court of justice. A basilica is a rectangular hall with rows of columns.
3. The Basilica Aemilia contained a shopping plaza.

❖ What architectural features were found in many of the buildings in the Forum?

The Middle Ages

In the late A.D. 300s and the 400s, powerful tribes from the north and east were a threat to the Roman Empire. Rome could not protect its borders. Disagreements among Roman leaders also threatened unity in the government. As a result of these problems, the Roman Empire began to break apart. By A.D. 500 much of Western Europe was no longer part of any empire.

In time, many of the advances made by the Romans and earlier civilizations disappeared in Western Europe. Art, education, industry, and trade were nearly forgotten. Only Christianity in the form of the Roman Catholic Church held the region together. This period from about 500 to 1500 marks Western Europe's Middle Ages, or the medieval (mee•DEE•vuhl) period.

With no strong government to unite Europe, as the Romans had done, the region broke up into small kingdoms. Each kingdom was ruled by a wealthy landowner. These landowners, or nobles, also ruled the people who worked on their land.

During the Middle Ages farming was the most important economic activity. Towns lost their importance, and people migrated to large farms called manors to live and work. The people did not buy the land, however. They used it and paid for its use with goods and services that they provided to the nobles. The people came to depend on the nobles for protection. This economic system of exchanging land use and protection for goods and services came to be called **manorialism**.

By about the 1300s people in Western Europe began exploring different ways of doing things. Some of these ways came from the past because people began studying the ancient civilizations of Greece and Rome. Other ideas came from other sources. Encounters with the Muslim Empire, for example, had given Europeans the system of Arabic numerals still used in many countries. These developments, sparked by a renewed interest in learning, mark a new period in European history. This period is called the **Renaissance** (REH•nuh•sahns), a French word meaning "rebirth."

The Renaissance began in Italy and spread throughout most of Europe during the 1400s and 1500s. It spread with the help of a German printer named Johannes Gutenberg (GOO•tuhn•berg). In about 1450 he invented a new way to print books that was easier and less costly. As a result, more books were printed and information spread more quickly.

By the 1500s nation-states, such as England, France, the Netherlands, Spain, and Portugal, began to form in Western Europe. A **nation-state** consists of a people with a common culture and a common

Farm workers on a manor

Johannes Gutenberg   c. 1400–1468

Character Trait: Inventiveness

In about 1450 Johannes Gutenberg became the first European to print with movable type. Movable type is a series of letters or numbers made from individual pieces of metal. These metal pieces can be positioned to form rows of words. Movable type made printing books easier and faster. Gutenberg's printing press and movable type changed communication forever. By the end of the 1400s, books had become available to more people. Gutenberg's invention helped begin an age in which even the poorest people had access to information in books.

MULTIMEDIA BIOGRAPHIES
Visit The Learning Site at www.harcourtschool.com/biographies
to learn about other famous people.

government. The rise of nation-states brought an end to manorialism. In its place was a new economic system called mercantilism.

Mercantilism was based on the idea that a nation's power was measured by its wealth. To gain wealth, a nation's exports had to be greater than its imports. For many nations the best way to make this happen was to set up colonies where their goods could be readily sold. From about the 1500s to the 1800s, Western Europe's leading nations set up colonies in Africa, Asia, and the Americas. More trade brought more wealth to Western Europe.

REVIEW How did the Renaissance change the people of Western Europe?

Into Modern Times

In the 1700s the nations of Western Europe competed fiercely for wealth. At the same time, advances in science and technology sparked the beginning of the Industrial Revolution. This was a time when power-driven machinery was first used and new ways of manufacturing were introduced. As a result, factories were built and people began moving from farms to work in cities.

During the Industrial Revolution many nations in Europe set up more colonies. By the 1900s the colonial powers of Western Europe ruled most of Africa and about one-third of Asia. Competition for colonies and wealth led to strong feelings of nationalism.

An iron factory in the 1800s

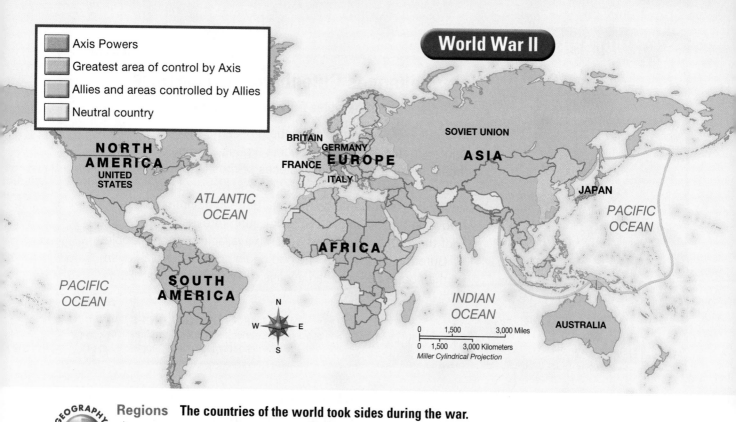

World War II

Axis Powers

Greatest area of control by Axis

Allies and areas controlled by Allies

Neutral country

NORTH AMERICA
UNITED STATES

ATLANTIC OCEAN

PACIFIC OCEAN

SOUTH AMERICA

BRITAIN

FRANCE

GERMANY

EUROPE

ITALY

AFRICA

SOVIET UNION

ASIA

JAPAN

PACIFIC OCEAN

INDIAN OCEAN

AUSTRALIA

N W E S

0   1,500   3,000 Miles
0 1,500 3,000 Kilometers
Miller Cylindrical Projection

GEOGRAPHY THEME

Regions **The countries of the world took sides during the war.**

◈ Which side—the Allies or the Axis—held more of Europe?

National pride in many European countries also led to war.

The Great War, or World War I as it was later known, was fought from 1914 to 1918. Britain, France, Russia, and other nations, including the United States, made up the Allied Powers. They fought the Central Powers. These included Germany, Austria-Hungary, and their allies.

World War I destroyed much of Western Europe. It also caused many economic problems. These troubles helped bring dictators to power in several European nations. In Germany the dictator Adolf Hitler blamed his nation's economic problems on its Jewish citizens. As a result, he took away their property and their rights.

Hitler planned to expand Germany into a great empire.

In 1938 Hitler took control of Austria and part of Czechoslovakia. In 1939 he invaded Poland.

To stop Hitler's conquests, Britain and France declared war on Germany. This war became World War II as more than 40 countries, including the United States, joined the conflict.

Meanwhile, Hitler continued to deal harshly with Germany's Jewish citizens. In 1942 he began a government policy of **genocide**, the mass murder of whole groups of people. Hitler's aim was to kill Jews and other people he found to be undesirable. This genocide during World War II is called the **Holocaust**. The word *holocaust* means "widespread destruction." By the time World War II

A United States soldier during the time of World War II

A window display featuring German dictator Adolf Hitler was used to persuade Austrians to vote for German rule in their country.

ended in 1945, more than 11 million people had been killed in the Holocaust, including 6 million Jews. World War II ended with the defeat of Germany and its allies.

World War II brought an end to Western Europe's world influence. After the war many European nations lost control of almost all their African and Asian colonies.

The war also had destroyed much of Western Europe and weakened its economies. With the help of the United States, however, the nations of Western Europe recovered. By the early 1950s their economies were stronger than before the war.

REVIEW How did World War II affect Western Europe?

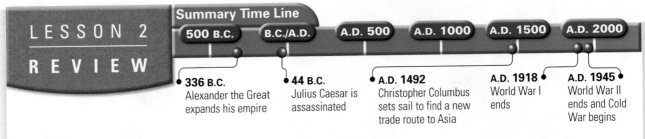

LESSON 2
REVIEW

Summary Time Line

| 500 B.C. | B.C./A.D. | A.D. 500 | A.D. 1000 | A.D. 1500 | A.D. 2000 |

336 B.C.
Alexander the Great expands his empire

44 B.C.
Julius Caesar is assassinated

A.D. 1492
Christopher Columbus sets sail to find a new trade route to Asia

A.D. 1918
World War I ends

A.D. 1945
World War II ends and Cold War begins

1 MAIN IDEA   In what ways are the Middle Ages and the Renaissance connected to each other?

2 WHY IT MATTERS   What are some groups, individuals, and events in the history of Western Europe that influenced present-day societies? Explain your answer.

3 VOCABULARY   Compare the economic systems of **manorialism** and **mercantilism**.

4 TIME LINE   How many years after World War I ended did World War II end?

5 READING SKILL—Identify Cause and Effect   What brought an end to manorialism?

6 HISTORY   Who helped spread the Renaissance throughout Europe?

7 GEOGRAPHY   On what islands were Western Europe's earliest civilizations located?

8 CRITICAL THINKING—Synthesize   How did the colonization of Asia, Africa, and the Americas lead to Europe's economic growth?

PERFORMANCE—Make a Diorama   Work in a group to make a diorama of a manor in the Middle Ages. Find out more about manors, and label the parts of your diorama.

PRIMARY SOURCES

Postage Stamps

The smallest countries in Europe are sometimes called postage stamp countries. They include Andorra, Liechtenstein, Monaco, San Marino, and Vatican City. The name *postage stamp* refers to their tiny size. It also points out that these countries earn much of their incomes from the sale of postage stamps to collectors. Postage stamps can tell you a lot about countries of the world—their histories, their geographies, their governments, their economies, and their cultures.

 FROM THE SMITHSONIAN INSTITUTION NATIONAL POSTAL MUSEUM

A letter carrier in France

HELVETIA 40

MASSICCIO DEL SAN GOTTARDO   EDI HAURI

25,00 MONACO
SLANIA

——— Value ———

——— Picture, portrait, or symbol ———

——— Country ———

A.

B.

E.

Analyze the Primary Source

1 From which European country is each stamp? How can you tell?

2 Which language is used for the first word of Stamp B?

3 What does each stamp show about the country's people, places, or activities?

F.

I.

C.

G.

J.

D.

H.

K.

ACTIVITY

Research and Explain Choose a stamp above. Use a reference source to find out more about the stamp. Write a paragraph explaining what it tells about the country.

RESEARCH

GO ONLINE

Visit The Learning Site at **www.harcourtschool.com/primarysources** to research other postage stamps.

3

Culture Unites and Culture Divides

MAIN IDEA
Read to find out how the cultures in Western Europe are similar to and different from each other.

WHY IT MATTERS
The diversity of the cultures in Western Europe can serve to both unite and divide the people who live there.

VOCABULARY

dialect
accent
bilingual
terrorism
institution
masterpiece

People of many different ethnic groups live close together in Western Europe, one of the smallest world regions. The mix of languages, religions, and ways of life has created a rich cultural mosaic. However, it also has led to conflict, often setting one ethnic group against another.

Land of Many Languages

A traveler in Western Europe today can hear more than 20 different languages. Some might be familiar, such as French or Spanish. Others might not be as familiar. For example, Basque (BASK) is an ancient language spoken in northern Spain.

Most countries have an official language set by the national government. A country's official language is often the language of its largest ethnic group. Some countries have more than one large ethnic group. As a result, there may be more than one official language. Switzerland has three—French, German, and Italian.

A parade in Brussels, Belgium

LOCATE IT

Brussels

BELGIUM

Romansh (roh•MAHNCH), which is spoken by a small number of Swiss people in rural areas, is a semiofficial language of Switzerland. Romansh includes two dialects that are spoken in different areas. A **dialect** is a form of a language and is used only in a certain region or by a certain group of people. Each dialect of a language may have its own words and sayings. However, speakers of different dialects usually understand each other.

In addition to languages and dialects, a traveler in Western Europe might hear a variety of accents. An **accent** is a special way of pronouncing words and phrases that is unique to a region or a group of people. In the United Kingdom, for example, people speak English with a variety of accents. In Scotland many people speak with an accent called a burr. The burr can be heard in words with an *r* sound, as a long or rolled form of the sound.

Many people in Western Europe are **bilingual**. They learn a second language as well as their official language. English is by far the most popular choice of a second language because it is widely used in business. In this way, English is helping to unify people of different cultures.

Language can also divide. In Belgium divisions have long existed between Dutch-speaking Flemings and French-speaking Walloons. In the 1830s a war with the Netherlands required the Flemings and the Walloons to put their differences aside and join forces. This led to the end of Dutch rule and helped make Belgium an independent nation. Despite this cooperation in the past, divisions

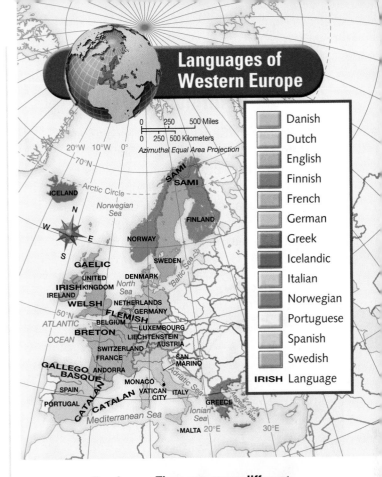

Regions There are many different languages spoken in Western Europe. Some countries have more than one official language.

❓ Which language is spoken in Austria and Switzerland?

based on language continue today. In 1994 Belgium revised its constitution to give more self-government to its various language communities. The largest of these remain the Flemings and the Walloons.

REVIEW Where have languages caused both division and unity in Western Europe?

Religion and Conflict

Western Europe also has many religions. Jewish people have long lived throughout Western Europe.

Each part of this sign is in both Spanish and Basque.

Reformation Day

Protestant Christians usually celebrate Reformation Day on the last Sunday of October. They attend church services to honor Martin Luther and others whose protests against the Roman Catholic Church gave rise to the Protestant Reformation. The Reformation began in Germany with Luther. It then spread to other parts of Europe, including England, Scotland, the Netherlands, and Scandinavia, where hundreds of new Christian churches were founded.

Wittenberg Cathedral, Germany

In recent years many immigrants from Asia have brought Islam and the Hindu religion to the region. Most of the people in Western Europe, however, are Christians. About 70 percent belong to the Roman Catholic Church. The others are members of the Eastern Orthodox and various Protestant Churches.

The Protestant Church began in the 1500s as an attempt by a small group of people to bring reform, or change, to the Roman Catholic Church. Instead, the Protestant Reformation led to the creation of many new Christian churches. The Protestant Church is an important part of life in Western Europe today. Conflict between Catholics and Protestants continues in Northern Ireland.

The dispute between Catholics and Protestants has been one of Northern Ireland's major problems. The problem started in the 1600s, when the first group of Protestants moved to the northern part of Ireland. Ireland was a Catholic country. The Protestants had come from England, which was a Protestant country.

Over the years the Catholics and the Protestants fought often for control of the government of Ireland. Then in 1920 the British Parliament finally divided Ireland into two separate government units. These were Northern Ireland and the Irish Free State, later called the Republic of Ireland. The Protestants accepted the division, but the Catholics did not.

Problems have continued into recent times. Sometimes **terrorism**, or acts of violence to further a cause, has been used in the conflict. Leaders, however, continue to work for peace. As Prime Minister Tony Blair of the United Kingdom said, "We only make progress if people give up violence for good."

REVIEW What past events have caused conflicts in Northern Ireland?

LOCATE IT

Bilbao

SPAIN

North American architect Frank O. Gehry designed the Guggenheim Art Museum in Bilbao, Spain. Many different shapes and materials were used in its construction.

Cities of Western Europe

Western Europe has some of the best-known cities in the world. They include Paris, Rome, and London.

Paris is a center for art, culture, and education in Western Europe. It is also the industrial center of France. Factories in and near the city produce a variety of goods, including automobiles.

Like many cities in Western Europe, Paris is a mix of the old and the new. Churches built during the Middle Ages stand next to modern skyscrapers. The sights of Paris include the Eiffel Tower and sidewalk cafés (ka•FAYZ). Cafés in Paris have become centers of urban life, where people meet to eat and talk.

The city of Rome in Italy dates back to the time of the ancient Roman civilization. Because its history is so long, it is called the Eternal City. The ruins of ancient buildings, such as the Colosseum, stand today as symbols of Rome's past.

Rome also became the center of the Roman Catholic Church. Vatican City, which is headquarters for the Church, is located within the city of Rome. During the Middle Ages and during the Renaissance, when there were few nation-states, the Church was the most

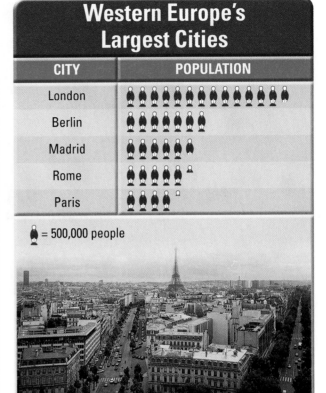

Western Europe's Largest Cities

CITY	POPULATION
London	
Berlin	
Madrid	
Rome	
Paris	

= 500,000 people

Analyze Graphs Three of every four Western Europeans live in cities.

◈ Which city is the largest?

important **institution**, or established organization, in Western Europe. Leaders of the Church, called popes, made Rome a center for art and education as well as religion. Today people come from all over the world to enjoy Rome's **masterpieces**, or great works of art.

The Globe Theater in London was built in 1599 and rebuilt in 1996. Most of Shakespeare's plays were first presented there.

Samuel Johnson, a writer in the 1700s, said of London,

> **When a man is tired of London, he is tired of life; for there is in London all that life can afford.**

London remains a lively city, known for its art galleries, museums, and theaters. It was the capital of Britain's former vast colonial empire and has become a center for international finance. London's bankers, insurance writers, and shippers do business with almost every country in the world.

Cities in Western Europe show influences from other cultures of the past and present. In Cordoba, Spain, for example, the architecture shows the influence of the Muslims who ruled parts of Spain for more than 700 years. Most of Europe's cities, however, are like other modern cities. They have high-rise buildings and public transportation systems that resemble those in the United States. For this reason, some people speak of the "Americanization" of Europe's cities.

REVIEW What are three of the best-known cities in Western Europe?

Western Europe's People

Almost 75 percent of the people in Western Europe live in cities. The movement from rural to urban areas started in the 1700s during the Industrial Revolution. It continues today. The growth of business and industry in many cities has drawn people from Africa, Asia, and other places outside Western Europe.

The number of immigrants began to increase after World War II. In the United Kingdom, for example, many arrived from countries that were once British colonies. They came from Australia, Pakistan, India, and the Caribbean. Immigrants, however, make up only a small part of Western Europe's population.

A sidewalk café in Lisbon, Portugal

Cyclists race in the streets of Florence, Italy.

Immigrants have added cultural diversity to an already diverse population in Western Europe. With more diversity, however, has come more distrust and conflict between different ethnic groups. Many people look for ways to unite. For some, unity can be achieved as people begin to think of themselves less as members of an ethnic group and more as members of a national group, such as British, French, or German. Others have begun to think of themselves simply as Europeans.

REVIEW Where do most people live in Western Europe?

LESSON 3
REVIEW

1 **MAIN IDEA** How are the cultures of the countries in Western Europe similar to each other? How are they different?

2 **WHY IT MATTERS** What links and what separates people of different cultures in Western Europe?

3 **VOCABULARY** Write a sentence about **dialects** in Western Europe.

4 **READING SKILL—Identify Cause and Effect** How did immigration contribute to the conflict between Catholics and Protestants in Northern Ireland?

5 **HISTORY** Which two groups in Belgium put their differences aside to cooperate and form a new country?

6 **CULTURE** Which culture had an influence on the architecture of Cordoba, Spain?

7 **CRITICAL THINKING—Analyze** Why do you think some countries have more than one official language?

PERFORMANCE—Make a Web Make a web with five parts. Label the center circle of your web *The Cultures of Western Europe*. Label the four circles that surround the center *Languages*, *Religions*, *Cultural Attractions*, and *Customs*. Then research the information to fill in your web.

4

MAIN IDEA
Read to find out how cooperation is changing the lives of the people in Western Europe.

WHY IT MATTERS
Western Europe has an important role in the world economy.

VOCABULARY

common market
postwar
euro
specialize
constitutional monarchy

Unity in Europe

For hundreds of years the nations of Western Europe fought over the region's land and resources. They built strong economies only to have them weakened by wars and conflicts. Today many of the governments of Western Europe are working together to improve their economies. Because of this spirit of cooperation, Western Europe is once again an economic leader in the world.

The European Union

After World War II the nations of Western Europe worked together to rebuild their war-torn economies. The first step took place in the early 1950s with the formation of a common market. A **common market** is an economic union of nations. Members of a common market work to make it easier to trade with one another. They do this by eliminating tariffs and other barriers to free trade. They also work to promote the free movement of workers and of investment money—human and capital resources—among the member nations.

The European Parliament, part of the European Union, meets in this building in Strasbourg, France.

LOCATE IT

Strasbourg

FRANCE

This first **postwar**, or after the war, common market in Western Europe was called the European Economic Community (EEC). Six nations belonged to the EEC—Belgium, France, Germany, Italy, Luxembourg, and the Netherlands. Later, the EEC joined together with two other economic groups to form a new group that became known as the European Community (EC). Over time, the EC expanded to include Denmark, Greece, Ireland, Portugal, Spain, and the United Kingdom.

In 1993 the members of the European Community expanded their cooperation. In addition to economic matters, they cooperated in areas such as law and immigration. That year, the European Community also reorganized to form the European Union, or EU. At that time, the union had 12 members. Today, 25 European nations are members of the EU.

The European Union is one of the most important economic units in the world. Together, its member nations have more people than the United States. In addition, the total GDP produced by its members is also greater than the value of goods and services produced by the United States. The United States, however, is the European Union's chief trading partner.

To show their unity, the members of the European Union have a flag. It is a circle of 12 gold stars on a blue background. The stars stand for the first 12 member nations. The European Union also has a currency, called the **euro**, which is used in many of the member nations.

REVIEW How do common markets, such as the European Union, remove trade barriers?

The euro coin (left) and the European Union flag (right) show 12 stars. Each star represents one of the first 12 member nations.

POINTS OF VIEW
The European Union

Should new members be allowed to join the EU?

JOSCHKA FISCHER,
German Foreign Minister

66 Enlargement is in the European interest and not a German project . . . 99

BENITA FERRERO-WALDNER,
Austrian Foreign Minister

66 Austria is the only country surrounded by four candidate countries. . . . We have to protect our employees. 99

GEORGE W. BUSH,
President of the United States

66 I believe the stronger Europe is, the better for America. . . . I believe that the EU ought to expand . . . 99

GIULIO TREMONTI,
Italian Finance Minister

66 If there are no compensations for Mezzogiorno (Italy's poor southern region), then Italy will ask that enlargement eastwards be slowed down. 99

Analyze the Viewpoints

1 What view does each person hold?

2 **Make It Relevant** Learn more about debate over enlargement of the EU. Write a paragraph explaining why new countries should or should not be allowed to join.

Italy is known for its hand-made glass objects (left), and Portugal is known for its painted ceramic tiles (right).

A Region of Strong Economies

Apart from the European Union, the individual economies in Western Europe are as diverse as their cultures. Different industries produce a wide range of goods and services.

The region is rich in natural resources. Germany, for example, has large deposits of coal and iron ore, which are used to make steel. The United Kingdom also has large deposits of coal on land, as well as oil and natural gas off its coast in the North Sea. The fertile soil of France on the Great European Plain supports a large agricultural industry.

Manufacturing is important throughout Western Europe, especially for producing means of transportation. Finland's shipyards build ferries and cruise ships. Germany and France both have large automobile industries. French factories also produce airplanes and high-speed trains. The

French TGV, which stands for *train grande vitesse*, or "very fast train," can travel at more than 200 miles per hour (322 kmph).

As with most developed economies, those in Western Europe have large numbers of service industries. Some countries specialize. For example, Luxembourg and Switzerland specialize in banking and finance. To **specialize** is to work at only one kind of job. These countries can specialize because they can depend on other countries for the goods they need.

Every country in the region benefits from tourism. People from all over the world travel to see Western Europe's many cultural and historical sites. Some smaller countries, such as Monaco, depend on tourism almost entirely for their national incomes.

Although most of Western Europe's industries benefit from free enterprise, some industries have come under government

A Finnish-designed armchair

A train emerges from the Chunnel, or Channel Tunnel. This railroad tunnel lies beneath the English Channel and connects Britain and France.

control. This is particularly true for the transportation services industry. In France, for example, a government agency called the French National Railway runs the French railroad system.

REVIEW Why are the economies of Western Europe considered to be diversified?

Governments

For much of Western Europe's history, monarchs have ruled its nations. Its citizens have had little say in how their governments were run. Then in 1215, the king of England accepted the Magna Carta. This list, or charter, was a first step in protecting the rights of citizens.

DEMOCRATIC VALUES
Constitutional Government

In 1215 a group of English nobles forced King John to sign a contract listing 63 demands. Later, this contract became known as the Magna Carta, or "Great Charter." By signing the Magna Carta, King John promised to follow the same rules that others had to follow. For example, the king could no longer take property without paying for it. To be sure that King John kept his promise, the Magna Carta gave English nobles the right to go to war against the king if he broke the charter's rules. At the time, the Magna Carta mainly protected the rights of nobles. Later, the Magna Carta became the basis for laws in Europe that protected the rights of everyone. Even the Constitution of the United States has its roots in ideas first expressed in the Magna Carta. For example, like the Magna Carta, the United States Constitution gives people the right to trial by jury.

Analyze the Value

1. Why do you think English nobles wanted to limit the power of the king?

2. **Make It Relevant** Think about some of the rights held by American citizens today. How do these rights limit the power of the United States government and protect the freedom of American citizens? How might life in the United States be different if people did not have these rights?

Today most of the nations in Western Europe are democracies. Monarchs, however, are still a part of some governments. Most of these nations do not allow their monarchs much authority. Rather, they are constitutional monarchies. In a **constitutional monarchy**, elected representatives run the government, and the king or queen plays a ceremonial role as leader. That is, the monarch represents the country to other nations. Many monarchs today are also symbols of their nations' histories. Some monarchies, such as the United Kingdom's, can be traced back more than 1,200 years.

Not all monarchs in Western Europe have only ceremonial roles. The monarch of Spain is considered the commander-in-chief of the military. In Belgium, Denmark, Luxembourg, and the Netherlands, the monarch selects the head of the government. The parliament in these countries, however, must approve the choice. In this way, the citizens have a voice in who leads their nation.

Many governments in Western Europe are republics. In nations such as France, Germany, Italy, and Greece, citizens elect their national leader. In Iceland citizens elect their president directly. In Switzerland citizens elect legislators. These legislators elect a council, and the council appoints the president. In Austria citizens elect a president, but the office of president is mainly ceremonial.

Many of the governments in Western Europe provide support to their citizens. Some offer free or low-cost health care and programs to help citizens who are unemployed or retired. In these countries taxes are used to pay for these government services. The more services the government provides, often the higher the tax paid by the citizens.

REVIEW What kinds of governments do most nations in Western Europe have?

The nineteenth-century Royal Palace in Brussels, Belgium, was once the home of the Belgian monarch.

Germany's Government

Executive Branch

President (Head of State)

Chancellor (Head of the Government)

Chancellor's Cabinet

Legislative Branch

Parliament

Bundestag (Lower House)

Bundesrat (Upper House)

Judicial Branch

Federal Constitutional Court

Federal Court of Justice

Federal Courts

State Courts

Local Courts

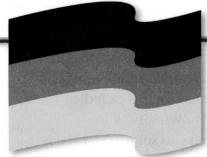

Analyze Diagrams The executive branch of the German government includes both a chancellor and a president. The chancellor is head of the government. The president represents the German people to other countries. Germany's government is similar to Canada's parliamentary democracy. The chancellor is elected by a majority of the Bundestag. German chancellor Gerhard Schroeder (left, in light-colored shirt) is shown riding a bicycle to promote alternate forms of transportation.

How is German government similar to and different from the governments of the United States, Canada, and Mexico?

LESSON 4 REVIEW

1 MAIN IDEA How has cooperation helped the economies of Western Europe?

2 WHY IT MATTERS What are some Western European industries that have had an influence on the world's economy?

3 VOCABULARY Use **common market** and **euro** in a sentence about the European Union (EU).

4 READING SKILL—Identify Cause and Effect Why do citizens in some countries pay high taxes?

5 ECONOMICS How can a common market help a nation's economy?

6 GOVERNMENT How is the role of monarch different in some constitutional monarchies?

7 CRITICAL THINKING—Evaluate Would you vote for or against letting more nations join the EU? Explain your answer.

PERFORMANCE—Make an Outline
Learn more about the Magna Carta at your library and on the Internet. Use the information you find to make an outline of this historic document. Draw illustrations of life in Europe during the 1200s to decorate your outline.

·SKILLS·

Read an Editorial Cartoon

READING

VOCABULARY

editorial cartoon

▶ WHY IT MATTERS

Many cartoons make us laugh, but some cartoons have a serious message to make us think. A cartoon on the editorial page of a newspaper usually presents the artist's point of view about people, current events, or politics. This kind of cartoon is called an **editorial cartoon**. Knowing how to read an editorial cartoon can sometimes help you better understand political and cultural issues.

▶ WHAT YOU NEED TO KNOW

Benjamin Franklin created one of the first editorial cartoons, in 1754. In his

cartoon, Franklin urged the British colonies in North America to unite for protection against the French and the American Indians. Franklin's cartoon shows the colonies as parts of a cut-up snake. The caption *Join, or Die* appears with the cartoon.

By the middle of the 1800s, drawing cartoons had become a popular way for artists to express their ideas and opinions. Honoré Daumier (ah•nuh•RAY dohm•YAY) became a leading cartoonist in France in the years after Napoleon's rule. Daumier often criticized the French government with his cartoons. For example, in the cartoon shown below he

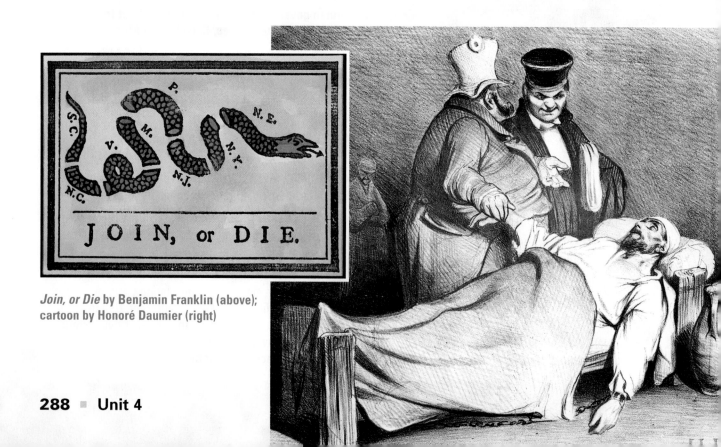

Join, or Die by Benjamin Franklin (above); cartoon by Honoré Daumier (right)

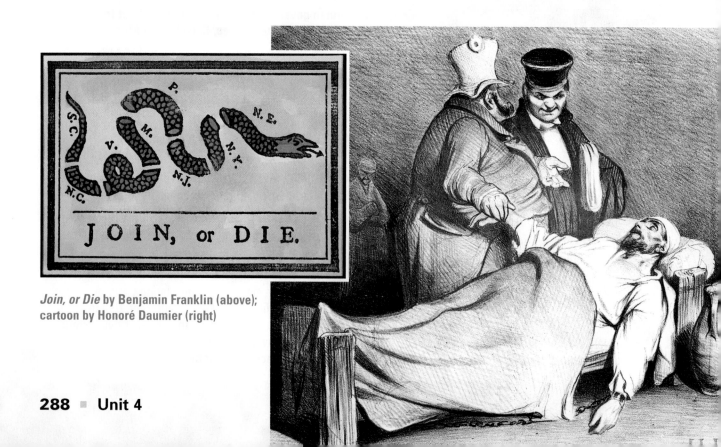

JOIN, or DIE.

attacked the French hospital system. Daumier's cartoon carried a caption that translates as *It's safe to release this one!*

To understand the meaning of an editorial cartoon, you first need to identify its details. Look for a caption or any writing on the drawing that can help you identify the people or the setting.

Many cartoonists use symbols, like Franklin's snake. Symbols often express the artist's ideas or opinions. To understand an editorial cartoon, you will need to identify what the symbols stand for. In Franklin's cartoon, the snake represents the colonies. Franklin believed that the colonies needed to unite to avoid being defeated by the French and their Native American allies. The statement below the cartoon reinforces his opinion.

The way people are drawn in a cartoon can also help you determine the artist's opinion or viewpoint. Daumier drew the hospital officials in a way that shows that he did not like them. As a result, we can tell that Daumier felt the officials did not care about the patient.

▶ PRACTICE THE SKILL

Look at the cartoon on this page. It was drawn recently by an artist who was expressing his opinion about Great Britain. Unlike other European Union countries, Great Britain did not want to adopt the euro as its currency. The circle of stars is a symbol for the European Union. Think about the cartoon's message. Then use the cartoon to answer the following questions.

This editorial cartoon is by Martin Guhl.

❶ What does the *GB* on the ostrich stand for?

❷ Why would the artist represent Great Britain as an ostrich sticking its head in the ground?

❸ How do you think the artist feels about Great Britain's not wanting to use the euro?

▶ APPLY WHAT YOU LEARNED

Choose a current event that you have a strong opinion about. Write a paragraph describing your feelings about it. Then draw your own editorial cartoon that shows your opinion.

Review and Test Preparation

Summary Time Line

500 B.C.   B.C./A.D.

● 338 B.C.
Alexander the Great
expands his empire

● A.D. 400s
Invaders threaten
the Roman Empire

USE YOUR READING SKILLS

Complete this graphic organizer to show that you understand how to identify causes and effects about Western Europe. A copy of this graphic organizer appears on page 79 of the Activity Book.

Cause-and-Effect Relationships in Western Europe

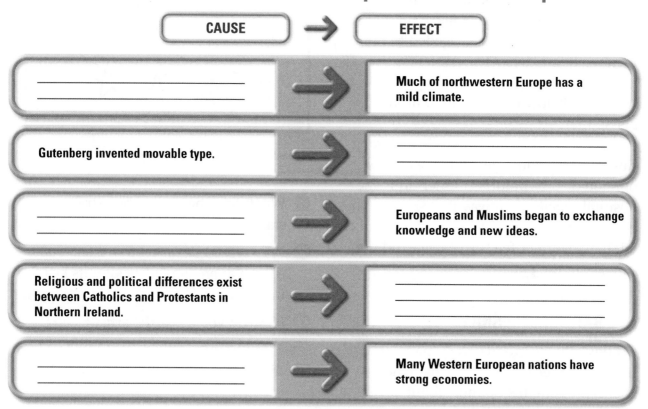

CAUSE → EFFECT

CAUSE		EFFECT
_____ _____	→	Much of northwestern Europe has a mild climate.
Gutenberg invented movable type.	→	_____ _____
_____ _____	→	Europeans and Muslims began to exchange knowledge and new ideas.
Religious and political differences exist between Catholics and Protestants in Northern Ireland.	→	_____ _____ _____
_____ _____	→	Many Western European nations have strong economies.

THINK & WRITE

Write a Travel Journal Think of some places you would like to visit on a trip to Western Europe. Write a travel journal listing each place and the things you might see there. Describe each site in detail and tell why it is important to history and culture in Western Europe. Share your travel journal with your classmates.

Write a Persuasive Letter Imagine that you are a citizen of a Greek city-state. Women are not allowed to take part in Greek democracy. Write a letter to a government leader explaining why women should be allowed to take part in the government. In your letter, also explain why it is important for all citizens to participate.

A.D. 500		A.D. 1000		A.D. 1500		A.D. 2000

A.D. 500
The Roman
Empire declines

A.D. 1400
The Renaissance
begins in Italy

A.D. 1500s
Nation-states formed
in Western Europe

A.D. 1918
World War I ends

A.D. 1945
World War II
ends

USE THE TIME LINE

Use the chapter summary time line to answer these questions.

1 When did the Roman Empire decline?

2 Did nation-states form in Western Europe before or after the start of the Renaissance in Italy?

USE VOCABULARY

Use each term in a sentence that explains both what the term means and how that meaning relates to Western Europe.

bog (p. 262)

city-state (p. 269)

genocide (p. 272)

Holocaust (p. 272)

dialect (p. 277)

RECALL FACTS

Answer these questions.

3 About how many people live in Western Europe?

4 Which emperor spread Greek culture throughout his empire?

5 At which theater were many of Shakespeare's plays first produced?

Write the letter of the best choice.

6 **TEST PREP** Visitors to Western Europe can hear more than 20 different—
 A radio stations.
 B dialects.
 C languages.
 D symphony orchestras.

7 **TEST PREP** In 1938 Hitler took control of—
 F Britain.
 G Austria.
 H Russia.
 J Germany.

THINK CRITICALLY

8 There were many factors that led to the start of World War II, including economic problems. Do you think the war would have started without these problems? Why or why not? What other problems might have led to the war?

9 Do you think that government aid programs in some European countries are worth the cost to taxpayers? Explain.

APPLY SKILLS

Land Use and Products

10 Look at the land use map of Western Europe on page 267. Which parts of the region are used mostly for manufacturing? What areas do you think are probably the most heavily populated? Why?

Read an Editorial Cartoon

11 Find an editorial cartoon in a recent newspaper or magazine. Does it focus on a political, a cultural, or an economic issue? What point was the artist trying to make? Share your cartoon with the class. Do any of your classmates have cartoons that illustrate a different point of view about the same issue?

Bridges span the Vltava River as it weaves its way through the city of Prague, the capital of the Czech Republic. Famous as a cultural center, Prague has been home to many artists, writers, and musicians over the centuries.

LOCATE IT

Prague

CZECH REPUBLIC

Eastern Europe

> **" Prague is . . . a city that exists as vividly in poetry and painting . . . as it does in brick and stone. "**
>
> —Paul Wilson, from *Prague: A Traveler's Literary Companion*, 1995

CHAPTER READING SKILL

Point of View

A person's **point of view** is his or her set of beliefs. Point of view may be influenced by a person's age, gender, culture, religion, and race.

As you read the chapter and the point of view feature on page 311, analyze the different viewpoints.

What the   →   How You
Point of View Is   Know This

SPEAKER	REASON FOR MAKING STATEMENT	POINT OF VIEW	WORDS THAT SIGNAL POINT OF VIEW

Varied Lands and Varied Resources

Today 16 independent countries make up the region of Eastern Europe. It stretches from the Baltic Sea in the north to the Balkan Peninsula in the south. Western Europe lies to the west and Russia to the east. Eastern Europe is made up of four separate subregions. They are Central Europe, the Baltic States, the Western Balkans, and the Eastern Balkans.

Central Europe

The subregion known as Central Europe is made up of Poland, the Czech (CHEK) Republic, Slovakia (sloh•VAH•kee•uh), and Hungary. These countries are in the center of Europe.

Poland is the largest country in Central Europe. North of it lies the Baltic Sea. Thousands of lakes dot the landscape of northern Poland. The Great European Plain covers both northern and central Poland. The Vistula (VIS•chuh•luh) River cuts through central Poland. It brings water to Poland's agricultural areas and provides transportation for Poland's industries.

Family members (inset) harvest grapes in one of the many vineyards (below) in Hungary.

FAST FACT

Seedless grapes cannot be grown from seeds because they produce no seeds to plant. They are grown by cutting and planting a small section of a seedless grape plant.

In southern Poland rolling hills break up the flat land of the Great European Plain. The Carpathian (car•PAY•thee•uhn) Mountains form Poland's southern border. These mountains are home to a variety of wildlife, such as brown bears, wolves, and lynxes, a kind of wildcat.

Most of the people in Poland live in cities. Many people in the cities work in service or manufacturing jobs. Factories in such cities as Lódź (LOOJ) and Katowice (kah•tuh•VEET•suh) make machinery and steel. Poland's capital city, Warsaw, has a large automobile factory. Workers outside the cities of southwestern Poland mine coal. Still, about one-fourth of the economy comes from agriculture.

Like many countries in Eastern Europe, Poland has a pollution problem. It is caused chiefly by burning coal. The air pollution sometimes builds up to levels that are dangerous to people's health.

Bordering Poland to the southwest is the Czech Republic. The economy of the Czech Republic is based mainly on the steel, plastic, machinery, and iron industries. In addition, people in the Czech Republic produce cement, textiles, wood and paper products, and pottery.

Prague, the capital city of the Czech Republic, is a popular stop for visitors. The Czech Republic's natural features are also popular. The Bohemian Forest, the Elbe (EL•buh) River, and the Sudety (SU•deh•tee) Mountains are just a few of the country's natural attractions.

To the southeast the Czech Republic touches Slovakia. The Carpathian and Tatra Mountains form Slovakia's northeastern border with Poland. The Danube River forms part of Slovakia's southern border.

Slovakia has some industries, but agriculture is the largest part of its economy. Slovakians depend on the fertile soil around the Danube River for farming.

Regions Over the years the number of countries in all parts of Eastern Europe has increased.

◈ Which of these countries are on the Baltic Sea?

South of Slovakia is the country of Hungary. Like Slovakia, Hungary has rich farmland. Hungarian farmers grow fruits, vegetables, and peppers for making paprika, a traditional Hungarian spice. Hungary's rivers supply its farmland with water. The largest rivers in Hungary are the Danube and Tisza (TIH•saw). Both rivers flow parallel to each other from north to south, dividing the country into thirds.

Acid Rain

When air pollution caused by burning fossil fuels combines with moisture in the air, it can form an acid. When it falls to the ground, the moisture is called acid rain. It can kill plants and animals and damage buildings. Acid rain can pass from one country to another, even one continent to another. Acid rain is an international problem.

This factory in Poland uses special equipment to fight acid rain.

Hungary also has more than 1,000 lakes and thermal springs. **Thermal springs** are sources of warm water that bubble up from the ground. Tourists travel to Hungary to bathe and relax in the springs to benefit their health. Travelers also go to Budapest (BOO•duh•pest), Hungary's capital city.

REVIEW What industries are important to the Czech Republic?

The Baltic States

Lithuania (lih•thuh•WAY•nee•uh), Latvia, and Estonia border the Baltic Sea. As a result, these three countries are sometimes called the Baltic States. The Baltic States share a low-lying coastal plain and a mild climate. Thick forests cover the interior of the Baltic States. Cows graze on the grass of the coastal plain. The soil is good for growing sugar beets, potatoes, and grain. Farming, forestry, and fishing are important to the economies of the Baltic States.

Lithuania is the largest of the Baltic States. Lithuania is famous for its **amber**, or tree sap that has hardened over thousands of years. Found on the shores of the Baltic Sea, this golden substance is made into jewelry. Lithuania has exported amber to other countries for centuries. Nearly 90 percent of the world's amber comes from Lithuania.

Latvia's forests cover about 40 percent of the land. These forests are home to elk, deer, brown bears, and wolves. The forests are also important to the economy. Latvia sells much of its timber and wood products to other countries.

The country of Estonia is known for its forests, waterways, and wildlife. This small country has more than 1,400 lakes. Ten percent of Estonia's land area is made

LOCATE IT

Budapest
HUNGARY

Danube River

A view of Budapest, Hungary, on the Danube River

The Skocjanske Caves (left) in Slovenia are famous for their unique formations (above).

up of 800 islands in the Baltic Sea. Most of Estonia's income comes from mining **oil shale**, a rock that produces oil when heated.

REVIEW What renewable resource is important to Latvia's economy?

The Western Balkans

The countries on the western part of the Balkan Peninsula are called the Western Balkans. The Balkan Peninsula sits between the Adriatic and Black Seas. The word *Balkan* means "mountain" in Turkish. As the name suggests, these countries are mountainous. Most share the rocky shoreline of the Adriatic Sea.

Slovenia (sloh•VEE•nee•uh) is the north-ernmost country in the Western Balkans. Nearly half of Slovenia is covered with forests. Farmers use most of the remaining land to grow crops. Slovenia's limestone caverns and caves are a dramatic contrast to the country's rugged green landscape.

South and east of Slovenia is Croatia (kroh•AY•shuh). Croatia is curved in shape with a long stretch of land along the Adriatic coast. Travelers moving west through Croatia will notice the Pannonian (puh•NOH•nee•uhn) Plains change into rolling hills. The hills give way to the rocky Dinaric (duh•NAR•ik) Alps.

Triangular in shape, the country of Bosnia (BAHZ•nee•uh) and Herzegovina (hert•suh•goh•VEE•nuh) fits neatly within the curve of Croatia. In the north Bosnia and Herzegovina is made up of forested mountains. The southern part is flat farmland. Along the southwestern border rise the Dinaric Alps.

East of Bosnia and Herzegovina are Serbia and Montenegro (mahn•tuh•NEE•groh).

The city of Dubrovnik, Croatia, on the Adriatic Sea

Monastery from the 1600s

Festival of the Roses

A seaside walkway

Scenic mountains

A European wolf

Serbia and Montenegro were once part of the former country of Yugoslavia. Much of Serbia is flat while Montenegro is mountainous. Along the Adriatic coast of Montenegro is Eastern Europe's only fjord.

Macedonia (ma•suh•DOH•nee•uh) is the only landlocked country in the Western Balkans. It is just south of Montenegro. Macedonia's warm climate is ideal for growing fruit, rice, and cotton. Its landscape is one of rivers, mountains, and forests.

Macedonia's western neighbor is Albania (al•BAY•nee•uh). Albania's inland mountains are not suitable for growing crops. Along the Adriatic coast, however, farmers grow such crops as corn and fruit.

REVIEW From where do the Balkans get their name?

The Eastern Balkans

The Eastern Balkans are clustered around the western shore of the Black Sea. These countries are Romania (ru•MAY•nee•uh), Bulgaria (buhl•GAR•ee•uh), and Moldova (mahl•DOH•vuh). Romania and Bulgaria border the Black Sea. Moldova is inland, but it is just 62 miles (100 km) away from the Black Sea coast.

Rivers define the borders of these countries. The Danube runs along the boundary between Romania and Bulgaria. The Dniester (NEES•tuhr) and Prut (PROOT) form Moldova's eastern and western borders. These waterways also help keep the land fertile and provide transportation.

Located between Europe and Asia, the Black Sea has long been important in the histories, cultures, environments, and economies of the people living in the region.

The smallest country, Moldova, is mostly flat plains and gentle rolling hills. Several rivers run through Moldova, helping to make the country's rich soil. Farmers grow corn, wheat, and vegetables. Factories produce various consumer goods.

REVIEW **What physical features do the countries in the Eastern Balkans share?**

Most of the land in the Eastern Balkans is mountainous. The Carpathians cut across Romania, becoming the Transylvanian Alps. In the southeast the land turns into flat plains. Farmers grow a variety of crops on these plains. Romania is rich in natural resources, such as gold, silver, and **lignite**, a soft brown coal.

Many kinds of wildlife are found all over Romania. In fact, 60 percent of Europe's bears and 40 percent of its wolves live there. More than 250 kinds of birds and 90 kinds of fish live near the mouth of the Danube River. This spot is a major stop for birds migrating from Africa to Asia.

In northern Bulgaria the Danube River creates excellent farmland. The Balkan Mountains run through the center of the country, giving way to rolling lowlands and then rising again. Along the foothills of the Balkan Mountains lies the Valley of the Roses. The fragrant flowers that grow there are harvested for their oil, which is used to make perfume.

LESSON 1 REVIEW

1 **MAIN IDEA** In what ways does the Danube River both unite and divide the countries in Eastern Europe?

2 **WHY IT MATTERS** What kinds of products from Eastern Europe could play an important part in the world's economy?

3 **VOCABULARY** Use the terms **oil shale**, **amber**, and **lignite** to write a paragraph describing Eastern Europe's natural resources.

4 **READING SKILL—Determine Point of View** How might a farmer's view of Poland differ from that of a factory worker?

5 **GEOGRAPHY** What major river runs though much of Eastern Europe?

6 **ECONOMICS** How does the Danube River affect the economies of the countries surrounding it?

7 **CRITICAL THINKING—Evaluate** Burning coal has caused major air pollution in Poland. Why do you think the Polish people continue to burn coal despite the pollution? Explain your answer.

PERFORMANCE—Make a Map Use the information in the text and additional sources to make a three-dimensional relief map of economic activities in Eastern Europe. Be sure to label all of the kinds of industries.

MAIN IDEA
Read to find out how the land in Eastern Europe has been ruled by many different governments throughout history.

WHY IT MATTERS
The political changes in Eastern Europe show how easily peace between countries can be broken.

VOCABULARY

Iron Curtain
collective
satellite nation
buffer zone

Centuries of Change

Imagine living in a country that had several different governments over the last 100, or 50, or even 20 years. Many people in Eastern Europe live in countries that are younger than they are! Recent conflicts in Eastern Europe have caused new countries to form. This is not unusual in these regions. Throughout history the land in Eastern Europe has been invaded and conquered. Borders have been redrawn over and over again. All of this conflict and change has affected the way people live in the region.

Early Settlers and Conquerors

The Romans colonized the Balkans as early as 133 B.C. By A.D. 117 they had conquered many Balkan peoples. The Romans added much of Eastern Europe to their empire.

As time passed, Rome's strength began to fade. In A.D. 395 the Roman Empire split into the Eastern Roman Empire and the Western Roman Empire. The Eastern Roman Empire controlled Greece, the Balkans, and Asia Minor in what is today Turkey. In the A.D. 400s the eastern region of the old Roman Empire became known as the Byzantine (BIH•zuhn•teen) Empire. The Byzantine Empire lasted nearly 1,000 years. A strong army, good government, and a productive economy helped the Byzantine Empire last.

Beginning in the A.D. 400s, migrating groups from Asia traveled to Eastern Europe. These groups included the Huns, the Visigoths (VIH•zuh•gahths), and the Ostrogoths (AHS•truh•gahths). These groups moved through the southern part of Eastern Europe. They sometimes fought with the Romans already living there. Yet they did not stay to settle in the region. Soon a people called the Slavs began to migrate from the Carpathian Mountains. The Slavs settled in what are now

A statue of an ancient warrior in Budapest, Hungary

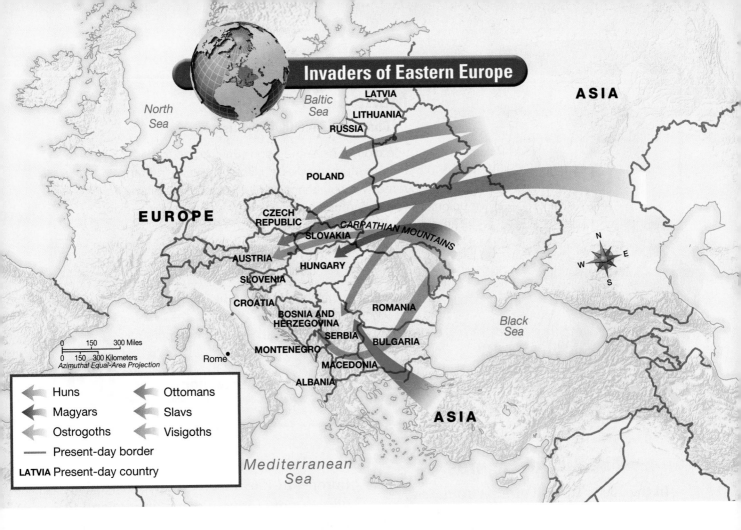

Invaders of Eastern Europe

ASIA

EUROPE

LATVIA
LITHUANIA
RUSSIA
POLAND
CZECH REPUBLIC
SLOVAKIA
CARPATHIAN MOUNTAINS
AUSTRIA
HUNGARY
SLOVENIA
CROATIA
BOSNIA AND HERZEGOVINA
ROMANIA
SERBIA
MONTENEGRO
BULGARIA
MACEDONIA
ALBANIA
ASIA

North Sea
Baltic Sea
Black Sea
Mediterranean Sea
Rome

0 150 300 Miles
0 150 300 Kilometers
Azimuthal Equal-Area Projection

← Huns   ← Ottomans
← Magyars   ← Slavs
← Ostrogoths   ← Visigoths
— Present-day border
LATVIA Present-day country

GEOGRAPHY THEME

Movement   **Several Asian peoples invaded and settled the region.**
❖ Where did the Magyars settle?

Poland, the Czech Republic, Slovakia, and the Western Balkan countries. Slowly, the Slavs moved north and east into the Baltic region and Russia.

The next major invasion of Eastern Europe came at the end of the A.D. 800s. People called the Magyars (MAG•yahrs) traveled from the east through a pass in the Carpathian Mountains into what is now Hungary. Nearly 60,000 Magyars settled on this

Hungarian golden vessel from the A.D. 800s

land. The newcomers forced the Slavs who were already living there to leave.

As new groups moved into Eastern Europe, many peoples fought for control of the land. By A.D. 1100 most of the fighting between groups had calmed down. The Byzantine Empire controlled all of the Balkans. The Magyars held what is now Hungary. The Slavs lived in places all over Eastern Europe. But a new group would soon invade and control the region for hundreds of years to follow.

REVIEW In what areas of Eastern Europe did the Slavs and the Magyars settle?

Marie Curie 1867–1934

Character Trait: Individualism

In Poland, Marie Curie did not have the opportunity to go to college. So, she moved to France to study medicine. While she was in France, Curie discovered two substances that she named radium and polonium. Curie named polonium after her homeland, Poland. The discovery of these substances was one of the most important advances ever made in science. They helped with the development of the X-ray machine and were later used to treat cancer.

Curie won two Nobel Prizes for her work. She was the first woman to win a Nobel Prize and the first person ever to win two Nobel Prizes. She is remembered as one of the greatest scientists in history.

MULTIMEDIA BIOGRAPHIES
Visit The Learning Site at www.harcourtschool.com/biographies
to learn about other famous people.

GO ONLINE

The Rise of Empires

In the 1300s Turkish groups from Asia, the Ottomans, were well on their way to establishing an empire in Asia Minor. First they took land from the Byzantines. Then they expanded into Eastern Europe.

As the Ottomans continued to add to their empire in the south, Poland took control of the northern part of Eastern Europe. In 1569 Poland gained control of what is now Lithuania, making Poland the largest kingdom in Europe. Poland did not remain strong. After the mid-1500s, poor leadership and a weak government led to Poland's decline. In 1772 the countries of Austria, Prussia, and Russia seized parts of Poland's land, dividing it among themselves. By 1795 Austria, Prussia, and Russia controlled all of the land in Poland.

Beginning in 1863 the government of the part of Poland under Russian rule tried to forbid Polish culture. Some of Poland's greatest thinkers lived and worked during this time. One of the best known was Marie Curie. She was born in 1867 in Warsaw and became one of the most important scientists in history. Even through troubling times, Curie's parents taught her to always be proud of her Polish heritage.

The Hapsburg family is one of the most famous families in Eastern Europe. The Hapsburg family (also spelled Habsburg) ruled for nearly 400 years.

When Poland first began to pick up strength, another empire grew in Eastern Europe. In 1526 the Austrian Hapsburg family took over Bohemia, in what is now the western Czech Republic. The Hapsburgs seized Hungary from the Ottomans in the early 1700s. Though the Hungarians rebelled, the Hapsburgs remained in complete control until the late 1800s.

In 1867 Hungary and Austria joined to become Austria-Hungary. Once united, Austria-Hungary ruled over people of many different nationalities, including Slavs and Romanians. By the early 1900s, however, the spirit of nationalism among these groups led to war.

REVIEW What different groups controlled Eastern Europe between the early 1300s and the early 1900s?

War Redraws the Map

In 1908 Austria-Hungary seized Bosnia and Herzegovina. This angered the Serbs who lived there. They thought Bosnia and Herzegovina should be part of Serbia. On June 28, 1914, Archduke Francis Ferdinand, who was to be ruler of Austria-Hungary, arrived in the Bosnian capital of Sarajevo (sar•uh•YAY•voh). As the archduke and Sophie, Duchess of Hohenberg, his wife, rode through the streets in an open car, a young Serbian nationalist shot and killed them. The leaders of Austria-Hungary thought that the Serbian government was to blame for the killing. One month later Austria-Hungary declared war on Serbia.

Soon other countries joined the fight. By early August 1914 most of Europe was at war. By 1917 the war had spread to countries outside Europe, in what became known as World War I. In that same year the United States entered the war and helped bring it to a close in November 1918.

Austrian Archduke Francis Ferdinand and Sophie, his wife, just before their assassination on June 28, 1914

As a result of the war, Austria-Hungary split into two countries again—Austria and Hungary. In addition, the countries of Poland, Finland, Czechoslovakia (cheh•kuh•sloh•VAH•kee•uh), Estonia, Latvia, Lithuania, and Yugoslavia were formed.

Many people were unhappy with the new borders and the way the land was divided. Different ethnic groups each wanted to have their own country, but many people claimed the same land. People who seemed to be closely related but were really very different were grouped together to form one country. Yugoslavia, for example, was formed from the provinces of Slovenia, Croatia, Bosnia and Herzegovina, Serbia, Montenegro, and Macedonia. Though the people in these provinces spoke different languages and practiced different religions, they were forced to be part of the same country.

Following World War I, countries all over Europe faced serious economic problems. Europeans also began taking tremendous pride in their own nation. These factors contributed to the start of World War II.

A World War II poster of British Prime Minister Winston Churchill

In 1938 Germany invaded Czechoslovakia. In 1939 it attacked Poland. Germany wanted to take control of the countries in Eastern Europe. Britain and France sought to stop Germany. They declared war on the country, beginning World War II. At first, it seemed Germany's army could not be beat. Then, in 1941, things began to turn around. The United States and the Soviet Union joined the fight on the side of Britain and France. With the help of the United States and the Soviet Union, the war in Europe ended in 1945. Germany was finally defeated.

REVIEW How did World War I lead to the start of World War II?

The Iron Curtain

After World War II the Soviet Union took control of Eastern Europe and set up communist governments in Poland, Hungary, Czechoslovakia, Bulgaria, Romania, Albania, and Yugoslavia. In 1946 the former British Prime Minister Winston Churchill said that an "iron curtain" had "descended across the continent." The term **Iron Curtain** meant that the countries controlled by the Soviet Union were closed off from contact and trade with countries in the west. Eastern and Western Europe were sharply divided. This happened because the leader of the Soviet Union, Joseph Stalin, did not want people under his control to be influenced by Western political and economic ideas.

Once in control, the Soviet Union quickly built up industries in Eastern Europe. It also converted small farms into **collectives**, in which many people worked together as a group to produce more food. The government owned the land and the machinery. Major cities grew into large industrial regions.

Troops march in the streets of Poland after Germany's invasion of the country in September 1939.

Soviet-controlled countries in Eastern Europe were called satellite nations. A **satellite nation** is one whose economy and government are controlled by another, more powerful country. These satellite nations served as a **buffer zone**, land that separates two or more areas.

One country in Eastern Europe freed itself from Soviet control. Under the leadership of Josip Broz Tito (YOH•sip BRAWZ TEE•toh), Yugoslavia gained its independence from the Soviet Union. Tito ruled Yugoslavia with an iron hand. As a result, the different ethnic groups in Yugoslavia lived together fairly peacefully.

As time went on, people grew tired of communism and Soviet rule. People working to change the government began to weaken the Soviet Union. By the 1980s Eastern Europe was about to change once more.

REVIEW Why did the Soviet Union establish the Iron Curtain?

In 1961 the Soviet-backed communists of East Germany built the Berlin Wall, a symbol of the Iron Curtain.

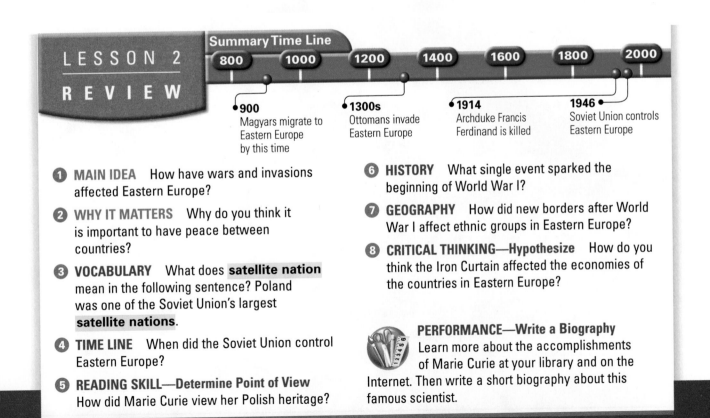

LESSON 2 REVIEW

Summary Time Line

| 800 | 1000 | 1200 | 1400 | 1600 | 1800 | 2000 |

900 Magyars migrate to Eastern Europe by this time

1300s Ottomans invade Eastern Europe

1914 Archduke Francis Ferdinand is killed

1946 Soviet Union controls Eastern Europe

1. **MAIN IDEA** How have wars and invasions affected Eastern Europe?

2. **WHY IT MATTERS** Why do you think it is important to have peace between countries?

3. **VOCABULARY** What does **satellite nation** mean in the following sentence? Poland was one of the Soviet Union's largest **satellite nations**.

4. **TIME LINE** When did the Soviet Union control Eastern Europe?

5. **READING SKILL—Determine Point of View** How did Marie Curie view her Polish heritage?

6. **HISTORY** What single event sparked the beginning of World War I?

7. **GEOGRAPHY** How did new borders after World War I affect ethnic groups in Eastern Europe?

8. **CRITICAL THINKING—Hypothesize** How do you think the Iron Curtain affected the economies of the countries in Eastern Europe?

PERFORMANCE—Write a Biography Learn more about the accomplishments of Marie Curie at your library and on the Internet. Then write a short biography about this famous scientist.

Identify Changing Borders

WHY IT MATTERS

At one time the empire of Austria-Hungary controlled a large part of Eastern Europe. After World War I Austria-Hungary was divided up, changing the borders in Eastern Europe. By comparing maps from different time periods, you can learn how the borders of countries have changed and how different parts of the world looked in the past.

WHAT YOU NEED TO KNOW

Maps of different time periods can be found in historical atlases and history books. The title or map key usually tells which time period is shown on a map. Color is often used to show the lands controlled or claimed by different countries.

Look at the map on this page. It shows Austria-Hungary before the beginning

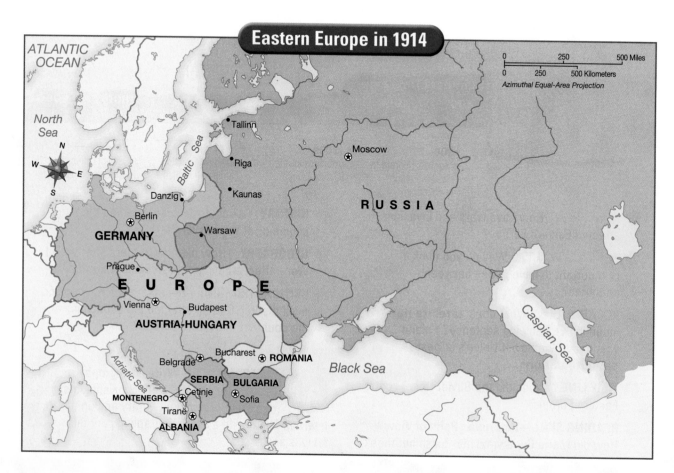

Eastern Europe in 1914

ATLANTIC OCEAN

North Sea

Baltic Sea

Tallinn

Moscow

Riga

Kaunas

Danzig

RUSSIA

Berlin

GERMANY

Warsaw

Prague

E U R O P E

Vienna

Budapest

AUSTRIA-HUNGARY

Caspian Sea

Bucharest · ROMANIA

Belgrade

Black Sea

SERBIA · BULGARIA

Cetinje

MONTENEGRO · Sofia

Tiranë

ALBANIA

Adriatic Sea

0   250   500 Miles
0   250   500 Kilometers
Azimuthal Equal-Area Projection

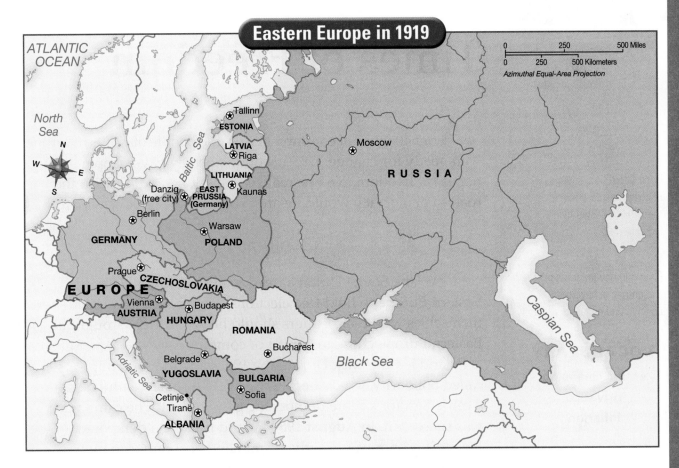

Eastern Europe in 1919

ATLANTIC OCEAN

North Sea

Baltic Sea

Tallinn
ESTONIA

Moscow

LATVIA
Riga

R U S S I A

LITHUANIA
Danzig (free city)
EAST PRUSSIA (Germany)
Kaunas

Berlin

Warsaw

GERMANY

POLAND

Prague
CZECHOSLOVAKIA

E U R O P E

Vienna
AUSTRIA
Budapest

HUNGARY

ROMANIA

Bucharest

Belgrade

Black Sea

Caspian Sea

YUGOSLAVIA

BULGARIA
Sofia

Adriatic Sea

Cetinje
Tiranë

ALBANIA

0   250   500 Miles
0   250   500 Kilometers
Azimuthal Equal-Area Projection

---

of World War I. The pink area on the map shows all the land controlled by the empire in 1914. The lands controlled by countries surrounding the empire are represented by different colors.

Now look at the map on this page. It shows how the same area looked after World War I. Notice that many new countries were formed by the treaties that ended the war.

▶ PRACTICE THE SKILL

Study the maps on these pages to answer the following questions.

1 After World War I, which new countries were formed in Eastern Europe?

2 After World War I, which countries no longer existed?

3 Which new countries were formed completely from land that was once part of Austria-Hungary?

4 Which other countries gained some land that was once part of Austria-Hungary?

▶ APPLY WHAT YOU LEARNED

Use a historical atlas or history book to find maps that show the growth of the United States. Then write a paragraph that describes how and when your state became part of the United States. Draw your own map to illustrate your paragraph. Use different colors to show how the United States looked before and after your state became part of the country. Share your paragraph and map with the class.

Practice your map and globe skills with the **GeoSkills CD-ROM**.

MAIN IDEA
Read about how changes
in governments affected
the lives of people living
in Eastern Europe.

WHY IT MATTERS
Changing governments in
a country can have both
positive and negative effects.

VOCABULARY
ethnic cleansing
privatize
inflation

Times of Freedom

After 40 years of communist rule, the people of Eastern Europe were ready for change. Dreams of democracy gave people new hopes for freedom. No one realized how long and difficult the road to democracy would be after the collapse of Soviet control.

The End of Communism

In 1989 the Soviet Union agreed to allow the countries in Eastern Europe to hold free elections. They could now decide for themselves who their leaders should be. Countries throughout Eastern Europe chose to get rid of communism.

Poland led the way. During the 1980s a workers' group called Solidarity, led by Lech Walesa (LEK vah•LEN•suh), began a campaign for a more democratic government. The campaign was successful. In August 1989 Poland became a democracy. Poland's economy, formerly a command economy run by the government, became a market economy.

Peaceful demonstrations in 1989 brought new freedoms for people in Bulgaria, Hungary, and Czechoslovakia, too. Their communist governments promised changes and peaceful elections. In fact, the changes in Czechoslovakia happened so peacefully that they are often called the "velvet revolution."

Change in Romania did not go as smoothly. President Nicolae Ceaușescu (chow•SHES•koo) ordered the Romanian army to stop

Citizens in Poland (below) and Lithuania (left) show their solidarity, or unity, for independence from communism.

People in the Baltic States showed their unity by holding hands to form a 310-mile (500-km) human chain.

any rebellion against the government. Instead, many soldiers sided with the people. By the end of 1989, Romania was on its way to becoming a democracy, too.

After Yugoslavian leader Tito died in 1980, religious, ethnic, and national differences that had been kept in check now surfaced. The citizens of Yugoslavia wanted to break up the country according to the three main groups living there— Muslims, Serbs, and Croats (KROH•ats).

In 1991 people in the Yugoslavian republics of Slovenia and Croatia voted for independence. Serbs living in Croatia did not want to live under the control of the Croats. They asked the Yugoslavian republic of Serbia for help. Under the leadership of the Serbian president, Slobodan Milosevic (SLAW•boh•duhn mee•LOH•shev•itch), Serbia attacked Croatia in 1991. By 1992 Serbia had taken over about one-third of Croatia's territory.

That same year Bosnia and Herzegovina declared its independence. The Serbs then tried to take a large part of Bosnia and Herzegovina and make it part of Serbia. Milosevic encouraged the Serbs to practice ethnic cleansing in Bosnia and Herzegovina. **Ethnic cleansing** is the forcing out or killing of ethnic minorities. Then Croatia began taking over areas of Bosnia and Herzegovina where many

Croats lived. The United Nations stepped in to bring back peace. In 1995 Serbs, Croats, and Muslims agreed to work for peace in Bosnia and Herzegovina.

In 1997 Milosevic became president of Yugoslavia. Later that year the Yugoslavian province of Kosovo (KAW•suh•voh) began to fight for its independence.

A United States soldier gives money to school-children in Serbia.

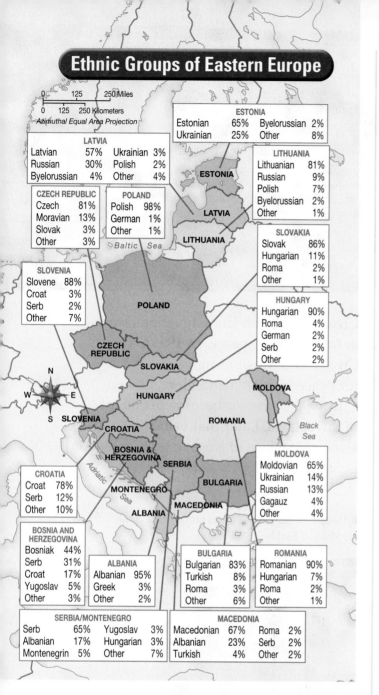

Ethnic Groups of Eastern Europe

0 125 250 Miles
0 125 250 Kilometers
Azimuthal Equal Area Projection

ESTONIA
Estonian	65%	Byelorussian	2%
Ukrainian	25%	Other	8%

LATVIA
Latvian	57%	Ukrainian	3%
Russian	30%	Polish	2%
Byelorussian	4%	Other	4%

LITHUANIA
Lithuanian	81%
Russian	9%
Polish	7%
Byelorussian	2%
Other	1%

CZECH REPUBLIC
Czech	81%
Moravian	13%
Slovak	3%
Other	3%

POLAND
Polish	98%
German	1%
Other	1%

SLOVAKIA
Slovak	86%
Hungarian	11%
Roma	2%
Other	1%

SLOVENIA
Slovene	88%
Croat	3%
Serb	2%
Other	7%

HUNGARY
Hungarian	90%
Roma	4%
German	2%
Serb	2%
Other	2%

CROATIA
Croat	78%
Serb	12%
Other	10%

MOLDOVA
Moldovian	65%
Ukrainian	14%
Russian	13%
Gagauz	4%
Other	4%

ALBANIA
Albanian	95%
Greek	3%
Other	2%

BOSNIA AND HERZEGOVINA
Bosniak	44%
Serb	31%
Croat	17%
Yugoslav	5%
Other	3%

BULGARIA
Bulgarian	83%
Turkish	8%
Roma	3%
Other	6%

ROMANIA
Romanian	90%
Hungarian	7%
Roma	2%
Other	1%

SERBIA/MONTENEGRO
Serb	65%	Yugoslav	3%
Albanian	17%	Hungarian	3%
Montenegrin	5%	Other	7%

MACEDONIA
Macedonian	67%	Roma	2%
Albanian	23%	Serb	2%
Turkish	4%	Other	2%

GEOGRAPHY THEME

Place This map shows the many different ethnic groups living in each country of Eastern Europe. Notice the largest group in each country.

❖ Which ethnic groups are found in the country of Moldova?

About 80 percent of the people living in Kosovo have Albanian ancestors. Milosevic sent in forces to stop the rebellion, killing thousands of people. Under world pressure Milosevic agreed to withdraw his troops from Kosovo. Then, on April 1, 2001, the

United Nations arrested Milosevic for his cruel acts against non-Serbs. Today, people in Kosovo continue to work for freedom.

Problems between ethnic groups were not limited to the Balkans. Czechs and Slovaks living in Czechoslovakia also wanted to break apart. These two groups believed that they were too different from each other to stay together. In 1992 Czechoslovakia divided into the Czech Republic and Slovakia. The division caused some problems. Czechs and Slovaks had agreed to split the country along ethnic lines. By doing this, the Czech Republic gained almost all of the industry and the strongest part of the economy. The Slovaks were left with little but agriculture to support themselves. Still, both sides were happy that the breakup took place peacefully.

Today more Europeans enjoy freedom than ever before. Even so, the peace between the countries of Eastern Europe remains fragile. People throughout these regions hope to rebuild their nations, free from violence, pollution, and economic hardship.

REVIEW How did Tito's death lead to fighting in Yugoslavia?

Forming New Governments

After the fall of communism, countries in Eastern Europe had to form new governments. Some countries chose the same kinds of governments used in other democratic nations. Other countries invented their own kinds of democratic governments.

The Czech Republic, Slovakia, Hungary, Bulgaria, and the Baltic States of Latvia, Lithuania, and Estonia all became parliamentary democracies. In a parliamentary democracy, the people elect the parliament and the parliament elects the president. In contrast, Poland, Romania, Yugoslavia, and Moldova became republics.

Bosnia and Herzegovina created a unique kind of government. After years of fighting, ethnic groups in Bosnia and Herzegovina faced the difficult job of planning a government that was fair to everyone. In 1995 representatives from Bosnia and Herzegovina reached an agreement. They decided the people should elect one Bosniac, one Serb, and one Croat to a four-year presidential term. The person who receives the most votes becomes chairperson of the presidency. Every eight months the job of chairperson goes to one of the other two who were elected. In this way, no one group gains too much power.

In forming traditional or nontraditional democratic governments, the countries in Eastern Europe have faced many challenges. After 40 years of communist rule, changing old systems was more difficult than expected. Change has been slow. Today the countries in Eastern Europe are still struggling to reach their democratic dreams.

REVIEW How did Bosnia and Herzegovina's past conflicts lead to its present government?

People who had been forced to leave their homes in Kosovo wait in line for food.

POINTS OF VIEW
Crisis in Kosovo

In 1999, the North Atlantic Treaty Organization (NATO) began air-strike bombings in Serbia in hopes of ending fighting in Kosovo.

BILL CLINTON, President of the United States

66 If the European community and its American and Canadian allies were to turn away from and therefore reward ethnic cleansing in the Balkans . . . we would be creating a world of trouble for Europe and for the United States in the years ahead. 99

DOUG HOSTETTER, International Secretary of the Fellowship of Reconciliation

66 I can only think of the terrible waste of material and human resources—for NATO, Serbia, and Kosovo. We need to learn to use our brains rather than our substantial brawn when dealing with dictators. 99

Analyze the Viewpoints
1 What viewpoint did each person hold?
2 **Make It Relevant** Write a persuasive essay that gives your opinion on this topic.

Changing Economies

As new democracies took hold in Eastern Europe, many industries were **privatized**. That is, they changed from government control to private ownership. Most of the factories had old equipment and sent harmful pollution into the air, water, and soil.

Even if private citizens wanted to buy old factories, they could not afford them. With no one to take control of the factories, many of them closed. The closings brought about much unemployment.

Another problem facing countries in Eastern Europe was inflation. **Inflation** is a continuing rise in the price of goods and services. With fewer jobs available, the average income of people in Eastern Europe dropped. In addition, fewer goods were produced, and more items had to be imported. This caused the price of goods to increase. Few people could afford to buy even the most basic products.

An automobile factory in Mladá Boleslav, Czech Republic

The countries in Western Europe saw that democracy would not survive in Eastern Europe if this trend continued. They stepped in to help by sending financial aid. In addition, some countries in Western Europe began to import goods from Eastern Europe. With money from exports, Eastern European countries improved their factories, built new roads and railways, and stepped up production.

Investors from other countries have also helped to bring new life to the economies

LOCATE IT

BOSNIA AND HERZEGOVINA

Sarajevo

An employee (left) of the National Library in Sarajevo, Bosnia and Herzegovina, stands among its ruins as a worker (right) plans to rebuild. Nations from all over the world are providing money for reconstruction of this war-torn land.

Source: CIA World Factbook

Analyze Diagrams The value of the money from Romania and Poland (below) has increased since the end of communist influence.

◆ Which country in Eastern Europe has the highest GDP?

of Eastern Europe. The outside companies provide jobs and bring new technology. In turn, the countries in Eastern Europe offer cheap labor, low taxes, and few government rules. Automobile makers, computer companies, and even cellular phone makers have brought their businesses to Eastern Europe.

Today unemployment is still high in Eastern Europe. Even so, the economies there are growing stronger. As several countries in Eastern Europe move to become members in the European Union (EU), they can expect more economic growth in the future.

REVIEW How has Western Europe helped strengthen the economies of Eastern Europe?

Economies of Eastern Europe

COUNTRY	GDP (Gross Domestic product)
Albania	🪙
Bosnia and Herzegovina	🪙
Bulgaria	🪙🪙🪙🪙
Croatia	🪙🪙🪙
Czech Republic	🪙🪙🪙🪙🪙🪙🪙🪙🪙🪙 🪙🪙🪙🪙
Estonia	🪙
Hungary	🪙🪙🪙🪙🪙🪙🪙
Latvia	🪙
Lithuania	🪙🪙
Macedonia	🪙
Moldova	🪙
Poland	🪙🪙🪙🪙🪙🪙🪙🪙🪙🪙 🪙🪙🪙🪙🪙🪙🪙🪙🪙🪙 🪙🪙🪙🪙🪙🪙🪙🪙🪙🪙
Romania	🪙🪙🪙🪙🪙🪙🪙🪙🪙
Slovakia	🪙🪙🪙🪙
Slovenia	🪙🪙🪙
Serbia/Montenegro	🪙🪙🪙

🪙 = 10 billion dollars

LESSON 3 REVIEW

1 MAIN IDEA How do you think the political changes in Eastern Europe affected the lives of the people living there?

2 WHY IT MATTERS What are the positive and negative effects of the change to democracy in Eastern Europe?

3 VOCABULARY Describe some challenges facing attempts to **privatize** the economy in Eastern Europe.

4 READING SKILL—Determine Point of View How did Lech Walesa's view of government for Poland differ from Nicolae Ceauşescu's view of government for Romania?

5 GEOGRAPHY Which two countries were created after the breakup of Czechoslovakia?

6 GOVERNMENT In what way is Bosnia and Herzegovina's government unique?

7 ECONOMICS How do outside investors help the economies of the countries in Eastern Europe?

8 CRITICAL THINKING—Evaluate How do you think the countries in Eastern Europe will change? Explain your answer.

PERFORMANCE—Write a TV News Story Look in your local newspaper, in a magazine, or on the Internet for a news article about Eastern Europe. Then write a one- or two-paragraph TV news story about the article you chose. Read your story to the class.

MAIN IDEA
Read to find out how the people of Eastern Europe have held on to their cultures despite their difficult past.

WHY IT MATTERS
As times change, keeping alive the cultures of their ancestors helps people in Eastern Europe hold on to their own identity.

VOCABULARY
Roma
homogeneous

Folk dancers from Romania perform at a Hungarian festival.

Varied Cultures

The countries in Eastern Europe are located close together, but mountains, valleys, and rivers divide the land. As a result, the region has many different cultures. Over time, wars and invasions have threatened these cultures. Many people in Eastern Europe follow traditions, or ideas that have been handed down from the past. In this way, the different groups have held on to their heritage.

Cultural Heritage

One way Eastern Europeans express their cultures is through art. The most common art form in these regions is folk, or traditional, art. Folk art includes music, dance, visual art, and stories that have been handed down among the common people of a region or country.

Folk music is celebrated at festivals in all parts of Eastern Europe. People at the festivals wear costumes and sing songs that have been taught for generations. In addition, they play a variety of musical instruments. In Moldova, for example, one might listen to the *cobza*. In Latvia one might hear the *kokle*. Both are kinds of stringed instruments.

Painting Easter eggs (below) is a tradition in Poland. Latvian women (right) in traditional dress share their country's music.

Sometimes the people of several different countries join together to share their cultures at one folk festival. In the Baltic States the Baltika folk festival is a time to celebrate the culture of all the Baltic peoples. Each summer thousands of people from Lithuania, Latvia, and Estonia gather to enjoy folk songs and dances.

The music in Eastern Europe is not only folk music. Opera singers, orchestras, and choirs from Eastern Europe perform in countries throughout the world.

Classical composers such as Frédéric Chopin (SHOH•pan), from Poland, and Franz Liszt (LIST), from Hungary, called Eastern Europe home.

Folktales are a large part of Eastern Europe's storytelling heritage. Several famous authors have also come from this region. Elie Wiesel (EH•lee vee•ZEL), born in 1928 in what is now Romania, wrote more than 30 books. One of his most famous books is *Night*. It tells of Wiesel's real-life experiences in a Nazi concentration camp during World War II. On writing about the Holocaust, Wiesel said,

> ❝I decided to devote my life to telling the story because I felt that having survived I owe something to the dead . . . and [because] anyone who does not remember betrays them again.❞

Wiesel received the Nobel Peace Prize in 1986. Other writers from Eastern Europe include Joseph Conrad and Franz Kafka, both of whom lived in the early 1900s.

Visual art in Eastern Europe varies from simple crafts to detailed paintings and pottery. A person who is traveling through Eastern Europe will see handmade objects not made anywhere else in the world.

People in the Baltic States use natural resources to create art. Wood carving is a popular art form there. Carefully carved wooden masks, crosses, and furniture are found in all the Baltic States.

Bohemian glass figure of a tropical fish

Harvesting red peppers is a tradition in Hungary. Paprika is one of the many spice products made from red peppers. Paprika is one of the richest sources of vitamin C found in a plant.

In Slovenia pottery making is one of the oldest and most beloved crafts. Slovenian potters make useful objects as well as artistic ones. In the Czech Republic glassblowers use their great skills to make glass objects. Bohemian glass, made from the fine sand found in the Czech Republic, has been made for hundreds of years. It is some of the finest glass in the world.

In all of Eastern Europe, handmade rugs and traditional costumes are a special kind of visual art. The patterns on these objects show each country's heritage. They have a special meaning to the people who live there.

Another way the people of Eastern Europe celebrate their cultural heritage is by preparing and eating traditional foods. Each country has its own kind of foods. A favorite dish among Hungarians is goulash (GOO•lahsh), a spicy stew made of meat, potatoes, onions, paprika, and sour cream. A Polish dinner may include cheese-filled potato dumplings called pierogi (puh•ROH•gee), followed by jam-filled donuts called paczki (PUHN•shkee). Lamb, pita bread, and rice are popular in the western Balkans, and Bulgarians enjoy a traditional salad called shopska (SHAHP•skuh).

Today visitors can find pizza in Bosnia and Herzegovina and hamburgers in the Czech Republic. However, traditional foods remain an important part of Eastern European culture.

REVIEW What kinds of visual art can be found in Eastern Europe?

Ethnic Identity and Ethnic Conflict

Conflict has been part of Eastern Europe's culture for hundreds of years. The seeds of conflict were planted there centuries ago. In A.D. 1054 the Byzantines made Eastern Orthodox Christianity the main religion in Eastern Europe. In the years that followed, the Ottoman Turks took over more and more of these regions. The Ottomans were Muslims. Many people changed their religion to Islam and became Muslims under Ottoman rule. This made people of the Eastern Orthodox faith angry. Today people with different religious views are still fighting in Eastern Europe.

Religious differences are not the only problem in Eastern Europe. Because the borders have changed so many times, some people identify more with their ethnic group than with their country. People of the same ethnic group want to have their own countries. This has caused conflict among ethnic groups.

One ethnic group living in Eastern Europe does not have its own country at all. The **Romas**, sometimes called Gypsies, have been living in Eastern Europe since the fourteenth century. During World War II, Adolf Hitler tried to get rid of the Romas by putting them in concentration camps. Even today some people discriminate against the Romas. They have tried to force out the Romas, or to make them assimilate into, or adopt, the cultures of their host country. Despite many troubles, the Romas have kept their cultural traditions throughout history. These cultural traditions include their distinct music and the Romany language. The Romas brought this language with them from India a long time ago.

REVIEW What kinds of conflicts in Eastern Europe resulted from historical events?

The Romas maintain their cultural traditions. Here a Roma musical group makes its way to a traditional wedding in Slovakia.

Rebuilding Cultures

The people of Eastern Europe have held on to their heritage despite many difficulties. When the Soviet Union took control of Eastern Europe, the communist government tried to end religious practice. Some churches became factories or warehouses. Valuable pieces of religious art were destroyed. The Soviet government believed that religion kept a country from developing into a modern state. The government also discouraged cultural traditions that might unite people. People who objected to the new ways were punished. Even so, many people refused to give up their religion and forget their heritage.

Since the fall of communism, people have begun to rebuild their cultures.

Countries in Eastern Europe also share their cultures with one another. People from many different countries gather at international folk festivals to celebrate different cultures. They enjoy the dance, music, and food of people from around the world.

One of the largest festivals in Eastern Europe is the Prague Spring International Music Festival. People gather in Prague, the Czech Republic's capital city, each May for three weeks of music. Orchestras, choirs, and singers from around the world perform at the festival. The festival is a celebration of the importance of music as a part of culture.

Sharing cultures helps people of different countries and ethnic groups better understand each other. It can make people's lives richer by giving them a new view of the

LOCATE IT

Prague

CZECH
REPUBLIC

Prague attracts tourists from around the world. Many stop to see the architecture of the city's Old Town Square.

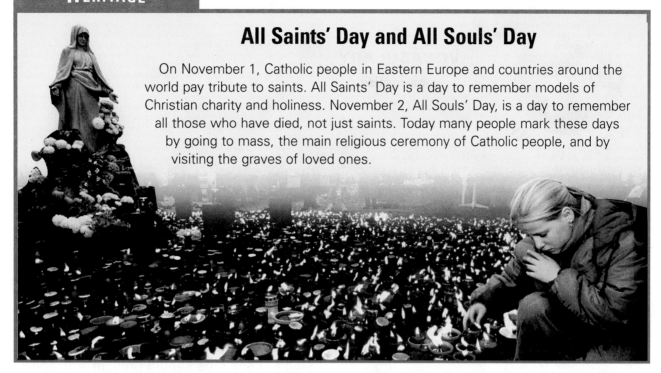

All Saints' Day and All Souls' Day

On November 1, Catholic people in Eastern Europe and countries around the world pay tribute to saints. All Saints' Day is a day to remember models of Christian charity and holiness. November 2, All Souls' Day, is a day to remember all those who have died, not just saints. Today many people mark these days by going to mass, the main religious ceremony of Catholic people, and by visiting the graves of loved ones.

world. Sharing cultures can also cause different groups to become **homogeneous**, or the same.

Today many people in Eastern Europe wear clothing similar to that worn by people in Western Europe and in the United States. Western music and movies are also popular in Eastern Europe. While older generations try to keep Eastern Europe's cultural heritage alive, younger people are developing new cultural traditions.

REVIEW How do people in Eastern Europe share their cultural heritage with others?

LESSON 4
REVIEW

1 MAIN IDEA How do people in Eastern Europe celebrate their rich history?

2 WHY IT MATTERS How might practicing traditions unite people within a country?

3 VOCABULARY Use **homogeneous** in a sentence about culture in Eastern Europe.

4 READING SKILL—Determine Point of View How do many people in Eastern Europe view the Romas?

5 CULTURE What author wrote the book *Night*? What is its subject?

6 CULTURE Why did the Soviets want to put an end to religious practice in Eastern Europe?

7 GEOGRAPHY In what country is the Prague Spring International Music Festival held?

8 CRITICAL THINKING—Synthesize Why do you think people in Eastern Europe tried to preserve their culture during Soviet rule?

9 CRITICAL THINKING—Evaluate Do you think cultural borrowing has had a positive or a negative effect on the cultures of Eastern Europe? Why?

 PERFORMANCE—Write a Song Work with a group of three or four students to write a folk song celebrating the cultures of Eastern Europe. Be sure to include in your song ideas that are important to people in the region.

·SKILLS· Resolve Conflicts

VOCABULARY

compromise

WHY IT MATTERS

People often disagree. Disagreements, or conflicts, are part of everyday life, but there are many ways to handle disagreements with other people. You can walk away and give strong feelings time to fade. You can try to show other people your way of thinking. You can also **compromise**, or give up some of what you want in order to reach an agreement. Knowing how to compromise gives you another way to resolve, or settle, disagreements.

Ethnic conflicts have always been among the most difficult disagreements to resolve. The Roma, Europe's largest minority, continue to suffer prejudice and discrimination. In Eastern Europe the Roma often live in poverty. Many Roma are without jobs because employers refuse to hire them. In addition, Roma often are not allowed in restaurants and nightclubs. Some Eastern European countries are working with Roma organizations to resolve the problems of discrimination by writing new laws and policies.

WHAT YOU NEED TO KNOW

When you disagree with someone, you might use the following steps that can help work out a compromise.

Step 1 Identify what each side wants. If possible, find a common goal.

Step 2 Each side should explain to the other side its wants and needs. Each side should listen carefully and politely to the wants and needs of the other side.

Step 3 Both sides should be prepared to compromise.

Step 4 Each side should present a compromise plan.

Step 5 The two sides should discuss the differences between the plans. The sides should be patient and willing to keep talking until they reach a compromise.

Step 6 Once the compromise has been put into action, it should be evaluated to see whether it resolved the conflict.

PRACTICE THE SKILL

In 1996 several Czech nightclub owners in a Prague neighborhood posted signs on the doors of their clubs. These signs said that Roma were not allowed in the clubs. It was the club owners' opinion that Roma were the cause of fights in their clubs. Many people, especially Roma, were very angry. Tensions in the neighborhood flared, and violence increased. To resolve the conflict, some members of the Roma and the Czech community met. Both sides agreed that they had the same goal—a quiet and peaceful neighborhood.

Workers tear down a wall built to separate Roma from the rest of Usti nad Labem, Czech Republic.

Roma festival in the Czech Republic

Next, the people from the meeting decided to ask the Czech club owners and the leaders of the Roma to meet to try to resolve the conflict. When the club owners finally agreed to a meeting, they suggested a compromise. They would allow no more than 10 Roma at a time in their clubs.

The Roma pointed out that only a few of their people, not the entire Roma community, had been responsible for the fighting.

The leaders of the Roma offered a different compromise. If the Czechs would take the signs down, the Roma would make sure that the people responsible for the trouble would behave.

The Czech club owners agreed, and they took down the signs. Since then, few fights have occurred.

Now reread the paragraphs about the Czechs and the Roma, and answer these questions.

1. What common goal did both the Roma and the Czechs have?
2. What was the compromise plan offered by the Czech club owners?
3. What did the Roma offer to do in their compromise plan?
4. Do you think the compromise resolved the conflict? Explain.

▶ **APPLY WHAT YOU LEARNED**

Think about a disagreement you have heard about in the news. Review the steps for resolving conflicts. Then write a paragraph that suggests two different compromises the people involved could agree upon to settle the problem.

9 Review and Test Preparation

Summary Time Line

800   1000

900
Magyars migrate
to Eastern Europe
by this time

USE YOUR READING SKILLS

Complete this graphic organizer to show that you understand
how to determine point of view about events in
Eastern Europe. A copy of this graphic organizer appears
on page 89 of the Activity Book.

Determine Point of View About the Fighting in Kosovo

SPEAKER	REASON FOR MAKING STATEMENT	POINT OF VIEW	WORDS THAT SIGNAL POINT OF VIEW
Bill Clinton, President of the United States	NATO's involvement in the bombings in Serbia		
Doug Hostetter, International Secretary of the Fellowship of Reconciliation	NATO's involvement in the bombings in Serbia		

THINK & WRITE

Write an Invitation Imagine that you are
helping organize the Baltika folk festival. Write
an invitation to a group of friends, asking them
to attend the festival. In your invitation, include
a schedule of events.

Write a Poem Think about some of the
different cultures you have read about in
this chapter. Then write a poem that celebrates
the different aspects of cultures in Eastern
Europe.

1300s
Ottomans invade
Eastern Europe

1526
The Hapsburgs
come to power

1569
Poland becomes
the largest kingdom
in Europe

1914
Archduke Francis
Ferdinand is killed

1946
Soviet Union controls
Eastern Europe

USE THE TIME LINE

Use the chapter summary time line to answer these questions.

1 Did the Hapsburgs come to power before or after the assassination of Archduke Francis Ferdinand?

2 When did the Magyars migrate to Eastern Europe?

USE VOCABULARY

For each pair of terms, write a sentence or two to explain how they are related.

3 **oil shale** (p. 297), **lignite** (p. 299)

4 **satellite nation** (p. 305), **buffer zone** (p. 305)

5 **ethnic cleansing** (p. 309), **homogeneous** (p. 319)

6 **inflation** (p. 312), **privatize** (p. 312)

RECALL FACTS

Answer these questions.

7 What kinds of jobs attract many people to Poland's cities?

8 What are some natural features that draw visitors to the Czech Republic?

9 To which Eastern European countries does the Danube River bring water and provide transportation?

Write the letter of the best choice.

10 **TEST PREP** An important natural resource in Lithuania is—
  A oil shale.
  B timber.
  C amber.
  D lignite.

11 **TEST PREP** The British leader who used the phrase "iron curtain" to describe the Soviet Union's control of Eastern Europe was—
  F Marie Curie.
  G Winston Churchill.
  H Francis Ferdinand.
  J Slobodan Milosevic.

THINK CRITICALLY

12 Do you think that many of the present-day ethnic problems in Eastern Europe have their roots in past conflicts? Explain.

13 What do you think are some things that will help democracy and freedom survive in Eastern Europe?

APPLY SKILLS

Identify Changing Borders

14 Use the maps on pages 306–307 to compare Eastern Europe before and after World War I. Which countries lost land to the new countries that were formed?

Resolve Conflicts

15 Find an article in a newspaper or magazine that describes a conflict between two groups. First, identify the disagreement. Then, use the steps on page 320 to come up with possible solutions for the disagreement.

RED SQUARE, MOSCOW, RUSSIA

Red Square lies just outside the walls of the Kremlin, Russia's center of government. The square covers about 800,000 square feet (74,320 sq m). The most famous structure in Red Square is St. Basil's Cathedral. With its colorful towers and domes, the cathedral has become a familiar symbol of Russia.

LOCATE IT

RUSSIA

Red Square, Moscow

Russia and the Eurasian Republics

“ Moscow . . . its buildings of pastel hues and white trim . . . appear to be the work of confectioners. **”**

—Warren Hoge on the
funeral of Premier Chernenko, 1985

CHAPTER READING SKILL

Categorize

When you **categorize,** you group people, places, events, or ideas that have something in common.

As you read this chapter, categorize people, places, events, or ideas from the chapter.

Similar Ideas → Category

IDEA

IDEA — CATEGORY — IDEA

IDEA   IDEA

Landforms and Climates

MAIN IDEA

Read to find out how different life can be in each region of Russia and the Eurasian republics.

WHY IT MATTERS

Even though people in Russia and the Eurasian republics live in the same world region, they live in a variety of environments.

VOCABULARY

permafrost
taiga
steppe
chromium

Imagine one country so large that it could almost cover the surface of the moon. Not long ago Russia and the Eurasian republics made up just such a country. This huge country was the Union of Soviet Socialist Republics, or the Soviet Union. The Soviet Union was so big that people in the west were getting up in the morning when people in the east were going to bed at night. In 1991 the Soviet Union broke apart to form 15 independent countries. Today 12 of these countries form a loose alliance called the Commonwealth of Independent States, or CIS.

The Land of Russia

The largest country in the CIS is Russia. Covering more than 6.5 million square miles (17 million sq km) and large parts of two continents, Russia is also the largest country in the world. Russia has more than 10 percent of all the land on Earth. This enormous country can be divided into five land regions—the Great European Plain, the Ural Mountains, the West Siberian Plain, the Central Siberian Plateau, and the East Siberian Uplands.

The Great European Plain covers much of Russia's land in Europe. This is the country's heartland where most Russians live. Russia's largest cities—Moscow and St. Petersburg—are there.

Travelers on a trail through the Russian steppe near the southern border of Russia

Russia and the Eurasian Republics

Regions **Twelve independent countries make up the CIS.**

Which country is second-largest in size?

East of the plain are the Ural Mountains. They form the traditional boundary between the European and Asian parts of Russia. The Urals run north and south from the Arctic Ocean to Kazakhstan (kuh•zahk•STAHN). The peaks of the Urals are rounded and worn. Their average elevation is only about 2,000 feet (610 m).

East of the Urals is the vast West Siberian Plain. It is the largest level region in the world. This huge, marshy plain covers more than 1 million square miles (2.6 million sq km), but it rises no higher than 500 feet (150 m) above sea level.

To the east of the lowland, the Central Siberian Plateau and the mountainous East Siberian Uplands rise to higher elevations. Many peaks are more than 10,000 feet (3,000 m) high. About 25 active volcanoes are on the Pacific coast.

FAST FACT The Siberian tiger lives in eastern Russia as well as in northern China. A large tiger can measure up to 10 feet (3 m) in length and weigh more than 700 pounds (320 kg). Siberian tigers are endangered animals.

327

As Russia's landforms vary from west to east, its climate varies from north to south. Northernmost Russia is mostly tundra with short summers and long, cold winters. Much of the tundra is treeless with permanently frozen soil called **permafrost**.

A belt of forest lies south of the tundra. The northern part of this belt is called the **taiga**. It is made up of coniferous trees, such as cedar, pine, and spruce.

South of the taiga is a grassland known as the **steppe**. Russia's best soils are located there, and it is the center of the country's farming. South of the steppe is an arid zone, where soil varies in richness by elevation.

REVIEW What regions make up the vast area of Russia east of the Urals?

Marshlands make up most of southern Belarus. The marshes shown here are near the city of Pinsk.

Ukraine and Belarus

About the size of Texas, Ukraine (yoo•KRAYN) covers more than 233,000 square miles (603,000 sq km). Ukraine has mostly level to gently rolling land, filled with steppes. Ukraine's steppes are part of a large plain that spreads from southern Ukraine into central Asia. While some of the plains in central Asia are dry, those in Ukraine are covered with a dark, rich soil.

Ukraine also has plenty of fresh water. Many rivers and streams flow through it. The Soviet Union allowed Ukraine's rivers to become badly polluted. This condition remains a problem today.

The Black Sea also has pollution problems. Almost all of the 26 kinds of fish once found there have died out. According to Dr. Lawrence Mee, a scientist who works to solve environmental problems that occur in the ocean,

66 If the habitats of these species can be protected and further damage avoided, the sea may slowly recover from the bottom up . . . if we act now. 99

· **GEOGRAPHY** ·

Chernobyl

Understanding Environment and Society

On April 26, 1986, an explosion at a nuclear power plant in Chernobyl (chuhr•NOH•buhl), Ukraine, became the worst nuclear accident in history. Tons of radioactive materials blew into the air. Strong winds carried these materials across Ukraine and Belarus, poisoning their environments. More than 15,000 people died as a result of the accident.

CHERNOBYL
Kiev
Kharkiv
Dnieper R.
Donets R.
UKRAINE
Carpathian Mts.
Dnipropetrovs'k
Donetsk
Sea of Azov
Crimean Peninsula
Black Sea

0   100   200 Miles
0 100 200 Kilometers

N W E S

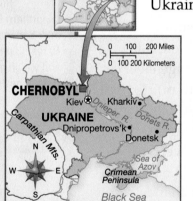

Today people from Ukraine are working to clean up the Black Sea and restore its marine life.

To the north of Ukraine is Belarus (bee•luh•ROOS). Like Ukraine, Belarus has plenty of water. Belarus's streams, rivers, and lakes are an important natural resource. The people of Belarus use the rivers to produce hydroelectric power.

Nearly one-third of Belarus is covered with forests. Several forests are nature preserves, where plants and animals are protected. More than 10,000 different kinds of animals and plants can be found in Belarus's forests.

REVIEW What important natural resource is plentiful in both Ukraine and Belarus?

The Caucasus Region

The high, snow-covered Caucasus (KAW•kuh•suhs) Mountains cut across 700 miles (1,100 km) of land between the Black and Caspian Seas. These mountains include Mount Elbrus, the highest point in Europe, at 18,510 feet (5,642 m). This region of the former Soviet Union includes the countries of Georgia, Azerbaijan (a•zuhr•by•JAHN), Armenia, and part of southern Russia.

The Caucasus Mountains cover northern and eastern Georgia. Many of Georgia's rivers begin in the Caucasus and provide hydroelectric power for the country. Near the Black Sea, mountains give way to flat land. Warm, moist air blowing off the Black Sea brings rain and warmth to Georgia's lowlands. Crops that cannot grow in colder places thrive in Georgia. Georgia's two most important crops are tea and citrus fruits.

The Caucasus Mountains extend into Armenia and Azerbaijan. Armenia is a land of rugged mountains and dormant volcanoes. Three features mark Azerbaijan's landscape—the Caucasus Mountains to the north, a wide lowland in the country's center, and the Caspian Sea in the east. Along the shores of the Caspian Sea, workers drill for oil.

Mount Elbrus in the Caucasus Mountains is an extinct volcano.

Azerbaijan is also rich in natural gas. People in Azerbaijan call their country the "land of fire." Early visitors to this land saw bursts of fire caused by natural gas coming from the ground. Many people believe that upon seeing this, the visitors gave Azerbaijan this name.

REVIEW What causes Georgia's land to be better for farming than land in many other places in the former Soviet Union?

Dry mountain ranges in Kyrgyzstan

Desert Countries

Across the Caspian from Azerbaijan are Kazakhstan, Turkmenistan, Uzbekistan (uz•beh•kih•STAHN), Tajikistan (tah•jih•kih•STAHN), and Kyrgyzstan (kir•gi•STAHN). These countries have more in common with each other than they do with the rest of the Commonwealth of Independent States. Many CIS countries have large areas of fertile plain ideal for farming. In sharp contrast, Turkmenistan, Uzbekistan, Tajikistan, and Kyrgyzstan are covered mostly with deserts and mountains.

Kazakhstan, however, is different. Half the size of the United States, it is the second-largest country in the CIS. Only eight countries in the world have more land.

Kazakhstan's climate is harsh, with cold winters and extremely hot summers. Scarce rainfall leaves little grassland for grazing. Because of the climate, few people made permanent homes in Kazakhstan. For thousands of years, nomadic groups traveled through the land, moving in search of scarce vegetation. The country's rich natural resources remained untouched.

Today most of Kazakhstan's natural resources have been put to use. In addition to its oil, Kazakhstan has the world's largest chromium (KROH•mee•uhm) mine. **Chromium** is a hard metal that does not rust easily. It is used to make objects such as car bumpers. Kazakhstan also has one of the world's largest deposits of gold.

Kazakhstan also faces a special environmental problem. It is the destruction of the

LOCATE IT

Aral Sea

KAZAKHSTAN

UZBEKISTAN

Aral Sea. This shallow sea is located on the border between Kazakhstan and Uzbekistan. The Aral Sea was once the world's fourth-largest inland body of water. Changes in the direction of the Syr Darya (SIR DAHR•yuh) and Amu (AH•moo) Darya Rivers caused much of the Aral Sea to dry up. Engineers drained water from these rivers to irrigate nearby farmland. At one time, the two rivers emptied into the Aral Sea. Because it no longer received water from the rivers, more than 60 percent of the Aral Sea dried up. Today ships sit in the middle of what appears to be a desert. This desert shipyard is actually the dry part of the Aral Sea's floor. The once-healthy fishing industry of this region is now out of business.

REVIEW What kinds of environmental problems do the desert countries of the CIS face?

Abandoned ships are common along the Kazakhstan-Uzbekistan border. A desert formed after the Aral Sea lost more than half its water from drought and from overuse because of irrigation needs.

Above, children play in an ancient city in Uzbekistan. The desert country of Uzbekistan is now part of the Commonwealth of Independent States, or CIS.

LESSON 1 REVIEW

1. **MAIN IDEA** How is the Great European Plain different from Siberia?

2. **WHY IT MATTERS** How might life on the plain differ from life in Siberia?

3. **VOCABULARY** Describe a **steppe**.

4. **READING SKILL—Categorize** The countries of Russia and the Eurasian republics are divided into five land regions. Make a chart listing each of the countries in the proper regional category.

5. **GEOGRAPHY** In what ways do the Ural Mountains differ from the Caucasus Mountains?

6. **CRITICAL THINKING—Analyze** What effect might changing the direction of rivers have on a country?

PERFORMANCE—Write a Travelogue Imagine you are traveling from east to west through the Commonwealth of Independent States. Write a travelogue of your experiences in at least five countries there. Be sure to describe the natural features and climate in each country you visit.

Read a Climograph

VOCABULARY

climograph

▶ WHY IT MATTERS

Moscow, the capital of Russia, is farther north than most other major cities of the world. As a result, the climate there is much different than in cities farther south. One way to learn about the climate of a place is to study a climograph. A **climograph** is a kind of graph that shows the average monthly temperature and precipitation for a place. Knowing about the climate of a place can help you understand more about that place and its people.

A cold, snowy day in Moscow, Russia

▶ WHAT YOU NEED TO KNOW

A climograph is a combination of a line graph and a bar graph. Along the bottom of a climograph are the months of the year.

The line graph part of a climograph shows temperatures. Along the left-hand side is a temperature scale. A dot is used to show the average temperature for each month, and all the dots are connected with a line. By studying the line, you can see which months are warmest and which are coolest.

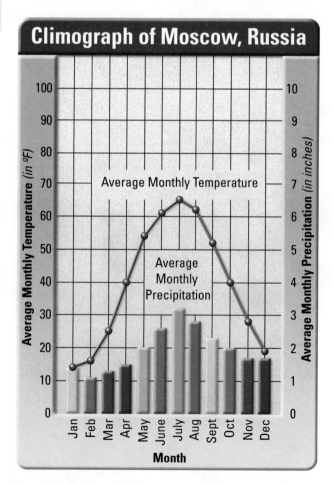

Climograph of Moscow, Russia

Average Monthly Temperature (in °F)

Average Monthly Precipitation (in inches)

Average Monthly Temperature

Average Monthly Precipitation

Jan Feb Mar Apr May June July Aug Sept Oct Nov Dec

Month

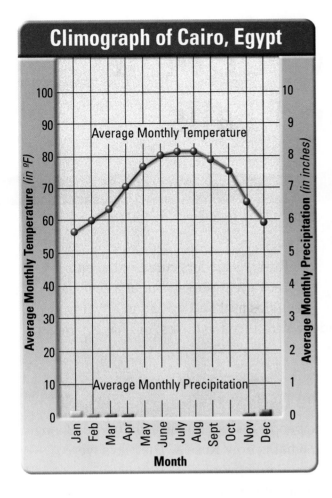

Climograph of Cairo, Egypt

Average Monthly Temperature (in °F)

Average Monthly Precipitation (in inches)

Average Monthly Temperature

Average Monthly Precipitation

Jan Feb Mar Apr May June July Aug Sept Oct Nov Dec

Month

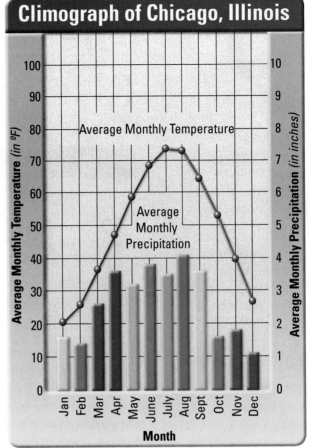

Climograph of Chicago, Illinois

Average Monthly Temperature (in °F)

Average Monthly Precipitation (in inches)

Average Monthly Temperature

Average Monthly Precipitation

Jan Feb Mar Apr May June July Aug Sept Oct Nov Dec

Month

The bar graph part of the climograph shows precipitation. Along the right-hand side is a precipitation scale. A bar is drawn up to the average amount of precipitation for each month. By studying the heights of the bars, you can see which months are drier and which months have more rain or snow.

▶ PRACTICE THE SKILL

The climographs on these pages show weather averages for Moscow, in Russia; Cairo, in Egypt; and Chicago, Illinois, in the United States. Study the climographs. Then use them to answer these questions.

1 Which are the warmest and coolest months in Moscow? in Cairo? in Chicago?

2 Which are the wettest and driest months in Moscow? in Cairo? In Chicago?

3 Which city has the lowest average temperature in January? Which city has the highest average temperature in August?

4 Which city has the most precipitation in January? Which city has the most precipitation in July?

▶ APPLY WHAT YOU LEARNED

Use an almanac to create a climograph for your city or a city near you. Compare your climograph with those for Moscow, Cairo, and Chicago. Share your climograph with a classmate or a family member. What does the climograph tell you about the area where you live?

CHART AND GRAPH SKILLS

MAIN IDEA
Read to find out how changes in Russia and the Soviet Union had both positive and negative effects.

WHY IT MATTERS
Forcing people to change without allowing them to take part in the process can sometimes have a harmful effect.

VOCABULARY

reform

czar

abdicate

totalitarian

purge

Cold War

perestroika

glasnost

LOCATE IT

RUSSIA

Novgorod

The Soviet Union Rises and Falls

| B.C./A.D. | 500 | 1000 | 1500 | 2000 |

For hundreds of years Russia's leaders ruled with complete authority. They brought Russia great power, but at a cost. The people suffered many hardships and had no say in government. By the 1900s new leaders introduced **reforms**, or changes meant to make things better.

The Early Russians

In the A.D. 400s Slavic people settled in Eastern Europe. Soon, they made their way to what is now Russia. The Slavs were farmers, cattle herders, and craftspeople. They built towns and settlements along the Dnieper River and throughout the land.

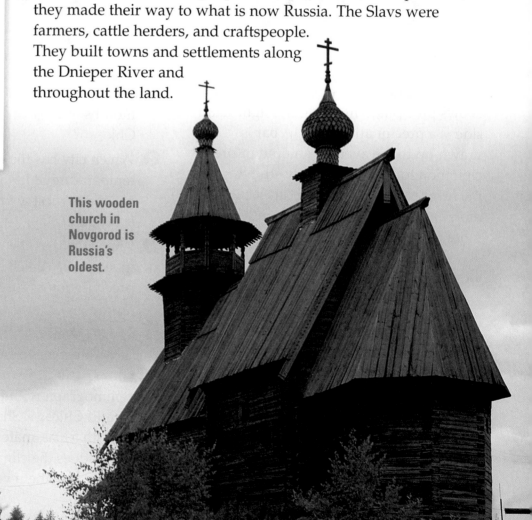

This wooden church in Novgorod is Russia's oldest.

Catherine the Great   1729–1796

Character Trait: Responsibility

Educating people was important to Catherine the Great. During Catherine's time most people in Russia had never been to school. To change this, Catherine built schools in every Russian town. These schools offered free education for the boys and girls of Russia's noble class. In time, there were more than 300 schools and 20,000 students in Russia. Catherine set up a college where teachers received training. She formed a committee to make sure that these advances in education were carried out all across Russia.

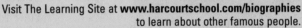

MULTIMEDIA BIOGRAPHIES
Visit The Learning Site at www.harcourtschool.com/biographies
to learn about other famous people.

One of these settlements, Novgorod (NAHV•guh•rahd), was a trading center. Novgorod is near what is today the Russian city of St. Petersburg. German and Scandinavian merchants traveled there to trade goods with the Slavs.

In A.D. 862 a Viking named Rurik led an invasion of Novgorod. The Vikings were sailors and warriors from Scandinavia. Rurik established the kingdom of Kievan Rus (KEE•ef•uhn ROOS). The city of Kiev later became its capital.

In 1222 the Mongols invaded Kievan Rus. These warriors conquered and took control of Kievan Rus. The Mongols ruled Kievan Rus for the next 200 years, until 1480. In that year a Slav prince named Ivan III won control of Kievan Rus. Ivan, sometimes called Ivan the Great, was the first true leader of Russia. Ivan's grandson, Prince Ivan IV, later became the first czar of Russia. **Czar** (ZAHR) is the Russian word for *Caesar*, or ruler. A series of czars ruled Russia for many years.

REVIEW Who was Russia's first czar?

The Czars and the Revolution

During the early 1600s Russia suffered from political and economic problems. Few leaders held power for long. Russia also faced invasion and civil war. This hard period, called the Time of Troubles, slowed Russia's growth. By the end of the 1600s, Western Europe was becoming a modern society. Meanwhile, Russia had changed little since the Middle Ages.

A new leader, Peter the Great, became czar in the late 1600s. His primary goal was to modernize Russia. Peter introduced European ideas, art, and architecture into Russian culture. He built schools, libraries, museums, and factories. Peter also expanded Russia's borders. Now the Russian people had access to new trade routes. Russians began trading goods with other countries.

Peter's grandson, Peter III, later became the leader of Russia. Peter III was a poor ruler. Many people wanted to get rid of him. He was assassinated, and Catherine, his wife, became the new leader of Russia.

This photograph taken in the early 1900s shows the last Russian czar, Nicholas II (second from left), with his family.

As ruler she became known as Catherine the Great.

Catherine encouraged Russians to work in industries, instead of farming. She also supported education and the arts. Catherine wanted Russians to receive proper health care. She was the first person in Russia to get a smallpox vaccination.

By the end of Catherine's rule, however, most Russians had seen little change. The czars and the nobles had all of Russia's wealth and power. The serfs lived little better than slaves did. The coming century brought an end to the rule of the czars.

Vladimir Lenin helped control the revolution by controlling what people read in the Russian newspapers.

The last czar, named Nicholas II, came to power in 1894. In January 1905 thousands of angry people gathered at the czar's Winter Palace. They asked Nicholas to improve their living conditions. Soldiers surrounding the palace fired at the crowd, killing or wounding hundreds of people. This day became known as Bloody Sunday.

In response to the killings, the Russian people went on strike. They refused to work until their demands were met. Nicholas gave in to a few of the people's demands. The government adopted a constitution. It also formed a lawmaking body called the Duma (DOO•muh). Still, Nicholas had total control over the Duma and over Russia. Some Russians started to think about a whole new kind of government.

Soon political parties were formed. One of these political parties was called the Bolsheviks (BOHL•shuh•viks). The leader of the Bolsheviks was Vladimir Ilyich Lenin (VLAH•duh•meer EEL•yich LEH•nuhn). The Bolsheviks wanted to establish a communist system of government. Lenin believed only a violent revolution would change the government. In early 1917 the Russian Revolution began. On March 2, 1917, the Bolsheviks forced Czar Nicholas II to **abdicate** (AB•dih•kate), or give up, his control of the Russian government. In July 1918 Lenin ordered Nicholas II and his family put to death. After 300 years, the rule of the czars ended.

REVIEW What kinds of changes did Catherine the Great bring to Russia?

The Soviet Union

In 1922 the Bolsheviks formed the Union of Soviet Socialist Republics. The Soviet Union stretched from the Baltic and Black Seas in the west to the Pacific Ocean in the east. Eventually, it ruled 15 republics. The largest of them was Russia.

Posters

Analyze Primary Sources

Posters such as these were used in the Soviet Union to convey political messages.

1 The poster on the left urges Soviet citizens to teach their children by using government-published textbooks.

2 The poster on the right honors the seventh anniversary of the Russian Revolution in 1924.

❖ Without knowing the Russian language, how can you tell the message of each poster?

When Lenin died in 1924, Joseph Stalin became the new leader of the Soviet Union. Stalin was a fierce totalitarian dictator. A **totalitarian** (toh•ta•luh•TER•ee•uhn) leader is someone who has complete control over a country and its people.

Stalin set up collectives in Russia. He ordered people to give up their land to the government. Those who refused were killed. Soon Stalin controlled everyone in the Soviet Union. The people could not protest, for fear of losing their lives.

Stalin ordered his agents to get rid of, or **purge**, the people that he saw as a threat to communism. Millions of Soviet citizens died under Stalin's rule.

Shortly before World War II, the Soviet Union formed an alliance with Nazi Germany. Stalin and Hitler agreed to divide Poland between them. Then Hitler went against the agreement, and his army invaded Russia. Stalin decided to join the Allied Powers in the fight against Hitler. However, before the end of the war, the Soviets and their allies began to disagree.

The other Allied Powers did not want the Soviet Union to spread communism.

When World War II ended, the Soviet Union took control of Eastern Europe. Stalin did not let these countries rule themselves. He put communist governments in control that obeyed him. Several of these countries tried to rebel. In each case Stalin ordered his army to stop those who fought for independence.

REVIEW Why did Stalin order his agents to purge his opponents?

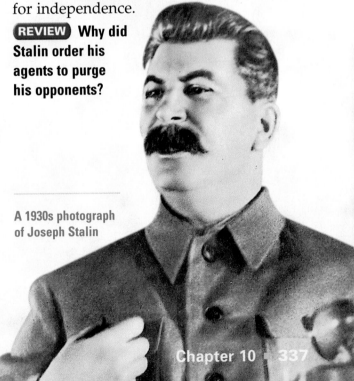

A 1930s photograph of Joseph Stalin

The Fall of the Soviet Union

Mikhail Gorbachev

Leaders who came after Stalin tried to extend communism beyond Eastern Europe. As a result of the United States and other countries working to stop communism from spreading, a new kind of war began. This time it was a war of words and ideas between the Soviet Union and the United States and its allies. This war came to be known as the **Cold War**.

Each side feared being attacked by the other. They built large supplies of dangerous weapons. The Soviet Union spent about one-third of its country's GDP on the military. Precious natural resources had to be sold to pay for food and other necessities. Even so, these remained in short supply.

By the late 1970s the Soviet Union was in trouble. Heavy military spending, failed reforms, and years of low pay for workers finally brought the Soviet economy to a standstill. The communist system was failing. Once again, the Soviet people wanted change.

In 1985 Mikhail Gorbachev (mee•KAH•eel GAWR•buh•chawf) became the leader of the Soviet Union. Gorbachev introduced some democratic principles in the Soviet Union. Still, he kept communism in place. Gorbachev announced two new reforms, called *perestroika* (per•uh•STROY•kuh) and *glasnost* (GLAZ•nohst). Gorbachev described these reforms as

> 66 **a thorough renewal of every aspect of Soviet life.** 99

Perestroika was a process of rebuilding government and economic systems. It allowed many farmers and factory managers the freedom to make their own business decisions. **Glasnost**, or openness, gave Soviet citizens the freedom to speak out without fear of being punished.

Boris Yeltsin speaks from a tank (below). Statues of former leaders are toppled (bottom).

Meanwhile, communist countries in Eastern Europe also wanted more freedom. Gorbachev realized that the Soviet Union could no longer control these countries. Beginning in 1989 the people finally got their way. In that year communism ended in Poland. Soon other countries in Eastern Europe became independent, too.

People in the Soviet Union wanted more than just reforms in communism, however. They wanted democracy, but many communists feared this idea. The communists fought to keep control of Russia.

In December 1991 Gorbachev stepped down as the leader of the Soviet Union. The president of the Russian republic, Boris Yeltsin, became the new leader of the central government. Yeltsin was the first democratically elected leader in the Soviet Union or in Russia.

In May 2000 Vladimir Putin won election as the new leader of Russia. Putin's primary goal was to increase wealth and the standard of living for all Russian people.

REVIEW **What factors led to the collapse of the Soviet Union?**

Russians shop in a department store in St. Petersburg.

LESSON 2 REVIEW

Summary Time Line

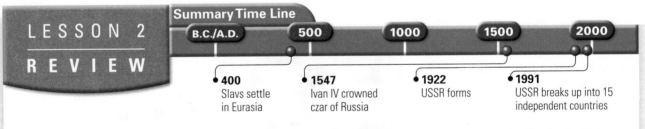

| B.C./A.D. | 500 | 1000 | 1500 | 2000 |

400 Slavs settle in Eurasia

1547 Ivan IV crowned czar of Russia

1922 USSR forms

1991 USSR breaks up into 15 independent countries

1. **MAIN IDEA** What were some positive and negative effects of Catherine the Great's rule?

2. **WHY IT MATTERS** Why do you think forcing people to change without allowing them to take part in the decisions can sometimes be harmful?

3. **VOCABULARY** Define the words **glasnost** and **perestroika** in your own words.

4. **TIME LINE** How many years passed between the formation and breakup of the Soviet Union?

5. **READING SKILL—Categorize** What have been the systems of government of Russia and the Soviet Union over the years?

6. **HISTORY** What was life like in the Soviet Union before the introduction of perestroika and glasnost?

7. **CRITICAL THINKING—Synthesize** Why do you think Gorbachev wanted to reform the Soviet Union?

PERFORMANCE—Write a Speech Write a speech as the newest leader of Russia. Make sure you include your hopes and plans for Russia's future. Read your speech to the class.

·SKILLS·
MAP AND GLOBE

Read a Time Zone Map

VOCABULARY
time zone

▶ WHY IT MATTERS

Because the sun rises and sets at different times in different places, clock times are not kept the same everywhere on Earth. A person in one part of the world might be going to bed at 10 P.M., exactly when a person in another part of the world is waking up at 7 A.M. Time differences like this can make communication difficult for people living in different parts of the world or even within a large country, such as Russia. Knowing how to read a time zone map can help you plan the best times to communicate with people in different places.

▶ WHAT YOU NEED TO KNOW

You know that a globe is divided by meridians, or lines of longitude. The prime meridian, at 0°, passes through Greenwich, in Britain. It is the starting point for the world's time zones. A **time zone** is a division of Earth in which all the places share the same clock time.

The world is divided into 24 standard time zones, 12 of them to the east of the prime meridian and 12 to the west. Each time zone covers 15 degrees of longitude. For every 15 degrees you move east, the time

changes by plus one hour. Every 15 degrees you move west, the time changes by minus one hour. All the time zones to the east of the prime meridian use later clock times than Greenwich time. All the zones to the west use earlier clock times than Greenwich time. The meridian where the eastern and western time zones meet is known as the international date line. This imaginary line is 12 time zones away from the prime meridian. So, when it is 12 noon in Greenwich, it is 12 midnight at the international date line, the place where each calendar day begins.

The map on page 341 shows all of the 24 time zones. The times at the top of the map show what time it is in each zone when it is 12 noon at the prime meridian.

You can also see from the map that in many places, the boundary between time zones does not follow the meridian exactly. The boundary may zigzag in places so that neighboring cities or countries can use the same clock time. In some places the people have chosen to use some other clock time. Such places are shown on the map as having nonstandard times.

This clock made in Russia features the figure of Saint George.

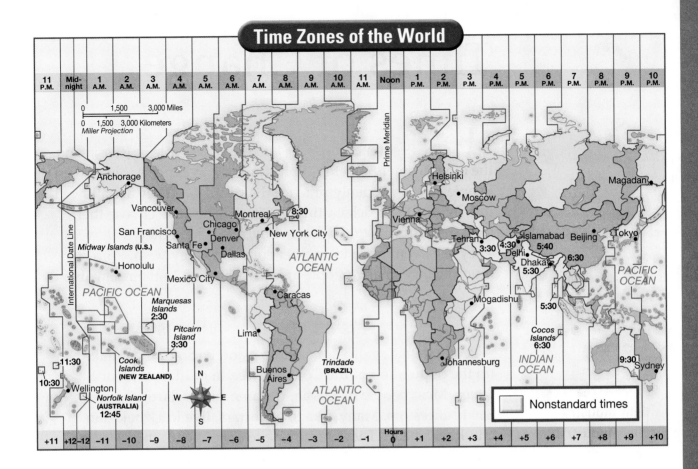

Time Zones of the World

▶ PRACTICE THE SKILL

Study the map above, and answer these questions.

1. When it is 12 noon in Greenwich, what time is it in Mexico City, Mexico?

2. When it is 12 noon in Greenwich, what time is it in Helsinki, Finland?

3. How many hours earlier is the time in Sydney, Australia, than the time in Johannesburg, South Africa?

4. How many hours later is the time in Beijing, China, than the time in Tokyo, Japan?

▶ APPLY WHAT YOU LEARNED

Write five word problems about time zones, and give them to a classmate to solve. Here is an example: "At 9 P.M. Victor, who lives in Moscow, Russia, telephones his sister in New York City, in the United States. What time is it in New York City?"

Practice your map and globe skills with the **GeoSkills CD-ROM**.

3

Times of Change

For the first time in nearly 1,000 years, people in Russia and the other former Soviet republics are free to express themselves. People can now openly practice their religion. They are allowed to celebrate their rich cultural heritage. They can choose their jobs, the products they wish to buy, and where they will live. They can even move to another country if they wish. With so much change, many people are still adjusting to their new lives.

A Land of Many Cultures

People of many different cultures and backgrounds make up the population of the Commonwealth of Independent States. Most people in Russia, Ukraine, and Belarus have Slavic ancestors. Many Tatars, or Tartars, live in Uzbekistan and Kazakhstan. The Tatars came to Russia with the invading Mongols. Other people in the CIS belong to one of more than 100 other ethnic groups.

At least 70 percent of the people living in the CIS speak the Russian language. Nearly every country in the CIS has its own language and dialects. People in Georgia speak Georgian, a language that dates back to the A.D. 400s. People in Tajikistan have strong cultural ties to Iran. They speak a dialect of the Iranian language of Farsi. Other languages spoken in the CIS include Armenian, Kazak, Ukrainian, and Turkic.

FAST FACT
The people in the country of Georgia claim to have long life spans. This motorcycle rider says he is 115 years old.

Boy prepared for Siberian cold

Russians in traditional dress

342   Unit 4

The countries of the CIS have a rich cultural history. Folk art and traditional music are common. A well-known kind of Russian folk art is the *matryoshka*. The *matryoshka* is a series of wooden dolls that vary in size. Each doll can be stored inside a larger doll in the series.

Handmade clothing, rugs, and wall hangings show the culture of a particular region. These items are usually brightly colored with detailed patterns. Some people in the former Soviet countries wear traditional clothing on special occasions.

Folktales are passed down through generations. One traditional tale in Ukraine is similar to the story of Robin Hood. According to the folktale, a man comes from his home in the Carpathian Mountains to steal from the rich and give to the poor. This character is a hero in Ukrainian folklore.

The performing arts are an especially important part of Russia's history. Russian ballet and theater have had an effect on the performing arts around the world. The Moscow Art Theater has been putting on plays since 1898. Several plays from the Russian writers Anton Chekhov and Leo Tolstoy first opened there. Plays first performed at the Moscow Art Theater are popular all over the world.

Each small *matryoshka* doll nests inside a larger one. These folk art figures are a popular souvenir sold in Russia.

Some people in the CIS enjoy the performing arts, but others prefer sports. The leaders of the former Soviet Union encouraged people to play sports. The Soviets built large sports arenas, where people went to play sports and watch sporting events. Today many of these arenas are closed.

Soccer is one of the most popular sports in the CIS. Most countries have their own teams. Large crowds gather to watch soccer competitions as well as wrestling, hockey, and horse racing.

Many people consider chess to be a game, but people in the former Soviet countries think of it as a sport. Children learn to play chess at an early age. They compete with each other to become great chess players. Chess players from Georgia and Russia are international chess champions.

Young woman of Turkmenistan

Boys in Ukraine

Children of Kazakhstan

Eastern Orthodox Church

Jewish Synagogue

Muslim Mosque

Buddhist Temple

Under the Soviets, many people had to worship in secret. Today the people in Russia have freedom of religion.

Food in the region varies from country to country. A dinner guest in Russia will probably eat borscht, a soup made of red beets and meat. People in Azerbaijan eat a variety of breads, fruits, and grains, and Ukrainians are fond of sausages and other meats. Potatoes are also an important part of the diet of many people.

Religious practice is on the rise in Russia and the former Soviet republics. The Soviets did not allow people to practice their religion openly. After the collapse of the Soviet Union, the government treated religion differently. For the first time in almost 100 years, people may worship openly. Freedom of religion led to a renewed interest in faith. Today more than 100 million people practice the Russian Orthodox religion. Others practice the Catholic or Eastern Orthodox branches of Christianity. Buddhism, Islam, and Judaism are also practiced.

Russia's diversity of cultures and religions has led to some conflicts. After the collapse of the Soviet Union, people of similar ethnic backgrounds wanted to group together. People with common heritages have tried to form their own countries. For example, many Tatars voted to form an independent republic. Their republic is now called Tatarstan.

People in Chechnya (chech•NYAH) also want independence. Most of the people of Chechnya are Muslims. They believe that their religion and ethnic identity have little in common with Russian beliefs. In 1994 Russian president Boris Yeltsin sent troops into Chechnya to stop the fight for independence. Yeltsin's actions started a war. Many people have died in this conflict.

REVIEW What caused a renewed interest in religion in Russia and the former Soviet republics?

A New Economy

The end of communism brought changes in the economy. The government sold many of its factories, farms, and other businesses to private owners. Most of these businesses were part of the country's light industry. **Light industry** businesses manufacture and sell consumer goods, such as appliances and clothing.

Soviet **heavy industry** factories produced large commercial items, such as military equipment and machinery. Privately owned companies now own many of these factories. Some sell military equipment to other countries. Others sell cars, boats, and farm equipment to consumers.

With new opportunities, the people also face new problems. Under communism, all citizens were guaranteed jobs. Even so, most people had no choice about what job they took. After the end of communism, people could choose where they wanted to work. Many found that the old system had not prepared them for the jobs they wanted. Now that communism has ended, many people in the CIS are unemployed.

The government also faced new challenges. After privatizing its businesses,

Russian office workers use technology to gather information.

the government had less money. There was not enough money to pay all of the government workers. As a result, more people lost their jobs. By the mid-1990s nearly 12 percent of the population—or about 18 million people—could not find jobs.

The economy finally began to improve in the early 2000s. More people have jobs, and there is less inflation. Small businesses are growing. Some factories, made private only a few years ago, manufacture affordable and well-made goods. Private farms are also making money.

Oil workers in Baku use technology to gather one of Azerbaijan's plentiful resources.

LOCATE IT

Baku

Caspian Sea

AZERBAIJAN

Bronze relief of space workers

Russian cosmonauts in space

Even Russia's space program is making new advances. More than 40 years ago, Russians were leaders in space exploration. Late in the Soviet period, there was little money for such an expensive program. Today skilled Russian **cosmonauts**, or space explorers, and American astronauts work together at the International Space Station.

The road to a better economy has not been easy for the people in the CIS. Still, many people see the difficulties faced by their countries as a small bump on the road to a better future. Young people, especially, look forward to changing times.

REVIEW Why was there so much unemployment after the end of communism?

Changing City Life

Russia's urban areas are home to people of many cultures. Originally, people moved to large towns and cities in search of work. Later, the communist government **displaced** large numbers of people. That is, the Soviets moved people against their will. They removed people from their rural land to make room for collectives. During World War II, people left their homes to escape the fighting. Many came to live in Moscow and other large cities.

Today cities continue to grow. The Russian capital of Moscow has become a fast-paced, modern city. About 10 million people live there and earn more than 70 percent of Russia's income. Moscow has become an important center of world trade and finance. Businesspeople from around the world meet there to discuss investments and Russia's future.

This monument to Russian space exploration was built in 1964 to honor the launch of *Sputnik*, the first human-made satellite to orbit Earth.

LOCATE IT

RUSSIA

Moscow

Gorki Park, along the Moskva River, is a popular recreation area in Moscow.

While many Russians still suffer economically, some are very successful. They import and sell consumer goods. Others buy and sell real estate, run factories, and invest in other businesses. Selling natural resources, such as oil, also brings wealth to people and the government. The success of Russians in business has led to something that could never have existed under communism—a new social class of wealthy citizens, sometimes called the "New Russians."

Traditional life in Moscow has not been lost. Neighborhoods, such as the Arbat, have cafés where Russians eat borscht, black bread, sausage, and other favorites. Street vendors and performers draw crowds of people. The busy streets of Moscow's business district, the markets of the Arbat, and the tree-lined paths of Gorki Park are filled with Russians who are finally free. They face problems, but many are optimistic. Each year on June 12, Russians celebrate their independence from the Soviet Union.

REVIEW How much of Russia's earnings come from the people in Moscow?

LESSON 3
REVIEW

1. **MAIN IDEA** How have the economies in Russia and the former Soviet republics changed since the fall of communism?

2. **WHY IT MATTERS** What are some challenges faced by the countries in the former Soviet Union since the collapse of communism?

3. **VOCABULARY** Explain the difference between **heavy industry** and **light industry**.

4. **READING SKILL—Categorize** What are some of the ethnic groups of Russia and the Eurasian republics?

5. **CULTURE** What kinds of sports are popular in the countries of the CIS?

6. **CULTURE** Who are the "New Russians"? What makes them different from other Russians?

7. **CRITICAL THINKING—Analyze** How do you think life in Moscow today is different from life there under Soviet rule?

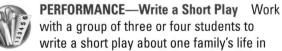 **PERFORMANCE—Write a Short Play** Work with a group of three or four students to write a short play about one family's life in Russia after communism. Your play should be about ten minutes long. Be sure to include details about religion, the economy, and culture. Perform your play for the class.

10 Review and Test Preparation

Summary Time Line

B.C./A.D.   500

400s
Slavs settle
in what is
now Russia

USE YOUR READING SKILLS

Complete this graphic organizer to show that you understand how to put the people, the places, and the ideas found in Russia and the Eurasian Republics into categories. A copy of this graphic organizer appears on page 98 of the Activity Book.

Landforms of Russia

THINK & WRITE

Write a Speech   Imagine that you are a Soviet leader of the past. Write a speech to explain why government reforms, such as *perestroika* and *glasnost,* are necessary to improve the Soviet way of life.

Write an Obituary   Use library or electronic resources to research Peter the Great or another Russian leader from the past. Then write an obituary that includes a description of this leader's life and accomplishments.

1222
Mongols invade
Kievan Rus

1547
Ivan IV is crowned
czar of Russia

1917
The Russian
Revolution begins

1922
The Soviet
Union is formed

1991
USSR breaks up into
15 independent republics

USE THE TIME LINE

Use the chapter summary time line to answer these questions.

1 How many years after the beginning of the Russian revolution was the Soviet Union formed?

2 Where did the Slavs settle in the 400s?

USE VOCABULARY

Write a story about Russia and the Eurasian republics using these terms.

reform (p. 334)

czar (p. 335)

abdicate (p. 336)

totalitarian (p. 337)

purge (p. 337)

RECALL FACTS

Answer these questions.

3 Why are the peaks of the once-jagged Ural Mountains rounded today?

4 Why do few people live in Siberia?

5 Who was the last czar of Russia?

Write the letter of the best choice.

6 **TEST PREP** Russia's two largest cities are located—
  A in the West Siberian Plain.
  B on the Central Siberian Plateau.
  C on the Great European Plain.
  D in the taiga.

7 **TEST PREP** In 1985 Mikhail Gorbachev introduced two government reforms called—
  F glasnost and perestroika.
  G matryoshka and Novgorod.
  H borscht and Chechnya.
  J Yeltsin and Putin.

THINK CRITICALLY

8 How do you think political decisions during the Cold War affected the use of technology in the Soviet Union?

9 Do you think Russian workers were better off under the command economy of the former Soviet Union than they are today? Explain.

APPLY SKILLS

Read a Climograph

10 Use the climographs on pages 332–333 to draw conclusions about the climates in Moscow, Russia; Cairo, Egypt; and Chicago, Illinois. Write a paragraph describing what the climate in each place is probably like.

Read a Time Zone Map

11 Find your time zone on the map on page 341. How many hours ahead or behind is your time zone compared to Wellington, New Zealand; Moscow, Russia; and Caracas, Venezuela?

VISIT

Neuschwanstein *Castle*

Neuschwanstein (NOY·shvahn·shtyn) Castle in Füssen, Germany, was built in the late 1800s by King Ludwig of Bavaria. The king's vision for the castle was inspired, in part, by a castle in one of his favorite operas. Perched high on a rocky hill, Neuschwanstein Castle rises over the Bavarian countryside. Visitors to Neuschwanstein are impressed by its elaborate detail. Intricate wood carvings, tapestries, and murals cover the walls and ceilings. The ornate castle looks as if it comes from the pages of a fairy tale.

Neuschwanstein Castle is set in the Bavarian Alps in southern Germany.

LOCATE IT

GERMANY

Füssen

When visitors pass through the gate, they enter the castle's grand courtyard.

Stained-glass windows in King Ludwig's bedroom depict family crests.

Singer's Hall, a large concert hall, was the first room planned for the castle.

TAKE A FIELD TRIP

GO ONLINE

A VIRTUAL TOUR
Visit The Learning Site at **www.harcourtschool.com/tours** to take virtual tours of other castles and palaces.

CNN
Turner Le@rning

A VIDEO TOUR
Check your media center or classroom library for a videotape tour of Neuschwanstein Castle.

4 Review and Test Preparation

VISUAL SUMMARY

Write a Newspaper Headline On the visual summary time line below, find the event that marks the decline of Communism. Look at the picture and write a newspaper headline for this event.

USE VOCABULARY

For each group of terms, write a sentence or two that explains how the terms are different.

1 **polder** (p. 264), **taiga** (p. 328)

2 **loch** (p. 265), **thermal spring** (p. 296)

3 **constitutional monarchy** (p. 286), **totalitarian** (p. 337)

RECALL FACTS

Answer these questions.

4 From what civilization did the ancient Greeks borrow?

5 Where in Eastern Europe did the Magyars settle?

6 How did the opportunities for Russian citizens to participate in government change after the collapse of the Soviet Union?

Write the letter of the best choice.

7 **TEST PREP** An early document that protected the rights of citizens was—
A the Magna Carta.
B glasnost.
C perestroika.
D NATO.

8 **TEST PREP** French-speaking Belgians are called—
F Flemish.
G Walloons.
H Romansch.
J Scots.

9 **TEST PREP** All of the following are groups that invaded Eastern Europe except—
A the Visigoths.
B the Romans.
C the Slavs.
D the Basques.

Visual Summary

| 800 B.C. | 500 B.C. | B.C./A.D. | A.D. 500 |

800 B.C. **Earliest Greek city-states form** p. 269

336 B.C. **Alexander the Great expands his empire,** p. 269

A.D. 400s **Slavs settle in Eastern Europe and what is now Russia** p. 334

THINK CRITICALLY

10 How do you think Johannes Gutenberg's invention of a new kind of printing press has affected present-day cultures around the world?

11 How do you think religious ideals have affected cultures in Northern Ireland?

12 Do you think that the new borders after World War I added to ethnic tensions in Eastern Europe? Explain.

13 Do you think that Russia should allow the people of Chechnya to have their independence? Explain.

APPLY SKILLS

Identify Changing Borders
Use the two maps on this page to answer the following questions.

14 Which country is united today that was not united in 1980?

15 Which present-day countries were once part of Yugoslavia?

16 Which countries in Europe were once part of the Soviet Union?

17 What countries once made up Czechoslovakia?

Present-Day Europe

Europe, 1980

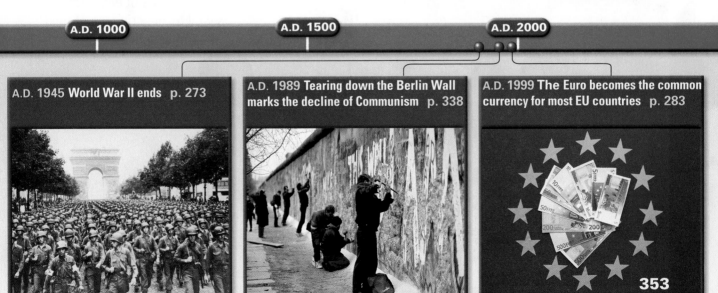

A.D. 1000   A.D. 1500   A.D. 2000

A.D. 1945 **World War II ends** p. 273

A.D. 1989 **Tearing down the Berlin Wall marks the decline of Communism** p. 338

A.D. 1999 **The Euro becomes the common currency for most EU countries** p. 283

Unit Activities

Visit The Learning Site at www.harcourtschool.com/socialstudies/activities for additional activities.

Create a Hall Of Fame

Choose some figures from European history that you admire. Include them on a poster called Important Europeans. Research each person's life, and write a short biography to include on the poster. Then download or copy pictures to illustrate your poster, or draw your own pictures. Add captions to each picture explaining why that figure is important to European history. Present your poster to the class.

Draw a Graphic Organizer

Compare a map of the former Soviet Union with a map of the same region today. Draw a graphic organizer that displays all of the countries that were once part of the Soviet Union.

VISIT YOUR LIBRARY

■ *Daily Life in Ancient and Modern Moscow* by Patricia Toht. Runestone.

■ *Celtic Fairy Tales* retold by Neil Philip and illustrated by Isabelle Brent. Viking.

■ *Zlata's Diary: A Child's Life in Sarajevo* by Zlata Filipović. Penguin.

COMPLETE THE UNIT PROJECT

Plan a Festival Work with a group of classmates to complete the unit project—plan a festival. On a piece of paper, create a schedule of activities that will occur during your festival. On the schedule, include descriptions of each activity as well as descriptions of food and costumes.

Southwest Asia and North Africa

Phoenician vase,
fifth century B.C.

Kasbah near Timidert in the Dra River Valley of Morocco

Southwest Asia and North Africa

66 The well shall not dry up . . . so long as we are clouds and our hopes are drops of rain. **99**

—Fouzi El-Asmar, from "Expectation," 1998

Preview the Content

Quickly scan the unit. Use what you see to answer these questions: *Who* and *what* is the unit about? *When* did the events occur? *Where* are the locations found in photos throughout the unit? *Why* is what happened important? Make a chart to record your responses.

	WHO?	WHAT?	WHEN?	WHERE?	WHY?
Chapter 11					
Chapter 12					

Preview the Vocabulary

Context Clues   Context clues are the words in sentences that help you figure out the meanings of unfamiliar words. Find these words: *Torah, Ten Commandments, Gospels, Five Pillars, minaret, muezzin,* and *hajj.* Then write a sentence that explains what the words have in common. Do the same for these words: *oasis, aquifer, desalinization, wadi, qanat, dike,* and *cataract.*

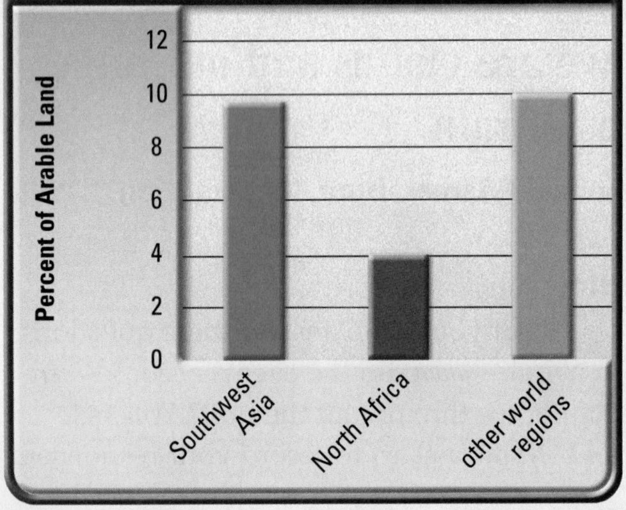

Southwest Asia and North Africa

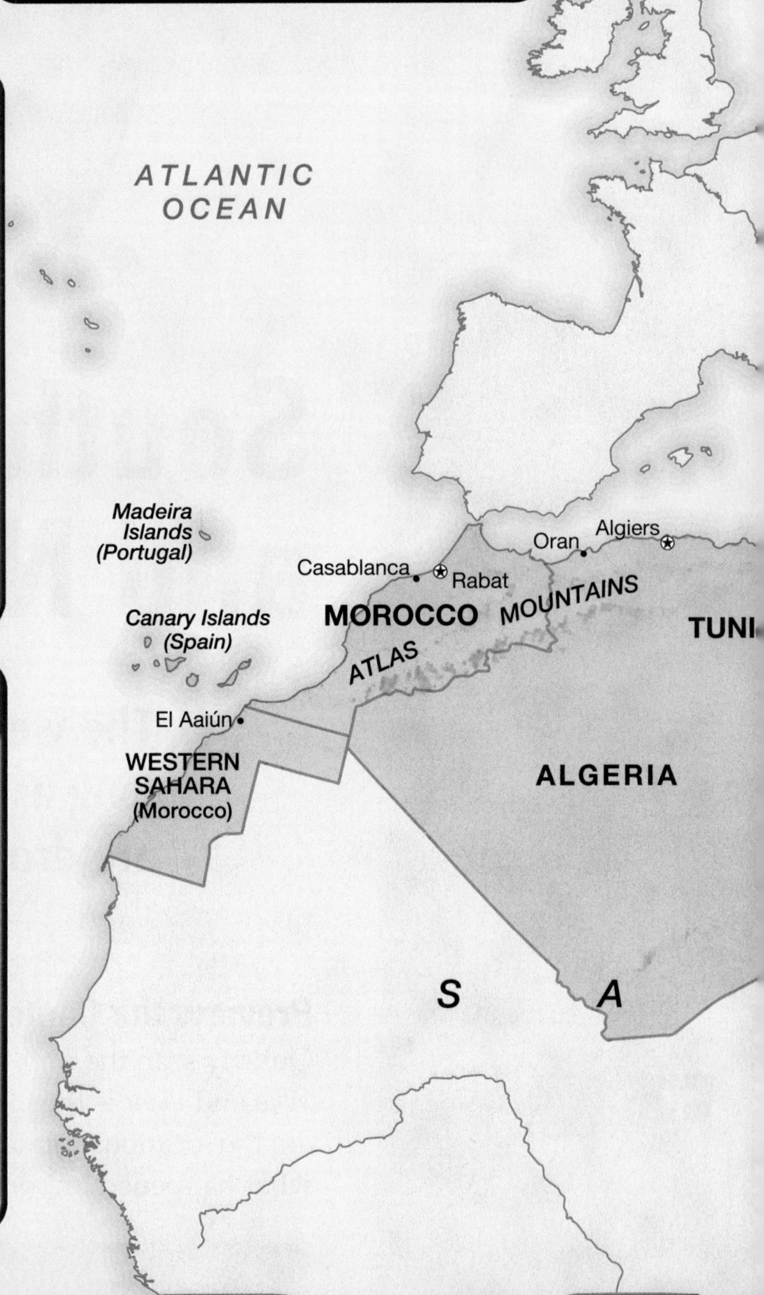

World Oil Supply

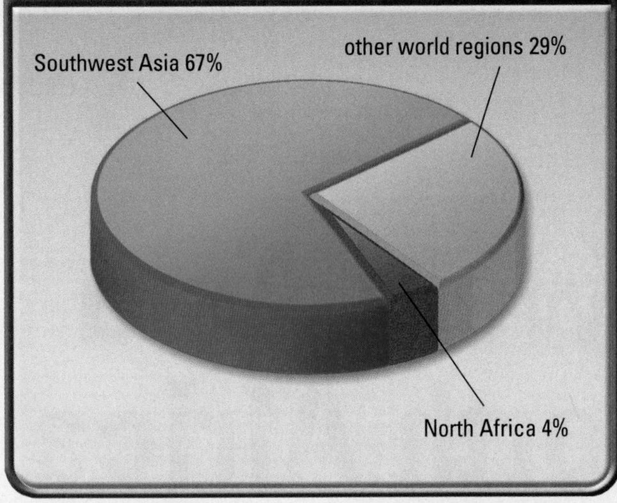

Southwest Asia 67%

other world regions 29%

North Africa 4%

Arable Land

Percent of Arable Land

12
10
8
6
4
2
0

Southwest Asia

North Africa

other world regions

ATLANTIC OCEAN

Madeira Islands (Portugal)

Casablanca • ⊛ Rabat

Oran • Algiers ⊛

MOROCCO MOUNTAINS

TUNI

Canary Islands (Spain)

ATLAS

El Aaiún •

WESTERN SAHARA (Morocco)

ALGERIA

S   A

Key Events

| 4000 B.C. | 3000 B.C. | 2000 B.C. | 1000 B.C. |

3500 B.C. **Sumerians build city-states in Mesopotamia** p. 372

3000 B.C. **Egypt becomes the world's first nation-state** p. 408

1300 B.C. **Judaism develops in Southwest Asia, the first of three major religions founded in this region** p. 374

356

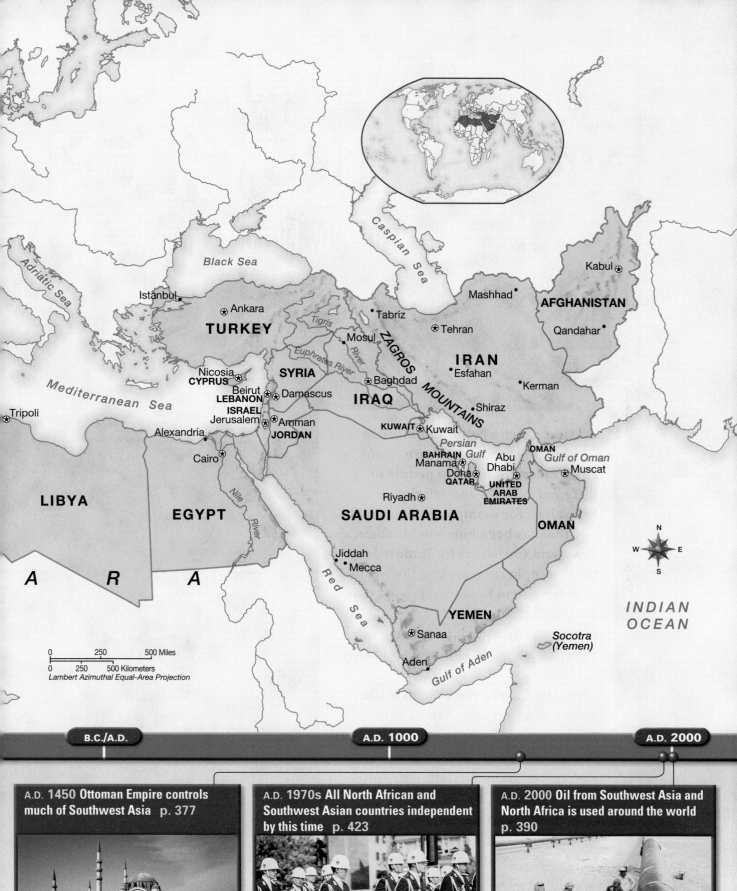

Black Sea

Caspian Sea

Adriatic Sea

Mediterranean Sea

Istanbul

Ankara

TURKEY

Tigris

Mosul

Euphrates River

Nicosia
CYPRUS

SYRIA

Beirut
LEBANON
ISRAEL
Jerusalem

Damascus

IRAQ

Baghdad

River

ZAGROS MOUNTAINS

Amman
JORDAN

Alexandria

Cairo

LIBYA

EGYPT

Nile River

A R A

Tabriz

Mashhad

Tehran

AFGHANISTAN

Kabul

Qandahar

IRAN

Esfahan

Kerman

Shiraz

KUWAIT Kuwait

Persian Gulf

BAHRAIN
Manama
Doha
QATAR

Abu Dhabi

OMAN

Gulf of Oman

Muscat

UNITED ARAB EMIRATES

Riyadh

SAUDI ARABIA

OMAN

Jiddah
Mecca

Red Sea

YEMEN

Sanaa

Aden

Gulf of Aden

Socotra
(Yemen)

INDIAN OCEAN

N
W E
S

0   250   500 Miles
0   250   500 Kilometers
Lambert Azimuthal Equal-Area Projection

B.C./A.D.

A.D. 1000

A.D. 2000

A.D. 1450 **Ottoman Empire controls much of Southwest Asia** p. 377

A.D. 1970s **All North African and Southwest Asian countries independent by this time** p. 423

A.D. 2000 **Oil from Southwest Asia and North Africa is used around the world** p. 390

357

A WALK THROUGH JERUSALEM

written by Elizabeth Crooker

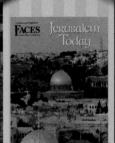

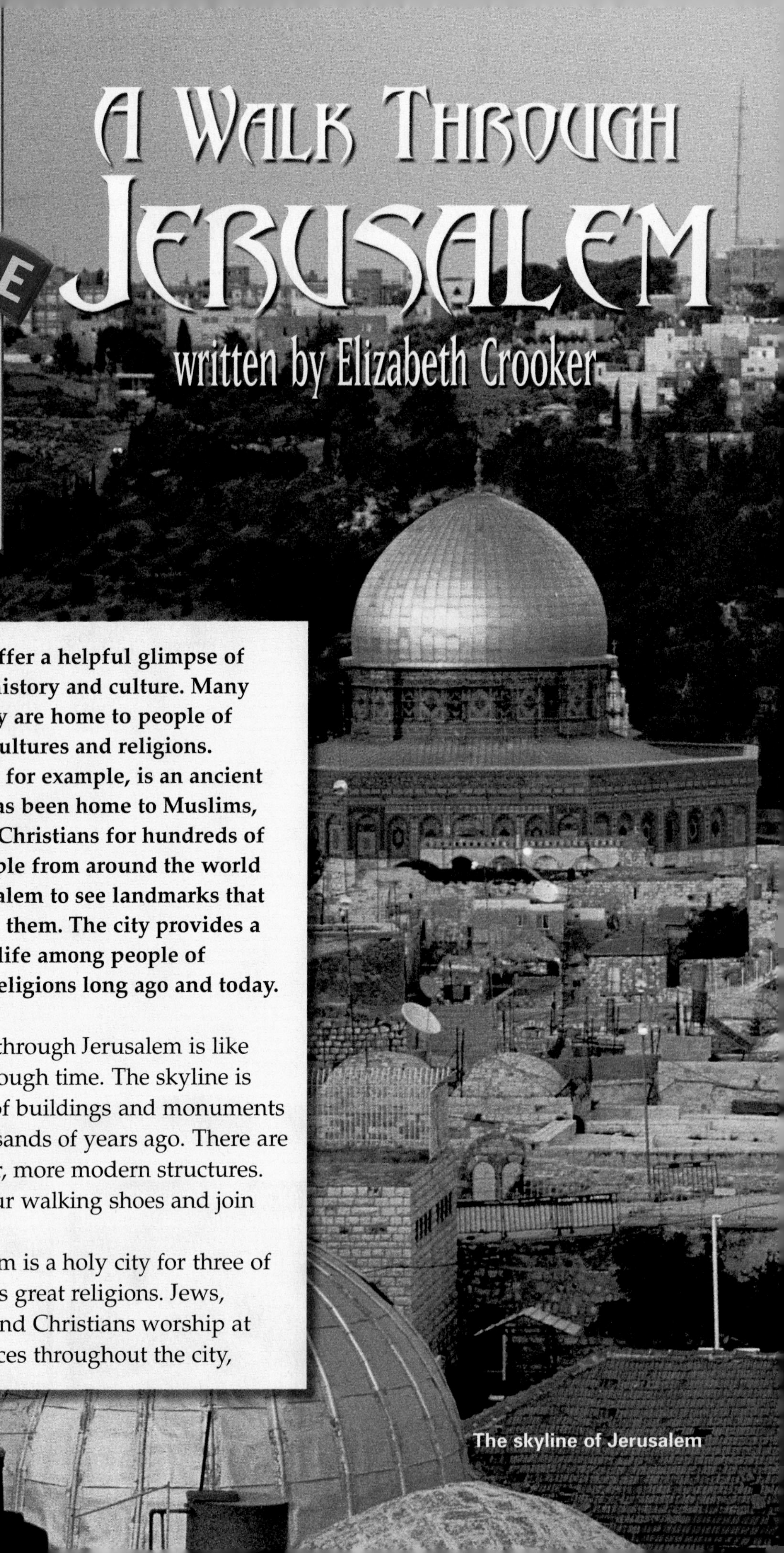

FACES Jerusalem Today

Cities offer a helpful glimpse of both history and culture. Many cities today are home to people of different cultures and religions. Jerusalem, for example, is an ancient city that has been home to Muslims, Jews, and Christians for hundreds of years. People from around the world visit Jerusalem to see landmarks that are holy to them. The city provides a picture of life among people of different religions long ago and today.

A walk through Jerusalem is like a walk through time. The skyline is made up of buildings and monuments built thousands of years ago. There are also newer, more modern structures. Put on your walking shoes and join the tour!

Jerusalem is a holy city for three of the world's great religions. Jews, Muslims and Christians worship at sacred places throughout the city,

The skyline of Jerusalem

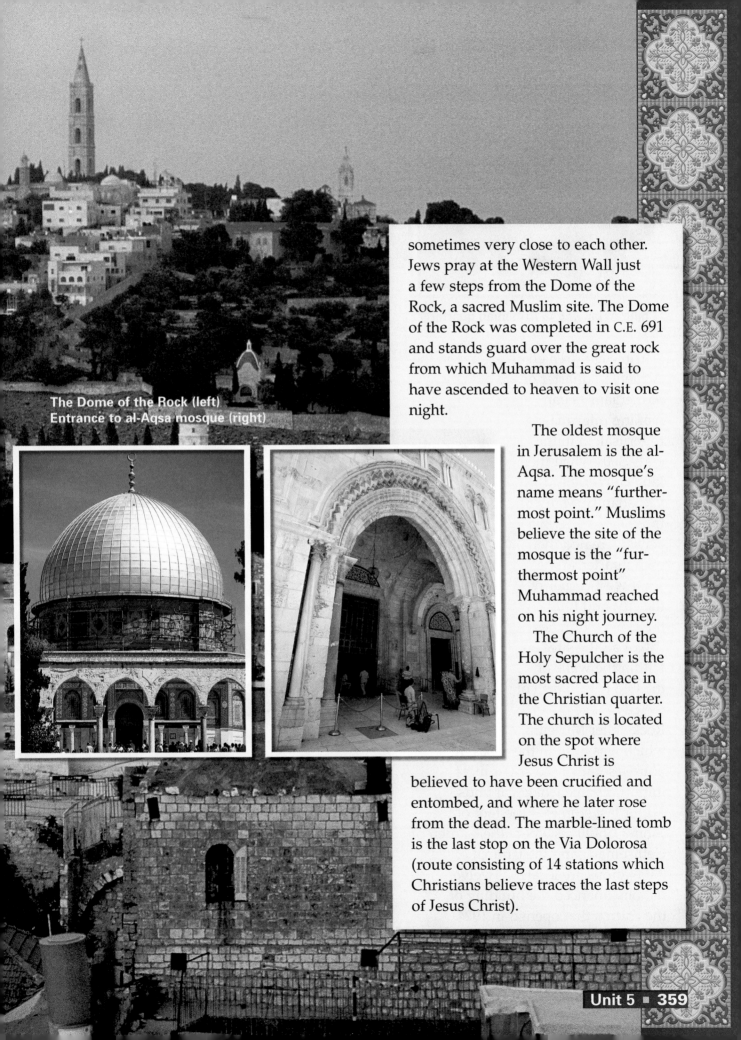

The Dome of the Rock (left)
Entrance to al-Aqsa mosque (right)

sometimes very close to each other. Jews pray at the Western Wall just a few steps from the Dome of the Rock, a sacred Muslim site. The Dome of the Rock was completed in C.E. 691 and stands guard over the great rock from which Muhammad is said to have ascended to heaven to visit one night.

The oldest mosque in Jerusalem is the al-Aqsa. The mosque's name means "furthermost point." Muslims believe the site of the mosque is the "furthermost point" Muhammad reached on his night journey.

The Church of the Holy Sepulcher is the most sacred place in the Christian quarter. The church is located on the spot where Jesus Christ is believed to have been crucified and entombed, and where he later rose from the dead. The marble-lined tomb is the last stop on the Via Dolorosa (route consisting of 14 stations which Christians believe traces the last steps of Jesus Christ).

Children playing in Armenian quarter

Three children enjoy a game in the Armenian quarter of the old city. Armenians began making pilgrimages to Jerusalem in the early 300s when their king converted to Christianity. Many of those early pilgrims stayed, created their own quarter in the southwest corner of the city, and built their own churches.

Not all the sites are within the walls of the Old City. North of the city is the Rockefeller Museum, which was built in the 1930s. It houses some of the area's most important archaeological finds.

Our last stop is at the foot of the Mount of Olives where the Garden of Gethsemane and the Church of All Nations are located. Twelve nations financed the building of the church that opened in 1924.

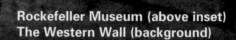

Rockefeller Museum (above inset)
The Western Wall (background)

Church of All Nations

Also known as the "Basilica of the Agony," the building was designed by Antonio Barluzzi. The garden that surrounds the building is said to have been the location of the Last Supper. Olive trees more than two thousand years old still bear fruit.

The sights and sounds of Jerusalem are unique to the city. Where else can each step take you back 5,000 years?

Garden of Gethsemane

Analyze the Literature

1 Why is Jerusalem important to people living in other parts of the world?

2 What places in your city or state might be meaningful to people around the world? Write a magazine article about landmarks found in your city or town.

READ A BOOK

START THE UNIT PROJECT

Make a Travel Guide As you read this unit, take note of places you would like to visit in Southwest Asia and North Africa. Include these places in a travel guide of the region.

USE TECHNOLOGY

Visit The Learning Site at **www.harcourtschool.com/ socialstudies** for additional activities, primary sources, and other resources to use in this unit.

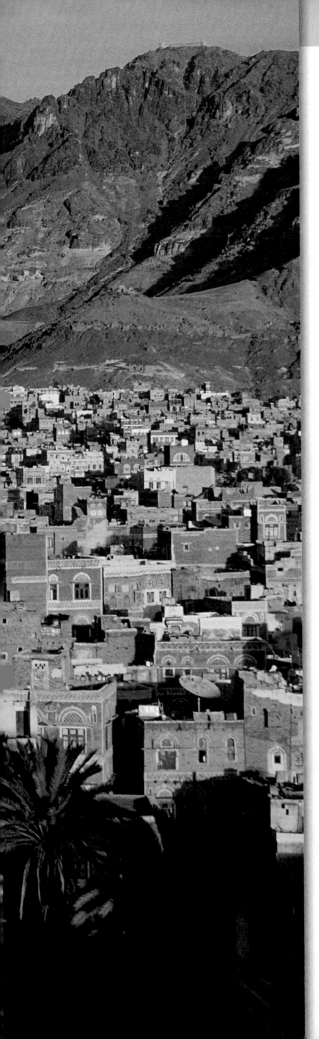

Southwest Asia

" I fly to you, I roam over
my Yemen, my Damascus
in winter, in summer
my village, my city
my minarets, my rivers… "
—Mohja Kahf, from "You Are My Yemen," 1998

CHAPTER READING SKILL

Compare and Contrast

To **compare** people, places, events, or ideas, identify their similarities. To **contrast** people, places, events, or ideas, identify their differences.

As you read this chapter, look for similarities and differences. Note them in a chart.

How are the topics the same?
How are the topics different?

TOPIC A	TOPIC B

Land of Contrasts

MAIN IDEA

As you read, think about how the physical features and natural resources of Southwest Asia affect the lives of the people who live there.

WHY IT MATTERS

No matter where they live, people find ways to adapt to or change their environment to meet their needs.

VOCABULARY

alluvial soil
oasis
exotic river
wadi
aquifer
qanat
desalinization

Southwest Asia is one of the driest regions in the world, but it is more than a land of deserts. Fertile valleys, wide plains, high plateaus, and rugged mountains combine with arid deserts to make Southwest Asia a region of contrasts.

This land of contrasts even has two names. Europeans have often thought of themselves as being in the West and Asia as being in the East. Because it is between Europe and Asia, however, they called Southwest Asia the Middle East. Many people today still refer to the region as the Middle East.

Land and Sea

Southwest Asia has long been considered the crossroads of the world. It is the place where the continents of Asia, Africa, and Europe meet. Southwest Asia is near both North Africa and Eastern Europe. For hundreds of years the central location of Southwest Asia has made it a center of trade.

Seas surround much of Southwest Asia. Of the region's 16 countries, only Afghanistan is completely landlocked. To the west of Southwest Asia lie the Mediterranean Sea and the Red Sea. To the south is the Arabian Sea, which is part of the Indian Ocean. To the east are the Persian Gulf and the Gulf of Oman. To the north is the Caspian Sea. Despite its name, the Caspian Sea is actually the world's largest saltwater lake.

The Dead Sea is the lowest body of water on Earth. Although called the Dead Sea, it is actually a salt lake. Because the Dead Sea is seven times as salty as the ocean, people can easily float in the water.

LOCATE IT

ISRAEL

JORDAN

Dead Sea

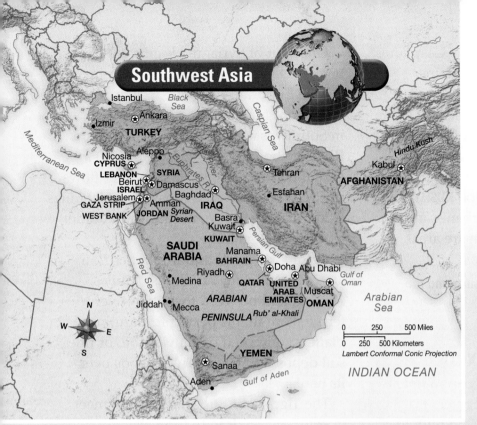

Southwest Asia

GEOGRAPHY THEME

Place Sixteen countries make up Southwest Asia, an area often called the crossroads of the world. Southwest Asia is close to both Europe and Africa. People have thrived here for thousands of years, largely due to their ability to adapt to the different environments of the region.

❓ **What bodies of water border the Arabian Peninsula?**

Not far from the Caspian Sea lies the Black Sea. Like all true seas, the Black Sea connects to other bodies of water. A set of narrow straits that cut through the country of Turkey links the Black Sea to the Aegean Sea, which is an arm of the Mediterranean. On the eastern side of the straits is the continent of Asia. On the western side is Europe. Turkey and Russia are the only countries in the world that are located on two different continents.

Much of Southwest Asia is made up of two peninsulas. The Arabian Peninsula is surrounded by five bodies of water. The Red Sea borders it on the west, and the Persian Gulf and the Gulf of Oman border it on the east. To the south is the Arabian Sea and Gulf of Aden. The other peninsula is called Asia Minor, or Anatolia (an•uh•TOH•lee•uh). Today the country of Turkey occupies the peninsula. It is surrounded by the Black Sea to the north and the Mediterranean Sea to the south. The two bodies of water are joined by the Bosporus, a strait that is 19 miles (31 km) long.

In many places the seas in the region give way to coastlines of high mountains and rolling hills. Along Turkey's coastline are the Pontic Mountains in the north and the Taurus Mountains in the south. Separating these ranges is a high area of land called the Plateau of Anatolia. Many volcanic peaks add to Turkey's rough and rocky landscape.

FAST FACT

Southwest Asia's Dead Sea is so salty that few plants can survive along its banks. Any fish that swim into the Dead Sea from the Jordan River die immediately.

Along the southern edge of the Caspian Sea, in Iran, are the Elburz Mountains. Along Iran's western border stand the Zagros Mountains. Between these two chains of mountains is an area of high land known as the Plateau of Iran.

East of Iran, a large mountain range called the Hindu Kush (HIN•doo KUSH) cuts through northeastern Afghanistan. At the base of the Hindu Kush are areas of plains, foothills, and plateaus.

REVIEW **What bodies of water surround the countries of Southwest Asia?**

A Tale of Two Rivers

The Tigris and Euphrates (yu•FRAY•teez) Rivers are the most important rivers in Southwest Asia. Both rivers begin high in the mountains of Turkey as small, snow-fed streams.

After leaving Turkey, the Euphrates River flows southeast through Syria. There, the Euphrates provides water for farming. It is also the only river in Syria free of rapids and deep enough for boat travel.

Once out of Syria, the Euphrates begins its long journey across Iraq. In all, the Euphrates is about 1,740 miles (2,800 km) long, making it the longest river in Southwest Asia. In contrast, the Tigris River is about 1,180 miles (1,900 km) long. Like the Euphrates, the Tigris River flows south out of Turkey. It runs for just 20 miles (32 km) along Syria's northeastern border and then enters Iraq.

In Iraq the Tigris and Euphrates flow almost parallel for hundreds of miles. Around and between these two rivers lies a fertile plain that is perfect for farming. The plain is composed of **alluvial soil**, or fine soil deposited when a river floods over its banks.

The Tigris and Euphrates Rivers meet in southeastern Iraq to form a single river called the Shatt al Arab (SHAHT ahl AR•uhb). The Shatt al Arab flows southeast until it empties into the Persian Gulf.

Throughout history the fertile area between the Tigris and Euphrates has been called Mesopotamia, or the "land between the rivers." For 5,000 years, most of Iraq's

For centuries, people have depended on the Tigris and Euphrates Rivers to irrigate the land. The satellite photo (inset) shows where the two rivers meet. People still rely on these two rivers for food, water, and transportation. Several bridges now cross the Tigris River in Baghdad, Iraq (below).

The section of the Rub' al-Khali, or Great Sandy Desert, in Yemen (left) contains soft sand dunes. In contrast, the Syrian Desert in Wadi, Jordan (above), has hard, rocky terrain.

people have settled on or near this plain between the two rivers. This is where Baghdad, Iraq's capital and largest city, is located. Past and present farmers on the plain have found a variety of ways to bring water to the rich but dry soil. Along the banks of the rivers, people have built dams and canals as ways to save and carry water. Irrigation was invented there.

REVIEW How are the Tigris and Euphrates Rivers important to the people of Syria and Iraq?

Sand, Steppes, Oases, and Mountains

Vast stretches of desert cover much of Southwest Asia. The two largest deserts in this region are the Syrian Desert and the Rub' al-Khali (RUB al•KAHL•ee).

The Syrian Desert covers parts of Syria, Saudi Arabia, Iraq, and Jordan. Like most deserts, the Syrian Desert has a rocky land-scape. Sandy areas are rare. These parts of the desert receive almost no rain. Strong winds that blow across the desert cause huge dust storms throughout the year.

Other parts of the desert area are con-sidered to be steppe. These steppes receive enough rainfall to have different kinds of vegetation, depending on the seasons. Although these places are very dry, nomadic tribes known as Bedouins (BEH•duh•wuhnz) live there by migrating from place to place. They graze their herds on whatever plant life is available during the different seasons.

On the southeastern and southwestern edges of the Arabian Peninsula, mountains receive enough rain for farming. Such farmland can be found in Oman, Yemen, and parts of Saudi Arabia.

People have also settled in places in Southwest Asia where there are oases. An **oasis** (oh•AY•suhs) is a place in a desert that has a dependable supply of water. Most of the water at an oasis comes from underground springs. Oases often provide the water needed for farmers to grow their crops and care for their animals.

Most people think of deserts as being hot all the time. This is true of the Syrian Desert and the Rub' al-Khali during the day in summer. Daytime temperatures can reach 130°F (54°C). Nighttime temperatures can drop to a freezing 32°F (0°C).

REVIEW What different landscapes can be found in Southwest Asia?

Cars, buses, and trucks powered by oil travel across the Galata Bridge in Istanbul, Turkey, every day. Oil in Southwest Asia is pumped out of the ground using machines called pumpjacks (below).

Desert Resources

Southwest Asia is rich in many natural resources. Iron ore, coal, copper, phosphates, and rock salt are just a few of the mineral riches. Yet for many countries of Southwest Asia, the most important natural resources are natural gas and oil.

Both natural gas and oil are kinds of fossil fuels that are found deep within Earth. Like other natural resources, natural gas and oil are distributed unevenly around the world. While scarce in many places, natural gas and oil are abundant in Southwest Asia. The countries that produce large amounts of natural gas and oil cluster around the Persian Gulf. Saudi Arabia is one of the world's largest oil producers. Kuwait, Iraq, and Iran also produce large amounts of oil.

Oil is an important source of energy around the world. People use oil to power automobiles, planes, and boats and to heat homes and generate electricity. Often where there is a large supply of oil, there is also natural gas. Like oil, natural gas is used for heat and to generate electricity.

The people of Southwest Asia are working to develop new industries because natural gas and oil are not renewable resources and will not last forever. Many planners in Southwest Asia argue that oil must be saved for uses other than fuel. Oil is a valuable resource for making plastics, medicines, and other products.

REVIEW Why is oil an important resource?

Scarcity of Fresh Water

Fresh water is a rare and precious resource for the people of Southwest Asia. To many it is a resource far more precious than oil.

Much of Southwest Asia is arid. Because rain seldom falls, many areas are too dry to grow crops. Crops grow only if farmers use irrigation, or human-made methods to move water to dry areas. Irrigation adds needed farmland, but it may not be the most economical use for water that cannot be replaced.

You might think that all the bodies of water surrounding Southwest Asia could provide the region with more than enough water for drinking and irrigation. However, all this water is salt water, not fresh water. Salt water cannot be used for drinking or for watering crops.

Although fresh water is not plentiful in Southwest Asia, various sources do exist. These sources are both on the surface and underground. Each source is important, but each has its advantages and disadvantages.

Rivers are vital but limited because surface water evaporates quickly in desert regions. The sources of rivers that bring fresh water to the dry land are outside the desert, where water results from melting snow. Rivers that start in a wetter area and flow into a drier area are **exotic rivers**. Many people live along these rivers. The people who live upstream can affect the river as it flows through their territory. They can use it up or pollute it, leaving little for those who live downstream.

Another surface source of fresh water is in **wadis** (WAH•deez), or riverbeds that

A well farmer in Abu Dhabi, in the United Arab Emirates, pumps fresh water out of the ground.

are usually dry. In the southwestern part of the United States, these dry riverbeds are called arroyos (uh•ROY•ohs). During the rainy season, wadis fill with rainwater. However, they are not a reliable source of water. The dry river basins soak up much of the rainwater, and rains are unpredictable.

• SCIENCE AND TECHNOLOGY •

Farming in the Desert

Many Southwest Asian countries need more farmland to feed their growing populations. Creating new farmland from desert is difficult because there is already a shortage of water. To solve this problem, farmers and scientists are working together to grow more food on existing farmland.

In Israel some farmers now grow crops year-round in greenhouses. Other farmers apply "drip" irrigation. This system uses less water by delivering water and fertilizer directly to the roots of plants through small holes in underground pipes.

Water towers like these dominate the skyline of Kuwait City, the capital of Kuwait.

Aquifers (A•kwuh•ferz) are far more reliable sources of fresh water. **Aquifers** are underground layers of rock or sand that hold water. Water in aquifers may be thousands of years old yet still be pure and fresh. For this reason, it is often called fossil water. Fossil water, like fossil fuel, is a nonrenewable resource.

Some people of Southwest Asia have found an interesting way to move fresh water to where it is needed. For 2,500 years people in Iran have built **qanats** (kuh•NAHTS), or underground canals. The qanats tap into springs in mountains or hills to bring water to the valley floor.

Today many Southwest Asian countries collect seawater and use a process called **desalinization** to remove the salt. People use this water for drinking or for irrigation. Desalinization requires a great deal of energy, and the process is costly. Only countries rich in oil, such as Saudi Arabia, Kuwait, and the United Arab Emirates, are able to use this process on a large scale.

REVIEW What natural sources of water can be found in Southwest Asia's deserts?

LESSON 1 REVIEW

1 MAIN IDEA Why can Southwest Asia be described as a land of contrasts?

2 WHY IT MATTERS What are three ways people today have adjusted to the physical environment of Southwest Asia?

3 VOCABULARY Write a paragraph about Southwest Asia's natural resources. Use these terms—**alluvial soil**, **oasis**, **wadi**, **desalinization**, **aquifer**.

4 READING SKILL—Compare and Contrast Compare and contrast the various kinds of landscapes in the Arabian Peninsula. How are they alike? How are they different?

5 GEOGRAPHY What is the world's largest saltwater lake? Why is its name somewhat misleading?

6 GEOGRAPHY Through which three countries does the Euphrates River flow?

7 TECHNOLOGY What process removes the salt from seawater to make it drinkable?

8 CRITICAL THINKING—Evaluate Why are countries around the world interested in the resources of Southwest Asia?

PERFORMANCE—Make a Game Design a board game based on the physical features and natural resources of the deserts of Southwest Asia. Play your game in class.

Southwest Asia Long Ago

| 4000 B.C. | 3000 B.C. | 2000 B.C. | 1000 B.C. | B.C./A.D. | A.D. 1000 | A.D. 2000 |

MAIN IDEA
Read to find out how the early people of Southwest Asia found new ways of doing things.

WHY IT MATTERS
The people who lived in Southwest Asia long ago introduced many ideas that remain important today.

VOCABULARY
domesticate
dike
ziggurat
cuneiform
code
Torah
Ten Commandments
Gospels
Qur'an
Crusades

The region known as Southwest Asia has had a long and varied history. Early farmers there planted some of the world's first crops. It was also the home of the world's earliest cities. This region gave birth to three religions. People living there probably etched the first writing into clay and rolled the first wheels.

Ancient Mesopotamia

One area of land particularly important to the early people of Southwest Asia was the fertile plain between the Tigris and Euphrates Rivers. People found that plants grew well in Mesopotamia. The Mesopotamians probably learned about agriculture from the early farmers of Asia Minor. In the foothills of the Zagros and Taurus Mountains, people had learned to **domesticate** wild plants, or change them for human use. The people began picking seeds from the healthiest and best-tasting wild plants and planting them to get more of the same plants. In doing so, they became some of the world's first farmers. These early farmers built year-round shelters not far from their fields, forming some of the world's earliest communities. Soon, people in other parts of Southwest Asia learned about this way of getting food.

Southern Mesopotamia, or Sumer, proved to be particularly good for farming. The plains there provided the rich soil needed for growing crops. The rivers provided the water required to keep the crops alive.

The same rivers that helped Sumerian farmers survive also brought danger. No one knew just when the Tigris and Euphrates Rivers would overflow their banks. Sudden floods wiped out crops, destroyed houses, and sometimes brought death.

This bronze sculpture of a chariot was made in ancient Sumer almost 5,000 years ago.

The Sumerians found ways to control the unpredictable rivers. They built **dikes**, or high walls of dirt, to keep the rivers from overflowing. They also dug ditches, or canals, to carry water to their dry fields. These innovations, or new ways of doing things, allowed the Sumerians to grow large amounts of grain and dates.

By 3500 B.C. the Sumerian communities had grown into city-states. In the center of each city-state stood a huge temple called a **ziggurat** (ZIH•guh•rat). The Sumerians believed in many gods, and the ziggurat honored a city-state's most important god. The Sumerians built their ziggurats using bricks made from mud. They made the mud by mixing their clay soil with river water.

The demands of city life led the Sumerians to introduce more innovations. The need to move things caused the Sumerians to build both wheeled carts and sailboats. The need to keep trade records led to the world's first writing system. At first, the Sumerians used picture symbols. As time passed, the symbols became less picturelike. Today the Sumerian symbols are known as **cuneiform** (kyu•NEE•uh•fawrm).

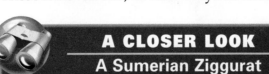

A CLOSER LOOK
A Sumerian Ziggurat

Some historians believe ziggurats were built to represent mountains. Others think ziggurats were built as bridges between heaven and Earth. These mud-brick structures towered over Sumerian cities like skyscrapers. To build such a structure required teamwork and skill.

1. Builders constructed a ziggurat in layers, each one smaller than the one below.

2. All the walls of a ziggurat sloped. These sloping walls may have been covered with trees and bushes.

3. Sumerians built smaller buildings around the base of the ziggurat. Some of these buildings had workshops where workers made clothing, tools, and other items. In others, priests performed religious ceremonies.

❓ Why do you think a temple was built to the city's special god at the very top of the ziggurat?

This Sumerian weight is shaped like a goose and inscribed with cuneiform.

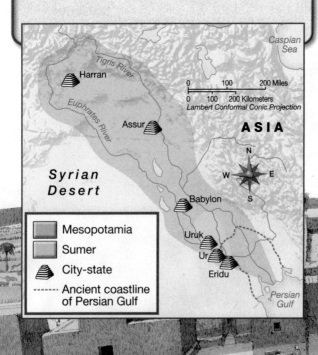

Caspian Sea

Tigris River

Harran

Euphrates River

Assur

ASIA

Syrian Desert

Babylon

Uruk

Ur

Eridu

Persian Gulf

0   100   200 Miles
0   100   200 Kilometers
Lambert Conformal Conic Projection

Mesopotamia
Sumer
City-state
Ancient coastline of Persian Gulf

In about 2500 B.C. a king known as Sargon conquered the Sumerian city-states. He then formed one of the world's first empires. It was known as the Akkadian (uh•KAY•dee•uhn) Empire.

The Akkadian Empire lasted long after Sargon's death but eventually weakened. For hundreds of years no one leader ruled the area. Then, in about 1790 B.C., a leader named Hammurabi (ha•muh•RAH•bee), king of the city-state of Babylon (BA•buh•luhn), began a time of conquest. By 1750 B.C. Hammurabi had conquered much of Mesopotamia, forming the Babylonian Empire.

Hammurabi is perhaps best known for organizing and rewriting the region's **codes**, or laws. This collection of laws has become known as the Code of Hammurabi.

REVIEW What were two innovations that helped the Mesopotamians control their rivers?

The Mediterranean Coast in Ancient Days

The people known as Phoenicians once lived in what today is Lebanon and at other places along the Mediterranean coast. They are best known as traders whose ships sailed as far as West Africa. They exchanged goods and ideas with their trading partners. They also developed an early alphabet made up of symbols that stood for sounds. Most other early writing systems before this one used pictures to stand for words. The Phoenician alphabet influenced many later writing systems, including those many people use today.

South of Lebanon is a region that has been home to many different peoples. It is often called the Holy Land because three of the world's major religions—Judaism,

Christians march in prayer during the Christmas season.

Christianity, and Islam—began here. Parts of the region have also been called both Palestine and Israel.

Judaism is one of the oldest major religions and the first to teach the belief in one God. The basic laws and teachings of Judaism come from the **Torah**, the first five books of the Hebrew Bible. The Hebrews, who came to be called Israelites, were the ancestors of the present-day Jewish people.

The Torah describes God's covenant, or special agreement, with Abraham, the founder of the Jewish religion. The Torah also tells how God gave the Jewish people a set of laws for responsible behavior. These laws are called the **Ten Commandments**. The Torah contains other commandments as well. It also tells how the kingdom of ancient Israel was divided and conquered by other peoples.

By 37 B.C., the land that had been the kingdom of Israel had fallen under Roman control. It became the province of Judaea. During this time a Jewish teacher named Jesus traveled throughout Judaea. He taught the Ten Commandments and belief in one God, as other Jewish teachers did. Jesus also told people to stop sinning, or doing wrong, so that they could be part of God's kingdom. He explained that God loved and forgave sinners. He urged his listeners to love one another.

Christians, Jews, and Muslims around the world all consider Jerusalem to be a holy place. Muslims visit the Dome of the Rock, and Jews pray at the Western Wall.

374

As more people followed Jesus and came to believe his teachings, Roman leaders became concerned. They thought that Jesus might take over their empire and set up his own kingdom. They did not want to risk loosing control of the region. In about A.D. 30, the Roman governor of Judaea allowed his soldiers to put Jesus to death. Jesus was nailed to a cross and left to die.

Within days, Jesus' followers reported that he had risen from the dead, or had been resurrected. To them, this proved that Jesus was the Son of God. Jesus' followers came to be known as Christians, and their religion was called Christianity.

As followers spread Jesus' teachings and established churches, more people became Christians. They learned about Jesus from stories in the **Gospels**, the first four books of the Christian Bible's New Testament. The Christian Old Testament includes the Hebrew Bible.

The Roman leaders, who wanted people to worship their emperor, punished both Christians and Jews for their belief in one God. Some Jewish people revolted against the Romans and were forced to leave the Holy Land in about A.D. 70. Years later, in A.D. 313, Christianity was accepted in the

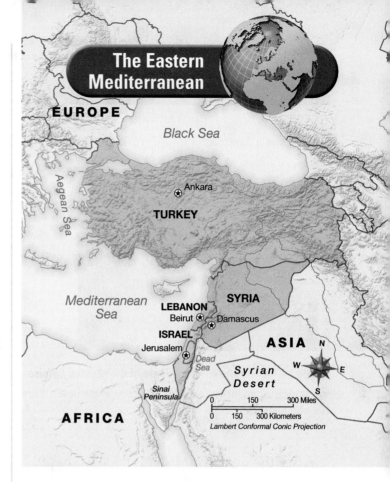

The Eastern Mediterranean

Location The lands along the Mediterranean Sea are important to Southwest Asia's history.

❖ Why do you think many groups settled along the coast of the Mediterranean?

Roman Empire. In A.D. 392 Christianity became the Empire's official religion. Today Christians around the world celebrate Jesus' birth at Christmas and his resurrection at Easter.

During the A.D. 600s an Arab teacher named Muhammad (mah•HA•muhd) preached that there is only one God and that he, Muhammad, was God's messenger. Muhammad's messages form the holy book of the religion of Islam, known as the **Qur'an** (kuh•RAN). Followers of Islam are called Muslims.

This illuminated manuscript shows Christians and Muslims meeting during the Crusades.

Achievements of the Muslim Empire

700	725	750	775	800

705
Great Mosque at Damascus built

About 750
Astrolabe improved

760
First known Arabic numbers, in Arabia

782
Advances in the study of chemistry

785
Mosque at Cordoba built

Analyze Time Lines **The people of the Muslim Empire made many advances.**

◆ Which event took place first, improvements in the astrolabe or advances in chemistry?

After the death of Muhammad, Arab Muslims took control of the lands along the Mediterranean. These included the Holy Land. By about A.D. 750 Islam had spread from present-day Spain and North Africa in the west to China and India in the east. The people of the Muslim Empire built a civilization that made important advances in science, mathematics, and technology. They created the most accurate maps of their day. They also collected great libraries.

Between the years 1095 and 1291, European Christians sent armies to take the Holy Land from Muslim control. Christian leaders had said that Muslims would not let Christians visit Jerusalem and other sacred places in the Holy Land. The battles that were fought between Christians and Muslims in the Holy Land are known as the **Crusades**.

The Crusades caused much loss of life among both Christians and Muslims. Yet they also brought the two peoples closer together. During the Crusades, Christians and Muslims learned about each other's ways of life and each other's resources. They traded goods and borrowed ideas and technology.

REVIEW **What do Judaism, Christianity, and Islam have in common?**

Ancient Empires in Iran and Turkey

In the 500s B.C., long before the Muslim Empire, an empire was built by the Persians, the ancestors of today's Iranian people. The Persian Empire was almost as large as the 48 joined United States. It stretched from Eastern Europe and North Africa in the west to India in the east. It went from the Gulf of Oman in the south to the Caucasus Mountains in the north. Under leaders such as Cyrus the Great and Xerxes (ZERK•seez), the Persian Empire built a great civilization. One of its innovations was a pony-express system for sending messages. This system stretched from one end of the vast empire to the other.

The Persian Empire lasted only 200 years. In 331 B.C. Greek armies led by Alexander the Great conquered the Persian Empire and introduced Greek culture. During the middle A.D. 600s, Arabs made Persia a part of the Muslim Empire. Over time the Arab rulers gradually converted the Iranians to Islam. However, most Iranians continued to follow Persian culture and to speak the Persian language.

During the mid-1000s Arab rule weakened in what is now Iran. Seljuk Turks from Central Asia took control and ruled an empire that included most of Iran, the Holy Land, and parts of Eastern Europe. During their rule the Seljuk Turks introduced Islam to the people of Eastern Europe.

In the 1300s another group of Turks, the Ottomans, began to build a mighty empire of their own. The Ottoman Empire reached its greatest influence in the region in the 1500s. During this time the Ottomans controlled much of Southwest Asia and parts of North Africa and Eastern Europe. More

A frieze painting (right) shows one of the royal guards who protected the Persian kings. The sculpture of a horse's head (left) was once a decoration on a throne made of silver and gold.

importantly, the Ottoman Empire also controlled much of the Mediterranean Sea. Because of this, it controlled trade in the region.

REVIEW What empires were once centered in what is now Iran and Turkey?

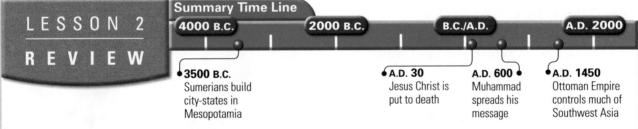

LESSON 2 REVIEW

Summary Time Line

4000 B.C.	2000 B.C.	B.C./A.D.	A.D. 2000

3500 B.C. Sumerians build city-states in Mesopotamia

A.D. 30 Jesus Christ is put to death

A.D. 600 Muhammad spreads his message

A.D. 1450 Ottoman Empire controls much of Southwest Asia

1 MAIN IDEA What Southwest Asian innovations from long ago do you think are most important?

2 WHY IT MATTERS Which innovations of the ancient people of Southwest Asia are still in use today?

3 VOCABULARY Write a sentence that describes **cuneiform** as an innovation.

4 TIME LINE When did the Sumerians build city-states in Mesopotamia?

5 READING SKILL—Compare and Contrast What changed in Sumer after dikes and canals were built?

6 CIVICS AND GOVERNMENT What laws did Hammurabi write for his empire?

7 CULTURE Why do Christians around the world celebrate Christmas and Easter?

8 CRITICAL THINKING—Evaluate Why do you think the Romans punished those who believed in one God?

PERFORMANCE—Make a Book Write and illustrate a page or two for a picture book. Describe at least three innovations of the early people of Southwest Asia.

·SKILLS·
MAP AND GLOBE

Compare Historical Maps

VOCABULARY

historical map

▶ WHY IT MATTERS

One way to learn about history is to use historical maps. A **historical map** gives information about a place at a certain time in history. Some historical maps show where events in the past took place. Others show how places looked at a certain time in the past. Knowing how to compare historical maps can help you discover how a place was and how it has changed over time.

▶ WHAT YOU NEED TO KNOW

Often, the title or the map key tells what year or time period is shown on the map. Colors on a map key can show you the areas claimed by different cities, states, or countries. These colors can also indicate the time period in which the land was controlled by a certain group.

The first map on page 379 shows the different civilizations that arose in Southwest Asia from 3500 B.C. to 650 B.C. One of the earliest civilizations, Sumer—bordered in purple—arose about 3500 B.C. About 2300 B.C. Sargon built the Akkadian Empire, bordered in green on the map. The lands of the Babylonian Empire in 1750 B.C. are bordered in red. The yellow areas show the lands of the Assyrian Empire in 650 B.C.

The cream-colored areas show lands controlled by other groups.

The second map shows the lands of the Persian Empire under Darius in about 500 B.C. At that time the Persian Empire controlled much of Southwest Asia. The cream-colored areas show lands controlled by other groups.

These gypsum statues show how one early artist pictured the Sumerians.

PRACTICE THE SKILL

Compare the maps and study the map keys to learn what each color means. Then use the maps to answer these questions.

1 What color is used to show the lands of the Sumerians? the Akkadians? the Assyrians? the Babylonians? the Persians?

2 Which empire controlled much of Southwest Asia by 500 B.C.?

3 Which is the earliest civilization shown on the first map?

4 Which civilizations controlled lands along the Nile River?

APPLY WHAT YOU LEARNED

Find Southwest Asia on a map or globe that shows present-day borders. Compare that map to the map of Southwest Asia c. 500 B.C. How have the borders in Southwest Asia changed since the days of the Persian Empire? How many countries exist today on the lands that were once controlled by the Persians? Make a list with the names of these countries and their capitals.

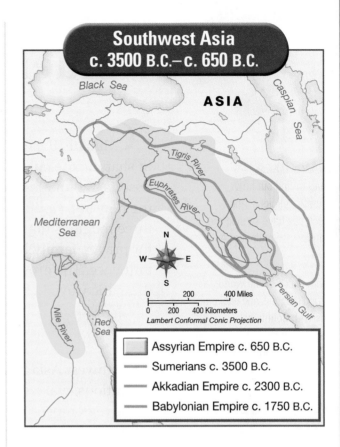

Southwest Asia c. 3500 B.C.–c. 650 B.C.

0 200 400 Miles
0 200 400 Kilometers
Lambert Conformal Conic Projection

- Assyrian Empire c. 650 B.C.
- Sumerians c. 3500 B.C.
- Akkadian Empire c. 2300 B.C.
- Babylonian Empire c. 1750 B.C.

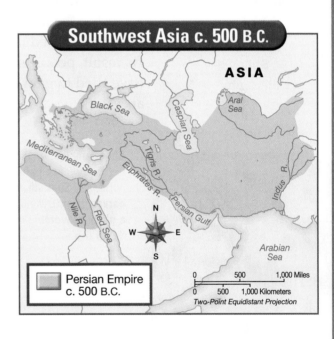

Southwest Asia c. 500 B.C.

Persian Empire c. 500 B.C.

0 500 1,000 Miles
0 500 1,000 Kilometers
Two-Point Equidistant Projection

Statue of Darius, a ruler of the Persian Empire

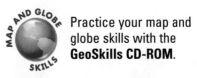

Practice your map and globe skills with the **GeoSkills CD-ROM**.

Chapter 11 ▪ **379**

MAIN IDEA
Read to find out how climate, religions, and resources have shaped the cultures of Southwest Asia.

WHY IT MATTERS
Today much of the world has strong religious and economic ties with Southwest Asia. Because of these ties, people around the world feel a close connection to this region.

VOCABULARY
refugee
Five Pillars
hajj
Sunni
Shi'i
calligraphy

Influences on Cultures

Climate, beliefs, and resources each played a critical role in shaping the cultures of Southwest Asia. Over the centuries deserts, mountains, coasts, and other landscapes have affected the housing, clothing, and food of the people who live there. The three religions that developed in the region have provided rules for prayer, family life, and artistic expression. Oil is a more recent influence. The growth of the oil industry has changed life in dramatic ways in some parts of Southwest Asia.

People of Southwest Asia

Southwest Asia has been a crossroads for thousands of years. Migrations, wars, invasions, religion, and trade have brought to the region people from Africa, Asia, and Europe. Some came to set up colonies and build empires. Others came out of love for the land and its religious meaning.

During the last two centuries, wars, treaties, and European colonization carved many separate nations out of Southwest Asia. As result, people such as the Afghans, Kurds, and Palestinians have tried to gain new homelands in this region where their ancestors lived.

Christians in Jerusalem observe Good Friday (left). Jews use palm branches to honor the holiday of Sukkoth, which celebrates the harvest (right). Muslims make a pilgrimage to a place of worship called the Ka'ba in Mecca, Saudi Arabia.

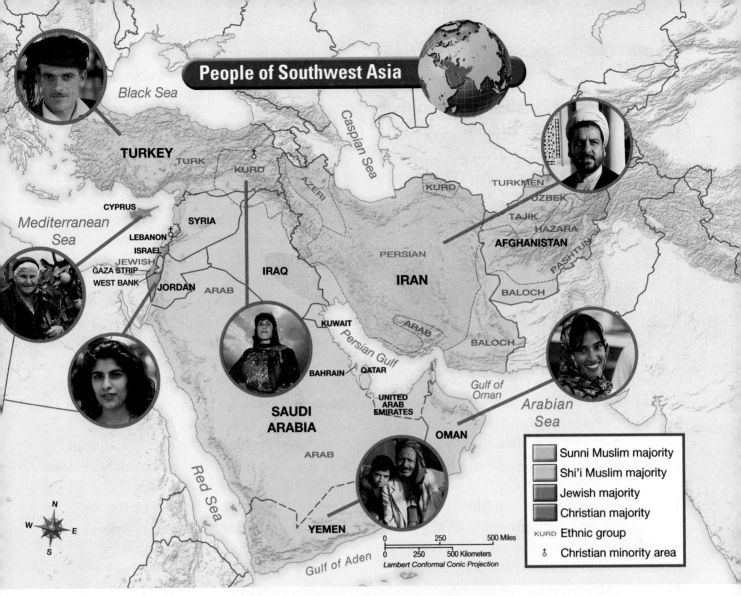

People of Southwest Asia

Black Sea

TURKEY

TURK

KURD

CYPRUS

Mediterranean Sea

SYRIA

LEBANON

ISRAEL

JEWISH

GAZA STRIP

WEST BANK

JORDAN

ARAB

IRAQ

KUWAIT

BAHRAIN QATAR

SAUDI ARABIA

ARAB

Red Sea

YEMEN

Gulf of Aden

Persian Gulf

UNITED ARAB EMIRATES

Caspian Sea

AZERI

KURD

TURKMEN

UZBEK

TAJIK

HAZARA

AFGHANISTAN

PASHTUN

PERSIAN

IRAN

BALOCH

ARAB

BALOCH

Gulf of Oman

OMAN

Arabian Sea

N
W E
S

	Sunni Muslim majority
	Shi'i Muslim majority
	Jewish majority
	Christian majority
KURD	Ethnic group
☦	Christian minority area

0   250   500 Miles
0 250 500 Kilometers
Lambert Conformal Conic Projection

GEOGRAPHY THEME

Location Many ethnic groups live throughout Southwest Asia. However, most people are either Sunni or Shi'i (also spelled Shiite) Muslims. The Sunni is the largest branch of Islam, and the Shi'i is the second-largest branch.

❖ In which country are the majority of people followers of the Shi'i branch in the religion of Islam?

Many Jews now living in Israel are descendants of those who settled there in the late 1800s and 1900s. Some went there because of their desire to live in the Holy Land. Others went to escape discrimination in other countries. Many European Jews went to the region as refugees from the Holocaust. A **refugee** is a person who flees from his or her home or country to find refuge, or a safe place to stay. Jews also moved to Israel from Arab countries after the nation of Israel was established in 1948.

The people of Southwest Asia are diverse in culture and religion. However, most of the people there are Arab Muslims. Arabs are a group of people whose language is Arabic and who have a common history and culture. Muslims are followers of the religion of Islam. Their beliefs are based on the Qur'an, the holy book of Islam. The Qur'an teaches Muslim wisdom, laws, and duties. The main duties, or the **Five Pillars**, are acts of worship that Muslims are expected to perform.

Rosh Hashanah and Yom Kippur

An important holiday that Jews in Israel and around the world celebrate is Rosh Hashanah (RAHSH uh•SHAH•nuh), the Jewish New Year. Rosh Hashanah is the first day of a ten-day period of worship. The tenth day, Yom Kippur (YOHM kih•POOR), is the holiest day of the Jewish year. On Yom Kippur, Jewish people pray and fast.

The Five Pillars are (1) stating their faith, (2) praying five times a day, (3) giving to charity, (4) fasting during Ramadan (RAH•muh•dahn), the Muslim holy month, and (5) making a pilgrimage to Mecca, Saudi Arabia, the holiest city of Islam. This journey is called a **hajj** (HAJ).

There are two main groups within the religion of Islam. They are the **Sunni** (SOON•nee) Muslims and the **Shi'i** (SHEE•uh) Muslims. Most Muslims in Southwest Asia are Sunni. Of the 15 percent of Shi'i Muslims in the world, most live in Iran, Iraq, and Lebanon.

Judaism, Christianity, and Islam began in Southwest Asia. From there they spread throughout the world. Today, Cyprus is the only country in Southwest Asia where Christianity is the main religion. The Greek people of Cyprus follow the Eastern Orthodox branch of Christianity. Christian minorities are found in Jordan, Lebanon, Syria, Israel, Turkey, Iraq, and Iran. Some Palestinians are Christians as well. Today most of the Jews in Southwest Asia live in Israel.

Southwest Asia is a region where many languages can be heard. Hebrew and Arabic are among the oldest languages that are still spoken today. Hebrew has been modernized and is now the official language of Israel. Today Arabic is the main language spoken in every country in Southwest Asia except Afghanistan, Iran, Cyprus, Israel, and Turkey. Greek is spoken in Cyprus. Iranians speak Farsi (FAR•see), or Persian. Afghans speak Dari or Pashto. Kurds in Iran, Iraq, and Turkey speak Kurdish. Colonial nations of Europe brought their languages to the region. Today, immigrants from many other regions of the world bring with them their own languages.

REVIEW What is the largest ethnic group in Southwest Asia, and what religion do they follow?

Educational opportunities for women in some parts of Southwest Asia are expanding. These young girls sing songs in English at an all-girls' school in Iran.

Boys pick apples on a kibbutz in Israel (left). A kibbutz is a farm where many families live together and share what they produce. Vendors sell fresh produce in a street market in Istanbul, Turkey (right).

Ways of Life in Southwest Asia

Strong family life is valued in all the societies of Southwest Asia. Parents and children often share their homes with other relatives. The oldest male in the household has the most say in making a decision. Women play a major role in taking care of their children and homes.

In some Arab countries a woman's freedom may be limited outside the home. In Saudi Arabia women are not allowed to drive cars and must be accompanied by a male relative wherever they go. At the same time women in nearly every country in Southwest Asia may have careers and can vote in elections.

The people of Southwest Asia have always made the most of their limited resources. In small villages some people still make sun-dried bricks out of mud or gather stones to use for their houses. However, in urban areas, builders use cement, brick, glass, and steel. Skyscrapers rise in cities such as Dubai (doo•BY) in the United Arab Emirates, Beirut (bay•ROOT) in Lebanon, Kuwait City in Kuwait, and Tel Aviv in Israel.

Since ancient times men and women throughout the region, including early Jews and Christians, have worn long, loose robes and some kind of head covering. Today many people still wear this traditional clothing. It conforms to religious teachings that require Muslims to dress modestly. Also, the clothing offers protection from the strong sun of the region. However, western clothing has become popular in many parts of Southwest Asia. European-style suits and sneakers can be seen throughout the region.

In such countries as Afghanistan, Iran, Iraq, and Saudi Arabia, laws for public dress have been written according to the customs and views of Islam. These laws require women to be almost completely covered, with only their eyes exposed. Women in other Muslim countries wear a variety of styles of Arabic and Western dress.

Even though there is little fertile farmland in Southwest Asia, nearly half of the people of the region still grow crops for a living. Farmers usually live in villages near their fields. The farmers grow grains, olives, cotton, fruits, and vegetables.

Crops that are not used by farmers and their families are often sold at markets. These lively places are located in villages and in older sections of cities, on narrow streets lined with shops and stalls.

The discovery of oil brought many changes to some of the traditional ways of life in Southwest Asia. With the growth of the oil industry came the growth of cities. About 50 percent of Southwest Asia's people now live in cities. Government profits from oil also have brought improved health care, education, and other social services.

In recent times the oil industry has created more nonfarming jobs. Jobs in construction, manufacturing, and the service industries are increasing. As a result, more people are moving into urban areas. Sometimes people even come from other countries to work in the oil-rich countries. These guest workers come mainly from poor countries, including Egypt, India, and the Philippines.

REVIEW What discovery has caused many changes to the ways of life of Southwest Asians?

Arts in Southwest Asia

Beginning in the seventh century, the spread of Islam began to influence the arts and architecture of Southwest Asia. As Islamic teachings spread, they changed the content of the arts and brought about new styles. Islamic beliefs do not allow the use of holy images in worship and forbid images of animals and people. Instead, Islamic artists use designs that have geometric shapes. These designs are important in Islamic art and architecture.

Calligraphy, or decorative writing, is the most respected form of art in Islam. This writing was used to make beautiful copies

Arabic calligraphy

of the Qur'an in Arabic, the language in which all Muslims recite it. In time, calligraphy became an art form used to decorate public spaces, personal objects, and books of all kinds.

When Islam spread with the growth of the Muslim Empire, Arabic literature spread with it. Poems and stories were ways that the Arab people shared their culture and way of life with other people. Today, many Arabs enjoy listening to and reciting poetry. Stories, novels, and plays are also published in great numbers.

These musicians in Oman play the Arab drum (left) and the oud, a stringed instrument (right).

In recent years western styles of literature have influenced writers in Southwest Asia. Also, growing Internet use is exposing the Arab people to western literature and western news media more than ever before.

Western music and movies have also influenced the region. At the same time, music and films from Southwest Asia have gained audiences and awards around the world.

Islamic religious beliefs and customs sometimes conflict with western ideas, however. Some governments in Southwest Asia take action to limit western influence.

For centuries building designs in Southwest Asia have been shaped by Islam. Mosques, or Islamic houses of worship, are good examples of this. Columns, domes, arches, and towers for calls to prayer can be found in the mosques of Southwest Asia. Over time, Islamic architecture came to be used for courts of law, government buildings, and palaces.

Countries of Southwest Asia are known for their beautiful handicrafts. Turkey, Iran, and Iraq are famous for their hand-woven carpets and rugs. Craftworkers in Lebanon and Syria create amazing glassware.

Arab music was influenced by Persian and Greek music. Arab music often uses stringed instruments called ouds (OODZ). It usually has long repeated rhythms.

REVIEW **Why does Islamic art feature geometric shapes and patterns?**

LOCATE IT

OMAN

Bawshar

LESSON 3
REVIEW

1 **MAIN IDEA** Describe one way the cultures of Southwest Asia have been influenced by each of the following—climate, religion, and resources.

2 **WHY IT MATTERS** What do you think is the strongest economic tie that Southwest Asia has with the rest of the world? Why?

3 **VOCABULARY** Explain the importance of the **Five Pillars** and the **hajj** to Muslims.

4 **READING SKILLS—Compare and Contrast** What are three ways in which life is different for people living in rural areas and in urban areas in Southwest Asia?

5 **CULTURE** How are Rosh Hashanah, Yom Kippur, and Ramadan important to the people of Southwest Asia?

6 **CRITICAL THINKING—Evaluate** What do you think are the advantages and disadvantages of being a guest worker in an oil-rich country?

PERFORMANCE—Make a Table Create a table that lists the major religions and languages of at least five countries in Southwest Asia.

Schoolbooks

Schoolbooks, or textbooks, contain information for students studying subjects such as literature, mathematics, science, and social studies. Schoolbooks are written in many languages. Your schoolbooks might be used anywhere the English language is used. The schoolbook shown on these pages might be used anywhere Modern Standard Arabic (MSA) is used. MSA serves as the main form of Arabic in all Arab lands. It is the language used in most schools and in radio and television broadcasts throughout the Arab world.

FROM HARCOURT SCHOOL PUBLISHERS
TEXTBOOK COLLECTION

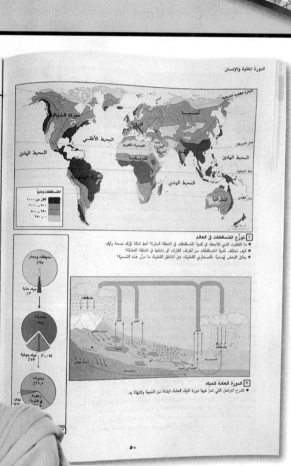

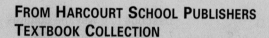

Palestinian students study Arab history and geography.

Analyze the Primary Source

1 How is this Arabic-language schoolbook like those you use in school?

2 How is the Arabic schoolbook different from yours?

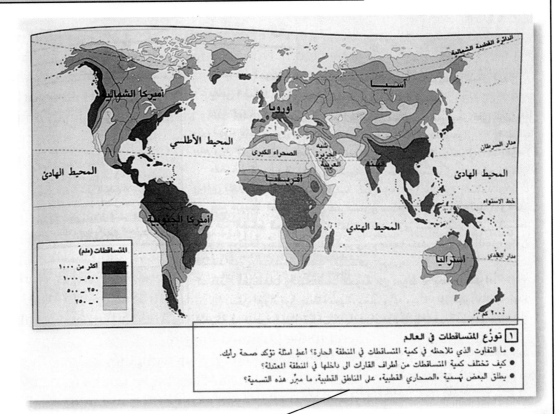

TRANSLATION:

Precipitation distribution around the globe

- What variations do you observe in precipitation in the hot regions? Provide examples.
- How does the amount of precipitation toward the inside of warmer regions vary with the size of a continent?
- Some call the Polar Region the Polar Desert. What is the explanation for this name?

ACTIVITY

Compare and Contrast Find a map in this book that is similar to the one on this page. Compare and contrast the different parts of each of the maps.

RESEARCH

Visit The Learning Site at **www.harcourtschool.com/primarysources** to research other primary sources.

New Governments and Strong Economies

MAIN IDEA
Read to find out about the wide range of governments and economies found in Southwest Asia.

WHY IT MATTERS
The governments and economies of Southwest Asia affect other parts of the world.

VOCABULARY

Zionism
mixed economy
absolute monarchy
embargo

FAST FACT

Independence Day in Turkey is celebrated in every city. In Ankara there is a military show. Everywhere people carry flags and flames and sing songs. At night fireworks paint the sky.

Almost every country found on a political map of Southwest Asia today would be missing from a map of just 100 years ago. Although the once-mighty Ottoman Empire had lost most of its former glory by the early 1900s, it still ruled parts of Southwest Asia. After World War I ended, the Ottoman Empire and other world empires were broken up.

The Birth of New Nations

World War I pitted the Central Powers—the Ottoman Empire, Germany, and Austria-Hungary—in a fight against the Allied Powers—France, Britain, Russia, and later the United States. The involvement of the Ottoman Empire in World War I brought fighting to Southwest Asia. In 1918, World War I ended in a victory for the Allied Powers. The end of the war also brought an end to the Ottoman Empire.

After the Allied Powers won, they redrew the maps of Europe and Southwest Asia. They broke up the former Ottoman Empire. New countries were established, and more territory in Southwest Asia came under the control of France and Britain. All that was left of the Ottoman Empire was the country known today as Turkey. In 1923 a leader known as Kemal Ataturk (kuh•MAHL

A•tuh•terk), or "Father of the Turks," declared Turkey an independent republic. French and British territories received independence after yet another world war.

A new organization called the League of Nations was given the responsibility for the former Ottoman lands. Representatives from countries all over the world had come together to create the league. Its main purpose was to help solve future conflicts peacefully. Later, the United Nations replaced the League of Nations as a world organization.

The League of Nations created a system called mandates to govern the former Ottoman lands. Britain and France were given control over the newly divided land. These lands were to become independent later. Iraq, which had been under British control, gained independence in 1932. Syria and Lebanon, which had been under French control, gained independence in 1941. The independence of British-controlled Palestine turned out to be much more complicated.

Before World War I, a movement called **Zionism** developed among Jews in Europe and Russia. Mistreatment of Jews in those places led to the idea of having a homeland where Jews could settle and govern themselves. Zionist leaders asked the British for their support for a homeland in Palestine. The British had also promised the territory to the Arabs because of their help fighting the Ottomans. More and more Jewish settlers came. Hoping to keep each group happy, Britain promised both Jews and Palestinians a homeland in Palestine.

After World War II and the horrors of the Holocaust, Zionists' demand for an independent Jewish state grew. Unable to govern Palestine, Britain turned the whole problem over to the newly formed United Nations.

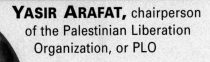

In 1947 the United Nations decided to divide Palestine into a Jewish state and an Arab state. Jerusalem—holy to three religions—was to become an international city not controlled by any one group. In 1948, when Jewish leaders announced the creation of Israel as an independent country, Arab armies attacked Israel. The Arabs aimed to destroy the new nation. By 1949, however, Israel defeated the Arabs and gained control of about half of the land planned for the new Arab state of Palestine.

Over the years Israel and the Arab nations have fought several more wars.

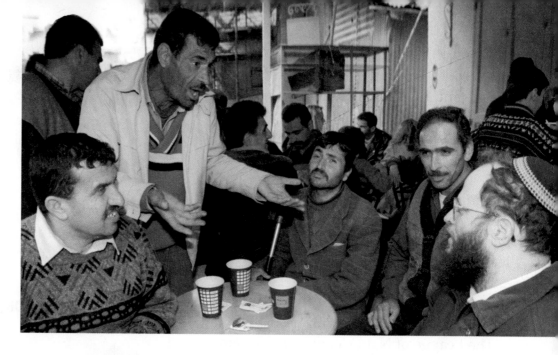

Israeli and Palestinian artists peacefully discuss issues of the day in the West Bank city of Hebron.

As a result of these wars, Israel gained control over more of the land that had been set aside for the Palestinian state. Without a homeland, some Palestinians now live under the rule of the Israeli army or have become citizens of Israel. Others live as refugees in neighboring Arab countries. To achieve the goal of a Palestinian homeland, the people have organized into many different groups. The best known is the Palestine Liberation Organization, or PLO.

The PLO has used both peaceful and violent means. In 1987 the PLO supported a violent series of protests called the intifadas in the West Bank and the Gaza Strip. However, in 1993 the PLO worked together with Israeli leaders to achieve a peace plan. The plan gave back to the Palestinians control of some of the land lost in past wars. Since that time, however, there has been more violence and conflict.

Conflict has occurred in other parts of Southwest Asia as well. When Cyprus gained independence from Britain in 1960, many people whose ancestors had come from Turkey and Greece lived there. Turkish and Greek Cypriots, or people from Cyprus, began to fight over control of the island. Since 1974 the northern part of the island has claimed to be a separate Turkish state.

From 1980 to 1988 Iran and Iraq fought a war over oil-producing territory along their shared border. Today the Kurdish people of Turkey, Syria, Iraq, and Iran continue to fight for freedom to preserve their own language and culture.

REVIEW How did the Ottoman Empire lose its lands in Southwest Asia?

A Wide Range of Economies

A wide range of economies works together in Southwest Asia. Some countries, such as Israel, have market economies that work with government participation. Others, such as Iraq, have command economies. Most of Southwest Asia's countries have **mixed economies**, with varying degrees of free enterprise and governmental control.

Before the discovery of oil, most of Southwest Asia's countries depended on farming and trade. Oil changed Southwest Asia's economies dramatically. Countries such as Saudi Arabia, Iran, Iraq, and Kuwait suddenly had money to improve public school systems, universities, and health care. Money from the sale of oil also made it possible to import food from countries with stronger agricultural industries. However, even in the oil-rich countries, not everyone has shared in the wealth that this valuable natural resource has brought.

In 1960 several major oil-producing countries, including Venezuela in South America, joined to form the Organization of Petroleum Exporting Countries (OPEC). Today, the Southwest Asian countries of Iran, Iraq, Kuwait, Qatar, Saudi Arabia, and the United Arab Emirates belong to OPEC. OPEC provides its members with scientific and economic aid for oil production. OPEC also tries to control the price of oil. To make sure prices do not dip too low, the organization decides how much oil each country can produce.

Many oil-producing countries, such as Bahrain, have worked to diversify their economies. They do not want to be dependent on any one resource or product. Today Bahrain serves as a shipping and banking center for Southwest Asia.

Southwest Asia's non–oil-producing countries have had to find ways other than the sale of oil to help their people earn a living. Without oil, Israel has managed to create one of Southwest Asia's strongest economies. Israel exports cut diamonds, high-tech equipment, and fruits and vegetables. Agriculture is important in many non–oil-producing countries. On the

Oil Production in Southwest Asia

Rest of the world about 33%
Saudi Arabia 27%
Iraq 10%
Bahrain less than 1%
Syria less than 1%
Yemen less than 1%
Oman less than 1%
Qatar less than 1%
Kuwait 10%
Iran 9%
United Arab Emirates 7%

Analyze Graphs The countries of Southwest Asia produce much of the world's oil.

❖ How does Saudi Arabia's oil production compare with that of the rest of the world?

island of Cyprus, farmers grow wheat and barley. In Lebanon natural springs provide farmers with water to grow olives, grapes, figs, and sugar beets. Vineyards, orchards, and olive groves dot the Turkish landscape. Turkish farms grow large crops of grains, cotton, and sugar beets. The economies of other countries without oil, such as Jordan and Afghanistan, have not done as well.

REVIEW In what kind of economy do both individuals and governments make economic decisions?

Money from a country is sometimes decorated with symbols that are important to its people. These coins are from Israel and Iran. This paper money is from Saudi Arabia.

Sultan Qaboos bin Said rules the country of Oman.

Jordan's King Abdullah II and Queen Rania lead the royal motorcade through Jordan's capital of Amman.

A Wide Range of Governments

A wide range of governments exists in the countries of Southwest Asia. Many of these governments are either republics or monarchies. One kind of monarchy found in Southwest Asia is an absolute monarchy. In an **absolute monarchy**, the monarch has absolute, or complete, authority. In Oman an absolute monarch holds all of the power to make and enforce laws.

In most of today's monarchies, the monarch shares power with elected officials. This kind of government is called a constitutional monarchy. Jordan has a constitutional monarchy with a parliamentary system. Citizens in Jordan elect the lower house of the parliament, and the king appoints the upper house. Jordan's King Abdullah II also appoints a prime minister, who runs the government.

The United Arab Emirates has a monarchy that is different from the others found in Southwest Asia. This country is divided into seven different parts, or emirates. A ruler called an emir, or prince, rules each of these parts.

Until the late 1970s Iran was a monarchy. A shah, or king, ruled Iran. In 1979 the shah was overthrown during a revolution. Soon after the revolution the Ayatollah Khomeini (eye•uh•TOH•luh koh•MAY•nee) took absolute control of Iran's government. An ayatollah is the highest authority on Islamic law in Iran. The government of Iran became an Islamic republic, or a government based on the religious laws of Islam. Khomeini died in 1989, but control by an ayatollah remains strong. The present ayatollah oversees and has the final word on all decisions made by the government.

Many Southwest Asian leaders consider their countries republics. Only some of these countries are true republics. In recent years, Iraq has struggled to become a republic. For many years, dictator Saddam Hussein (suh•DAHM hoo•SAYN) ruled with an iron hand.

In 1990 disputes over money and oil led Iraqi military forces under Saddam Hussein to occupy nearby Kuwait. The United Nations placed an **embargo**—a limit or ban on trade—on goods entering Iraq. The United Nations also placed an embargo on Iraq's oil exports. These actions

Democratic Republic

In Israel people elect a prime minister and a legislative branch called the Knesset.

Republic Under Military Rule

Members of the Syrian People's Assembly raise their hands in support of a new law.

were meant to stop Iraq, but Saddam Hussein did not give up. Soon a war called the Persian Gulf War started. This war ended after a coalition of forces, led by the United States, took military action against Iraq and took back control of Kuwait.

The 2000s saw more conflict between the United States and Iraq. President George Bush believed that Iraq's Saddam Hussein was a threat to world peace. The United States and its allies attacked Iraq in 2003. Their goal to topple Hussein's government was a success. Even so, violence there continued.

Southwest Asia also has several true republics. In countries such as Turkey, Lebanon, and Israel, the people elect the members of their government.

REVIEW What kinds of monarchies are found in Southwest Asia?

LESSON 4
REVIEW

1 **MAIN IDEA** What kinds of governments and economies are found in Southwest Asia?

2 **WHY IT MATTERS** How do disagreements between governments in Southwest Asia affect the rest of the world?

3 **VOCABULARY** What is the difference between a mixed economy and a market economy?

4 **READING SKILL—Compare and Contrast** How is the monarchy in Jordan different from the monarchy in Oman?

5 **HISTORY** What happened to the Southwest Asian lands still controlled by the Ottoman Empire after World War I?

6 **ECONOMICS** How does OPEC control the price of oil in the world?

7 **GOVERNMENT** How is the monarchy of the United Arab Emirates different from others found in Southwest Asia?

8 **CRITICAL THINKING—Analyze** How do you think the borders established by the Allied Powers affected the lives of people in Southwest Asia?

PERFORMANCE—Make a Postcard
Make a postcard for a Southwest Asian country of your choice. On the front of this postcard, draw a picture that shows some aspect of this country's economy or government. On the back, write a message to a friend about this country. In your message, include facts about the government, industries, and natural resources found there.

Identify Frames of Reference

VOCABULARY

frames of reference

➡ WHY IT MATTERS

Why did the Persian Gulf War start? Who started it? Why did the United Nations get involved? These are questions that many people around the world asked on January 17, 1991, when the United Nations, led by the United States, attacked Iraq. **Frames of reference** are the different viewpoints from which an issue can be seen. The Iraqi frame of reference led them to claim some of Kuwait's land as their own, and they wanted Kuwait's oil resources to help pay off Iraqi debt. Of course, Kuwait had a completely different viewpoint.

Understanding the frames of reference of different people and countries helps us understand why things such as the Gulf War happen.

➡ WHAT YOU NEED TO KNOW

Time and place can be important in understanding different frames of reference. Historians have to be careful not to interpret things from a present-day frame of reference. Frames of reference can also differ based on where a person may live, on their religion, or on their values.

When evaluating frame of reference, ask yourself these questions:

- What does the person or group want?
- What is important to them? How have they been taught? What is their culture?
- Where do they live?
- How will different solutions to the problem affect them or their lifestyle?

❝ **The President [George Bush] listened carefully and the President said, 'Now Colin, you are really sure that air power alone can't do it?' And my response was, 'Mr. President, I wish . . . I could assure you that air power alone could do it . . . there'll be no guessing . . . we're going to be successful with this plan'. . . when the meeting had gone on long enough for the President . . . he simply looked up and he said, 'Do it.'** ❞

—Colin Powell, Chairman of the U.S. Joint Chiefs of Staff

66 We were facing two options, either to stop servicing our debts and then being declared bankrupt in the international arena . . . or . . . stop living well . . . but our country needs several billion dollars a year to buy food, medicine, [and] spare parts, and to take into consideration that after eight years of war [with Iran], the people wanted a better living. 99

—Tariq Aziz, Foreign Minister of Iraq

66 I remember you always ask for Allah's advice, because this is what you have started our meeting with. Let me use the opportunity of this meeting to give a piece of advice to you—reconsider your position, because it is dangerous. Pass this message . . . to Saddam Hussein— the path you have chosen means trouble for Iraq, the world community would never agree . . . to let a conflict with such dangerous consequences . . . start as a result of your adventure. That was our tough, but absolutely just, position. It was in everybody's interest, and most of all to the interest of Iraq. 99

—Mikhail Gorbachev, President of the Soviet Union

▶ **PRACTICE THE SKILL**

Read these different frames of reference on the Persian Gulf War. Then use the quotes to answer the following questions.

1 What is the frame of reference of Tariq Aziz?

2 How does the frame of reference of Tariq Aziz compare to Mikhail Gorbachev's frame of reference? How does Gorbachev acknowledge Aziz's religious frame of reference? What was the advantage of acknowledging it?

3 What is Colin Powell's frame of reference? How is it different from Aziz's and Gorbachev's frames of reference?

▶ **APPLY WHAT YOU LEARNED**

Think of a recent conflict or problem that you have had with a family member or a friend. At the top of a piece of paper, write down what the problem was. Now, list the people who were involved. Be sure to list yourself. Beside each person's name, write her or his frame of reference. Ask yourself the questions in **What You Need to Know**. What was each person's point of view? How did he or she see the problem? Show this paper to the people you listed. Do they agree with your opinion of their frames of reference? Do they think that you understand their points of view? When you have a problem, think about the other person's frame of reference. It may help you have fewer conflicts in the future.

11 Review and Test Preparation

Summary Time Line

4000 B.C.   3000 B.C.

3500 B.C.
Sumerians build
city-states in
Mesopotamia

USE YOUR READING SKILLS

Complete this graphic organizer to show that you understand how to compare and contrast different topics, such as life in Southwest Asia before and after the discovery of oil. A copy of this graphic organizer appears on page 107 of the Activity Book.

Oil in Southwest Asia

TOPIC A
_____
_____

TOPIC B
_____
_____

LIFE BEFORE THE DISCOVERY OF OIL

_____
_____
_____

People farmed and sold crops in markets.

_____
_____
_____

Food was sometimes in short supply.

LIFE AFTER THE DISCOVERY OF OIL

Urban areas and cities began to grow.

_____
_____
_____

Governments were able to pay for improved health care and education.

_____
_____
_____

THINK & WRITE

Write an Opinion   Do you think that the discovery of oil changed life in Southwest Asia for the better? List the reasons for your opinion.

Write to Compare   The countries of Southwest Asia have a wide range of governments. Write a paragraph that compares and contrasts these governments.

1750 B.C.
Babylonian
Empire forms

500 B.C.
Persian Empire develops
pony-express system

A.D. 1500s
Ottoman Empire
controls much of
Southwest Asia

A.D. 1991
Persian Gulf
War begins

USE THE TIME LINE

Use the chapter summary time line to answer these questions.

1 By which year had the Babylonian Empire formed?

2 About when was a pony-express system started in the Persian Empire?

USE VOCABULARY

Identify the term that correctly matches each definition.

oasis (p. 367)

wadis (p. 369)

ziggurat (p. 372)

hajj (p. 382)

embargo (p. 392)

3 riverbeds that are usually dry

4 a huge temple

5 in a desert, a place that has a dependable supply of water

6 ban on trade

7 a pilgrimage to Mecca, Saudi Arabia

RECALL FACTS

Answer these questions.

8 Why were the Tigris and Euphrates Rivers dangerous to the Sumerians?

9 What were some needs that led to innovations in Sumer?

10 How is a woman's freedom limited in some Arab countries?

Write the letter of the best choice.

11 **TEST PREP**   Because rain seldom falls in Southwest Asia,—
   A many areas are too dry to grow crops.
   B crops grow easily in most areas.
   C it is easy to create new farming areas.
   D most people live in deserts.

12 **TEST PREP**   In most of the monarchies in Southwest Asia today,—
   F the monarch has complete authority.
   G the monarch has been overthrown.
   H the monarch shares power with elected officials.
   J the government is based on religious laws.

THINK CRITICALLY

13 What do you think was the most important achievement of the Mesopotamians?

14 Imagine that you live in Southwest Asia. How has your life changed since the discovery of oil?

APPLY SKILLS

Compare Historical Maps

15 Use the maps on page 379 to name the civilizations that at different times controlled Southwest Asia. Tell which empire had the greatest amount of land.

Identify Frames of Reference

16 Find an article about a problem in your community. Identify who is involved and what each person's frame of reference is. Offer possible solutions, and determine how the different frames of reference might affect each solution to the problem.

NILE RIVER, EGYPT

Egyptian feluccas, or sailboats, glide down the Nile River at sunset. Throughout history, the waters of the Nile have been essential to travel, trade, and agriculture in Egypt.

LOCATE IT

EGYPT

Nile River

North Africa

" It flows through old
hushed Egypt
and its sands

Like some grave
mighty thought
threading a dream . . . "

—Leigh Hunt, from "A Thought
of the Nile," 1818

CHAPTER READING SKILL

Sequence

The order in which events, processes, or ideas happen is **sequence**. Sequence tells what happens first, next, and last.

As you read this chapter, tell what events, processes, and ideas happened and in what order they happened.

FIRST → NEXT → LAST

MAIN IDEA
Read to find out how North Africa's mostly desert climate affects the way people live.

WHY IT MATTERS
Learning about the climate of North Africa will give you a better understanding of how people adapt to their physical surroundings.

VOCABULARY
cataract
reg
erg
draa
depression

A Region of Deserts

A vast desert called the Sahara lies just across the Red Sea from Southwest Asia. This desert stretches across Africa from the shores of the Atlantic in the west to the Suez Canal and the Red Sea in the east. Parts of the Sahara can be found in Morocco, Algeria, Tunisia, Libya, and Egypt. These five countries make up the region called North Africa. Few people live in the Sahara, for it has little water. Most of North Africa's people live along the Atlantic coast in the west, the Nile Valley in the east, and the Mediterranean coast in the north. These coastal areas have fertile lands, rainfall, and cities. Other people live near another supply of water, such as an oasis within the Sahara.

North Africa's Landscape

The Atlantic Ocean, the Mediterranean Sea, and the Red Sea make up the long coastline of North Africa. All of the desert countries touch the sea, but parts of Algeria, Libya, and Egypt are far from the sea. The Mediterranean Sea separates North Africa from Europe. At the Strait of Gibraltar, Africa is separated from Europe by only 8 miles (13 km) of water!

In the distant past, Europeans often called the land across the Mediterranean Sea the Barbary Coast, after the Berbers. The Berbers were nomads and were the earliest-known people to live in the lands that are today Morocco, Algeria, Tunisia, and Libya. Today, people call the northwestern part of North Africa the Maghreb (MAH•greb). *Maghreb* means "the west" in Arabic. To the Arabs the Maghreb is the western part of their world. The Maghreb includes Morocco, Algeria, and Tunisia.

Imagine that you are traveling the Maghreb from north to south. Your journey starts on a large plain that stretches from Morocco's Atlantic coast to the Mediterranean coast in Algeria and Tunisia. This coastal plain has most of the region's fertile farmland. Farmers there grow citrus fruits, dates, olives, and tomatoes. The majority of the Maghreb's people live on this coastal plain.

This man picks dates from a palm tree in Egypt. He places the dates in a straw basket and uses ropes to support him as he climbs.

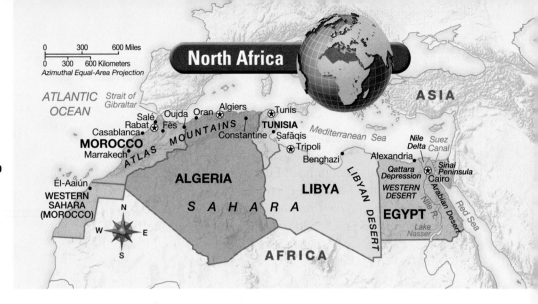

North Africa

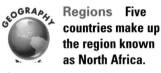

Regions Five countries make up the region known as North Africa.

❖ What geographical feature do the countries of North Africa share?

The coastal plain is a good place for crops to grow and people to live because of its mild climate. It is warm and wet in winter and hot and dry in summer.

Toward the south the coastal plain gives way to hills and then to a mountain range, the Atlas Mountains. In Algeria this hilly coastal area is called the Tell. In Arabic, *tell* means "hill." The hills and low mountains along Algeria's coast are known as the Tell Atlas. The snow-capped Atlas Mountains stand more than 13,000 feet (3,962 m) tall at their highest point in Morocco. The Atlas mountain range extends from southwestern Morocco northeast into northern Algeria and Tunisia.

Travel to the other side of the Atlas Mountains and you find the rocky and arid landscape of the Sahara. A large part of Egypt and Libya is also covered by the Sahara. Much of the land in Libya is too dry for farming. However, palm, olive, and orange trees grow in the desert oases.

In the 1990s the Libyan government began a project to bring fresh water from oases to the coast. A pipeline will provide water for Libya's cities.

Traditional mud-brick buildings in Dades Valley, Morocco, lie beyond lush palm trees and wheat fields. This area is an oasis in the desert.

Suez Canal

Understanding Human Systems

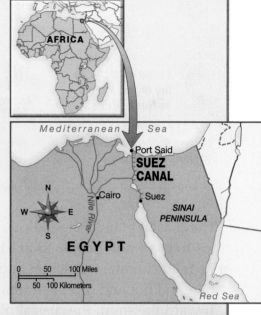

For centuries, traders from Europe traveled overland across Asia to reach the Mediterranean Sea from the Red Sea. In 1858 a French engineer named Ferdinand de Lesseps got permission from Sa'id Pasha, the leader of Egypt, to build a canal. This canal opened with a great ceremony on November 17, 1869. The Suez Canal cost about $100 million to build. The Suez Canal is a shortcut for ships traveling from the Mediterranean Sea to the Indian Ocean. In recent years the Suez Canal was made deeper and wider so that bigger ships could pass through. Tolls collected from ships using the canal add money to Egypt's economy.

This water will also be used to irrigate Libya's land, turning dry coastal plains into valuable farmlands. While parts of this massive pipeline project are already complete, the year 2007 is the date set for completion of the total project.

In Egypt a natural waterway called the Nile River divides Egypt's desert region into two parts—the Eastern Desert and the Western Desert. Between the two desert regions is a strip of fertile land fed by the waters of the Nile.

In Egypt's northeastern corner is the Sinai (SY•ny) Peninsula. Although the Sinai has water on three sides, much of the peninsula consists of rocky desert and rugged mountains. This part of Egypt is actually on the continent of Asia. A human-made waterway called the Suez Canal separates the Sinai Peninsula and the main part of Egypt. The canal enables ships to travel from the Mediterranean Sea to the Indian Ocean without having to sail around the southern part of Africa.

REVIEW What mountain range runs through Morocco, Algeria, and Tunisia?

The Nile River

The Nile River, the world's longest river, runs through Egypt from south to north. Without its waters Egypt would be all desert. For this reason, the Nile River was called the "giver of life" by the Egyptians who lived alongside its banks long ago. For thousands of years the Nile has provided

These farmers plow the fertile soil near the Nile River in Luxor, Egypt.

farmers in Egypt with the water and rich soil needed for growing crops. These farmers lived and worked on the narrow ribbon of fertile land along the Nile. This land is known as the Nile Valley.

The Nile Valley once got its rich soil from the Nile's annual flooding. The river overflowed during the rainy season, from May to August. When the floodwaters drained away, they left behind rich silt, made up of tiny particles of soil and sand. This silt made the farmlands of the Nile Valley especially fertile.

The waters of the Nile River have their sources in the highland regions of Central and East Africa. From there, the Nile flows northward into Egypt. During this journey, the Nile passes through six **cataracts**, or series of rapids. The Nile twists and turns for more than 4,000 miles (6,437 km). At its mouth the Nile flows into the Mediterranean Sea. The land near the mouth is called the Nile River Delta. A delta is low land formed at the mouth of some rivers by the silt the river drops there. The Nile River Delta fans out in a huge triangle where the Nile enters the Mediterranean Sea.

The flooding of the Nile brought rich soil to Egypt. Yet at the same time, it caused many problems. Sometimes floodwaters destroyed homes and farms. To control the waters of the Nile, the Egyptians built several dams during the past century.

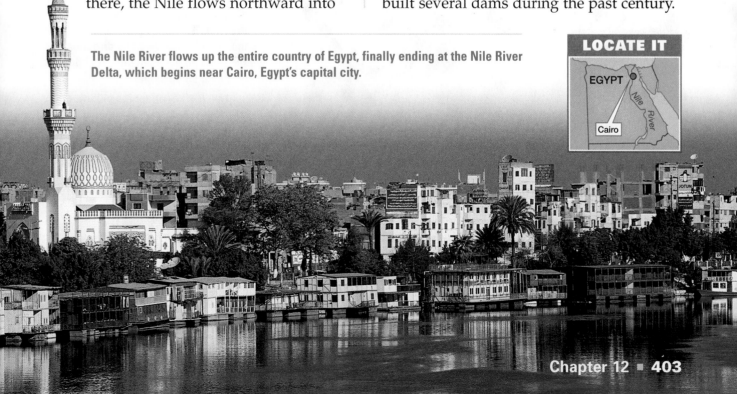

The Nile River flows up the entire country of Egypt, finally ending at the Nile River Delta, which begins near Cairo, Egypt's capital city.

LOCATE IT

EGYPT

Cairo

Nile River

The largest dam is the Aswan High Dam in southern Egypt. The floodwaters are captured in Lake Nasser behind the dam. Engineers maintain a steady flow of water through the dam's gates during the planting season. The completion of the Aswan High Dam in 1971 changed Egyptian ways of life and Egyptian agriculture forever. The dam brought an end to the yearly flooding. Farmers build reservoirs and canals near their villages to irrigate their fields. The Aswan Dam generates large amounts of electricity.

Most of Egypt's population lives along the Nile River and the Suez Canal. Many live in Egypt's largest city, Cairo, at the southern edge of the Nile River Delta. Others live in the port city of Alexandria, located at the point where the Nile River Delta meets the Mediterranean Sea.

REVIEW Why is the Nile River so important to the people of Egypt?

The Sahara

In Arabic, *sahara* means "desert." The Sahara is made up of shifting white sands, rocky plains, plateaus, and mountains. The air all around is dry. Temperatures in this region average about 90°F (32°C) during the day. Temperatures can drop below 40°F (4°C) at night.

The Sahara stretches through most of North Africa from the Atlantic Ocean in the west to the Red Sea in the east. The Sahara is so large that almost all of the United States would fit inside of it. Mountain ranges and a variety of natural landscapes divide the Sahara into smaller areas.

The Western Sahara is a land area south of Morocco that is made up of areas of rocky, windswept plains called **regs**. These plains of loose rock cover much of the Sahara. Beneath the dry regs of the Sahara, underground water often flows. Where this water rises to the desert's surface, it

How Sand Dunes Form

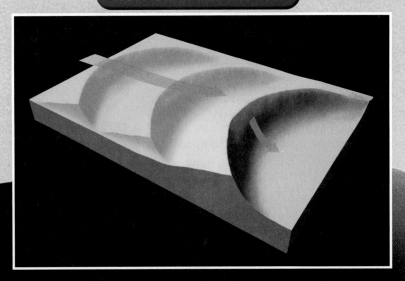

Analyze Diagrams Dunes are piles of sand shaped into patterns by the wind. Different dune patterns form depending on the speed and direction of the wind. In the diagram the arrows show the wind direction. This dune pattern forms when the wind blows from one direction. When the sand piles up too high, it slides down to form a steep slope.

? What two factors affect the pattern of a sand dune?

forms an oasis. The waters of oases create fertile areas in the desert.

Because the Sahara receives an average rainfall of little more than 3 inches (8 cm) a year, oases are important to life in the region. Much of the plant and animal life in the Sahara can be found near oases. Farmers who live in these areas direct water from the oases into canals and ditches for irrigation. Saharan farmers grow dates, citrus fruits, figs, peaches, apricots, vegetables, and grains.

In the eastern part of the Sahara is the Libyan Desert. The Libyan Desert receives almost no rainfall, and it is considered to be one of the driest parts of the Sahara. Most of the Libyan Desert is covered with **ergs**, or large areas of sand dunes. These "seas" of sand make the Libyan Desert dangerous and difficult to cross. The sand in ergs lies in loose sheets that shift with the wind. The wind blows this loose sand into large piles called dunes. Some sand dunes, or **draas**, can reach more than 400 feet (122 m) in height.

The lowest point of the Sahara is at the Qattara (kuh•TAHR•uh) Depression in northwestern Egypt. A **depression** is a land area lower than the land around it. The deepest point of the Qattara Depression is 436 feet (133 m) below sea level.

The Sahara is the largest desert in the world. Large sand dunes, like this one in Morocco, stretch for hundreds of miles.

Long periods of drought have also caused areas south of the Sahara to turn to desert. In this case, the climate as well as overfarming and overgrazing brought about desertification of the land.

REVIEW What different kinds of landforms can be found in the Sahara?

LESSON 1 REVIEW

1. **MAIN IDEA** In which areas do most North Africans live? Why is this so?

2. **WHY IT MATTERS** How do the people of North Africa survive in the desert?

3. **VOCABULARY** Describe the Sahara, using the words **reg**, **erg**, **draa**, and **depression**.

4. **READING SKILL—Sequence** Describe the path the Nile River takes from its sources to its mouth.

5. **GEOGRAPHY** Where is most of Morocco's agricultural land located?

6. **ECONOMICS** What kinds of crops are grown near desert oases?

7. **CRITICAL THINKING—Synthesize** How do you think the Sahara affects travel between North and Central Africa?

PERFORMANCE—Draw a Scene Draw a scene showing life around an oasis. In your scene, include plants, animals, and people. Show an underground river as the source of the oasis. Show water being directed into ditches and canals to irrigate fields.

Follow Routes on a Map

▶ WHY IT MATTERS

For thousands of years explorers tried to find the quickest way to get from Europe to Asia. Early traders from Europe had to either travel great distances by land or sail around Africa to reach Asia. To sail around Africa was a long and dangerous journey. You can imagine the excitement when the Suez Canal opened in 1869. This new waterway through the Isthmus of Suez cut 6,000 miles off the journey from Europe to Asia. An isthmus is a narrow strip of land connecting two larger areas of land. The Isthmus of Suez connects the Sinai Peninsula to Egypt. By learning to follow routes on a map, you will understand how far early traders had to travel to get from Europe to Asia.

▶ WHAT YOU NEED TO KNOW

The map shows the trade routes or paths that traders used as they exchanged goods between Europe and Asia. Notice how long the journey is between these two continents. The solid lines show the routes people may have used traveling over land. The dashed lines show water routes. Answer the questions as though you were a European trader.

▶ PRACTICE THE SKILL

Study the map keys to learn about some of the different trade routes from Europe to Asia. Then use the map keys, compass rose, and scale bar to answer the questions on the next page.

Opening celebration for the Suez Canal

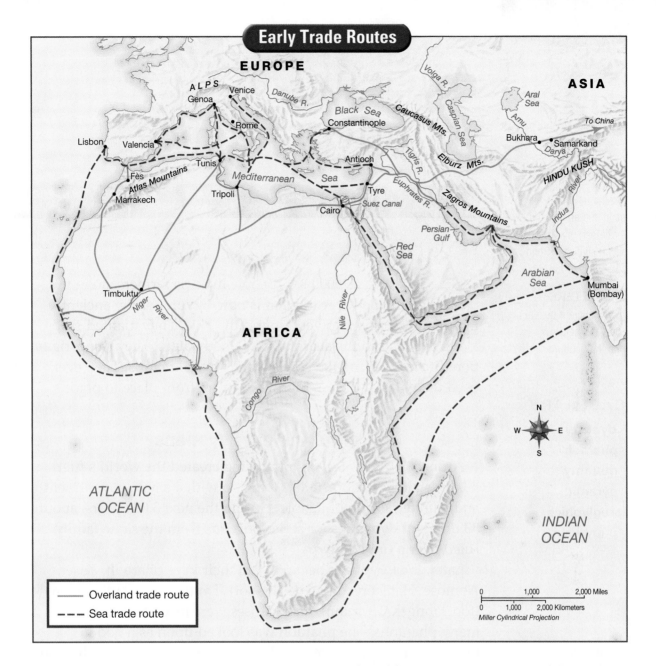

Early Trade Routes

Overland trade route

- - - Sea trade route

0   1,000   2,000 Miles
0 1,000 2,000 Kilometers
Miller Cylindrical Projection

1 If you lived in Genoa and wanted to begin your sea voyage in Lisbon, in which direction would you travel?

2 You have heard that India has spices and perfumes that many wealthy Europeans will buy. Based on the map, what is the best route to follow? Why? Remember that the Suez Canal has not been built.

3 About how far is it from Lisbon to India, traveling mainly by land? How far is it by sea without using the Suez Canal? How far is it by sea using the Suez Canal?

▶ APPLY WHAT YOU LEARNED

Using an atlas, plot a route for a trip you would like to take. Choose where to begin and end your trip. Use the compass rose and scale bar to help you plot your route. As you plot your route, list the directions in which you need to travel and the distances between the stops along your route.

Practice your map and globe skills with the **GeoSkills CD-ROM**.

MAP AND GLOBE SKILLS

2

MAIN IDEA
Learn how the natural resources in and around the Nile River helped give birth to an ancient civilization and affected its ways of life.

WHY IT MATTERS
Knowing why ancient people lived as they did helps us understand their culture better.

VOCABULARY

dynasty
pharaoh
mummy
pyramid
hieroglyphics
papyrus

Ancient Days to Independence

| 3000 B.C. | 2000 B.C. | 1000 B.C. | B.C./A.D. | A.D. 1000 | A.D. 2000 |

As long ago as 5000 B.C., people lived as farmers along the banks of the Nile River in what is now Egypt. For the ancient Egyptians, all life revolved around the Nile. They planted crops along the river in the silt left by its floodwaters. They dug irrigation ditches to bring the Nile's waters to their crops. They even used the Nile as a river "highway" to get from place to place.

The Ancient Egyptians

Around 3000 B.C., an Egyptian king created the world's first nation-state. A nation-state is a region with a single government and a united group of people. During the next 3,000 years, about 33 different **dynasties**, or series of rulers from the same family, ruled over a united Egypt.

Later, the Egyptians began to call their king **pharaoh**. Zoser, Ahmose, Hatshepsut (hat•SHEP•soot), Thutmose, Tutankhamen (too•tahng•KAH•muhn), and Ramses were just a few of Egypt's many pharaohs. The pharaoh was looked upon as a god in human form. The pharaoh had total power. Because the pharaoh had final say in all matters, Egyptian society did not change much through the years.

The Egyptians believed in many gods. Each god was said to control a different part of nature and human life. The god Re ruled the sun. Thoth was the god of wisdom. Hathor was the goddess of love. Isis ruled over motherhood.

By praying to their gods, the Egyptians believed that they could ensure happy lives for themselves. They prayed for healthy crops and for the flood that renewed the land, making it ready for planting once again.

This wooden model from about 2000 B.C. shows an Egyptian farmer plowing the land after it is no longer flooded.

Hatshepsut   1503 B.C.–1458 B.C.

Character Trait: Courage

Most pharaohs were men. An exception was Queen Hatshepsut, who ruled as pharaoh from 1473 B.C. to 1458 B.C. After her husband, Pharaoh Thutmose II, died, Hatshepsut claimed the throne. She knew that the Egyptians might not accept a woman as pharaoh, but she was willing to take a chance. Just to be safe, she lived much of her life as a male pharaoh would. She dressed in traditional clothing and even wore a false beard. During Hatshepsut's rule, Egypt developed trade instead of conquering other people.

This statue of Hatshepsut is in the form of a sphinx—a creature half-human and half-animal.

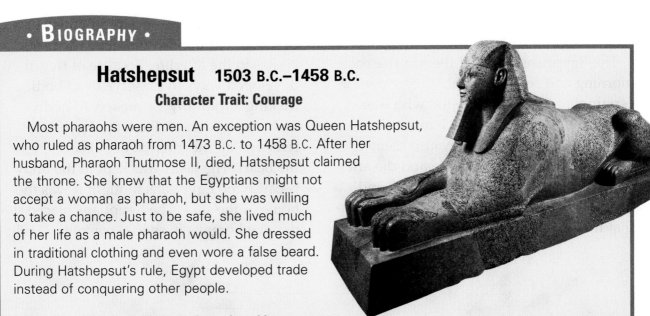

MULTIMEDIA BIOGRAPHIES

Visit The Learning Site at **www.harcourtschool.com/biographies** to learn about other famous people.

GO ONLINE

Egyptians waited eagerly for the yearly flood. However, farmers could not plant crops during the flood. Instead, they finished any building projects that the pharaoh had ordered. Only when the land emerged from beneath the water could they plant. In a good year the harvest provided more than enough food.

The Egyptians depended on nature for more than just food. They made their houses out of sun-dried mud brick. They used clay to make pottery. Reeds found along the Nile were used to weave baskets. Egyptian craftworkers used fibers from flax plants to weave a cloth called linen. Egyptian women wore long, sleeveless linen dresses. Men wore knee-length linen skirts, with or without short-sleeved shirts.

REVIEW **What were three ways the ancient Egyptians depended on nature?**

GEOGRAPHY THEME

Movement **The Nile River flows from higher land in the south to lower land in the north. It passes through six cataracts where the water runs fast over rocks.**

⟐ **Why is the Nile said to flow "up" Egypt?**

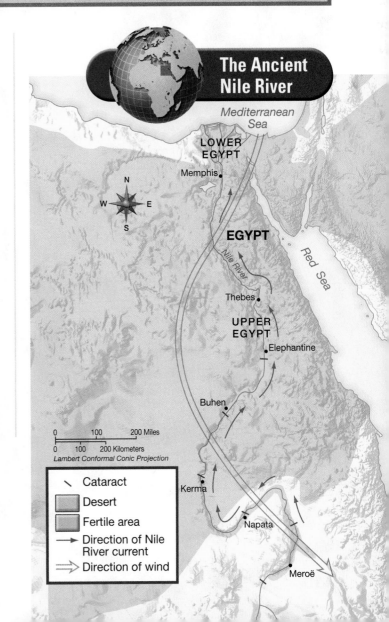

The Ancient Nile River

Mediterranean Sea

LOWER EGYPT

Memphis

EGYPT

Nile River

Red Sea

Thebes

UPPER EGYPT

Elephantine

Buhen

Kerma

Napata

Meroë

0   100   200 Miles
0   100   200 Kilometers
Lambert Conformal Conic Projection

⟍ Cataract
▢ Desert
▢ Fertile area
→ Direction of Nile River current
⟹ Direction of wind

Egyptian Ideas

The Egyptians watched the sun rise each morning and set each night. They grew certain that the sun was a god who was born each day and died each night. The farmlands of the Nile Valley also seemed to come alive during flooding and die after the harvesting of crops. Seeing birth and death in nature led the Egyptians to believe that they, too, would have an afterlife, or life after death. The ancient Egyptians believed that they would need their bodies in the afterlife. Because of this, they developed ways to preserve dead bodies. Making a **mummy**, or preserved body, took about 70 days. First, the Egyptians removed all the internal organs except for the heart. The heart was kept in the body because the Egyptians thought it was the home of the soul. The Egyptians placed the removed organs in special containers called

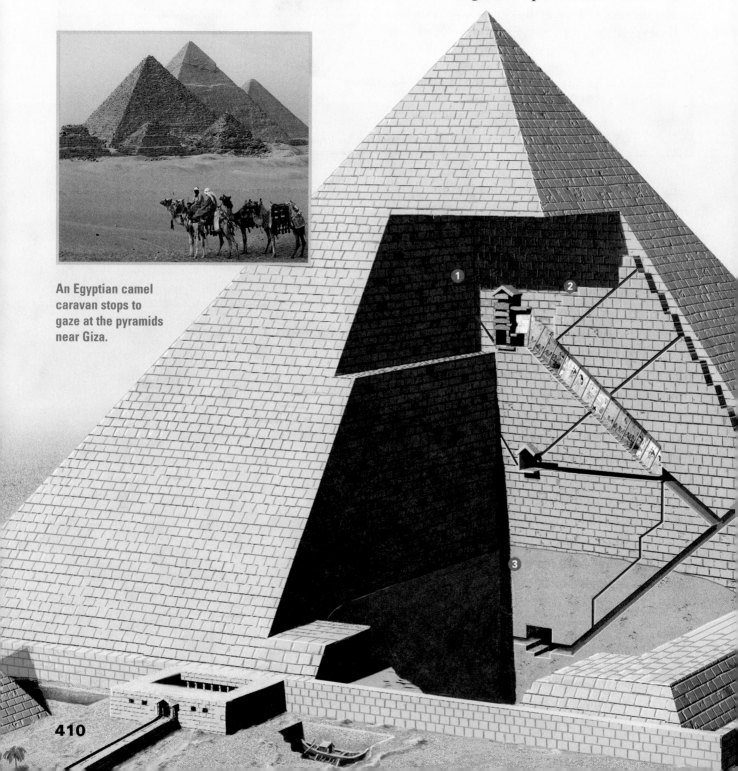

An Egyptian camel caravan stops to gaze at the pyramids near Giza.

canopic jars. Next, they covered the body with powdered salt to dry it out. Then the Egyptians rubbed the dried-out body with special oils to protect it from decay. Finally, they wrapped the body from head to toe in linen cloth. The mummy was then ready to be placed in its tomb.

Egyptian tombs came in different sizes. The biggest were four-sided structures called **pyramids**. Only pharaohs and their families could be buried in these huge stone monuments. One of the largest pyramids ever built is the Great Pyramid at Giza. Its builders used about 2 million limestone blocks, each weighing more than 2 tons (about 2,000 kg). The huge stone blocks had to be cut by hand and dragged to the construction site. Pyramids like the Great Pyramid at Giza took thousands of people many years to build.

To keep records of harvests, trade, and government decisions and to express religious ideas, the ancient

Mummy cases were made to look like the person they held. This one was made for Paankhenamun, an Egyptian who lived sometime between 900 B.C. and 700 B.C.

Egyptians came up with another innovation. They developed a writing system that is known as **hieroglyphics** (hy•ruh•GLIH•fiks). Egyptian hieroglyphics used more than 700 different picture symbols, which stood for whole words. In time hieroglyphic symbols came to stand for sounds, too. Not all Egyptians learned to write hieroglyphics. Learning the many symbols took years of training.

Egyptians wrote their hieroglyphs on **papyrus** (puh•PY•ruhs), a paperlike material made from reeds that grew in the Nile. For the Egyptians, a "book" was a scroll—a roll made of papyrus sheets joined end to end. One of the most important of all Egyptian writings was the *Book of the Dead*. It contained prayers and maps to help a person's spirit find its way to the afterlife.

REVIEW How did nature influence the religious ideas of the ancient Egyptians?

A CLOSER LOOK
Pyramids

Experts estimate that more than 20,000 people helped build the Great Pyramid. The architect who designed it included more inner chambers and passageways than in any other pyramid. Because the Great Pyramid was entered by grave robbers, archaeologists cannot be sure exactly what was once inside it. Mysteries continue to surround the construction of the Great Pyramid and its functions.

➊ The King's Chamber is hidden close to the center of the pyramid. The pharaoh Khufu's sarcophagus still remains inside the chamber.

➋ Air shafts from the King's Chamber line up with the star constellation of Orion. Egyptians believed the king's soul would ascend to the stars.

➌ Some secret underground rooms remain mysterious. They resemble burial chambers, but for some reason were never completed.

❖ Why do you think the Egyptians buried treasures and statues with their pharaohs?

Times of Conquest

As a land of rich agriculture and famous kings, Egypt attracted the attention of conquerors. It was well protected by deserts and the sea, but still it faced invasion by several empires. In about 525 B.C. the Persians conquered Egypt and ruled it for the next 200 years. Later, Alexander the Great of Greece added Egypt to his growing empire.

After Alexander's death the lands fell into the hands of Ptolemy, one of Alexander's generals. Ptolemy and his descendants ruled Egypt for about 300 years. The reign of their last leader, Cleopatra, ended around 31 B.C., when her army was defeated by the Romans.

When the Roman Empire split in A.D. 395, Egypt became part of the eastern half, later known as the Byzantine Empire.

While civilization developed in ancient Egypt, a group of nomadic people called

This Roman coin reads, "Captive Egypt."

the Berbers lived to the west. The Berbers were the earliest-known people to occupy what is today Morocco, Algeria, Tunisia, and Libya. The Berbers did not settle in any one place but traveled the desert and mountain regions of North Africa. They knew where to find grazing areas for their livestock.

In about 1100 B.C. Phoenicians arrived in North Africa from Southwest Asia. The seafaring Phoenicians built many colonies along Africa's Mediterranean coast. The Berbers stayed mostly inland. They had little contact with the culture and beliefs of the Phoenicians.

The Phoenicians built the city of Carthage in what is today Tunisia. From there, they controlled much of the North African coast for about 500 years. Carthage became an important trading center. The Phoenicians traded goods and ideas with many of the different peoples who lived along the Mediterranean Sea.

The Rosetta Stone

Analyze Primary Sources

After the ancient Egyptians were conquered, their written language—hieroglyphics—was no longer used. In time, no one could read it. For thousands of years, the meaning of ancient Egyptian writings remained a mystery. Then, in A.D. 1799, a French army officer found a large black stone near the city of Rosetta, Egypt—today known as Rashid. On the stone's shiny surface were three different kinds of writing—two ancient Egyptian and one ancient Greek. The ancient Greek gave scholars the key to one of the Egyptian scripts, but the Egyptian hieroglyphics still could not be understood. Then, in 1822, Jean-François Champollion decoded the hieroglyphics, using the other forms of writing as a guide.

1 This is hieroglyphic writing.

2 This writing, also used by the ancient Egyptians, is called demotic writing. Demotic writing was a short form of hieroglyphic writing. It used symbols rather than pictures.

3 This writing is ancient Greek.

◈ Why do you think decoding hieroglyphic writing was such an important discovery?

Carthage's main rival was the Roman Empire. Carthage and the Roman Empire fought several wars for control of trade in the Mediterranean Sea. After many difficult battles, Carthage lost the last of the wars. By 146 B.C. the Romans had gained complete control of Carthage. The Romans also conquered parts of what is today Algeria, Libya, and Morocco as well as Egypt. Around A.D. 500, the Byzantine Empire took control of the region.

In about A.D. 643, Arab Muslims invaded North Africa. The Muslim armies conquered lands as far west as Morocco. All along the way, they spread the religion of Islam. The independent Berbers resisted this change to their way of life. It took a long time for Arab culture to blend into Berber society. Within 400 years most people in North Africa had become Muslims. Arabic had also become the main language of the region. Today, Berber languages are also spoken in many parts of the Maghreb.

Beginning in the 1500s, most of North Africa except Morocco came under the con-

Ruins of an ancient Roman city in Libya show the influence of Roman culture in North Africa.

trol of the Ottoman Empire. By the 1800s Europeans began looking toward Africa as a source of wealth and natural resources. As the Ottoman Empire began to lose its hold over the region the Europeans arrived.

Countries such as Britain, France, Spain, and Italy built colonies in North Africa. During World War II, these colonies were the sites of fierce fighting. After the war, parts of North Africa gained independence.

REVIEW What European Empire was the rival to Carthage?

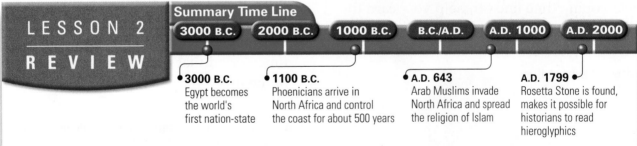

LESSON 2
REVIEW

Summary Time Line

| 3000 B.C. | 2000 B.C. | 1000 B.C. | B.C./A.D. | A.D. 1000 | A.D. 2000 |

3000 B.C.
Egypt becomes the world's first nation-state

1100 B.C.
Phoenicians arrive in North Africa and control the coast for about 500 years

A.D. 643
Arab Muslims invade North Africa and spread the religion of Islam

A.D. 1799
Rosetta Stone is found, makes it possible for historians to read hieroglyphics

1. **MAIN IDEA**   How did the Nile River affect the way of life of the ancient Egyptians?

2. **WHY IT MATTERS**   How does knowing about life in ancient North Africa help you understand the region?

3. **VOCABULARY**   Write a sentence describing why the ancient Egyptians built pyramids. Use the terms **pharaoh** and **mummy** in your sentence.

4. **TIME LINE**   Who arrived in North Africa first—the Phoenicians or the Arab Muslims?

5. **READING SKILL—Sequence**   Describe the process the ancient Egyptians used to preserve a body.

6. **HISTORY**   Which North African city at one time controlled much of the trade in the Mediterranean Sea?

7. **CRITICAL THINKING—Interpret**   What led the ancient Egyptians to believe in an afterlife?

PERFORMANCE ACTIVITY—Write Using Hieroglyphs   On a sheet of paper, draw your own hieroglyphs. Then, beside each hieroglyph, write the English word for the idea, sound, or object shown by the hieroglyph. On the same sheet of paper, write a sentence using your hieroglyphs.

· SKILLS ·

CHART AND GRAPH

Read a Telescoping Time Line

 *(VOCABULARY box)*

VOCABULARY

telescoping time line

➡ WHY IT MATTERS

A time line allows you to look at history chronologically, or in time order. For example, the time line on page 415 puts the reigns of important Egyptian pharaohs in order from earliest to latest.

Sometimes you may want details about a specific section on a time line. A **telescoping time line** helps you take a closer look at a specific event or time period, such as the reign of a particular pharaoh. Just as a telescope helps you take a closer look at a faraway object, a telescoping time line lets you take a closer look at history. Knowing how to read a telescoping time line can help you learn the details of historic events and time periods.

Statue of Ramses II

➡ WHAT YOU NEED TO KNOW

Use the following tips to help you read a telescoping time line.

- Find out what time period is being covered. The time line on page 415 covers the period from 1600 B.C. to 1200 B.C. It is divided into spans of 100 years.

- Look at the telescoping part of the time line and determine which years it covers. The telescoping time line on page 415 covers the years 1280 B.C. to 1200 B.C. It is divided into spans of 20 years.

- The key difference between the main time line and the telescoping time line is the difference in the time span. Remember that the telescoping part of the time line shows in greater detail a time period that occurs on the main part of the time line.

Box that holds ushebtis, servants for the pharaoh in the afterlife

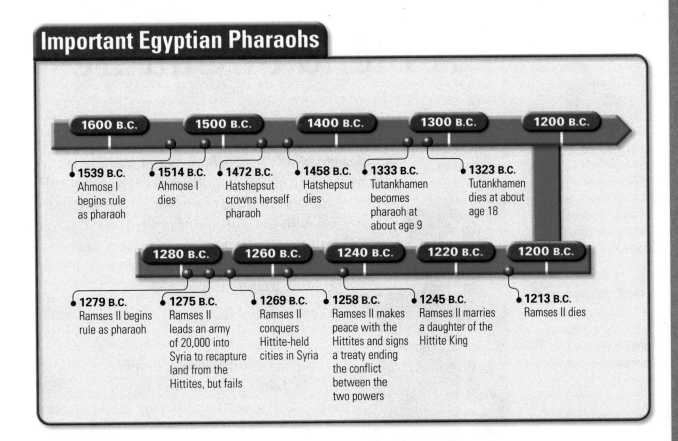

Important Egyptian Pharaohs

1600 B.C.   **1500 B.C.**   **1400 B.C.**   **1300 B.C.**   **1200 B.C.**

1539 B.C.
Ahmose I begins rule as pharaoh

1514 B.C.
Ahmose I dies

1472 B.C.
Hatshepsut crowns herself pharaoh

1458 B.C.
Hatshepsut dies

1333 B.C.
Tutankhamen becomes pharaoh at about age 9

1323 B.C.
Tutankhamen dies at about age 18

1280 B.C.   **1260 B.C.**   **1240 B.C.**   **1220 B.C.**   **1200 B.C.**

1279 B.C.
Ramses II begins rule as pharaoh

1275 B.C.
Ramses II leads an army of 20,000 into Syria to recapture land from the Hittites, but fails

1269 B.C.
Ramses II conquers Hittite-held cities in Syria

1258 B.C.
Ramses II makes peace with the Hittites and signs a treaty ending the conflict between the two powers

1245 B.C.
Ramses II marries a daughter of the Hittite King

1213 B.C.
Ramses II dies

▶ PRACTICE THE SKILL

Study the telescoping time line above. Then use it to answer the questions.

1 Which pharaoh had the shortest reign? How short was it?

2 What time period does the telescoping part of the time line show?

3 Which event took place first, Hatshepsut's reign or Ramses II's peace treaty with the Hittites? How do you know?

4 What was different about Ramses II's relationship with the Hittites after 1258 B.C.?

▶ APPLY WHAT YOU LEARNED

Which year in your life has been particularly eventful or exciting? Make a time line of your life so far, using spans of one year. Make a telescoping section for the particularly eventful or exciting year using spans of one month. Include at least three events in the telescoping section.

Tomb of Nefertari; Nefertari was the wife of Ramses II.

A Blend of Cultures

MAIN IDEA

Read to find out how the cultures of Europe, Asia, and Africa have blended to shape the way people live in North Africa today.

WHY IT MATTERS

Advances in communication have brought cultures closer together. Today people around the world need to appreciate the cultures of others.

VOCABULARY

minaret
muezzin
overpopulation
medina

LOCATE IT

Casablanca

MOROCCO

Many groups of people have taken their cultures and ideas to North Africa. Some went to trade while others came to settle. Still others went to conquer. Over time, the cultures of the early North Africans merged with the cultures of newcomers. Customs and ideas from parts of Europe, Asia, and Central Africa blended with Berber and Egyptian traditions and customs.

Religions and Languages

Islam is the official religion of Morocco, Tunisia, Libya, Algeria, and Egypt. More than 90 percent of the people living in these countries are Muslims, or followers of Islam.

The cry *"Allahu akbar! Allahu akbar! la ilaha illa'llah . . ."* begins a call heard across North Africa five times every day. The call often comes from **minarets** (mih•nuh•RETS), towers attached to every mosque. The words called by a **muezzin** (moo•EH•zuhn), or prayer caller, ring through the streets of every North African city and town. Today recordings played over loudspeakers have replaced many muezzins. Some Muslims even receive the call to prayer on their cell phones.

No matter how they are called to prayer, all Muslims pray at sunrise, noon, mid-afternoon, sunset, and night. Islamic law requires Muslims to face in the direction of the holy city of Mecca when they pray. In North Africa, Muslims face east.

Islamic law also influences daily life. Muslim women and men are required to dress modestly. Traditionally, both men and women have worn long robes over their clothing. Some women cover their heads; others cover their faces. Many North African men wear a scarf, called a kaffiyeh (kuh•FEE•uh), around their heads. In Morocco both men and women wear a long, hooded robe called a djellaba (juh•LAH•buh). Many Algerian women wear long robes, or hijabs (hih•JABZ), over their clothing and cover their hair and faces as well. Berber men wear a long, loose-fitting robe called a burnous (ber•NOOS).

The style and strictness of dress vary from place to place. In cities such as Tunis and Casablanca, some men and women

Ramadan

Ramadan is a monthlong holiday. It marks the month when, according to Muslim belief, Muhammad received the verses of the Qur'an sent by God. During Ramadan, healthy adult Muslims do not eat or drink during the day. To prepare for the fast, they eat a pre-dawn breakfast. At sunset the day's fast is broken with a meal that usually begins by eating a date. Ramadan is a time for prayer and charitable acts.

wear less-traditional clothing. The people there might dress in business suits or sportswear.

Before Islam came to North Africa, many Egyptians were Christians. Today many of the descendants of these early people are members of the Coptic Church.

The Hassan II Mosque in Casablanca is one of the world's largest mosques (left). A muezzin calls the prayer (left inset). Muslims pray at a mosque (middle inset), and along a city street (right inset).

Coptic Christians are Egypt's largest minority. Other Christian groups in Egypt are Roman Catholic, Anglican, and Eastern Orthodox. A small number of Jews live in North Africa, mostly in Morocco.

Arabic is the official language of all the North African countries. It has been spoken by most North Africans for about 1,000 years. Arabic, however, is not the region's only language. Berber languages have also survived in rural areas and in parts of the Sahara. When Europeans claimed North Africa, they added their languages. Today the European languages French and Spanish are spoken in Morocco. Libyan schools prepare children to work in business by teaching English.

REVIEW What is the main religion of countries in North Africa?

People of the Desert

For centuries some North Africans lived nomadic lives in the desert. Three groups—the North African nomads, the Bedouins and the Tuaregs (TWAH•regz)—still carve out a life in the Sahara. In the twenty-first century, desert people make up a small but very important part of North Africa's population. A few desert

Some Tuaregs still trade by camel caravan.

people still follow their nomadic ways of life. Others settle and build communities near oases.

Berbers have lived in the Sahara for thousands of years. Many continue to live as nomads. While most Berbers have become Muslims, some follow an older religion.

Bedouins, or Bedu as they call themselves, are Arabs who live in the desert and raise camels, sheep, and goats. Bedouin people have been in Southwest Asia since at least the 200s B.C. They migrated into North Africa with the Arab Muslims. Today many live in the Sinai Peninsula and other parts of Egypt. Nomadic Bedouins live in tents made from goat hair. Other Bedouins who have settled and become farmers often build permanent homes out of stone. Both kinds of Bedouins live in tribes led by a shaykh, or chief.

In ancient times Tuaregs led camel caravans carrying precious goods across the desert to trade in village marketplaces. They were the main traders of the Sahara. Tuaregs still keep camels to help carry their belongings, but airplanes and trucks carry most goods to market.

REVIEW Which group of desert nomads lives in the Sinai Peninsula?

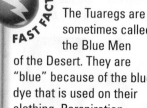

FAST FACT The Tuaregs are sometimes called the Blue Men of the Desert. They are "blue" because of the blue dye that is used on their clothing. Perspiration causes the blue dye to color their skin.

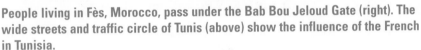

People living in Fès, Morocco, pass under the Bab Bou Jeloud Gate (right). The wide streets and traffic circle of Tunis (above) show the influence of the French in Tunisia.

People of the City

Cities grew up along the North African coast in ancient times. Some were early Phoenician port cities, such as Carthage. Others were ancient cultural centers, such as Alexandria, where Greek and Jewish scholars shared knowledge. There were also Roman cities where early Christians preached their faith. As time passed, North African cities grew. In modern times, cities have swelled as North Africans have left the countryside to look for jobs or to get an education. Some came to enjoy the fast-paced life of North African cities.

So many people live in North Africa's cities that **overpopulation**, or too many people living in one place, has become a problem. In Egypt almost half of the population shares the resources of the urban areas along the Nile River and the Suez Canal. In Cairo, crowded conditions mean that many Egyptians live in small apartments. Others live on the streets, on rooftops, or on boats. One large community of people lives in a huge cemetery called the City of the Dead, where sultans are buried.

City dwellers, however, have more opportunities for jobs than do people in rural areas. Tunis, the capital of Tunisia, has an important tourist industry. There are jobs in hotels, shops, restaurants, and other service industries.

Most cities also offer other attractive business opportunities. People in Cairo and other large cities find a ready market for their goods and services. More people with more money make their living in these cities.

Many of North Africa's cities are a mixture of the old and the new. In some North African cities, skyscrapers stand on the edge of the **medina**, or the old section of the city. *Medina* actually means "city" in Arabic. The medina in Tunis is a busy area with narrow streets, shops, bakeries, and private houses.

The modern part of Tunis is the workplace of doctors, teachers, salesclerks, and computer technicians. In the medina, however, workers carry on a variety of traditional crafts, such as carpet making, pottery, and metalworking. People visiting shops in the medina might be offered a glass of hot mint tea while they shop.

Moroccan salads

REVIEW Why have many of North Africa's nomads and farmers moved to cities?

Cultural Life in North Africa

Over the years North Africans have borrowed many cultural traits from societies in other regions. The blending of cultures in North Africa can be seen most in the way people live.

Many North Africans watch television shows and listen to radio broadcasts in many languages. Half of all Moroccan television programs are in French, while the other half are in Arabic. In Cairo there are more than 70 movie theaters, where people can watch films from around the world.

The mixture of many cultural influences can also be seen in the architecture of North Africa. In Casablanca, in the former French colony of Morocco, the cities have wide streets lined with white villas. These streets are like many found in France. There are also French-inspired parks and sidewalk cafés. Many Moroccans often gather at cafés to talk and share meals.

North Africans eat foods similar to those found in Southwest Asia. Many of the nutritious, filling dishes are based on beans and grains. A mixture of herbs and spices, including garlic, cinnamon, cumin, saffron, cloves, and ground pepper, gives the foods a distinctive flavor. Couscous is a popular dish in Morocco, Algeria, and Tunisia. It is made from wheat that is sprinkled with water and oil, rolled into tiny pieces, and steamed.

Mint tea is a popular drink in North Africa. At a market in Morocco this man (below) sells the mint used to make mint tea. A Berber woman (right) pours tea in a traditional way, from high above the glass.

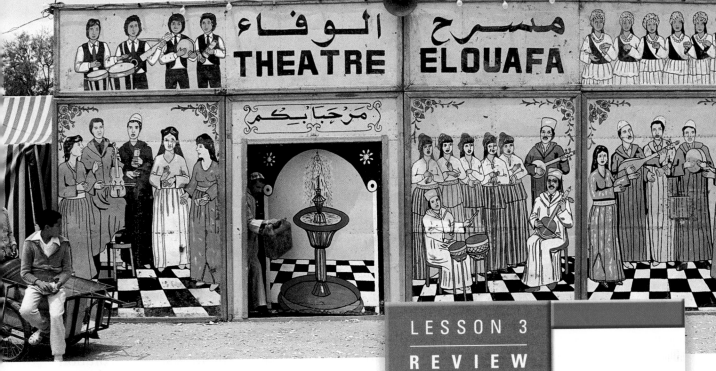

This theater near Marrakech, Morocco, shows the presence of the French and Arabic languages in North Africa.

North Africans also create traditional works of art. Since Islamic teachings discourage the display of people and animals in works of art, geometric patterns decorate jewelry, carpets, metals, and leather. Complex designs of curving lines are called *arabesque* in style. These colorful designs in tiles decorate fountains, floors, and walls in mosques, public buildings, and homes.

Leisure activities are an important part of cultural life in North Africa. Soccer—or football, as it is called there—is popular in the region. Teams from Libya and Morocco have represented their countries in the Olympics. Camel racing remains popular in Tunisia. Algerians take advantage of their coastal climate to enjoy water sports.

People enjoy a rich cultural life in North Africa. In its cities and villages, they find a blend of cultural influences that makes the region unique.

REVIEW How have other regions influenced parts of North Africa?

LESSON 3 REVIEW

1 **MAIN IDEA** How have the ideas of other cultures blended with the cultures of North Africa?

2 **WHY IT MATTERS** How have the cultures of North Africa's desert people been influenced by other groups? How have their cultures remained the same?

3 **VOCABULARY** Using the term **minaret**, describe the role performed at a mosque by a **muezzin**.

4 **READING SKILL—Sequence** Which did Berbers do first, practice their traditional religions or practice Islam?

5 **CULTURE** How is the Tuareg culture different from other desert cultures in North Africa?

6 **ECONOMICS** What job opportunities do people find in North African cities?

7 **CULTURE** What kinds of sports do people in North Africa enjoy?

8 **CRITICAL THINKING—Hypothesize** How does an arid environment cause people to adapt?

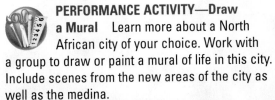

PERFORMANCE ACTIVITY—Draw a Mural Learn more about a North African city of your choice. Work with a group to draw or paint a mural of life in this city. Include scenes from the new areas of the city as well as the medina.

4

Present-Day Concerns

MAIN IDEA
Read to find out how colonialism and religion have influenced the various governments and economies of present-day North Africa.

WHY IT MATTERS
Governments and economies of countries around the world are affected by a variety of influences.

VOCABULARY

sanction
fellahin

Today the North African countries of Morocco, Algeria, Tunisia, Libya, and Egypt are independent. The road to independence was not smooth. These North African countries also hit many bumps in the years following independence. Because of this, the countries have witnessed many changes in government and faced many economic challenges.

Governments in North Africa

In the 1800s the Ottoman rulers of North Africa began to lose control of the region to the Europeans. The Industrial Revolution made it possible for Europeans to make products faster and at less cost than ever before. To continue making so many products, the Europeans needed more raw materials. They also wanted new markets in which to sell their products. North Africa, a short distance from Europe across the Mediterranean Sea, provided both. Britain, France, Spain, and Italy began to compete for possession of North Africa. Soon Europeans began shipping raw materials from Africa across the sea to European factories.

North Africa's mostly Muslim population suffered under European colonialism. Europeans, instead of North Africans, profited from the sale of North African resources.

From the 1800s through World War II, colonialism continued in North Africa. During this time only Egypt made progress toward freedom. In 1922 Britain gave Egypt limited self-rule. The British army remained in Egypt to protect Britain's interests there. The British were especially concerned about the Suez Canal. The canal was important to them because they traveled through it to get to their other colonies.

King Mohammad VI of Morocco (at right) meets with French president Jacques Chirac.

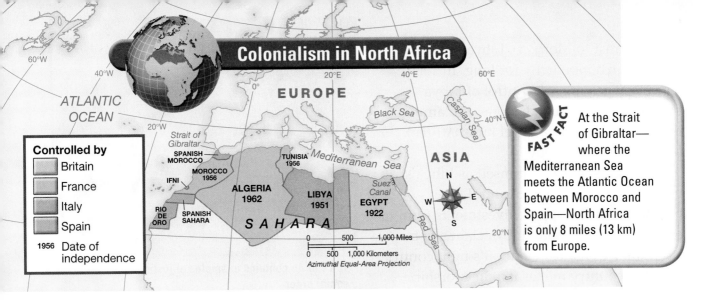

Colonialism in North Africa

Controlled by
- Britain
- France
- Italy
- Spain

1956 Date of independence

EUROPE

ATLANTIC OCEAN

Strait of Gibraltar
SPANISH MOROCCO
IFNI
MOROCCO 1956
RIO DE ORO
SPANISH SAHARA
ALGERIA 1962
TUNISIA 1956
Mediterranean Sea
LIBYA 1951
EGYPT 1922
Suez Canal
SAHARA
Red Sea

ASIA

Black Sea
Caspian Sea

0 500 1,000 Miles
0 500 1,000 Kilometers
Azimuthal Equal-Area Projection

GEOGRAPHY THEME

Human-Environment Interactions The former colonial empires of Western Europe once stretched across the globe. In the past, North Africa was controlled by European powers.

❖ Which European country controlled Egypt?

FAST FACT At the Strait of Gibraltar—where the Mediterranean Sea meets the Atlantic Ocean between Morocco and Spain—North Africa is only 8 miles (13 km) from Europe.

Following World War II, all of North Africa gained independence as colonialism came to an end. After wars of independence, the North African countries had to create new governments. Egypt, Tunisia, and Algeria became democratic republics. Today the citizens of each of these countries elect a president, a prime minister, and members of a legislature. Since becoming fully independent, Egypt has had three presidents. Each of these presidents— Gamal Abdel Nasser (NAH•suhr), Anwar as-Sadat (suh•DAHT), and Hosni Mubarak (mu•BAHR•uhk)—have all worked to improve life in Egypt.

Unlike their North African neighbors, Morocco and Libya set up monarchies. At first Morocco's government was an absolute monarchy. Later it became a constitutional monarchy with a multiparty system. Unlike most modern monarchs, Morocco's king still holds much power. The Moroccan king can overrule any decisions of the legislature.

In 1999 the people of Morocco mourned the death of King Hassan II, who had ruled the country for more than 38 years. His son King Mohammad VI currently rules the country.

Egyptian citizens wave miniature flags and cheer during the election of their president, Hosni Mubarak.

In contrast to Morocco, Libya did not remain a monarchy for long. In 1969 a military group took control of Libya from the Libyan king. Colonel Mu'ammar al-Qaddafi (MOH·ah·mar el kuh·DAH·fee) led the military takeover.

Qaddafi established himself as Libya's new ruler. Qaddafi took control of all businesses and stopped investments from other countries. Today Libya claims to be a republic. In reality, Qaddafi's tight control over the country makes it a dictatorship.

Under Qaddafi's rule, Libya has had poor relationships with western countries. Qaddafi has spoken out against Israel and countries that support Israel's right to exist. He has also questioned western ways. Many countries suspect Qaddafi of encouraging terrorism to further his causes.

In 1992 the United Nations placed a trade **sanction**, or penalty, on Libya. Such sanctions punish countries for violations of international law. The UN placed the sanction on Libya for refusing to release suspects in an airplane bombing. The UN lifted the sanctions in 1999 after Libya turned over the bombing suspects.

REVIEW What three kinds of government are found in North Africa today?

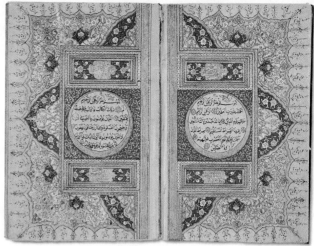
The Qur'an contains examples of justice and social order.

Religion and Government

Although Europe's control over North Africa ended with colonialism, its influence on the region's laws remains. Today the laws in North Africa are based on European, Islamic, and Ottoman laws.

Islam is the faith of the majority of North Africans. For more than 1,000 years, governments in the region incorporated Islamic law into their systems of rule. Over centuries, Muslim scholars developed a complex system of Islamic law. It was based on the Qur'an and the example of how Muhammad had ruled and acted as a judge. The Qur'an contains principles for

The palace in Tripoli, Libya

Some North African farmers use traditional farming techniques. Moroccan farm workers tend to a field near Rabat (above). A man living in an Egyptian village practices a traditional irrigation technique (right).

governing fairly and for relationships between individuals in society. Ottoman laws and legal traditions developed by tribal leaders and kings also played a role in North African governments.

In the 1800s Europeans began to replace Islamic laws with their own traditions of law. The colonial governments made European laws a permanent part of North African governments. Islamic law is today limited to family and personal matters.

Both Islamic laws and European laws vary from country to country. Today Libyan laws are based on a mixture of Islamic laws, Ottoman laws, and Italian laws, since Italy once held Libya as a colony. Morocco combines Islamic, French, and Spanish laws with a traditional monarchy.

In Algeria and Egypt some citizens want to strengthen the role of Islamic law in governing their countries. This reflects increasing interest in Islam's role in culture, education, the arts, and government.

Since Egypt gained independence, its leaders have set out to develop and change the country. Many have not ruled democratically, and critics have spoken out against them. While some protest the government through peaceful means, a few groups have turned to terrorism.

REVIEW What sources are the laws of North Africa based on today?

Changing Economies

Before Europeans arrived in North Africa, the region had no national economies. Many North Africans practiced subsistence farming. They produced just enough to feed their families. In rich agricultural areas, no crops such as cotton, rice, wheat, and sugarcane were grown on large, commercial farms for export.

When Europeans established colonies in North Africa, they made all of the decisions. They decided which crops should be grown and where they should be sold. They wanted North Africans to export as much as they could to Europe.

Europeans also began shipping North Africa's mineral resources to factories in Europe. European companies turned the raw materials into finished products. The products were then sold in both Europe and North Africa. The finished products were worth far more than the raw materials, so the Europeans made tremendous profits.

The Europeans left the region of North Africa in the 1900s. Even so, the economies of North Africa and Europe remain connected. This connection is a result of colonialism and the fact that the countries are so close to each other. The countries of Europe remain North Africa's biggest trading partners.

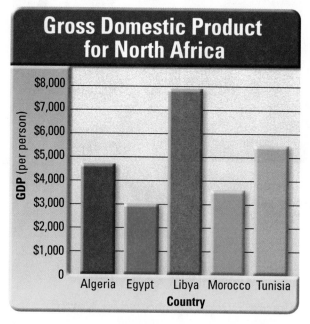

Gross Domestic Product for North Africa

GDP (per person)

$8,000
$7,000
$6,000
$5,000
$4,000
$3,000
$2,000
$1,000
0

Algeria Egypt Libya Morocco Tunisia

Country

Analyze Graphs This graph shows the GDP per person. The bars show the amount each person would make if the country's economy was divided evenly among its citizens.

◆ Although Algeria makes more money overall than Tunisia, its GDP per person is lower. Why do you think this is so?

Today Egypt, Morocco, and Tunisia are described as developing countries. Leaders of these countries are working to build strong market economies. Their goal is for North Africa to be a region of developed countries with a high standard of living.

Since the 1990s Egypt has moved slowly away from the command economy it once had. Private companies are buying industries formerly owned by the government. Egypt's market economy has become more diversified as it develops.

The growth of Egypt's economy is a result, in part, of the Suez Canal. Ships from around the world pay a toll to use the canal. They willingly pay the toll to avoid having to sail around the southern tip of Africa to get from the Mediterranean Sea to the Indian Ocean.

Morocco and Tunisia have a developing economy based mainly on farming and mining. About half of Morocco's workers are farmers, who raise such crops as barley, wheat, citrus fruits, and olives. Tunisia's main farm exports are sugar beets, dates, and almonds. Morocco is one of the world's largest exporters of phosphate rock, which is used as fertilizer.

Service and manufacturing industries are growing. Clothing, electronics, and appliances are put together by North African workers in manufacturing centers owned by companies from around the world. Many North Africans also migrate to work in Europe temporarily or permanently.

Because of the rich Nile soil and the vast Nile River Delta, farming still plays a major role in the Egyptian economy. Egyptian farmers are known as **fellahin** (feh•luh•HEEN). They use a mixture of modern machines, animal power, and hand tools to grow such crops as cotton, rice, wheat, and vegetables. Owners of tractors and other large farm machines often rent out their equipment to farmers in a village as it is needed.

Algeria and Libya both have command economies. Their governments own all businesses except small farms and factories. Oil resources make Algeria and Libya two of Africa's richest countries. However, not all the citizens of these countries benefit from the sale of oil. When oil prices are high, their economies are strong. When oil prices drop, their economies suffer.

Postage stamps often contain images of things that are important to a country. These stamps show some important industries in Algeria (left) and Egypt (below).

Throughout North Africa, tourism has become an important part of the economy. People come from all over the world to see Egypt's pyramids. They also visit North Africa for its warm climate and its Mediterranean beaches. Visitors to Tunisia can enjoy viewing historic mosques as well as French architecture. The Moroccan cities of Tangier, Marrakesh, and Casablanca offer a wide variety of activities. Some tourists even come to Morocco to climb its highest mountain, Jebel Toubkal.

North African countries are working to diversify their economies. They face many challenges. Among these challenges are improving education and training workers to use advanced technology in their careers.

REVIEW **What industries are most important to North Africa's economies?**

Money from foreign tourists helps to strengthen the Egyptian economy.

LESSON 4
REVIEW

1 **MAIN IDEA**   How have both colonialism and Islam shaped the governments of North Africa?

2 **WHY IT MATTERS**   How have history and religion affected the government and economy of North Africa?

3 **VOCABULARY**   Explain the purpose of a **sanction**.

4 **READING SKILL—Sequence**   Which came first for the people of North Africa— the influence of Europe or the influence of Islam?

5 **HISTORY**   Why did European countries colonize North Africa?

6 **CIVICS AND GOVERNMENT**   How are the governments of Morocco and Libya different? How are they similar?

7 **ECONOMICS**   How are Algeria's economy and Tunisia's economy different?

8 **CRITICAL THINKING—Evaluate**   How do you think North Africa might be different today if colonialism had not taken place?

PERFORMANCE ACTIVITY—Design a Flag   Imagine that you have been asked by a North African government at the time of independence to design the country's flag. Include symbols of the country's main export, national religion, and form of government on the flag. Next to your design, explain what ideas the symbols and colors on the flag mean.

Summary Time Line

3000 B.C. ——————————— **2000 B.C.**

3000 B.C.
Egypt becomes
the world's first
nation-state

USE YOUR READING SKILLS

Complete this graphic organizer to show that you understand the
sequence of the various conquests of Egypt. A copy of this
graphic organizer appears on page 117 of the Activity Book.

Conquerors of Egypt

FIRST → NEXT → Last

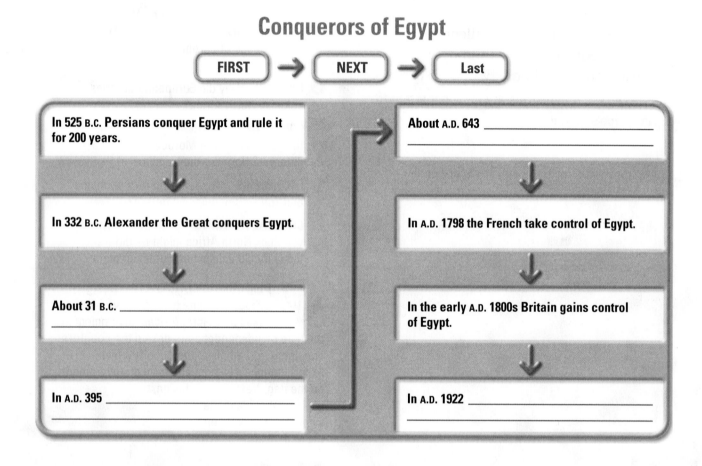

In 525 B.C. Persians conquer Egypt and rule it
for 200 years.
↓
In 332 B.C. Alexander the Great conquers Egypt.
↓
About 31 B.C. _____
_____
↓
In A.D. 395 _____
_____

About A.D. 643 _____
_____
↓
In A.D. 1798 the French take control of Egypt.
↓
In the early A.D. 1800s Britain gains control
of Egypt.
↓
In A.D. 1922 _____
_____

THINK & WRITE

Write a Description Imagine that you are
a farmer living beside the Nile River in about
the year 2000 B.C. Describe what your life
is like. Use library resources to learn more
about what life was like along the Nile.

Write an Advertisement Tourism has
become important to North Africa's economy.
Write an advertisement in which you describe
what North Africa has to offer tourists and
encourage people to visit the area.

1000 B.C.		B.C./A.D.		A.D. 1000		A.D. 2000

1100 B.C.
Phoenicians arrive in North
Africa and control the coast
for about 500 years

A.D. 643
Arab Muslims invade
North Africa and spread
the religion of Islam

A.D. 1500
The Ottoman
Empire controls
much of North
Africa

A.D. 1799
Rosetta Stone is
found, makes it
possible for
historians to read
hieroglyphics

A.D. 1962
Algeria becomes
the last country
in North Africa
to gain independence

USE THE TIME LINE

Use the chapter summary time line to answer these questions.

1 When did Egypt become a nation-state?

2 How many years after Arab Muslims invaded North Africa did the Ottomans control the region?

USE VOCABULARY

Write a word from this list to complete each of the sentences that follow.

reg (p. 404)

dynasty (p. 408)

medina (p. 419)

fellahin (p. 426)

3 A series of rulers from the same family is called a _____.

4 An old section of a city is called a _____.

5 An area of rocky, windswept plains is known as a _____.

RECALL FACTS

Answer these questions.

6 Why was the Nile River called the "giver of life" by Egyptians who lived near its banks?

7 How has traditional North African culture blended with cultures of other continents?

Write the letter of the best choice.

8 **TEST PREP** Ancient Egyptians preserved dead bodies because they believed—
  A the heart was the soul of the body.
  B it was the best way to honor their gods.
  C their gods ordered it.
  D they would need their bodies in the after-life.

9 **TEST PREP** Although European nations no longer control North Africa, their economies remain connected because—
  F Europeans need North African resources.
  G European countries are North Africa's largest trading partners.
  H European countries have always controlled farmland.
  J it is difficult for North Africans to trade with other countries.

THINK CRITICALLY

10 How did the pharaohs of Egypt make sure that life in Egypt would remain unchanged?

11 How do you think the Industrial Revolution and colonialism affected North Africa?

APPLY SKILLS

Follow Routes on a Map

12 Look at the map on page 407. In which direction would you go to travel from Rome to Cairo?

Read a Telescoping Time Line

13 Use the information on the time line on page 415. Why is there a telescoping view of the time period for 1280 B.C. to 1200 B.C.? What important events occurred?

Chapter 12 ▪ 429

Turkey

Turkey is a large country that is rich in history and culture. It is also geographically varied. The combination of these qualities makes Turkey an interesting country to visit.

Thermal springs set high in a cliff have been a popular attraction since ancient times at the city of Pamukkale (puh•MOO•kuh•lay). Terraced pools of mineral-rich water overlook the striking beauty of the surrounding plains.

If you visit Cappadocia (ka•puh•DOH•shuh), you can see unique ancient dwellings. The area of Cappadocia was formed by years of volcanic activity followed by many years of erosion. Over time, people carved intricate communities and elaborate underground cities out of the volcanic mountains.

Istanbul is Turkey's largest city. If you visit, you can go shopping at a large bazaar, or street market, that has over 4,000 shops. You can enjoy the unique architecture of the many mosques, or places of worship. You can tour the cobblestone streets of the city and gather a taste of its rich history.

This man stands outside a cave dwelling in Cappadocia.

LOCATE IT

Istanbul

TURKEY

Cappadocia

Pamukkale

The Blue Mosque in Istanbul (above), thermal springs at Pamukkale (left), and a copper goods shop in Istanbul (right) are a few of Turkey's sights.

GO
ONLINE

A VIRTUAL TOUR
Visit The Learning Site at
www.harcourtschool.com/tours
to take virtual tours of other
world cities.

CNN
Turner
Le@rning

A VIDEO TOUR
Check your media
center or classroom library
for a videotape tour highlighting
several areas of Turkey.

5 Review and Test Preparation

Write a Paragraph Look closely at each picture, and read the captions to help you review Unit 5. Then imagine that you are at one of the places shown. Write a paragraph that describes what you are doing.

USE VOCABULARY

For each pair of terms, write a sentence or two that explains how the two terms are related.

1 **aquifer** (p. 370), **qanat** (p. 370)

2 **dike** (p. 372), **cuneiform** (p. 372)

3 **hieroglyphics** (p. 411), **papyrus** (p. 411)

RECALL FACTS

Answer these questions.

4 Why is the country of Iraq under Saddam Hussein not a true republic?

5 What were the things ancient Egyptians depended on nature to provide?

6 How is Egypt's economy changing from a command economy to a market economy?

Write the letter of the best choice.

7 **TEST PREP**   To move things from one place to another, Sumerians built—
A ziggurats and mosques.
B canals and dikes.
C wheeled carts and sailboats.
D qanats and wadis.

8 **TEST PREP**   The growth of the oil industry in Southwest Asia caused—
F a loss of job opportunities.
G people to move to small villages.
H a decline in government services.
J cities to grow.

9 **TEST PREP**   Bedouins are the group of desert nomads who live—
A in the City of the Dead.
B on the Sinai Peninsula.
C in Cairo.
D near the Atlas Mountains in Morocco.

Visual Summary

| 4000 B.C. | 3000 B.C. | 2000 B.C. | 1000 B.C. |

3500 B.C. **Sumerians build city-states in Mesopotamia** p. 372

3000 B.C. **Egypt becomes the world's first nation-state** p. 408

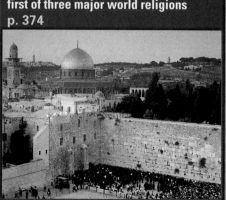

1300 B.C. **Southwest Asia develops its first of three major world religions** p. 374

10 Why do you think the resources found in Southwest Asia are important to people throughout the world?

11 The Egyptians believed in an afterlife. Why do you think they may have believed this?

APPLY SKILLS

Compare Historical Maps
Use the two historical maps on this page to answer the following questions.

MAP AND GLOBE SKILLS

12 What time period does each map show?

13 Which map shows land Egypt controlled on two continents?

14 On what two continents did Egypt control this land?

15 What color is used to show Egyptian land during the New Kingdom? Egyptian land during the Old Kingdom?

16 What cities existed during the Old Kingdom?

17 What cities existed during the New Kingdom?

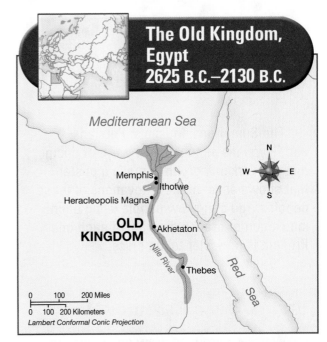

The Old Kingdom, Egypt 2625 B.C.–2130 B.C.

Mediterranean Sea

Memphis
Ithotwe
Heracleopolis Magna
OLD KINGDOM
Akhetaton
Nile River
Thebes
Red Sea

N W E S

0 100 200 Miles
0 100 200 Kilometers
Lambert Conformal Conic Projection

The New Kingdom, Egypt 1539 B.C.–1075 B.C.

Mediterranean Sea

Memphis
NEW KINGDOM
Thebes
Abu
Buhen
Nile River
Red Sea
Napata

N W E S

0 200 400 Miles
0 200 400 Kilometers
Lambert Conformal Conic Projection

B.C./A.D.   A.D. 1000   A.D. 2000

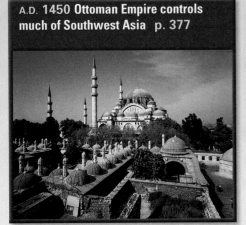

A.D. **1450** Ottoman Empire controls much of Southwest Asia p. 377

A.D. **1970s** All North African and Southwest Asian countries independent by this time p. 423

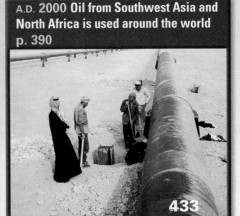

A.D. **2000** Oil from Southwest Asia and North Africa is used around the world p. 390

433

Unit Activities

 Visit The Learning Site at www.harcourtschool.com/socialstudies/activities for additional activities.

Make an Innovations Poster

The Sumerians, Muslims, Persians, and Egyptians all found new ways of doing things. Work in a group to make a poster that shows some of the innovations of these peoples. You can show people using each innovation or draw a diagram of each one. Present your poster to the class.

Draw a Resource Map

Work in a group to draw an outline map of Southwest Asia and North Africa on a large sheet of paper. Refer to maps in your textbook and in encyclopedias. Label the major land areas and bodies of water. Then draw symbols to show resources found in the countries of Southwest Asia and North Africa. Use your textbook and other reference sources to identify these resources. Use the resource map as you take turns explaining about the resources found in each area.

VISIT YOUR LIBRARY

- **The Stars in My Geddoh's Sky** by Claire Sidhom Matze. Albert Whitman & Company.

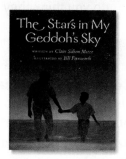

- **If You Could Be My Friend: Letters of Mervet Akram Sha'ban and Galit Fink** presented by Litsa Boudalika. Orchard.

- **The Space Between Our Footsteps: Poems and Paintings from the Middle East** selected by Naomi Shihab Nye. Simon & Schuster.

COMPLETE THE UNIT PROJECT

Make a Travel Guide   Work with a group of classmates to complete the unit project—a travel guide about Southwest Asia and North Africa. In this travel guide, include information about each country's people, cultures, and landforms. In the guide, include information about historic sites you think people might want to visit. Illustrate your travel guide with drawings or pictures from magazines.

Africa South of the Sahara

Leopard throne,
Cameroon, 1800s

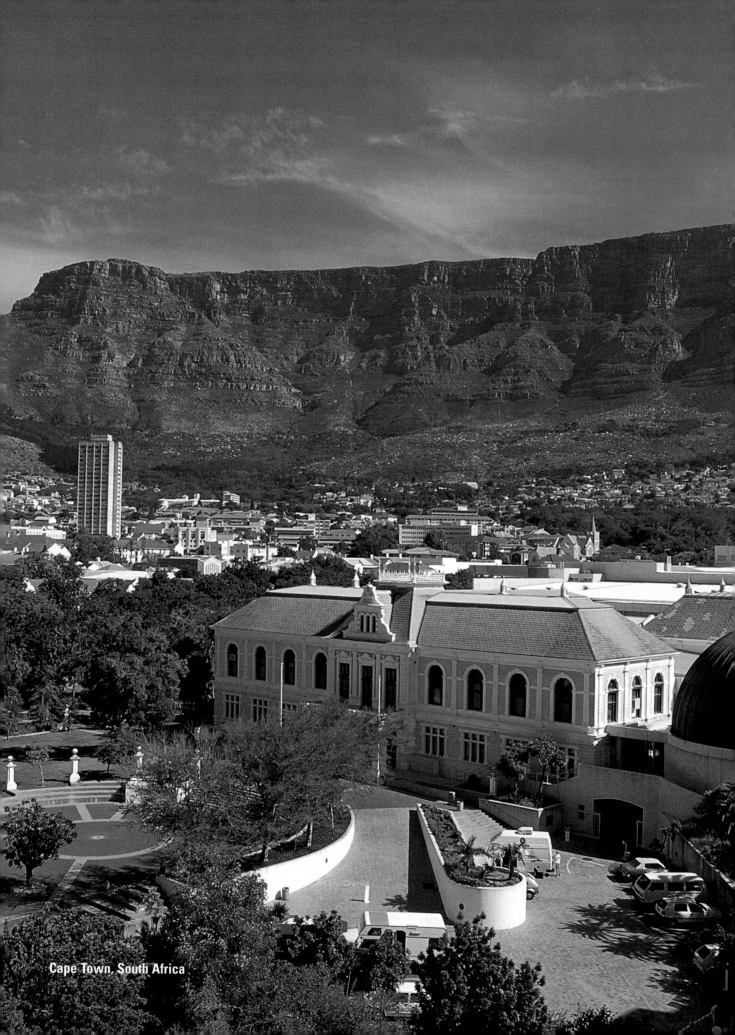

Cape Town, South Africa

Africa South of the Sahara

> " All that you have given me Africa
> Makes me walk
> With a step that is like no other. "
>
> —Anoma Kanié, from "All That You
> Have Given Me Africa," 1978

Preview the Content

Read the titles of the chapters and lessons in this unit. Use them to make an outline. Write any questions you have about Africa.

Preview the Vocabulary

Synonyms   Synonyms are words that have the same or similar meaning as other words. Copy the chart below, and identify a unit Vocabulary Word to match each synonym. Then write a sentence using each Vocabulary Word.

SYNONYM	VOCABULARY WORD	SENTENCE
singer		
trade route		
sailboat		
grassy plain		

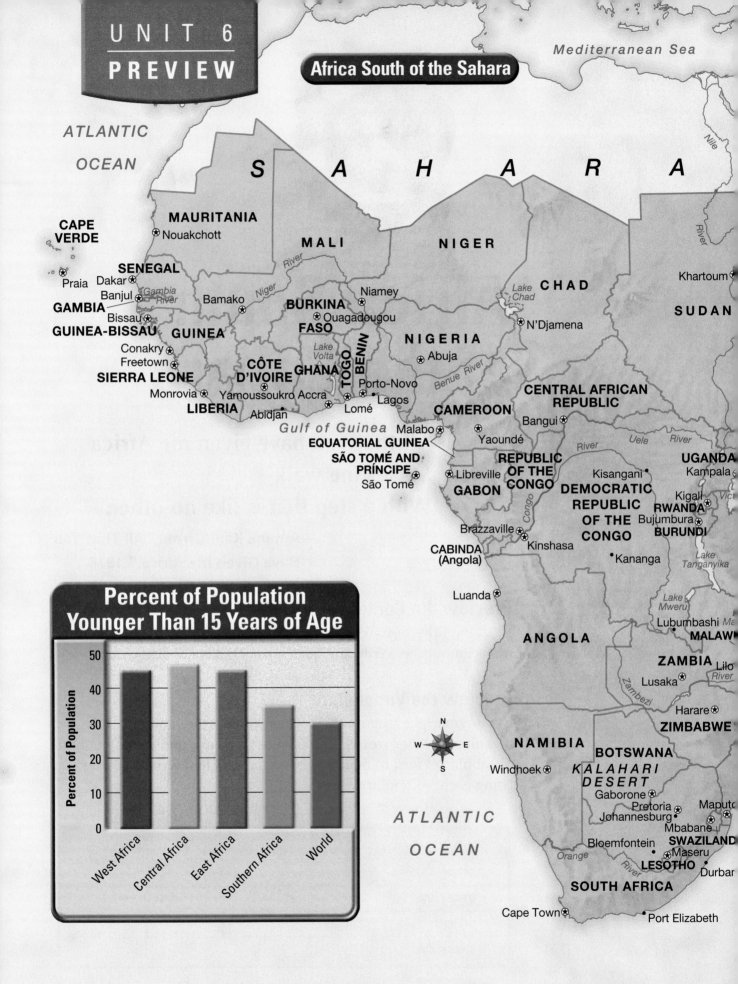

Africa South of the Sahara

Mediterranean Sea

ATLANTIC OCEAN

S A H A R A

Nile River

MAURITANIA
⊛ Nouakchott

CAPE VERDE

M A L I

N I G E R

C H A D

Khartoum ⊛

SUDAN

SENEGAL
Praia • Dakar ⊛
Banjul ⊛
Gambia River
GAMBIA
Bissau ⊛
GUINEA-BISSAU

Bamako ⊛
Niger River

Niamey ⊛

Lake Chad

N'Djamena ⊛

BURKINA FASO
⊛ Ouagadougou

NIGERIA
Abuja ⊛

GUINEA
Conakry ⊛
Freetown ⊛
SIERRA LEONE

CÔTE D'IVOIRE

Lake Volta

GHANA

TOGO

BENIN

Benue River

CENTRAL AFRICAN REPUBLIC

Monrovia ⊛
LIBERIA
Yamoussoukro ⊛ Accra ⊛
Abidjan ⊛
Lomé
Porto-Novo •
Lagos •

CAMEROON
Bangui ⊛

Gulf of Guinea
Malabo ⊛
EQUATORIAL GUINEA

Yaoundé ⊛

Uele River

UGANDA
Kampala ⊛

SÃO TOMÉ AND PRÍNCIPE
São Tomé ⊛

• Libreville ⊛
GABON

REPUBLIC OF THE CONGO

River

Kisangani •

DEMOCRATIC REPUBLIC OF THE CONGO

Kigali ⊛
RWANDA
Bujumbura ⊛
BURUNDI

Vict

Brazzaville ⊛
Congo River

Kinshasa •

CABINDA (Angola)

Kananga •

Lake Tanganyika

Luanda ⊛

Lake Mweru

Lubumbashi •

MALAWI

ANGOLA

ZAMBIA
Lusaka •

Lilo

River

Zambezi

Harare ⊛

NAMIBIA

ZIMBABWE

BOTSWANA

KALAHARI DESERT

Windhoek ⊛

Gaborone ⊛

Pretoria ⊛
Johannesburg •

Maputo

Mbabane

SWAZILAND
Maseru •
LESOTHO
Durbar

ATLANTIC OCEAN

Bloemfontein •
Orange River

SOUTH AFRICA

Cape Town ⊛
• Port Elizabeth

Percent of Population Younger Than 15 Years of Age

Percent of Population

50
40
30
20
10
0

West Africa • Central Africa • East Africa • Southern Africa • World

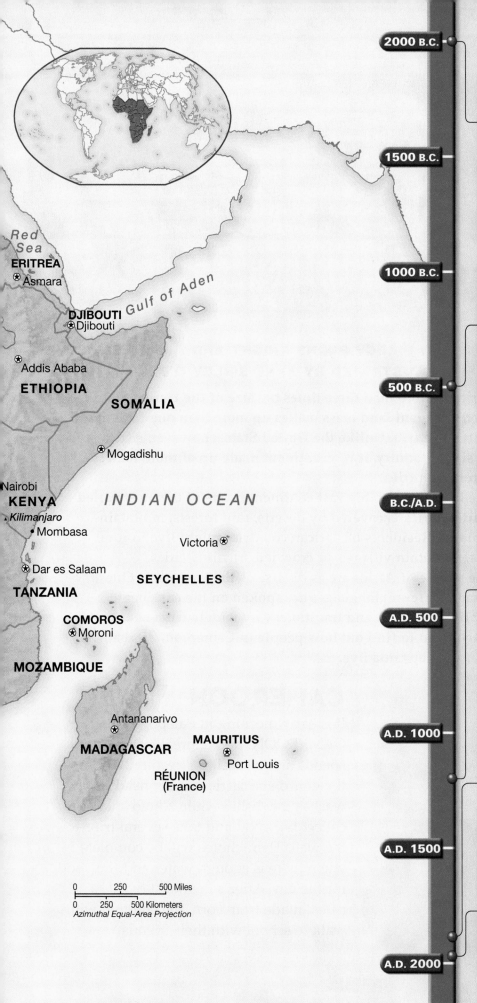

2000 B.C. First African empire south of the Sahara develops p. 485

500 B.C. Nok people become the first West Africans to use iron tools p. 452

A.D. 1200 Shonas build Great Zimbabwe p. 489

A.D. 1900 Most of Africa is colonized by this time p. 455

A.D. 1990 Apartheid ends in South Africa p. 497

2000 B.C.
1500 B.C.
1000 B.C.
500 B.C.
B.C./A.D.
A.D. 500
A.D. 1000
A.D. 1500
A.D. 2000

Red Sea
ERITREA
⊛ Asmara
Gulf of Aden
DJIBOUTI
⊛ Djibouti
⊛ Addis Ababa
ETHIOPIA
SOMALIA
⊛ Mogadishu
Nairobi
KENYA
▲ Kilimanjaro
• Mombasa
INDIAN OCEAN
Victoria ⊛
⊛ Dar es Salaam
SEYCHELLES
TANZANIA
COMOROS
⊛ Moroni
MOZAMBIQUE
Antananarivo ⊛
MAURITIUS
⊛ Port Louis
MADAGASCAR
RÉUNION (France)

0   250   500 Miles
0   250   500 Kilometers
Azimuthal Equal-Area Projection

437

STORY

AFRICA IS NOT A COUNTRY

WRITTEN BY MARGY BURNS KNIGHT AND MARK MELNICOVE
ILLUSTRATED BY ANNE SIBLEY O'BRIEN

Africa is more than three times the size of the United States. In fact, this giant land mass makes up more than one-fifth of all the land on Earth. Unlike the United States, however, Africa is not a single country. It is a continent made up of more than 50 different countries.

The landscape of this vast continent is one of the most varied on Earth. Africa is covered by deserts, rain forests, mountains, and plains. Residents of African countries might live in rural towns, mountain villages, or crowded, bustling cities.

The people of Africa are as diverse as the landscape. One thousand different languages are spoken on the continent. Daily life, histories, and traditions vary widely from country to country. Read to find out how people in Cameroon, Zimbabwe, Benin, and Tanzania live.

CAMEROON

It is early morning in Palepo, a village in CAMEROON. Before breakfast, Mantoh spends an hour selling fresh milk from the gourd she carries on her head. Tepe washes the dishes while Nkolo and Folla collect firewood and take several trips to the well. Their chores will be complete when there is enough water and firewood for the day. After a breakfast of *pap*, a cereal made from corn, the children will walk to school with their friends.

ZIMBABWE

Chip, Farai, Rudo, and the other children are practicing for a choir concert later today in another part of Harare. They will sing two songs: one about the seasonal rains that help the crops to grow, and the other about the abundance of wildlife in ZIMBABWE. Each song will be sung in English and Shona. Zimbabwe means "stone enclosure" in Shona, which is both the name and language of the people who built the kingdom of Great Zimbabwe about 700 years ago.

BENIN

Sena, Celeste, and Darine have come to the market in Cotonou, BENIN'S busiest city, to buy beans and tomatoes for lunch. As Sena holds her cousin's hand, she greets each vendor. When she says *"Mifonya,"* or *"Mifonan,"* or *"Mifonday,"* or *"Edjidada,"* or *"Bonjour,"* she hears two little voices repeat each greeting.

The *"Mi-"* greetings are in the Fon, Guon, and Mina languages. Sena speaks Fon at home. It is similar to Guon and Mina, which Sena has learned to speak from friends and relatives.

Edjidada is Yoruba. Sena's grandmother is Yoruba, so she speaks the language well. The French *Bonjour* is not heard as often as other greetings, but Sena speaks it every day in school.

TANZANIA

Priscilla and Mary have been traveling for several hours, so they are hungry. They poke their heads out of the window to buy some bananas, of which there are at least seventeen varieties in TANZANIA. Today the girls have two choices.

Their uncle has gone into the *duka* to buy them cold drinks. The girls hope that the man who drives the *basi* will soon tell all of the passengers to get back on board. They want to get to their grand-mother's in time to play with their cousins before supper.

Analyze the Literature

1 What are some similarities and differences in the ways people live, work, and play in these African countries?

2 Why do you think the people of Africa speak many different languages?

3 Choose an African country not mentioned in the passage to research. Draw a picture and write a paragraph about what daily life is like in that country.

READ A BOOK

START THE UNIT PROJECT

Prepare a Multimedia Presentation With the class, prepare a multimedia tour of Africa south of the Sahara. As you read this unit, you will learn about people and places in Africa. Start to think of ways you will use the information you gather to prepare a multimedia presentation.

USE TECHNOLOGY

Visit The Learning Site at **www.harcourtschool.com/ socialstudies** for additional activities, primary sources, and other resources to use in this unit.

MOPTI, MALI

At the place where the Bani and Niger Rivers meet lies the city of Mopti. Spread out on three islands, Mopti is one of Mali's largest cities. Many of the city's buildings, such as the mosque in the photograph, are made from mud brick. The wooden posts that stick out from the walls allow workers to climb to apply additional mud for any needed repairs.

LOCATE IT

Mopti

MALI

West Africa and Central Africa

❝ Africa is never the same to anyone who leaves it and returns again. **❞**

—Beryl Markham, from
West with the Night, 1942

CHAPTER READING SKILL

When you **summarize**, you restate the most important ideas, or key points, in your own words.

As you read this chapter, think about the key points of each lesson. Then summarize each lesson.

(KEY POINTS)   →   (SUMMARY)

Desert, Savanna, and Rain Forest

MAIN IDEA
Read to find out how different climate and vegetation regions can affect the way people live and where they live.

WHY IT MATTERS
Many West and Central Africans find life in rural areas so difficult that they move to crowded cities.

VOCABULARY

savanna
transition zone
cacao
bauxite
copper belt
cobalt

South of the Sahara, yellow desert sands give way to the dry, rocky soil of West and Central Africa. Herds of camels and goats graze on thorny bushes. Farther south lie miles of waving grass, dotted with flat-topped acacia (uh•KAY•shuh) trees and neatly planted farm plots. Still farther south, grasslands give way to thick forests. In the dim shadows of the rain forest, birds chirp while chattering monkeys scamper through the branches overhead.

Three Different Regions

A journey through West and Central Africa is a journey through three different climate and vegetation regions. Along the southern edge of the Sahara lies the Sahel (SAH•hil), a hot, dry region where little rain falls. The second region is the **savanna** (suh•VA•nuh), a grassy plain with scattered trees where everything is green during the summer rainy season. The savanna forms a wide belt between the Sahel and the third climate and vegetation region. This is the rain forest. The tall trees there are green year-round and grow so close together that their leaves form a canopy, or rooflike covering.

Climate and Vegetation Regions

FAST FACT Farmers in the Sahel face many problems. There is either too little rain or too much rain. Other problems include diseases that affect people and livestock, attacks by locusts that destroy crops, and wind erosion that wears away the region's scarce amount of fertile soil.

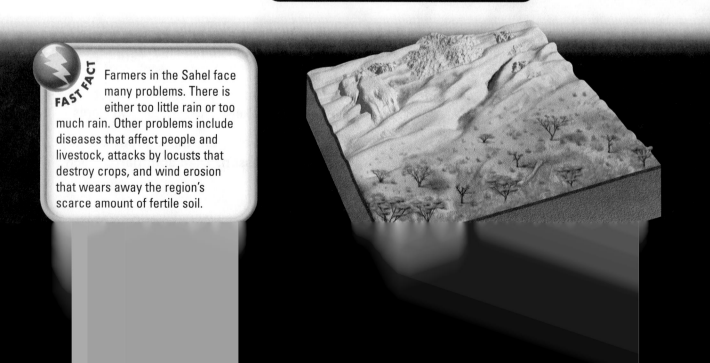

The weather is hot all year in West and Central Africa. That is in part because the region lies along the equator, between the Tropic of Cancer and the Tropic of Capricorn. These imaginary parallel lines mark the tropics. During most of the year, the sun strikes the tropics straight on.

Another reason the region is so hot is that, unlike other parts of Africa, most of West and Central Africa does not rise very far above sea level. Only a few scattered mountains in Cameroon and Guinea and the highland plateaus of Angola and Zambia reach greater heights. Most of the region is less than 3,000 feet (914 m) above sea level.

Farmers in West and Central Africa depend on the amount of rain that falls in their area. Rainfall affects both the type and the amount of crops that grow in each climate and vegetation region.

Rainfall and temperature also affect the fertility of the soil. Much of the soil is very dry in areas of little rain. The high temperatures cause the little rain that does fall to evaporate too quickly. The dry soil cannot support crops. As a result, there are few large farms other than large commercial plantations where crops are grown for

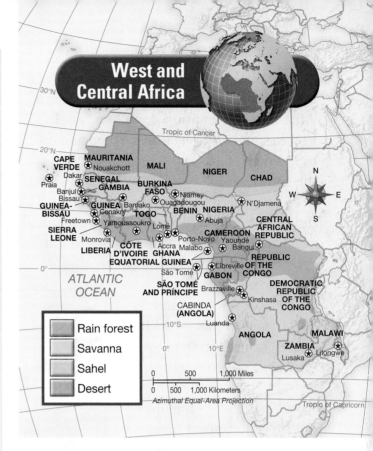

West and Central Africa

Rain forest
Savanna
Sahel
Desert

Regions The Sahel is between the desert and the savanna.
❓ **Which countries are in the Sahel?**

export. Most farms are more like large gardens that provide food for the farmers and their families.

REVIEW What are the three climate and vegetation regions of West and Central Africa?

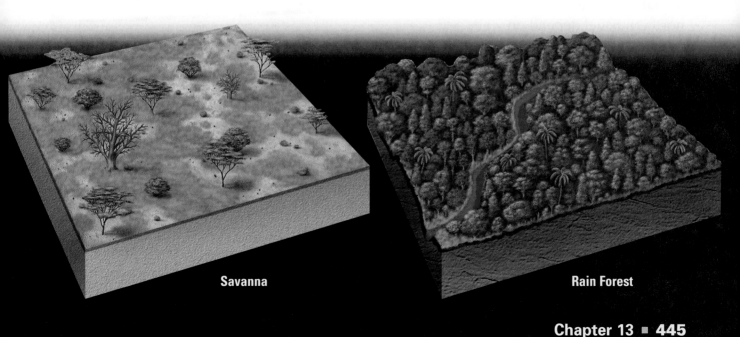

Savanna

Rain Forest

The Sahel

The Sahel is the transition zone between the desert and the grasslands in northern Africa. As a **transition zone**, the Sahel shares some of the features of the Sahara to the north and the savanna grasslands to the south.

The northern Sahel is made up of sand dunes and gravel-covered plains. So much swirling sand fills the air at times that it is often difficult to see and to breathe. A few low mountains and plateaus break the flatness of the land in places. As in a desert, rainfall in the northern Sahel is infrequent and unpredictable. When the rains finally do come, they fall for only a short time. The Sahel has long periods of drought, during which its few rivers and lakes dry up.

The only major bodies of water in the Sahel are the northern bend of the Niger River and Lake Chad. Lake Chad lies at the point where the countries of Chad, Niger, Nigeria, and Cameroon all meet. Lake Chad is thought to have been much larger hundreds of years ago. Today as the climate in the Sahel has become drier, the lake is almost empty. People in the northern Sahel depend on wells and springs for their water. Because many people live far from these places, they must travel great distances to get water.

From the central to the southern Sahel, the landscape is savanna grassland. Farther to the south, there are trees, and the soil can support some kinds of crops. Farmers in the southern Sahel are able to grow dry-climate crops such as peanuts and dates. Most people in the region, however, earn their living by herding livestock.

As a result of the Sahel's harsh environment, its population is fairly small. There

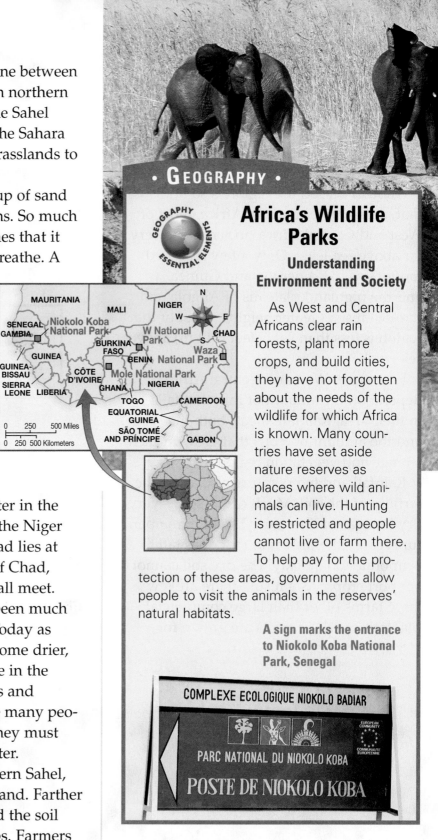

· GEOGRAPHY ·

Africa's Wildlife Parks

Understanding Environment and Society

As West and Central Africans clear rain forests, plant more crops, and build cities, they have not forgotten about the needs of the wildlife for which Africa is known. Many countries have set aside nature reserves as places where wild animals can live. Hunting is restricted and people cannot live or farm there. To help pay for the protection of these areas, governments allow people to visit the animals in the reserves' natural habitats.

A sign marks the entrance to Niokolo Koba National Park, Senegal

COMPLEXE ECOLOGIQUE NIOKOLO BADIAR

PARC NATIONAL DU NIOKOLO KOBA

POSTE DE NIOKOLO KOBA

are few large cities. Most people live in small settlements or villages. Often they have to travel from place to place with their herds to find grazing land and water.

REVIEW Why is the Sahel considered a transition zone?

A herd of elephants on the move after bathing in Waza National Park, Cameroon

The Savanna

To the south of the Sahel, a huge plateau stretches across Africa into Nigeria and Guinea. The savannas of West and Central Africa lie on this landform. Much of the plateau is covered with grasses and some trees. The most important of these is the baobab (BAY•oh•bab) tree. Both its leaves and its fruit are edible. They are used in making medicines. Its bark can be made into paper, rope, and cloth. Its seeds can be made into fertilizer and soap.

The climate of the savanna region consists of regular wet and dry seasons. The dry season is almost completely dry, but it is brief. At Ouagadougou (wah•gah•DOO•goo), the capital city of Burkina Faso, there is almost no rain from October to February.

During the wet season, rain falls almost daily. During this time, farmers grow a variety of crops, including potatoes, onions, okra, tomatoes, corn, yams, and peanuts. The major economic activity of the region is farming. As in many parts of the world, most of the farmers subsist on what they grow. There are also large plantations where crops, including palm oil, coffee, rubber, and cacao, are raised for export. **Cacao** beans are used in making chocolate.

The highest parts of the plateau are where the region's most important rivers begin. Draining the highlands to the west are the Senegal and Gambia Rivers. The Volta and Niger Rivers drain the highlands to the south. Most of the people who live in the savanna live along the rivers. Some live on small farms and in villages, but many find life in rural areas too difficult.

A village in the savanna region of West and Central Africa

447

In recent years the region has experienced migrations of people from the countryside to urban areas.

REVIEW Why can the savanna region support more people than the Sahel?

The Rain Forest

South of the savanna is the rain forest region of West and Central Africa. It is one of the largest rain forests in the world. Its major physical feature is the Congo River basin. This huge area in Central Africa lies mainly in the Democratic Republic of the Congo, but parts are also in the Central African Republic and the Republic of the Congo. Highlands and mountains to the east and lowlands to the west border the rain forest.

The Congo River, known also as the Zaire, is Africa's second longest river, after the Nile. The Congo River is more than 2,900 miles (4,700 km) long, with many rapids and waterfalls along its course. Because of this, ocean-going ships can travel fewer than 100 miles (161 km) up the river from the Atlantic coast.

Many plants grow in the wet, tropical climate, where it rains as much as 200 inches (508 cm) a year. Thick forest covers the land, with some trees growing as high as 150 feet (46 m). Rain forest trees provide a variety of resources. Some trees, such as mahogany, teak, and ebony, provide lumber. The fluffy white flowers that grow on the kapok (KAY•pahk) tree are used to fill mattresses and pillows.

Although more than 80 percent of the people in the rain forest earn a living by farming, only about two percent of the land is farmed. The large, lush forest leaves little space for large farms and grazing lands. Insects that inhabit the rain forest can destroy crops and cause sickness among people and livestock.

REVIEW What is the main physical feature of the rain forest region?

Rich in Minerals

Minerals are among the most important natural resources in West and Central Africa. Coastal areas produce iron ore, phosphates, uranium, and bauxite. **Bauxite** is the main ingredient in aluminum.

Farmers have small plots along the banks of the Congo River (right). The tsetse fly (above) lives along riverbanks and lakeshores. It causes disease in people and livestock.

Copper

Diamond

Cobalt

Bauxite

Farther inland, the highlands hold large amounts of gold and diamonds. Straddling the border of Zambia and the Democratic Republic of the Congo lies a **copper belt**, an area rich in the mineral used as a conductor of heat and electricity. The region also produces nearly three-fourths of the world's cobalt. **Cobalt** is a mineral that is mixed with other minerals to make metals harder.

Petroleum is another important resource. Africa's Atlantic coast from Nigeria south to Angola has large oil deposits. Nigeria's huge supply of this resource makes it one of the world's leading producers.

Mineral resources have become the region's most important trade items. They provide money needed for its countries' developing economies and jobs for people in a growing population.

REVIEW What kind of natural resource in the region is important for trade?

LESSON 1
REVIEW

1 **MAIN IDEA** What characterizes the tropical climate of West and Central Africa?

2 **WHY IT MATTERS** How does living in the tropics affect the lives of West and Central Africans?

3 **VOCABULARY** How is the **savanna** different from the Sahel?

4 **READING SKILL—Summarize** In what ways does the rain forest make life hard for people living in the Congo River basin?

5 **GEOGRAPHY** What are two reasons the weather in West and Central Africa is hot?

6 **ECONOMICS** What is the major economic activity of the Sahel?

7 **CRITICAL THINKING—Evaluate** How can the mineral resources of West and Central African countries help the economies and the people of those countries?

 PERFORMANCE—Make a Model
Use the Internet or print references to gather information about the rain forest. Find out about the climate, vegetation, wildlife, diseases, and economic activities. Gather your information in a chart or database. Then use your database to create a rain forest model with labels. Display your model in your classroom.

·SKILLS·

MAP AND GLOBE

Compare Map Projections

VOCABULARY	
projection	equal-area projection
distortion	conformal projection

▶ WHY IT MATTERS

Cartographers, or mapmakers, have developed different ways to show the round Earth in the form of flat maps.

Cartographers must change Earth's shape by splitting or stretching it to make it lie flat. These different views of Earth are called **projections**. Every map projection has **distortions**, or parts that are not accurate. Some map projections distort the shape or the size of the area shown. Cartographers classify map projections by what is distorted the least. By learning about the distortions, you will understand how different map projections can best be used.

▶ WHAT YOU NEED TO KNOW

Maps A and B show the same area. Map A shows an equal area on either side of the prime meridian and on either side of the equator. This is an **equal-area projection**. The sizes of regions are correct in relation to one another, but the shapes are distorted. An equal-area projection is useful for comparing information about different parts of the world.

Map B is a **conformal projection**, which is useful for showing directions correctly even though it distorts sizes. Sizes are especially distorted for places near the poles. On a conformal projection, the lines of longitude are all an equal distance apart.

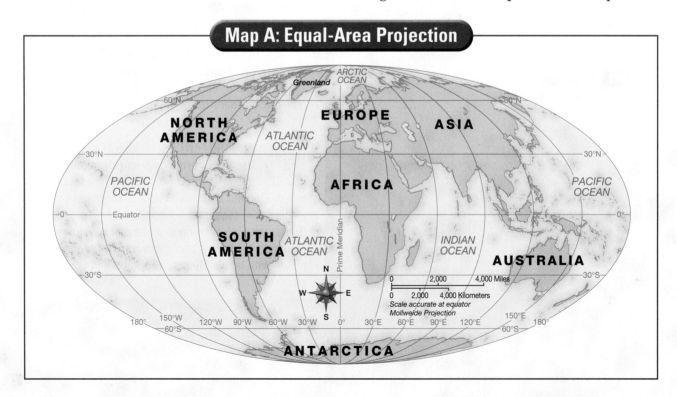

Map A: Equal-Area Projection

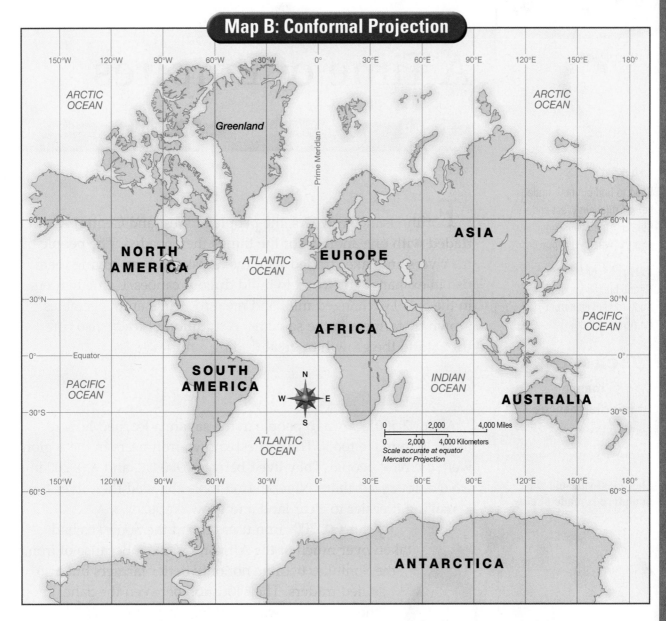

Map B: Conformal Projection

On a globe, these lines would get closer together as they neared the poles, where they meet. On a conformal projection, the lines of latitude get farther apart closer to the poles. On a globe they are an equal distance apart.

▶ PRACTICE THE SKILL

Look at each map projection, and notice the differences. Think about the best uses for each projection. Then use the maps to answer these questions.

1 In reality, Africa is much larger than Greenland. Which projection shows Greenland's size more accurately?

2 The greatest east-west distance in Africa is about the same as the greatest north-south distance. Which projection shows Africa's shape more accurately?

▶ APPLY WHAT YOU LEARNED

Write a paragraph about the advantages and disadvantages of using an equal-area projection and a conformal projection.

Practice your map and globe skills with the **GeoSkills CD-ROM**.

MAIN IDEA

Read to find out how trade helped rulers in West and Central Africa build kingdoms of great wealth and power.

WHY IT MATTERS

Nation building and trade remain important for Africans today.

VOCABULARY

mansa
middle passage

This 2,000-year-old Nok sculpture is made of clay.

A Time of Empires

| 1000 B.C. | B.C. / A.D. | A.D. 1000 | A.D. 2000 |

For thousands of years, the people of West and Central Africa traded with one another for the things they needed. The people of the rivers and lakes traded with the forest dwellers, giving them fish in exchange for wood to build dugout canoes. Cattle herders in the Sahel exchanged milk and meat for fruits and vegetables grown by farmers in the savanna. A tradition of trade also contributed to the growth of great trading empires.

A Tradition of Trade

About 2,500 years ago people in the savanna learned how to use iron to make tools. The earliest known iron users in the region were the Nok people. They lived between 900 B.C. and A.D. 200 in what is today northern Nigeria. Iron tools changed their lives by making it easier to clear land and grow crops.

By the A.D. 700s iron users called the Soninkes had taken over much of the African savanna. Because of iron, the Soninkes became not only better farmers but also skilled traders. Their location between the Sahel and the rain forest was ideal for a center of trade. North African merchants crossed the Sahara to trade with the Soninkes. The North Africans were interested in gold from the Soninkes.

The Soninkes traded with the Wangara people of the rain forest to get gold, which they then traded with merchants from North Africa. Gold was scarce in the savanna, but the Wangaras had access to it in the rain forest. In exchange for gold, the Soninkes traded salt, which they had gotten from the North African merchants. Because the Wangaras had very little salt, they were willing to trade it for gold.

The Soninkes benefited from the trading cycle. They soon grew powerful and rich with profits from their trading partners. Their wealth led to the development of a great trading empire.

REVIEW For the Soninkes, what was the result of trade?

Ghana, Mali, and Songhai

The Soninke trading empire soon became known by the title also used by its rulers—*Ghana* (GAH•nuh), meaning "war chief." Ghana, which was located between the Senegal and upper Niger Rivers, began its rise to power about A.D. 700. Over the next 300 years the empire grew to cover more than 100,000 square miles (about 260,000 sq km).

In the A.D. 1000s quarrels between Ghana and one of its trading partners led to war. Ghana lost the war and never became powerful again. By 1203 the empire had broken up into small kingdoms.

In time, the people of the fallen Ghana Empire came under the rule of other African empires. The first of these was Mali. The people who founded Mali were called the Malinkes (muh•LING•keez). Under their leader Sundiata (sun•JAHT•ah), the

A bracelet from the Ghana Empire

Malinkes conquered many of the small kingdoms that Ghana once held, including those rich in gold. Mali's riches, like Ghana's, came from the gold and salt trade.

The **mansas**, or rulers, who followed Sundiata won more land for the Mali Empire. Mali grew to be nearly twice as large as the empire of Ghana had been. Mali's greatest growth came during the rule of Mansa Musa, from 1307 to 1332. During his rule Mansa Musa extended the empire to include the rich trading markets of Gao (GOW) and Timbuktu (tim•buhk•TOO). After his death, however, Mali's leaders could not hold on to the land that he had gained. Because of this, Mali's power slipped away.

As Mali weakened, another empire began to grow. By the late 1400s much of what had been Mali had become the Songhai (SAWNG•hy) Empire. Like Ghana and Mali before it, Songhai grew rich from its control of trade routes across the Sahara.

Map of the Mali Empire

Analyze Primary Sources

This section of a map from the 1300s shows the great Mali Empire. The map is part of the *Catalan Atlas*, a Muslim reference book.

1. The seated, crowned figure is Mansa Musa.
2. The small buildings are symbols for cities.
3. The lines on the map show the importance of a city. The important cities have more lines than others.

◆ What do you think the golden wall at the top of the map shows?

Songhai also took control of the trading centers along the Niger River—Jenné (jeh•NAY), Timbuktu, and Gao.

Songhai's control of trade lasted only until the 1590s. In 1591, the ruler of Morocco attacked Songhai with a new weapon not known before in Africa—guns, which the Moroccans of North Africa had gotten from Southwest Asia.

REVIEW What three large empires flourished in West Africa before the 1600s?

The Slave Trade

Besides gold, the North Africans traded for cotton goods, animal skins, and ivory with the West African empires. They also bought slaves, whom they later sold to owners of salt mines or large farms. The slave trade was not new in Africa when the Europeans arrived.

The Portuguese were the first Europeans to establish settlements in West and Central Africa in the late 1400s. The Africans were willing to trade, and they allowed the Portuguese to set up stations all along the Atlantic coast. At first, the Portuguese traded for spices, gold, and ivory. As time went on, slaves came to be the main export of African trade.

During the 1500s, events in the Americas brought about an increased demand for slaves. Europeans had started mines and plantations in their American colonies. To do the work, they used slave labor. At first, the Europeans had used Native Americans as slaves, but as their numbers fell, the Europeans looked to Africa as a source for new labor. First the Portuguese and then other Europeans took part in what became the transatlantic slave trade.

Because the demand for slaves was so great, African traders needed more slaves. They often went into the countryside, capturing anyone they could. They then sold their captives to European traders at stations along the coast. So many slaves were traded that part of Africa's coast became known as the Slave Coast.

At the stations, slave traders loaded the captives onto ships for the journey to the Americas called the **middle passage**. During the middle passage, enslaved people faced terrible conditions. Many died before they even reached the Americas. Some died fighting against the chains and cruel treatment. Others died of diseases that quickly passed from person to person on the crowded ships.

For more than 300 years, before slavery was abolished, West and Central Africa was the focus of the transatlantic slave trade.

This tomb from the 1500s is a reminder of the Songhai Empire.

Gorée Island

Two miles (about 3 km) off the coast of Dakar, the capital of present-day Senegal, lies Gorée Island. This island was once one of the major slave-trading ports on the Atlantic coast of Africa. Visitors to the small island today can see the Maison des Esclaves, or "House of Slaves." It is one of the many places where people who had been captured to be sold as slaves were held while waiting to be shipped overseas.

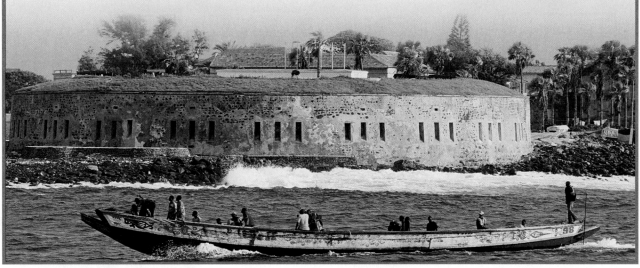

During that time as many as 11 million enslaved Africans were taken to the Americas. The slave trade had a terrible effect on the African economy. In some places so many people were taken that the land was left almost empty. There were few people to farm or care for the herds. By the time the slave trade ended, the descendants of the people who had created the once-great African trading empires were left with little.

REVIEW How did the slave trade affect West and Central Africa?

The Colonial Period

When the slave trade ended in the 1800s, Europeans remained interested in Africa for its natural resources instead of for its slaves. By the 1880s European interest in Africa became so strong that one British newspaper called it the "scramble for Africa." The scramble to control parts of Africa went on until 1884, when representatives from 14 European nations met in Germany to divide Africa among themselves. No African representatives were invited to the meeting. Because of this, borders were drawn that often separated people of the same language and culture.

By 1900 the Europeans had colonies almost everywhere in Africa. They built mines, factories, and plantations. Often the Europeans treated the African workers in these places as slaves.

During the colonial period Europeans introduced Christianity. They also brought their languages and forms of government to Africa. This, combined with earlier influences by North African traders who introduced Islam and Arab culture, changed Africa greatly.

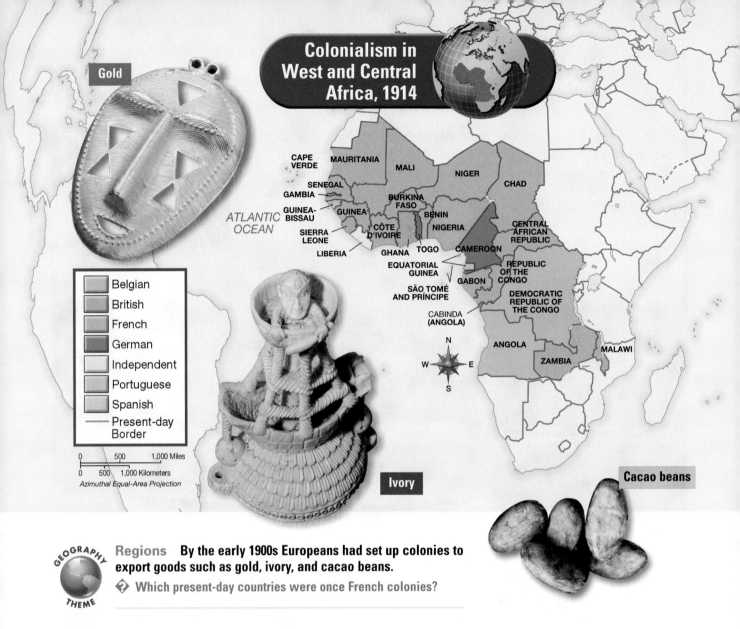

Gold

Colonialism in West and Central Africa, 1914

CAPE VERDE
MAURITANIA
MALI
NIGER
CHAD
SENEGAL
GAMBIA
BURKINA FASO
GUINEA-BISSAU
GUINEA
BENIN
ATLANTIC OCEAN
CÔTE D'IVOIRE
NIGERIA
CENTRAL AFRICAN REPUBLIC
SIERRA LEONE
LIBERIA
GHANA
TOGO
CAMEROON
EQUATORIAL GUINEA
REPUBLIC OF THE CONGO
GABON
SÃO TOMÉ AND PRÍNCIPE
DEMOCRATIC REPUBLIC OF THE CONGO
CABINDA (ANGOLA)
ANGOLA
MALAWI
ZAMBIA

N W E S

Belgian
British
French
German
Independent
Portuguese
Spanish
Present-day Border

0   500   1,000 Miles
0 500 1,000 Kilometers
Azimuthal Equal-Area Projection

Ivory

Cacao beans

GEOGRAPHY THEME

Regions By the early 1900s Europeans had set up colonies to export goods such as gold, ivory, and cacao beans.

❓ Which present-day countries were once French colonies?

Some Africans accepted change, but others fought to keep their lands and culture. In West and Central Africa, Samori Touré and his well-trained soldiers held off the French for more than 15 years. In 1898, however, the French took Samori prisoner and took control of much of the region. For the next 50 years, Europe controlled almost every part of African life.

It was not until after World War II ended in 1945 that African leaders began to push for independence. Inspired by the independence movement in India, African leaders had just one demand of their own—freedom now!

REVIEW Why did European nations divide Africa into colonies?

Independence

While some African colonies fought for their independence, others gained it peacefully. In the British colony of the Gold Coast, a young leader named Kwame Nkrumah (KWAH•mee en•KROO•muh) persuaded the British to hold an election. As a result of the vote, the British granted full independence to the colony in 1957. The new nation took the name Ghana, after the great trading empire of earlier times.

Whether or not they won their independence peacefully, the new nations faced problems left over from colonial days. When the Europeans created Nigeria, for

Lagos, Nigeria, is the largest city in Africa. Like many modern cities in the world, Lagos is a mix of the past (left) and the present (right).

example, they grouped together people from more than 250 different ethnic groups.

In some cases the Europeans encouraged fighting among groups within their colonies. They believed that if Africans fought one another, they would never be able to unite against colonial rule. In the Democratic Republic of the Congo, which had been known as the Belgian Congo, the

people set aside their differences to work together for independence, which they gained in 1960.

Today these nations face two great challenges. They struggle to stay united and to raise the standard of living above the subsistence level.

REVIEW What problems did colonization cause for the newly independent nations?

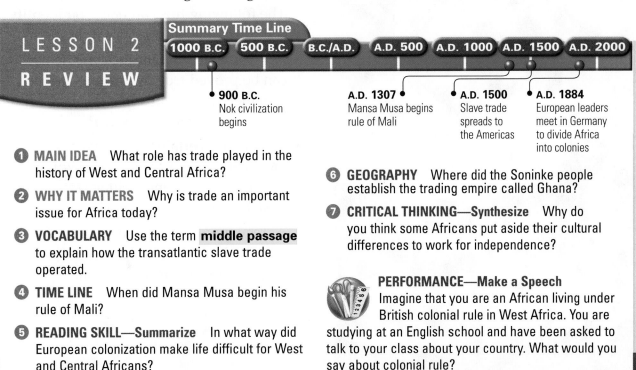

LESSON 2
REVIEW

Summary Time Line

| 1000 B.C. | 500 B.C. | B.C./A.D. | A.D. 500 | A.D. 1000 | A.D. 1500 | A.D. 2000 |

900 B.C.
Nok civilization begins

A.D. 1307
Mansa Musa begins rule of Mali

A.D. 1500
Slave trade spreads to the Americas

A.D. 1884
European leaders meet in Germany to divide Africa into colonies

1 **MAIN IDEA** What role has trade played in the history of West and Central Africa?

2 **WHY IT MATTERS** Why is trade an important issue for Africa today?

3 **VOCABULARY** Use the term **middle passage** to explain how the transatlantic slave trade operated.

4 **TIME LINE** When did Mansa Musa begin his rule of Mali?

5 **READING SKILL—Summarize** In what way did European colonization make life difficult for West and Central Africans?

6 **GEOGRAPHY** Where did the Soninke people establish the trading empire called Ghana?

7 **CRITICAL THINKING—Synthesize** Why do you think some Africans put aside their cultural differences to work for independence?

PERFORMANCE—Make a Speech
Imagine that you are an African living under British colonial rule in West Africa. You are studying at an English school and have been asked to talk to your class about your country. What would you say about colonial rule?

Identify Fact and Opinion

WHY IT MATTERS

When you read, it is important to identify whether what you are reading is a statement of fact or a statement of opinion. A statement of **fact** can be proved either true or untrue. An **opinion** is a statement that cannot be proved or disproved. Opinions express beliefs, attitudes, and viewpoints.

Nigerian President Olusegun Obasanjo

The following statement is a fact: "Many African nations became independent in the 1950s and 1960s." By checking a history book or an encyclopedia, you could prove the statement true or untrue. However, the following statement is an opinion: "Independence was the best thing that ever happened to the nations of Africa." The sentence expresses a belief or viewpoint, but it cannot be proved.

Knowing the difference between facts and opinions can help you make judgments about the reliability of what you read.

WHAT YOU NEED TO KNOW

The following tips can help you identify whether statements are facts or opinions.

- Ask yourself whether the statement can be proved true or untrue. Can the statement be checked in a reliable, up-to-date reference source?

- Sometimes, certain words signal statements of opinion. Words that signal feelings or emotions include *best, worst, good, bad, wonderful,* or *terrible.*

- Agreeing with an opinion does not make it a fact. If a statement cannot be proved true or untrue, it is an opinion.

This building in Porto-Novo, Benin, shows a European influence.

▶ PRACTICE THE SKILL

Read the following statements, and decide whether they are statements of fact or opinion.

❶ During the 1800s European nations began building colonies in Africa.

❷ Ethiopia and Liberia were the only African countries that remained independent.

❸ The British ruled their African colonies better than the French ruled their colonies.

❹ The Congo was a Belgian colony.

❺ For most Africans colonial rule was worse than slavery.

❻ European nations should not have allowed African colonies to gain independence.

▶ APPLY WHAT YOU LEARNED

Reread the section in Lesson 2 titled "The Slave Trade." What are your opinions about the information presented?

Write six statements about the information in the section—three that state facts from the section and three that are your own opinions. Trade papers with a classmate, and challenge each other to identify which statements are facts and which are opinions.

MAIN IDEA
Read to find out about the rich diversity of West and Central African cultures.

WHY IT MATTERS
By appreciating cultural differences, you can learn how groups of people can contribute to a society.

VOCABULARY
animism
kinship
griot
folktale

Many Cultures

People in Africa belong to many different ethnic groups. In West and Central Africa alone, there are hundreds of groups, each with its own culture. People belonging to a culture may wear distinctive clothing, speak a common language, and enjoy foods prepared in a particular way. Each African culture also has its own history and way of thinking about life.

Cultural Layers

The many cultures of West and Central Africa changed over thousands of years as early peoples migrated to and settled in different regions. They adapted their lives to what the environment had to offer. They became herders, hunters and gatherers, farmers, or fishers. They built homes and made clothes from locally available materials. They also changed by learning from people of other cultures.

Today savanna dwellers such as the Malinke still make houses out of woven grass. Mbuti homes are made of branches and leaves from the rain forest in which they live. The nomadic Baggara, who live on the desert's edge in Chad, build tents with wooden frames and animal skins.

Groups often traded with one another or moved around as resources changed. Even farmers migrated to new areas, looking for more fertile soil or more rainfall. As groups came in contact with one another, they learned and sometimes adopted new ways of doing things. This can be seen in their languages, artwork, customs, and beliefs.

REVIEW How did West and Central Africa's many ethnic groups develop?

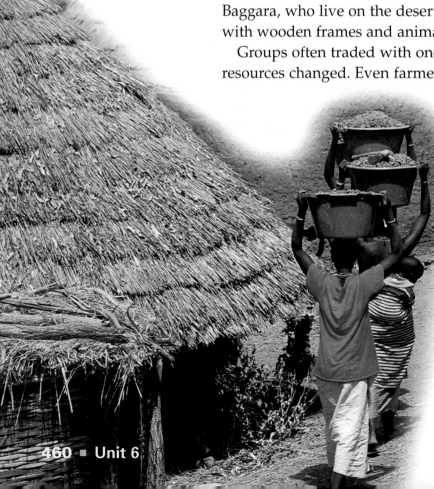

People in rural areas often live in small villages made up of houses woven from grass.

Many Languages

Similarities in many of the languages spoken in West and Central Africa may have been the result of a group of farmers migrating 3,000 years ago. These languages use the word *bantu*, or a word similar to it, to mean "people." Historians believe that farmers from the savanna moved to the rain forest at a time of drought. Besides their language, they carried tools to the forest people and taught them how to raise yams and bananas. Today people from eastern Nigeria to Kenya and southward to South Africa speak Bantu languages.

People living in West and Central Africa do not share a single language, however. Most people grow up speaking the language of their ethnic group, a language such as Ibo (EE•boh), Kikongo, or Fang. Some also know the languages of other ethnic groups. Hausa (HOW•suh) and Malinke are widely spoken in West Africa by people who do not belong to those ethnic groups. Lingala is a Bantu language spoken by many Central Africans.

Contact with the world outside Africa has added to the number of languages spoken. Because few of the countries have only one ethnic group, the official language of a country most often is that of the coun-try that ruled it during the colonial period. English, Portuguese, French, and Spanish are official languages of countries through-out West and Central Africa.

Official Languages in West and Central Africa

LANGUAGES	COUNTRIES
Arabic	Chad, Mauritania
Chichewa	Malawi
English	Cameroon, The Gambia, Ghana, Liberia, Malawi, Nigeria, Sierra Leone, Zambia
French	Benin, Burkina Faso, Cameroon, Central African Republic, Chad, Democratic Republic of the Congo, Republic of the Congo, Côte d'Ivoire, Equatorial Guinea, Gabon, Guinea, Mali, Niger, Senegal, Togo
Portuguese	Angola, Cape Verde, Guinea-Bissau, São Tomé and Príncipe
Spanish	Equatorial Guinea
Wolof	Mauritania

Analyze Tables **This table shows the official languages spoken in West and Central Africa.**

◈ **Which languages are least common?**

Dakar, the capital of Senegal, is a city filled with modern and French colonial architecture. This large port city is a major trade center in the region.

LOCATE IT

Dakar

SENEGAL

Not all official languages come from the European colonial rulers. In Chad and Mauritania, where many Muslims live, Arabic is an official language. Arabic first reached Africa in the A.D. 700s, and today many African Muslims learn the language as part of their religious education. Two African languages are official languages. One is Chichewa in Malawi, and the other is Wolof (WOH•lawf) in Mauritania.

Millions of people around the world use languages such as English, French, Spanish, and Arabic. These global languages are useful for international trade and understanding. Some native African languages, however, have as few as 1,000 speakers. Some of these languages may someday disappear. Others will survive, probably with the addition of many words and phrases from the official languages of modern Africa.

REVIEW **Why do many West and Central Africans speak more than one language?**

Religious Beliefs

Just as the people living in West and Central Africa do not share a single language, they do not all practice the same religion. Many observe one of the traditional African religions, while others are Christians, Jews, or Muslims. Unlike Christianity, Judaism, and Islam, however, traditional African religions have no sacred books, and their origins are not known.

Many of the traditional African religions believe in a world of spirits. Some of these spirits are associated with nature—the sky, the stars, the moon, trees, mountains, rivers, or other natural objects. The belief that a spirit lives within a natural object is called **animism**. Sacred mountains and caves serve as shrines to these spirits. Other spirits are believed to be the souls of dead ancestors. Some Africans believe these spirits watch over them.

Traditional religions have the greatest number of followers in the West African

Zuma Rock is located near Abuja, the capital city of Nigeria. Many people who follow traditional African beliefs in animism consider the rock to be a holy place.

LOCATE IT

NIGERIA

Zuma Rock

A Muslim mosque in Mali (left) and a Roman Catholic church in Côte d'Ivoire (right)

countries of Liberia, Togo, and Benin. In other parts of West and Central Africa, many people have adopted religions brought to Africa by other cultures. After a number of West African kings converted to Islam in the eleventh century, many African people accepted Islam.

Catholic missionaries first brought Christianity to West and Central Africa during the 1400s and 1500s. Protestant missionaries arrived later, especially during the colonial period of the 1800s and 1900s. Today the fastest growing Christian churches are new denominations or sects started in Africa as independent churches. In Angola, the Democratic Republic of the Congo, the Republic of the Congo, Equatorial Guinea, Gabon, Malawi, Nigeria, and Zambia, about half of the people practice Christianity.

REVIEW What are the main religions practiced in West and Central Africa?

A wedding party at a Methodist church in Ghana

Family First

Although they are divided in many ways, West and Central African people all believe in the importance of family. Extended families, in many cases, live in neighboring houses. Families share whatever they own, and the oldest man usually makes decisions for the entire family. When a daughter marries, she leaves her original family and goes to live with her husband's family.

Kinship, or the relationship among people with the same ancestors, is important in Africa. Family members support one another. They share work, food, and property. Families often plan marriages, hoping to create useful ties between two families.

Families are the most important part of almost all cultural groups. The heads of families in each village become the elders who make decisions and settle disputes within that village. In some cultures, one family is more important than the others and a ruler is selected from that family. A council of elders, made up of the heads of all the families, decides which member of the ruling family should become their ruler. The elders then advise the ruler.

Today many Africans have left their villages to find work in large cities. Although they live apart from their families, family

A nomad in Niger plays a flute.

ties remain important. City workers send money home to their rural kin. They help find jobs for family members who go to the city. In times of crisis, it is often the families and not the government that aid the people hurt by a disaster.

REVIEW What role do family and kinship play in traditional African society?

Keeping Traditions Alive

The many ethnic groups of West and Central Africa want to keep their traditions alive in a world where many different cultures compete for attention. Present-day communications carry music, television programs, and films from around the world into African homes. Modern commerce and trade bring consumer goods from distant countries.

A griot shares the oral history of his village in Côte d'Ivoire (left). A grass painting (insert) shows a griot from Senegal doing the same.

One way in which African cultures seek to preserve their traditions is by remembering the past. One source of information about the past is oral history, or the stories that people tell about themselves and their origins. Storytellers recite epic poems that keep alive the memory of ancient rulers. The poems tell of leaders who first united a people through heroic deeds.

These storytellers are called by different names in the many cultures of West and Central Africa. Among the Wolof, who live mostly in Senegal, Mauritania, and Gambia, the storyteller is known as a griot (GREE•oh). A **griot** is a person who tells traditional stories on the radio or in villages.

Not all the stories are about the past. A griot may also entertain children with riddles and folktales. A **folktale** is a traditional story that often teaches a lesson. These tales may be about heroes, common people, or animals.

Other arts also help preserve ethnic traditions. Music, dancing, singing, and drumming are popular pastimes.

REVIEW How do Africans preserve their cultural traditions?

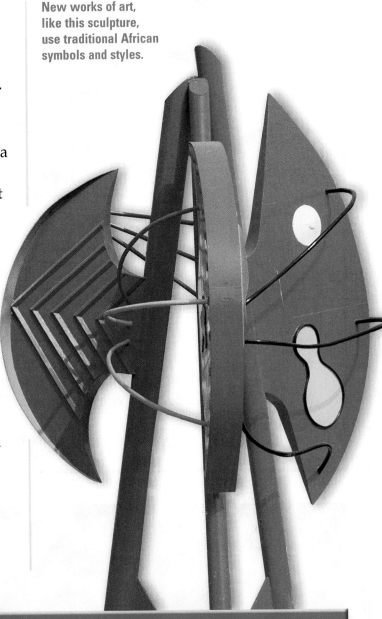

New works of art, like this sculpture, use traditional African symbols and styles.

LESSON 3 REVIEW

1. **MAIN IDEA** Why are there many different cultures in West and Central Africa?

2. **WHY IT MATTERS** What are some of the traditional West and Central African cultures, and what can we learn from them?

3. **VOCABULARY** Write a sentence about Wolof storytellers in Senegal. Use the word **griot**.

4. **READING SKILL—Summarize** How did Africans become Christians, Jews, and Muslims?

5. **CULTURE** What is an official language?

6. **CULTURE** Why do believers in many traditional African religions pray to their ancestors?

7. **CRITICAL THINKING—Evaluate** You are the leader of an African nation where 72 different languages are spoken. The colonial rulers made English the official language. What language would you urge your country to adopt as its official language? Why?

PERFORMANCE—Write a Folktale Folktales are often told about heroes. Find out more about a hero from Africa. Then write a folktale that includes ideas about what makes a person a hero.

Colors and Patterns of Africa

Kente is a multicolored cloth recognized around the world as being African. The Ashanti people of Ghana in West Africa make the best-known kente. Ashanti kente, like the examples shown on page 467, is identified by its colorful patterns of bright colors, geometric shapes, and bold designs. It is worn as clothing during important social and religious events, but it is also used to decorate drums, shields, umbrellas, fans, and other objects. The different designs of Ashanti kente carry different meanings. Study the colors and patterns of the kente shown on these pages. Some patterns represent proverbs.

 FROM THE NEWARK MUSEUM IN NEWARK, NEW JERSEY

Ewe cloth, unlike Ashanti kente, includes symbols.

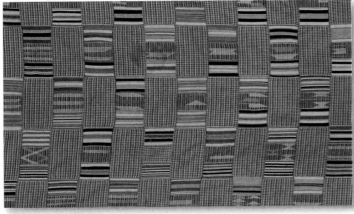

"I walk alone"
(individualism)

The word *kente* comes from the Ashanti word *kenten*, meaning "basket."

"Working together" (common good)

"I have exhausted my skill" (do your best)

Analyze the Primary Source

1. What messages do some of the cloths represent?

2. What do you think the symbols mean on the Ewe cloth?

3. Why do you think people wear messages on their clothing?

ACTIVITY

Design and Draw Design and draw your own cloth pattern. Use different colors, shapes, and symbols to represent a democratic value or character trait of your choice.

RESEARCH

Visit The Learning Site at **www.harcourtschool.com/primarysources** to research other kinds of clothing.

4

Developing Nations

MAIN IDEA

Find out about the problems West and Central Africans face as they strive for economic independence and political stability.

WHY IT MATTERS

Economic independence and political stability may help the countries of West and Central Africa create a better future for Africans.

VOCABULARY

staple

millet

sorghum

People board a train in the West African town of Lomé in Togo.

As the countries of West and Central Africa began to win independence from the European colonial powers after World War II, they faced many problems. They needed to form new governments. They also had to earn money to pay for their governments and the services the governments would provide. Today many West and Central Africans are still seeking political stability and economic independence.

Colonial Economies

In the late 1800s the nations of Europe were the economic leaders of the world. The Industrial Revolution had made them rich by enabling them to manufacture large amounts of goods cheaply. When the Europeans began to colonize Africa, they wanted to use Africa's natural resources as raw materials for their factories. They also wanted to sell finished European goods to Africans.

With these goals in mind, European companies planted crops such as cotton, coffee, tea, tobacco, sugar, and cacao in Africa to export to Europe. They developed gold, copper, diamond, iron, bauxite, phosphate, cobalt, and manganese mines in Africa. Crops grown on African plantations and products from African mines were shipped to European factories.

Colonial policies turned many Africans into wage earners or cash-crop farmers. These people needed money to pay the taxes to their colonial rulers. They also wanted cash to buy the goods that the colonial powers wanted to sell them. But most Africans earned very little money.

As a result of colonial rule, many Africans became economically dependent on European trade. Africans worked for European-owned businesses, but their low-paying jobs did not teach them any useful skills. They learned nothing about the skills needed for running large businesses. The profits of all the trade and manufacturing during the colonial period were not invested in Africa. Most of the benefits went to Europeans instead of to Africans.

REVIEW How did the colonial powers use Africa's resources?

Independent Economies

Political independence did not bring economic independence to West and Central Africa. Some countries continued to export agricultural and mineral products to their former rulers. They did so because it was what they were used to doing and because of the high profits they could earn. Often the new countries exported a single crop or mineral, as they had under colonial rule. Chad and Burkina Faso, for example, have depended on cotton for most of their export earnings. Nigeria and Angola have relied chiefly on exporting crude petroleum rather than refining the petroleum at home.

Depending on a single crop for export earnings is risky. A poor growing season hurts the whole economy of a country. By not diversifying, a country also leaves itself open to large losses when the price of a product falls on the world market.

· SCIENCE AND TECHNOLOGY ·

Africa's Railroads

When colonial rulers built railroads in Africa, the tracks almost always ran between the African coast and the interior of the continent. That way goods and resources could be sent to ports in North Africa for quick transport to Europe. Few rail lines went from the interior to ports on the coasts of East or West Africa. African leaders saw the importance of improving the rail system soon after their countries gained independence. Today the Organization of African Unity is working to improve the railways. It recognizes the importance of a modern rail system to Africa's economy. Along with the Union of African Railways and other groups, it is repairing old tracks, putting in new ones, and linking tracks in different countries. These rail lines will bring resources and crops from rural areas to factories and ports in coastal towns and cities.

Top Trading Countries in West and Central Africa

Billions of Dollars

14
13
12
11
10
9
8
7
6
5
4
3
2
1
0

Angola · Cameroon · Rep. of the Congo · Côte d'Ivoire · Gabon · Ghana · Nigeria · Senegal · Zambia

Country

■ Imports ■ Exports

Analyze Graphs Some countries in the region have more successful economies than others.

❖ Which country has the most exports?

When African leaders tried to start new industries in Africa, they faced many other problems. Their countries lacked skilled workers and trained managers. Roads and railroads were in poor condition. There was little money to build factories. Even so, some West and Central African countries now produce foods and beverages, assemble automobiles, and make many different consumer goods. These include textiles, clothing, shoes, medicines, and tires. Today some countries have factories that make cement and steel and refine oil.

Several other factors have hurt Africans in their search for economic independence. The population is growing quickly. Some countries are politically unstable. Many countries have large debts on which they must pay interest to international financial organizations. The economic problems in West and Central African countries are so great that there is even more poverty since they won independence from the colonial powers.

REVIEW What happened to West and Central African economies after independence?

· HERITAGE ·

Civic Participation

The idea of electing representatives to rule a country came partly from the parliamentary governments of Western Europe. These had taken their inspiration from the democracies of ancient Greece. Democratic rule, however, was not new in Africa. In African villages, elders met to discuss problems and to agree on solutions. Even in many cultures where a king acted as the head of the government, a council of advisers made the most important decisions. Taking part in political life was an African tradition as well as a European one.

New Governments

The first leaders of the newly independent countries were often those who had brought people together to fight for freedom from colonial rule. After independence was won, however, the leaders were faced with building a single nation from many different ethnic groups.

Leaders tried to unify their countries by centralizing the government. In some countries, democratically elected leaders made political opposition unlawful after gaining power. Their countries became one-party states. Other countries became autocracies, or governments in which one person has complete control.

In many cases only the army was powerful enough to oppose the ruler. After taking control of the country, army officers usually promised to hold elections. They said they would turn the government over to a civilian government. However, some military leaders became dictators.

Dictators often abused their power. Some took government money for their own personal use. Some rewarded their supporters with important positions in the government. Others gave government jobs to family members and political supporters. In some cases the number of government workers grew so large that their salaries took up much of the country's money. Little money was left for education, building roads, or other government services.

Many dictators also took control of businesses such as factories, mines, farms, airlines and railroads, banks, and even retail stores. As a result, many businesses became inefficient or dishonest.

REVIEW What three kinds of government were formed in West and Central Africa?

· **BIOGRAPHY** ·

Kwame Nkrumah
1909–1972
Character Trait: Responsibility

As a student at the London School of Economics, Kwame Nkrumah heard about the Italian invasion of Ethopia in 1935. He later said that the event stirred his anger at colonialism. He prayed that he would play a part in bringing about the end of such an unfair system. He became active in student politics and in the movement that sought to overthrow colonial rule in all of Africa. When he returned to his home in the Gold Coast, he founded a political party to campaign for freedom from British rule. His party later won the first elections in the new country of Ghana, and he became Ghana's first prime minister. He continued to strive for freedom for all Africans. He urged Africans to unite to fight foreign rule and trade policies that favored Europe.

Ghana's memorial to Kwame Nkrumah

GO ONLINE

MULTIMEDIA BIOGRAPHIES
Visit The Learning Site at
www.harcourtschool.com/biographies
to learn about other famous people.

Self-Reliance

African leaders had different goals after their countries gained independence. Kwame Nkrumah of Ghana hoped that all the countries of Africa would join together to form a single united African government. Not everyone shared Nkrumah's dream. Instead, 32 newly independent African countries founded the Organization of African Unity, or OAU, in 1963. Its purpose is to promote trade among African nations and to prevent conflict among its members.

The OAU has little authority, but it has become an important organization for planning Africa's future. During the 1980s

The Organization of African Unity has its headquarters in Addis Ababa, Ethiopia.

A monument to African unity in Cameroon

LOCATE IT

Yaoundé

CAMEROON

the OAU began to look for ways to make Africa less dependent on overseas trade. Its first major goal is for Africa to produce enough food to feed its own growing population.

The OAU hopes to make Africa more self-reliant in industry as well. The biggest goal of the OAU is to create an African Economic Community like the European Economic Community. Today members of the OAU are working to change that organization into one called the African Union, or AU.

In West Africa, 16 nations have united to form the Economic Community of West African States. Today 10 Central African countries are members of the Economic Community of Central African States. At the southern rim of Central Africa, Angola, Zambia, and Malawi have joined forces with 8 countries in southern and southeastern Africa to create the Southern African Development Community.

Countries are taking several steps to become self-sufficient in food production. One important step is to promote agriculture. Government programs help farmers irrigate their fields. They ask farmers to plant a variety of staple foods for use at home instead of a single crop for export.

A **staple** is any article of food or other common item that is used regularly and is kept in a large amount.

Two important staples are millet and sorghum. **Millet** is a quick-growing grass that produces grain in just 6 to 12 weeks. **Sorghum**, another grass that produces grain, grows in climates too hot for other grain crops. Both millet and sorghum grow well in dry areas and are used to make porridge and flat breads.

Senegal has succeeded in growing many different crops. Senegal produced mainly peanuts during colonial rule and in the early years after independence. During the 1990s, Senegal began to grow other crops, including millet, sorghum, rice, corn, beans, yams, and cassava. In spite of improvements in their country's economy,

Senegal's people still suffer from poverty, disease, and other problems.

Neighboring countries have worked together to build railroads and dams that help their region. Shared projects include a railway between Benin and Nigeria. The same two countries also jointly own a sugar-processing factory and a cement factory.

Africa will become self-reliant as nations continue to work together to solve problems. Thomas Sankara, a president of Burkina Faso, said of the difficulties Africa faces,

66 **Africa must invent the future.** 99

REVIEW How could Africa become economically independent?

A girl carries a basket of mangoes for sale at a market in Burkina Faso.

LESSON 4
REVIEW

1 MAIN IDEA What are some of the problems West and Central Africans faced after independence?

2 WHY IT MATTERS How will stronger economies improve the lives of West and Central Africans?

3 VOCABULARY Explain why **millet** and **sorghum** are important crops in West and Central Africa.

4 READING SKILL—Summarize How do organizations like the OAU help Africans plan for the future?

5 ECONOMICS Why did the European nations colonize Africa?

6 ECONOMICS What problems make it hard for African nations to improve their economies?

7 CRITICAL THINKING—Evaluate Should African countries continue to export food crops when they must import food to feed their people?

PERFORMANCE—Make a Bibliography Use the library and the Internet to locate primary and secondary sources about African leaders. Use these sources to make a bibliography about governments in Africa.

13 Review and Test Preparation

Summary Time Line

1000 B.C.   500 B.C.

900 B.C. The Nok people settle in northern Nigeria

500 B.C. The Nok people begin using iron tools and weapons

USE YOUR READING SKILLS

Complete this graphic organizer to show that you understand how to summarize key points about West and Central Africa. A copy of this graphic organizer appears on page 127 of the Activity Book.

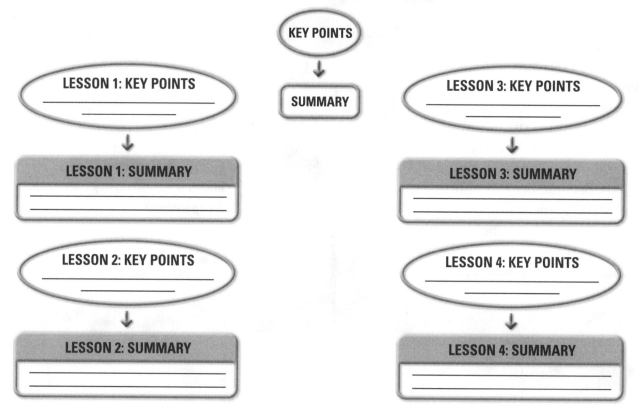

Summarize Key Points About West and Central Africa

KEY POINTS

SUMMARY

LESSON 1: KEY POINTS

LESSON 1: SUMMARY

LESSON 2: KEY POINTS

LESSON 2: SUMMARY

LESSON 3: KEY POINTS

LESSON 3: SUMMARY

LESSON 4: KEY POINTS

LESSON 4: SUMMARY

THINK & WRITE

Write a Plan Think about some of the problems faced by countries in West and Central Africa after independence. Imagine that you are the leader of a newly independent African nation. Write a plan describing how your government will be organized.

Write a Poem Think about the different climate and vegetation regions found in West and Central Africa. Write a poem that describes the Sahel, the savanna, and the rain forest of West and Central Africa. Use poetry to describe how the landscapes are alike and different.

● A.D. **1307**
Mansa Musa begins
rule of Mali

● A.D. **1400**
Decline of the
Mali Empire

● A.D. **1500**
Slave trade
spreads to the
Americas

● A.D. **1884**
European leaders
meet in Germany
to divide Africa
into colonies

USE THE TIME LINE

Use the chapter summary time line to answer these questions.

1 In what year did the slave trade spread to the Americas?

2 How long after the start of Mansa Musa's rule did the Mali Empire decline?

USE VOCABULARY

For each pair of terms write a sentence or two that explains how the terms are related.

3 **bauxite** (p. 448), **cobalt** (p. 449)

4 **griot** (p. 465), **folktale** (p. 465)

5 **millet** (p. 473), **sorghum** (p. 473)

RECALL FACTS

Answer these questions.

6 Why are there few large farms in West and Central Africa?

7 How did the Wangaras' need for salt benefit the Soninkes?

8 How did the division of Africa by Europeans affect West and Central African cultures?

9 How have countries and cultures in West and Central Africa worked together to improve the economy and way of life?

Write the letter of the best choice.

10 **TEST PREP** The baobab tree is important to the people who live on the savannas of West and Central Africa because—
  A it provides cacao.
  B its leaves and fruit are edible.
  C it flowers are used to fill mattresses and pillows.
  D it is a major export.

11 **TEST PREP** All of the following are trading empires that existed in West and Central Africa except—
  F Mali.
  G Ghana.
  H Songhai.
  J Congo.

THINK CRITICALLY

12 Why do you think trade was so important to the empires of West and Central Africa?

13 Why do you think kinship is so important to the societies of West and Central Africa?

14 Do you think the conditions in West and Central Africa are a result of past problems and conflicts? Explain.

APPLY SKILLS

Compare Map Projections

15 Use the maps on pages 450–451 to create a quiz about map projections. For this quiz, write three questions that ask students to compare map projections.

Identify Fact and Opinion

16 Find an article in a newspaper or magazine about a recent event. Read through this article, and highlight all statements of opinion in one color and all statements of fact in another. How much of the article was fact? How much was opinion?

VICTORIA FALLS BETWEEN ZIMBABWE AND ZAMBIA

At Victoria Falls the waters of the Zambezi River plunge more than 300 feet (91 m) into a large canyon. Because of the broad mist and loud roar, the Kalolo-Lazi people gave the falls the name Mosi-oa-Tunya, or "The Smoke That Thunders." The first European explorer to see the falls was David Livingstone. He named them Victoria Falls for Queen Victoria, then queen of Britain.

LOCATE IT

Victoria Falls

ZIMBABWE

14

East Africa and Southern Africa

" Africa has always walked in my mind upright, an African giant among continents . . . "

—Laurens Van der Post, from *Flamingo Feather*, 1955

CHAPTER READING SKILL

Generalize

When you **generalize**, you make a broad statement about what you have read. The generalization is based on facts and details. Then the statement can be applied to related situations.

As you read this chapter, use facts and details from each lesson to generalize.

FACTS + DETAILS → GENERALIZATION

Plains and Plateaus

The landscape of East and Southern Africa offers dramatic variety. Inviting beaches line the warm waters of the Indian Ocean. A short distance from the coast, steep stone cliffs rise up like walls protecting the interior. Beyond the cliffs are mountains and plateaus. Toward the center of Southern Africa, the land dips down into the Kalahari Desert and then rises to form plateaus. To the west, the land drops off suddenly into the Namib Desert. This desert is so dry that animals and plants get moisture only from fog rolling in off the cold Atlantic Ocean.

A Supercontinent Breaks Up

All the continents on Earth were once joined as one huge supercontinent that many geologists, or scientists who study Earth and its rocks and minerals, call Pangaea (pan•JEE•uh). Pangaea means "all land." About 250 million years ago, pressure from Earth's hot, molten core cracked the surface. Pangaea split into two large continents, Laurasia (law•RAY•zhuh) and Gondwana (gahn•DWAH•nuh). Over many millions of years, the same pressure split these two continents into the seven that we know today.

Location This map shows the 21 countries that make up the region of East and Southern Africa.

❖ Which country lies between Botswana and Mozambique?

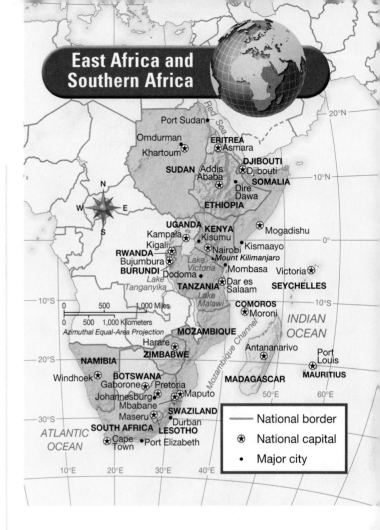

East Africa and Southern Africa

Port Sudan
Omdurman
Khartoum
SUDAN
ERITREA
⊛Asmara
DJIBOUTI
⊛Djibouti
Addis
Ababa
SOMALIA
Dire
Dawa
ETHIOPIA
UGANDA KENYA
Kampala⊛ •Kisumu
Kigali •Nairobi⊛ •Kismaayo
RWANDA Mount Kilimanjaro
Bujumbura⊛ Lake
BURUNDI Victoria
Dodoma •Mombasa Victoria⊛
Lake TANZANIA⊛Dar es SEYCHELLES
Tanganyika Salaam
Lake COMOROS
Malawi ⊛Moroni INDIAN
MOZAMBIQUE OCEAN
Harare Antananarivo
NAMIBIA ⊛ZIMBABWE ⊛ Port
Windhoek⊛ BOTSWANA Louis
Gaborone⊛ •Pretoria MADAGASCAR MAURITIUS
Johannesburg⊛ ⊛Maputo
Mbabane SWAZILAND
Maseru⊛ Durban
ATLANTIC SOUTH AFRICA LESOTHO
OCEAN ⊛Cape •Port Elizabeth
Town

National border
⊛ National capital
• Major city

In East Africa about 40 million years ago, forces inside Earth stretched its crust so thin that it broke. Huge blocks of land sank. Magma from Earth's center flowed in to seal the cracks. The result of this breakage was a rift, or a long valley.

The African rift is part of the Great Rift Valley. This valley extends about 3,500 miles (5,600 km) from Djibouti (juh•BOO•tee) to Malawi. Its width varies from about 24 to almost 40 miles (about 40 to 65 km). In some places the steep cliffs on either side rise more than 10,500 feet (3,200 m) above the valley floor.

The Great Rift Valley has two branches. The eastern rift passes from Djibouti through Ethiopia, Kenya, and Tanzania. The western rift travels along the border between the Democratic Republic of the Congo and Uganda, Rwanda, Burundi, and Tanzania. The two branches meet in Malawi.

FAST FACT
The Drakensberg Mountains, or "Dragon Mountains," lie in Southern Africa. The Zulu people call the range the Barrier of Spears because of its spearlike formations.

Much of Africa has only narrow coastal plains and few natural harbors. In East and Southern Africa, only Somalia and Mozambique have wide coastal plains. In most places a narrow coastal strip is lined with sharp, steep escarpments. This line of imposing cliffs is known as the Great Escarpment. The Drakensberg Mountains of eastern South Africa and Lesotho form part of this great natural wall.

The Great Escarpment creates a barrier to transportation. Ships cannot travel very far inland on the rivers here. Roads and railroads are difficult to build. Early explorers from outside Africa found it hard to reach the highlands where most Africans lived. To the explorers Africa seemed a mysterious continent.

REVIEW What stopped some explorers from reaching the highlands of Africa?

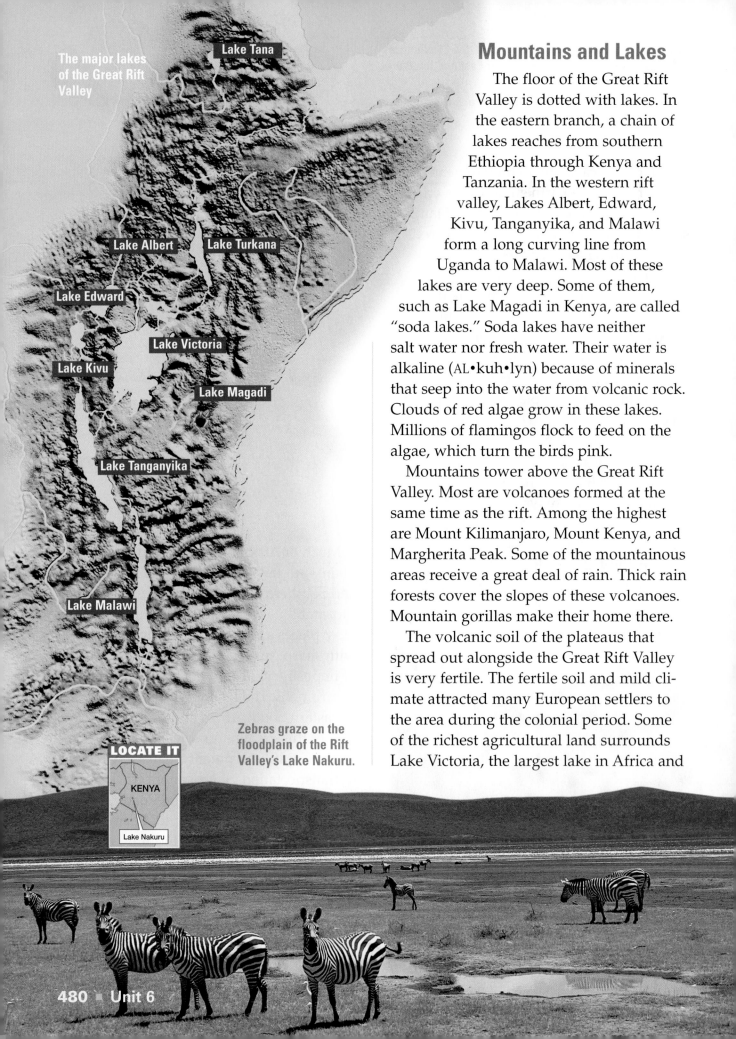

The major lakes of the Great Rift Valley

Lake Tana

Lake Albert

Lake Turkana

Lake Edward

Lake Victoria

Lake Kivu

Lake Magadi

Lake Tanganyika

Lake Malawi

LOCATE IT

KENYA

Lake Nakuru

Zebras graze on the floodplain of the Rift Valley's Lake Nakuru.

Mountains and Lakes

The floor of the Great Rift Valley is dotted with lakes. In the eastern branch, a chain of lakes reaches from southern Ethiopia through Kenya and Tanzania. In the western rift valley, Lakes Albert, Edward, Kivu, Tanganyika, and Malawi form a long curving line from Uganda to Malawi. Most of these lakes are very deep. Some of them, such as Lake Magadi in Kenya, are called "soda lakes." Soda lakes have neither salt water nor fresh water. Their water is alkaline (AL•kuh•lyn) because of minerals that seep into the water from volcanic rock. Clouds of red algae grow in these lakes. Millions of flamingos flock to feed on the algae, which turn the birds pink.

Mountains tower above the Great Rift Valley. Most are volcanoes formed at the same time as the rift. Among the highest are Mount Kilimanjaro, Mount Kenya, and Margherita Peak. Some of the mountainous areas receive a great deal of rain. Thick rain forests cover the slopes of these volcanoes. Mountain gorillas make their home there.

The volcanic soil of the plateaus that spread out alongside the Great Rift Valley is very fertile. The fertile soil and mild climate attracted many European settlers to the area during the colonial period. Some of the richest agricultural land surrounds Lake Victoria, the largest lake in Africa and

117°F
(47°C)

8°F
(-13°C)

Analyze Graphs Animals of the Kalahari, such as this gazelle, have to adapt to the desert's hottest summer temperatures (left) and coldest winter temperatures (right).

❖ What is the difference in degrees Fahrenheit between the summer high temperature and the winter low temperature?

the second-largest freshwater lake in the world. Uganda, Kenya, and Tanzania all border this lake. Large numbers of people live in the area. They fish and grow bananas, coffee, tea, and other crops along the shore and in the nearby highlands.

The plains atop these plateaus support sizable herds of large animals, including giraffes, antelope, and zebras. Lions, leopards, and cheetahs prey on these herds. Parts of this land have been set aside as game preserves where animals are protected. Parks such as the Serengeti National Park in Tanzania and Tsavo National Park in Kenya attract tourists and scientists who study wildlife.

REVIEW Where is some of the richest farmland in East Africa?

Deserts

The climate of East and Southern Africa is influenced by the amount of rain that falls. Southern Africa has two deserts, the Kalahari and the Namib. These arid lands receive little or no rainfall.

The Kalahari Desert stretches across much of Botswana, the northeast corner of Namibia, and part of west-central South Africa. Small, scattered populations of San, Khoikhoi (KOY•koy), and Tswana (TSWAH•nuh) people live here. Giraffes, lions, impalas, and wildebeests (WIL•duh•beests) thrive in large game preserves.

Most of the Kalahari Desert is flat land at an altitude of 3,000 to 4,000 feet (about 915 to 1,220 m). Summers are very hot, with temperatures often over 100°F (38°C). On the other hand, during the winter it can be quite chilly, with temperatures falling below the freezing mark.

When rain does fall in the Kalahari, it fills thousands of shallow holes or ditches called pans. A **pan** is a shallow pond or lake that forms during rainy seasons. The water dries up during the dry seasons, leaving behind a crust of salt and other minerals. In the Kalahari, both animals and people depend on pans. Pans provide water when it rains and are a source of salt and minerals during the long dry season.

The Namib Desert on the Atlantic coast of Southern Africa is even drier than the Kalahari Desert. In the language of the Nama people, *Namib* means "area of nothingness."

Few animals and only some people can survive in this hostile environment. A cold ocean current cools the air along the shore. It creates fog that provides enough moisture for some plants to live. Animals get the moisture they need from the leaves of the plants they eat. To escape the desert heat, some animals also burrow under the sand and come out only at night.

REVIEW What two deserts are found in Southern Africa?

The Veld

Early Dutch settlers called the grasslands of Southern Africa the **veld**, which in Dutch means "field." The veld of Southern Africa is like the savanna of West Africa. However, the veld's climate is more varied because it is spread across a wider range of elevations.

The veld region runs from the southwest to the northeast through South Africa and Zimbabwe. The highest plains lie more than 4,000 feet (about 1,220 m) above sea level and are known as the high veld. Because of the high altitude, the high veld has cool nights and warm, sunny days. The altitude of the middle veld,

Cattle graze on the veld near the southern part of the Drakensberg Mountains. Besides land for grazing, the veld also provides fertile farmland.

which surrounds the high veld, varies between about 3,000 and 4,000 feet (about 915 and 1,220 m). Areas below 3,000 feet (about 915 m) are called the low veld.

The veld is made up of gently rolling hills. Plant life varies with the rainfall. The western part of the veld receives little rain. There, plant life consists of sparse grass and thorny bushes. In wetter areas to the east, there are grassy plains with a few trees. Thick clay soil makes this part of the veld good farmland. Still farther east, in Lesotho, even more rain falls. Scattered timber forests climb the slopes of the Drakensberg Mountains there.

The high veld of Southern Africa attracted many European settlers during the 1800s. They raised cattle in the drier plains and farmed the wetter eastern areas.

REVIEW What is the veld?

Mineral Riches

East and Southern Africa, like West and Central Africa, have many mineral resources. The country of South Africa is particularly rich in minerals. Of all the countries in this part of Africa, South Africa has the largest amounts of minerals. It is Africa's largest producer of minerals.

Diamonds and gold are South Africa's best-known minerals. South Africa's diamonds are mined both for jewelry and for industrial use. South Africa has about one-half of the world's deposits of gold and has long been the world's leading producer of gold.

In addition, South Africa is a major source of the world's chromium, manganese, platinum, titanium, and vanadium. Industries in the United States depend on South Africa for minerals used in many types of manufacturing. South Africa's large coal deposits provide fuel for making electricity. Uranium, copper, and iron ore

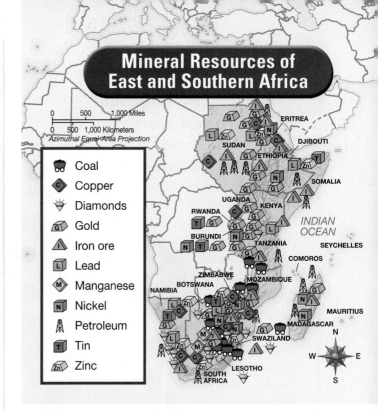

Mineral Resources of East and Southern Africa

Coal
Copper
Diamonds
Gold
Iron ore
Lead
Manganese
Nickel
Petroleum
Tin
Zinc

Location Mineral resources as well as fossil fuels are found throughout East and Southern Africa.

❖ Which mineral resources are found in the country of Somalia?

are also found in South Africa.

Several other countries in East and Southern Africa are rich in mineral resources. Namibia has diamonds, uranium, tin, copper, rock salt, lead, and zinc. Botswana, another large producer of diamonds, has deposits of gold, silver, uranium, copper, nickel, and coal. One of the smallest countries in Africa, Swaziland is rich in coal, gold, and diamonds. Zimbabwe produces more than 40 minerals, gold being the most important. Tanzania, too, has reserves of many minerals and gems, including tanzanite, a dark blue stone used in making jewelry. It is named for the country where it is found.

Rivers in East and Southern African countries provide moving water that can be used to generate electricity. This allows the countries located in the region to provide electricity for people and businesses.

Madagascar
Understanding Places and Regions

Madagascar is a continental island, or a piece of a continent that has separated from the mainland. About the size of Texas, Madagascar is the fourth-largest island in the world. Geologists think that Madagascar broke off from southeastern Africa about 65 million years ago. The island of Madagascar is home to at least 200,000 plant and animal species. These include lemurs like the one pictured here.

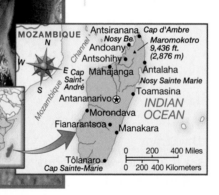

MOZAMBIQUE
N
Mozambique Channel
W E
S
Cap Saint-André
Antananarivo ⊛
Morondava
Fianarantsoa
Tôlanaro
Cap Sainte-Marie
Antsiranana Cap d'Ambre
Nosy Be
Andoany
Antsohihy
Mahajanga
Antalaha
Nosy Sainte Marie
Toamasina
INDIAN OCEAN
Manakara
Maromokotro 9,436 ft. (2,876 m)
0   200   400 Miles
0 200 400 Kilometers

It also allows Africa's countries to improve their economies by powering equipment for mining and other industries.

The longest river in Southern Africa is the Zambezi. On this river two major dams have been built. They harness the river's energy as it streams down from high plateaus to the Indian Ocean. The Kariba Dam on the border between Zambia and Zimbabwe makes electricity shared by those two countries. The Cabora Bassa Dam in Mozambique supplies power to both Mozambique and South Africa.

The many dams of the Orange River Project on South Africa's Orange River add to South Africa's electrical production. The Nile flows over the Owen Falls Dam in Uganda, providing power for that country's copper industry.

REVIEW Which country in the region has the greatest variety of and produces the most minerals?

LESSON 1
REVIEW

1 MAIN IDEA What kinds of landscape are found in East and Southern Africa?

2 WHY IT MATTERS What are some of the natural resources found in East and Southern Africa?

3 VOCABULARY Use the words **pan** and **veld** to describe Southern Africa.

4 READING SKILL—Generalize What might be the reason that South Africa has a stronger economy than other countries in East and Southern Africa?

5 GEOGRAPHY Which two countries on the east coast of Africa have wide coastal plains?

6 GEOGRAPHY What is the largest lake in Africa?

7 CRITICAL THINKING—Analyze How have rivers that flow through countries of East and Southern Africa helped people and industries?

PERFORMANCE— Make a Chart Use the information in this lesson to make a chart showing each country's mineral resources.

Ancient Cultures

| 1000 B.C. | 500 B.C. | B.C./A.D. | A.D. 500 | A.D. 1000 | A.D. 1500 | A.D. 2000 |

MAIN IDEA
Read to learn about how cultures developed in East and Southern Africa.

WHY IT MATTERS
Learning about how different cultures began helps you understand the differences between East and Southern Africans today.

E uropean traders and explorers who arrived in Africa in the early sixteenth century were no doubt surprised to find such well-developed and diverse cultures. Africans in the northern and eastern parts of the continent had been trading with the Arab people for hundreds of years. Christianity spread into Africa as early as the A.D. 300s. Influences from these three cultures had been blending for centuries by the time Europeans met Africans living south of the Sahara. Advanced cultures existed in many parts of Africa during the time Europe was in the Middle Ages.

VOCABULARY
flax
dhow
Afrikaans
Boers

Ancient Kush

The earliest empire in Africa south of the Sahara began as a farming and trading community. This empire lay in the Nile River Valley, south of the first set of rapids in the Nile River. The Egyptians, who lived north of these rapids, called the land Nubia. The history of Nubia is closely tied to that of Egypt.

Egyptian rulers traded with the Nubians for gold, granite, ebony, and ivory. After 1991 B.C. the Egyptians tried to annex, or take over, northern Nubia and make it part of Egypt. They built forts near the second cataract of the Nile and mined gold for themselves in the desert. The Nubians fled southward, where they formed a kingdom known as Kush. They set up a capital at Kerma, which became a trading center famous for its fine ceramics, copper, jewels, ivory, and woodcarving.

The ancient ruins of Meroë in present-day Sudan

The Queens of Nubia

Queens played an important role in Nubian society. Nubian kings traced their line through their mothers. This system gave the queen mother a position of great power and respect. When a king died, his successor was chosen from among those of royal blood. The queen mother and the leading men of the kingdom chose the new king. If the chosen ruler was still a minor, the queen mother ruled in his place. Ruling queens were known as Kandakes (kahn•DAH•kays). Some queens ruled together with their husbands.

Queen Shanadakhete was one of the most powerful rulers of Meroë. She is credited with building stone temples and palaces. This silver and gold mask shows Queen Malaqaya of Kush. The mask was made about 2,500 years ago.

In time, Kush grew stronger and won back control of northern Nubia. When Egypt weakened, Kushite kings attacked. During the 700s B.C., King Piankhi (PYANG•kee) conquered all of Egypt, and Kushite kings ruled Egypt for the next half-century.

When Assyrians invaded the Nile River Valley in the 600s B.C., Kush lost control of the lower Nile. Around 300 B.C., Kushite leaders moved their capital still farther south to Meroë (MAIR•oh•wee) on the east bank of the Nile.

The land around Meroë was rich in iron ore. It also had many trees to supply wood for fires used to melt the iron. Meroë became an important ironworking center. The savanna was also good for farming and raising cattle. Irrigation canals watered fields along the river. In addition to millet and other food crops, people grew cotton and **flax**, the plant from which linen is made, and wove cloth.

Meroë's location gave its people an advantage in their trading businesses. A caravan route from the Red Sea met the Nile River at Meroë. From Meroë, gold, slaves, ivory, and tropical produce traveled to the Mediterranean and Southwest Asia. Goods came to Meroë from as far away as India and China.

For six hundred years Meroë prospered. The Kushites built many stone palaces and a great stone temple to their principal god, Amon. In royal cemeteries, pyramids marked the burial sites of Kushite kings and queens. Carved stones and painted ceramics depicted scenes from Kushite life. Inscriptions were also carved on many Kushite monuments, but today we cannot read what they say. Kushite writing has not yet been deciphered.

REVIEW What gave Meroë an advantage in trading?

The Axumite Empire

Around 500 B.C. people from southern Arabia crossed the Red Sea and began settling along the African coast. They inter-married with African people in the area and slowly spread inland to the nearby highlands. They set up their capital at Axum around A.D. 50.

Axumite kings controlled several seaports along the Red Sea. The busiest was Adulis (AH•joo•luhs). Africans brought ivory, gold, incense, hides, and slaves to Adulis to trade for Mediterranean wine, olive oil, cloth, iron and brass, and tools and weapons.

Axum soon became a wealthy city. People from many parts of the world lived there. King Zoscales, who ruled Axum during the first century A.D., read Greek literature. Many people spoke Greek as well as the local language, Ge'ez (GAY•uhz).

Over the next 200 years, Axum expanded its power over the horn of Africa. Axumites also conquered Yemen on the Arabian Peninsula. During the A.D. 300s, King Ezana led his troops against the Nubians. This warlike king defeated the Kushites and destroyed their capital at Meroë.

In his later years King Ezana converted to Christianity. He

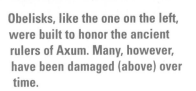

Obelisks, like the one on the left, were built to honor the ancient rulers of Axum. Many, however, have been damaged (above) over time.

declared Axum a Christian city, and the city became an important center for Christian learning.

Axum lost control of the Red Sea ports during the A.D. 600s when Islam spread across Arabia and into northern Africa. As neighboring kingdoms converted to Islam, Christian rule in the Ethiopian highlands survived. With only a brief period as a colony of Italy from 1936 to 1941, Ethiopia remained an independent Christian kingdom until the monarchy fell from power in 1975. Then a totalitarian government established a command economy and made Ethiopia a communist state.

REVIEW What religion was adopted by King Ezana?

The crown of a nineteenth-century king of Ethiopia

City-States on the Indian Ocean

Beginning in the A.D. 600s, Arab merchants became the most active traders on the coast of East Africa. During the winter Arab sailboats known as **dhows** sailed out of the Red Sea and southward along the African coast into the Indian Ocean.

Arab traders prospered as their trading networks spread across the Indian Ocean between the 900s and the 1400s. Their dhows arrived in Africa loaded with porcelain, spices, silk, and other goods from India, China, and Persia. They sailed away carrying ivory, gold, iron, and slaves.

Some Arab merchants settled in East Africa. They lived in trading towns with local people of Bantu (BAN•too) heritage. The local people spoke a dialect called Swahili (swah•HEE•lee). They shared traditions and language with many people across East and Southern Africa. The Arab merchants learned Bantu customs and began calling both the language and the people they lived among Swahili.

The Swahili trading towns grew into wealthy city-states. Among the largest were Lamu, Malindi, Mombasa, Zanzibar, Dar es Salaam, and Kilwa. The richest cities had large mosques, palaces, and tall houses built of coral stone with finely carved wooden doors. When the world traveler Ibn Battuta visited Kilwa in 1331, he thought it was "one of the most beautiful and best constructed towns in the world."

The Swahili city-states lost power during the late 1400s. Portuguese explorers reached the east coast of Africa in 1498. They attacked and looted Kilwa and other trading centers. Then they built their own fortified trading posts, which disrupted the Indian Ocean trade as they tried to take it over.

REVIEW Which two cultures blended with trading towns on the coast of East Africa?

Kingdoms of the Interior

The Swahili traders who lived on the east coast of Africa did not make many of the goods that they sold in their cities. Instead, they depended on people who lived inland. People who spoke Bantu languages had moved across Central Africa and Southern Africa many centuries earlier. Settling along river valleys and lakes, they farmed and raised cattle. They also hunted wild animals that lived on the plains. They traded ivory tusks for cloth and glass beads imported by the Swahili traders.

By the A.D. 900s the people living inland discovered minerals in the rocky ridges bordering the plateaus. They began to mine iron, copper, and gold. To mine the gold,

The ancient wall still stands around the ruins of the stone palace at Great Zimbabwe.

women and children were sent down narrow shafts as much as 100 feet (30 m) deep. The metals became valuable trade goods.

A Bantu-speaking group called the Shona (SHOH•nuh) gained control of the gold mines in about 1200. As their wealth grew, they came to rule a large empire east of the Kalahari Desert, between the Zambezi and Limpopo Rivers. They built their impressive capital at Great Zimbabwe.

A CLOSER LOOK
The Arab Dhow

Arab boat builders designed their dhows to be fast and easy to maneuver.

❶ Each mast supported an efficient triangle-shaped sail.

❷ A curved bow, or front, allowed the dhow to move easily through the water.

❸ The hold, or cargo deck, was the area that held the trader's goods.

❖ Why might this dhow have had two sets of masts?

On a hilltop overlooking the city stood a stone palace. Around the palace a stone wall, 30 feet (9 m) high, was built without mortar. It enclosed an area as long as a football field and about four times as wide.

Great Zimbabwe flourished from the 1200s to the 1400s. Other kingdoms arose later in the interior of East and Southern Africa. The Monomotapan Empire succeeded Shona rule on the Zimbabwe plateau. To the north, in the area around Lake Victoria and the lakes of the western part of the Great Rift Valley, the kingdoms of Buganda, Rwanda, and Burundi took shape during the 1600s and 1700s.

REVIEW **What was Great Zimbabwe?**

The First European Settlers

European ships first sailed to East and Southern Africa in the late 1400s. Portuguese explorers rounded the Cape of Good Hope in 1488. They were searching for a sea route to the spice markets of India. Along the way they discovered the fine stone buildings and the busy ports of the Swahili city-states and heard about the gold mines in the interior. Their tales of wealth awakened the Portuguese king's interest in southeastern Africa.

Military forces sent from Portugal marched up the Zambezi River valley, hoping to take over the gold fields on the Zimbabwe plateau. The expedition failed. The steep land, malaria, and native warriors kept the Portuguese from reaching the gold mines. However, Portuguese missionaries and settlers established large plantations called *prazos* on the broad coastal plains of what is today Mozambique.

Ships from France, Britain, and the Netherlands also sailed around the Cape of Good Hope. The journey lasted several months. Sailors needed bases in East and Southern Africa where they could stop for repairs, fresh water, and supplies.

During the 1600s the Dutch claimed the uninhabited island of Mauritius, 500 miles (about 800 km) east of Madagascar. In 1652 they also started a settlement at Table Bay near the Cape of Good Hope. They built a fort, planted vegetables and grapevines, and traded for cattle with the Khoisan (KOY•sahn) people, who lived at the nearby cape.

The Dutch colony at the cape became more than a place for merchants to get supplies for their ships as new settlers arrived from Europe. Many of these settlers came from the Netherlands. Others were Germans and Huguenots, or French Protestants, who came to Africa to escape religious persecution in their own countries.

The descendants of these early settlers called themselves Afrikaners because they had been born in Africa. They no longer thought of themselves as Europeans. They

This painting shows Khoisan people visiting the Dutch settlement at Table Bay.

spoke **Afrikaans**, a language based on Dutch that included Khoisan, French, and German words.

Some Afrikaners were merchants who lived in Cape Town, but most Afrikaners lived on farms, where they raised grain, grapes, and livestock. They were known as **Boers**, which is the Dutch word for "farmers," but they did not till the soil themselves. The Boers owned slaves, who worked their large farms. As their numbers grew, the Boers traveled on foot and by oxcart into the Southern African veld to claim more land. The Khoisan people who lived in the veld moved into the less fertile land of the Kalahari Desert.

REVIEW **What is Afrikaans?**

Vineyards near Cape Town

LESSON 2 REVIEW

Summary Time Line

| 1000 B.C. | 500 B.C. | B.C./A.D. | A.D. 500 | A.D. 1000 | A.D. 1500 | A.D. 2000 |

700s B.C.
Kingdom of Kush conquers Egypt

A.D. 600s
Arab merchants begin to build trading empires along the East African coast

A.D. 1200
Shonas begin building Great Zimbabwe

A.D. 1488
Portuguese explorers reach Eastern Africa

1 **MAIN IDEA** What people from outside Africa had a strong influence on the ancient cultures of East and Southern Africa?

2 **WHY IT MATTERS** How is the Arabic influence shown in East and Southern Africa today?

3 **VOCABULARY** Use the words **Afrikaans** and **Boer** to write a paragraph about the Dutch influence on Southern Africa.

4 **TIME LINE** Which group came to the region first—the Arabs or the Portuguese?

5 **READING SKILL—Generalize** Why did many groups of outsiders hope to control the lands of East and Southern Africa?

6 **HISTORY** Which Kushite king conquered Egypt?

7 **ECONOMICS** Control of what resource enabled the Shona to build a large empire?

8 **CRITICAL THINKING—Analyze** How did the Islamic religion spread in East and Southern Africa?

PERFORMANCE—Write a Scene Write a short scene of a meeting between an Arab trader and an African merchant that would make clear some of the differences between them. For example, what things would they offer each other? After you have finished writing, perform your scene with a partner for the class.

MAIN IDEA
Read to find out about East and Southern Africa's long struggle against invasion and domination.

WHY IT MATTERS
Only as citizens of independent nations can Africans gain a voice in their own future.

VOCABULARY
apartheid
Pan Africanism

From Colonies to Countries

In the late 1800s Kikuyu messengers brought exciting news from the coast to Chief Wangombe's home in the highlands of Kenya. On "the big water" that stretched "like a vast treeless plain," they had seen "large animals that spat fire and smoke" with "people coming out of these animals' stomachs." Before long, the strangers came to settle in Chief Wangombe's territory. The chief welcomed them and gave them building sites. He advised his elders: Learn their clever ways, "for it is by using your wisdom that you may safeguard your country."

Europe Divides Africa

In the early 1800s Britain had the world's most powerful navy. Britain was building a huge empire on which, people said, "the sun never set." Cape Town, today part of South Africa, was a busy seaport that was well located to protect British trade routes. The British took over Cape Town from the Dutch in 1806. British

The statue of a mother and her children, before a relief wall of wagons, is at the Voortrekker Monument in Pretoria, South Africa. The monument honors Afrikaners who took part in the Great Trek.

settlers soon followed. They came into conflict with the Afrikaners, who did not want English to be the official language and who disagreed with British laws. In 1834 many of the Afrikaners moved in a "Great Trek," or trip, inland to areas north and east of the cape.

Crossing the Drakensberg Mountains, the Boers entered the land of the Zulu people. The Boers and the Zulu fought many battles over the land. In the end the Boers pushed the Zulu and other African kingdoms onto less desirable, mountainous land.

When diamonds were discovered in 1867 and gold in 1885, European interest in Southern Africa soared. These minerals were found on land claimed by the Boers and by the Tswana and other African people. The British, however, quickly added these lands to their Cape Colony. British companies paid for the deep mines that were needed to dig out the new-found wealth. They grew rich from the profits.

In 1899 a bitter war broke out between the British and the Boers. They fought for rights to the gold-rich land beyond the Vaal River, an area known as the Transvaal. The war finally ended in a British victory in 1902. In 1910 lands claimed by the Boers and the British were joined to form the Union of South Africa, a British colony.

Not all of the Europeans who came to East and Southern Africa came for business reasons. During the 1800s explorers and missionaries from several European countries went farther inland than earlier Europeans had gone. There they found lakes and mountains, fertile soil, and a pleasant, highland climate. Many of these settlers stayed to farm, raise cattle, run businesses, and raise their families.

Thousands of British people moved to the highlands of Kenya, to what is

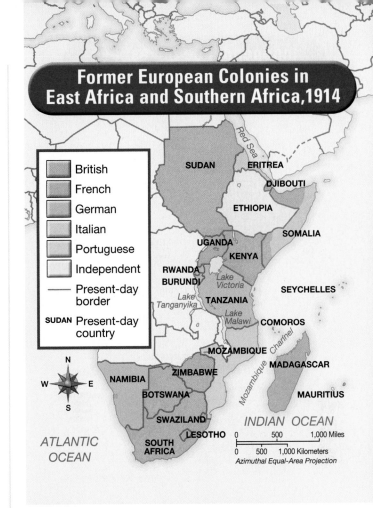

Former European Colonies in East Africa and Southern Africa, 1914

British
French
German
Italian
Portuguese
Independent
— Present-day border
SUDAN Present-day country

Regions Africa in 1914 had only two independent countries, Liberia in West Africa and Ethiopia in East Africa. The rest of the continent was under European colonial rule.

❷ Which European nation ruled present-day Uganda?

now Zimbabwe, and to South Africa. Germans settled in what is now Tanzania. Many French people settled in Madagascar.

Under the colonial system, European settlers were treated better than the people who already lived in East and Southern Africa. New settlers could buy large pieces of the best land at low prices. In contrast, Africans were moved to "reserves" that had less-fertile land. The settlers hired Africans to work for them at low wages.

REVIEW Which groups fought over land that is now South Africa?

Independence in East and Southern Africa

Regions Today all of the nations of East and Southern Africa are independent.

❓ Which nation in the region gained independence first, Kenya or Sudan?

Map labels:

SUDAN 1956
ERITREA 1993
DJIBOUTI 1977
ETHIOPIA
SOMALIA 1960
UGANDA 1962
KENYA 1963
RWANDA 1962
BURUNDI 1962
TANZANIA 1964
SEYCHELLES 1976
COMOROS 1975
Lake Victoria
Lake Tanganyika
Lake Malawi
MOZAMBIQUE 1975
ZIMBABWE 1980
NAMIBIA 1990
BOTSWANA 1966
MADAGASCAR 1960
MAURITIUS 1968
SWAZILAND 1968
SOUTH AFRICA 1910
LESOTHO 1966
Red Sea
Mozambique Channel
ATLANTIC OCEAN
INDIAN OCEAN

0   500   1,000 Miles
0   500   1,000 Kilometers
Azimuthal Equal-Area Projection

N W E S

Independence for East Africa

Colonial rule ended in East and Southern Africa in much the same way as it did in other parts of the continent. After World War II, Britain and France were prepared to give their colonies independence after a period of self-rule. The first African colony south of the Sahara to win independence was Sudan, which voted to become independent from Britain in 1956. In 1959 and 1960 two Somali territories that had been colonies of Britain and Italy were joined to form Somalia. In 1960 people living in Madagascar, including many French settlers, voted in favor of independence from France. Ugandans chose freedom from British rule in 1962.

Belgium, which had taken charge of several of Germany's colonies after World War I, did not want to give up its colonies at first. Faced with rebellion, however, Belgium finally backed down. In Burundi and Rwanda rival ethnic groups, the Tutsi and the Hutu, battled for control of the new governments. The Tutsi minority, favored by the Belgians, had long held power over the Hutu majority in both territories. The Hutu won out in Rwanda and formed a republic. The Tutsi kept control of Burundi, which became a monarchy. Both countries gained independence in 1962.

At first, Britain proposed a slow change from European to African rule. They

Every December 12 the people of Kenya parade through the streets as part of Jamhuri Day. This holiday marks Kenya's independence.

Children stand in front of the Wall of Independence in Windhoek, the capital of Namibia. Namibia gained its independence in 1990.

introduced what they called a multiracial constitution. Each racial group would elect the same number of representatives, regardless of the size of the group. Under this plan, the European minority and the African majority would have the same representation.

Africans in Kenya did not want to accept this compromise. Many were angry because they lacked enough land to grow food for themselves. In 1951 Africans formed small, armed bands known as Mau Mau and began attacking farms, hoping to scare British settlers into leaving. The Mau Mau burned farms and crops, and killed livestock and settlers. British troops fought back, killing many of the Mau Mau and jailing political leaders such as Jomo Kenyatta. The Mau Mau rebellion lasted five years and cost many lives, but it led the British to grant self-rule to Kenya. In 1963 Kenya gained independence.

Tanganyika also had many European settlers, but it took a less violent path to independence. Tanganyika had a well-organized nationalist movement, started in 1954 by Julius Nyerere (nyuh•RAY•ray). Using Swahili as a common language, Nyerere's party helped unite the more than 120 ethnic groups. When a new constitution was introduced in 1958, even many Europeans supported the African political party. Tanganyika became independent in 1961, with Julius Nyerere heading the government. After Zanzibar achieved independence from Britain in 1963, the island republic voted to unite with Tanganyika to form Tanzania in 1964.

REVIEW Which two European countries prepared their colonies for independence?

Gaining Freedom in Southern Africa

The road to independence took the longest in Southern Africa. Botswana, Lesotho, and Swaziland became independent nations in the 1960s, but Africans in neighboring Namibia and Zimbabwe had to wait much longer.

South Africa had the largest white settler community of any African colony. About 4 million people of European descent lived there in 1950, and they did not want to give up the good life they enjoyed when South Africa was a colony.

Black Africans in South Africa had battled for years to gain equal rights.

The African National Congress, or ANC, a political party founded in 1912, took an active role in seeking rights for South Africans of color. After World War II, the ANC asked the United Nations for support. It also encouraged workers to strike for better wages and working conditions.

White South Africans voted the National party into power in 1948. The National party thought blacks and whites should have little contact. They believed in **apartheid**, or separateness. This policy separated black Africans, people of mixed races, and Asians from whites. The new government passed laws requiring all non-whites to live on the outskirts of towns and in areas called townships.

Townships were often crowded clusters of tiny homes without electricity or running

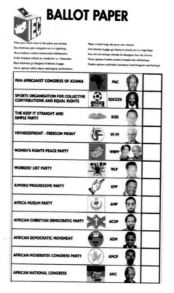

BALLOT PAPER

Ballot from 1994 election

water. They were located far from the jobs in the cities and mines. The people could leave the townships only to go to their jobs. They had to return after work.

When the people protested against apartheid, the government often responded harshly with arrests. In 1960 a violent protest in the township of Sharpeville resulted in the deaths of many people. The South African government blamed the ANC for the violence and declared it and other opposition political parties illegal.

The ANC and other opponents of apartheid continued their protests, however. Some were violent. In 1962 the government arrested Nelson Mandela and five ANC leaders in an attempt to stop the protests. They were sentenced to life in prison on Robben Island, off the coast of Cape Town.

DEMOCRATIC VALUES
Individual Rights

In 1989 two people could scarcely have been living more differently than Nelson Mandela and F. W. de Klerk. Mandela had been in jail more than 25 years when F. W. de Klerk became leader of the National party and president of South Africa in 1989. Although he was a member of the same political party that earlier imprisoned Mandela, de Klerk ordered his release. The two leaders began working together to bring an end to apartheid and to make South Africa a truly democratic country. Their efforts brought great changes to the country, especially to those who had suffered unfair treatment for so long. In 1993 Mandela and de Klerk were awarded the Nobel Peace Prize for their work together in South Africa. Just three years after their lives had been so very different, the two men were recognized by the world for their shared goal of social equality.

Analyze the Value

❶ How was ending apartheid important to social equality?

❷ **Make It Relevant** Find out more about how world leaders work together. Write an article about what you learn.

South Africa prospered under National party rule. However, countries around the world were shocked by the brutal enforcement of apartheid and began to limit trade with South Africa. The economy and the government began to weaken.

By 1989 many white South Africans started to speak out against apartheid. In 1990 President F. W. de Klerk lifted the ban on the ANC and other political parties. He also freed Nelson Mandela. Negotiations began for free elections in which all adult citizens, regardless of race, would be allowed to vote. In April of 1994 Nelson Mandela became South Africa's president.

REVIEW Which country had a policy of apartheid?

Working Together

European rulers established the boundaries of many of the countries of East and Southern Africa, paying little attention to ethnic and religious differences. For example, the expansion of Ethiopia divided the Somali people among five different countries. The Masai, too, were split by the artificial boundaries drawn by the colonial powers. Some now live in Kenya, and the rest live in Tanzania.

Not all of Africa's ethnic conflict comes from colonial interference. Religious and ethnic conflicts existed for centuries before Europeans or Arabs arrived in Africa. In the north of Sudan, most people are Muslim and speak Arabic. In the south, most people are Christians or animists. More than 2 million Christian and animist Sudanese in the south have been killed by northern Sudanese. At least 4 million have become refugees, and many suffer from disease and hunger. Thousands of Sudanese in the south, including many children, have been forced to work as slaves.

POINTS OF VIEW
Unite or Divide?

Zimbabwe's leader believes that life for many of his people will improve if the descendants of British settlers leave his country. He allows his supporters to take the land and homes belonging to these British descendants. In contrast, South Africa's leader wants citizens of British descent to stay in his country. He believes his country will improve if all its citizens work together.

THABO MBEKI, leader of South Africa

❝This conflict is wrong. This approach, this occupation of farms, the disregard for the law, these things are wrong, these things must be addressed.❞

ROBERT MUGABE, leader of Zimbabwe

❝Let the British pay for the land. We should not even be defending our position. This country is our country and this land is our land.❞

Analyze the Viewpoints

1 Does Thabo Mbeki believe that the actions of Zimbabwe's leader should be allowed to continue?

2 Who does Robert Mugabe believe should pay the descendants of British settlers for the land that is taken from them?

3 **Make It Relevant** Read the newspaper to find out about a problem in your community or state. Is it a problem that affects everyone? Would it be easier or harder to solve if only some of the people worked on it? Write a paragraph explaining how you would like people to work together to solve the problem.

These children leaving their school reflect the future hope for African unity.

Border wars and civil wars are another result of regional, cultural, and ethnic divisions. For nearly 20 years, Ethiopia received military aid from the Soviet Union to help it fight the people of the area of Eritrea (er•uh•TREE•uh). The Eritreans wanted to be free of Ethiopian rule. Independence for Eritrea came after the collapse of the Soviet Union ended its support for Ethiopia. Unfortunately, conflict continues.

The problems caused by nationalism will continue to challenge East and Southern Africa. One solution may be the revival of the idea of **Pan Africanism**, a movement that envisioned all African nations politically united in one federation. The Organization of African Unity proposed an African Common Market, with free trade and a common currency within Africa that would provide a kind of economic Pan Africanism.

Many countries wrote new constitutions during the 1990s. These constitutions established multiparty elections. If successful, these constitutions will help Africans build strong, politically stable nations during the twenty-first century.

Resolving the ethnic and religious conflicts in Africa will not be an easy task. To do so, old prejudices must be put aside for the sake of the common good of the region. All people need to realize that they are Africans, and their help is needed to solve Africa's problems together. No Africans can be considered outsiders if they are to live in harmony with their neighbors and contribute together to Africa's future.

REVIEW What two challenges face East and Southern Africans as they build nations?

LESSON 3
REVIEW

1 MAIN IDEA For how long were East and Southern Africans subjected to European domination?

2 WHY IT MATTERS What problems has independence brought to East and Southern Africa?

3 VOCABULARY Using the word **apartheid**, explain how the National party segregated South Africa.

4 READING SKILL—Generalize Why did people from Europe think that they could take resources and land in East and Southern Africa?

5 ECONOMICS The discoveries of what minerals attracted British businesspeople to Southern Africa?

6 CULTURE What cultural differences caused problems in Sudan after it won independence?

7 CRITICAL THINKING—Analyze How did having many European settlers affect the struggle for independence?

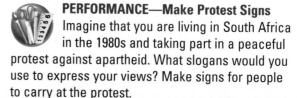

PERFORMANCE—Make Protest Signs
Imagine that you are living in South Africa in the 1980s and taking part in a peaceful protest against apartheid. What slogans would you use to express your views? Make signs for people to carry at the protest.

Facing the Future

MAIN IDEA
Read to find out about the challenges East and Southern Africa face today.

WHY IT MATTERS
Political stability and economic independence will improve life for East and Southern Africans.

VOCABULARY
Harambee
migrant worker
foreign debt
debt service
malnutrition
poacher

When Jomo Kenyatta campaigned for president of Kenya in 1962, many whites feared losing their farms and having no say in the new government. Some Luo and Masai people worried that Kenyatta would favor his own Kikuyu people. Kenyatta's adopted name, after all, was the Kikuyu word for a traditional beaded belt that Kenyatta always wore as a symbol of his ethnic pride. To show his desire for national unity, however, Kenyatta began wearing a Luo hat as well. He also gave his country a new rallying cry. It was **Harambee**! (har•ahm•BAY). The slogan was an old Swahili loggers' work chant meaning "Let's pull together!" The Harambee spirit helps all Africans as they face the many challenges of the twenty-first century.

Economic Development

The two richest countries in East and Southern Africa are very different. The tiny island of Mauritius has a thriving economy based on sugar, textiles and clothing, and banking. The country of South Africa has an even stronger economy based on a much wider variety of industries. In a recent year South Africa placed twenty-ninth among the world's leading economies. No other African country appeared on that list.

South Africa's economic strength helps its neighbors as well. Nearby countries depend on South Africa for much of their foreign trade. Some of these countries send **migrant workers**, or people who have jobs outside their home countries, to work in South Africa's mines. They extract gold, platinum, diamonds, and other minerals that are then sold on the world market. Mining is one of the most important industries in South Africa and an important source of jobs for people there and in nearby countries.

A printing plant worker in South Africa

499

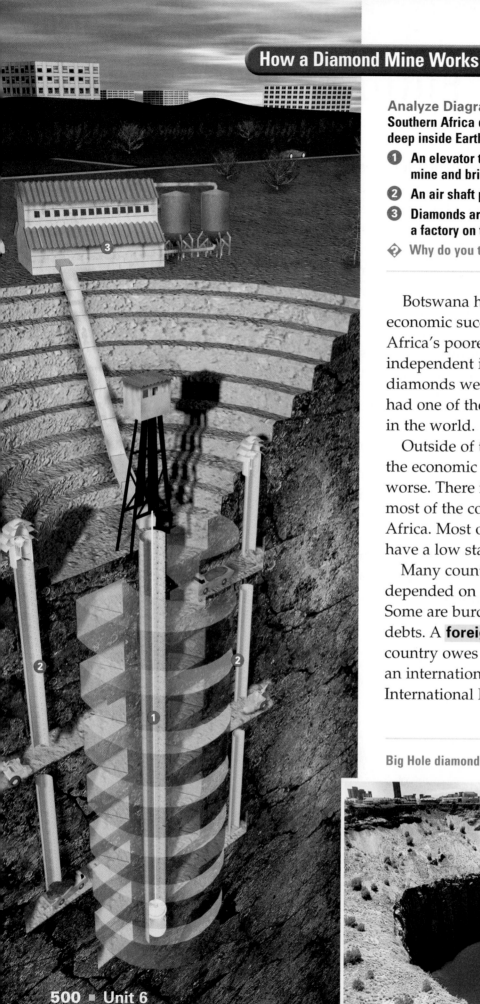

How a Diamond Mine Works

Analyze Diagrams Some diamond mines in Southern Africa can be more than 1 mile (1.6 km) deep inside Earth.

1 An elevator transports workers into and out of the mine and brings up rock material.

2 An air shaft provides fresh air inside the mine.

3 Diamonds are separated from the rock material in a factory on the surface.

◈ Why do you think mining diamonds is so difficult?

Botswana has also achieved some economic success. Botswana was among Africa's poorest countries when it became independent in 1966. Then in the 1970s diamonds were discovered. Soon Botswana had one of the fastest-growing economies in the world.

Outside of the country of South Africa, the economic outlook for the region is worse. There is little economic growth in most of the countries of East and Southern Africa. Most of the people who live there have a low standard of living.

Many countries in East Africa have depended on foreign aid for decades. Some are burdened with large foreign debts. A **foreign debt** is money that a country owes to another country or to an international organization such as the International Monetary Fund (IMF) or

Big Hole diamond mine in South Africa

LOCATE IT

Kimberley

SOUTH AFRICA

The Flying Doctors organization, based in Kenya, provides emergency medical care across Africa in areas without health services.

the World Bank. **Debt service**, or the repayment on a loan, takes up as much as half of some African countries' earnings.

Organizations such as the IMF and the World Bank offer suggestions to help African countries improve their economies. They often advise poorer nations to work against illegal financial practices in their governments and businesses. For example, they suggest that foreign aid money should not disappear into the bank accounts of government officials. Aid money and foreign loans should be spent on projects that will provide jobs and improve the people's standard of living. Some suggest that wealthy countries can help poorer nations by canceling their debts or by waiting to be repaid so the countries that owe them money have more time to improve things for their people.

REVIEW Which country in East and Southern Africa has the strongest economy?

Health and Welfare

Government problems and poverty make it difficult for many East and Southern African countries to provide such services as health care and education.

These problems will be important and difficult challenges of the twenty-first century.

Many people in East and Southern Africa suffer from health problems. For example, AIDS, HIV, and malaria, or sleeping sickness, are common throughout the region. Other diseases and health conditions that are easy to prevent or cure in other parts of the world often cause death in Africa. Many children suffer and die from **malnutrition**. It is an unhealthy condition caused by not getting enough healthful food to eat. A general lack of clean water for drinking, cooking, and bathing also causes many of the region's health problems.

The high cost of medicines to treat many diseases that are widespread in Africa is another problem. International charities such as Doctors Without Borders are working with drug companies to lower the price of medicines needed to treat patients in Africa.

Free education is not yet offered everywhere in the region. Improved literacy will help these countries meet many of the challenges they face. Health education will increase life expectancy.

Dr. Matthew Lukwiya
1958–2000

Character Trait: Compassion

Matthew Lukwiya grew up in one of Uganda's poorest regions, but he excelled in school. Lukwiya won scholarships that paid his way to England, where he earned a master's degree in tropical medicine. Instead of remaining abroad, he returned to Uganda to work in a missionary hospital.

When three student nurses at the hospital fell sick and died of a mysterious illness, Dr. Matthew, as he was called, realized it was an outbreak of Ebola. He notified the authorities. Then he isolated the Ebola patients. He and several nurses cared for them around the clock.

Dr. Matthew fell ill a few days later. Within two weeks he, too, died of the disease. His quick response had prevented the epidemic from spreading farther. Thousands more lives would have been lost had it not been for the caring work of Dr. Lukwiya.

One of the greatest challenges to human welfare is how to feed the growing population. Years of drought, or too little rain, have brought starvation to Somalia and other areas. Civil wars within African countries have also caused groups of people to go without enough to eat.

Food sent from the United States and other countries has saved many Africans from starvation. In the past, however, there have been problems getting food to those who needed it most. Government officials in some African countries stole food intended to help their people. Others refused to give the food to their citizens because of disagreements with the countries that donated it. Also, food donations sometimes lessened the amount of food grown on farms in African countries. Some farmers saw no reason to plant crops when food was being given away. Today, most groups that distribute food take steps to avoid these problems.

It is difficult not to ask for help when there is so much suffering. In a recent meeting with United States President George W. Bush, South Africa's leader, Thabo Mbeki (TAY•boh m•BEK•ee), asked for help from the United States:

> **The moment has come for us . . . to deal with problems of . . . poverty [and] disease [in Africa].**

REVIEW What are some of the major health problems in East and Southern Africa?

F. W. de Klerk, South Africa's former president, often spoke about the importance of education in dealing with serious health problems: "Our enemy cannot be defeated by medicines, but it can be defeated by communication. Education is not only the key to economic growth and development, it is the first requirement in the war against AIDS."

South African leader Thabo Mbeki

Protecting the Environment

The African environment is very fragile. Tropical rains, which fall heavily for a short period, carry away soil that is not held in place by tree roots. However, trees are quickly disappearing. Tropical woods have become a valuable cash crop for many countries. Farmers also clear woodlands to grow food, and most African people use firewood for cooking.

Two-thirds of Africa is very dry. Along the edges of the deserts, dry lands can support only a few people, small herds, and small amounts of grain. Crops cannot grow on most of the land.

People crowd to the few areas that have good soil and enough rain. As the population increases, farmers face two choices. They can either clear more land for farming or plant too many crops on the land they have already cleared. Clearing more land does not give trees a chance to grow back. Farmers will then lose all the valuable products trees provide, such as firewood, fruit, nuts, dyes, medicines, and building materials. Planting too many crops makes the soil less fertile and even more likely to be washed away.

In Ethiopia, clearing trees and overplanting have created serious erosion problems. During the short rainy season, water carries topsoil off the hillside farms. Tanzania and Mozambique have similar problems. When soil loss turns fertile land into desert, a process called desertification has begun.

Increasing the amount of farmland also affects African wildlife. As in West and Central Africa, the people in East and Southern Africa have established many large game preserves. These parks protect animals and also attract tourists, who pay to see them. Tourism brings much-needed money to countries in East and Southern Africa.

• HERITAGE •

The Uganda Women's Tree Planting Movement

As elsewhere in Africa, women in Uganda have the job of gathering firewood for cooking. This chore may take as much as three hours a day. Aware of the scarcity of wood, a group of Ugandan women decided to form a national organization known as the Uganda Women's Tree Planting Movement (UWTPM).

With advice from forestry experts, small groups of women and children, with 10 to 35 members in each group, have been planting seedlings in many parts of Uganda. They raise money for their project by selling seedlings along main roads. Their fund-raising has increased public awareness of the need for environmental protection.

An international ban on trading ivory has helped solve the problem of **poachers**, or people who kill wild animals illegally. In Southern Africa, however, the elephant population has grown so large that several countries need to make the herds smaller.

The debate on how best to protect the environment will continue. By working together, the countries of the region will find new ways to balance today's need for economic progress with preserving the environment for future generations.

REVIEW Why are Africa's forests disappearing?

Culture and Conflict

"Africa is not a country!" became a popular saying in recent years. For many people, it stresses the importance of Africa's many different cultures.

The people living in the tiny country of Djibouti speak one or more of four languages. Arabic is the official language there, but French has been a second language since France ruled Djibouti. Many Djiboutians also speak the Afar and Somali languages of their ancestors.

Nine or more languages can be heard in Eritrea, another small country. It is also home to a variety of religions. About half of all Eritreans are Muslim. Most other Eritreans are members of the Ethiopian Orthodox Church. Some Christian Eritreans became Roman Catholics when the Italians settled in their country. Some still attend Catholic churches.

Most people in Kenya and Tanzania are Christian. The Masai, an ancient people who live in both countries, continue to follow their traditional religion. Their faith is strongly related to cattle. In fact, the Masai still raise cattle for their livelihood. Today some Masai have settled onto permanent farms, where they raise wheat and other crops. Others raise such birds as ostriches. The Masai have adapted to changes in Kenya and Tanzania, while keeping much of their culture.

The Malagasy people on the island of Madagascar have a rich and diverse culture. People from islands in the Pacific settled there. Today their culture is a blend of Indonesian, Polynesian, Indian, Spanish, Portuguese, French, and African influences.

Masai

Malagasy

Kenyans

Many Malagasy are Christian. Others are Muslims, and some practice the traditional religion of the Malagasy culture.

Rwanda is another small country that is home to several cultures. The two largest groups are the Hutu and the Tutsi. Most Rwandans speak the Kinyarwanda language. Some also speak French or German. People in Rwanda practice Christianity, Islam, and traditional African religions.

For centuries the Hutu and the Tutsi lived side by side in what is now Rwanda. Yet they did not govern the area equally. The Tutsi ruled the Hutu, even though the Hutu outnumbered them.

At the end of the 1800s, Rwanda came under European control. First Germany and then Belgium ruled Rwanda. During this time the Tutsi were allowed to maintain power over the Hutu.

However, the Hutu began to seek a voice in government. Fighting broke out. In 1962 Rwanda became independent, with the Hutu as the rulers. Conflict between the

A view of the city of Nairobi in Kenya

two groups continued on and off during the rest of the 1990s. Both groups wanted to lead Rwanda. Finally, the year 2000 brought peace. Today both the Hutu and the Tutsi take part in Rwanda's government.

REVIEW **What is one reason why the Hutu and the Tutsi fought in Rwanda?**

LESSON 4
REVIEW

① **MAIN IDEA** What challenges face the countries of East and Southern Africa in the twenty-first century?

② **WHY IT MATTERS** How will political stability and economic independence affect East and Southern Africa?

③ **VOCABULARY** Write a short paragraph that explains why **Harambee** would make a good slogan for Pan Africanism.

④ **READING SKILL—Generalize** How has help from Europe and the United States brought harm to East and Southern Africans?

⑤ **ECONOMICS** How does South Africa's economic strength help neighboring countries?

⑥ **CULTURE** How have the Masai changed, and how have they kept their culture over the centuries?

⑦ **CRITICAL THINKING—Apply** What causes desertification?

⑧ **CRITICAL THINKING—Evaluate** If some elephants are killed because the herd has grown so large that it threatens to destroy the environment, should people be allowed to sell the ivory from the elephants' tusks?

PERFORMANCE—Make a Graph
Choose four countries from East and Southern Africa. On a double bar graph, show the per capita GDP of each country in relation to the number of people who are affected by disease each year. You may wish to use some information from the graphs on page 507 to help you with this task. Can you make any generalizations about the relationship between economy and disease?

Compare Tables

SKILLS

CHART AND GRAPH

VOCABULARY

table

row

column

▶ WHY IT MATTERS

It can be a challenge to learn about the similarities and differences in the countries of a large continent like Africa. It is much easier to understand information if it is sorted into categories. A **table** organizes facts, statistics, and other information into categories.

Tables are especially useful for comparing and contrasting facts and statistics. For example, the tables on page 507 allow you to compare political, social, and economic facts and statistics for several countries in East and Southern Africa. By reading and comparing the tables, you can quickly see how the nations are alike and how they are different.

▶ WHAT YOU NEED TO KNOW

The tables on page 507 compare the forms of government, literacy rate, important farm products, and Gross Domestic Product (GDP) for countries in East and Southern Africa. Literacy rate refers to the percentage of a country's people who can read and write. Use the following tips when you are comparing tables.

• Read the titles of the tables to find out what each one compares.

• Tables are organized in rows and columns. A **row** is horizontal, and a **column** is vertical. Each row in the tables on page 507 is labeled with a category for comparison. The top of

King Mswati III of Swaziland (bottom row, center) became the youngest ruling monarch in 1986 at age 18.

Southern Africa			
	BOTSWANA	**LESOTHO**	**SWAZILAND**
Form of Government	democratic republic	constitutional monarchy	constitutional monarchy
Literacy Rate	70%	83%	77%
Important Farm Products	sorghum, corn, millet	corn, wheat, sorghum	sugarcane, corn, citrus
Gross Domestic Product	$10.4 billion	$5.1 billion	$4.4 billion

East Africa			
	ETHIOPIA	**KENYA**	**SUDAN**
Form of Government	democratic republic	democratic republic	military dictatorship
Literacy Rate	36%	78%	46%
Important Farm Products	sugarcane, corn, potatoes	sugarcane, corn, wheat	sugarcane, sorghum, wheat
Gross Domestic Product	$39 billion	$45.6 billion	$35.7 billion

each column is labeled with the name of a country.

- To enable you to compare information in the two tables, the same categories of information must be represented in the tables. Notice that the categories in the two tables are the same.

▶ PRACTICE THE SKILL

Study the tables above, and then answer these questions.

❶ Which region of Africa has leaders who are kings or queens?

❷ Which country has the highest percentage of people who can read and write?

❸ Which country has the lowest Gross Domestic Product?

❹ Which farm products are important in both East Africa and Southern Africa?

▶ APPLY WHAT YOU LEARNED

Research the governments and economies of two of the countries you read about in Lesson 4. Then make two tables similar to the ones above. You may use the same categories or choose other categories. Remember that you must use the same categories in both tables. When you have finished your tables, use them to write a paragraph comparing and contrasting the two nations.

Review and Test Preparation

Summary Time Line

1000 B.C. | B.C./A.D.

700s B.C.
Kingdom of Kush
conquers Egypt

600s B.C.
Assyrians invade
the Nile River Valley

USE YOUR READING SKILLS

Complete this graphic organizer to show that you understand how to use facts and details to make generalizations about East and Southern Africa. A copy of this graphic organizer appears on page 136 of the Activity Book.

Make Generalizations About East and Southern Africa

FACTS + DETAILS → GENERALIZATION

Many East and Southern African countries have weak economies. They must deal with ethnic conflicts, famine, disease, and large amounts of foreign debt. Also, protecting the environment is a major concern.

_____
_____
_____
_____
_____

People from the many different world regions, including the Arabian peninsula and Europe, have settled in Africa. Each group brought with it new cultural ideas and influences, such as languages, religions, and customs.

_____
_____
_____
_____
_____

THINK & WRITE

Write an Explanation In some areas of Africa, it is difficult for farmers to feed growing populations in their communities. Farmers must either clear more land for farming or plant too many crops on the land already cleared. Explain how over time these methods can make the problem worse.

Write a Newspaper Headline Imagine that you are a newspaper reporter in the United States. Write a headline announcing the end of apartheid in South Africa. Your headline should quickly grab a reader's attention. You may wish to include a subhead that mentions the *who, what, where, why,* and *how* of the story.

A.D. 300s
Christianity spreads into Africa

A.D. 600s
Arab merchants become active traders along the East African coast

A.D. 1200
Shonas begin building Great Zimbabwe

A.D. 1488
Portuguese explorers reach East and Southern Africa

USE THE TIME LINE

Use the chapter summary time line to answer these questions.

1 When did Christianity spread into Africa?

2 Which occurred first, the building of Great Zimbabwe or the Assyrian invasion of the Nile River Valley?

USE VOCABULARY

Identify the term that correctly matches each definition.

pan (p. 481)

flax (p. 486)

debt service (p. 501)

malnutrition (p. 501)

poacher (p. 504)

3 repayments on a loan

4 a person who kills wild animals illegally

5 a shallow pond or lake that forms during the rainy season

6 the plant from which linen is made

7 not getting enough food

RECALL FACTS

Answer these questions.

8 How has the geography of the Great Escarpment affected the people of Africa?

9 How did natural resources affect the ancient capital of Meroë?

10 Under the colonial system, how were European settlers in East and Southern Africa treated in relation to the people who already lived there?

11 What do some leaders believe is the best way to meet the challenges faced by many East and Southern Africans?

Write the letter of the best choice.

12 **TEST PREP** Many geologists think that at one time all the Earth's continents were joined into a supercontinent called—

　A Gondwana.
　B Pangaea.
　C Laurasia.
　D the Great Escarpment.

13 **TEST PREP** The first country south of the Sahara to win independence was—

　F South Africa.
　G Kenya.
　H Sudan.
　J Mozambique.

THINK CRITICALLY

14 Do you think it would be a good idea for Africa to unite under one federation? Why or why not?

15 Countries around the world limited trade with South Africa to help end apartheid. What are the advantages and disadvantages of this method?

APPLY SKILLS

Compare Tables of Information

16 Make a table of the information below. For these countries, what is the relationship between GDP per capita and life expectancy?

Somalia: GDP per capita—$600
Life expectancy—46 years
Seychelles: GDP per capita—$7,500
Life expectancy—70 years
South Africa: GDP per capita—$6,900
Life expectancy—51 years

A Wildlife PARK

GET READY

Each year millions of people from all over the world visit South Africa to see its breathtaking landscape. In addition to its rugged scenery, South Africa has many protected wildlife areas and national parks. In these areas visitors can see animals in their natural environments. There are many different animals to see, but the most popular ones to spot are known as the Big Five. This group consists of the elephant, the rhino, the leopard, the lion, and the cape buffalo. With the help of a guide, you can follow the tracks of a leopard, see lions drinking at a water hole, or watch a herd of grazing cape buffalo.

LOCATE IT

SOUTH AFRICA

WHAT TO SEE

Zebra

Rhinos

Cape buffalo

Lion

Elephant

Leopard

Giraffes

TAKE A FIELD TRIP

GO ONLINE

A VIRTUAL TOUR
Visit The Learning Site at **www.harcourtschool.com/tours** to take virtual tours of other parks and scenic areas.

CNN Turner Le@rning

A VIDEO TOUR
Check your media center or classroom library for a videotape tour of a South African Wildlife Park.

6 Review and Test Preparation

VISUAL SUMMARY

Write a Journal Entry Look closely at each picture and read the captions to help you review Unit 6. Then write a journal entry about each picture and tell how it relates to the social studies ideas presented in this unit.

USE VOCABULARY

Describe the lands of Africa south of the Sahara using these terms.

savanna (page 444), **transition zone** (page 446),

bauxite (page 448), **copper belt** (page 449),

cobalt (page 449), **staple** (page 473),

pan (page 481), **veld** (page 482)

RECALL FACTS

Answer these questions.

1 What different climate and vegetation regions are found in West and Central Africa?

2 What European countries had colonies in Africa south of the Sahara?

3 What organization in Africa was formed to promote trade and prevent conflict among African nations?

Write the letter of the best choice.

4 **TEST PREP** Each of the following was a leader in West and Central Africa *except*—
A Mansa Musa.
B Kwame Nkrumah.
C Sundiata.
D Nelson Mandela.

5 **TEST PREP** The religion that is native to Africa is—
F Islam.
G animism.
H Christianity.
J Judaism.

6 **TEST PREP** Afrikaans is a language based on Dutch. It includes words from all of the following languages *except*—
A German.
B French.
C Portuguese.
D Khoisan.

7 **TEST PREP** The country in Africa south of the Sahara with the strongest economy is—
F Zimbabwe.
G Rwanda.
H Ghana.
J South Africa.

THINK CRITICALLY

8 Why do you think so many Africans speak European languages? Explain.

9 How do the achievements of an individual such as Kwame Nkrumah or Nelson Mandela affect contemporary society? Describe.

10 How do natural resources affect the economies of countries in Africa south of the Sahara?

APPLY SKILLS

Compare Map Projections

Use the Robinson and the Equidistant Projection maps on this page to answer the questions.

MAP AND GLOBE SKILLS

11 The North Pole is a single point. Which projection shows the North Pole accurately?

12 Often the central point shown on a map is one of the poles. Which map can be called a polar projection?

13 On which map do the lines of longitude get closer together toward the poles?

14 On which map are the lines of longitude parallel, or equally far apart?

15 Antarctica is a single continent. Which map more accurately shows the shape of Antarctia?

Equidistant Projection

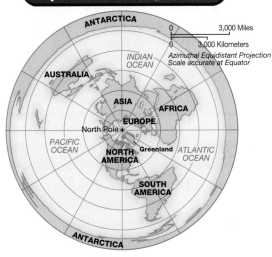

Robinson Projection

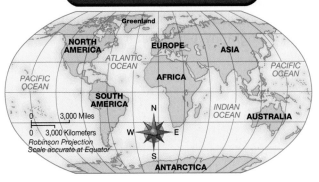

513

Unit Activities

 Visit The Learning Site at
www.harcourtschool.com/
socialstudies/activities
for additional activities.

Create an Almanac

Almanacs list information about different countries, such as population, type of government, and cultural groups. Use what you have learned about Africa to make an almanac of its countries. Pick one country for which to create an almanac entry. Illustrate your almanac with a drawing of the country's flag. You may wish to work with classmates to compile an almanac of all the countries in Africa south of the Sahara.

Tell a Story

One way Africans preserve their culture is by telling stories about the past. Some storytellers and griots tell of African heroes. Research a hero from Africa. This person can be a doctor, an artist, or a leader. Use what you find out about this person to write a story about him or her. Then perform your story for the class. You should tell your story using movements and descriptive language.

VISIT YOUR LIBRARY

- **A family from Ethiopia** by Julia Waterlow. Steck-Vaughn.

- **West Africa** by Tony Binns and Rob Bowden. Steck-Vaughn.

- **Journey to Jo'burg: A South African Story** by Beverly Naidoo. Harper Trophy.

COMPLETE THE UNIT PROJECT

Prepare a Multimedia Presentation

Work with the class to complete the unit project—a multimedia tour. First, gather the parts of your presentation, such as sound recordings, pictures, costumes, and video. Then, organize all your materials into a presentation that will give a tour of Africa. Your tour should include information about Africa's geography, people, and wildlife.

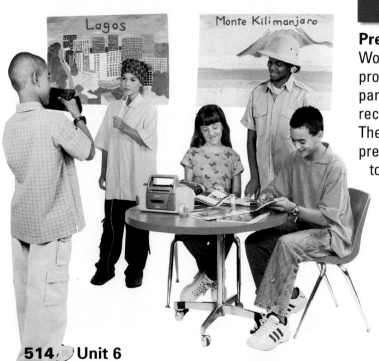

Asia

Japanese porcelain,
1615–1868 Edo period

Bullet train speeds past Mount Fuji, Japan

Asia

> **" My souvenir from Edo [Tokyo]
> Is the refreshingly cold wind
> Of Mount Fuji
> I brought home on my fan. "**
>
> —Matsuo Basho, haiku about Edo, 1676

Preview the Content

Read the lesson titles and the Main Ideas throughout the unit. Use them to develop a web for each chapter. Write words or phrases to help you identify the main topics to be covered.

Preview the Vocabulary

Related Words   Related words are words that share a relationship. Decide how the Vocabulary Words below are related. Make a web like the one below, and in the center, write the relationship that the words share. Make similar webs for other related words in this unit.

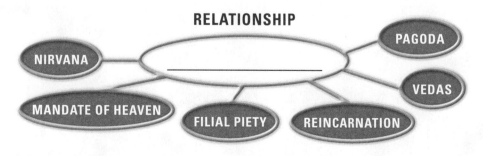

RELATIONSHIP

PAGODA

NIRVANA

VEDAS

MANDATE OF HEAVEN

FILIAL PIETY   REINCARNATION

Asia

MONGOLIA
Ulaanbaatar
Harbin
Changchun
Shenyang
ALTAI SHAN
TIAN SHAN
GOBI
NORTH KOREA
Beijing
P'yongyang
TAKLA MAKAN
KUNLUN MOUNTAINS
Taiyuan
Tianjin
Seoul
SOUTH KOREA
Islamabad
Huang He
Xi'an
Yellow Sea
Nanjing
Shanghai
PAKISTAN
Lahore
HIMALAYA MOUNTAINS
CHINA
Wuhan
East China Sea
Indus R.
Mount Everest
Chengdu
Chongqing
Delhi
New Delhi
NEPAL
Brahmaputra R.
Chang Jiang
Taipei
Karachi
Kathmandu
BHUTAN
Thimphu
Mekong R.
TAIWAN
Kanpur
Ganges R.
Kunming
Xi R.
Ahmadabad
BANGLADESH
Guangzhou
Hong Kong
Arabian Sea
INDIA
Kolkata (Calcutta)
Dhaka
Irrawaddy R.
Macao
Mumbai (Bombay)
DECCAN
Hyderabad
EASTERN GHATS
Mandalay
Hanoi
South China Sea
WESTERN GHATS
PLATEAU
MYANMAR (BURMA)
LAOS
Vientiane
Bay of Bengal
Da Nang
Manila
Chennai (Madras)
Yangon (Rangoon)
THAILAND
VIETNAM
PHILIPPINES
Andaman Sea
Bangkok
CAMBODIA
Ho Chi Minh City
SRI LANKA
Phnom Penh
Gulf of Thailand
Colombo
MALDIVES
Male
Bandar Seri Begawan
BRUNEI
MALAYSIA
Medan
Kuala Lumpur
Singapore
SINGAPORE
Borneo
INDIAN OCEAN
Banjarmasin
Palembang
INDONESIA
Jakarta
Java Sea
Surabaya
Bandung

Visual Summary

3000 B.C.   2000 B.C.   1000 B.C.

2500 B.C. First cities in the Indus River valley of South Asia p. 530

1600 B.C. First Chinese dynasty p. 561

500 B.C. Buddhism emerges in South Asia p. 532

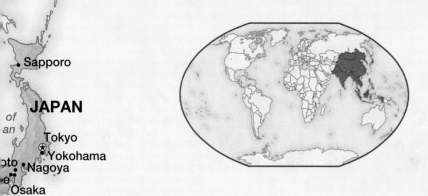

Sapporo

JAPAN

of
an

Tokyo
Yokohama
Nagoya
Osaka
kyushu

0   500   1,000 Miles
0   500   1,000 Kilometers
Lambert Azimuthal Equal-Area Projection

PACIFIC OCEAN

New Guinea

Dili

EAST TIMOR

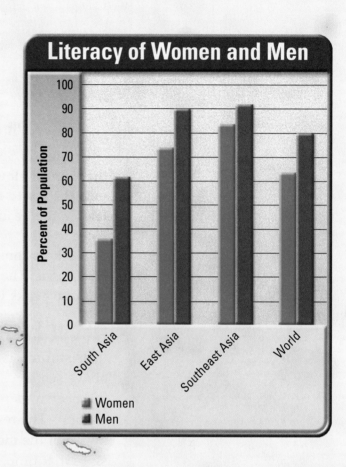

Literacy of Women and Men

Percent of Population

| | South Asia | East Asia | Southeast Asia | World |

■ Women
■ Men

B.C./A.D.   **A.D. 1000**   **A.D. 2000**

A.D. 100 Indian-influenced kingdoms develop in Southeast Asia p. 592

A.D. 1949 China becomes a communist nation p. 575

A.D. 2000 Asian economies experience many changes p. 599

517

THE TOP OF THE WORLD
CLIMBING
MT. EVEREST

THE TOP OF THE WORLD
Climbing
Mount Everest

written and illustrated by Steve Jenkins

Located in South Asia, the Himalaya Mountains are the highest mountain range on Earth. People from all over the world travel to the Himalayas. Some come to take in the beauty of their peaks and valleys. Others come to hike, or trek, the lower mountains of the range. Still others come to climb the higher peaks of the Himalayas. The most famous—and most challenging—of these peaks is Mount Everest.

Mount Everest

Its summit is the highest point on earth, $5\frac{1}{2}$ miles above sea level. For thousands of years, the mountain has been a sacred place for those who live in its shadow. The rest of the world, however, wasn't really aware of the mountain until about 180 years ago. Ever since that time, climbers, scientists, and adventurers have been fascinated by this peak. Many have tried to climb it. Some have succeeded, but many more have failed. Some have died trying.

Mount Everest is a place of great beauty, adventure, and danger. If you ever want to climb it, here are a few things to think about.

The Roof of the World

Rising between India and China, the Himalayas are the highest mountain range on earth. More than 1,500 miles long, the range includes many of the world's tallest peaks. The highest of them all, Mount Everest, stands on the border of Nepal and Tibet. Its summit is 29,028 feet above sea level.

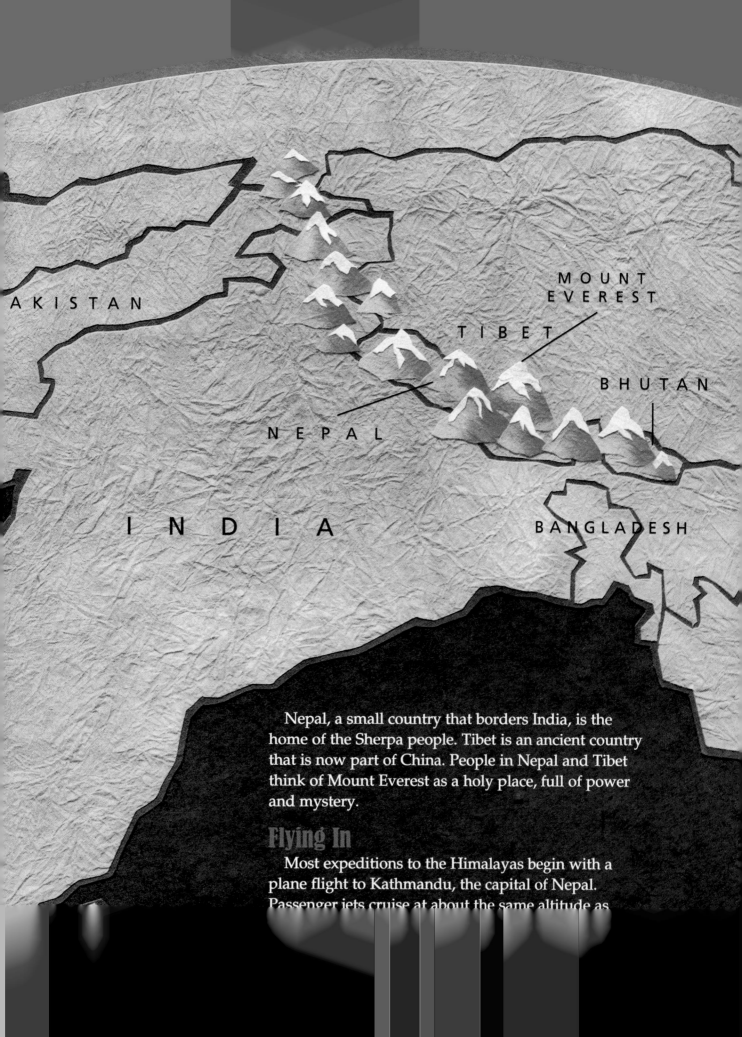

AKISTAN

MOUNT
EVEREST

TIBET

BHUTAN

NEPAL

INDIA

BANGLADESH

Nepal, a small country that borders India, is the home of the Sherpa people. Tibet is an ancient country that is now part of China. People in Nepal and Tibet think of Mount Everest as a holy place, full of power and mystery.

Flying In

Most expeditions to the Himalayas begin with a plane flight to Kathmandu, the capital of Nepal. Passenger jets cruise at about the same altitude as

Kathmandu

When you arrive in the bustling capital city of Nepal, you'll collect your gear, meet your guides, and pay for your climbing permit. If you're lucky, you'll have time to pay a visit to the Monkey Temple, one of the many Buddhist religious sites in the city. Sherpas and other climbers often make offerings here before beginning an expedition.

Kathmandu is also where you'll begin the long trek to Everest.

The Sherpas

Since the first British adventurers came to Nepal, a group of native people known as Sherpas have worked with climbers as guides and partners. They are famous for their strength, climbing skill, and honesty. Sherpas are born and raised in the mountains, so they are accustomed to the altitude and can work well high on the mountain.

READ A BOOK

TIME For Kids READERS
The People of India
Harcourt

TIME For Kids READERS
Climbing HIGH
Harcourt

TIME For Kids READERS
Changing the Face of China
Harcourt

First to the Top

The British expedition of 1921 was the first organized attempt to climb Mount Everest. Sickness and exhaustion kept the climbers from reaching the top, but they did discover a route to the summit. Many attempts by climbers of different nationalities followed, but no one succeeded until May 29, 1953, when Edmund Hillary and Tenzing Norgay reached the summit. Hillary was from New Zealand and Tenzing Norgay was a Sherpa from Nepal. Both men became international heroes.

Analyze the Literature

1 What are some of the challenges of climbing Mount Everest?

2 What are some reasons climbers risk their lives to climb Mount Everest?

3 Imagine you are trekking in the Himalayas. Write a journal entry describing the things you see and the challenges you face.

START THE UNIT PROJECT

Plan a Web Page Think about what you might like to include in a Web page about Asia. As you read this unit, take notes about Asia's geography and people. Your notes will help you decide what to include on your Web page.

USE TECHNOLOGY

Visit The Learning Site at **www.harcourtschool.com/ socialstudies** for additional activities, primary sources, and other resources to use in this unit.

TAJ MAHAL, INDIA

The Taj Mahal in Agra, India, was built by the Mogul emperor Shah Jahan as a monument to his wife, Mumtaz Mahal. She died in 1631. Made of white marble inlaid with gold and precious stones, the Taj Mahal took 20,000 workers more than 22 years to complete.

LOCATE IT

Agra

INDIA

15

South Asia

" One solitary tear . . . on the cheek of time. In the form of this white and gleaming Taj Mahal. "
—Rabindranath Tagore, from *"Shah-Jahan,"* 1914

CHAPTER READING SKILL

Fact and Opinion

A **fact** is a statement that can be proved to be true. An **opinion** is a person's judgment or feeling. An opinion cannot be proved to be true.

As you read this chapter, identify facts about topics. Then write your opinion about something related to the topic.

| If you can prove it | → | it is a FACT. |
| If it is a judgment or feeling | → | it is an OPINION. |

1

MAIN IDEA

Read to learn how the rivers of South Asia make trade and transportation possible in an otherwise isolated region.

WHY IT MATTERS

The waterways of South Asia connect the region with the rest of the world.

VOCABULARY

subcontinent
irrigation canal
atoll
monsoon

Great Rivers, Mighty Monsoons

South Asia is made up of seven countries—India, Pakistan, Bangladesh, Nepal (nuh•PAWL), Bhutan (boo•TAHN), Sri Lanka (sree LAHNG•kuh), and the Maldives (MAWL•deevz). The Himalayas and several other mountain ranges separate parts of South Asia from the rest of the Asian landmass. Geographers call the part of South Asia that lies to the south of the Himalayas the Indian **subcontinent**.

Great Rivers in South Asia

The rivers of the Indian subcontinent provide its farmers with water to produce crops. The rivers also make possible the transportation of goods to the rest of the world. Bangladesh alone has more

FAST FACT The Ganges is considered by Hindus to be a holy river and has no fewer than 108 names.

than 700 rivers. These rivers provide much-needed water, but they also cause damage and suffering when they overflow their banks. India's Ganges (GAN•jeez) River is one of the longest rivers in the world. It begins high in the Himalayas, some 10,000 feet (about 3,050 m) above sea level. Water from melting snows and glaciers winds through deep mountain gorges as the river grows wider and deeper. The river enters a plain at the town of Haridwar. It then runs southeast across northern India and Bangladesh. It joins with the Brahmaputra (brah•muh•POO•truh) River finally to form the vast Ganges Delta.

The Indus River begins its course of more than 1,900 miles (about 3,060 km) in the Himalayas of southwestern Tibet. It flows through the Hindu Kush mountains and then enters the Punjab Plain. Here the Indus is joined by its main tributaries. South of Pakistan's city of Hyderabad (HY•duh•ruh•bad), the river divides into several branches that empty into the Arabian Sea.

REVIEW What is formed when the Ganges joins the Brahmaputra?

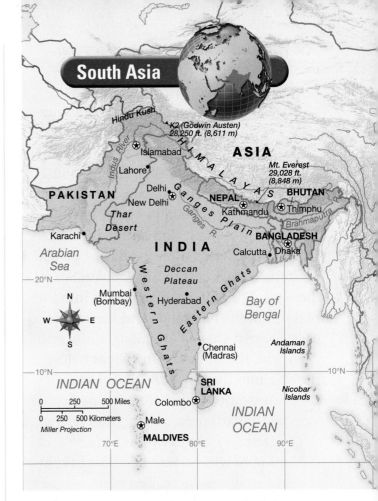

South Asia

Regions The region of South Asia is made up of these seven countries.

❖ What landform separates South Asia from the rest of the continent?

The Subcontinent

South Asia's landscape is so varied that some geographers divide it into three regions. The first is the Northern Mountain Rim. To its south is the Ganges Plain, where India's rivers come out of the mountains and flow to the sea. From the plain, the Deccan Plateau stretches across India.

The Himalayas dominate the Northern Mountain Rim. This vast mountain chain rises in western China and stretches across India's northern border with Pakistan. Ninety-five Himalayan peaks are higher than 24,600 feet (7,500 m). Mount Everest, the world's highest mountain, reaches nearly 5.5 miles (about 9 km).

Chapter 15 ▪ **525**

The Himalayas are made up of several mountain ranges. Together they cover Nepal, Bhutan, northern India, and northeastern Pakistan. The highest mountains are found mainly in the north. Their peaks are snow-covered all year. To the south the Himalayas descend into foothills that border the Ganges Plain.

India's Ganges Plain lies between the Northern Mountain Rim and the Deccan Plateau. It extends from the Bay of Bengal on India's east coast to the Arabian Sea in the west. The Ganges River flows into the plain from the highlands and then turns east. There it crosses into Bangladesh and joins with the Brahmaputra River before flowing into the Bay of Bengal. The land rises where the Ganges River turns east, sloping upward onto the Deccan Plateau.

The Deccan Plateau averages 1,968 feet (600 m) in height and covers most of central and southern India. The plateau offers fertile soil and wide, grass-covered plains where herds can graze. Most of India's mineral resources, including oil, gold, and iron ore, are found on the Deccan Plateau. Four mountain ranges border it. To the west, past the Aravalli Range, lies the Thar (TAHR) Desert. This desert stretches northwest to the border with Pakistan.

Five of South Asia's seven countries lie on the subcontinent. In addition to India, they are Pakistan, Bhutan, Nepal, and Bangladesh. The four smaller countries are arranged in a shallow semicircle across India's northern border. Much of this border follows the Northern Mountain Rim and the Himalayas.

Pakistan, to India's northwest, stretches from the Arabian Sea in the south to the Himalayas in the north. Pakistan often has too little rainfall to grow crops. Its farmers must use a large network of **irrigation canals**, or human-made waterways that carry water from a source to where it is needed. Drawing water from the Indus River and its main tributaries, these canals are part of the world's largest irrigation system.

Farmland in India

Where these waterways flow through Kashmir, land lying between India and Pakistan, there is conflict. Both countries need this important source of water.

Nepal, to the north of India, is almost all in the Himalayas. Most of its people live in the city of Kathmandu (kat•man•DOO) or in small mountain villages between the towering Himalayan peaks. The southern part of Nepal, known as the Terai (tuh•RY), has broad plains and excellent farmland. Nepal also has regions of swamp and rain forest. Central Nepal, the region the people call "hill country," is mountainous and crossed by many rivers and valleys. In the north are the Himalayas. Along the border between Nepal and Tibet is Mount Everest.

Bhutan lies between India's northern plains and Tibet, a part of China. It is less than 100 miles (161 km) wide and 200 miles (322 km) long and is very mountainous. Some of the highest mountains of the Himalayas can be found in northern Bhutan. Bhutan's border with Tibet stretches along peaks covered with snow, some of which have never been reached by humans. As in Nepal, Bhutan's valleys and plains are densely populated. Central Bhutan contains several fertile valleys that are the most populated parts of the country. The Duars Plain, near Bhutan's border with India, is a hot, humid, rainy area. Deer, tigers, elephants, and other wildlife live here, including golden langurs, some of the rarest monkeys in the world.

Bangladesh, meaning "Bengal nation," lies along the Bay of Bengal, where its coastline runs for 357 miles (575 km).

The Pokhara Valley and the Machhapuchhare Mountain in Nepal

Desert in India

LOCATE IT
Pokhara Valley
NEPAL

Most of Bangladesh lies within the large Ganges Delta. Three rivers—the Ganges, the Brahmaputra, and the Meghna—empty into the Bay of Bengal here. During the flood season these waterways deposit fertile soil in farmers' fields across the delta.

REVIEW What are the three regions of the subcontinent?

Island Countries

Sri Lanka, formerly known as Ceylon, is an island in the Indian Ocean. It lies 22 miles (35 km) from India on the other side of the Palk Strait. The country rises from lowland rice fields plowed by water buffalo to grass-covered mountains about 7,000 feet (2,100 m) high. The south-central region of Sri Lanka is mountainous, and rolling plains cover the surrounding areas. Sri Lanka has long been known for its physical beauty and all that the land yields—tea, rubber, coconuts, spices, and gemstones.

The Maldives lie about 400 miles (645 km) southwest of Sri Lanka in the Indian Ocean. This country consists of more than 1,000 coral islands, or atolls. An **atoll** forms where coral grows around a volcano.

A landmark in Male, the capital city of the Maldives

Many of these coral islands are rings that surround lagoons or ponds. None of the atolls in the Maldives are larger than 5 square miles (13 sq km). People use boats to travel between the many islands. Most people use bicycles rather than cars for transportation on the islands. The islands are low, rising no higher than 8 feet (2.4 m) above sea level. The climate is mostly warm and humid.

REVIEW How big is the largest atoll in the Maldives?

Mighty Monsoons

Each year between April and October, winds blowing from the Indian Ocean bring warm air and heavy rains to South Asia. These winds, called **monsoons**, blow in the opposite direction in winter. Monsoon rains flood low-lying areas, but they provide much of South Asia's water. As much as 90 percent of India's fresh water comes from monsoon rains.

Almost half the world's population lives in areas affected by the monsoons. Most of these people are farmers. Too much or too little rain from the monsoons can

None of the Maldives' 1,190 atolls rise more than a few feet above sea level.

Summer monsoon winds blow cool, moist air over South Asia. The cool air is heated by the land and produces heavy rain.

mean disaster to South Asia's people in the form of flood or famine.

In the winter months, monsoon winds blow from the northeast and carry the rain clouds out to sea. Without the heavy rains that come each year with the summer monsoons, farmers in South Asia could not feed the growing population. Just one season with too little rain can mean a whole year of hunger for the people of South Asia.

REVIEW What large body of water is responsible for the formation of summer monsoons in South Asia?

LESSON 1
REVIEW

1 **MAIN IDEA** What divides South Asia from the rest of Asia?

2 **WHY IT MATTERS** Why are the rivers and waterways of South Asia important to its people?

3 **VOCABULARY** Use the word **subcontinent** to describe the unique landform that is South Asia.

4 **READING SKILL—Identify Fact and Opinion** This sentence is found in the lesson: "Sri Lanka has long been known for its physical beauty and all that the land yields—tea, rubber, coconuts, spices, and gemstones." Which part is fact, and which part is opinion?

5 **GEOGRAPHY** Into what three distinct regions do geographers divide South Asia?

6 **HISTORY** What is the former name of Sri Lanka?

7 **CRITICAL THINKING—Analyze** Why is it difficult to grow enough food to feed the people in Himalayan countries such as Nepal?

PERFORMANCE—Write a Travel Plan Find South Asia on a globe. Imagine you are planning a trip to the region for students who are interested in geography. On a sheet of paper, list at least three types of landforms you think they should see. Which parts of South Asia would you include as an example of each type?

MAIN IDEA
Read to learn how people from many different lands settled in South Asia over the centuries.

WHY IT MATTERS
South Asia's history helps us understand the people and cultures of South Asia today.

VOCABULARY
urban planning
caste system
stupa
puppet ruler

Through the Ages

3000 B.C.	2000 B.C.	1000 B.C.	B.C./A.D.	A.D. 1000	A.D. 2000

Thousands of years ago people settled in the Indus Valley of South Asia. Some historians believe these people came across the Himalayas from other parts of Asia. Other newcomers, possibly from northern Africa, settled on India's southern peninsula. Later, conquerors pushed people living in northern India southward and finally onto islands in the Indian Ocean. Today more than 1 billion people live in South Asia, in areas as diverse as tiny farming villages in the Himalayan foothills and bustling cities on the coast.

Life in the Indus Valley

Between around 3000 B.C. and around 1700 B.C., people established a civilization in the Indus Valley, in what is now Pakistan. By about 2500 B.C. they had built an amazing civilization along a 1,000-mile (1,609-km) section of the fertile Indus Valley. These people developed an empire based on agriculture. They worked and lived in comfort in a number of large towns. The remains of

FAST FACT Indus Valley merchants tagged their goods with clay seals. Some of these seals have been found as far away as Mesopotamia.

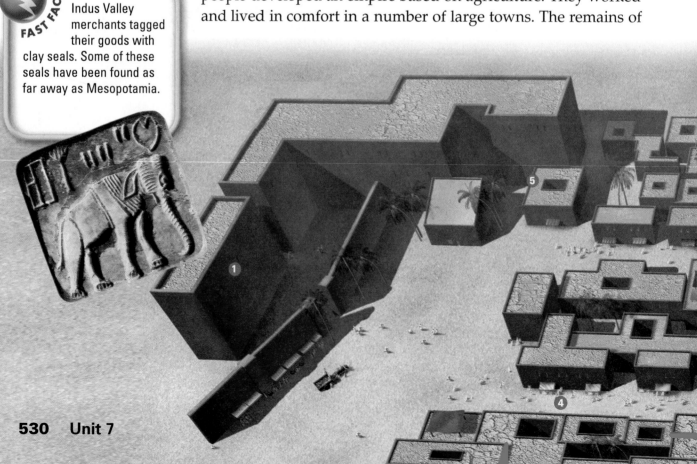

two great cities, Mohenjo-Daro (moh•HEN•joh DAR•oh) and Harappa (huh•RA•puh), show that the people who settled in the Indus Valley understood **urban planning**, or how to plan cities. Mohenjo-Daro was built on a grid design about 3 miles (5 km) around. It had wide avenues with homes and shops. Its buildings were made of baked brick and had stairways, bathrooms, and underground drainage systems. Harappa and other ancient cities followed a similar grid design.

Archaeologists have unearthed a variety of objects from this civilization. These included jewelry set with gemstones, pottery, and kitchen tools made of lead and silver. Some of these objects came from other places, such as Mesopotamia, the ancient civilization between the Tigris and Euphrates Rivers in what is today Iraq. Such objects tell scholars that the people of the Indus Valley traded with people in other parts of the world.

REVIEW **What two Indus Valley cities are examples of urban planning?**

Aryans Bring Changes

Another group of people, called Aryans (AIR•ee•uhnz), came to South Asia from central Asia near what are now parts of southern Russia and northern Iran. They were nomads and had little use for towns. From 1700 B.C. to 1500 B.C., they drove the people of the Indus Valley to the south and east, along the Ganges Plain. The Aryans made slaves of many of them. They placed them at the bottom of their social system. As Aryan culture blended with that of other people living there, this social system grew into what is today the caste system that many people in India still follow. A **caste system** divides people in a society into different social classes.

Some scholars believe that the religions of the Aryans and other early South Asians blended to become the religion known as Hinduism. Hinduism has remained important to people living in India and some other South Asian countries for at least 3,500 years.

A CLOSER LOOK
Mohenjo-Daro

Mohenjo-Daro was a carefully planned settlement in the Indus Valley. Its streets were laid out in rectangular blocks for houses and shops. More than 40,000 people may have lived in Mohenjo-Daro.

1. Fortress
2. Palm trees
3. Tents provide shade.
4. City streets were paved.
5. Buildings were made of bricks baked in ovens.

❖ Why do you think the streets were laid to form rectangular blocks?

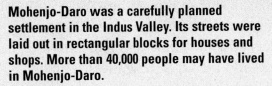

Vishnu (left), Brahma (center), and Shiva (right) are the three main gods of Hinduism.

Hinduism is a religion in which life is thought of as a cycle of death and rebirth. Hindus worship many gods and are known for their tolerance of other faiths.

The Aryans influenced South Asia in ways other than religion, too. Descendants of the Aryans settled throughout India and contributed to a culture known for its poetry, science, and other accomplishments.

The Macedonian warrior Alexander the Great conquered Afghanistan around 328 B.C. He then moved into India and occupied it for two years. Early Indian rulers adopted some of the invaders' ideas and blended these ideas with their own.

LOCATE IT

Sanchi

INDIA

The Great Stupa at Sanchi, India

In 322 B.C. Chandragupta Maurya (chuhn•druh•GUP•tuh MOW•ree•uh) began what would be known as the Maurya Empire. His son, Bindusara, expanded the Maurya Empire. Asoka (uh•SHOH•kuh), Chandragupta's grandson, brought almost all of India under his control by the end of his rule in 232 B.C.

REVIEW **What religion did the Aryans help form in South Asia?**

Buddhism Begins in India

During the 500s B.C., an Indian prince, Siddhartha Gautama (sid•HART•ah GOW•tuh•muh), gave up a life of luxury for one of meditation and teaching. Soon the religion known as Buddhism was born. Gautama's followers began calling him "the Enlightened One," or Buddha.

Asoka, the Mauryan ruler of the third century, turned to Buddhism near the end of his life. Earlier in his rule he expanded the Maurya Empire by military conquest. He killed and enslaved many thousands of people. He claimed these actions were right, saying:

66 **Any power superior in might to another should launch into war.** 99

After turning to Buddhism, Asoka helped spread the religion in India and Sri Lanka. He sent Buddhist missionaries to countries as far away as Egypt. He had cave temples built for Buddhist monks, and he ordered the construction of thousands of stupas. A **stupa** is a curved mound of brick that holds statues of Buddha. Asoka is sometimes credited with helping to make Buddhism a world religion.

Buddhism spread in India from the time of Asoka's rule until around A.D. 1200. Hinduism never died out, but hundreds of years passed before it became the official religion of India. During the A.D. 1200s, Muslim sheikhs forbade all religions except Islam. Buddhism nearly died out in India. The few Buddhists left in India, less than 1 percent of the Indian population, live in the north near Nepal and Bhutan. Yet Buddhism still flourishes in some South Asian countries.

REVIEW What leader is sometimes credited for having made Buddhism a world religion?

The Last Empires

The golden, or classical, age of ancient India lasted from about A.D. 320 to 500. It was the period of the Gupta Empire, when literature, arts, and science flourished. During this period Hinduism became the chief religion of the Indian people.

During the 500 years after the downfall of the Guptas, many small kingdoms fought one another for control. During this time both Arabs and Turks invaded India. They saw the conflict among Indian people as a chance to gain control of India.

In A.D. 711, Arab Muslims conquered Sind, today part of Pakistan. Muslim Turks and Afghans swept into the region in 1206. In 1526 Babur, a Muslim king from Afghanistan, led an army into India. He set up Agra as the Indian capital. Babur also

Babur (on horseback) was a Muslim ruler who founded the Mogul Empire in 1526.

An ancient coin shows Chadragupta II.

formed what would become known as the Mogul Empire.

The Mogul Empire flourished until the early 1700s, when its rulers expanded their rule to the south. The high taxes on Hindus sparked revolts that weakened the Mogul Empire. Britain moved into the region in 1757. The British kept the Moguls on as **puppet rulers**, or rulers without power, for the next 100 years.

REVIEW Who established the Mogul Empire in South Asia?

Mohandas Gandhi
1869–1948
Character Trait: Perseverance

By 1920 Mohandas Gandhi was greatly admired among the people of India. They called him *Mahatma*, which among Hindus means "Great Soul." Gandhi played a role in making the Indian National Congress party stronger. When Indians began to push for independence, he used his leadership to avoid violence. Instead, he called for the Indian people to stop buying British goods and services. As a result, the British arrested Gandhi along with other leaders in the independence movement.

While Gandhi was in prison, the Indian National Congress split into two groups. The strong bond that had grown between the Hindus and Muslims when they protested together had broken apart. Upon his release, Gandhi continued working for independence as well as trying to resolve problems between Hindus and Muslims.

MULTIMEDIA BIOGRAPHIES
Visit The Learning Site at
www.harcourtschool.com/biographies
to learn about other famous people.

GO ONLINE

Indians Work for Independence

In 1498 Vasco da Gama (VAS•koh dah GAH•muh), a Portuguese explorer, landed on Indian shores. He and other Western Europeans had been looking for a route to the trading ports of Asia. Wanting to avoid the long, difficult overland route used by Italian merchants, the Portuguese were very excited by da Gama's success.

Soon European businesses began to compete for control of the trade in such Asian goods as spices and pearls. During the 1600s the British East India Company set up trading posts in India at Chennai (Madras), Mumbai (Bombay), and Kolkata (Calcutta). However, as the British moved inland, both the French and local Indian rulers blocked them. Several wars resulted.

By the late 1700s the British had become the chief colonial power in India. British troops defeated local armies and slowly gained control over the whole subcontinent. About one-third of the area was left in the control of 562 "native states." These tiny kingdoms relied on the British for defense, postal service, railroads, and other needs. Puppet rulers who followed British directions led these native states.

Indian nationalism grew during British rule. In 1919 Mohandas Gandhi became the leader of the Indian National Congress political party. Gandhi organized many nonviolent protests against British rule. For example, he urged Indians to buy only Indian products or make their own clothing and other goods. Gandhi encouraged Indians to avoid trading with the British.

Slowly, the British began to give Indians greater representation in the legislature and increased the power of Indian local governments. They finally agreed to end their rule in 1947. Religious differences between Hindus and Muslims in the former colony

Victoria Terminus is a railroad station in Mumbai, India. The station was named to honor Queen Victoria of Britain when it was built in the 1800s.

LOCATE IT

Mumbai (Bombay)

INDIA

led the British to form two countries when they granted independence—Hindu India and Muslim Pakistan.

A poor economy, a great population increase, ethnic and regional conflicts, and religious differences have continued to trouble the Indian government in the years after winning independence. The government has tried to slow population growth, expand industry and trade, and increase food production. One of the government's most important goals is to provide an education to more of its citizens.

REVIEW Where did the British East India Company set up trading posts?

LESSON 2 REVIEW

Summary Time Line

| 3000 B.C. | 2000 B.C. | 1000 B.C. | B.C./A.D. | A.D. 1000 | A.D. 2000 |

2500s B.C. First cities built in the Indus Valley

1700s B.C. Aryans invade South Asia

A.D. 320 Hinduism becomes the dominant religion in India

A.D. 1757 Britain gains control of much of South Asia

A.D. 1947 India gains independence

① **MAIN IDEA** How did early settlers influence Indian civilization?

② **WHY IT MATTERS** Why did India and Pakistan become separate countries?

③ **VOCABULARY** Use the term **puppet ruler** to describe how the British controlled South Asia.

④ **TIME LINE** When did India gain independence?

⑤ **READING SKILL—Identify Fact and Opinion** Write a fact about the formation of India and Pakistan as separate countries. Give your opinion about what the British should have done.

⑥ **GEOGRAPHY** Why did South Asia interest European traders of the 1600s?

⑦ **CRITICAL THINKING—Analyze** Why do you think the Gupta Empire period is called a golden age in India's history?

PERFORMANCE—Make an Outline First, locate primary and secondary sources about the history of India at your library and on the Internet. Then, make an outline of India's history that includes information about important people and events. Illustrate your outline with pictures and drawings.

MAIN IDEA
Read to find out about religious and cultural differences among the people of South Asia.

WHY IT MATTERS
The cultures and religions of all of South Asia's people contribute to the subcontinent's uniqueness.

VOCABULARY
reincarnation
nirvana
Vedas
tandoor
purdah

People and Culture

Winston Churchill once said, "India . . . is no more a single country than the equator." He was speaking of the rich and varied cultures, religions, languages, and customs of India. That same richness and diversity can be found in all of South Asia.

Religions and Languages

Many religions of the modern world started in Asia. Today South Asia is home to Hindus, Muslims, Christians, Buddhists, Sikhs, and Jainists. Religion often determines peoples' names, their food and clothing, their ideas on the roles of women and men, and many other behaviors. In the case of India and Pakistan, religion has even influenced their nationalities. They are separate countries today because of their people's religious differences.

Hinduism began more than 4,000 years ago. Most Hindus believe in the existence of many gods. They also believe in a cycle of birth, death, and **reincarnation**, or rebirth. They believe that a person who lives a moral life may be reborn as a more advanced being. Eventually that person is thought to reach the highest stage, called nirvana. **Nirvana** is an enlightened state in which the cycle of death and rebirth ceases.

Temples such as this Jain temple (left) and Hindu temple (right) are found throughout South Asia.

Hindus also believe in the wisdom contained in the **Vedas**, a collection of writings about the history of their faith. Today almost 1 billion Hindus live in India and Nepal.

Sikhism came into being around 1500. It started as a blend of Hindu and Muslim beliefs. Many Hindus who became Sikhs wanted a religion that did not have Hinduism's caste system. Jainism arose about the same time as Buddhism. Unlike believers of many other religions, followers of Jainism believe in no god or supreme being. They follow the ways of one of their early leaders, who taught the value of kindness and charity.

Many people at the bottom of the Hindu caste system have chosen to become Christians. However, Christians in India and some other parts of South Asia suffer discrimination and sometimes violence.

Many South Asians speak the traditional languages of their people. There are far more South Asian languages than there are South Asian countries. India and Pakistan alone have almost 20 official languages!

In Pakistan, Punjabis (puhn•JAH•beez) are the largest ethnic group. Punjabi is the name of the most widely spoken language. Urdu (UR•doo) is the language of a smaller number of Pakistanis. People in government and business usually learn Punjabi as well. Urdu and English are the official languages of Pakistan.

In India there are 16 major languages. All are considered national languages of India, although Hindi, spoken by about 30 percent of all Indians, is an official language. English is also an official language. The English language is used mostly in business and government communications.

REVIEW How many national languages does India have?

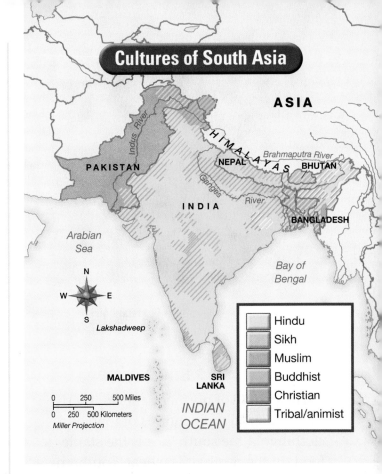

Cultures of South Asia

- Hindu
- Sikh
- Muslim
- Buddhist
- Christian
- Tribal/animist

GEOGRAPHY THEME

Movement In 1947 the British relocated most of India's Muslims into Pakistan.

❓ What became India's major religion?

Languages of South Asia

COUNTRY	LANGUAGE
Bangladesh	Bangla (Bengali), English
Bhutan	Dzongkha
India	Hindi, English, Bengali, Telugu, Marathi, Tamil, Urdu, Gujarati, Malayalam, Kannada, Oriya, Punjabi, Assamese, Kashmiri, Sindhi, Sanskrit
Maldives	Dhivehi, Arabic, Hindi
Nepal	Nepali, Newari, Bhutia
Pakistan	Urdu, English, Punjabi, Sindhi
Sri Lanka	Sinhala, Tamil, English

Analyze Tables More than 1,000 different languages are spoken in South Asia.

❓ What are the major languages of Bangladesh?

Pakistani girl

Sri Lankan man

Tastes and Styles

The people of northern and southern India differ in their choices of food and clothing. In the south, rice is the staple food. In the north, it is wheat. Southerners like spicy foods, while northerners use milder spices. Hindus do not eat beef, and some very strict Hindus eat no meat at all.

Wheat bread is Pakistan's staple food. Chapati (chuh•PAH•tee) is a flat wheat bread baked in a **tandoor** (tahn•DUR), a clay or brick oven. It is eaten at nearly every meal. Breads are eaten with meats and vegetables. Muslims do not eat pork.

In Pakistan the shawar kameez (shuh•VAHR kuh•MEEZ) is the common type of clothing for both men and women. The outfit consists of baggy, pajamalike pants called the *shawar* and a long tunic called the *kameez*. In keeping with the Islamic idea of modesty, women cover their heads with a dupatta (doo•PAH•tuh), a long scarf draped across the chest and hanging down the back on two sides.

It is Islamic custom for women to live in **purdah** (PUHR•duh), or "behind the veil." When they go out, these women cover their faces with a veil called a *chadder* (CHAH•duhr). Some wear a hooded gown called a *burka* (BUHR•kuh), which covers the entire body and allows vision only through a net screen.

Clothing in Nepal is varied and colorful. Women wear blouses and long skirts, while men wear knee-length robes and tight pants. Sri Lankan men often wear western-style clothing, such as a loose shirt or jacket. They wear this above the native sarong, a long piece of cloth wrapped around the body and fastened at the waist. Women in Sri Lanka and

A wedding in Jaipur, India

Indian dancer

Indian musician

other South Asian countries wear a garment similar to a sarong, with a blouse or jacket. Some wear a sari, which is a cloth draped so that one end forms a long skirt and the other a head or shoulder covering.

REVIEW What foods are eaten in South Asia?

Arts and Education

South Asians enjoy old and new art forms. Traditional dance remains popular in India. Performers use movements of their hands to provide meaning for their audience. Musicians such as the sitar player Ravi Shankar have made Indian music known throughout the world.

Each language spoken in South Asia has its own literature. Classics in the ancient Indian language of Sanskrit are among the great achievements in world literature. They include two epic, or hero, poems, the *Ramayana* and the *Mahabharata*. Modern writers are also popular. They include Arundhati Roy, Kazi Islam, and Rabindranath Tagore. Tagore, an Indian poet, won the Nobel Prize for literature in 1913.

Culture in most South Asian countries is influenced by the religions their people practice. This influence can be seen first in the architecture. Among the best examples of Islamic influence is India's Taj Mahal. The Taj Mahal was built as a tomb for Mumtaz Mahal, the wife of the Mogul emperor Shah Jahan, in the 1600s. The Taj Mahal took 22 years and more than 20,000 workers to complete. Sri Lanka is home to many examples of Buddhist architecture. They include beautiful temples and monasteries, many of them decorated with statues and other stone carvings.

Education is an important part of preserving the culture of South Asian countries, as well as of improving their economies. Tiny Sri Lanka actually has one of the highest literacy rates in South Asia. Nearly 90 percent of its citizens can read and write. The people of Sri Lanka value education and provide schooling, including college, for all citizens. Unfortunately, many South Asian governments cannot provide good schools for all of their citizens.

In Pakistan less than half the people can read and write. One problem is that cultural and religious traditions make it difficult for women to get an education. One-fourth or fewer women are literate.

Benazir Bhutto (BEN•uh•zir BOO•toh) was once Pakistan's prime minister. She was the first woman to lead the elected government of a Muslim country. Bhutto went to college in the United States and in England. She did so, in part, because of the education problems in Pakistan, especially those faced by women.

As prime minister, Benazir Bhutto increased funding for universities and helped set up private schools for girls throughout the country. Nawaz Sharif (nah•VAHZ shah•REEF), prime minister until 1999, ordered plans for 100,000 new schools that would provide education for girls and women in Pakistan. A new government ended the plan, however.

Abida Farheen (AH•bee•duh far•HEEN), who leads one of Pakistan's regional education offices, states,

66 We think women's education is equally important. When women become literate, they can help build a better nation. 99

REVIEW What government leader became the first woman to lead a Muslim country?

Former Pakistani Prime Minister Benazir Bhutto delivers a speech in Islamabad, Pakistan, urging the Indian and Pakistani governments to settle their disputes.

LESSON 3
REVIEW

1 MAIN IDEA What effect did religious differences have on the nationalities of some South Asians?

2 WHY IT MATTERS How do culture and religion make South Asia unique?

3 VOCABULARY Use the words **reincarnation** and **nirvana** to describe two important Hindu beliefs.

4 READING SKILL—Fact and Opinion Which of the following sentences is a fact, and which is an opinion? Explain.

"The Taj Mahal is a beautiful example of architecture in India."

"It took the work of more than 20,000 laborers more than 20 years to build the Taj Mahal."

5 HISTORY What two religions influenced the beliefs of Sikhs?

6 CRITICAL THINKING—Analyze Why would some Indian people choose to practice religions other than Hinduism?

 PERFORMANCE—Make a Menu Imagine that you are going to invite some people from India and Pakistan to share a meal with your class. On a piece of paper, list the foods you would serve. What dishes would you include? Be sure to offer foods that people of the different cultural and religious backgrounds found in India and Pakistan can eat.

Predict a Likely Outcome

Aurangzeb

WHY IT MATTERS

Have you ever heard people say that "history repeats itself"? It means that events in history often follow patterns. For example, in your study of history, you have probably noticed that empires tend to flourish for a while and then eventually fall. Sometimes, the same kinds of events lead other empires to fall.

You can use what you have already learned about history to make predictions about other events you may read about. When you make a prediction, you are combining what you already know with new information to predict a probable, or likely, outcome.

WHAT YOU NEED TO KNOW

A Mogul ruler named Aurangzeb reigned from 1658 to 1707. He was a very strict Muslim and attempted to force Hindus to convert to Islam. Aurangzeb taxed Hindus heavily, while Muslims paid few taxes. He also ordered that Hindu schools and

Vase from India in the seventeenth century

temples be destroyed. During Aurangzeb's rule, the only way for a Hindu to obtain a government job was to convert to Islam.

To make a prediction, follow these steps.

Step 1 Review new information you have learned.

Step 2 Think about what you already know.

Step 3 Look for patterns that may help you predict an outcome.

Step 4 Make a prediction.

PRACTICE THE SKILL

Answer the following questions.

1 What have you read about the Mogul Empire? What do you already know about the rise and fall of empires?

2 What do you think happened to the Mogul Empire after Aurangzeb's death?

APPLY WHAT YOU LEARNED

Lesson 2 ends with a summary of the problems India faced after it won independence in 1947. Use the steps listed above to predict how leaders in independent India might deal with such problems. As you read the next lesson, use the new information you learn to check or revise your prediction.

4

South Asia Today

MAIN IDEA
Read to find out how South Asians faced new problems after their countries gained independence.

WHY IT MATTERS
The influence of colonization can last long after a country gains independence.

VOCABULARY
diplomat
green revolution
urban center

Britain's long rule in India had an effect on the kind of democracy India would become. In 1858 the British government took control of India. Before that the British East India Company controlled the country. From 1858 until 1947 India was ruled by a British governor-general. The governor-general also acted as a **diplomat**, or adviser, in Britain's relations with the hundreds of separate Indian states. Since India spent nearly 100 years under British rule, the British model of democracy was the one its leaders knew best.

Government in South Asia

India gained full independence from Britain in August 1947. The sweet victory of independence, however, was made bitter by Britain's decision to divide the subcontinent into two countries along religious lines—Hindu India and Muslim Pakistan. It was the only way, the British said, to end the violence between Hindus and Muslims.

Pakistan was created out of northeastern and northwestern India. The two sections of the new nation—East Pakistan and West Pakistan—were more than 1,000 miles (1,600 km) apart.

The partition, or division, of India led to the largest migration of people in history. More than 17 million Hindus and Muslims became refugees as they fled across the borders to escape conflicts among themselves. Armed conflict also broke out over rival claims in the area of Jammu and Kashmir in northern India. Conflict

Indian voters are shown how to use an electronic voting machine.

over control of the present-day Indian territory of Kashmir continues today.

The government of the new nation of India was set up as a parliamentary democracy, similar to governments in Britain, Germany, and other western nations. India's first prime minister was Jawaharlal Nehru (juh•WAH•huhr•lahl NER•oo), a nationalist leader and head of the Congress party. It was the same party once led by Mohandas Gandhi. Gandhi was assassinated in 1948 by a Hindu angry about Gandhi's tolerance toward Muslims.

In 1949 a constitution similar to the United States Constitution was approved, making India a federal republic. Like citizens in the United States, Russia, and other republics, citizens in India elect officials who make the laws and run the government. Under India's federal structure, India's "native states" were reorganized based on language. Today India has 25 states and 7 territories.

In 1956 Pakistan, too, became a republic. Major General Iskander Mirza became the first president. Mirza faced problems in uniting his nation. The great distance between East Pakistan and West Pakistan, as well as the lack of common cultural and social traditions, other than religion, separated the two regions. The people in East Pakistan also did not like it that West Pakistan became the country's political and economic center. This rivalry between East Pakistan and West Pakistan eventually led to civil war and division. In 1971 East Pakistan became a democratic republic known as Bangladesh.

Military rule has prevailed in Pakistan since its independence. Pakistan's first free elections under civilian rule did not take place until 1977. In 1999 military rule returned.

REVIEW Which country on the subcontinent is not a democracy?

In July 2001 leaders from India and Pakistan met to discuss disputes between their two countries, including their positions on Kashmir, which both countries claim. The meeting ended without an agreement.

PERVEZ MUSHARRAF, President of Pakistan

66The hope I have is, now I feel nobody can stop this process from moving forward. 99

POINTS OF VIEW
Kashmir

ATAL BEHARI VAJPAYEE, Prime Minister of India

66We want to continue talking and continue the process of peace with Pakistan. But we will not spare in effort in defeating terrorism. Pakistan could not take Kashmir through wars. There should be no illusion that it could get it through supporting terrorism . . . 99

NAVEED BASHIR, student

66Unfortunately the failure of talks means more violence, death, and destruction. 99

Analyze the Viewpoints

1 What is each person's point of view?
2 **Make It Relevant** Find out more about Kashmir. Write a paragraph about the disputes.

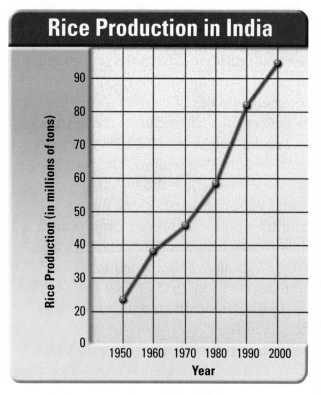

Rice Production in India

Rice Production (in millions of tons) vs **Year**

90
80
70
60
50
40
30
20
0

1950 1960 1970 1980 1990 2000

Analyze Graphs This graph shows rice production in India from 1950 to 2000.

❖ What trend in rice production does the graph indicate?

Village Life

South Asia is mainly a land of villages. More than 500,000 villages dot the countryside, and most of the population lives in them. Most of these villages have fewer than 1,000 people. They live in groups of houses surrounded by farms and grazing areas. Most villages are connected to one another by dirt paths that become impossible to walk on during the rainy season. Most of the houses are built of mud. Their roofs

are covered with the leaves of palms and other trees.

Although more than half of India's people are farmers, in the past large amounts of food had to be brought to India to feed the many hungry people. To solve this problem, the Indian government introduced a long-range program known as the **green revolution** to increase the country's food supply. Indian farmers developed new kinds of rice and wheat seeds that could double or even triple grain output. However, these seeds required more careful irrigation, insect control, and fertilization than traditional types of seeds do. So, the government began to teach farmers throughout India how to grow the new seeds. As a result of the green revolution, India's production of food, especially grain, began to increase. During the late 1960s and early 1970s, for the first time in decades, food production grew more rapidly than the population.

In Nepal's villages farmers grow rice, wheat, millet, maize, sugarcane, and jute, which is used to make burlap and string. Sheep and goats graze on the lower hillsides. At higher altitudes people raise cattle and yaks, a kind of ox. Tourism is

Every village has a few wells that supply water for drinking, cooking, and bathing.

Mumbai is the movie capital of South Asia. It is often called "Bollywood."

Every year the Indian film industry makes more than 1,000 movies and sells about 5 billion tickets.

also on the rise in Nepal. Money from tourism has helped the government provide schools, electricity, industry, roads, and many other services that its citizens need.

Almost half of all Pakistani workers are farmers. Nearly a fourth work in mining, manufacturing, and construction. Seven out of ten Pakistanis live in the lowlands near the Indus River and its tributaries. The plentiful water there helps farming and industry flourish.

Wealthy Pakistani landowners, industrialists, and others may live in large, comfortable houses filled with modern conveniences. Middle-income families often live in apartments or small homes. In the villages, most houses are built of mud or unbaked bricks and have flat roofs. Housing conditions in Pakistan have slowly improved over the years.

REVIEW What is the major economic activity of South Asia?

City Life

About 20 percent of India's people live in towns or cities. India's cities have always played an important part in the nation's history. As early as 2000 B.C., India had two large **urban centers**, or cities—Mohenjo-Daro and Harappa. Each of these cities had more than 40,000 residents.

Today India's major cities—Kolkata (Calcutta), Mumbai (Bombay), Delhi, and Chennai (Madras)—have 2 million or more residents. Many of Kolkata's 10 million people live in poor conditions. Some are unable to find work and do not have money for food. Others suffer from disease and have no medical care. Mother Teresa, a Roman Catholic nun, won the Nobel Peace Prize in 1979 for her work with the poor and sick in Kolkata.

The cities are centers of India's cultural life. Mumbai, Chennai, and Kolkata have hotels, restaurants, museums, theaters, and universities.

A colorful bus in Karachi, Pakistan's largest city

India has one of the biggest movie industries in the world. Studios in Mumbai, Kolkata, Chennai, and elsewhere produce more than 1,000 films a year. Movies are popular with the people living in India's cities, so there is always a great demand for new films.

Pakistan's newest and most modern city is Islamabad, the capital. Its name means "place of Islam." Faisal Masjid, the world's largest mosque, is located in Islamabad.

Pakistan's largest city is Karachi. It dates to the early 1700s, when a fort was built there to protect the sea trade that was attracted by its excellent harbor. The harbor makes Karachi one of the only outlets to the sea for Pakistan and for neighboring Afghanistan. Karachi has grown into a large industrial center, producing textiles and many consumer goods.

In Bangladesh the cities of Chittagong, Dhaka, and Khulna are becoming crowded with people looking for work and a better way of life. Kathmandu is Nepal's capital and largest city. In the old part of the city, streets are lined with ancient temples and monuments. Each year thousands of visitors travel through Kathmandu. Many of them come to Nepal to hike and climb in the Himalayas. The Sherpas of Nepal are skilled climbers and often work as their guides.

REVIEW What are some of South Asia's largest cities?

Worshipers at the Buddhist Boudhanath Stupa in Kathmandu, Nepal's capital

LOCATE IT

Kathmandu

NEPAL

Island Life

The climate of South Asia's island countries is affected by monsoons, the shifting winds that bring heavy rainfall. For example, the weather in the Maldives is generally warm and humid. Coconut palms and breadfruit trees grow everywhere. The waters are filled with fish, and there are beautiful tortoises.

Many of the people of the Maldives are skilled sailors, and fishing employs 80 percent of the workers. It also supplies about 75 percent of the nation's exports. Clothing made in the Maldives also accounts for a large part of the nation's exports. People in countries throughout the world buy these products.

Tourists, drawn by the warm weather and beautiful scenery, are also good for the economy. Money from tourism and exports such as clothing helps the people of the Maldives purchase food, consumer goods, and petroleum products.

Tourism and farming are important to the economy of Sri Lanka. Farmers grow coconuts, rubber trees, rice, and tea. The

Workers harvest tea leaves on a plantation near Nuwara Eliya, Sri Lanka.

island is known for gemstones, such as sapphires, rubies, topazes, amethysts, and garnets. These gems, found in Ratnapura, the "City of Gems," are made into beautiful jewelry. Visitors to Sri Lanka find tropical beaches, varied wildlife, and Buddhist temples and monuments. The beauty of this land has inspired its name, which means "shining land."

REVIEW How do monsoons affect the climate of the Maldives?

LESSON 4 REVIEW

1. **MAIN IDEA** Why did India form a government like Britain's after gaining independence?

2. **WHY IT MATTERS** How have the governments of South Asia worked to solve some of the problems faced by people there today?

3. **VOCABULARY** Use the word **diplomat** to describe the duties of Britain's governor-general in colonial India.

4. **READING SKILLS—Identify Fact and Opinion** State your opinion: Would you rather live in a city in South Asia or in one of its villages? What facts influence your opinion?

5. **GEOGRAPHY** Why is Karachi an important city for Pakistan and Afghanistan?

6. **HISTORY** Who won the Nobel Peace Prize in 1979 for helping India's sick and poor?

7. **CRITICAL THINKING—Analyze** How does India's government function compared to the governments of the United States and Russia?

PERFORMANCE—Design a Brochure Imagine you are working on a committee in the Maldives to increase tourism. On a sheet of construction paper make a tourist brochure for the Maldives. Describe some of the things about the country that would make people want to visit.

·SKILLS·

CHART AND GRAPH

Read a Population Pyramid

VOCABULARY

population pyramid

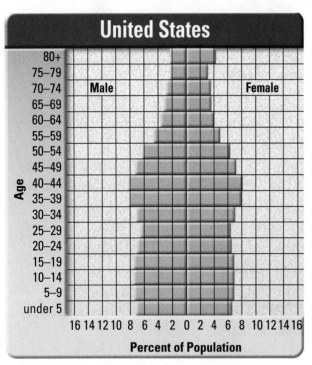

United States

Age

80+	
75–79	
70–74	Male
65–69	
60–64	
55–59	
50–54	
45–49	
40–44	
35–39	
30–34	
25–29	
20–24	
15–19	
10–14	
5–9	
under 5	

Female

16 14 12 10 8 6 4 2 0 2 4 6 8 10 12 14 16

Percent of Population

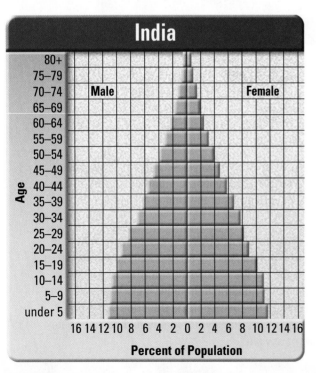

India

Age

80+	
75–79	
70–74	Male
65–69	
60–64	
55–59	
50–54	
45–49	
40–44	
35–39	
30–34	
25–29	
20–24	
15–19	
10–14	
5–9	
under 5	

Female

16 14 12 10 8 6 4 2 0 2 4 6 8 10 12 14 16

Percent of Population

▶ WHY IT MATTERS

Did you know that the population of India is more than one billion people? Pakistan's population is about 141 million, and Sri Lanka's people number around 19 million. If you wanted to find out how each country's population is divided by age and by gender (male and female), you could use a special graph called a **population pyramid**.

A population pyramid's shape depends on the country's birth rate (the number of births each year for every 1,000 people) and the death rate (the number of deaths each year for every 1,000 people). The shape of the pyramid also depends on the amount of immigration to and from the country. Knowing how to read a country's population pyramid can provide you with a lot of information about that country.

▶ WHAT YOU NEED TO KNOW

The population pyramids on these pages show the populations of the United States, India, Pakistan, and Sri Lanka by age groups. The bars that make up each pyramid show the percentage of males and of females in each age group.

The shape of the United States' pyramid shows that its population is growing very slowly. The United States has a high percentage of people over the age of 50 (about 55 percent), while India, Sri Lanka, and Pakistan have more young people. The bars of these pyramids show that the populations of India, Pakistan, and Sri Lanka are very young.

▶ PRACTICE THE SKILL

Look at each population pyramid, and notice the differences. Use the information to answer these questions.

1 What percentage of the population of the United States is in your age group? Are there more males or more females in this group?

2 Compare this percentage to those of the other countries. Are the percentages of people in your age group higher or lower in India, Pakistan, and Sri Lanka?

3 Which of the four countries has the largest percentage of people between 15 and 19 years old?

▶ APPLY WHAT YOU LEARNED

Think about the similarities and differences in these population pyramids. Write some questions of your own about the populations of these four countries. Make an answer key, and exchange questions with another classmate.

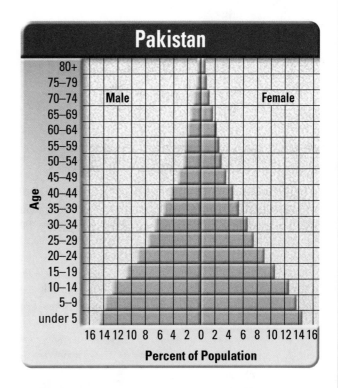

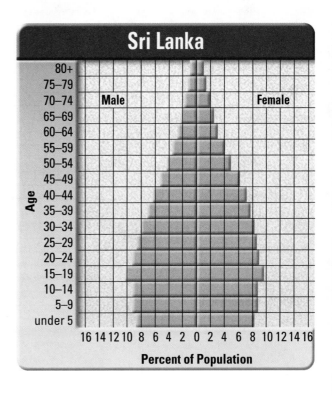

CHART AND GRAPH SKILLS

15 Review and Test Preparation

2500s B.C.
First cities built in
the Indus Valley

1700s B.C.
Decline of the
Indus Valley
civilization

USE YOUR READING SKILLS

Complete this graphic organizer to show that you understand
how to identify facts and opinions about South Asia. A copy
of this graphic organizer appears on page 145 of the Activity
Book.

Write Facts and Opinions About South Asia

TOPIC	FACT	OPINION
The Ganges River		
Sri Lanka		
Mohandas Gandhi		
Religions in South Asia		
India's Cities		
Clothing in South Asia		

THINK & WRITE

Write a Description   Encyclopedias
contain facts and descriptions about many
subjects. Write a description of the Ganges
River that might appear in an encyclopedia.
Draw an illustration to go with your description.

Write an Opinion   The people of India
speak many languages. Is it better for a
country to have many languages or just one?
Write a paragraph about your opinion. In your
paragraph list reasons for your opinion.

A.D. 320
Gupta Empire begins and Hinduism becomes the dominant religion in India

A.D. 711
Muslim Arabs invade Pakistan

A.D. 1757
Britain gains control of much of South Asia

A.D. 1947
India gains independence and splits into two states—India and Pakistan

USE THE TIME LINE

Use the chapter summary time line to answer these questions.

1 In about what year did the Indus Valley civilization decline?

2 How much time passed between Britain's taking control of much of South Asia and India's independence from Britain?

USE VOCABULARY

Fill in each blank with the correct vocabulary word.

> atoll (p. 528)
>
> caste system (p. 531)
>
> stupa (p. 533)
>
> Vedas (p. 537)

3 The collection of writings about the history of Hinduism is the _____.

4 An _____ forms where coral grows around a volcano.

5 A curved mound of brick that holds statues of Buddha is called a _____.

6 A _____ divides people in a society into different social classes.

RECALL FACTS

Answer these questions.

7 In what ways were ancient cities in the Indus Valley advanced?

8 Why does Sri Lanka have one of the highest literacy rates in South Asia?

Write the letter of the best choice.

9 **TEST PREP** Most people in India live in—
A cities with fewer than 500,000 people.
B cities with more than 500,000 people.
C villages with fewer than 1,000 people.
D villages with more than 1,000 people.

10 **TEST PREP** Eighty percent of the workers in the Maldives are employed in—
F farming.
G fishing.
H manufacturing.
J tourism.

THINK CRITICALLY

11 Sri Lanka used to be called Ceylon. Why might the name of a country change?

12 By unearthing ancient artifacts, archaeologists discover many clues about past civilizations. What artifacts might be found at an archaeological site? What could be discovered about past civilizations from those artifacts?

APPLY SKILLS

Predict a Likely Outcome

13 How might Pakistan and India be different today if the British had not controlled much of South Asia?

Read a Population Pyramid

14 Review the population pyramids on pages 548 and 549. What are the percentages of people over the age of 65 for each country?

THE GREAT WALL OF CHINA

The Great Wall that visitors see today is a result of construction started around 1400. This construction lasted for about 200 years and extended the wall to more than 2,500 miles (4,020 km). The Great Wall stands between 30 feet (9 m) and 35 feet (11 m) high and has 40-foot (12-m) towers. The wall is so thick that two wagons traveling on top of it can pass each other.

LOCATE IT

Great Wall

CHINA

16

East Asia

" China is a long caravan, longer and stronger than the Wall. "

—Genevieve Taggard, from *Turn to the East*, 1938

CHAPTER READING SKILL

Draw Conclusions

To **draw a conclusion**, use evidence from what you read as well as what you already know about the subject.

As you read this chapter, use what you read and what you already know to draw conclusions about places and ideas.

WHAT YOU READ + WHAT YOU KNOW → CONCLUSION

1

MAIN IDEA
Read to find out about the various environments of East Asia.

WHY IT MATTERS
The people of East Asia have adapted to the region's different environments.

VOCABULARY

loess

typhoon

tsunami

FAST FACT

Bactrian camels are found in China's deserts, including the Takla Makan. Even in the world's driest desert, these camels can go for a week without water.

Mountains, Deserts, Rivers, and Seas

Mountains, deserts, rivers, and seas separate East Asia from the rest of the continent. For thousands of years these physical barriers also separated the early people of East Asia from the rest of the world. Within East Asia lie some of the world's tallest mountains, highest plateaus, driest deserts, longest rivers, and most fertile valleys. The region also has destructive storms, earthquakes, and volcanic eruptions. Over time, the people of East Asia have learned to adapt to their challenging environments.

The Lands of China and Mongolia

China covers about 85 percent of East Asia. Slightly larger than the United States, China is the third-largest country in the world after Russia and Canada. Two-thirds of China is made up of mountains or deserts.

To understand the landscape of this huge land, imagine stairs with three steps. Moving across China from west to east, each step would become lower. The top step, the highest, would

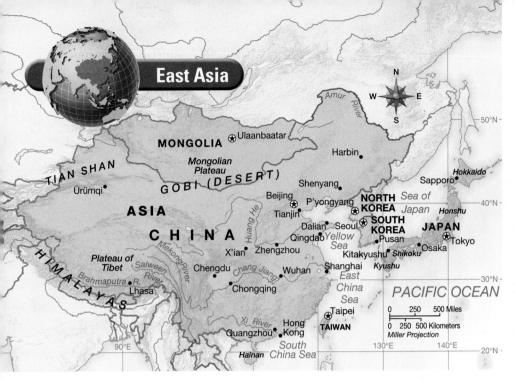

East Asia

GEOGRAPHY THEME

Location The countries of China, Japan, Mongolia, North Korea, South Korea, and Taiwan make up the region of East Asia.

◈ **What is the capital of Mongolia?**

be western China. There are the tall Himalayas, the highest mountain range on Earth.

North of the Himalayas lies the Plateau of Tibet. This cold, dry plateau is the largest and highest plateau in the world. The snow-fed streams of its mountains give rise to the Huang He (HWANG HUH) and Chang Jiang (CHANG JYAHNG)—two of the world's longest rivers. The western side of the Plateau of Tibet is called the Roof of the World because elevations there average more than 16,000 feet (4,877 m).

Even farther north are more tall mountains and deserts. The Takla Makan (tah•kluh muh•KAHN), one of the world's largest and driest deserts, stretches across this area. Few people live in this climate of little rainfall, hot summers, and very cold winters.

The middle step, or central China, is made of more mountains but at lower elevations. Unlike the high peaks of western China, these mountains have elevations between 3,000 and 6,000 feet (914 and 1,829 m). More people live here than live in western China.

Flowing down to the lower elevations, the Huang He and Chang Jiang cross central China. As the Huang He crosses central China's northern plateau, it picks up a yellow, fertile soil known as **loess** (LES). The loess colors the river yellow. For that reason, the river is called the Huang He, or "Yellow River." A third major river of China, the Xi (SHEE), flows in the south.

CHINA

Jinghong

The bottom step, or eastern China, has China's lowest elevations. Eastern China's hills and plains are less than 1,500 feet (457 m) high. In the east, China's border is a long coastline. The country's major rivers pass through eastern China on their way to the Pacific Ocean.

Both the Huang He and Chang Jiang have carved valleys that open to large fertile plains. China's earliest agricultural settlements spread from the Huang He valley, not far from where the Huang He flows into the Yellow Sea. The valley's soils are fertile from the loess deposited there. Together, the Huang He and Chang Jiang valleys make up China's most important agricultural area. Crops such as rice, wheat, and corn grow well in their rich soils.

Crops are shipped by river to the major trading centers of Shanghai (shang•HY) and Guangzhou (GWAHNG•joh). Shanghai lies near the mouth of the Chang Jiang, where it empties into the East China Sea. Guangzhou is to the south on the South China Sea at the mouth of the Xi.

As do people in much of East Asia, most people of China live in the fertile valleys and coastal plains of the lower elevations. These lowlands have the country's best farmland, and the weather is milder than in the mountains. Many people also live in coastal cities, which are near fertile farmlands. The seas and rivers that flow to these cities provide the people with good transportation.

Mongolia is China's neighbor to the north. It is a landlocked country. Russia lies to the north of Mongolia and China to the east, west, and south. A wide, high plateau called the Mongolian Plateau

A Chinese woman carries water buckets along a flooded rice field.

makes up much of this northern country. Mongolia's landscape is like that of the northern part of central China. The Gobi extends from northern China into southern and eastern Mongolia. Dry, cold winds blow across much of Mongolia. Nomads use the region's grasslands for herding cattle, sheep, goats, and horses.

REVIEW What kind of landforms are found in western China?

Most of the lowland of the mountainous Korea Peninsula is along the coastline.

The Korea Peninsula

South of northeastern China is the mountainous Korea Peninsula. The country of North Korea takes up the northern half, and the country of South Korea takes up the southern half. Rugged mountains form the border between China and North Korea. Mountains run through the peninsula, too.

Rivers on the Korea Peninsula begin high in the mountains. They flow either west to the Yellow Sea or south to the Korea Strait. Rivers flowing to the Yellow Sea bring fertile soil to the wide river valleys and coastal plains of the western lowlands. Lowlands to the south and east of the mountains are narrower.

Only about 20 percent of North and South Korea's land is arable, or usable for farming. In the river valleys of North Korea, farmers grow corn, potatoes, and

wheat. Farmers in South Korea plant fields on hillside terraces. Mild summers in the south make it a good area for growing rice, barley, and onions.

REVIEW What kind of landform separates China and the Korea Peninsula?

The Islands of Japan and Taiwan

Japan is an archipelago made up of four main islands and about 6,000 smaller islands. Mountains running from north to south divide the four main islands of Hokkaido (hoh•KY•doh) in the north, Honshu (HAHN•shoo) in the middle, and Shikoku (shih•KOH•koo) and Kyushu (kee•OO•shoo) in the south.

The Japanese islands are actually the peaks of a long underwater mountain range. The bottom of the mountain range lies deep in the Pacific Ocean.

The islands of Japan, such as Miyaka-Jima (right), are the tops of mountains rising from the ocean floor.

Japan lies along the Ring of Fire, the circle of volcanoes around the Pacific Ocean. Japan has more than 200 major volcanoes. About 85 of these volcanoes are still active. Mount Fuji, in the southern part of central Honshu, is Japan's tallest mountain at 12,388 feet (3,776 m). Mount Fuji last erupted in 1707.

Hokkaido is one of Japan's coldest areas. Its long, snowy winters and beautiful, cool summers attract many tourists, and more than 5 million people live there. In contrast, Kyushu lies in the warm subtropics. Kyushu has short, mild winters and hot, humid summers.

Winds affect the climate of Japan. Winter winds from Asia pick up moisture as they pass over the warm waters of the Sea of Japan. This brings heavy snowfalls to the western side of the mountains, while the eastern side tends to be dry. In the summer, winds from the Pacific Ocean bring warm, humid air and rain to Japan's eastern side.

One hundred miles southwest of Japan is the island of Taiwan. The mountainous eastern half of Taiwan is covered with dense forests. The western part of the island is a broad coastal plain suitable for farming. Rice, vegetables, and fruits grow well in Taiwan's warm climate.

REVIEW Which of the four main islands is one of Japan's coldest areas?

An earthquake on the ocean floor off the coast of Japan caused a tidal wave that destroyed much of this port community.

Volcanoes, Earthquakes, and Storms

The Pacific Ocean provides the people of East Asia with important resources for fishing, trade, and transportation. The ocean currents also bring dangerous winds and much rain to the region's eastern coasts. Only landlocked Mongolia is not affected.

Summer monsoons bring heavy rains to the coastal areas of Asia. During the winter months, monsoon winds blowing off the mainland toward the ocean can cause drought, or lack of rain. **Typhoons**, the

Located on the east coast of Taiwan, Taroko Gorge is famous for its forests, hot springs, and wildlife.

Three Gorges Dam

Once built, the dam, which will be 1.2 miles (1.9 km) wide, will hold back the waters of the Chang Jiang. People are concerned about the effects of the dam. The 370-mile (595-km) lake created by the dam will force people to move. The lake will also cover the natural habitats of many native animals. However, others believe the dam will have a positive effect on China. It will control flooding of the Chang Jiang and provide China with much-needed electricity.

western Pacific name for hurricanes, also bring strong, damaging winds and heavy rains.

The location of East Asia on the Ring of Fire presents other challenges to the people who live there. Volcanic eruptions and earthquakes threaten life and destroy property. They also can cause **tsunamis** (soo•NAH•meez), or huge tidal waves, to crash upon the shore. Tsunamis can reach 100 feet (30 m) or higher!

East Asia's rivers are important for trade and transportation. However, the rivers often flood, destroying homes and farmland. The Huang He is sometimes called China's Sorrow because of the destruction its flooding brings. To help control flooding of the Chang Jiang, China began building the Three Gorges Dam. When finished, it will be the largest dam in the world.

REVIEW What dangerous natural disasters can occur in East Asia?

LESSON 1
REVIEW

1 **MAIN IDEA** What are some of the different physical features found in East Asia?

2 **WHY IT MATTERS** How does geography affect where people live in East Asia?

3 **VOCABULARY** Describe how **typhoons** and **tsunamis** affect life in East Asia.

4 **READING SKILL—Draw Conclusions** In general, what is the relationship between elevation and population in East Asia?

5 **ECONOMICS** What crop is well suited to the climate of southeastern China?

6 **CRITICAL THINKING—Evaluate** How can people and countries prepare themselves for hazardous weather conditions?

 PERFORMANCE—Draw a Map Research to find the five cities with the largest populations in China. Draw a map that shows the outline of China. Mark and label the cities on the map. Explain to the class any patterns of the cities' locations.

Long-Lasting Civilizations

MAIN IDEA
Read to find out how Chinese culture spread to other East Asian civilizations.

WHY IT MATTERS
Today parts of Chinese culture are found throughout East Asia.

VOCABULARY

Mandate of Heaven
virtue
standardization
khan
clan
samurai
shogun

| 2000 B.C. | 1000 B.C. | B.C./A.D. | A.D. 1000 | A.D. 2000 |

Physical barriers and great distances separated ancient China from other civilizations. This separation made the Chinese believe they lived in the center of the world, or the Middle Kingdom. As China developed into an advanced civilization, merchants and warriors carried Chinese ideas to other parts of East Asia. Civilizations in Tibet, Mongolia, Korea, and Japan adopted some parts of Chinese life. Later, travelers and merchants from Europe, hearing about a rich land to the east, arrived in China. They, too, carried Chinese ideas back to their countries.

Civilization Develops in China

Historians study ancient writings to learn more about early Chinese civilization. Bronze containers hold some of China's oldest written records. Ancient writings have also been found on turtle shells and animal bones. Many of these writings were made more than 4,000 years ago. At that time the Chinese already had

a very organized society. They lived in walled villages and developed irrigation and flood control. They also planted grains such as millet and rice and raised livestock.

China's early villages grew into towns and large city-states. Monarchs ruled the city-states. By 1600 B.C. the Shang family governed much of northeastern China around the Huang He valley. This powerful family formed China's first dynasty, called the Shang dynasty. A dynasty is a series of rulers from the same family. Many different families would rule China after the Shang. In fact, dynasties would rule over China for most of the next 3,500 years.

In 1122 B.C. the Zhou (JOH) family defeated the Shang family and began a new dynasty. The Zhou believed Tian (TYEN), or Heaven, gave a Chinese ruler the right to govern. This right was known as the **Mandate of Heaven**. As long as the ruler had **virtues**, or good qualities, Heaven allowed the ruler to govern. The Chinese believed that war, disease, or a lack of food or rain meant that Heaven had taken away

This bronze-and-jade statue of a child is from the time of the Zhou dynasty.

favor from the ruler. Then power would go to another family.

Halfway through its rule, the Zhou dynasty began to face problems. The Zhou family had allowed other rulers to govern new Zhou states outside the area directly ruled by its dynasty. Over time, these rulers fought for control of all of China. This period of war is known as the Warring States period.

Two important Chinese philosophers, or thinkers, lived during the Zhou dynasty. Confucius (kuhn•FYOO•shuhs) taught the importance of good behavior in society. The ideas of Lao-tzu (LOWD•zuh) said that a person should live a simple life in harmony with nature. The teachings of both Confucius and Lao-tzu guided Chinese life for more than 2,000 years.

REVIEW What was the Mandate of Heaven?

A CLOSER LOOK
Ancient Chinese City

This illustration shows how most Chinese cities might have looked during the Shang and Zhou dynasties.

❶ A wall and gate protected the city from invaders.

❷ Rulers, priests, and other wealthy citizens lived inside the city walls.

❸ Peasants and farm workers lived outside the city walls.

❓ Where do you think the peasants went during times of invasion or other danger?

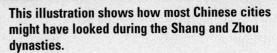

Empires Rise and Fall

In 221 B.C. the Qin (CHIN) dynasty took control of China from the Zhou dynasty and the rulers of the warring states. Even though the Qin dynasty was short-lived, its results were long-lasting. In fact, the name China comes from the word *Qin*. More importantly, the Qin family was the first dynasty to unite China as an empire under a strong central government. This made the Qin founder, Shi Huangdi (SHIR HWAHNG•DEE), China's first emperor, or ruler of an empire.

Shi Huangdi called for **standardization**, or making all things of a certain type alike. Under this system his government standardized coins, weights, and writing. This helped make trade and communication easier all over China.

Shi Huangdi also watched over the building of China's Great Wall. The wall was built along China's northern border to protect the Qin Empire from the Mongols. These fierce warriors from the north rode horses and used bows and arrows.

The Qin dynasty survived attacks from outsiders but not rebellions within the empire. In 202 B.C. the Han dynasty took over control of the weakened empire.

During 400 years of Han rule, the empire grew and culture flourished. The people of China set up universities, advanced the study of mathematics, and developed compasses. Arts and literature grew, too. Travelers and traders, as well as military conquerors and diplomats, spread Chinese culture throughout East Asia. Korea and Japan looked to China for ideas about writing, arts, philosophy, agriculture, science, and government. Trade routes linked China to the Roman Empire in Europe.

The people of China were proud of their empire under Han rule. They even began calling themselves Hans, as they do today. Power struggles in the empire, however, brought Han rule to an end. Over the next 1,000 years, the Chinese empire rose and fell, but Chinese culture continued to advance.

REVIEW Who was the first emperor of China?

Chinese Ideas Spread

In the early 1200s one **khan**, or ruler of the Mongols, known as Genghis Khan (JENG•guhs KAHN), began to build a huge empire. By the late 1200s his grandson, Kublai Khan (KOO•bluh KAHN), had expanded the Mongol Empire from

East Asia to Eastern Europe. The Mongol Empire was the largest empire in history.

Under Mongol rule, news of China's advanced culture continued to spread in Asia and Europe. A traveler from Venice, Italy, named Marco Polo traveled to China. He returned to Europe with Chinese silks, jewels, and porcelain. Polo wrote a book about his travels in China and the riches he had seen there. Soon after, European merchants searched for sea routes to China.

In time, the Ming family drove the Mongols out of China. Under the Ming dynasty China began a period of isolation, or separation from others. To further protect the empire, the Mings added on to the Great Wall. At more than 4,000 miles (more than 6,437 km), much of the Great Wall today is a result of their work.

REVIEW Who took information about China back to Europe?

Conflicts in China

In 1644 the Manchus from northeastern Asia took control of China and began the Qing (CHING) dynasty. Their rule was peaceful until the 1800s. Then European powers began spreading their empires into Asia. Much of China fell under European influence. At the same time, many Chinese wanted an end to rule by dynasties. They wanted a republic.

In 1911 European influence remained, but a revolution ended Qing rule. In 1912, under the new Republic of China, 2,000 years of rule by emperors ended.

Soon the people of China split into two political groups—the Nationalists and the Communists. The Nationalists wanted China to remain a republic based on democracy. The Communists believed that communism was the best governing and economic system for China.

The Great Wall was built over many centuries. Construction required millions of workers and mountains of stone, brick, and dirt.

LOCATE IT

Great Wall

CHINA

During the 1930s Japan seized large parts of China. By World War II, China was in chaos. The Europeans were mostly gone, but the country was now divided among the Japanese, the Nationalists, and the Communists.

REVIEW When did Chinese dynasties end?

Samurai armor was made of bamboo, cloth, and metal.

The Empire of Japan

The early Japanese probably came from the Asian mainland. People lived in **clans**, or groups of related families. The people felt great loyalty to their clans and their clan leaders. In A.D. 645 one family declared itself Japan's imperial family. Its head, Kotoku, became emperor.

Chinese influences in the Japanese empire were strong. In fact, many Chinese ways of life can still be found in Japanese culture today. Chinese influences reached Japan mainly from the Korea Peninsula.

The Japanese adopted Chinese methods of art, music, writing, and architecture. To strengthen their power, Japanese emperors adopted the Chinese idea of a centralized government. The teachings of Confucius and Buddha also reached Japan.

In the early 1100s noble families in Japan gained power and wealth by controlling large private estates. To protect their lands, the nobles hired warriors known as **samurai** (SA•muh•ry). Many samurai also gained power and land.

Late in the 1100s the Minamoto (mee•nah•MOH•toh) family became Japan's strongest family. Their military leader, Minamoto Yoritomo, convinced the emperor to give him the title of **shogun**, or leading general. The shogun and his advisers ruled Japan for the emperor.

Built about 400 years ago, Himeji Castle in Japan provided an important military location for the shogun.

LOCATE IT

JAPAN

Himeji

In 1603, after a long period of wars over land ownership, Japan came under the control of Tokugawa, a shogun. To keep Japan united, Tokugawa stopped most contact with foreigners, including traders. Japan's isolation brought peace. It was not until the 1850s that Japan opened up to the outside world again.

In 1868 Japan entered the Meiji period. The Meiji period marked a return of power to the emperor and a building of Japan's industries. By the late 1800s Japan was Asia's most powerful nation. With this new power Japan expanded its empire into China and Korea and throughout Asia. The building of Japan's empire would eventually lead it into World War II.

REVIEW **Who was the first shogun?**

A Divided Korea

Early in Korea's history Chinese and Mongols invaded its land. The invaders left, but much of Chinese culture remained. Over the centuries Korea adopted many of China's ways of life.

In 1392 General Yi started the Yi dynasty, which lasted until 1910. It ended when Japan made Korea part of its empire. Japan

Korean and Chinese Writing

KOREAN	ENGLISH	CHINESE
봄	Spring	春
여름	Summer	夏
가을	Autumn	秋
겨울	Winter	冬

Analyze Charts Ancient Koreans borrowed Chinese writing and later developed their own alphabet.

❖ How do you think these alphabets are alike and different?

built industries in Korea to aid the Japanese military in World War ll. After the war the Japanese left. Soviet forces took control of northern Korea, and United States forces occupied the south. In 1948 the nations of North Korea and South Korea were created.

REVIEW **What dynasty ruled Korea?**

LESSON 2 REVIEW

Summary Time Line

| 2000 B.C. | 1000 B.C. | B.C./A.D. | A.D. 1000 | A.D. 2000 |

1600 B.C.
Shang family becomes China's first ruling dynasty

A.D. 1392
General Yi establishes the Yi dynasty in Korea

A.D. 1868
Japan begins to build its industries

① **MAIN IDEA** Who helped spread Chinese culture in East Asia?

② **WHY IT MATTERS** Which parts of Chinese culture spread in East Asia?

③ **VOCABULARY** What is the difference between a **khan** and a **shogun**?

④ **TIME LINE** How much time passed between China's first dynasty and Korea's first dynasty?

⑤ **READING SKILL—Draw Conclusions** Why did Chinese culture spread in East Asia?

⑥ **HISTORY** Why was the Meiji period important?

⑦ **CRITICAL THINKING—Synthesize** What were two causes for the fall of empires in East Asia?

 PERFORMANCE—Trace a Route Research the route Marco Polo traveled to reach China. Draw it on a map of East Asia.

Musical Instruments of Korea

Despite influences from China and Japan, the traditional music of Korea is distinctive from the music of other Asian cultures. This is the result of the large number of musical instruments Korean musicians use. More than 45 different kinds of instruments are commonly played. The three instruments shown here are the ones most frequently used.

FROM THE NATIONAL CENTER FOR KOREAN TRADITIONAL PERFORMING ARTS IN SEOUL, KOREA

The *changgo,* or hourglass drum, is heard in almost all forms of Korean music.

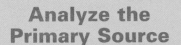
1. Identify each instrument as a wind instrument, a percussion instrument, or a stringed instrument.

2. Do any of the instruments look like ones you have seen before? Explain.

3. What might the variety of musical instruments used by a culture tell you about the importance of music in that culture?

The *wolgum,* or moon guitar, has four strings stretched over 13 frets.

The *saenghwang,* or mouth organ, has 17 slender pipes that produce a soft, dry tone.

ACTIVITY

Collect and Compile
Gather several recordings of music from around the world. Identify ways in which each example is similar to and different from music that you are familiar with.

RESEARCH

Visit The Learning Site at **www.harcourtschool.com/primarysources** to research other musical instruments.

Read a Cartogram

VOCABULARY

cartogram
population cartogram

▶ WHY IT MATTERS

With the exception of China, the countries of East Asia are not very large in size. The population of most of these small countries, however, is greater than that of some countries that are large in size. Population is not spread evenly around the world. Some areas are almost empty, while other areas are very crowded. Factors such as resources, elevation, climate, historical events, and ways of life affect an area's population. One way to show population

is to use a cartogram. A **cartogram** is a diagram that gives information about places by the size shown for each place. A **population cartogram** shows which countries have many people and which have few people.

▶ WHAT YOU NEED TO KNOW

On most maps, the size of each country or continent is based on the size of its land area. On a cartogram, the size of the country or continent is

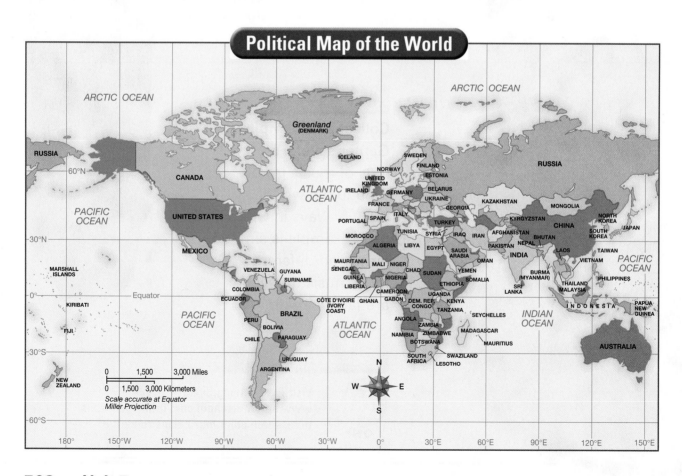

Political Map of the World

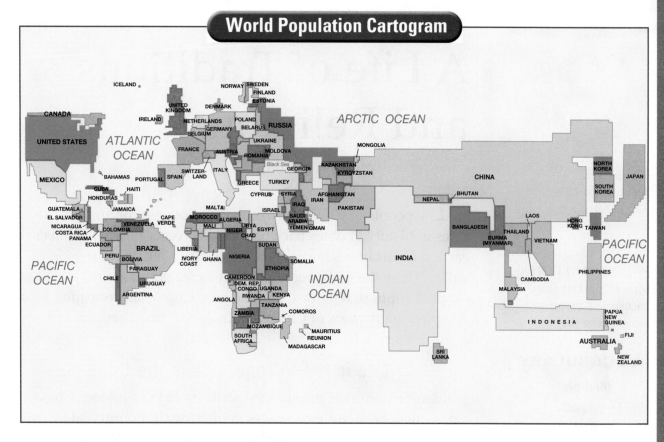

World Population Cartogram

based on a statistic, such as population. A population cartogram shows the size of each country according to the size of its population. A country with a large population would be shown much larger than a country with a small population. When countries are shown in this way, you can quickly compare populations around the world.

The map on page 568 is a political map of the world. It shows each country based on the size of its land area. Compare the sizes of China and Russia. Which is larger? The cartogram on this page is a population cartogram. The size of each country is based on its population. Compare the sizes of China and Russia again. Although China has a smaller land area than Russia, it is shown larger than Russia on the cartogram because it has more people.

▶ PRACTICE THE SKILL

Answer these questions. Use the map and the cartogram to compare land areas and populations.

1 Compare Taiwan and Australia. Which country has the larger land area? Which country has the larger population?

2 Which continent on the cartogram has the largest population? the smallest population? Explain.

▶ APPLY WHAT YOU LEARNED

With a partner, brainstorm other statistics that could be shown on a cartogram. Decide on one kind of statistic, and choose one continent, such as Asia. Use reference sources or the Internet to locate the statistics, and make a cartogram for the countries of your continent.

Next, write questions that can be answered by looking at your cartogram. Exchange cartograms and questions with another pair of students, and answer each other's questions.

A Life of Traditions and Religions

MAIN IDEA
Read to find out about the ways of life, religions, and traditions of East Asian cultures.

WHY IT MATTERS
Many ancient East Asian traditions are an important part of modern life.

VOCABULARY
filial piety
pagoda
haiku

The people of China have one of the longest continuous cultures in history. It dates back nearly 4,000 years to when China's earliest civilizations formed in the country's fertile Huang He valley. There the early people of China created ideas and practices for philosophies, religions, and the arts. East Asians outside China accepted many parts of Chinese culture and tradition.

Life in the Village, Life in the City

Taking a train ride through the fertile valleys of eastern China, a passenger sees endless villages peppering the countryside. While China has many large cities, most of the people of China live outside the city centers. Of China's 1.3 billion people, nearly 75 percent live in rural villages or small towns. Many villages and towns in northeastern China are surrounded by walls, just as they were in ancient times. Rural homes are usually built of bricks or stones with roofs made of straw or tile.

Families of up to three generations often live in the same house. Older members of the household take care of the children while other family members work, mostly on state-owned farmland.

Many families in China live and work together.

Farmers work long hours to raise food for China's huge population. Many farmers plant fields of rice. Rice is eaten regularly at every meal. Tofu, or soybean cheese, is also well liked. Chinese like fish, chicken, duck, pork, and vegetables, too.

A typical rural family in China has a radio and a sewing machine and uses bicycles for transportation. Some may own a television, a washing machine, and a motorcycle.

While most Chinese live in rural areas, many are moving to China's cities for jobs and opportunities. Many city people live in housing much like that seen in the rural areas. Others live in large apartment buildings. The living spaces in the city are much smaller than those of the

countryside. Households in the city, however, are usually made up of only parents and their children.

Unlike the people of China, most people in the rest of East Asia live in urban areas. Cities in Japan, Taiwan, and South Korea are modern, with busy streets, high-rise apartment buildings, and a wide variety of entertainment.

Rural housing in Japan and South Korea is similar. Houses there have tile roofs. In contrast to most rural areas around the world, in North Korea the government provides apartment housing to many of the country's farmers. The rural housing in Mongolia is also different. There, yurts, or domed tents of felt, dot the grasslands.

• GEOGRAPHY •

Seoul, South Korea
Understanding Human Systems

Seoul is South Korea's largest city. South Koreans are attracted to it because of the opportunities there. Businesses and factories provide jobs. Seoul has colleges and universities, good health-care facilities, and a variety of entertainment.

571

Confucius   551 B.C.–479 B.C.

Character Trait: Self-Discipline

Confucius believed in order and respect. He taught that a person must learn self-control in order to develop good relationships with others. One of the most important virtues stressed in his wise sayings is "Do not do to others what you do not want them to do to you." This and other sayings of Confucius can be found in a collection called the *Analects*.

GO ONLINE

MULTIMEDIA BIOGRAPHIES
Visit The Learning Site at www.harcourtschool.com/biographies to learn about other famous people.

The people of most East Asian countries have diets similar to that of the people in China. Fish is very popular in Japan. In Mongolia, which has little fertile farmland, huge grasslands support large herds of sheep, goats, and cattle. These herds supply the people of Mongolia with milk and meat. Tea is East Asia's most popular drink.

REVIEW What do most rural families in China use for transportation?

The Spread of Teachings and Religions

The teachings of both Confucius and Lao-tzu began to form the center of Chinese tradition and thought around the sixth century B.C. Confucianism, or the teachings of Confucius, stressed the importance of education, good manners, and respect for tradition. People should be kind and show respect to others. **Filial piety** (FIH•lee•uhl PY•uh•tee), the respect and honor owed to one's parents, was an important virtue.

To bring peace to a person's life and to society, Daoism (DOW•ih•zuhm), or the teachings of Lao-tzu, called for living a simple life in harmony with nature. People should be kind, humble, and thrifty.

In the first century A.D., merchants and Buddhist monks from India carried Buddhism to China. Buddha's teachings included charity, virtues, and wisdom.

By the A.D. 500s Confucianism, Daoism, and Buddhism had spread from China to Korea and then to Japan. Christianity arrived in East Asia during the 1600s.

Influences from Confucianism and Daoism are still seen in East Asia. A good education remains a goal for many East Asians. The people of East Asia are also known for their politeness and the care given to older people. Not showing too

A Buddhist monk spins a wheel with a prayer written inside the wheel. Every turn of the wheel repeats the prayer.

much pride and saving money are part of the East Asian character, too. Other influences can be seen in the art forms of East Asia.

Buddhism has followers in all the countries of East Asia. While the Chinese government does not encourage religion, Buddhism is strong in its Tibetan region. Buddhist prayer flags and prayer wheels are often seen there.

For religion, the people of Japan look to Buddhism and to their own native religion, Shintoism, based on nature spirits. A Japanese family usually has a Buddhist priest oversee the funeral of a family member. The same family will have a Shinto shrine in the home to pray and offer gifts to the spirits.

REVIEW **What virtue did Confucius emphasize?**

Lasting Traditions

Modern culture has developed in parts of East Asia, but the region remains rich in tradition. The people of East Asia show a respect for tradition in their art, ceremonies, and healing methods. These activities often center on nature, religion, and simple ideas.

Opera performances have a long tradition in China.

Art's ties to the nature of East Asia can be seen in beautiful paintings. Paintings of misty mountains reflect the region's landscape. A Japanese garden is often arranged like a tiny scene of mountains, lakes, waterfalls, and forests.

The influence of Buddhism appears in the architecture of East Asia. The curved, tiled roofs found on Buddhist temples also cover stadiums and other public buildings. **Pagodas**, or towers with many levels, can be found as well.

For hundreds of years artists of East Asia have expressed themselves through calligraphy. Calligraphy was at first copied from China, but Japanese and Korean artists have developed their own styles. Much practice and skill are needed to write in calligraphy.

The performing arts of East Asia are full of tradition. They range from folktales and plays about history to music played with old types of flutes, stringed instruments, and gongs. These traditional performances still attract sellout crowds.

LOCATE IT

JAPAN

Matsue

Japanese gardens reflect Japanese views on nature and religion.

SADAKO
and the Thousand Paper Cranes

Origami (awr•uh•GAH•mee) is the Japanese art of folding paper into shapes. In the story *Sadako and the Thousand Paper Cranes* by Eleanor Coerr, a young girl named Sadako is seriously ill. Her friend Chizuko visits her with an idea to help her get well. Chizuko folds a piece of gold paper over and over into a crane, the Japanese symbol for good health.

Sadako was puzzled. "But how can the paper bird make me well?" "Don't you remember that old story about the crane?" Chizuko asked. "It's supposed to live for a thousand years. If a sick person folds one thousand paper cranes, . . . [it will] make her healthy again." She handed the crane to Sadako. "Here's your first one."

Another respected Japanese art form is the haiku. A **haiku** is a poem arranged in three lines. Each line has a set number of syllables. The first line has five syllables, the middle line has seven, and the last line has five. Poets often use nature as the subject of their haiku.

Ceremonies make up an important part of East Asian traditions—for example, the Japanese tea ceremony. The ceremony is held in complete silence. The host dressed in a kimono, or traditional short-sleeved robe tied with a sash, serves tea. During the ceremony a number of steps must be followed exactly. After the ceremony the host and guests discuss subjects such as art.

Chinese healing methods, traditional ways of practicing medicine, are based on nature. For example, the use of herbs is common in Chinese medicine. While herbs have long been used in East Asia, only recently have they been used by western countries.

REVIEW What are three ways that East Asians show a respect for tradition?

LESSON 3
REVIEW

1 MAIN IDEA Which teachings and religions influenced most of the cultures of East Asia?

2 WHY IT MATTERS How do East Asian teachings and religions affect the ideas and behaviors of the people?

3 VOCABULARY How are **filial piety** and Confucianism related?

4 READING SKILL—Draw Conclusions How might Confucianism have benefited the large population of China?

5 CULTURE Why are many rural Chinese moving to China's cities?

6 CULTURE Why is the diet of Mongolia's people different from that of the rest of East Asia's people?

7 HISTORY When did Confucianism, Daoism, and Buddhism spread throughout East Asia?

8 CRITICAL THINKING—Analyze In what general direction did the ideas of Buddhism, Confucianism, and Daoism spread? Why is this so?

 PERFORMANCE—Write a Haiku Write a haiku about your favorite season of the year. Remember to follow the syllable pattern of 5, 7, 5, on lines 1, 2, and 3.

A Region of Contrasts

MAIN IDEA
Read to find out how the governments in East Asia work.

WHY IT MATTERS
The success of a country's economy often depends on the success of the country's government.

VOCABULARY
politburo
censor
Diet
keiretsu
Special Economic Zone
most-favored-nation status

Worrld War II and the Cold War changed East Asia. By the middle of the twentieth century, two very different forms of government—communism and democracy—dominated the region. The governments of China, North Korea, and Mongolia were influenced by the communism of the former Soviet Union and its command economy. The democracy of the United States shaped the governments of Japan, South Korea, and Taiwan and their market economies.

Post-War Governments

After China endured World War II and Japanese occupation, the Chinese Communist party defeated the Chinese Nationalist party. In 1949 China became a communist country, the People's Republic of China. Its leader was Mao Zedong (MOW zuh•DUNG). The Nationalists fled the Chinese mainland and set up a democracy on the island of Taiwan.

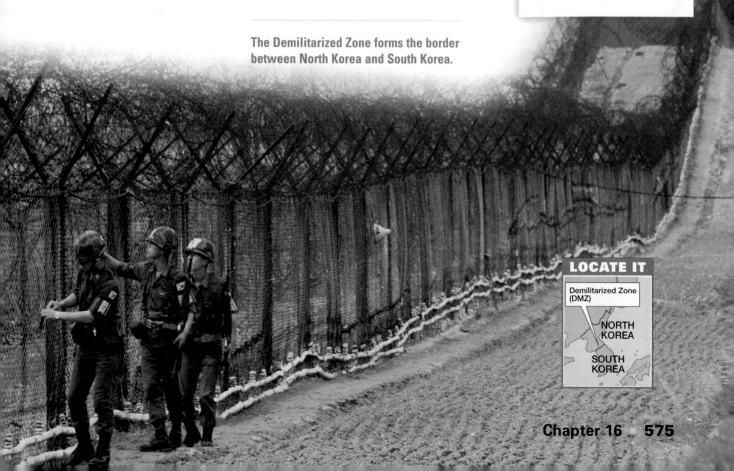

The Demilitarized Zone forms the border between North Korea and South Korea.

LOCATE IT

Demilitarized Zone (DMZ)

NORTH KOREA

SOUTH KOREA

Even though the Cold War has ended, China remains the world's largest nation ruled by communists. China's Communist party controls the country's government, military, and economy in a strict manner.

Only citizens who are members of the Communist party can elect the National People's Congress, China's legislature. Members of the congress elect the **politburo**, or political bureau. The politburo sets policy for the national government. This system enables the Communist party to stay in power and control policy in China.

China's national government is made up of the National People's Congress and the State Council. The National People's Congress has little power. It mostly follows the policies set by the Communist party. A premier heads the State Council, which is also controlled by the Communist party and oversees the national government.

China's government rules every part of life in the country, and its citizens have few freedoms. Newspapers and television

Emperor Akihito inherited the Japanese throne in 1989.

stations are **censored**—that is, they cannot print or broadcast anything the government does not allow.

After World War II North Korea became a communist nation influenced by the Soviet Union. At the same time South Korea became a democracy with support from the United States. In the 1950s North Korea tried to take over South Korea in what became known as the Korean War. Neither country won the war. As a result, however, North Korea began to follow a policy of isolation. Today it has little contact with other countries.

Like South Korea, Japan became a democracy after World War II. Japan's government includes a two-house legislature known as the **Diet**. Members of the Diet are chosen in elections. The Diet chooses the country's prime minister. Japan's emperor no longer has authority in governing. The emperor is only a symbol of Japan's people and its past.

Built in 1651, Tiananmen Square is one of the largest public squares in the world. Mao Zedong's portrait hangs over Tiananmen Gate in the square.

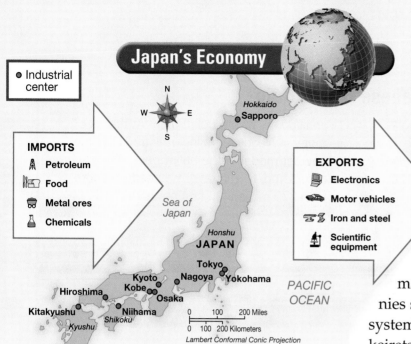

Japan's Economy

Industrial center

IMPORTS
- Petroleum
- Food
- Metal ores
- Chemicals

Sea of Japan

Hokkaido
Sapporo

Honshu
JAPAN

Tokyo
Kyoto Nagoya
Kobe   Yokohama
Hiroshima
Osaka
Kitakyushu Niihama
Shikoku
Kyushu

0   100   200 Miles
0 100 200 Kilometers
Lambert Conformal Conic Projection

EXPORTS
- Electronics
- Motor vehicles
- Iron and steel
- Scientific equipment

PACIFIC OCEAN

GEOGRAPHY THEME

Human-Environment Interactions
Japan imports raw materials and exports finished products.

❖ What products does Japan export?

electronics, machinery, and chemicals. Japanese brands are respected around the world.

Many Japanese manufacturers maintain strong ties with other companies such as banks and suppliers under a system called **keiretsu** (kay•RET•soo). In a keiretsu the member companies own parts of each other. This ownership makes the members of the group very loyal to each other.

Japan's economic growth has also helped other countries in East Asia. Through investments from Japan and partnerships with Japanese companies, China, South Korea, and Taiwan have improved their economies. While the United States is still Japan's largest trading partner, China, South Korea, and Taiwan make up much of the rest of its trade.

Both Taiwan and South Korea have economies that work much like the economy of Japan. They import raw materials and energy resources. Then they turn the materials into high-quality products and export these products around the world.

Mongolia was a communist country before and after World War II. It became a republic in 1992 after its people asked for more freedoms. Mongolia now elects a president and has many political parties.

REVIEW What is the Diet?

Connected Economies

Few economic success stories can match the growth of Japan's economy since World War II. It succeeded because the Japanese were willing to listen and to learn from others. Japan followed the advice of foreign bankers and economists. In addition, its people, businesses, and government worked together in rebuilding the economy.

Manufacturing is a major part of Japan's economy. Since Japan has few raw materials and energy resources, the country imports these to make products for export. Japan produces automobiles,

LOCATE IT

CHINA

Hong Kong

Hong Kong International Terminal is one of the world's largest ports.

EVERGR

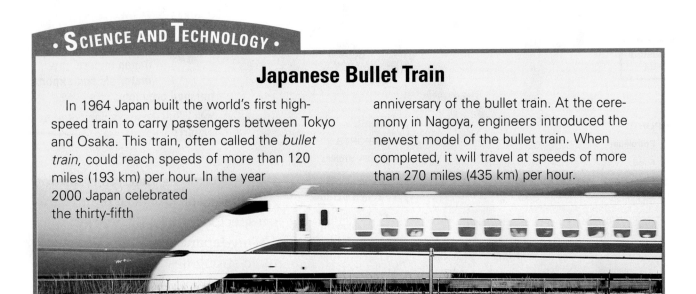

Japanese Bullet Train

In 1964 Japan built the world's first high-speed train to carry passengers between Tokyo and Osaka. This train, often called the *bullet train*, could reach speeds of more than 120 miles (193 km) per hour. In the year 2000 Japan celebrated the thirty-fifth anniversary of the bullet train. At the ceremony in Nagoya, engineers introduced the newest model of the bullet train. When completed, it will travel at speeds of more than 270 miles (435 km) per hour.

Taiwan and South Korea export many electronic products such as televisions, radios, VCRs, and toys.

The economy of North Korea has remained far behind the rest of East Asia. Its command economy is one of the most controlled and closed off in the world. North Korea mainly exports minerals and metal products. Japan, South Korea, and China are among its trading partners.

Two hundred years ago Napoleon stated:

❝China is a sleeping giant.❞

The giant appears to be awakening. In recent years the economy of China has greatly increased. Today the economy of China, like the economy of Japan, is one of the world's largest. However, the standard of living in Japan remains much higher than in China. The per capita GDP in China is only $3,800, compared to Japan's $23,400. The growth and improvement in China's economy is due largely to the government's introduction of free enterprise. While China's leaders want the country to remain communist, they realize the benefits of a market economy.

To improve China's economy without stirring up a desire for democracy, the government has set up **Special Economic Zones** (SEZs). These modern manufacturing areas lie along the country's eastern coast. The SEZs are more like the market

The city of Pudong is one of China's SEZs. It was built on land that was a swamp only a few years ago.

economies of democratic nations. So far the experiment has been successful.

REVIEW What is a keiretsu?

Economies at Risk

While most East Asian economies have improved over time, they do face many challenges. These include maintaining economic growth, handling growing populations, and resolving tensions in the region.

At the start of the twenty-first century, the growth of Asian economies has slowed. To help its economy, Japan has slowly begun to move away from the keiretsu system. When a company is not forced to buy from a keiretsu, it can search for the lowest prices. China, too, has continued to reform and open its economy. As a result, the United States renewed the **most-favored-nation status** of China. This status, or position, helps China by lowering taxes that Chinese companies

A North Korean and a South Korean show unity by carrying a flag with the image of the Korea Peninsula.

must pay to trade with the United States.

Both Japan and China also face population problems. Since much of Japan's economy is centered in Tokyo, the capital city is becoming too crowded. One way to solve this problem has been for the Japanese government to create new land from landfills. China has tried to slow its population growth by having a rule of one child per family. Many Chinese believe this is too much government control.

Almost all the countries of East Asia trade with each other, but there are political tensions between them. China says Taiwan is a part of China. Taiwan says it is independent. Both North Korea and South Korea claim the entire Korea Peninsula. With the support of other countries, these disagreements may be settled.

REVIEW What are three problems East Asia faces today?

LESSON 4
REVIEW

1. **MAIN IDEA** What different forms of government are found in East Asia?

2. **WHY IT MATTERS** Which economies of East Asia—command or market—have had more success?

3. **VOCABULARY** How might **politburo** and **censor** be related?

4. **READING SKILL—Draw Conclusions** Why might the countries of East Asia trade with each other even though there are political tensions between their governments?

5. **ECONOMICS** How are the economies of Japan, Taiwan, and South Korea similar?

6. **CULTURE** How has China tried to deal with its growing population?

7. **CRITICAL THINKING—Hypothesize** Why might the government of China want to remain communist?

PERFORMANCE—Make a Graph or a Chart Look in an almanac to find Japan's and China's most recent imports and exports. Choose three imports and three exports that the two countries have in common. Draw a chart or a graph to compare the value of these imports and exports.

16 Review and Test Preparation

1600 B.C.
Shang family becomes
China's first ruling dynasty

1122 B.C.
Rise of the Zhou
dynasty and the
"Mandate of Heaven"

USE YOUR READING SKILLS

Complete this graphic organizer to show that you understand
how to draw conclusions about East Asia. A copy of this graphic
organizer appears on page 153 of the Activity Book.

Draw Conclusions About East Asia

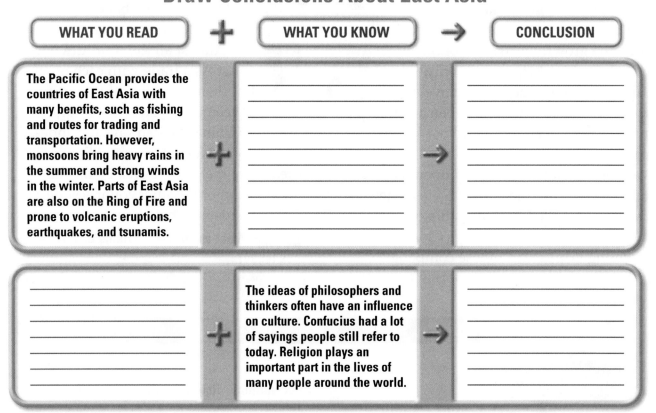

| WHAT YOU READ | + | WHAT YOU KNOW | → | CONCLUSION |

The Pacific Ocean provides the countries of East Asia with many benefits, such as fishing and routes for trading and transportation. However, monsoons bring heavy rains in the summer and strong winds in the winter. Parts of East Asia are also on the Ring of Fire and prone to volcanic eruptions, earthquakes, and tsunamis.

The ideas of philosophers and thinkers often have an influence on culture. Confucius had a lot of sayings people still refer to today. Religion plays an important part in the lives of many people around the world.

THINK  & WRITE

Write a "Packing for a Journey" List
The Takla Makan is one of the world's largest
and driest deserts. Make a list of the items you
might need to survive for a week in this desert.
Give a reason for bringing each item.

Write an Invitation Imagine that you are
the leader of democratic South Korea. Write
an invitation to the leader of communist North
Korea. Include a list of events the leader will
attend during his or her two-day visit.

B.C./A.D.   A.D. 1000   A.D. 2000

551 B.C.
Confucius born

A.D. 1200
Rise of the
Mongol Empire

A.D. 1392
General Yi establishes
the Yi dynasty in Korea

A.D. 1868
Japan begins to
build its industries

USE THE TIME LINE

Use the chapter summary time line to answer these questions.

1 In what year did China's first ruling dynasty form?

2 Was Confucius born before or after the rise of the Mongol Empire?

USE VOCABULARY

Fill in each blank with the correct vocabulary word.

> **loess (p. 555)**
>
> **virtues (p. 561)**
>
> **samurai (p. 564)**
>
> **pagoda (p. 573)**
>
> **most-favored-nation status (p. 579)**

3 _____ were warriors that Japanese nobles hired to protect their land.

4 A _____ is a tower with many levels.

5 Good qualities that a person has are called _____.

6 Countries that pay lower tariffs to trade with the United States have _____ .

7 _____ is a fertile yellow soil.

RECALL FACTS

Answer these questions.

8 Why were the people of China so proud of the Han dynasty?

9 Which culture influenced Korea more, Chinese culture or Japanese culture? Why?

10 How is the geography of Mongolia different from that of the other countries of East Asia?

11 How do ocean currents affect East Asia?

Write the letter of the best choice.

12 **TEST PREP**   In general, the elevation in China becomes lower from—
  A south to north.
  B north to south.
  C east to west.
  D west to east.

13 **TEST PREP**   Most people of East Asia live in urban areas *except* people in—
  F China.
  G Mongolia.
  H Japan.
  J North Korea.

THINK CRITICALLY

14 Newspapers and television stations in China are strictly censored by the Chinese government. What harm might citizens of a country experience if information they get is strictly censored?

15 China became a communist nation when the Chinese Communist party defeated the Chinese Nationalist party. How might China be different today if the Nationalist party had defeated the Communist party?

16 How does China's government function compared to the governments of Germany, India, Russia, and the United States?

APPLY SKILLS

Read a Cartogram

17 Look at the World Population cartogram on page 569. Which country in East Asia has the smallest population?

CHART AND GRAPH SKILLS

BANAUE, PHILIPPINES

The village of Banaue, Philippines, lies in the Cordillera Central mountain range on the island of Luzon. Long ago, the Ifugao people of this rugged region carved terraces into the slopes surrounding Banaue. The farmers of northern Luzon have been using these terraces to grow rice for more than 2,000 years.

LOCATE IT

PHILIPPINES

Banaue

Southeast Asia

" [We] ran up the hills where, as you looked down . . . the flooded rice fields lay shining like a broken mirror. "
—Colin McPhee on Bali, 1984

CHAPTER READING SKILL

Cause and Effect

A **cause** is an event or action that makes something else happen. An **effect** is what happens as a result of that event or action.

As you read this chapter, list the causes and effects of the key events.

What Caused → Event
the Event

CAUSE → EFFECT

Peninsulas, Islands, and Seas

MAIN IDEA
Read to find out what countries, landforms, and bodies of water come together to form the region of Southeast Asia.

WHY IT MATTERS
The region's main geographical parts have characteristics that are both similar and different.

VOCABULARY
insular
strait
paddy
biodiversity

Southeast Asia is a region rich in natural resources. It lies south of China, east of India, and north of Australia. It stretches between the South Pacific Ocean and the Indian Ocean. The region is home to Myanmar (MYAHN•mahr), Thailand, Laos (LAH•ohs), Cambodia, Vietnam (vee•et•NAHM), Malaysia (muh•LAY•zheeuh), Singapore, Indonesia (in•duh•NEE•zhuh), East Timor, Brunei (broo•NY), and the Philippines.

Varying Sizes and Populations

Southeast Asia covers an area of about 5 million square miles (13 million sq km). About two-thirds is water. The other one-third is a collection of peninsulas and archipelagoes. The region is home to more than 528 million people, not quite double the population of the United States.

Indonesia is the largest country in Southeast Asia. It also has the largest population. About two out of every five people in Southeast Asia, or more than 216 million people, live in Indonesia. Only China, India, and the United States have more people than Indonesia does.

Downtown Jakarta has many wide boulevards lined with modern buildings.

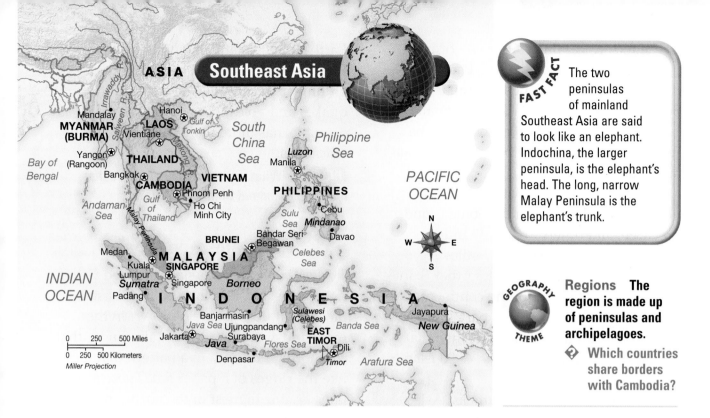

ASIA **Southeast Asia**

Mandalay
MYANMAR Hanoi
(BURMA) **LAOS**
Yangon Vientiane
(Rangoon)
THAILAND South
China
Sea Philippine
Sea
Luzon
Manila

Bay of
Bengal
Bangkok
CAMBODIA **VIETNAM**
Phnom Penh **PHILIPPINES** **PACIFIC
OCEAN**
Andaman Gulf Ho Chi
Sea of Minh City
Thailand Cebu
Sulu Mindanao
Sea Davao

BRUNEI Bandar Seri
Medan Begawan Celebes
MALAYSIA Sea

**INDIAN
OCEAN**
Kuala **SINGAPORE**
Lumpur
Sumatra Singapore Borneo
Padang **INDONESIA** Jayapura
New Guinea

Banjarmasin Sulawesi
(Celebes)
Java Sea Ujungpandang Banda Sea
0 250 500 Miles Jakarta Surabaya **EAST
TIMOR**
0 250 500 Kilometers Java Flores Sea Dili
Denpasar Timor Arafura Sea
Miller Projection

FAST FACT The two
peninsulas
of mainland
Southeast Asia are said
to look like an elephant.
Indochina, the larger
peninsula, is the elephant's
head. The long, narrow
Malay Peninsula is the
elephant's trunk.

**GEOGRAPHY
THEME**

Regions The
region is made up
of peninsulas and
archipelagoes.

❓ Which countries
share borders
with Cambodia?

About two-thirds of Southeast Asia's people live in rural areas. Most of them live in river valleys and deltas or on the sides of volcanic mountains. There the soil is good for farming. However, people are also moving to large cities in Southeast Asia, and the entire region is fast becoming more urban. Bangkok in Thailand, Jakarta in Indonesia, and Manila in the Philippines are the three largest cities in Southeast Asia.

Singapore, which covers only 225 square miles (583 sq km), is Southeast Asia's smallest country. Four countries the size of Singapore would fit inside an area smaller than the state of Rhode Island. However, Singapore is packed with people. With more than 4 million people, Singapore has a population density of more than 16,700 people per square mile (6,448 per sq km). The tiny European country of Monaco is the only independent nation in the world with a population density higher than that of Singapore.

REVIEW What is the largest country in Southeast Asia?

Where Land Meets Sea

Southeast Asia is made up of two parts. One part is mainland Southeast Asia, which is attached to the Asian continent. The other part is made up of islands. The island part of the region is often called insular (IN•su•luhr) Southeast Asia. **Insular** means "related to islands."

Mainland Southeast Asia has two peninsulas. The larger of the two is the peninsula called Indochina. Myanmar, Laos, Thailand, Cambodia, and Vietnam are located on the Indochina peninsula.

The smaller of the two peninsulas is the Malay Peninsula. The Malay Peninsula branches off from the western side of the Indochina peninsula, extending southward about 700 miles (1,127 km). On the narrowest part of the Malay Peninsula, called the Isthmus of Kra, are part of the countries of Myanmar and Thailand. The Isthmus of Kra connects Myanmar and Thailand to the mainland part of Malaysia. The island of Singapore is located just off the southernmost tip of the Malay Peninsula.

The four remaining countries—Brunei, Indonesia, East Timor, and the Philippines—make up the many islands of insular Southeast Asia. Brunei takes up a small part of a larger island called Borneo. The rest of Borneo is divided between Malaysia and Indonesia.

Indonesia is an archipelago made up of more than 17,500 islands. Some islands are large, and others are small. Indonesia stretches for more than 3,000 miles (4,828 km) from east to west, farther than the east-west distance of the continental United States. East Timor is part of an island between Indonesia and Australia. People live on only 400 of the 7,000 islands in the Philippines.

The islands of insular Southeast Asia were formed along the Pacific Ring of Fire.

Earth's plates that make up the Ring of Fire are still shifting. So, pressure deep within Earth continues to create earthquakes and volcanoes. Indonesia, for example, has more than 120 active volcanoes.

REVIEW What are the two peninsulas that make up mainland Southeast Asia?

Mountains and Tropics

Most of Southeast Asia is covered with mountains and rain forests. The coastal plains that do exist are narrow. On the mainland are several mountain ranges that run north and south in a pattern that looks like the ridges of a paper fan. These mountains are the highest in the northern part of the region.

GEOGRAPHY THEME

Place Mountains make up a large part of insular Southeast Asia.

Which mountains are found on the island of Sumatra?

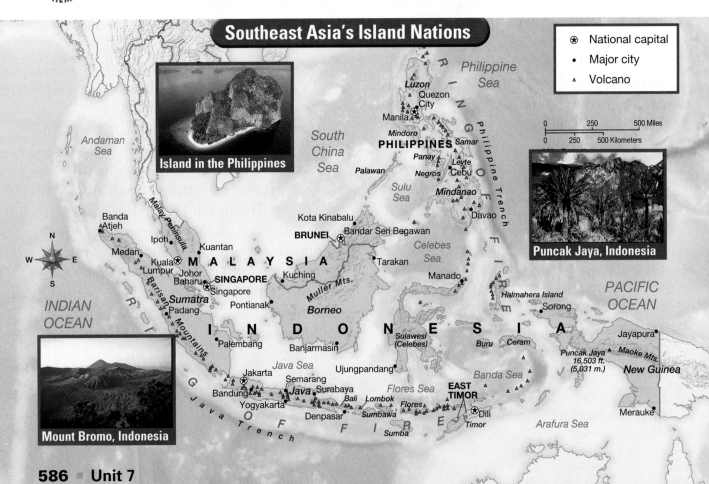

Southeast Asia's Island Nations

⊛ National capital
• Major city
▲ Volcano

Island in the Philippines

Puncak Jaya, Indonesia

Mount Bromo, Indonesia

The Mekong River is important for transportation, fishing, and providing water for farming.

The highest point in insular Southeast Asia is Indonesia's Puncak Jaya (PUN•chahk JAH•yuh) on the island of New Guinea. At 16,500 feet (5,030 m), Puncak Jaya is also the highest island mountain in the world. Its highest peaks are covered with snow year-round. At its lower elevations tropical plants grow, as they do in the rest of the region.

Almost all of Southeast Asia lies in a tropical climate zone, where the weather is hot and humid most of the year. In much of the region, it rains more than 60 inches (152 cm) a year. There are places that receive as much as 180 inches (457 cm) of rain each year.

When seasons change, the amount of rainfall usually changes more than the temperature. Two different monsoon winds affect the amount of rainfall in Southeast Asia. The northeast monsoon blows from November to March, and the southwest monsoon blows from May to September. The northeast monsoon blows toward the region from the Asian mainland. This monsoon crosses the South China Sea, where it picks up moisture and brings heavy rain to most parts of insular Southeast Asia.

The southwest monsoon brings dry air from Australia. East Timor is most affected by this wind and has a five-month-long dry season. The islands farthest from Australia have no dry season at all.

REVIEW What do the monsoons affect in Southeast Asia?

Water, Water Everywhere

For hundreds of years traders have passed through Southeast Asia while traveling between the Pacific and Indian Oceans. Invaders from other lands also were attracted by the region's location in a good passageway between the two oceans. Two bodies of water separate the mainland part of Southeast Asia from the insular part—the Strait of Malacca (muh•LA•kuh) and the South China Sea. A **strait** is a narrow waterway that connects two larger bodies of water.

If the mountains on Southeast Asia's mainland remind you of the ribs of a paper fan, then the rivers in the region might remind you of the creases of the fan. Several large river systems, including the Mekong (MAY•kawng), begin on the Asian mainland and flow to the southern coast.

Along the way these rivers deposit fertile soil in the valleys, lowlands, and wide deltas, where the rivers meet the sea.

As seasons change and rivers flood, rice farmers make use of the extra supply of water. Certain kinds of rice grow best in flooded fields. Farmers in Vietnam and Thailand use the wet season to grow this important crop. In areas that do not flood naturally, farmers build drainage ditches to direct water into special fields. Low earth walls, built to keep water from flowing away, often surround these fields. These walled fields are called **paddies**. In hilly areas, such as those on the Indonesian island of Bali, rice fields may follow the slopes of hills like large steps. This type of farming is described as terracing.

The rivers of Southeast Asia also provide transportation for people and goods. Rivers link Southeast Asians who might otherwise be kept apart by thick rain forests or rugged mountains. In Bangkok, the capital of Thailand, rivers have been made into a series of transportation canals called klongs. Today klongs serve as streets in parts of this busy city.

REVIEW What two bodies of water separate mainland Southeast Asia from insular Southeast Asia?

A Unique Environment

Many different plants and animals are found in Southeast Asia. Some of them are found in no other place on Earth. The rafflesia (ruh•FLEE•zhee•uh)—the largest flower in the world—is found only in a few rain forests of Indonesia. A rafflesia flower can measure up to 3 feet (0.9 m) across! Spices, such as cloves and nutmeg, grow in the Moluccas (muh•LUH•kuhz). These islands between Sulawesi and New Guinea were once known as the Spice Islands.

Sellers move their goods through klongs at Bangkok's floating market. Buyers on shore stop the boats that sell goods they want to buy.

LOCATE IT

THAILAND

Bangkok

For hundreds of years Asian, Arab, and European traders came to the area to take part in the spice trade.

The Indonesian island of Komodo (kuh•MOH•doh) is home to the world's largest lizard—the Komodo dragon. Found nowhere else, Komodo dragons number only in the thousands today. The largest ever found was more than 10 feet (3 m) long! The rain forests of Sumatra and Borneo are among the few places where orangutans (uh•RANG•uh•tangs) still live in the wild. Both Javan rhinoceroses and Sumatran rhinoceroses live nowhere else but in Southeast Asia.

In recent years Southeast Asian nations have become concerned about the growing population's effect on the environment. The cutting of forests has left many kinds of plants and animals endangered. This is reducing the region's **biodiversity**, or its number of different plants and animals.

Some countries are taking steps to save forests, control erosion, and create national parks that protect plant and animal life. Singapore is working to protect its biodiversity. It has set aside land for a nature

The Siamese Cat

Before 1938 Thailand was known as Siam (sy•AM). One of Siam's most famous exports was—and still is—the Siamese cat. The Siamese cat was said to be so highly prized that hundreds of years ago only the king of Siam, or his close family members, could own one. Siamese cats can be more aggressive than many other cats. Legend says that they may have been used to guard Siam's religious temples. The first Siamese cats arrived in the United States sometime between 1890 and 1909.

reserve. Smaller than 1 square mile (2.6 sq km), this reserve has more kinds of plants than are found in all of North America.

REVIEW What are three unique animals that live in Southeast Asia?

LESSON 1 REVIEW

1 MAIN IDEA What are the two parts of Southeast Asia?

2 WHY IT MATTERS How are the two parts similar? How are they different?

3 VOCABULARY Use the word **insular** in a sentence describing Southeast Asia.

4 READING SKILL—Cause and Effect How has population growth affected Southeast Asia's environment?

5 GEOGRAPHY Which of the world's countries have more people than Indonesia?

6 CULTURE In what kind of areas do most people in Southeast Asia live? Why?

7 GEOGRAPHY What is one route in Southeast Asia between the Pacific and Indian Oceans?

8 CRITICAL THINKING—Analyze Why has an abundance of water been important to Southeast Asia?

PERFORMANCE—Hold a Press Conference Imagine that you are the leader of a country that is an archipelago. Think of at least three advantages and three disadvantages of having lots of islands in your country. Then write a speech in which you explain your findings to the citizens of your country.

Compare Maps of Different Scale

VOCABULARY

scale

▶ WHY IT MATTERS

Southeast Asia is a region that is made up of the countries of Myanmar, Thailand, Laos, Cambodia, Vietnam, Malaysia, Singapore, Indonesia, East Timor, Brunei, and the Philippines. When you look at the map below, you can see that Singapore is the region's smallest country.

If you wanted to see different views of Southeast Asia, you could use maps with different scales. **Scale** refers to the size of

a map in relation to its content. Places are drawn larger or smaller on maps, depending on how much area is to be shown. Maps that show large areas must use small scales since places must be drawn small to fit everything in. Maps that show only small areas can use large scales. Drawing places large allows details to be shown. Knowing about maps of different scale can help you choose the best map for gathering the information you need.

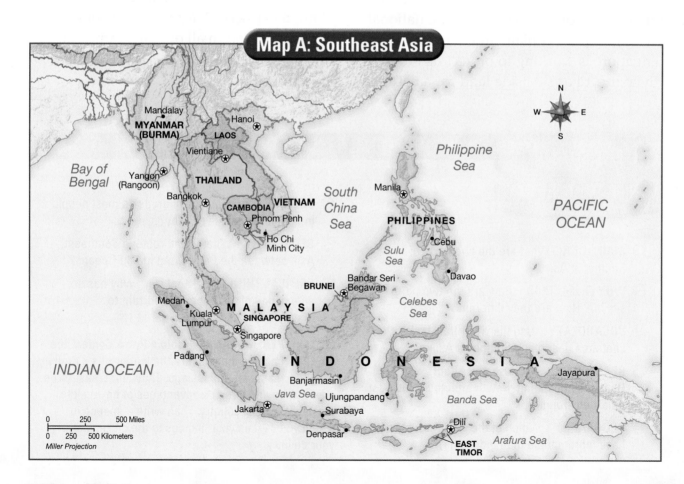

Map A: Southeast Asia

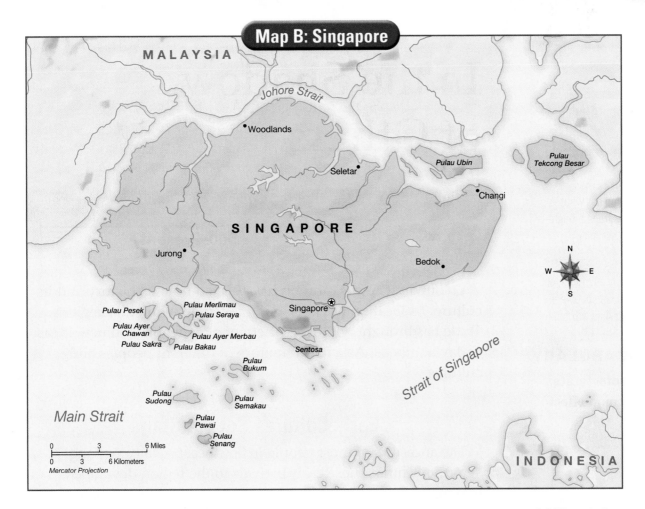

Map B: Singapore

MALAYSIA

Johore Strait

• Woodlands

Seletar•

S I N G A P O R E

Pulau Ubin

Pulau Tekcong Besar

•Changi

Jurong•

Bedok •

Pulau Pesek

Pulau Merlimau
Pulau Seraya

Singapore ✪

Pulau Ayer Chawan

Pulau Ayer Merbau

Pulau Sakra *Pulau Bakau*

Sentosa

Pulau Bukum

Strait of Singapore

Pulau Sudong

Pulau Semakau

Main Strait

Pulau Pawai

Pulau Senang

0   3   6 Miles
0   3   6 Kilometers
Mercator Projection

I N D O N E S I A

▶ WHAT YOU NEED TO KNOW

The maps on these two pages show how scale can change depending on whether the map shows a close-up or faraway view of an area. Map A is a small-scale map. It shows a large area of land with little detail. Map B is a large-scale map. It shows a small amount of land with a lot of detail. The map scale on each map compares the distance on the map to the distance in the real world.

▶ PRACTICE THE SKILL

Use the maps to answer these questions.

1 Find Singapore on both maps. Which map, A or B, shows more cities in Singapore?

2 Suppose you wanted to travel from Jurong to Changi. On which map, A or B, can you better measure the distance between them? What is it about the scale that helps you do this?

3 Suppose you want to measure the Johore Strait. Which map, A or B, would you use? What is its length?

▶ APPLY WHAT YOU LEARNED

Think about how you use maps when you travel. Find two road maps with different scales. One might be a road map of your state, and the other might be a road map of a large city within your state. Write a sentence explaining an instance when it would be more helpful to use the state map, with the smaller scale. Then write another sentence explaining an instance when it would be more helpful to use the city map, with the larger scale.

Practice your map and globe skills with the **GeoSkills CD-ROM**.

2

In the Shadow of Others

500–Present

Southeast Asia's location has affected both its history and its culture. Its location has been good for trade with other regions. Trade has brought with it a variety of new people and new ideas. Today Southeast Asia has a mixture of different peoples and cultures.

Early Cultures Set the Stage

The ancestors of most people in Southeast Asia came long ago from China. These early arrivals to the region developed into many different ethnic groups, such as the Mons, Khmers (kuh•MEHRS), and Malays.

A seafaring people called the Mons settled in present-day Cambodia. There they formed Southeast Asia's first kingdom—the Funan Kingdom—in the first century A.D. They controlled trade between China and India through the Strait of Malacca.

Before long, the cultures of India and China began to influence the people of the Funan Kingdom. The kingdom borrowed some Chinese ways, but it also adopted Hinduism, Buddhism, and other practices from India.

The temple of Angkor Wat was built in the 1100s to honor the Hindu god Vishnu. It was also used as an astronomical observatory.

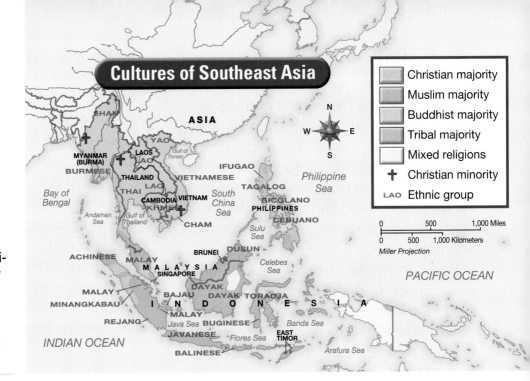

Cultures of Southeast Asia

Christian majority
Muslim majority
Buddhist majority
Tribal majority
Mixed religions
✝ Christian minority
LAO Ethnic group

ASIA

SHAN
YAO
MYANMAR (BURMA)
LAOS
LAO
BURMESE
IFUGAO
THAILAND
VIETNAMESE
THAI
TAGALOG
CAMBODIA VIETNAM
BICOLANO
KHMER
PHILIPPINES
CHAM
CEBUANO
Bay of Bengal
Andaman Sea
Gulf of Thailand
South China Sea
Sulu Sea
ACHINESE
MALAY
BRUNEI
DUSUN
Celebes Sea
MALAYSIA
SINGAPORE
DAYAK
MALAY
BAJAU DAYAK TORADJA
MINANGKABAU
INDONESIA
REJANG
MALAY
Java Sea BUGINESE
Banda Sea
JAVANESE
EAST TIMOR
INDIAN OCEAN
Flores Sea
BALINESE
Arafura Sea
PACIFIC OCEAN

Gulf of Tonkin

N W E S

0   500   1,000 Miles
0   500   1,000 Kilometers
Miller Projection

GEOGRAPHY THEME

Place The region's major religions are strongly tied to its past.

❖ In which part of the region is Islam found most?

The Funan Kingdom became the first of many kingdoms in the region that were influenced by India over the next 1,000 years.

In A.D. 650 the Khmers defeated the Funan rulers. About 240 years later the Khmers created the great Angkor-Khmer Kingdom. This kingdom included present-day Cambodia, Vietnam, Thailand, and parts of Laos. At the peak of the kingdom's power, the famous Hindu temple Angkor Wat was built.

At the same time that the Funan Kingdom fell to the Khmers, the Malays also formed a kingdom. It was on Indonesia's northern island of Sumatra along the Strait of Malacca. Since the Khmers were not a seafaring people, the Malays took over control of the trade between India and China. In time, the kingdom became a major center for studies in Buddhism. Lasting until 1290, the Malay Kingdom, or Srivijaya (sree•wih•JAW•yuh), existed longer than any other empire in Asia.

Descendants of these peoples still live in Southeast Asia and make up some of its many ethnic groups. Today about 90 percent of Cambodians are members of the Khmer ethnic group. Malays make up nearly one-fourth of Southeast Asia's population.

By the 1300s, Southeast Asia began to undergo major changes. One change was the decline of the region's kingdoms. Experts are not sure why they lost power.

Other changes took place as new kingdoms arose. These new kingdoms began mixing and uniting separate cultures into larger groups. Many of these changes have lasted. For example, today the people of Thailand write their language, which is related to Chinese, in a script based on the Indian language Sanskrit, which they got from the Khmers.

Change also came from newcomers to the region in the 1400s. As trade increased in Southeast Asia, Arab traders and settlers arrived from Southwest Asia and India. Some of these traders brought with them their religion, Islam. The Malays adopted Islamic teachings and culture. Islam remains the religion of most people in Indonesia and southern Malaysia.

REVIEW What group brought Islam to Southeast Asia in the 1400s?

Outside Influences

For many years Arab traders provided spices—black pepper, cloves, nutmeg, and cinnamon—to European consumers. The spices, however, sold at very high prices because the demand was so great. When supplies of spices from Arab traders were cut off in the 1400s, European explorers began searching for new routes to Southeast Asia.

Portugal was the first European country to arrive in "the Indies"—the name Europeans used to describe India, China, and Southeast Asia. By the 1500s, the Portuguese controlled much of the spice trade. They were followed by the Dutch, the French, the British, and the Spanish. Europeans introduced Christianity to the region.

By the 1800s European countries controlled almost all of Southeast Asia as colonies or protectorates. A **protectorate** is a country that maintains control of its own domestic policies but depends on another country to direct its foreign affairs. Only Thailand remained an independent country during this time.

During World War II all of Southeast Asia was taken over by Japan. The Japanese wanted the region's land and resources to help their economy. When Japan lost the war in 1945, Japanese forces left Southeast Asia.

After World War II most Southeast Asian countries that had been controlled by European nations before the war began to win independence. Some did so peacefully, but others had to fight for it. Independence brought struggles over what forms the governments should take. The old monarchies that had ruled before Europeans took control now competed for power with people who had been part of the European-run governments. New political parties appeared. Military groups sometimes took power by force.

Southeast Asia's nations struggled to govern themselves. In most of the nations, power changed hands quickly and often. Some of the most bitter battles were fought over the activities of communist groups and the harsh methods of dictators. Some of those conflicts continue today.

LOCATE IT

Hanoi — VIETNAM

This theater in Hanoi, Vietnam, shows the influence of French architecture.

During the Cold War the United States was one of many countries that aided groups fighting communism. United States President Dwight D. Eisenhower feared the domino effect in Southeast Asia. The **domino effect** is the idea that if one country in a region is taken over by communists, the same thing will probably happen to the other countries there. Like a line of dominoes, if one country fell to communism, so could all the others.

Fear of the domino effect was an important reason the United States became involved in the Vietnam War. In 1954 Vietnam was divided into North Vietnam and South Vietnam. Communists controlled North Vietnam. In South Vietnam the people, supported by the French, wanted democracy. The two groups battled for years. Starting in the mid-1960s, however, the United States military came to the aid of the South Vietnamese. United States troops withdrew from Vietnam in 1973. The war ended in 1975 with communist forces in charge of both North Vietnam and South Vietnam. Vietnam became one country.

REVIEW What did United States leaders fear would happen in Southeast Asia?

A Cultural Snapshot

Many languages are spoken throughout Southeast Asia. Across the many islands of Indonesia, people mainly speak Bahasa Indonesian. The people of Myanmar speak Burmese. Thai is the main language of Thailand. Filipino and English are spoken in the Philippines. Other languages, such as Tagalog, Ilocano, and Cebuano, are also heard in the Philippines. Some people in Vietnam, Laos, and Cambodia speak French. The language and culture were introduced when France controlled those countries. In Chinese and Indian communities across the region, people can be heard speaking languages and dialects that are also spoken in China and India.

• HERITAGE •

The Shwe Dagon Pagoda

A pagoda is a type of building, usually built as a Buddhist memorial or place of worship. One of the world's most famous pagodas is the Shwe Dagon Pagoda in Yangon, the capital city of Myanmar.

The Shwe Dagon Pagoda was built more than 2,500 years ago. It is made of brick and concrete. The whole outer surface is covered in gold. Parts of the surface contain diamonds and precious gems. Around the base are carvings of kings, praying figures, and animals. There are also places where worshipers can leave offerings to Buddha.

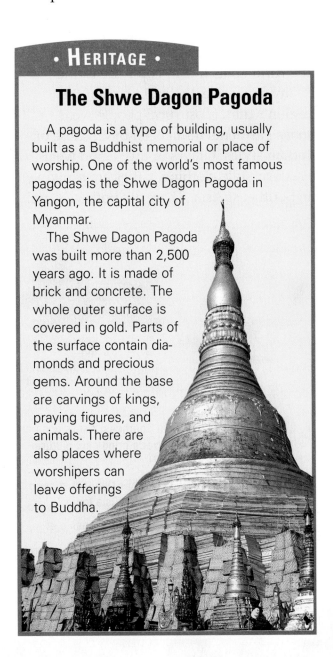

Traditional dancing in Bali, Indonesia

Southeast Asia is mostly rural. In the rural areas most people are farmers. Many grow rice, the main part of the region's diet. Most rural people wear loose garments influenced by Chinese or Indian styles. Others in the region wear western-style clothing. Cities are growing in Southeast Asia. There are both very rich and very poor cities, each with a variety of industries.

Religion is important to many Southeast Asians. Indonesia has the world's largest Muslim population. After Islam, Buddhism is the region's next most common religion, especially on the mainland. Christianity, brought by the Europeans, is common in the Philippines. Some people mix these major religions with traditional beliefs.

Music and dance are important art forms in the region. On the Indonesian islands of Java and Bali, people might go to see traditional dancing. A gamelan orchestra made up of drums, gongs, flutes, and stringed instruments plays for the dancers. In any Southeast Asian country, people might attend a concert to hear one of the new forms of music that merge traditional music with western pop or rock. People also watch television, shop in large malls, and use the Internet.

REVIEW What are some religions found in Southeast Asia?

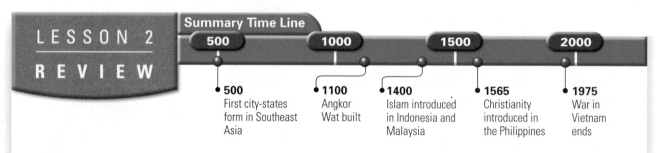

LESSON 2 REVIEW

Summary Time Line

| 500 | 1000 | 1500 | 2000 |

500 First city-states form in Southeast Asia

1100 Angkor Wat built

1400 Islam introduced in Indonesia and Malaysia

1565 Christianity introduced in the Philippines

1975 War in Vietnam ends

1 MAIN IDEA   How did Southeast Asia's position as a center for world trade bring new cultural influences to the area?

2 WHY IT MATTERS   How has the past shaped the way people live in Southeast Asia today?

3 VOCABULARY   What is the relationship of a country to its **protectorate**?

4 TIME LINE   When was Angkor Wat built?

5 READING SKILL—Cause and Effect   How can it affect a country to be controlled by another country?

6 HISTORY   What was the longest-lasting empire in Asia?

7 CRITICAL THINKING—Hypothesize   How might Southeast Asia be different today if the region had not been located along trade routes?

PERFORMANCE—Write a Report   Research the Malay Kingdom. Write a report about the kingdom. Include information about its history, influences, and achievements.

Varying Economies, Varying Governments

In the years since World War II, the countries of Southeast Asia have gained independence from countries outside the region. Some have been successful with self-rule. Others have struggled. With plentiful resources found throughout the region, the economies can do well. Much of the economic success will depend on the success of the governments.

Struggles with Independence

Myanmar (formerly Burma) has long struggled to create a stable economy with an effective government. Since 1937, when Myanmar became self-governing, it has had six complete changes of government. There have been rebellions, dictators, and military takeovers. Today a strict military dictatorship rules Myanmar.

MAIN IDEA
Read to find out how governments and economies work in each of the countries of Southeast Asia.

WHY IT MATTERS
In the countries of Southeast Asia, as in many countries around the world, a successful economy often depends on a stable, effective government.

VOCABULARY
human rights
sultan

People from Myanmar protest in favor of democracy.

I AM NOT AFRAID

Aung San Suu Kyi 1945–

Character Trait: Heroic Deeds

When Aung San Suu Kyi was only two years old, her father, General Aung San, was assassinated. General Aung San had been a leader in Burma's early struggle for democratic self-rule. In 1989 Burma's government was taken over by a military dictatorship that changed the country's name to Myanmar. Suu Kyi became a leader in the nonviolent struggle for a democratic government. In 1991 Suu Kyi won the Nobel Peace Prize for her work toward establishing democracy and human rights in Myanmar.

MULTIMEDIA BIOGRAPHIES
Visit The Learning Site at www.harcourtschool.com/biographies
to learn about other famous people.

That government watches its citizens carefully. Citizens with pro-democracy views, such as Aung San Suu Kyi (AWNG SAHN SOO CHEE), are sometimes arrested and jailed for sharing their ideas about freedom.

Even though Myanmar is rich in natural resources, the country has much poverty. The government, not the people, controls all profits from its resources. Most workers are subsistence farmers who produce only enough food to survive. The economy is also affected by trade sanctions. The United States put trade sanctions in place to punish Myanmar's government for its poor record in human rights. **Human rights** are the freedoms that all people should have. Experts believe that Myanmar's future will depend on whether it finds a more democratic government and takes advantage of its natural resources.

With a per capita GDP less than $750, Cambodia is among the poorest nations in the world. The Vietnam War, which spilled over into Cambodia and Laos, left all three countries heavily damaged. By the war's end, communists were in control of their governments and economies. Since then, Cambodia has become a constitutional monarchy. Laos and Vietnam remain communist states.

The Vietnam War greatly affected the people of Cambodia. During the war a group of Cambodian communists called the Khmer Rouge (ROOZH) took control of the country. The people suffered terribly under their rule. Nearly one-fourth of Cambodia's people are said to have died while the Khmer Rouge was in power.

The economies of Cambodia, Laos, and Vietnam are based mainly on agriculture. About three-fourths of the workers in these countries are farmers. Many grow rice along the Mekong River. With so many farmers who grow food only

The Friendship Bridge provides a transportation route across the Mekong River enabling Laos to trade more easily with neighboring Thailand.

LOCATE IT

LAOS
THAILAND
Mekong R.
Friendship Bridge

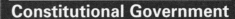

for their families, there is little money for improvements.

The future does look hopeful, however. In Cambodia visitors come to see Angkor Wat. This gives hope for tourism. Land-locked Laos can now increase trade with Thailand using the Friendship Bridge, paid for by Australia. Better relationships with the United States and the discovery of oil are helping Vietnam's economy.

REVIEW **What kind of government does Myanmar have today?**

Emerging from the Past

Thailand, Indonesia, and the Philippines are still working to build effective self-rule. Even so, these countries have developed fairly successful economies.

In recent years Thailand has had many different governments. Monarchies, dictatorships, and democracies are among them. The country's capital city of Bangkok has seen military takeovers and protests by the people. Since 1992 Thailand has been a constitutional monarchy.

Indonesia and the Philippines are both republics. However, the constitution of Indonesia provides for little balance of power. Most power rests in the hands of the president. Due to many differences with Indonesia, East Timor voted in 1999 to be independent from Indonesia. In 1987, after years of instability, the Philippines adopted a constitution similar to that of the United States.

Most workers in Thailand, Indonesia, and the Philippines are farmers. While farming makes the economies of these countries similar, there are many differences, too.

DEMOCRATIC VALUES
Constitutional Government

In 1973, under the rule of Philippine President Ferdinand Marcos, the Philippine constitution was replaced with a new one. This constitution gave Marcos almost unlimited power. It changed the Philippine government from a two-house legislature to a one-house legislature, gave the president power to dissolve the legislature, and allowed the president to appoint the prime minister. After Marcos was removed from power in 1986, a new constitution was written. Adopted in 1987, this constitution allowed for a two-house legislature of representatives elected by the people. It also stated that the president may serve only one term of six years.

Analyze the Value

1. Why do you think that the Philippine constitution of 1987 placed a limit on the number of years that the president may serve?

2. **Make It Relevant** Write a paragraph that explains why it is important to have a constitution that limits the power of government.

Thailand has the strongest of these economies. It is the world's largest rice exporter. Thailand's economy continues to depend on agriculture, but tourism and manufacturing are growing.

Indonesia has plenty of oil, natural gas, and forests. It is the largest exporter of plywood in the world. As in Myanmar, the government controls all profits. Because of this, many of Indonesia's people are poor. Much of the country's economic activity takes place in Jakarta, its capital.

A Buddhist monk uses an Internet kiosk in Thailand.

A busy port city, Jakarta must deal with a population that is growing faster than are jobs. The economy of the Philippines depends on exporting wood, fish, and gold.

A period of economic problems called the Asian Crisis began in Thailand in 1997. It spread to other countries in Southeast Asia and then around the world. With help from other countries, Thailand and its neighbors are slowly starting to recover.

REVIEW **Which country's constitution is similar to the United States Constitution?**

Stable Governments, Better Economies

Brunei is one of the world's smallest countries but one of Southeast Asia's richest countries. Brunei's stable government has allowed the country to build its economy. The government of Brunei is a kind of monarchy called a sultanate. A **sultan** is a name for a leader of a Muslim country. The country the sultan rules is a sultanate. The sultan of Brunei has a cabinet. There is no legislature, and the people do not vote.

Brunei is rich in petroleum and natural gas. The government provides the people with health care and helps supply them with food and housing. One problem that

Brunei faces is that its economy is limited. The wealth of the country depends on world oil prices. If prices are high, the economy does well. If prices are low, the economy suffers. As a result, Brunei is trying to develop more industries, such as banking, fishing, and agriculture.

The government of Malaysia, a constitutional monarchy, has not changed much since 1963. The national government has a house of representatives and a senate. A nine-member group of state rulers chooses a paramount ruler, or chief ruler, from among themselves. That ruler is considered a monarch, but the position is not inherited. The position of state ruler, however, is inherited.

Malaysia has a diverse economy made up of manufacturing, agriculture, forestry, and petroleum. Malaysia is the world's largest producer of rubber as well as a leading source of hardwoods. Besides these major exports, the country is beginning to manufacture electronics.

Singapore's stable government has allowed the country to prosper. The government keeps order with strict rules about public behavior. Littering, chewing gum, and crossing the street outside a crosswalk are unlawful and carry stiff fines. Many people say Singapore's rules are too harsh,

A worker collects the white liquid from a rubber tree in Malaysia.

but its crime rate is one of the lowest in the world.

Singapore has a strong economy. It has the highest GDP per capita in Southeast Asia at $27,800. Its economy is diverse, open, stable, and free of corruption. Unlike the rest of Southeast Asia, Singapore has almost no agriculture. Technology industries and banking are among its main economic activities. More than 3,000 international companies have offices there.

In 1967 Singapore, Thailand, Malaysia, Indonesia, and the Philippines formed the Association of Southeast Asian Nations (ASEAN). The purpose of the organization is to promote more stable governments and economies.

REVIEW **Which country has the highest GDP per capita in Southeast Asia?**

Stock trading (above) is a common economic activity in Singapore (below).

LESSON 3
REVIEW

1 MAIN IDEA How does the government of each Southeast Asian country influence its economy?

2 WHY IT MATTERS What do the economies of Brunei, Malaysia, and Singapore have in common?

3 VOCABULARY What is the difference between a **sultan** and a sultanate?

4 READING SKILL—Cause and Effect Myanmar is rich in resources. Why, then, are so many people in Myanmar poor?

5 ECONOMICS What event negatively affected the economies of Southeast Asia in 1997?

6 CIVICS AND GOVERNMENT How does the government of Brunei share the country's wealth with its people?

7 CRITICAL THINKING—Analyze What economic advantages might a country that is not landlocked have over a country that is landlocked?

PERFORMANCE—Create a Fact Sheet Imagine that you are taking a trip to Singapore. Create a fact sheet to carry with you on your travels. What do you need to know as you tour Singapore? Research the answers, and record them on your fact sheet. Share your completed sheet with a partner or group.

· SKILLS · Compare Circle Graphs

CHART AND GRAPH

VOCABULARY
circle graph

▶ WHY IT MATTERS

Malaysia and Brunei have two of Southeast Asia's strongest economies. The two economies, however, are very different. One of the major differences has to do with economic diversity. Looking at the percentages of people employed in different parts of an economy can tell you a great deal about how countries make money. The **circle graphs** on page 603 show the percentages of people working in different parts of the economies of Brunei and Malaysia. Circle graphs show information by means of a circle divided into parts. Like other graphs, circle graphs can help you make comparisons. They are often called pie charts, because they look like pies with a number of different-sized slices. The larger the slice is, the greater its percentage.

▶ WHAT YOU NEED TO KNOW

Listed below are some tips that will help you compare circle graphs.

- Read the titles of the graphs to find out what is being compared.

- The slices of a circle graph add up to 100 percent. The size of each slice represents part of the whole 100 percent. For example, if a slice takes up exactly half of the graph, it represents 50 percent. It is not always easy to estimate how large a slice is just by looking at it, so it is often labeled with its percentage.

- To find out what each slice represents, look for a label within or next to each slice. Sometimes circle graphs will have a legend, or key, instead of labels. For example, the legend on page 603 tells you that red represents the percentage of people with jobs in agriculture, forestry, or fishing.

- One of the most useful features of circle graphs is their ability to show information at a glance. For example, by just glancing at the Employment in Brunei graph, you can easily tell that nearly half of the jobs in Brunei are government jobs.

A worker puts together television sets in Malaysia.

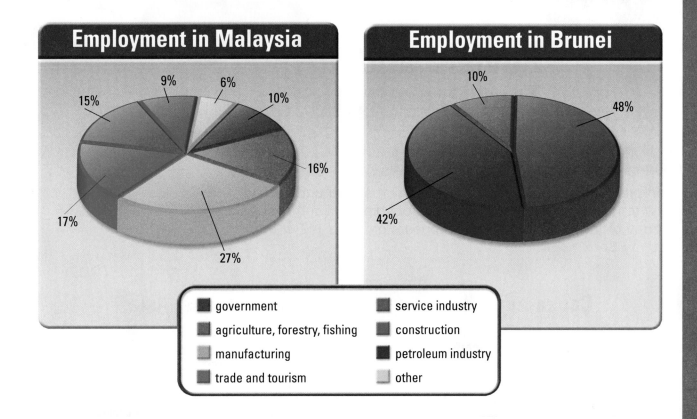

Employment in Malaysia

9%
6%
15%
10%
16%
17%
27%

Employment in Brunei

10%
48%
42%

Legend:
- government
- agriculture, forestry, fishing
- manufacturing
- trade and tourism
- service industry
- construction
- petroleum industry
- other

▶ PRACTICE THE SKILL

Study the circle graphs, and then answer the following questions.

1 Which nation has a more diversified economy? How do you know?

2 What kinds of jobs are important in Brunei but not in Malaysia?

3 In Brunei, which kind of job is held by the smallest percentage of people?

4 In Malaysia, which kind of job is held by the largest percentage of people?

▶ APPLY WHAT YOU LEARNED

Make your own circle graph that shows data about your classmates, such as gender (male or female), eye color, or hair color. First, use a calculator to find percentages. For example, take the number of male students in a class and divide it by the total number of students in the class. If there are 18 male students in a class of 30 students, then 60 percent of the students in the class are males. After you find all of the percentages, use them to make a circle graph.

USE YOUR READING SKILLS

Complete this graphic organizer to show that you understand
how to identify cause-and-effect relationships in Southeast Asia.
A copy of this graphic organizer appears on page 162 of the
Activity Book.

Cause-and-Effect Relationships in Southeast Asia

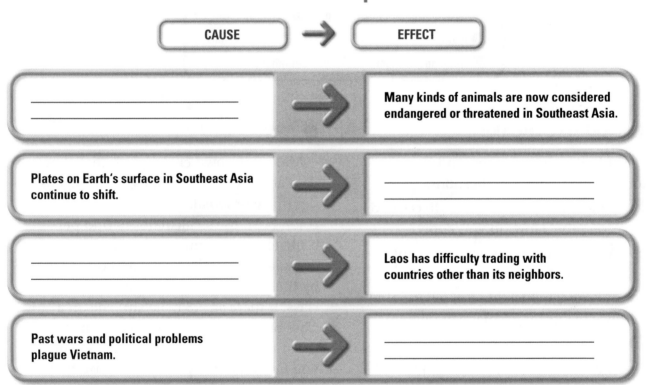

CAUSE ⟶ EFFECT

CAUSE		EFFECT
_____ _____	⟶	**Many kinds of animals are now considered endangered or threatened in Southeast Asia.**
Plates on Earth's surface in Southeast Asia continue to shift.	⟶	_____ _____
_____ _____	⟶	**Laos has difficulty trading with countries other than its neighbors.**
Past wars and political problems plague Vietnam.	⟶	_____ _____

THINK & WRITE

Write a Persuasive Letter   Think of ways
the lives of people in Myanmar might be
improved. Write a letter to Myanmar's leaders,
explaining how they might make the country's
government and economy better.

Write a Diary Entry   Imagine that you are
a visitor arriving in Indonesia for the first time.
Write a diary entry describing the unique plants
and animals you see there. Draw pictures to
illustrate your diary entry.

900s
Rise of the
Angkor-Khmer
Kingdom

1100s
Angkor Wat
built

1400s
Islam introduced
in Southeast Asia

1565
Christianity introduced
in the Philippines

1973
The United
States military
leaves Vietnam

1975
War in
Vietnam
ends

USE THE TIME LINE

Use the chapter summary time line to answer these questions.

1 Did Islam arrive in Southeast Asia before or after the rise of the Angkor-Khmer Kingdom?

2 In what year did the Vietnam War end?

USE VOCABULARY

Use each term in a sentence that explains both the meaning of the term and how the term relates to Southeast Asia.

3 **paddy** (p. 588)

4 **biodiversity** (p. 589)

5 **domino effect** (p. 595)

6 **human rights** (p. 598)

RECALL FACTS

Answer these questions.

7 What role has the Strait of Malacca played in Southeast Asia's history?

8 What factors make the countries of Cambodia, Laos, and Vietnam poor?

9 Why were Europeans interested in Southeast Asia in the 1500s?

Write the letter of the best choice.

10 **TEST PREP** Which is the correct chronological order for the arrival of religions in Southeast Asia?
A Islam, Christianity, Hinduism
B Hinduism, Islam, Christianity
C Christianity, Islam, Hinduism
D Hinduism, Christianity, Islam

11 **TEST PREP** Which country controlled Southeast Asia during World War II?
F Britain
G India
H Portugal
J Japan

THINK CRITICALLY

12 What challenges does the geography of Southeast Asia pose for the farmers of the region?

13 Singapore has many strict rules about public behavior. Many people criticize Singapore's government for its harsh rules; however, the country has one of the lowest crime rates in the world. What are the advantages and disadvantages of having so many rules?

APPLY SKILLS

Compare Maps of Different Scale

14 Draw a map of your school. Then draw a map of your school that includes the entire neighborhood. Which is small scale? Which is large scale?

Compare Circle Graphs

15 Use the following data to make a circle graph that shows the percentages of people working in different parts of the economy of Thailand.

> Agriculture: 54%
> Industry: 15%
> Services: 31%

Hue, Vietnam

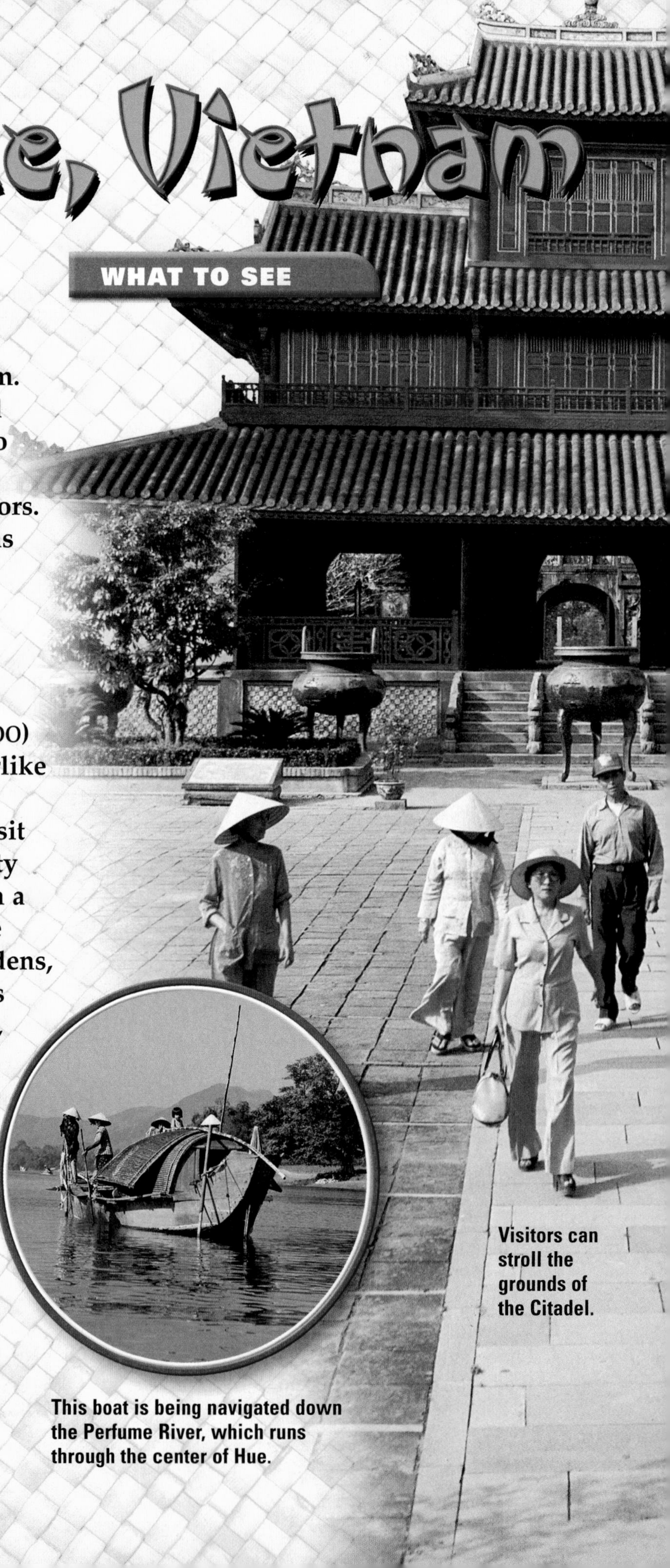

GET READY

The city of Hue (hoo·AY) is located in the center of Vietnam. It has a long and distinguished history. Hue is often referred to as an imperial city because it has been home to many emperors. Before World War II it served as the capital of Vietnam. When visitors tour this ancient city, Hue's history unfolds.

Hue has many examples of beautiful architecture. You can visit the Thien Mu (TEE·ehn MOO) Pagoda, or temple, a tall, towerlike building on the banks of the Perfume River. You can also visit the Citadel, a huge enclosed city where emperors once lived. On a tour of the Citadel, you can see palaces, theaters, libraries, gardens, and temples. The city of Hue is more than just these buildings, however. It is a living history of the culture of this region.

LOCATE IT

Hue

VIETNAM

WHAT TO SEE

This boat is being navigated down the Perfume River, which runs through the center of Hue.

Visitors can stroll the grounds of the Citadel.

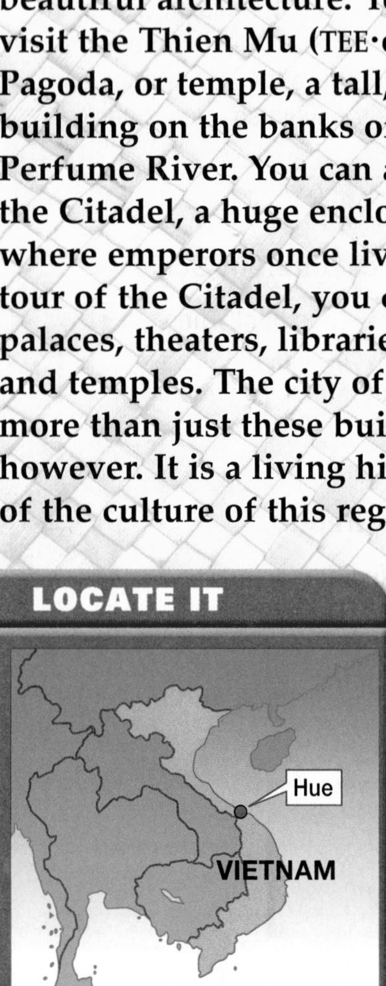

The Thien Mu Pagoda (top left) has seven tiers, or stories. Hue's emperors had very grand tombs. The interior of the tomb of Emperor Khai Dinh (KY DIN) (top right) is very decorative. Courtyard statues (bottom) guard the tomb of Emperor Khai Dinh.

This Buddhist monk worships in the Thien Mu Pagoda.

TAKE A FIELD TRIP

A VIRTUAL TOUR
Visit The Learning Site at **www.harcourtschool.com/tours** to take virtual tours of other world historical sites.

GO ONLINE

CNN Turner Le@rning.

A VIDEO TOUR
Check your media center or classroom library for a videotape tour of Hue, Vietnam.

VISUAL SUMMARY

Write a Paragraph Choose one of the events from the time line below. Write a paragraph that describes what happened during the event.

USE VOCABULARY

For each group of terms, write a sentence or two that explains how the terms are related.

1 **urban planning** (p. 531), **urban center** (p. 545)

2 **Mandate of Heaven** (p. 561), **virtue** (p. 561)

3 **irrigation canal** (p. 526), **paddy** (p. 588)

RECALL FACTS

Answer these questions.

4 Which country in South Asia makes up most of the subcontinent?

5 Who was China's first emperor? What dynasty did he found?

6 What is the purpose of ASEAN?

Write the letter of the best choice.

7 **TEST PREP** Thousands of years ago people in South Asia established a civilization in—
A the Himalayas.
B the Indus Valley.
C the Takla Makan.
D the Mekong Delta.

8 **TEST PREP** Daoism developed in—
F Thailand.
G India.
H China.
J Japan.

9 **TEST PREP** What country in Southeast Asia remained independent of colonialism?
A Thailand
B Cambodia
C the Philippines
D Brunei

10 **TEST PREP** In general, the economies of Japan, Taiwan, and South Korea—
F export diamonds.
G export raw materials.
H import raw materials and export products.
J do not import or export.

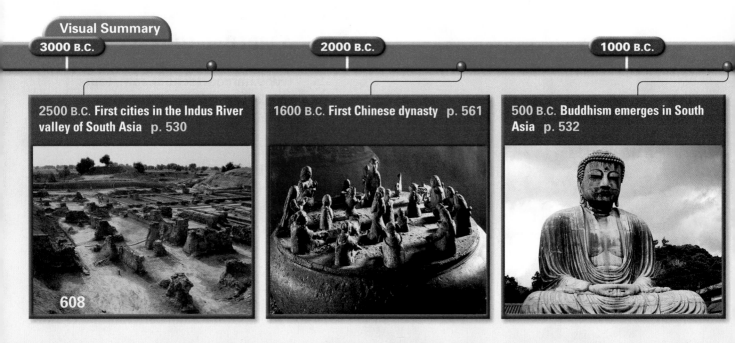

Visual Summary

3000 B.C.   2000 B.C.   1000 B.C.

2500 B.C. **First cities in the Indus River valley of South Asia** p. 530

1600 B.C. **First Chinese dynasty** p. 561

500 B.C. **Buddhism emerges in South Asia** p. 532

11 Why do you think many countries, including Asian countries, have struggled after independence from colonialism?

12 China has had some success combining its communist government with a market economy. Explain whether you think this system can last.

13 Do you think biodiversity is important? Why?

APPLY SKILLS

Bhutan

Compare Maps of Different Scale

Use the two maps on this page to answer these questions.

MAP AND GLOBE SKILLS

14 Suppose you want to describe the location of Bhutan to a friend. Which map would better show the country in relation to other countries?

15 Find Bhutan on both maps. Which map shows more cities?

16 Suppose you want to travel from Thimphu to Tongsa Dzong. On which map can you better measure the distance between the two? What is it about the scale that helps you do this?

17 On which map can you find rivers and towns?

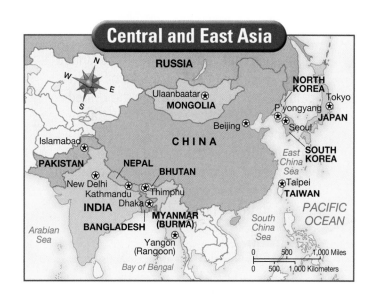

Central and East Asia

A.D. 100 Indian-influenced kingdoms develop in Southeast Asia p. 592

A.D. 1949 China becomes a communist nation p. 575

A.D. 2000 Asian economies experience many changes p. 599

B.C./A.D.   A.D. 1000   A.D. 2000

Unit Activities

Visit The Learning Site at
www.harcourtschool.com/
socialstudies/activities
for additional activities.

Create a Flag

After World War II, the Korea Peninsula was divided into communist North Korea and democratic South Korea. Many Koreans in both the north and south hope the two countries will unite again in the future. Imagine that you are in charge of designing the flag for a united Korea. Look at each country's present flag; then design a new flag that combines ideas from both.

Make a List

Imagine that you are head of the United States Department of Energy. An oil tanker accident has occurred outside the United States. The oil tanker accident has caused a temporary shortage of oil around the world, including in the United States. You must present a list of actions that American citizens can take to conserve oil. Present your list to the class.

VISIT YOUR LIBRARY

■ *A Family from Vietnam* by Simon Scoones. Steck-Vaughn.

■ *In Search of the Spirit: The Living National Treasures of Japan* by Sheila Hamanaka and Ayan Ohmi. Morrow.

■ *Gandhi: Great Soul* by John B. Severance. Clarion.

COMPLETE THE UNIT PROJECT

Plan a Web Page   Work with a group of classmates to complete the unit project—to plan a Web page. First, make a list of links to include on a home page. Use those links to organize information from the unit into categories, such as culture, geography, government, economics, and history. Then decide which people, events, and ideas to include under each category as links from your home page. Next, write a short description of each person, event, and idea that will appear on your Web page.

The Pacific Realm

Coral reef and fish in the South Pacific Ocean, Fiji

The Pacific Realm

> **" ...a mighty ocean ...a restless ever-changing, gigantic body of water that would later be described as Pacific. "**
>
> —**James Michener, from *Hawaii*, 1959**

Preview the Content

Read the titles of the chapters and lessons. Use them to fill in a K-W-L chart about the Pacific Realm.

K–What I Know	W–What I Want to Know	L–What I Have Learned

Preview the Vocabulary

Parts of Speech   Parts of speech include nouns, verbs, adjectives, and adverbs. Nouns formed by joining two or more words are called compound nouns. A compound noun can be written as one word, as two or more words, or as a hyphenated word. Scan the unit to find Vocabulary Words that are compound nouns. Write what you think each noun means. Then check the Glossary.

The Pacific Realm

Midway Islands

NORTH PACIFIC OCEAN

Honolulu • • HAWAII (U.S.)

MARSHALL ISLANDS
⊛ Majuro

FEDERATED STATES OF MICRONESIA ⊛ Palikir

⊛ Koror **PALAU**

NAURU ⊛
Yaren ⊛

⊛ Tarawa (Bairiki)

K I R I B A T I

PAPUA NEW GUINEA

SOLOMON ISLANDS
⊛ Honiara

TUVALU
⊛ Funafuti

Port Moresby

VANUATU
Port-Vila ⊛

SAMOA
Apia ⊛

Darwin •

Suva ⊛

FIJI

TONGA ⊛
Nuku'alofa

COOK ISLANDS (N.Z.)

NEW CALEDONIA (FRANCE)

Papeete •

AUSTRALIA

GREAT SANDY DESERT

GREAT DIVIDING RANGE

• Brisbane

FRENCH POLYNESIA (FRANCE)

GREAT VICTORIA DESERT

⊛ Sydney
⊛ Canberra

Auckland •

NEW ZEALAND
⊛ Wellington

Adelaide •

• Melbourne

INDIAN OCEAN

Perth •

• Hobart

SOUTH PACIFIC OCEAN

0 — 1,000 — 2,000 Miles
0 — 1,000 — 2,000 Kilometers
Lambert Azimuthal Equal-Area Projection

South Magnetic Pole +

South Pole +

TRANSANTARCTIC MOUNTAINS

ANTARCTICA

Key Events

1500 B.C. | **1000 B.C.** | **500 B.C.** | **B.C./A.D.**

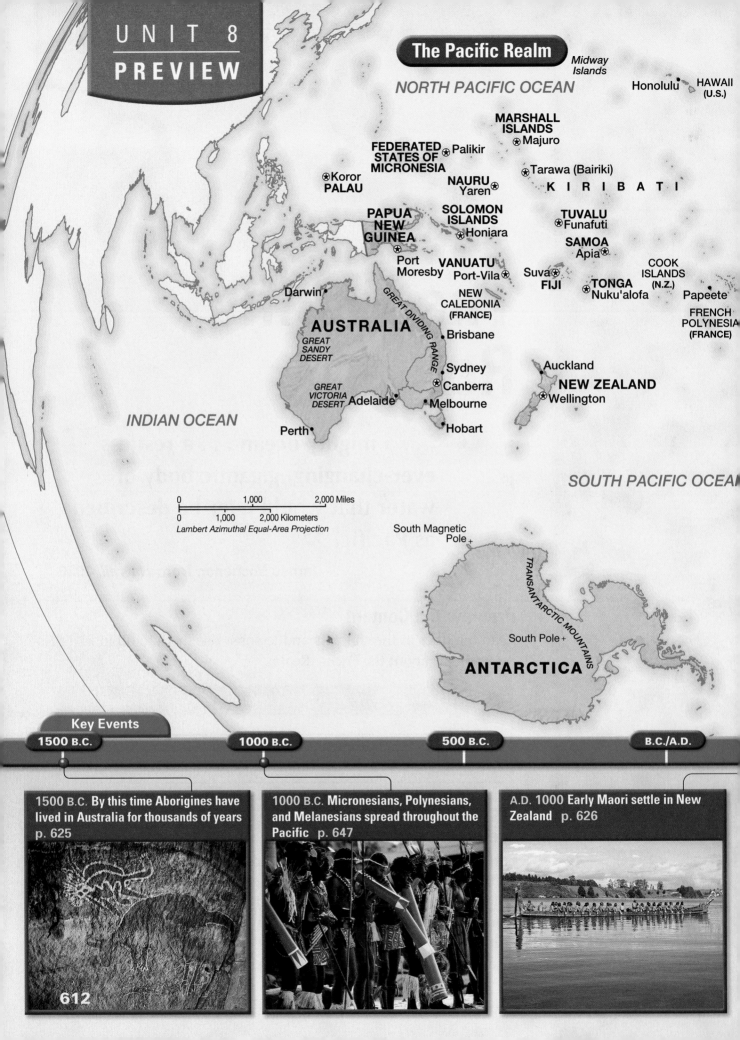

1500 B.C. By this time Aborigines have lived in Australia for thousands of years p. 625

1000 B.C. Micronesians, Polynesians, and Melanesians spread throughout the Pacific p. 647

A.D. 1000 Early Maori settle in New Zealand p. 626

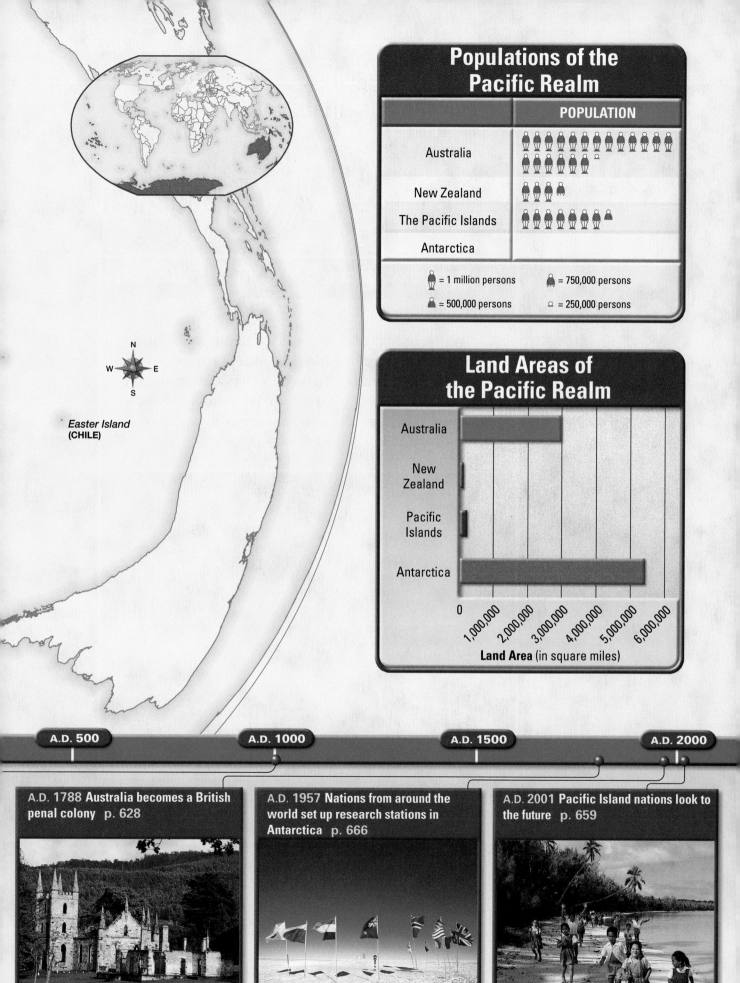

Populations of the Pacific Realm

	POPULATION
Australia	
New Zealand	
The Pacific Islands	
Antarctica	

= 1 million persons		= 750,000 persons	
= 500,000 persons		= 250,000 persons	

Land Areas of the Pacific Realm

Australia

New Zealand

Pacific Islands

Antarctica

0   1,000,000   2,000,000   3,000,000   4,000,000   5,000,000   6,000,000

Land Area (in square miles)

Easter Island (CHILE)

N
W · E
S

A.D. 500   A.D. 1000   A.D. 1500   A.D. 2000

A.D. 1788 Australia becomes a British penal colony p. 628

A.D. 1957 Nations from around the world set up research stations in Antarctica p. 666

A.D. 2001 Pacific Island nations look to the future p. 659

START
with a
SONG

Waltzing Matilda

by Andrew Barton "Banjo" Paterson

"Waltzing Matilda" was written in the late 1800s in the Australian countryside. The song is still popular throughout Australia. This song offers a glimpse of how people lived in rural areas of Australia about one hundred years ago. The song expresses the spirit and lingo that is still a part of Australia today.

Coulibah tree

Billabong in western Australia

Once a jolly swagman sat beside a billabong,
Under the shade of a coulibah tree,
And he sang as he sat and waited by the billabong
"You'll come a-waltzing, Matilda, with me."

"Waltzing Matilda , waltzing Matilda,
You'll come a-waltzing, Matilda with me."
And he sang as he sat and waited by the billabong,
"You'll come a-waltzing, Matilda with me."

Down came a jumbuck to drink beside the billabong,
Up jumped the swagman and seized him with glee.
And he sang as he talked to that jumbuck in his tucker-bag ,
"You'll come a-waltzing, Matilda with me!"

"Waltzing Matilda, waltzing Matilda,
You'll come a-waltzing, Matilda with me."
And he sang as he talked to that jumbuck in his tucker-bag,
"You'll come a-waltzing, Matilda with me."

swagman wanderer

billabong a river back-water or watering hole

coulibah a kind of eucalyptus tree

waltzing matilda carrying a swag, or a bundle of clothes and other possessions

jumbuck a sheep

tucker-bag a bag used to carry food

Near Alice Springs, Australia

Down came the stockman riding on his thoroughbred,
Down came troopers, one, two, and three.
"Where's the jolly jumbuck you've got in your tucker-bag?
"You'll come a-waltzing Matilda with me."

"Waltzing Matilda, waltzing Matilda,
You'll come a-waltzing, Matilda with me."
"Where's the jolly jumbuck you've got in your tucker-bag?"
"You'll come a-waltzing, Matilda with me."

Up jumped the swagman and plunged into the billabong,
"You'll never catch me alive," cried he,
And his ghost may be heard as you ride beside the billabong,
"You'll come a-waltzing, Matilda with me."

"Waltzing Matilda, waltzing Matilda,
You'll come a-waltzing, Matilda with me."
And his ghost may be heard as you ride beside the billabong,
"You'll come a-waltzing, Matilda with me."

Karijini National Park, Australia

Jumbucks drink beside the billabong

Andrew Barton "Banjo" Paterson
1864–1941

Andrew Paterson is one of Australia's best-loved writers. Paterson worked as a lawyer in Sydney, a city in southeastern Australia, but he always remembered the boyhood years spent on farms and ranches. Paterson became dissatisfied with his work as a lawyer and began working as a journalist. This job gave him the chance to travel and to learn. Paterson visited Europe, Asia, and Africa. He also visited Australia's vast "outback." It was in that rugged land that he met the people who inspired him to write "Waltzing Matilda."

This statue by Daphne Ma, called *Jolly Swagman*, was dedicated to Banjo Paterson.

Analyze the Literature

1. What does this song tell you about how people lived in rural Australia in the late 1800s?

2. There are many songs about early life in the United States. Pick one that you would like to learn more about. What does this song say about life during the time it was written? How have things changed since the song was written? How have they stayed the same?

READ A BOOK

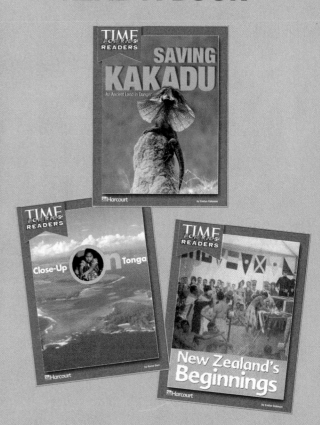

START THE UNIT PROJECT

The Travel Show With your classmates, create a travel show about the Pacific Realm. As you read the unit, take notes about the people and places. Your notes will help you decide what to include in your travel show.

USE TECHNOLOGY

Visit The Learning Site at **www.harcourtschool.com/ socialstudies** for additional activities, primary sources, and other resources to use in this unit.

Australia and New Zealand

" **The immense cities lie basking on the beaches of the continent like whales that have taken to the land.** "

—Arnold Toynbee, from *East to West*, 1958

CHAPTER READING SKILL

Make Inferences

To understand what you read, sometimes you need to make **inferences**, or educated guesses, based on details plus your own knowledge and experiences.

As you read, combine the details with your own knowledge to make inferences.

DETAILS + KNOWLEDGE → INFERENCE

The Lands Down Under

MAIN IDEA
Read to find out about the landscapes and resources of Australia and New Zealand.

WHY IT MATTERS
The land and resources of Australia and New Zealand affect where people live and work.

VOCABULARY

outback

marsupial

station

FAST FACT
Australia is the world's largest island. It is the only island that is also a continent, and the only continent that is also a nation. In terms of elevation above sea level, Australia is the world's flattest continent.

Australia and New Zealand are often called the "lands down under" because they are located in the Southern Hemisphere, south of the equator. Australia is the smallest continent, just one-third the size of North America. New Zealand consists of two large islands and a number of small islands. It is almost as big as the state of Colorado. Much of Australia is flat, and a large portion is desert. New Zealand is mountainous and enjoys abundant rainfall.

Land and Climate

Surrounded by the Pacific and Indian Oceans, Australia covers nearly 3 million square miles (nearly 8 million sq km). It has three major land regions. There are mountainous highlands along the Pacific coast, lowlands in the east-central interior, and a huge plateau to the west.

The Great Dividing Range stretches the length of the east coast from north to south. West of the highlands is low, flat, dry grassland. Australia's two major rivers, the Murray and the Darling, also flow through this region. Only the Murray has water year-round. Much of the region's water comes from wells that

Australia and New Zealand

trap water underground. When pressure builds up, water rises to the surface. It is often salty but still safe for livestock to drink.

To the west is a plateau that covers more than half the continent. The eastern part is sometimes called the "red center" because of the color of its landscape. In the middle of the red center is the world's largest rock. Called Uluru (OO•luh•roo), it is a mass of red stone 6 miles (10 km) around and more than 1,000 feet (300 m) high.

The rest of the plateau includes deserts and rocky plains. The deserts consist of vast sand dunes, occasional salt lakes, and a few waterholes. This is the sparsely settled, untamed region known as the **outback**. Along Australia's west coast, the plain is higher but is flat and rocky.

Near Australia is the world's largest coral reef. The Great Barrier Reef lies in the Pacific Ocean along Australia's east coast and includes many small islands.

• GEOGRAPHY •

The Great Barrier Reef
Understanding Environment and Society

The Great Barrier Reef is made up of billions of colorful living coral polyps and their skeletons. Its clear, warm, shallow waters are home to such an abundance and diversity of sea life that it is considered to be the world's richest marine resource. The reef is not a continuous structure but consists of more than 2,800 reefs and islands. Much of the reef is part of a marine park and is protected. It attracts tourists, many of them scuba divers and snorkelers, from all over the world.

Reef animals

The city center of Auckland, New Zealand

Like its land, Australia's climate varies. Coastal regions near the equator have a tropical climate. Near the coast it is hot year-round. The seasons are the opposite of those in the United States. The summer months of December and January are rainy, while the winter months of June through August are dry. Southern Australia has warm summers and cool winters.

Australia's central and western areas are dry, and long droughts are common. However, the southeast and southwest coasts receive plentiful precipitation during the rainy season. Because much of the country's environment is so harsh, more than 80 percent of Australians live in cities along the narrow coastal areas.

New Zealand's environment contrasts sharply with that of Australia. Lying 1,300 miles (2,100 km) southeast of Australia, New Zealand is made up of two large islands and a handful of smaller islands. The two largest islands, North Island and South Island, are separated by a narrow channel of water. Compared to Australia, New Zealand is small, covering only about 104,000 square miles (270,000 sq km). No place is more than 80 miles (129 km) from the coast.

The snow-capped Southern Alps run nearly the length of the western part of South Island. Along the east coast, lower mountains slope down to grassy plains. North Island is also mountainous, but its landforms are more varied. Low mountains rise along its east coast, and its central region is a mountainous plateau surrounded by foothills and plains. The mountains include several active volcanoes as well as geysers.

New Zealand has many rivers that rise in the mountains of both islands and flow all year long. The mountains of both islands also have waterfalls and deep lakes.

New Zealand, farther from the equator than Australia, has a mild marine climate. Except in South Island's mountains, summers are warm and winters are cool. In New Zealand rain falls year-round, and droughts rarely occur.

REVIEW How are the climates of Australia and New Zealand different?

Milford Sound in Fiordland National Park, South Island, New Zealand

Animals and Plants

Australia and New Zealand are home to many unique animals and plants. Because Australia and New Zealand were separated from other continents for millions of years, animals and plants from other places were never introduced.

The kangaroo is one of Australia's many marsupial species. **Marsupials** are mammals that carry their young in a pouch on the female's stomach. The koala is also a marsupial. The duck-billed platypus looks like a furry, web-footed beaver with a duck's bill. The platypus is unusual because it is a mammal whose young hatch from eggs.

Australia is also home to about 800 species of birds. They include the emu, a large, ostrichlike, wingless bird, and the kookaburra, nicknamed the "laughing bird" because of its odd, hysterical call.

Eucalyptuses and acacias are Australia's most abundant plants. The grayish green leaves of the eucalyptus, or gum tree, contain a fragrant oil. Acacias have brightly colored yellow or white flowers, and one type, the wattle, is the national floral emblem.

New Zealand has no native mammals. Scientists believe that birds, bats, and reptiles may have drifted to its shores on seaborne vegetation. Without mammals to hunt them, the birds eventually lost their wings and became ground dwellers. Among these birds is the kiwi, New Zealand's national symbol.

REVIEW Why are many of the animals of Australia and New Zealand unique?

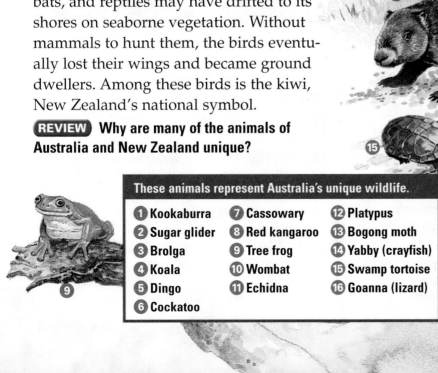

These animals represent Australia's unique wildlife.

❶ Kookaburra	❼ Cassowary	⓬ Platypus
❷ Sugar glider	❽ Red kangaroo	⓭ Bogong moth
❸ Brolga	❾ Tree frog	⓮ Yabby (crayfish)
❹ Koala	❿ Wombat	⓯ Swamp tortoise
❺ Dingo	⓫ Echidna	⓰ Goanna (lizard)
❻ Cockatoo		

Resources

Although Australia is dry, its land is a major natural resource. The country is famous for its vast sheep and cattle ranches called **stations**. Some stations cover thousands of square miles. Sheep graze on the dry, short grass and scrub from the highlands to the great deserts in the west. Cattle are raised close to the highlands, where rainfall is greater and grass is taller.

In the moister regions of Australia, particularly in the southeast and southwest, farmers are able to grow grains as well as fruits. Through the use of improved agricultural methods, Australia meets its own food needs and still has surpluses to export.

Beneath the surface of Australia's land is a vast array of mineral resources. Much of the world's bauxite, which is used in making aluminum, comes from northeastern Australia. In addition, some of the world's richest supplies of iron ore and coal are mined and exported to Japan. Gold, opals, copper, nickel, and uranium are important mineral resources. Offshore oil wells and natural gas are helping Australia become a self-sufficient, energy-producing nation.

Cattle ranchers in New Zealand move livestock across a floodplain.

New Zealand's land, like that of Australia, is not only able to produce ample food for its population, but it is able to produce great surpluses to be exported. Like Australia, New Zealand raises enormous flocks of sheep. Farmers produce wheat and other grains as well as many kinds of vegetables and fruits.

New Zealand's forests support a thriving lumber industry. Native trees supply some wood, but most comes from non-native trees brought in from both Europe and North America. New Zealand also has limited supplies of coal and natural gas.

REVIEW How do Australia and New Zealand use their land as a resource?

LESSON 1
REVIEW

1 **MAIN IDEA**   What physical features characterize the environments of Australia and New Zealand?

2 **WHY IT MATTERS**   How do the physical features of Australia and New Zealand affect where people live?

3 **VOCABULARY**   Use **outback** and **station** in a sentence that tells how they could be related.

4 **READING SKILLS—Make Inferences**   Rainfall varies widely in Australia, but eucalyptuses and acacias grow throughout the country. What inference can you make about these plants?

5 **GEOGRAPHY**   Why is water an important resource in Australia and New Zealand?

6 **ECONOMICS**   What minerals are mined in Australia?

7 **CRITICAL THINKING—Analyze**   What are the major differences between the land in Australia and in New Zealand?

PERFORMANCE—Write a Poem
An Australian poet wrote of her country, "I love a sunburnt country/A land of sweeping plains/Of rugged mountain ranges/Of droughts and flooding rains . . ." Write your own poem describing the land where you live.

Outposts in the Pacific

800   1000   1200   1400   1600   1800   2000

MAIN IDEA
Read to find out how people formed distinct cultures in Australia and New Zealand.

WHY IT MATTERS
People who have brought their customs and traditions from many lands have made Australia and New Zealand multicultural nations.

VOCABULARY
Aborigine
dreamtime
penal colony

The first people of Australia and New Zealand came from Asia and the Pacific Islands thousands of years ago. They adapted to their new environments and formed unique cultures. Europeans, who came little more than 200 years ago, affected those cultures. Over the years new cultures developed in both Australia and New Zealand.

Australia's First People

Scientists think that people from Southeast Asia began entering Australia over land and by sea as long as 40,000 to 60,000 years ago. These first settlers are known as Aborigines. **Aborigine** means "a person who was here from the beginning."

There were plenty of plants and animals then, and Aborigines lived in tribal groups of nomadic hunters and gatherers. The climate slowly began to change. As the climate changed, the landscape became increasingly dry. Ocean levels rose, isolating the continent.

Aborigines adapted to this changed environment. They got food from the land as they walked from place to place. They developed tools and weapons such as the boomerang, a curved club they threw to bring down birds and animals.

Each tribe lived in its own territory. A tribe was made up of smaller family groups, or clans. Wise elders who were familiar with the people's history were looked to as leaders. Each tribe knew the limits of its territory but could hunt in another territory with permission. Tribes also traded with one another.

An Aborigine ranger (below right) gives tours of Uluru, also called Ayers Rock (below left). The rock is sacred to the Aborigines.

Ancient cave paintings (far left) can be seen in Queensland, Australia. A present-day Aborigine artist (left) displays her colorful traditional work.

Aborigines believed that they were one with their "belonging place." This was the land where they were born, lived, and would die. They also believed that they had been in Australia since the dreamtime. The **dreamtime**, they believed, was an ancient time when spirits created the land and all things in it and gave it to the people. Each tribe's dreamtime spirits made that tribe the guardian of its land and all living things forever. Dreamtime stories and traditions were passed on in storytelling and ceremonies from one generation to the next. Today many Aborigines worship the dreamtime and their ties to their spirit creators.

Aborigines used art to show their beliefs and stories. Rock and cave paintings are found all over the continent in places sacred to the people. Aborigines believe that their art connects them to their ancestors and the dreamtime.

REVIEW What did Aborigines believe was their "belonging place"?

New Zealand's First Settlers

The first people in New Zealand came from a group of tropical islands known as Polynesia, in the central-western Pacific Ocean. They called themselves Maori (MOW•ree), which means "local people."

Scholars believe that from about A.D. 800 to A.D. 1000, groups of Maori came to New

A CLOSER LOOK
A Maori Village

Maori villages were among the most advanced that were built by early people of the Pacific.

1. Villagers grew foods such as sweet potatoes and taros.
2. Every village had a meeting house.
3. A palisade made of pointed stakes protected the villagers from attack.
4. Villagers carved canoes for transportation.

◈ Why do you think each village had a meeting house?

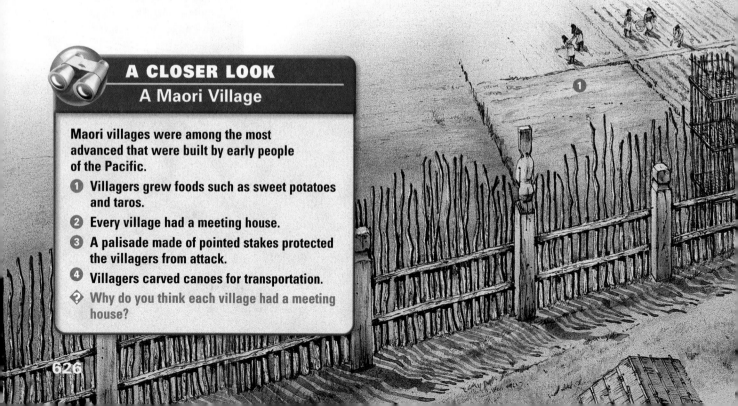

Zealand in large canoes. Most settled along the eastern coasts of North Island and South Island. There they grew crops and hunted.

The Maori made tools and weapons from rocks and wood. They turned timber from the forests into villages, canoes, and elaborate carvings.

The Maori formed tribes whose members believed that they came from the same ancient ancestor. Parts of these tribes lived together in villages of extended families. The people believed that tribal and village chiefs were closely tied to the group's ancestors. Everyone in a village worked. Men hunted and fished. Women planted crops, cooked, and wove clothing from the fibers of the flax plant.

The Maori honored not only their ancestors but also the many gods of nature that they believed in. Because they had no writing to record their past, they passed

A Maori hand-carved pendant

on the knowledge of their ancestors and their gods through stories and songs.

By the 1500s, as the number of people increased, resources were becoming scarce. Maori tribes had always protected their territories, sometimes through war. These wars now became more common. When Europeans began colonizing New Zealand, they met fierce warriors who fought to keep their tribal lands.

REVIEW What tied members of a Maori tribe together?

British navy Captain James Cook landed in New Zealand in 1769.

Europeans Arrive

Although other European explorers had visited parts of Australia, Captain James Cook claimed the land for Britain in 1770. Then in 1788 a group of ships landed at what is today Sydney. Among those on board were 750 prisoners in chains. Britain had decided to use remote Australia as a penal colony. A **penal colony** is a place where criminals were shipped to serve their sentences. Once their prison time was over, they could leave Australia or remain and settle there. Most of them chose to stay.

Despite early hardships, more prisoners and settlers followed. By the early 1800s colonists had killed many Aborigines in warfare. Many other Aborigines died of diseases brought by Europeans. Because Aborigines did not farm, mine, or build settlements, they had changed the land very little. The European colonists felt that the land was theirs to use and change as they wished. By the mid-1800s, Aborigine lands and culture had been nearly destroyed.

The first Europeans to see New Zealand were Dutch sailors. They sighted the islands in 1642 but did not land. The Dutch named the new land *Nieuw Zeeland* for a province in the Netherlands.

New Zealand attracted many European traders interested in the island's timber and in the whales that swam in the surrounding waters. In the early 1800s British settlers began migrating to the island. The British built communities on South Island, where there were already a few Maori settlements.

In 1840 the British and Maori agreed on land rights on the islands. As a result, the Treaty of Waitangi officially made New Zealand a British colony. It is one of the rare examples in history in which colonial expansion was negotiated between immigrants and indigenous people.

REVIEW Why was the Treaty of Waitangi unique?

Culture Today

Today Australia and New Zealand are multicultural nations. While there are small groups of Aborigines and Maori, most of the people in both nations are of British descent. However, immigrants from Europe, Asia, and the Pacific Islands have added to the original cultures.

In the past, Australian and New Zealand culture was much like that of Britain. Over the years, however, both countries have developed their own cultures. For example, Australians speak English, but in their own special way. *Bush* and *outback*, both meaning "back country," are words that fit their environment. They have also adopted Aborigine words such as *jumbuk*, which means "sheep," and *billabong*, which means "waterhole." In keeping with Australian ideas of friendliness, both friends and strangers are greeted as "mate."

Most Australians and New Zealanders live in single-family houses built in styles that would look familiar to people from the United States. There are very few apartment buildings except in New Zealand's largest cities.

Australia's foods show the tastes of its many cultures. Australians eat seafood, beef, and lamb, as well as less-familiar

On Anzac Day military veterans honor those who have died in wars.

foods such as water buffalo, crocodile, and kangaroo. Traditional British foods such as scones, a type of biscuit eaten with butter and jam, are often served at the meal called afternoon tea. In the cities Greek, Vietnamese, Thai, Indian, and Chinese restaurants are very popular. Another favorite Australian food is a thick strong-tasting paste made of yeast that is spread on toast.

New Zealanders eat a lot of lamb, beef, seafood, fruits, and vegetables. Tearooms are popular places for meals and snacks, such as pies filled with meat or vegetables.

Each year on January 26, Australians celebrate Australia Day to mark the day Britain colonized Australia. Australians and New Zealanders both celebrate Anzac Day on April 25 of each year. On that day they honor the memory of the Australia-New Zealand Army Corps soldiers who have died in wars.

Sydney is the largest city in Australia. The sail-like Sydney Opera house, which opened in 1973, stands on a peninsula in Sydney Harbor and is a city landmark.

LOCATE IT

AUSTRALIA

Sydney

Australian heroes, who remind people of the early settlers' independent spirit and determination, are still celebrated in popular songs. "Waltzing Matilda" is the tale of a man who died rather than give up his way of life roaming the bush. This song is familiar around the world as Australia's unofficial national song.

Sports figures who have won fame in tennis, swimming, track and field, and boat racing are another source of national pride. Australians were thrilled when runner Cathy Freeman became the first Aborigine to win a gold medal at the 2000 Olympics in Sydney.

Australians spend much of their free time camping, hiking, swimming, and sailing.

Gold-medal winner Cathy Freeman at the 2000 Summer Olympic Games in Sydney

Water sports are very popular because most people live along the coast. Aussies, as Australians call themselves, also like team sports, both as fans and as players. They play rugby, cricket, and netball, which is like basketball but is played without a backboard.

Australian artists take themes from their surroundings and their beginnings. Aborigine cave and rock paintings are now saved and protected as part of Australia's national heritage. Novels, short stories, and poetry celebrate Australian ways of life. These include works written by present-day Aborigine authors.

Rugby is a popular sport in the region. There are two forms of the game—rugby union for amateurs and rugby league for professionals.

New Zealanders call themselves Kiwis, after the bird that is their national symbol. Like Australians, most New Zealanders live in cities, but they too love the outdoors. Swimming, hiking, boating, and mountain climbing are favorite activities. Also like Australians, they like to play and watch team sports, especially rugby. Their national team, which includes Maori players, is one of the world's most successful rugby teams.

New Zealand strives to improve race relations. Along with English, Maori is an official language. Many schools teach the Maori language and Maori songs, dances, and literature. Traditional Maori painting and carving are important parts of New Zealand's culture. New Zealanders also value education highly. Education is free for all children, and nearly all New Zealanders can read and write. In recent

A Maori artist (above) carves wood. The didgeridoo (left) is an Aborigine musical instrument.

years many immigrants from Asia have found New Zealand a land of opportunity and equality. They have added their traditions and customs to New Zealand's cultural mix.

REVIEW Why are Australia and New Zealand considered multicultural nations?

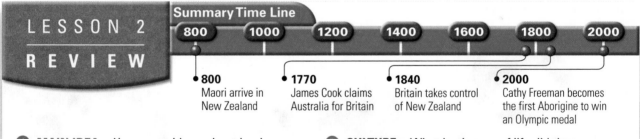

LESSON 2 REVIEW

Summary Time Line

800 — 1000 — 1200 — 1400 — 1600 — 1800 — 2000

800 Maori arrive in New Zealand

1770 James Cook claims Australia for Britain

1840 Britain takes control of New Zealand

2000 Cathy Freeman becomes the first Aborigine to win an Olympic medal

① **MAIN IDEA** How were ideas about land important in Australia and New Zealand?

② **WHY IT MATTERS** How have Australia and New Zealand developed as multicultural nations?

③ **VOCABULARY** In two sentences explain how the terms **Aborigine** and **dreamtime** are related.

④ **TIME LINE** Which country did the British first claim—Australia or New Zealand?

⑤ **READING SKILL—Make Inferences** How might the Aborigines' belief in the dreamtime help them in today's world?

⑥ **GEOGRAPHY** From which lands did the Aborigines and the Maori migrate to enter Australia and New Zealand?

⑦ **CULTURE** What basic way of life did the Aborigines and Maori follow?

⑧ **HISTORY** How did Europeans set up colonies in Australia and New Zealand?

⑨ **CRITICAL THINKING—Hypothesize** Why might Aborigines be unwilling to use technology to change the environment?

PERFORMANCE—Create a Symbol
People often create symbols such as flags to represent their nation, state, or community. Think about Australia and New Zealand. Create a symbol you feel best represents the culture of one of these countries. Explain why you chose that symbol. Display your symbol and explanation in the classroom.

· SKILLS · CITIZENSHIP

Act as a Responsible Citizen

WHY IT MATTERS

Responsible citizens stay informed about what is happening in their nation or community. They participate in their nation's government. When a nation faces problems, its citizens often need to take action if those problems are to be solved.

In a multicultural nation such as New Zealand, it is especially important to be well informed. New Zealand's citizens must work together to address the issues and concerns of all the members of its diverse population.

Maori children on their way to school

WHAT YOU NEED TO KNOW

Imagine that you are a citizen of New Zealand. You read the following paragraph in a newspaper.

New Zealand has made efforts to improve educational opportunities for the Maori, who make up about 20 percent of New Zealand's population. In general, however, the Maori continue to have fewer educational opportunities than the rest of the population. For example, only 6 percent of New Zealand's college students are Maori. Lack of education means that Maori often must take lower-paying, less-skilled jobs. The average Maori makes a wage that is only about 80 percent that of

NEW ZEALAND FIRE SERVICE

KAHUKURA

the average non-Maori. In addition, about 16 percent of the Maori are jobless, whereas the unemployment rate for non-Maori is only about 6 percent.

The following steps will help you act as a responsible citizen.

Step 1 **Keep informed about problems your nation or community faces.**

Step 2 **Think about ways to solve these problems.**

Step 3 **Decide how to bring about change in ways that would be good for the entire nation or community.**

Step 4 **Think about how you can help, either alone or with other citizens.**

You now know more about the Maoris in New Zealand. You also know the steps to follow to be a responsible citizen. Continue to imagine that you are a citizen of New Zealand. Do you feel better prepared to make decisions about New Zealand's problems?

▶ PRACTICE THE SKILL

Answer the questions below. Follow the steps for acting as a responsible citizen.

❶ What problem does New Zealand have?

❷ What is a possible solution to the problem?

❸ Would your solution benefit New Zealand as a whole? Explain.

❹ What could you do to help, as an individual or as a member of a school group?

▶ APPLY WHAT YOU LEARNED

Work with a small group of classmates to think of a problem facing your community or your school. Use the guidelines for acting as a responsible citizen to think of a plan for tackling the problem. Choose one person to present your group's idea to the rest of the class.

CITIZENSHIP SKILLS

3

Australia and New Zealand Today

Australia and New Zealand today have ties with countries around the globe. Like people all over the world, Australians and New Zealanders face great challenges in the twenty-first century.

Changing Economies Down Under

In the past Australia's economy was based on exporting agricultural and mining products. Today, however, manufacturing and service industries, such as tourism, are making that economy stronger and more diverse.

The use of modern farming methods has allowed Australia to become a major producer of agricultural goods. In addition to having enough to feed its people, the nation exports nearly two-thirds of those goods, including beef, wheat, dairy products, and wool. Australia leads the world in wool production. It provides more than 25 percent of the world's total supply.

Like the wool industry, mining has been important since colonial times, and Australia is one of the world's leading producers of minerals. Important mineral exports include iron ore, gold, coal, and bauxite. Gold brought Australia early wealth and growth as thousands of new settlers joined the gold rush of the mid-1800s. Today gold is still a major source of the nation's wealth and the second-largest export.

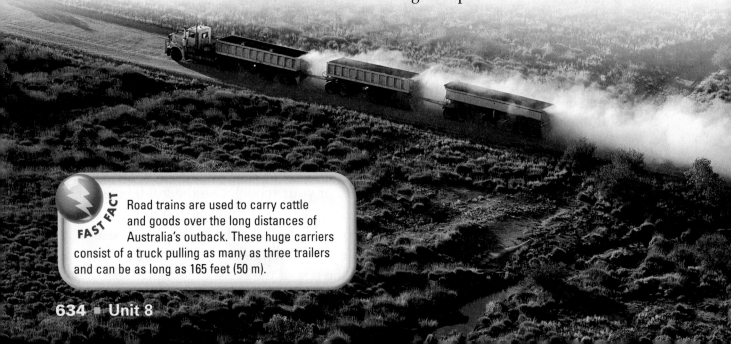

FAST FACT Road trains are used to carry cattle and goods over the long distances of Australia's outback. These huge carriers consist of a truck pulling as many as three trailers and can be as long as 165 feet (50 m).

Workers in New Zealand harvest kiwifruit for export. The fruit is also called a Chinese gooseberry.

Manufacturing is rapidly growing. Starting in the mid-1980s, the government began lifting trade barriers to encourage Australian industries to become more efficient and competitive. It also welcomed foreign investment. Today businesses manufacture products for Australians. They also export goods such as high-tech electronic equipment, software, chemicals, processed foods and minerals, paper and plastic, and cars. About 75 percent of Australians work in service industries. Of these, the fastest-growing is tourism. Tourist offices worldwide promote the nation's unique natural areas and friendly people.

Like that of Australia, New Zealand's economy depends heavily on agricultural exports, primarily meat, dairy products, and wool. New Zealand is the world's largest producer of lamb.

Although only 2 percent of the land is suitable for farming, New Zealanders have made it highly productive. The nation grows and exports an abundance of grains and fruits. It also exports forest products such as timber, paper, and pulp.

Natural gas is used to generate some electricity, but the nation relies mainly on hydroelectric power. Hot springs are also used to provide **geothermal power**, power that is generated from heat beneath the earth. Both geothermal and hydroelectric power are important economic resources, and they are renewable.

New Zealand's economy is not as diversified as that of Australia. Its manufacturing mainly centers on food processing and turning timber into wood products. As is the case with Australia, one of New Zealand's most important service industries is tourism.

In the past New Zealand's government protected industries and limited foreign investments. Taxes on imports were also high. In the 1990s the government changed its policies and began promoting an open market with other nations.

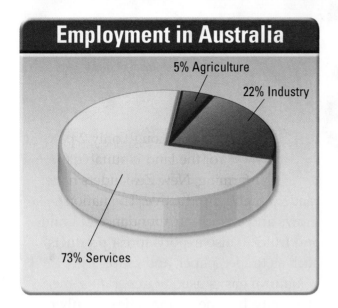

Employment in Australia

5% Agriculture

22% Industry

73% Services

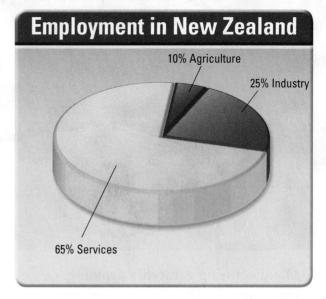

Employment in New Zealand

10% Agriculture

25% Industry

65% Services

Analyze Graphs These circle graphs show percents of employment by type in Australia and New Zealand.

◆ Which country relies more on primary industries?

For many years Britain was the major trading partner of both Australia and New Zealand. Britain favored both nations over others in trade agreements. Those ties weakened after World War II. As the United States increased its influence in the South Pacific, Australia and New Zealand forged closer ties with it. In 1972 Britain joined the European Economic Community. It no longer gave preference in trade to Australia and New Zealand. The two nations were forced to build stronger economic ties with each other and with their Asian and Pacific Islands neighbors. Instead of labeling the nations of eastern Asia the "Far East," Australians and New Zealanders more often speak of Asia as the "Near North."

Today Australia's largest markets for exports are Japan and China. More and more, Australia is aligning itself with Asia. While New Zealand's largest trading partner is Australia, it too is expanding its markets, especially to the Pacific Islands. With New Zealand's increasing population from the Pacific Islands, the nation recognizes its South Pacific ties. A former prime minister of New Zealand, David Lange, expressed the view of many New Zealanders when he said,

> **❝** We . . . accept what the map tells us, that we are a South Pacific nation. **❞**

REVIEW Which nation leads the world in the production of wool?

Conserving the Environment

European settlement had a devastating impact on the environments of Australia and New Zealand. Grazing animals, farming, mining, and logging destroyed plant and animal habitats. In addition to sheep and cattle, Europeans introduced dogs, cats, goats, pigs, rabbits, and weasels, which preyed on native animals and devoured native plants. Settlers hunted the kiwi bird and the koala, and both nearly became extinct.

Today Australians and New Zealanders are very aware of the importance of conserving their environments and unique wildlife. Environmentalists, sometimes called "greenies," have tried to influence governments to protect the land and endangered animals such as the platypus.

Since 1974, Australia has been a member of the United Nations World Heritage program, which identifies, protects, and encourages saving national treasures. Australia has ten national heritage sites including the Great Barrier Reef.

The government of New Zealand is a leader in conservation efforts. The Department of Conservation protects about 30 percent of New Zealand's land. It oversees 13 national parks and numerous nature preserves. An important government policy is the protection of whales and seals in the waters off New Zealand's coasts.

Since the mid-1980s New Zealand has not allowed nuclear-powered ships or ships carrying nuclear weapons to enter its ports. The policy at first caused a strain on relations with the government of the United States. New Zealand stood firm, however, and it is also a leader in opposing nuclear testing in the South Pacific.

REVIEW Which part of New Zealand's government protects land and wildlife?

Humpback whale

POINTS OF VIEW
Protecting the Whales

Members of the International Whaling Commission met to discuss the future of whale hunting. While some nations push for the right to hunt for whales, others are in favor of sanctuaries, or areas in which whales would be protected.

ROBERT HILL, Australia's environmental minister

❝ Over the past two centuries of industrial whaling, whale populations in the South Pacific collapsed. The animals require protection to allow them to recover to natural levels. ❞

MINORU MORIMOTO, Japanese representative for the International Whaling Commission

❝ Sanctuaries are not only unnecessary but also obstruct science. Japan considers the proposal irresponsible. ❞

HELEN CLARK, New Zealand's prime minister

❝ New Zealand is one of the strongest supporters of permanent sanctuaries for whales. ❞

RUNE FROVIK, spokesperson for the High North Alliance

❝ To hunt whale is one way of using natural marine resources, and whaling provides food for people and it provides a living for those that are involved in this activity. In the same way as we fish fish, then it's similar to hunt whales. ❞

Analyze the Viewpoints

1 What views about whale hunting does each person hold?

2 **Make It Relevant** Think about an issue that is important to your community. What is your viewpoint on that issue? Where do your classmates stand on that issue? Divide into two groups, and debate the issue.

Charles Perkins 1936–2000

Character Trait: Fairness

Growing up as an Aborigine, Charles Perkins faced many obstacles. Courageous and determined, he overcame discrimination at a time when Aborigines had few rights. He fought to become the first Aborigine to enter a university. A civil rights activist for decades, he was outspoken in criticizing the government's policies toward Aborigines. Even his critics praised him for his lifelong struggle for equality for Aborigines. At Perkins' funeral, a speaker compared him to Dr. Martin Luther King, Jr. Australia's prime minister called him a "tireless fighter" who was fearless in his struggle for civil rights.

MULTIMEDIA BIOGRAPHIES
Visit The Learning Site at **www.harcourtschool.com/biographies** to learn about other famous people.

Political Challenges

Australia and New Zealand are both parliamentary democracies within the Commonwealth of Nations. Although they are united with other members by common interests and problems, they are independent nations headed by a prime minister and a parliament.

Australia's government has elements of both the British and the United States systems. Like Britain, Australia's prime minister and cabinet are named from the majority party in parliament, and they are responsible to the parliament. If a majority of the parliament opposes the prime minister, he or she can lose that office. A new parliamentary election would then be held.

However, unlike Britain but like the United States, Australia has a written constitution. Another similarity to the United States is that the states of Australia have powers not given to the national government.

New Zealand's government follows the British pattern. Like Britain, New Zealand does not have a written constitution. Also, like those of Britain and Australia, its government is headed by a prime minister

Informally known as the Beehive, the Executive Wing is one of New Zealand's parliament buildings in Wellington.

and cabinet named from the majority party in the parliament.

The governments of Australia and New Zealand have made progress in improving relations with Aborigines and Maori. A major issue is that of land rights. Aborigine leaders such as activist Charles Perkins struggled for many years for rights to their sacred lands and compensation for those they lost. Through negotiations, Australia has returned to Aborigines the guardianship of sacred territories. In response to Aborigine demands, the courts have ruled that Aborigines are the original people of Australia. Whites had long declared that whites were the first people. In 1999, Australia's parliament made a formal apology to Aborigines for past mistreatment. Still, Aborigine groups

The Maori queen and the prime minister of New Zealand signed a 1994 land settlement agreement.

continue to demand ownership of many more of their original lands.

New Zealand, too, has faced the issue of land rights for Maori. Some lands have been returned, but most compensation is paid with money. In 1994 the government promised $1 billion over ten years to compensate Maori for lost land. The following year the government gave the Tainui tribe $170 million. Many Maori are active in politics, and groups continue to lobby the government not only for land rights but also for more equality in employment, health care, and housing.

REVIEW In what way is Australia's government like that of the United States?

LESSON 3
REVIEW

1 **MAIN IDEA** How have Australia and New Zealand faced economic, environmental, and political challenges in a modern world?

2 **WHY IT MATTERS** Why is it important for Australia and New Zealand to develop ties with nations around the world?

3 **VOCABULARY** Define and use **geothermal power** in a sentence that explains why it is a renewable resource.

4 **READING SKILL—Make Inferences** Australians and New Zealanders emphasize the importance of conserving the environment. What can you infer from their desire to protect their land and resources?

5 **ECONOMICS** How is Australia diversifying its economy?

6 **CIVICS AND GOVERNMENT** What are the roles of Australia and New Zealand within the Commonwealth of Nations?

7 **CRITICAL THINKING—Hypothesize** What might have happened if the governments of Australia and New Zealand had not protected the nations' industries against foreign competition?

8 **CRITICAL THINKING—Evaluate** What kinds of policies would you suggest to the governments of Australia and New Zealand to improve relations with Aborigines and Maori?

PERFORMANCE—Create a Bulletin
Think about an environmental issue in your community. It might be water, air, or land pollution, loss of animal or plant habitats, or destruction of open space. With a group of classmates, write a bulletin to alert your community to the problem and offer your solutions. Place your bulletin on the school or community bulletin board.

Compare Line Graphs

VOCABULARY

line graph
trend

▶ WHY IT MATTERS

Australia and New Zealand both have many resources, including livestock, grain, fruits, vegetables, lumber, gold, iron ore, coal, bauxite, and even some natural gas and petroleum. Suppose you are going to prepare a report on recent exports from Australia and New Zealand. You want to show this information in a way that makes comparisons easy. One way to do this is by drawing line graphs. A **line graph** is a diagram that can show change over time. It is useful in showing a **trend**, or the way something changes over time. Knowing how to read and draw line graphs will help you understand and compare information.

▶ WHAT YOU NEED TO KNOW

Line Graph A shows how the value of goods exported from Australia changed from 1995 to 1999. Each dot shows how much trade took place in a given year. A line connects all the dots. Depending on the information, the line may go up or down or stay at the same level. The general direction of the line shows the trend in Australia's exports.

Line Graph B is a double-line graph. It shows how the values of fresh fruits and fresh vegetables exported from New Zealand changed from 1995 to 1999. In addition to showing trends, the double-line graph makes it easy to compare the values of the two exports.

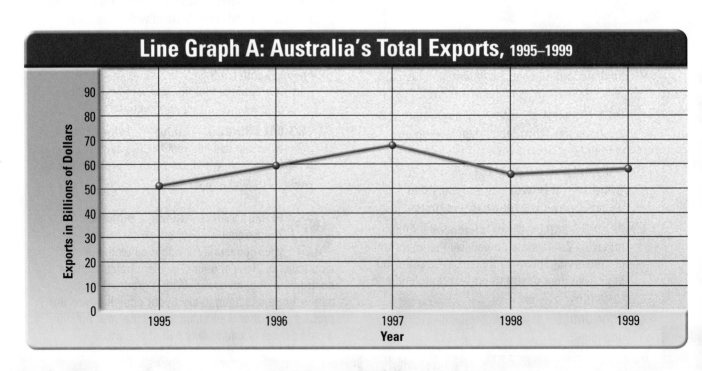

Line Graph A: Australia's Total Exports, 1995–1999

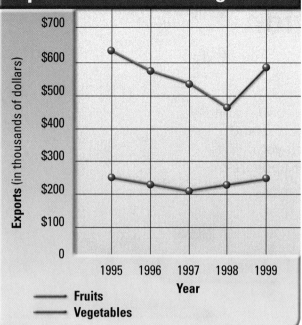

Line Graph B: New Zealand's Exports of Fruit and Vegetables

Exports (in thousands of dollars)

$700
$600
$500
$400
$300
$200
$100
0

1995   1996   1997   1998   1999

Year

—— Fruits
—— Vegetables

➡ PRACTICE THE SKILL

Compare the values in the line graphs by answering the questions that follow. Think about the advantages and disadvantages of using line graphs to show information.

1 In which year was the value of Australia's exports the greatest? In which year was it the least?

2 About how much growth in value did Australian exports have from 1995 to 1997?

3 In 1995 New Zealand's exports of fresh fruits and fresh vegetables brought in about how much money? how much in 1998?

4 Which export, fruits or vegetables, brought in the most income in New Zealand between 1995 and 1999? Explain your answer.

➡ APPLY WHAT YOU LEARNED

Using both line graphs on these pages, write a paragraph that summarizes trends in Australia's exports and New Zealand's exports in recent years. Share your paragraph with a partner, and compare your summaries.

CHART AND GRAPH SKILLS

18 Review and Test Preparation

USE YOUR READING SKILLS

Complete this graphic organizer to show that you understand how to make inferences about Australia and New Zealand by using the details from what you have read and your own knowledge. A copy of this graphic organizer appears on page 170 of the Activity Book.

Cultural Influences in Australia and New Zealand

DETAILS + KNOWLEDGE → INFERENCE

DETAILS

People from Southeast Asia settled in Australia. They became known as Aborigines. They had no formal government, and they believed in dreamtime spirits. In New Zealand the first people came from Polynesia and called themselves the Maori. They formed tribes and honored gods of nature and their ancestors. Unlike the Aborigines, they were fierce warriors. In 1788 Britain began using Australia as a penal colony. Eventually, British colonists settled in Australia and New Zealand. Immigrants from around the world have also come to Australia and New Zealand.

KNOWLEDGE

_____

INFERENCE

_____

THINK & WRITE

Write a Persuasive Letter Australia's government has returned some sacred lands to the Aborigines. However, many more lands have not been returned. Write a letter to the Australian government, explaining why you support or do not support the Aborigines' claims to sacred lands.

Write a Report Think about some of the plants and animals found only in Australia and New Zealand. Write a report about these plants and animals. In your report, describe each plant and animal, tell where it can be found, and say whether or not it is endangered. Draw pictures to illustrate your report.

1500s
Tribal wars among the Maori begin by this time

1788
Australia becomes a British penal colony

1800s
Aborigine lands and culture nearly destroyed in Australia

1840
British rule in New Zealand

2000
Cathy Freeman becomes the first Aborigine to win an Olympic medal

USE THE TIME LINE

Use the chapter summary time line to answer these questions.

1 When did the Maori arrive in New Zealand?

2 How many years after the Maori arrived in New Zealand did Britain take control of the island?

USE VOCABULARY

Use the terms at right to complete the sentences.

marsupial (p. 623)

station (p. 624)

Aborigine (p. 625)

dreamtime (p. 626)

3 In Australia there are vast sheep and cattle ranches called ____.

4 Scientists believe that the ____ first began to settle Australia as long as 40,000 to 60,000 years ago.

5 A kangaroo is a kind of ____.

6 The Australian Aborigine story of how the land was created is called ____.

RECALL FACTS

7 Why do most Australians live in cities along the coast?

8 How does the art of Aborigines connect them to their culture and beliefs?

9 How did the Maori pass on their history and beliefs?

10 How did European colonialism affect the land and people of Australia and New Zealand?

Write the letter of the best choice.

11 **TEST PREP** Scientists believe that Aborigines migrated to Australia from—
  A Southeast Asia.
  B Polynesia.
  C Africa.
  D South America.

12 **TEST PREP** New Zealand is the world's largest producer of—
  F wool.
  G timber.
  H lamb.
  J geothermal power.

THINK CRITICALLY

13 Why do you think Britain chose to set up a penal colony in Australia?

14 How are the cultures and history of Australia represented in its art, literature, and music?

15 How has the land in Australia and New Zealand influenced the economy in each country?

APPLY SKILLS

Act as a Responsible Citizen

16 Find a newspaper or magazine article about a group of people who solved a problem in their community or country. Write a report describing how these people acted as responsible citizens to solve the problem.

Compare Line Graphs

17 Make a line graph that shows your social studies test scores. What is the trend in your scores? Have your scores gone up over time? If not, what can you do to improve the trend?

EASTER ISLAND

Easter Island, also called Rapa Nui, was named by Dutch explorers who arrived on Easter Day 1722. Although it is a territory of Chile, Easter Island is considered a part of the Pacific Islands. Scientists believe that Pacific islanders arrived there around A.D. 400. These first settlers are credited with carving the island's giant stone statues called *moai*.

LOCATE IT

PACIFIC OCEAN

SOUTH AMERICA

Easter Island

NEW ZEALAND

19

The Pacific Islands and Antarctica

" The deep dark-shining
Pacific leans on the land, . . .
To the outmost margins. "

—Robinson Jeffers, from *Night,* 1925

CHAPTER READING SKILL

Predict a Likely Outcome

When you **predict a likely outcome,** you use what you already know and new information from what you have read.

As you read, use your knowledge and evidence from the text to predict likely outcomes.

WHAT YOU + KNOW	WHAT YOU = READ	PREDICTION	WHAT ACTUALLY HAPPENED

MAIN IDEA
Read to find out how people migrated to and settled the islands of the Pacific Ocean.

WHY IT MATTERS
As people from other lands came to the Pacific Islands, unique cultures developed.

VOCABULARY
outrigger
tabu
kastom
mana

Horseshoe-shaped Matangi is one of the hundreds of islands of Fiji.

LOCATE IT

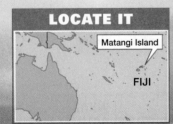
Matangi Island
FIJI

Island Migrations

In the 1800s geographers divided the islands of the Pacific Ocean into three groups. They are Melanesia, Micronesia, and Polynesia. Together they are called the Pacific Islands. Today's islanders are descendants of people from Southeast Asia who traveled across the Pacific Ocean thousands of years ago to settle there. Pacific islanders thus share a common heritage. Their island homes are small and far apart. On maps most look like tiny green dots on the huge blue sea. Because great distances separated them and because their environments differed, Pacific islanders developed different cultures and ways of life.

Melanesia

The islands of Melanesia lie north of Australia and east of Indonesia. They include New Guinea (GIH•nee), the Solomon Islands, Vanuatu (van•WAH•too), New Caledonia (ka•luh•DOH•nyuh), and Fiji (FEE•jee). Many scientists believe that New Guinea was the first to be settled because it is closest to Southeast Asia. The earliest Fijians were probably people who came from Southeast Asia, island-hopping through Indonesia about 40,000 years ago. Some also believe they may have been related to the Aborigines of Australia.

New Guinea's earliest settlers, called Papuans (PA•pyuh•wuhnz), were hunters and gatherers. Some of them settled in the forests of the highlands. They lived in small groups and used stone tools. Some Papuans stayed along the coast of New Guinea, where they lived by fishing and hunting. Over time, some Papuans who lived along the coast left to settle the nearby Solomon Islands.

For about 30,000 years there was no contact with people from other lands. Eventually, however, more people from Southeast

Asia began arriving in New Guinea and the Solomon Islands in oceangoing canoes. They brought new kinds of plants, such as yams and taro, a tropical plant used as food. The newcomers introduced animals such as pigs, chickens, and dogs, which they brought with them. They also introduced a new language.

The newcomers fished, farmed, and hunted in the coastal areas they shared with Papuans and Solomon Islanders. They taught their neighbors how to carve larger and more seaworthy canoes. Groups of islanders began traveling south and east about 3,500 years ago. They settled New Caledonia and the island chains of Vanuatu and Fiji. In time they became the people now known as Melanesians.

REVIEW What did newcomers contribute to the settlement of Melanesia?

Micronesia

Made up mostly of islands even smaller than those in Melanesia or Polynesia, most of Micronesia lies north of the equator. It includes different groups, or chains, of islands. These island chains are named Caroline, Marshall, Gilbert, and Mariana. The name *Micronesia*, which means "small islands," describes the region. While a few of its 2,000 or so islands have volcanoes, most are small, low-lying coral islands.

Micronesians include more than one group of people, each of whom settled over a period of many centuries. Experts believe that around 1500 B.C. people from the Philippine Islands, sailing east, landed on the Mariana Islands. To the south, Melanesians began their voyages once again. Around 1000 B.C. groups of people began traveling north from New Guinea, the Solomon Islands, and the Fiji island chain. Over the next few centuries, more Melanesians reached the Caroline, Gilbert, and Marshall Islands. Micronesians are the descendants of Melanesians and people from the Philippines.

To explore the widely scattered islands, Micronesians had to cross great distances. They built large single and double canoes with outriggers.

Outriggers are wooden beams that extend from the sides to keep the canoe stable. Micronesians also added sails to some of their canoes.

To be sure of reaching the right islands, Micronesians watched the directions of the winds, ocean currents, and migrating birds. Since most of Micronesia's islands were low-lying, they could not always be seen from a distance. Sailors learned to read the patterns of waves as they neared land. This made it easier for them to find distant islands. They constructed stick charts, which were actually navigation charts that helped them learn the locations of many islands. Sailors tied flat strips of cane together to show the patterns of waves. They used shells to show the locations of the islands. They also became experts in locating their position by studying the stars.

REVIEW How were Micronesians able to sail the great distances between their islands?

A CLOSER LOOK
A Micronesian Village

Life for the early people of Micronesia revolved around the sea.

1. Micronesians built dugout canoes and larger outrigger canoes for transportation.
2. Fishing provided an important food source.
3. Canoes with outriggers and sails were used for deep-sea fishing and long ocean journeys.

❖ What tools did the early Micronesians use to catch fish?

Polynesia

People known as Polynesians settled a huge triangle of scattered islands in the Pacific. The islands stretched from Hawaii to New Zealand and from Fiji to Easter Island. Scholars believe that groups of people, probably from Fiji, first settled the island chains of Tonga and Samoa about 1500 B.C. By 200 B.C. the Polynesians had settled Tahiti, the Society Islands, and the Marquesas Islands. They sailed north to Hawaii sometime near A.D. 400. About 600 years later they sailed south to New Zealand. Long before Europeans began voyages of discovery, much of the Pacific Islands had been settled by Polynesians.

Europeans could not believe that people who used stone tools, had no written languages, and did not use instruments such as the compass could possibly have sailed so far. Some Europeans said the Polynesians had come from India or the Americas. Others believed they reached the Pacific Islands by accident when they lost their way on fishing trips.

A voyage made in 1976 showed that Polynesians could indeed have sailed long distances. Sailors in a double canoe traveled from Hawaii to Tahiti and to New Zealand. In 1995 sailors crossed the ocean from the Cook Islands in the central Pacific to Tahiti, on to Hawaii, and back again, using only traditional navigation methods.

REVIEW How did Europeans once think Polynesians reached the Pacific Islands?

Pacific Island Cultures

As people from other lands arrived in the Pacific Islands over the centuries, the islanders developed cultures and ways of life that were borrowed and adapted. The landscape of the Pacific Islands also affected how cultures developed. For example, the mountains and forests of Melanesia's islands separated villages. This caused the Melanesians to develop different languages and ways of living.

Melanesian communities varied from small villages with a few families to large villages of people who were related to one another. Community leaders in the Pacific Islands gained power in different ways. In Fiji chiefs were considered sacred, and it was **tabu**, or forbidden, to touch them. Most Fijian chiefs inherited their positions, but anyone who showed great skill in warfare or who gained wealth could become a chief. In the Solomon Islands and Vanuatu, however, villages were governed by **kastom**, or custom. Village elders passed traditional beliefs from generation to generation. Breaking kastom was a serious offense.

Micronesians followed a different pattern. They created clans, or classes, of people who were related. People inherited land and a place in society through their clans. On some islands leadership was based on how long a clan's ancestors had lived on the land. Oral traditions passed down through generations were important because they told the history of ancestors.

Maui

A legendary figure in the Pacific Islands is Maui, a hero and trickster who was believed to be part god and part human. Stories said that he stole fire from the gods and gave it to humans and that he created the first dog. Maui was also said to be an expert at fishing who pulled from the sea fish so huge that they turned into the islands of the Pacific Ocean. Depending on which island they say Maui created, storytellers have different versions of the bait he used. Cook Islanders say he baited his hook with coconuts and leaves. Polynesians claim he used either his own ear or red feathers.

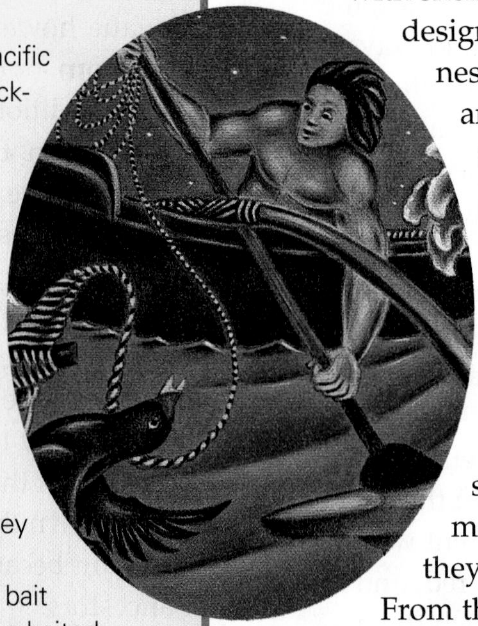

Some Micronesians were skilled in crafts. They made wooden bowls and boxes inlaid with shells, and they carved detailed designs on their canoes. Micronesians at first built their homes and temples of wood, but in time they began to use stone as well. Huge stones that held up houses still remain on the Mariana Islands.

The last Pacific Island culture to develop was that of the Polynesians. They settled in villages along the shores and in the valleys of mountainous islands. There they farmed, fished, and hunted. From the thick forests they cut timber for homes and for their great canoes. These were used for trade among their islands and for war. Polynesians were

The harbor and modern buildings at Papeete, the capital of French Polynesia, make the city a popular stop for ships crossing the Pacific Ocean.

LOCATE IT

Papeete

TAHITI

Crafts for ceremonies and for decorations have long been made in the Pacific Islands, including this bone carving (left), mask (center), and basket (right).

known as warriors, and rival groups fought for lands and positions of power.

Polynesians formed a clan society whose members were related to the same ancestor. The clan chiefs were older men who could show their direct relation to an ancestor. Since there was no written language, oral histories were very important for a chief to prove his ancestry. A chief also had to have **mana**, or personal power, which Polynesians believed came directly from the gods. In Samoa a chief's abilities were more important than who his ancestors were.

Pacific Island cultures grew and adapted slowly to change over the centuries. With the coming of Europeans, however, new conflicts, new technologies, and new threats to their cultures suddenly burst upon the islands.

REVIEW **What important elements of culture did Pacific islanders share?**

LESSON 1
REVIEW

1 MAIN IDEA How were early people able to travel over great distances and settle islands in the Pacific Ocean?

2 WHY IT MATTERS Why are the great migrations of Pacific islanders important?

3 VOCABULARY Use the words **tabu** and **mana** in a sentence about the position of a chief in Pacific Island culture.

4 READING SKILL—Predict a Likely Outcome How do you think Pacific Island culture will change as the influences of technology and outside cultures increase?

5 GEOGRAPHY What are the three main geographical divisions of the Pacific Islands?

6 HISTORY What factors may have caused some Pacific island people to live separately from others for thousands of years?

7 SCIENCE AND TECHNOLOGY What tools, skills, and other advancements helped make the long sea voyages of Pacific islanders possible?

8 CRITICAL THINKING—Analyze Why do you think Pacific Island cultures began to change after 30,000 years?

PERFORMANCE—Make a Model Pacific islanders built a variety of dwellings, ranging from small family homes to large meeting houses, homes for chiefs, and places for ceremonies. With a partner or group, select a culture and research its architecture. Then choose a building and construct a model. Write a description to go with your model, and explain how the building was used.

Marshall Islands Stick Charts

Living in a vast ocean, the sailors of the Marshall Islands were among the best in the world. They sailed by observing not only the stars but also the ocean. Experienced sailors recorded their observations of ocean waves and currents using stick charts like the ones shown on these pages. Stick charts were not used as maps but as teaching aids. They were used to explain the ocean patterns to young sailors, who memorized the charts. In addition to stick charts, the sailors of the Marshall Islands also studied cloud shapes, winds, and even the flight patterns of birds to find their way from island to island in the Pacific Ocean.

FROM THE CULTURAL HERITAGE STUDIES DEPARTMENT OF CHARLES STURT UNIVERSITY, AUSTRALIA

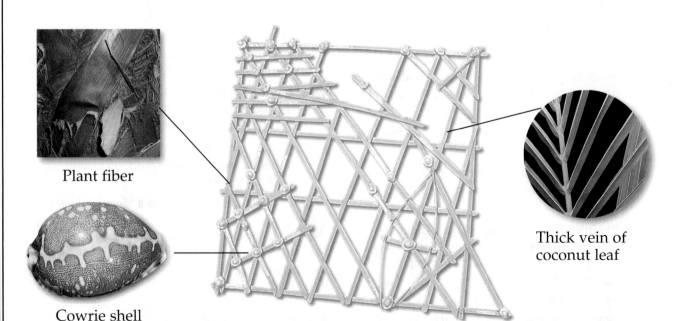

Plant fiber

Cowrie shell

Thick vein of coconut leaf

Analyze the Primary Source

1 **What are stick charts made of?**

2 **What do stick charts show?**

3 **How are stick charts similar to and different from maps?**

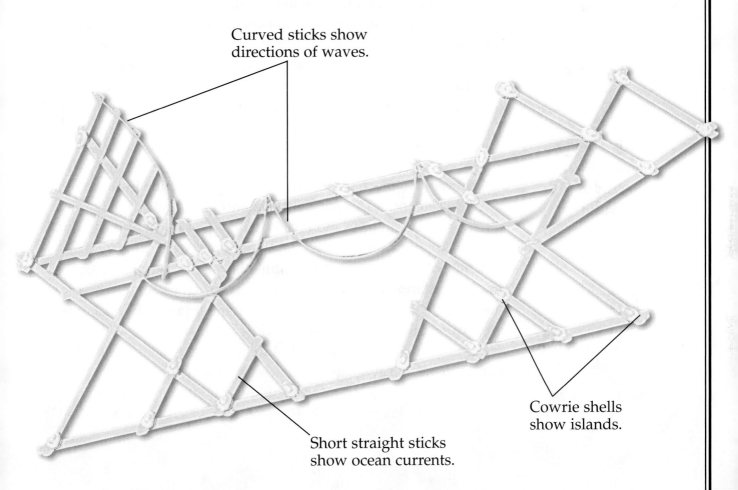

Curved sticks show
directions of waves.

Cowrie shells
show islands.

Short straight sticks
show ocean currents.

ACTIVITY

Make a Stick Chart With a partner, make a chart, like a stick chart, of your classroom or school. Use only materials found in the classroom. Then draw a map of the same area. Explain the advantages and disadvantages of the map and the stick chart for showing location, direction, and distance.

RESEARCH

Visit The Learning Site at **www.harcourtschool.com/primarysources** to research other maps and charts.

MAIN IDEA
Read to find out how
European exploration
affected the islands of
the South Pacific.

WHY IT MATTERS
The nations of the Pacific
Islands are no longer isolated
from the rest of the world.

VOCABULARY

continental island
high island
low island
copra
trust territory

The waters around the forest-covered Rock Islands of Palau are home to abundant marine life, including 350 kinds of coral and more than 1,400 kinds of fish.

Island Nations

It is estimated that as many as 20,000 islands are scattered across the South Pacific Ocean. These islands lie in groups, or chains. Many are separated by great distances. Some are large and mountainous. Others are low-lying specks in the ocean. Some have thousands of people, some have only a few hundred, and most have no people at all. Some islands in the Pacific are independent nations. Others are self-governing territories of countries in Europe, Asia, or North America. All must deal with the problems and opportunities faced by nations in the modern world.

An Ocean Environment

Geographers place the islands of the South Pacific in three physical categories. A **continental island** is one category. It refers to an island or island chain that lies just north of the continent of Australia and was probably once part of it. New Guinea and the Solomon Islands are continental islands. Another category is a **high island**. This kind of island formed when undersea volcanoes erupted and built up land to form mountains. High islands are located all over the South Pacific. Hawaii and New Zealand are high islands. New Guinea is a high island as well as a continental island. A **low island** is made up mostly of volcanic rock and coral reefs. Thousands of low islands dot the South Pacific Ocean. People live on some of these, such as the Marshall

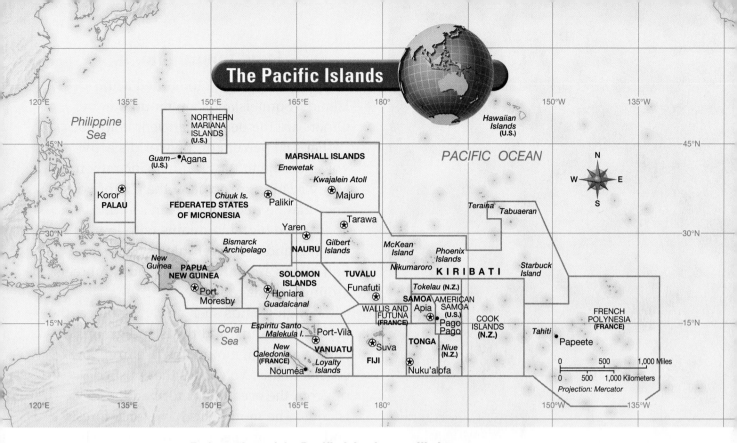

The Pacific Islands

Movement **Early settlers of the Pacific Islands most likely came from Southeast Asia.**

In which general direction did people move as they settled the Pacific Islands?

Islands, but most are not inhabited. Many barely rise above the ocean's surface.

The Pacific Islands share a warm and humid climate because almost all the islands lie in the tropics. On most islands the temperature seldom drops below 70°F (21°C) or rises above 80°F (27°C). In the highlands of Papua New Guinea, however, temperatures are somewhat cooler.

Rainfall varies throughout the region. Many of the low islands receive only a few inches of rain a year. Other islands,

especially the high islands in western Melanesia, often have more than 150 inches (381 cm) a year. Most places in the region have regular wet and dry seasons.

Typhoons often strike the Pacific Islands with violent winds and heavy rain. Like hurricanes in the Atlantic Ocean, typhoons in the Pacific sometimes cause property damage and loss of life. While typhoons may strike anytime, most occur between January and March.

REVIEW What are the major categories of islands in the South Pacific Ocean?

A fox bat

A bird of paradise

A skink

Cassowaries

A wide variety of animals are found on the Pacific Islands.

Land Environments

Landforms vary among the Pacific Islands. Some islands are mountainous. Others are the peaks of ancient volcanoes. Perhaps 80 percent of the world's active volcanoes lie in the South Pacific region. Many islands are actually the tips of volcanoes that lie under the ocean's surface. Some have high mountains with low beaches and coral reefs along their shores. Still others are only ring-shaped coral reefs around calm lagoons.

On high islands such as New Guinea, the Solomon Islands, and the island groups of Samoa and Fiji, mountains rise from low coastal plains. Volcanoes that pushed up from the ocean floor formed these islands. The mountains have thick forests and many high peaks. Although the climate is tropical, frost sometimes appears on the high peaks of Papua New Guinea.

Heavy rainfall on high islands supports rich vegetation. Mangrove trees and palms thrive in the low, swampy coastal areas of Papua New Guinea. Beech, pine, and oak trees grow in the mountains. Rain forests cover much of Fiji and the Solomon Islands. Both high and low islands have palm trees. They range from low, shrublike plants to the tall coconut palm. More than two-thirds of the world's palm trees grow in the Pacific Islands.

Most of the Pacific Islands are low-lying volcanic or coral-reef islands. Sandy beaches, tall palm trees, and clear blue waters ring thousands of the low islands. Although the climate is warm and humid, rainfall is not regular. The soil on many low islands is thin and not fertile. On islands with more rainfall, palm, banana, and breadfruit trees thrive.

Many kinds of birds, such as the flightless cassowary (KA•suh•wer•ee) and the brightly colored bird of paradise, live in the

Although coconuts are among the main export products of the Pacific Islands, fishing, tourism, and commercial farming are also important economic activities in the region.

Net fishing

Tourists on a boat

Harvesting sugarcane

Pacific Islands. Many seabirds, such as albatrosses and terns, are found in the islands. Rats, lizards, and bats are also common on many islands. Tonga has some of the world's largest bats. The Solomon Islands are home to a lizard called a skink, which catches food with its tail.

Trees are a major resource on many islands. Forests are heavily logged for lumber and other wood products. Oil, natural gas, and minerals such as gold, copper, and bauxite are found on many of the high islands. The coconut palm is an important food resource on all of the islands. Coconut meat, called **copra**, also provides oil that is very useful. It can be made into soap and other products.

The many fish found in the waters of the South Pacific are a major resource. The warm climate, blue waters, and scenic beauty of the Pacific Islands are resources, too. They attract thousands of tourists who, by visiting the islands, help the region's economy grow.

REVIEW What kind of trees are found in both high islands and low islands?

Colonial Rule

By the late 1800s Britain, Germany, France, Spain, and the United States were competing for control of the Pacific Islands. The impact of these nations on the region was great. They brought commercial farming, metal tools, and many new crops. They also introduced Christianity and western government.

After Spain's defeat in the Spanish-American War of 1898, Germany and the United States took over the Spanish possessions in Micronesia. By the early 1900s, Germany also held parts of Nauru, the Samoa Islands, and the northeastern part of New Guinea. The United States controlled Hawaii and the rest of the Samoa Islands. Meanwhile, France gained control of New Caledonia and French Polynesia and shared control of what is now Vanuatu with Britain. Britain held Fiji, Tonga, southeast New Guinea, and parts of present-day Kiribati, Tuvalu, and the Solomon Islands.

After Germany's defeat in World War I (1914–1918), New Zealand took over German Samoa and Australia received control of the northeastern part of New Guinea. Japan received control of the German possessions in Micronesia. Japan's occupation of the Pacific Islands resulted in great physical changes. Japan built roads, docks, and buildings whose remains can still be seen on the islands. Japan's control ended with its defeat in World War II (1939–1945).

During World War II many of the Pacific Islands became battlegrounds. Fierce fighting took place in particular on Guadalcanal (gwah•duhl•kuh•NAL) in the Solomon Islands, and on Iwo Jima, an island in the western Pacific. In 1945 Japan surrendered in the war and lost its Pacific empire.

REVIEW How did colonial rule affect the Pacific Islands?

Changes and Challenges

Through all the changes of rule in the 1800s and early 1900s, the Pacific islanders had little or no voice in their government. This continued after World War II. The United Nations decided that four areas in the Pacific should be governed as trust territories until they were ready for independence. A **trust territory** is an area placed under the temporary control of another country until it sets up its own government. New Zealand, Australia, Britain, and the United States governed the various trust territories in the Pacific.

This sunken battleship on the ocean floor is a reminder of the role of the Pacific Islands during World War II.

Since the 1960s many of the islands or island groups became independent nations. Samoa, for example, gained independence in 1962 and became a constitutional monarchy. In 1978 all of the Mariana Islands except Guam became a commonwealth of the United States. Guam remained a territory, or part, of the United States.

Building strong economies is the current challenge for these new nations. Many of them depend on tourism and primary industries, such as agriculture, logging, and mining.

No longer isolated from other regions, the Pacific Island nations are part of a global economy. Yet some islanders fear economic growth will destroy their traditional ways of life. These are problems only the islanders can solve. As a leader in Fiji said,

❝ Solutions for our problems in Fiji lie in Fiji. ❞

REVIEW What major challenges do the Pacific Island nations face?

Peacesat

Peacesat is a satellite communications network based at the University of Hawaii in Honolulu, Hawaii. Peacesat helps link the island nations of the Pacific. Because the Pacific Ocean is so large, island nations often have difficulty communicating with each other and with the rest of the world. Begun in 1971, Peacesat provides a way for island nations to share ideas, technology, and information that can benefit the people of the Pacific Islands.

A Peacesat satellite

LESSON 2
REVIEW

1 MAIN IDEA How did European exploration affect the development of the Pacific Islands?

2 WHY IT MATTERS How are Pacific Island nations connected to the rest of the world?

3 VOCABULARY How is a **trust territory** different from a colony?

4 READING SKILL—Predict a Likely Outcome What changes do you think would make Pacific islanders living in U.S. trust territories want to end their agreements with the United States?

5 GEOGRAPHY Why does rainfall vary on the low islands and the high islands?

6 HISTORY What impact did European and Japanese control have on the region?

7 CRITICAL THINKING—Hypothesize How might investment in more technology and high-tech skills benefit the economies of the Pacific Island nations?

PERFORMANCE—Write a Speech Protecting the environment and improving economies are major concerns in the Pacific Islands. Write a speech you would give as an island leader to explain how you would try to balance economic and environmental needs to the benefit of the islands.

·SKILLS·

Compare Different Kinds of Maps

▶ WHY IT MATTERS

There are many kinds of maps, and each kind shows different information. For example, political maps mark present-day cities, countries, and borders. Physical maps show physical features. Maps can also show economic and cultural information.

At 178,272 square miles (461,689 sq km), the country of Papua New Guinea covers slightly more than the area of California. It lies east of Indonesia. In fact, if you look at Map A, a political map, you will see that Papua New Guinea is connected to Irian Jaya (ir•ee•AHN JAH•yuh), a part of

Indonesia. Papua New Guinea includes 4 large islands and more than 600 smaller islands. From the physical map, Map B, you may be able to see that Papua New Guinea has both lowlands and mountainous regions. By studying Map C, a mineral resources map, you can learn about some of the resources of Papua New Guinea. Map D, a population map, shows where the people of Papua New Guinea live.

Using different maps together is helpful. It allows you to make connections between the history, geography, economics, government, and culture of a country or region.

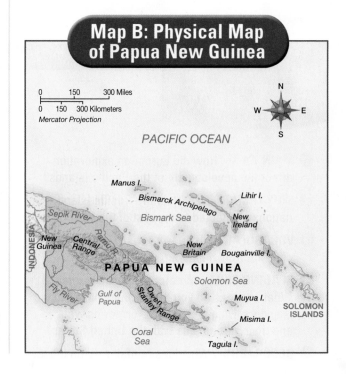

Map A: Political Map of Papua New Guinea

0 150 300 Miles
0 150 300 Kilometers
Mercator Projection

⊛ National capital
• City
— National border

PACIFIC OCEAN

Vanimo
Manus I.
Wewak
Kavieng Lihir I.
Rabaul New Ireland
New Guinea
Kimbe New Britain
Kundiawa
Mendi
Lae
Bougainville I. Arawa
PAPUA NEW GUINEA
Kerema
Daru
Popondetta
Muyua I.
Port Moresby ⊛
Misima I.
SOLOMON ISLANDS
Alotau
Tagula I.
INDONESIA

Map B: Physical Map of Papua New Guinea

0 150 300 Miles
0 150 300 Kilometers
Mercator Projection

PACIFIC OCEAN

Manus I.
Bismarck Archipelago Lihir I.
Sepik River Bismark Sea
New Ireland
New Guinea
Central Range Ramu R.
New Britain Bougainville I.
PAPUA NEW GUINEA
Solomon Sea
Fly River
Gulf of Papua
Owen Stanley Range
Muyua I.
Misima I.
SOLOMON ISLANDS
Coral Sea
Tagula I.
INDONESIA

▶ WHAT YOU NEED TO KNOW

Study the maps and compare them. When comparing maps, you can follow these steps:

Step 1 Look at each map's title to find out what kind of map it is.

Step 2 Study each map and map key to determine what information is being presented.

Step 3 Think about how the maps can be used together to provide more information.

▶ PRACTICE THE SKILL

Use the information on the maps to answer these questions:

1 Which cities are in mountainous areas?

2 In what body of water can you find a deposit of petroleum?

3 How many people per square mile are there in Papua New Guinea's capital?

4 Which minerals are found on Misima Island?

▶ APPLY WHAT YOU LEARNED

Use library resources to find a population map and a physical map of the United States. On the population map, find a large city and a small town. Then use the maps together to answer these questions:

A. What physical features surround the large city? Do you think these features affected the city's growth? Explain.

B. From the physical map, can you tell why the small town is not larger? What physical features may have limited its growth? Explain.

 Practice your map and globe skills with the **GeoSkills CD-ROM**.

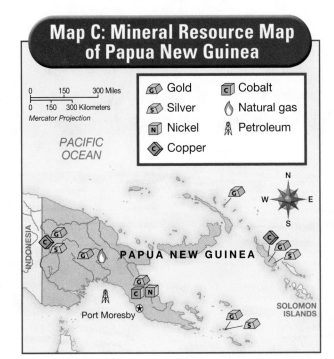

3

MAIN IDEA
Read to find out how Antarctica's environment has been formed and how the continent's resources are being used.

WHY IT MATTERS
Scientists from around the world work together in Antarctica.

VOCABULARY

ice shelf
pack ice
krill

FAST FACT Equipped with cameras and moving along on four wheels, a robot named Nomad recently made a technological breakthrough when it correctly classified the chemical makeup of a sample of meteorite rock in Antarctica.

Antarctica: A Continent Without a Population

For hundreds of years, Antarctica was unknown to and untouched by humans. Then twentieth-century explorers reached the continent as they competed to be the first to reach the South Pole. Today, many nations maintain year-round research bases where scientists study Antarctica's environment. Those who work in Antarctica face the challenges of living in this harsh environment. Together they are working to increase the world's scientific knowledge.

A Land of Ice and Cold

Antarctica is the most isolated of the continents. It covers the South Pole and is surrounded by the South Atlantic, South Pacific, and Indian Oceans. The continent is larger than the United States and Mexico combined, or more than 5 million

The Ross Sea is one of the most easily approached seas in Antarctica. It was first entered during an 1841 expedition by James Clark Ross.

square miles (13 million sq km) in area. Most of the world's ice and most of its supply of fresh water lie trapped in Antarctica's icy grasp.

High rocky mountain ranges divide Antarctica. The Transantarctic Mountains split the continent into the smaller area of West Antarctica and the larger area of East Antarctica. The Antarctic Peninsula, a finger of rocky and icy land, points toward the tip of South America. The Weddell Sea borders the Antarctic Peninsula on the west. The Ross Sea lies off the south coast of West Antarctica. Many islands lie off the coast of the peninsula and along the coast of West Antarctica.

Antarctica's interior is made up of thousands of miles of ice-covered plateaus. About 99 percent of Antarctica's surface is not land at all, but a massive ice cap. Plateau ice has built up so high that in some places it is as thick as 15,000 feet (4,572 m). This ice cap along with the Transantarctic Mountains are Antarctica's two major landforms.

Antarctica is a place of huge glaciers. Gravity and the sheer weight of the ice cap move ice from the interior to the sea. As the ice pushes through the mountains, it

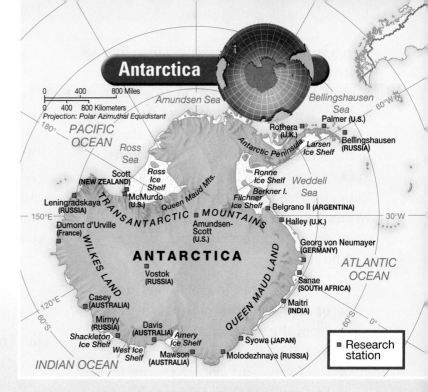

Human-Environment Interactions
The continent of Antarctica has no permanent population.

❖ **Why do you think there are no large cities or towns?**

often cracks, leaving huge splits in the mountains. When it reaches the sea, a glacier can form a massive, permanent **ice shelf** that hangs out over the water. The largest of the ice shelves, the Ross Ice Shelf, juts about 500 miles (805 km) from the coast into the Ross Sea. Smaller shelves are scattered along the coast of East Antarctica.

In a process called calving, large chunks of ice periodically break away from the ice shelves and the glaciers along the coast. An iceberg, a gigantic mountain of flat-topped ice, forms and moves slowly into the sea. In the Antarctic summer, which begins in December, the sun's rays reflect off icebergs. This reflection can change their whiteness into glowing colors. One observer wrote this about the icebergs that he saw:

> 66 They adapted to create feelings of awe and admiration. Not alone from the majesty of their size, but, likewise, by the variety of the forms and ever changing hues [colors] that they assume. 99

REVIEW What are two important features of Antarctica?

Antarctica's Resources

To early explorers, Antarctica seemed like a lifeless land. Although people have never lived there, its waters are home to many kinds of life. Lichens, or mosslike plants, and mosses cling to ice-free areas. Two flowering plants, hairgrass and pearlwort, also manage to survive. No large land animals are found on the Antarctic continent for an obvious reason. Neither food nor water is available to support them. Today, as scientists explore the dry valleys, they are finding life in the form of microscopic animals that live under the soil. Frozen microscopic worms called nematodes are collected and brought back to an active state by putting them in water.

It is the sea, however, that is rich in plant and animal life. Algae cling to the under-side of the great stretches of **pack ice**, or sea ice that forms into a large mass. These water plants are essential to animal and bird life in Antarctica. Algae have no roots, stems, or leaves, and they make their own food from nutrients in the seawater. Sea-weed is a form of algae. Algae provide food for krill. **Krill** are tiny shrimplike animals that gather in huge masses to feed on algae. Because seals, whales, birds, and fish in turn all feed on krill, they are important to animal life in Antarctica.

Many of Antarctica's birds, such as these king penguins, are found on the coast.

LOCATE IT

Port Martin

ANTARCTICA

Tourists explore a glacier on the Adélie Coast in the eastern part of Antarctica.

Many whales and seals live in the waters of Antarctica, along with porpoises and dolphins. Whales migrate to the waters to feed in the summer. Blue, humpback, and minke (MING•kuh) whales dine on krill. An average blue whale can eat 4 to 6 tons of krill a day. Other whales, such as killer whales and sperm whales, hunt fish and giant squid. Leopard, fur, and elephant seals spend most of their time in the seas eating krill and fish. On shore, seals by the thousands breed, give birth to their young, and feast and swim in the icy waters surrounding the continent.

Probably the most famous Antarctic creatures are the penguins, which include species such as the king, Adélie (uh•DAY•lee), chinstrap, and emperor. All are flightless, and all breed and nest along the coasts and on several of the islands. Though they look awkward when they hop and waddle on land, penguins are excellent swimmers. They dive into the icy waters and speed along beneath the surface, feeding on krill and fish. Scores of seabirds, such as petrels as large as geese, cormorants, albatrosses, and terns, migrate to the Antarctic during its summer to dive for fish and to nest. Antarctic animals have adapted to living in the severe environment. For example, a layer of fat under the skin protects whales and seals from the extreme cold.

Fossil fuels such as coal have been found in the Transantarctic Mountains. The mineral resources iron, gold, and uranium have also been found. Oil may lie under the Ross Sea. Fearful that any mining would harm the environment and the wildlife, the United States and 23 other nations signed an agreement in 1991 to ban any mining.

Although few people think of Antarctica as a place for a vacation, tourists do visit the continent. In the Antarctic summer, cruise ships carry tourists to see the icebergs, glaciers, and animal life. Some young people have also had a chance to visit the continent. Two Canadian students won a writing contest about what they thought life was like in Antarctica. As a prize, they were invited to join a 13-day expedition called Students on Ice. With scientists and historians as their guides, they studied glaciers and volcanoes in Antarctica. The students spotted whales, seals, seabirds, and other wildlife. They were especially impressed by the thousands of penguins they saw.

REVIEW Why are krill so important to the animal life of Antarctica?

On December 1, 1959, the United States, Argentina, Australia, Belgium, Britain, Chile, France, Japan, New Zealand, Norway, South Africa, and the former Soviet Union signed the Antarctic Treaty. In the treaty these 12 nations agreed to work together for peaceful uses of the continent. The treaty promoted scientific investigation of the Antarctic and protected the continent's environment. It also banned countries from building military bases or testing military weapons there. As part of the treaty states,

66 It is in the interest of all humankind that Antarctica shall continue to be used forever for peaceful purposes and shall not become the scene or object of international discord. 99

Analyze the Value

1 Why do you think it is important that Antarctica not belong to any one nation?

2 **Make It Relevant** Do some more research about scientific study in Antarctica. Then write a paragraph explaining why scientists from every country should have equal access to study in Antarctica.

Research in Antarctica

Antarctica does not belong to any one nation. Some, including Britain, Australia, and Argentina, have made claims. Other nations do not recognize these claims. In 1957–1958, scientists from 67 nations gathered in Antarctica to take part in the International Geophysical Year. Their purpose was to begin scientific study of the effect of the continent's ice masses on weather, oceans, and the atmosphere around the world. Twelve nations set up about 50 stations for research.

Scientist at the Amundsen-Scott Polar Station at the South Pole.

By the late 1990s, 18 nations were operating more than 40 stations in Antarctica, mostly on the Antarctic Peninsula. The United States Antarctic Program is paid for by the National Science Foundation and maintains three bases. McMurdo Station is on the edge of the Ross Ice Shelf. Palmer Station is on an island near the peninsula. The Amundsen-Scott Polar Station is at the South Pole. Most research is carried out during the summer season, although weather conditions can be difficult in both summer and winter. During the severe winter season, fewer people live and work on the stations. They mostly study weather patterns.

Getting in and out of stations is almost impossible in the winter. Ships have to struggle through the ice pack, and planes are turned back by the fog and high winds. Food, supplies, and scientific equipment must be delivered in the summer. People who work there are trained to survive in a world of ice. Those who work there know how to live in extreme cold and high altitudes, especially at the South Pole. The average temperature is –56°F (–48°C), and the air is thin. Station workers must also learn to avoid everyday hazards such as frostbite and dehydration when exploring dry valleys. They must be careful not to fall into cracks in glaciers.

Despite the extremely harsh conditions, experts are gathering valuable information. Scientists speculate that Antarctic life forms will give them clues to life on a cold, dry planet such as Mars. Astronomers at the South Pole use sophisticated infrared and radio telescopes to learn more about the effects of the sun and the formation of stars. In areas along the Antarctic coasts and in the seas, experts study the behavior of land and sea animals.

LOCATE IT

Amundsen-Scott Polar Station

ANTARCTICA

Inside the dome of this research station, residents have housing, food, and entertainment.

Scientists believe that the knowledge they gather from studying Antarctica will help them answer questions about environments around the world. Research in Antarctica has also shown that many nations can cooperate to share important information and knowledge.

REVIEW Why is it important for many nations to do scientific research in Antarctica?

LESSON 3 REVIEW

1. **MAIN IDEA** What physical features make Antarctica a unique continent?

2. **WHY IT MATTERS** Why is Antarctica an important place for scientists to study and explore?

3. **VOCABULARY** How are **pack ice** and **krill** related?

4. **READING SKILL—Predict a Likely Outcome** What scientific findings do you think will be made in Antarctica?

5. **GEOGRAPHY** What roles do algae and krill play in the food chain of Antarctica?

6. **SCIENCE AND TECHNOLOGY** How do scientists help people learn more about Antarctica's environment?

7. **CRITICAL THINKING—Synthesize** Why do you think countries agreed to share Antarctica's lands rather than fight to claim them?

 PERFORMANCE—Write an Essay Imagine that you want to join an expedition to visit and explore Antarctica as the two Canadian students did. Write an essay explaining why you want to go, what you want to investigate, and how such a trip will add to your knowledge of the continent. Share your essay with a classmate.

19 Review and Test Preparation

USE YOUR READING SKILLS

Complete this graphic organizer to show that you understand how to make predictions about the Pacific Islands and Antarctica by using the details from what you have read and your own knowledge. A copy of this graphic organizer appears on page 179 of the Activity Book.

Make Predictions About the Pacific Islands and Antarctica

WHAT YOU + KNOW	WHAT YOU = READ	PREDICTION	WHAT ACTUALLY HAPPENED

WHAT YOU KNOW +	WHAT YOU READ ⇌	PREDICTION	WHAT ACTUALLY HAPPENED
Europeans changed life for people living in the Americas, Africa, South America, Asia, and Australia.	Pacific Islanders lived in isolation from the rest of the world until early European exploration expanded into the Pacific Ocean.	_____	_____
The climate in Antarctica is very harsh and cold. This makes it difficult for plants to grow and people to live there. Seals, whales, penguins, and seabirds make Antarctica their home.	Antarctica is surrounded by the waters of the Atlantic, Pacific, and Indian Oceans. These waters support Antarctica's wildlife.	_____	_____

THINK & WRITE

Write an Opinion Letter Write a letter to your local newspapers expressing your opinion about the ownership of Antarctica. Should Antarctica be owned by one country? Explain why or why not. How might ownership by one country affect scientific discovery and the Antarctic environment?

Create a Bibliography Think about some Pacific Island cultures that interest you. Then create a bibliography of sources that give information about these cultures. Write a one- or two-sentence description of each source. Share your bibliography with classmates to help them learn more about the Pacific Islands.

200 B.C.
Polynesians settle in Tahiti

A.D.1000
Polynesians reach New Zealand

A.D.1700s
Captain Cook explores the South Pacific

A.D.1941
Japanese attack U.S. forces in the Pacific

A.D.1959
Antarctic Treaty is signed

USE THE TIME LINE

Use the chapter summary time line to answer these questions.

1 Did the Polynesians reach Tahiti before or after they reached New Zealand?

2 In what year was the Antarctic Treaty signed?

USE VOCABULARY

Identify the term that correctly matches each definition.

> kastom (p. 649)
>
> continental island (p. 654)
>
> high island (p. 654)
>
> low island (p. 654)
>
> krill (p. 664)

3 island made up mostly of volcanic rock and coral reef

4 a traditional form of government or rule in the Solomon Islands and Vanuatu

5 island that was probably once part of Australia

6 tiny shrimp-like animals

7 island made when volcanoes erupted from the ocean floor and rose to form mountains

RECALL FACTS

Answer these questions.

8 Which island in Melanesia do scientists believe was the first to be settled?

9 Which countries competed for control of the Pacific Islands?

10 How is an ice shelf formed?

Write the letter of the best choice.

11 **TEST PREP** Geographers divide the Pacific Islands into—
   A Melanesia, Micronesia, and Polynesia.
   B Polynesia, Micronesia, and New Zealand.
   C Hawaii, Melanesia, and Micronesia.
   D Papua, New Guinea, and Polynesia.

12 **TEST PREP** The Antarctic research station at the South Pole is the—
   F McMurdo Station.
   G Palmer Station.
   H Polar Research Station.
   J Amundsen-Scott Polar Station.

THINK CRITICALLY

13 Why do you think Europeans were so amazed by the accomplishments of early Polynesian sailors?

14 How have the people of the Pacific Islands used technology to travel and communicate over great distances?

15 Do you think it is important to protect the environment in Antarctica? Explain.

APPLY SKILLS

Compare Different Kinds of Maps

16 Study the maps on pages 660–661. Write a paragraph that describes each map and tells how the maps can be used to find out information about Papua New Guinea.

VISIT

Antarctica

Years ago travel to Antarctica was barely thinkable because of the grueling journey and extreme weather. Today, however, many people decide to visit the continent to enjoy its spectacular, natural beauty. Travel to Antarctica has become easier, though the trip there is still long and hard. If you travel to Antarctica, you must first take a long flight to Christchurch, New Zealand. This flight takes over 12 hours. In Christchurch you will collect and pack special clothing and supplies that will be needed to keep you warm. Next, you board a plane for the 8-hour flight that takes you to the town of McMurdo Station, Antarctica. On a visit here guides will help you experience the Antarctic wilderness of ice and snow.

Taking a walk on an enormous iceberg is one way visitors can enjoy the unusual beauty of Antarctica. Weddell seals, like the one below, live in the seas that surround the continent.

LOCATE IT

South Pole

ANTARCTICA

Icebergs take many forms. The bluer the iceberg, the less air that is trapped inside it.

Visitors (right) walk among a colony of king penguins. In the summer months penguins hatch their eggs and take care of their young.

TAKE A FIELD TRIP

GO ONLINE

A VIRTUAL TOUR
Visit The Learning Site at **www.harcourtschool.com/tours** to take virtual tours of other geographic locations.

CNN Turner Le@rning®

A VIDEO TOUR
Check your media center or classroom library for a videotape tour of Antarctica.

8 Review and Test Preparation

VISUAL SUMMARY

Write a Plan On the visual summary time line below, find the date when nations began to set up research stations in Antarctica. Suppose you are one of the first researchers who will go to Antarctica. Write a plan describing how your research station will be set up and what you will study there.

USE VOCABULARY

Write a story about Australia, New Zealand, the Pacific Islands, and Antarctica by using these terms.

outback (p. 621), **dreamtime** (p. 626),

outrigger (p. 648), **pack ice** (p. 664)

RECALL FACTS

Answer these questions.

1 Why are Australia and New Zealand called the "lands down under"?

2 What tool did Aborigines invent to hunt birds and other animals?

3 Why did Pacific islanders develop different cultures and ways of life?

Write the letter of the best choice.

4 **TEST PREP** Australia is the world's leading producer of—
  A gold.
  B wool.
  C paper.
  D geothermal power.

5 **TEST PREP** The earliest settlers of the island of New Guinea were the—
  F Polynesians.
  G Kiwis.
  H Papuans.
  J Aussies.

6 **TEST PREP** Most of the plant and animal life in Antarctica can be found—
  A in the Transantarctic Mountains.
  B on the Antarctic Peninsula.
  C on the Ross Ice Shelf.
  D in the seas surrounding Antarctica.

Visual Summary

| 1500 B.C. | 1000 B.C. | 500 B.C. | B.C./A.D. |

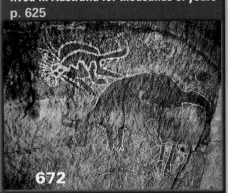
1500 B.C. By this time Aborigines have lived in Australia for thousands of years p. 625

1000 B.C. Micronesians, Polynesians, and Melanesians spread throughout the Pacific p. 647

A.D. 1000 Early Maori settle in New Zealand p. 626

7 Why do you think conservation is so important to the people of Australia and New Zealand?

8 How do you think the great distances between the islands of the Pacific have affected the economies there?

9 Why do you think it was important for the United States to stop Japan from controlling the islands of the Pacific during World War II?

10 Why do you think tourists might want to visit Antarctica?

APPLY SKILLS

Compare Different Kinds of Maps

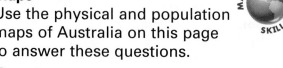

Use the physical and population maps of Australia on this page to answer these questions.

11 What is the largest city in Australia's interior?

12 Why do you think few people live in Australia's interior?

13 Which areas of Australia have the highest population density?

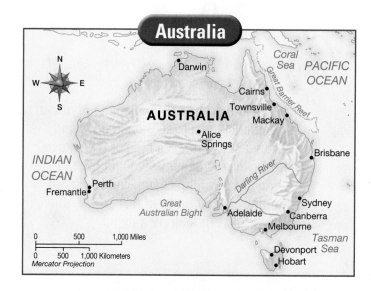

Australia

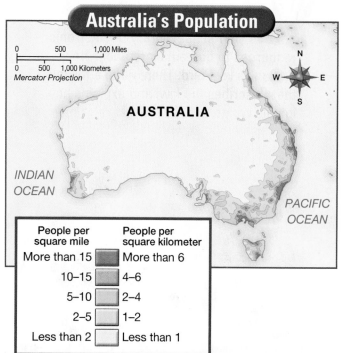

Australia's Population

People per square mile		People per square kilometer
More than 15		More than 6
10–15		4–6
5–10		2–4
2–5		1–2
Less than 2		Less than 1

A.D. 500   A.D. 1000   A.D. 1500   A.D. 2000

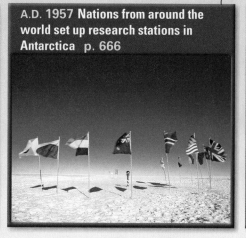

A.D. 1788 Australia becomes a British penal colony p. 628

A.D. 1957 Nations from around the world set up research stations in Antarctica p. 666

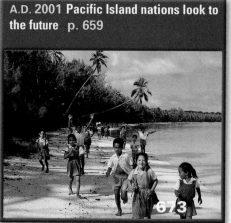

A.D. 2001 Pacific Island nations look to the future p. 659

Unit Activities

GO ONLINE Visit The Learning Site at www.harcourtschool.com/socialstudies/activities for additional activities.

Make a Map

Work in a group to make a map of one of the Pacific Islands. First, decide an island you would like to make a map of. Then, use online or library resources to find out the size and shape of the island. Next, find out the landforms and cities of this island. Use what you find out to draw a map.

Write a Folktale

Use your school library or electronic resources to find out more about New Zealand's kiwi bird. Then, write a folktale that describes the kiwi and explains how it lost its wings.

VISIT YOUR LIBRARY

- *Australia* by Robert J. Allison. Steck-Vaughn.

- *The Pacific Ocean* by David Lambert. Steck-Vaughn.

- *Antarctic Journal: Four Months at the Bottom of the World* by Jennifer Owings Dewey. HarperCollins.

COMPLETE THE UNIT PROJECT

The Travel Show Work with classmates to complete the unit project—the travel show. First, choose students to host the show. Then, write a script and create illustrations or costumes for scenes about the people and places of the Pacific Realm. Videotape your show and invite other students to watch it, or perform the show "live" for them.

For Your Reference

Almanac

Biographical Dictionary

Gazetteer

Glossary

Index

Country Flag	Country	Capital	Population*	Area (sq. mi.)	Economy
	**Algeria**	Algiers	31,736,053	919,590	oil, natural gas, light industry, food processing, grains, iron, mining, petrochemical
	**Angola**	Luanda	10,366,031	481,351	textiles, coffee, sugarcane, bananas, iron, diamonds, cement, fish processing, phosphates
	**Benin**	Porto-Novo	6,590,782	43,483	palm products, peanuts, cotton, corn, oil, construction materials, petroleum
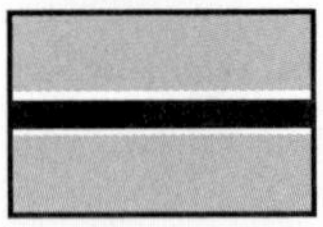	**Botswana**	Gaborone	1,586,119	231,803	livestock processing, corn, coal, copper, tourism, diamonds, salt, silver
	**Burkina Faso**	Ouagadougou	12,272,289	105,869	agricultural processing, textiles, millet, sorghum, manganese, soap, gold, beverages
	**Burundi**	Bujumbura	6,223,897	10,745	food processing, coffee, cotton, tea, nickel, soap, shoes
	**Cameroon**	Yaoundé	15,803,220	183,567	oil products, food processing, cocoa, coffee, lumber, textiles
	**Cape Verde**	Praia	405,163	1,557	bananas, coffee, sweet potatoes, salt, fish processing, ship repair
	**Central African Republic**	Bangui	3,576,884	240,534	textiles, cotton, coffee, diamonds, sawmills, footwear, assembly of bicycles and motorcycles

Africa

Country Flag	Country	Capital	Population*	Area (sq. mi.)	Economy
	Chad	N'Djamena	8,707,078	495,752	cotton, sorghum, millet, uranium, meat packing, soap, construction materials
	Comoros	Moroni	596,202	838	perfume, textiles, vanilla, coconut oil, plants, fruits, furniture, jewelry, construction materials
	Republic of the Congo	Brazzaville	2,894,336	132,046	oil, wood products, cocoa, coffee, potash, soap, sugar milling
	Côte d'Ivoire (Ivory Coast)	Yamoussoukro	16,393,221	124,502	food processing, coffee, cocoa, oil, diamonds, textiles, fertilizer, construction materials
	Democratic Republic of the Congo	Kinshasa	53,624,718	905,563	mining, food processing, sugar, rice, cobalt, cement, diamonds, textiles
	Djibouti	Djibouti	460,700	8,494	mainly service activities, dairy products, mineral water bottling
	Egypt	Cairo	69,536,644	386,660	textiles, tourism, chemicals, cotton, rice, beans, oil, gas, construction, cement, metals
	Equatorial Guinea	Malabo	486,060	10,830	fish, cocoa, coffee, bananas, oil, saw milling, natural gas
	Eritrea	Asmara	4,298,269	46,842	food processing, cotton, coffee, tobacco, gold, potash, textiles
	Ethiopia	Addis Ababa	65,891,874	435,184	food processing, textiles, coffee, grains, platinum, gold

* These population figures are from the most recent available statistics.

Country Flag	Country	Capital	Population*	Area (sq. mi.)	Economy
	Gabon	Libreville	1,221,175	103,346	textiles, cocoa, coffee, oil, manganese, uranium, cement
	Gambia	Banjul	1,411,205	4,363	tourism, peanuts, rice, fish, wood-working, metalworking
	Ghana	Accra	19,894,014	92,100	aluminum, cocoa, gold, manganese, food processing, lumbering
	Guinea	Conakry	7,613,870	94,925	mining, bananas, pineapples, iron, bauxite, diamonds
	Guinea-Bissau	Bissau	1,315,822	13,946	peanuts, cashews, cotton, rice, bauxite, agricultural processing
	Kenya	Nairobi	30,765,916	224,961	tourism, oil refining, coffee, corn, gold, limestone, cement, soap, textiles
	Lesotho	Maseru	2,177,062	11,720	food processing, textiles, corn, grains, diamonds, construction, tourism
	Liberia	Monrovia	3,225,837	43,000	mining, rice, cassava, coffee, iron, diamonds, gold, rubber, timber
	Libya	Tripoli	5,240,599	679,358	oil, food processing, dates, olives, gypsum, handicrafts, textiles, cement
	Madagascar	Antananarivo	15,982,563	226,656	textiles, meat processing, coffee, cloves, vanilla, chromite, graphite, soap, paper, petroleum, tourism
	Malawi	Lilongwe	10,548,250	45,745	agricultural processing, sugar, tea, tobacco, coffee

Country Flag	Country	Capital	Population*	Area (sq. mi.)	Economy
	Mali	Bamako	11,008,518	478,764	millet, rice, peanuts, cotton, gold, phosphates, construction
	Mauritania	Nouakchott	2,747,312	397,953	fish processing, dates, grains, iron ore, gypsum
	Mauritius	Port Louis	1,189,825	718	tourism, textiles, sugarcane, tea, metal products
	Morocco	Rabat	30,645,305	172,413	carpets, clothing, leather goods, grains, fruits, phosphates, iron ore, tourism
	Mozambique	Maputo	19,371,057	309,494	chemicals, petroleum products, cashews, cotton, sugar, coal, titanium, textiles, glass, cement
	Namibia	Windhoek	1,797,677	318,694	diamonds, copper, gold, fish, meat packing, dairy products
	Niger	Niamey	10,355,156	489,189	peanuts, cotton, uranium, coal, iron, gold, petroleum
	Nigeria	Abuja	126,635,626	356,667	oil, gas, textiles, cocoa, palm products, construction materials, chemicals, ceramics, steel
	Rwanda	Kigali	7,312,756	10,169	coffee, tea, tin, cement, soap, furniture, shoes, textiles
	São Tomé and Príncipe	São Tomé	165,034	386	cocoa, coconuts, textiles, soap, fish processing, timber
	Senegal	Dakar	10,284,929	75,749	food processing, fishing, peanuts, millet, phosphates, construction materials, fertilizer production

* These population figures are from the most recent available statistics.

Country Flag	Country	Capital	Population*	Area (sq. mi.)	Economy
	Seychelles	Victoria	79,715	176	food processing, tourism, coconut products, cinnamon, vanilla, fishing, boat building, printing
	Sierra Leone	Freetown	5,426,618	27,699	mining, cocoa, coffee, diamonds, titanium, textiles, footwear
	Somalia	Mogadishu	7,488,773	246,199	sugar, bananas, iron, tin, textiles
	South Africa	Cape Town/ Pretoria	43,586,097	471,008	steel, automobiles, corn, other grains, gold, diamonds, platinum, metalworking, textiles, chemicals
	Sudan	Khartoum	36,080,373	967,493	textiles, gum arabic, cotton, chromium, copper, cement, sugar, shoes, petroleum refining
	Swaziland	Mbabane	1,104,343	6,704	wood pulp, sugar, corn, cotton, asbestos, clay, coal
	Tanzania	Dar es Salaam	36,232,074	364,898	agricultural processing, cotton, tin, diamonds, textiles, fertilizer, salt
	Togo	Lomé	5,153,088	21,925	textiles, coffee, cocoa, yams, phosphates, handicrafts
	Tunisia	Tunis	9,705,102	63,170	food processing, textiles, oil products, grains, olives, dates, phosphates, tourism
	Uganda	Kampala	23,985,712	91,135	textiles, cement, coffee, cotton, tea, copper, cobalt, sugar

Country Flag	Country	Capital	Population*	Area (sq. mi.)	Economy
	Zambia	Lusaka	9,770,199	290,584	corn, cassava, sugar, cobalt, copper, zinc, emeralds, gold, silver, construction, chemicals
	Zimbabwe	Harare	11,365,366	150,803	clothing, steel, chemicals, tobacco, sugar, chromium, gold, nickel, wood products, steel

Asia

Country Flag	Country	Capital	Population*	Area (sq. mi.)	Economy
	Afghanistan	Kabul	26,813,057	251,737	textiles, furniture, wheat, fruits, copper, coal, wool, natural gas, oil, soap
	Armenia	Yerevan	3,336,100	11,506	vegetables, grapes, copper, gold, electric motors, tires, chemicals, trucks, watches, microelectronics
	Azerbaijan	Baku	7,771,092	33,436	oil, grains, cotton, iron, cattle, cement, textiles
	Bahrain	Manama	645,361	239	oil, gas, fruits, vegetables, ship repairing, tourism
	Bangladesh	Dhaka	131,269,860	55,598	jute, textiles, fertilizers, rice, tea, cement, chemical fertilizer
	Bhutan	Thimphu	2,049,412	18,147	rice, corn, timber, cement, processed fruits
	Brunei	Bandar Seri Begawan	343,653	2,228	petroleum, rice, bananas, cassava, construction

* These population figures are from the most recent available statistics.

Country Flag	Country	Capital	Population*	Area (sq. mi.)	Economy
	Cambodia	Phnom Penh	12,491,501	69,900	rice, wood, rubber, corn, gemstones, garments, wood and wood products, cement
	China	Beijing	1,273,111,290	3,705,386	iron, steel, textiles, tea, rice and other grains, cotton, coal, petroleum, cement, food processing, toys, footwear
	Cyprus	Nicosia	762,887	3,572	barley, grapes, olives, copper, tourism, metal products, wood products
	East Timor	Dili	800,000	9,266	coffee, mining, marble, fishing, tourism
	Georgia	Tbilisi	4,989,285	26,911	manganese, citrus fruits, potatoes, corn, steel, aircraft, machine tools, textiles
	India	New Delhi	1,029,991,145	1,269,338	textiles, steel, rice and other grains, tea, spices, coal, iron, chemicals, cement, mining, petroleum
	Indonesia	Jakarta	228,437,870	741,096	textiles, rice, cocoa, peanuts, nickel, tin, oil, petroleum, plywood, chemical fertilizers, rubber, tourism
	Iran	Tehran	66,128,965	636,293	sugar refining, carpets, rice and other grains, oil, gas, textiles, cement, construction materials
	Iraq	Baghdad	23,331,985	168,753	textiles, grains, dates, oil, chemicals, construction materials
	Israel	Jerusalem	5,938,093	8,019	diamond cutting, textiles, electronics, citrus fruits, copper, phosphates, tourism, chemicals, metal products
	Japan	Tokyo	126,771,662	145,882	electronics, automobiles, fishing, rice, potatoes, machine tools, ships, textiles

Country Flag	Country	Capital	Population*	Area (sq. mi.)	Economy
	Jordan	Amman	5,153,378	34,445	oil refining, cement, grains, olives, phosphates, tourism, potash
	Kazakhstan	Astana	16,731,303	1,049,150	steel, grains, cotton, oil, coal, phosphates, electric motors, construction materials
	Kuwait	Kuwait	2,041,961	6,880	oil, oil products, gas, food processing, construction materials
	Kyrgyzstan	Bishkek	4,753,003	76,641	textiles, mining, tobacco, cotton, sugar beets, gold, refrigerators, furniture, electric motors
	Laos	Vientiane	5,635,967	91,428	wood products, mining, sweet potatoes, corn, cotton, gypsum, construction
	Lebanon	Beirut	3,627,774	4,015	banking, textiles, oil refining, fruits, olives, vegetables, jewelry, wood and furniture products, metal fabricating
	Malaysia	Kuala Lumpur	22,229,040	127,316	rubber goods, logging, steel, electronics, palm oil, tin, iron, petroleum production
	Maldives	Male	310,764	115	fish processing, tourism, coconuts, sweet potatoes, corn, shipping, boat building, garments, handicrafts
	Mongolia	Ulaanbaatar	2,654,999	604,247	food processing, mining, grains, coal, oil, construction materials, copper
	Myanmar (Burma)	Yangon (Rangoon)	41,994,678	261,969	textiles, petroleum, rice, sugarcane, lead, gemstones, pharmaceuticals, copper, tin, fertilizer, construction materials

* These population figures are from the most recent available statistics.

Country Flag	Country	Capital	Population*	Area (sq. mi.)	Economy
	Nepal	Kathmandu	25,284,463	54,362	sugar, jute, tourism, rice and other grains, quartz, carpet, textiles, cement and brick production
	North Korea	P'yongyang	21,968,228	46,540	textiles, corn, potatoes, coal, lead, machine building, chemicals, mining, tourism
	Oman	Muscat	2,622,198	82,031	dates, vegetables, limes, oil, gas, construction, cement, copper
	Pakistan	Islamabad	144,616,639	310,403	textiles, petroleum products, rice, wheat, natural gas, iron ore, paper products, clothing
	Palau	Koror	19,092	177	tourism, fish, coconuts, copra, cassava, sweet potatoes, garment making
	Philippines	Manila	82,841,518	115,830	textiles, clothing, wood products, sugar, cobalt, copper, food processing, electronics, fishing
	Qatar	Doha	769,152	4,416	oil, petroleum products, fertilizers, cement
	Saudi Arabia	Riyadh	22,757,092	756,981	oil, oil products, gas, dates, wheat, cement, construction, fertilizer
	Singapore	Singapore	4,300,419	250	shipbuilding, oil refining, electronics, banking, tourism, rubber processing, biotechnology
	South Korea	Seoul	47,904,370	38,022	electronics, automobiles, textiles, clothing, rice, barley, tungsten, shipbuilding, footwear
	Sri Lanka	Colombo	19,408,635	25,332	clothing, textiles, tea, coconuts, rice, graphite, limestone, processing of rubber, cement, petroleum refining

Country Flag	Country	Capital	Population*	Area (sq. mi.)	Economy
	Syria	Damascus	16,728,808	71,498	oil products, textiles, cotton, grains, olives, phosphate, rock mining
	Taiwan	Taipei	22,370,461	13,892	textiles, clothing, electronics, rice, fruits, coal, marble, iron, steel, cement, machinery
	Tajikistan	Dushanbe	6,578,681	55,251	aluminum, cement, barley, coal, lead, chemicals and fertilizers, machine tools
	Thailand	Bangkok	61,797,751	198,455	textiles, tourism, rice, corn, tapioca, sugarcane, cement, furniture, plastics, tungsten, tin
	Turkey**	Ankara	66,493,970	301,380	steel, textiles, grains, mercury, food processing, mining, petroleum, lumber, paper
	Turkmenistan	Ashgabat	4,603,244	188,455	oil, mining, textiles, grains, cotton, coal, sulfur, salt, natural gas
	United Arab Emirates	Abu Dhabi	2,407,460	32,000	oil, vegetables, dates, fishing, construction materials, handicrafts
	Uzbekistan	Tashkent	25,155,064	172,741	machinery, natural gas, vegetables, cotton, textiles, food processing
	Vietnam	Hanoi	79,939,014	127,243	food processing, textiles, rice, sugar, phosphates, cement, fertilizer, steel, paper, oil, coal
	Yemen	Sanaa	18,078,035	203,849	oil, grains, fruits, salt, food processing, handicrafts

** in both Asia and Europe
* These population figures are from the most recent available statistics.

Country Flag	Country	Capital	Population*	Area (sq. mi.)	Economy

Australia and Oceania

Country Flag	Country	Capital	Population*	Area (sq. mi.)	Economy
	**Australia**	Canberra	19,357,594	2,967,893	iron, steel, textiles, electrical equipment, wheat, cotton, fruits, bauxite, coal, mining, food processing
	**Fiji**	Suva	844,330	7,055	tourism, sugar, bananas, gold, timber, clothing, silver
	**Kiribati**	Tarawa	94,149	277	fishing, coconut oil, breadfruit, sweet potatoes, handicrafts
	**Marshall Islands**	Majuro	70,822	70	agriculture, tourism, fish, crafts from shells, wood and pearls
	**Federated States of Micronesia**	Palikir	134,597	271	tourism, tropical fruits, vegetables, pepper, construction, fish processing
	**Nauru**	Yaren	12,088	8.5	phosphates, coconut products
	**New Zealand**	Wellington	3,864,129	103,736	food processing, textiles, machinery, fish, forest products, grains, potatoes, gold, gas, iron, coal, tourism
	**Papua New Guinea**	Port Moresby	5,049,055	178,703	coffee, coconuts, cocoa, gold, copper, silver, plywood production, construction, tourism
	**Samoa**	Apia	179,058	1,100	timber, tourism, coconuts, yams, hardwoods, fish

Country Flag	Country	Capital	Population*	Area (sq. mi.)	Economy
	Solomon Islands	Honiara	480,442	10,985	fishing, coconuts, rice, gold, bauxite, mining, timber
	Tonga	Nuku'alofa	104,227	289	tourism, fishing, coconut products, bananas
	Tuvalu	Funafuti	10,991	10	coconut products, coconuts, fishing, tourism
	Vanuatu	Port-Vila	192,910	5,700	fish processing, meat canneries, tourism, coconut products, manganese, wood processing

Europe

Country Flag	Country	Capital	Population*	Area (sq. mi.)	Economy
	Albania	Tiranë	3,510,484	11,100	cement, textiles, food processing, corn, wheat, chromium, coal, lumber, chemicals, mining
	Andorra	Andorra la Vella	67,627	180	tourism, sheep, tobacco products, iron, lead, timber
	Austria	Vienna	8,150,835	32,378	steel, machinery, automobiles, grains, iron ore, construction, lumber and wood processing, tourism
	Belarus	Minsk	10,350,194	80,154	manufacturing, chemicals, grains, vegetables, tractors, fertilizer, textiles
	Belgium	Brussels	10,258,702	11,781	steel, glassware, diamond cutting, automobiles, wheat, coal, engineering, textiles, petroleum
	Bosnia and Herzegovina	Sarajevo	3,922,205	19,741	steel, mining, textiles, timber, corn, wheat, berries, bauxite, iron, coal, vehicle assembly

* These population figures are from the most recent available statistics.

Almanac ▪ **R13**

Country Flag	Country	Capital	Population*	Area (sq. mi.)	Economy
	Bulgaria	Sofia	7,707,495	42,823	chemicals, machinery, metals, textiles, grains, fruits, bauxite, copper, zinc, construction materials
	Croatia	Zagreb	4,334,142	21,829	chemicals, plastics, steel, paper, olives, wheat, oil, bauxite, electronics, aluminum, textiles, petroleum, shipbuilding
	Czech Republic	Prague	10,264,212	30,450	machinery, oil products, glass, wheat, sugar beets, rye, coal, kaolin, motor vehicles, metal crafting
	Denmark	Copenhagen	5,352,815	16,639	food processing, machinery, textiles, furniture, grains, potatoes, dairy products, oil, salt, electronics, construction
	Estonia	Tallinn	1,423,316	17,462	shipbuilding, electric motors, potatoes, oil, phosphates, cement, furniture, paper, shoes
	Finland	Helsinki	5,175,783	130,128	metal, wood products, grains, copper, iron, paper, food stuffs, chemicals
	France	Paris	59,551,227	211,208	steel, textiles, tourism, wine, perfume, grains, fruits, vegetables, bauxite, iron, automobiles, electronics, mining
	Germany	Berlin	83,029,536	137,846	shipbuilding, automobiles, grains, potatoes, coal, potash, steel, iron, cement, machinery, electronics, food and beverages, textiles
	Greece	Athens	10,623,835	50,944	textiles, tourism, chemicals, wine, grains, olives, grapes, citrus fruits, bauxite, mining, petroleum
	Hungary	Budapest	10,106,017	35,919	iron, steel, wheat, corn, sunflowers, bauxite, coal, mining, construction materials, motor vehicles

Country Flag	Country	Capital	Population*	Area (sq. mi.)	Economy
	Iceland	Reykjavik	277,906	39,768	fish, aluminum, potatoes, tourism
	Ireland	Dublin	3,840,838	27,135	food processing, textiles, chemicals, tourism, potatoes, grains, zinc, lead, pharmaceuticals, machinery
	Italy	Rome	57,679,825	116,305	tourism, steel, machinery, automobiles, textiles, shoes, grapes, olives and olive oil, mercury, potash, sulfur, iron, food processing
	Latvia	Riga	2,385,231	24,938	machinery, train cars, grains, sugar beets, fertilizer, electronics, pharmaceuticals, processed foods
	Liechtenstein	Vaduz	32,528	62	electronics, textiles, ceramics, vegetables, wheat, metal manufacturing, tourism
	Lithuania	Vilnius	3,610,535	25,174	machinery, shipbuilding, grains, potatoes, vegetables, electric motors, petroleum refining, fertilizer
	Luxembourg	Luxembourg	442,972	999	steel, chemicals, food processing, grains, potatoes, grapes, metal products, tires, glass, aluminum
	Macedonia	Skopje	2,046,209	9,781	mining, textiles, wheat, rice, chromium, lead, coal, wood products
	Malta	Valletta	394,583	122	textiles, tourism, potatoes, tomatoes, electronics, shipbuilding and repair, construction
	Moldova	Chisinau	4,431,570	13,067	canning, wine, textiles, grains, lignite, gypsum, sugar, shoes, refrigerators and freezers

* These population figures are from the most recent available statistics.

Country Flag	Country	Capital	Population*	Area (sq. mi.)	Economy
	Monaco	Monaco	31,842	465 acres	tourism, chemicals, plastics
	Montenegro	Podgorica	620,145	5,333	steel, aluminum, coal mining, forestry, textiles, tourism
	Netherlands	Amsterdam/ The Hague	15,981,472	16,033	metals, machinery, chemicals, grains, potatoes, flowers, oil, gas, fishing
	Norway	Oslo	4,503,440	125,181	paper, shipbuilding, grains, potatoes, copper, petroleum, chemicals, timber, mining, textiles
	Poland	Warsaw	38,633,912	120,756	shipbuilding, chemicals, grains, potatoes, sugar beets, coal, copper, silver, iron, steel, food processing, glass
	Portugal	Lisbon	10,066,253	35,672	textiles, footwear, cork, fish, grains, potatoes, tungsten, uranium, iron, metal working, oil refining, chemicals, tourism
	Romania	Bucharest	22,364,022	91,699	mining, machinery, oil, oil products, grains, grapes, gas, coal, timber, chemicals, food processing
	Russia**	Moscow	145,470,197	6,592,735	steel, machinery, motor vehicles, chemicals, textiles, grains, sugar beets, mercury, manganese, potash, bauxite, cobalt, shipbuilding, handicrafts
	San Marino	San Marino	27,336	24	tourism, postage stamps, woolen goods, wheat, grapes, ceramics, cement, wine
	Serbia	Belgrade	9,975,991	34,116	steel, machinery, corn and other grains, oil, gas, coal, mining, footwear, chemicals, pharmaceuticals
	Slovakia	Bratislava	5,414,937	18,859	iron, steel, glass, grains, potatoes, chemicals, textiles, rubber products

** in both Asia and Europe

Country Flag	Country	Capital	Population*	Area (sq. mi.)	Economy
	Slovenia	Ljubljana	1,930,132	7,819	electronics, vehicles, coal, lead, zinc, wood products, chemicals, machine tools
	Spain	Madrid	40,037,995	194,896	machinery, textiles, grains, olives, grapes, lignite, uranium, lead, chemicals, shipbuilding, tourism
	Sweden	Stockholm	8,875,053	173,731	steel, machinery, vehicles, grains, potatoes, zinc, iron, lead, paper products, processed foods, motor vehicles
	Switzerland	Bern	7,283,274	15,941	machinery, chemicals, watches, cheese, chocolate products, tourism, salt
	Ukraine	Kiev	48,760,790	233,089	chemicals, machinery, grains, sugar beets, potatoes, iron, manganese, coal, food processing
	United Kingdom	London	59,617,790	94,525	steel, vehicles, shipbuilding, banking, textiles, grains, sugar beets, coal, tin, oil, gas, limestone, chemicals, petroleum, paper and paper products
	Vatican City	—	880	109 acres	tourism, postage stamps

North America

Country Flag	Country	Capital	Population*	Area (sq. mi.)	Economy
	Antigua and Barbuda	St. John's	66,970	171	manufacturing, tourism, construction
	Bahamas	Nassau	297,852	5,386	tourism, rum, banking, pharmaceuticals, fishing
	Barbados	Bridgetown	275,330	166	sugar, tourism, manufacturing

* These population figures are from the most recent available statistics.

Country Flag	Country	Capital	Population*	Area (sq. mi.)	Economy
	Belize	Belmopan	256,062	8,867	sugar, garment production, food processing, tourism
	Canada	Ottawa	31,592,805	3,851,809	nickel, zinc, copper, gold, livestock, fish, chemicals, wood and paper products, petroleum
	Costa Rica	San José	3,773,057	19,730	furniture, aluminum, textiles, fertilizers, coffee, gold, construction materials, plastic products
	Cuba	Havana	11,184,023	42,803	food processing, tobacco, sugar, rice, coffee, cobalt, nickel, iron, copper, salt, textiles, chemicals, petroleum
	Dominica	Roseau	70,786	289	tourism, bananas, citrus fruits, pumice, soap, furniture, cement blocks
	Dominican Republic	Santo Domingo	8,581,477	18,815	cement, tourism, sugar, cocoa, coffee, nickel, bauxite, gold
	El Salvador	San Salvador	6,237,662	8,124	food products, tobacco, coffee, corn, sugar, chemicals, fertilizer, textiles
	Grenada	St. George's	89,227	131	textiles, spices, bananas, cocoa, tourism, construction
	Guatemala	Guatemala City	12,974,361	42,042	furniture, rubber, textiles, coffee, sugar, bananas, oil, chemicals, petroleum, metals
	Haiti	Port-au-Prince	6,964,549	10,714	textiles, coffee, sugar, bananas, bauxite, tourism, cement

Country Flag	Country	Capital	Population*	Area (sq. mi.)	Economy
	Honduras	Tegucigalpa	6,406,052	43,277	textiles, wood products, bananas, sugar, gold, silver, copper, lead
	Jamaica	Kingston	2,665,636	4,243	tourism, sugar, coffee, bananas, potatoes, bauxite, limestone, textiles, rum, food processing
	Mexico	Mexico City	101,879,171	761,602	steel, chemicals, textiles, rubber, petroleum, tourism, cotton, coffee, wheat, silver, lead, zinc, gold, oil, gas, mining, motor vehicles
	Nicaragua	Managua	4,918,393	49,998	food processing, chemicals, textiles, cotton, fruits, coffee, gold, silver, copper, petroleum refining, beverages, footwear
	Panama	Panama City	2,845,647	30,193	oil refining, international banking, bananas, rice, copper, mahogany, shrimp, cement, sugar milling
	Saint Kitts and Nevis	Basseterre	38,756	96	sugar, tourism, cotton, salt, clothing, footwear
	Saint Lucia	Castries	158,178	238	clothing, tourism, bananas, coconuts, forests, beverages, cardboard boxes
	Saint Vincent and the Grenadines	Kingstown	115,942	150	tourism, bananas, arrowroot, coconuts, food processing, clothing, furniture
	Trinidad and Tobago	Port-of-Spain	1,169,682	1,980	oil products, chemicals, tourism, sugar, cocoa, asphalt, oil, gas, cotton textiles
	United States of America	Washington, D.C.	281,421,906	3,537,441	wheat, corn, coal, lead, uranium, iron, copper, gold, computers, electronics, machinery, motor vehicles, chemicals, lumber, mining

* These population figures are from the most recent available statistics.

South America

Country Flag	Country	Capital	Population*	Area (sq. mi.)	Economy
	Argentina	Buenos Aires	37,384,816	1,068,296	food processing, automobiles, chemicals, grains, oil, lead, textiles, printing, steel
	Bolivia	La Paz/Sucre	8,306,463	424,162	mining, tobacco, coffee, sugar, potatoes, soybeans, tin, tungsten, handicrafts, clothing
	Brazil	Brasília	174,468,575	3,286,470	steel, automobiles, textiles, coffee, soybeans, sugar, iron, manganese, shoes, chemicals, cement, lumber, aircraft
	Chile	Santiago	15,328,467	292,257	fish, wood, grains, grapes, beans, copper, cement, textiles
	Colombia	Bogotá	40,349,388	439,735	textiles, food processing, coffee, rice, bananas, emeralds, oil, gas, cement, gold
	Ecuador	Quito	13,183,978	109,483	food processing, bananas, coffee, oil, gas, copper, zinc, silver, gold, textiles, metal work, fishing
	Guyana	Georgetown	697,181	83,000	mining, textiles, sugar, bauxite, diamonds, gold, rice, fishing
	Paraguay	Asunción	5,734,139	157,043	food processing, textiles, cement, corn, cotton, iron, manganese, limestone, sugar, wood products
	Peru	Lima	27,483,864	496,222	fishing, mining, textiles, cotton, sugar, coffee, rice, copper, silver, gold, oil, auto assembly, cement, shipbuilding

Country Flag	Country	Capital	Population*	Area (sq. mi.)	Economy
	**Suriname**	Paramaribo	433,998	63,039	aluminum, food processing, rice, sugar, fruits, bauxite, iron, lumbering, fishing
	**Uruguay**	Montevideo	3,360,105	68,039	meat packing, textiles, wine, corn, wheat, oil refining, food processing, chemicals
	**Venezuela**	Caracas	23,916,810	352,143	steel, textiles, coffee, rice, corn, oil, gas, iron, petroleum, mining, motor vehicle assembly

* These population figures are from the most recent available statistics.

Biographical Dictionary

The Biographical Dictionary lists many of the important people introduced in this book. The page number tells where the main discussion of each person starts. See the Index for other page references.

A

Abdullah II *1962–* Became King of Jordan in 1999. p. 392

Acevedo-Vila, Anibal *1962–* Democratic member of Congress, representing Puerto Rico. p. 212

Ahmose (AHM•ohs) Name of two ancient Egyptian kings, King Ahmose I (*c. 1570–1546 b.c.*) and King Ahmose II (*570–526 B.C.*). p. 408

Akihito (ah•kih•HEE•toh) *1933–* Emperor of Japan from 1989. p. 576

Alexander the Great *356 B.C.–323 B.C.* Son of Philip II. He was tutored by Aristotle and became king of Macedonia in 336 B.C. As ruler, Alexander built a huge empire. p. 269

Alexander VI *1431–1503* Pope who was responsible for dividing the Americas between Spain and Portugal in 1493. p. 234

Angel, James C. *1899–1956* Discovered Angel Falls while searching for gold in Venezuela in 1935. p. 225

Annan, Kofi *1938–* Secretary-General of the United Nations since 1997; winner of 2001 Nobel Peace Prize. p. 87

Anthony, Susan Brownell *1820–1906* American reformer and one of the first leaders of the campaign for women's rights in the United States. p. 116

Arafat, Yasir (A•ruh•fat) *1929–* Palestinian political leader, chairperson of the Palestine Liberation Organization, and president representing the Palestinian people. p. 389

Asoka (uh•SHOH•kuh) *c. 200s B.C.* Maurya emperor, remembered as "the greatest and noblest ruler India has known." p. 532

Asturias, Miguel Angel (ahs•TOOR•yahs) *1899–1974* Guatemalan poet, novelist, and diplomat. p. 163

Ataturk, Kemal (A•tuh•terk, kuh•MAHL) *1881–1938* Turkish soldier and political leader. Known as "Father of the Turks." p. 388

Aung San (AWNG, SAHN) *1914–1947* Leader in the struggle for democratic self-rule in Burma (present-day Myanmar). p. 598

Aung San Suu Kyi (AWNG, SAHN SOO CHEE) *1945–* Daughter of Aung San and leader in the struggle for a democratic government in Myanmar. p. 598

Aurangzeb *1618–1707* Mogul ruler from 1658 to 1707. p. 541

B

Babur *1483–1530* Muslim king who founded the Mogul Empire in India. p. 533

Ballard, Robert *1942–* Oceanographer and designer of modern devices for exploring Earth's oceans. p. 30

Battuta, Ibn *1304–?* Moroccan world traveler. p. 488

Bhutto, Benazir (BOO•toh) *1953–* A prime minister of Pakistan. She was the first woman in modern times to lead a Muslim nation. p. 540

Blair, Tony *1953–* Became British prime minister in 1997. p. 278

Bolívar, Simón (boh•LEE•var, see•MOHN) *1783–1830* South American soldier, statesperson, and revolutionary leader. He freed Bolivia, Colombia, Venezuela, Ecuador, and Peru from Spanish rule. p. 240

Bush, George W. *1946–* Forty-third President of the United States. p. 149

C

Caboto, Giovanni (kah•BOH•toh) *c. 1450–c. 1499* Italian navigator and explorer. Also known as John Cabot. While seeking a western route to Asia, he reached North America and claimed it for England. p. 144

Cabral, Pedro (kah•BRAHL) *c. 1467–1520* Portuguese navigator who claimed Brazil for Portugal. p. 234

Cartier, Jacques (kar•TYAY, ZHAHK) *1491–1557* French sailor and explorer. His explorations gave France its claim to Canada. p. 144

Castro, Fidel *1926–* Cuban revolutionary leader, prime minister, and president. p. 211

Catherine the Great *1729–1796* Russian empress who supported learning and the arts but neglected the Russian peasant class. p. 335

Ceausescu, Nicolae (chow•SHES•koo) *1918–1989* Romanian dictator from 1974 to 1989. He was overthrown and executed by the Romanian people during their revolt. p. 308

Champlain, Samuel de (sham•PLAYN) *c. 1567–1635* French explorer who led a group of settlers in 1608 and founded Quebec. p. 145

Champollion, Jean-François *1790–1832* Professor of Egyptian antiquities. Deciphered Egyptian hieroglyphics by studying the Rosetta Stone. p. 412

Chandragupta Maurya (chuhn•druh•GUP•tuh MOW•ree•uh) *?–c. 297 B.C.* Emperor who united India. He gave up the throne to his son in 297 B.C. p. 532

Charles, Prince of Wales *1948–* Heir to the British throne. p. 151

Charles V *1500–1558* King of Spain from 1516 to 1556. p. 172

Chekhov, Anton *1860–1904* Russian playwright and author. p. 343

Chirac, Jacques (shir•AHK) *1932–* President of France since 1995. p. 422

Chopin, Frédéric (SHOH•pan) *1810–1849* Polish composer and pianist. p. 315

Chrétien, Jean (kray•TYAN) *1934–* Prime minister of Canada since 1993. p. 149

Churchill, Winston *1874–1965* British statesperson, author, and prime minister of Britain from 1940 to 1945. p. 304

Clark, Helen *1950–* Prime minister of New Zealand since 1999. p. 637

Cleopatra *69 B.C.–30 B.C.* Egyptian queen who, with Mark Antony, planned to set up an independent empire until the Roman leader Octavian defeated them. p. 412

Clinton, William *1946–* Forty-second President of the United States. p. 311

Coerr, Eleanor *1922–* Author of the famous children's book *Sadako and the Thousand Paper Cranes*. p. 574

Columbus, Christopher *1451–1506* Italian-born explorer for Spain. In 1492 he sailed from Spain, looking for a new route to Asia. Instead, he reached islands near the Americas, lands that were unknown to the Europeans. p. 107

Confucius (kuhn•FYOO•shuhs) *551 B.C.–479 B.C.* Philosopher considered to be the most revered person in Chinese history. His philosophy, known as Confucianism, became a guide for the way people lived. p. 561

Conrad, Joseph *1857–1924* British novelist born in Ukraine. p. 315

Cook, James *1728–1779* An English explorer, who sailed the world and charted the coasts of eastern Canada, Australia, New Zealand, and western North America. p. 628

Cortés, Hernando (kawr•TEZ, er•NAHN•doh) *1485–1547* Spanish conquistador who conquered the Aztec Empire. p. 172

Curie, Marie *1867–1934* Discoverer of radium and polonium. Her discoveries led to the development of the X-ray machine. p. 302

Cyrus the Great *c. 585 B.C.–529 B.C.* Leader who built the Persian Empire and conquered Babylon. p. 376

D

David-Neel, Alexandra *1868–1969* French author and adventurer. She traveled through Tibet on foot, entered its forbidden capital city, Lhasa, and wrote about her journeys. p. 19

de Klerk, Frederik Willem *1936–* Former president of South Africa. Although an Afrikaner, he lifted the bans on the African National Congress and freed Nelson Mandela and other political prisoners. p. 497

Díaz, Porfirio (DEE•ahz, pawr•FEER•ee•oh) *1830–1915* Mexican general and politician. p. 184

E

Eiffel, Alexandre-Gustave (EYE•fuhl, a•lāyks•AHN•druh goos•TAHV) *1832–1923* French engineer who built the Eiffel Tower in Paris in 1889. p. 263

Einstein, Albert (YN•styn) *1879–1955* American physicist and author of "The Meaning of Relativity." p. 51

Eisenhower, Dwight D. *1890–1969* Thirty-fourth President of the United States. p. 595

El-Asmar, Fouzi *1937–* Palestinan author, journalist, and poet. p. 355

Ezana (AY•zah•nah) Fourth-century A.D. king of Axum. He declared Axum a Christian city. p. 487

F

Farheen, Abida (far•HEEN, AH•bee•duh) Leader of Pakistani educational region. p. 540

Ferrero-Waldner, Benita *1948–* Austrian federal minister for foreign affairs. She informs on human rights and holocaust issues in Austria. p. 283

Figueres, José (fee•GAIR•ays) *1906–1990* Costa Rican landowner who fought in the civil war in 1948 and helped Otilio Ulate regain control of the Costa Rican government. p. 210

Fischer, Joschka *1948–* Federal foreign minister of affairs and vice-chancellor of the Federal Republic of Germany since 1998. p. 283

Ford, Henry *1863–1947* Founder and president of Ford Motor Co., the first automobile manufacturer to use the assembly-line method of production. p. 125

Fox Quesada, Vicente *1942–* Became president of Mexico in 2000. p. 185

Francis Ferdinand *1863–1914* Archduke of Austria, who was assassinated in 1914. This was considered the direct cause of World War I. p. 303

Freeman, Cathy *1973–* Australian athlete. At the 2000 Olympics in Sydney, Australia, she became the first Aborigine ever to win a gold medal. p. 630

Frovik, Rune Spokesperson for the High North Alliance. p. 637

G

Gama, Vasco da (GAH•muh, VAS•koh dah) *1460–1524* Portuguese navigator who completed the first voyage from Western Europe around Africa to Asia. p. 534

Gandhi, Mohandas (GAHN•dee, moh•HAHN•dahs) *1869–1948* Indian nationalist and spiritual leader. He was called *Mahatma*, or "Great Soul," by his followers and is considered the founder of independent India. p. 534

Gautama, Siddhartha (GOW•tuh•muh, sid•HART•ah) *563 B.C.–c. 483 B.C.* Philosopher known as *Buddha*, or "Enlightened One," who gave up worldly goods to search for enlightenment and truth. He founded the religion of Buddhism in India. p. 532

Genghis Khan (JENG•guhs KAHN) *c. 1162–1227* Mongol leader who began the Mongol Empire. p. 562

Gorbachev, Mikhail (GAWR•buh•chawf, mee•KAH•eel) *1931–* Secretary General of the Communist party of the Soviet Union from 1985 to 1991. He supported reform ideas that included restructuring the government and making it more open to Soviet citizens. p. 338

Gutenberg, Johannes (GOO•tuhn•berg, yoh•HAHN•uhs) *c. 1400–1468* German inventor who brought the idea of movable type to Europe. He printed Europe's first book, a 1,200-page Bible. p. 270

Guujaw President of the Council of the Haida Nation. p. 138

Hammurabi (ha•muh•RAH•bee) *c. 1792 B.C.–1750 B.C.* King of the city-state of Babylon. He compiled the set of laws known as the Code of Hammurabi. p. 373

Hapsburg (HAHPS•burk) Family whose members, for hundreds of years, were rulers of European countries and territories, including Austria and Hungary. p. 302

Hassan II *1929–1999* King of Morocco from 1961–1999. p. 423

Hatshepsut (hat•SHEP•soot) *c. 1503 B.C.–1458 B.C.* Female Egyptian pharaoh who expanded Egyptian trade routes. p. 408

Henry, Patrick *1736–1799* American revolutionary and orator. p. 108

Hidalgo, Miguel (ee•DAHL•goh) *1753–1811* Mexican priest and revolutionary leader who campaigned for Mexican independence. p. 183

Hill, Robert *1946–* Environmental minister of Australia. p. 637

Hitler, Adolf *1889–1945* German politician and *Führer*, or leader. As Nazi dictator of Germany, he planned to conquer the world, claiming that the German people were superior to others. During his time of power he ordered 12 million people killed. p. 272

Hostetter, Doug International Secretary of the Fellowship of Reconciliation. p. 311

Hunt, Leigh *1784–1859* An English journalist and poet. p. 399

Hussein, Saddam (hoo•SAYN, suh•DAHM) *1937–2006* Military ruler of Iraq and president from 1979 to 2003. His invasion of Kuwait in 1990 led to the defeat of Iraq in the Persian Gulf War. p. 392

Hyder, Zia *1936–* Professor of dramatic arts, poet, and playwright; born in Bangladesh. p. 11

Islam, Kazi *1899–1976* Modern Bangladeshi poet. p. 539

Ivan III *1440–1505* Slav prince who won control of Kievan Rus in 1480 and became the first true ruler of Russia. Also known as "Ivan the Great." p. 335

Ivan IV *1530–1584* Grandson of Ivan III. First czar of Russia. Also known as "Ivan the Terrible." p. 335

Jeffers, Robinson *1887–1962* An American poet. p. 645

Jefferson, Thomas *1743–1826* Third President of the United States and the main writer of the Declaration of Independence. p. 108

Jesus *c. 6 B.C.–c. A.D. 30* The person whose life and teachings are the basis of Christianity. Believing him to be the Son of God, his disciples proclaimed him the Messiah and the savior of humankind. p. 374

John *1167–1216* King of England who was forced by nobles to sign the Magna Carta. p. 70

Johnson, Samuel *1709–1784* English writer and critic. p. 280

Juárez, Benito (HWAH•rays) *1806–1872* Mexican revolutionary and statesperson. p. 184

Kafka, Franz *1883–1924* Austrian writer whose fiction expressed the anxiety of his time. p. 315

Kahf, Mohja *1967–* A professor at the University of Arkansas born in Yemen. p. 363

Kanié, Anoma Author from Côte d' Ivoire. p. 435

Kennedy, Robert F., Jr. *1954–* Environmental attorney and son of Robert F. Kennedy, former Attorney General of the United States. p. 138

Kenyatta, Jomo (ken•YA•tuh, JOH•moh) *1894–1978* First prime minister of independent Kenya. As leader of the Mau Maus, he freed Kenya from British rule. p. 495

Khomeini, Ruholla (koh•MAY•nee, roo•HOH•luh) *1900–1989* Leader of Shi'i Muslims in Iran known as the "Ayatollah." p. 392

Kim, Dae-Jung *1925–* Became president of South Korea in 1997. p. 68

Kim, Jong-Il *1941–* Became communist leader of North Korea in 1994. p. 68

King, Martin Luther, Jr. *1929–1968* American minister and reformer. Advocate of nonviolence and interracial brotherhood. p. 116

Kublai Khan (KOO•bluh KAHN) *1215–1294* Grandson of Genghis Khan. He expanded the Mongol dynasty from China to Eastern Europe. p. 562

Lange, David *1942–* Prime minister of New Zealand from 1984 to 1989. p. 636

Lao-tzu (LOWD•zuh) Sixth century B.C. Chinese philosopher. p. 561

Lazarus, Emma (LAZ•uh•ruhs) *1849–1887* American poet who wrote the poem carved on the base of the Statue of Liberty. p. 97

Lenin, Vladimir Ilyich (LEH•nuhn, vlah•duh•meer EEL•yich) *1870–1924* Russian leader of the Communist revolution of 1917 and first premier of the Soviet Union. p. 336

Lesseps, Ferdinand de (lay•SEPS) *1805–1894* French diplomat and promoter of the Suez Canal. p. 402

Lincoln, Abraham *1809–1865* Sixteenth President of the United States. p. 68

Liszt, Franz (LIST) *1811–1886* Hungarian piano virtuoso and composer. p. 315

Ludwig *1845–1886* King of Bavaria from 1864 to 1886. Also known as "King Louis II." p. 350

Lukwiya, Dr. Matthew *1958–2000* Doctor who worked in a Uganda misson. Helped isolate an Ebola breakout in 2000. p. 502

Luther, Martin *1483–1546* German religious reformer whose ideas led to the Protestant Reformation. p. 278

M

Madero, Francisco (mah•THAY•roh) *1873–1913* Mexican revolutionary and politician. p. 184

Madison, James *1751–1836* Fourth President of the United States. He was a leader in writing the Constitution and winning support for it. p. 113

Malaqaya Queen of Kush around 500 B.C. p. 486

Mandela, Nelson *1918–* South African leader of the African National Congress. He was imprisoned for 25 years for conspiracy to overthrow the South African government. In 1994 he became president of South Africa. p. 497

Mansa Musa *?–c. 1332* Emperor of Mali who is remembered for his pilgrimage to Mecca. During his rule, Mali became known as a wealthy state and a center of learning. p. 453

Mao Zedong (MOW zuh•DUNG) *1893–1976* Chinese soldier and statesperson. He was chairman of the Communist party and of the People's Republic of China. p. 575

Marcos, Ferdinand *1917–1989* Philippine president from 1965 to 1986. p. 599

Markham, Beryl *1902–1986* First woman pilot to fly solo across the Atlantic Ocean from east to west. p. 443

Matsuo, Basho (BAH•shoh) *1644–1694* Japanese poet. A former samurai, he revived and refined the haiku. p. 515

Mbeki, Thabo (m•BEK•ee, TAY•boh) *1942–* Became South African president in 1999. p. 497

McAllister, Ian *1969–* Rainforest Conservation Society activist. p. 138

Mee, Lawrence Scientist who specializes in ocean environments. p. 328

Michener, James *1907– 1997* Pulitzer prize-winning U.S. novelist. p. 611

Milosevic, Slobodan (mee•LOH•shev•ich, SLAW•boh•duhn) *1914–* Serbian president who led Serbia in an attack on Croatia in 1991. Elected president of Yugoslavia in 1997. Was arrested by the United Nations in 2001. p. 309

Minamoto Yoritomo (mee•na•MOH•toh yoh•rih•TOH•moh) *1147–1199* As shogun, he created a system that ended in Japan's being torn by civil war. p. 564

Mirza, Iskander *1899–1969* First president of Pakistan. p. 543

Momaday, N. Scott *1934–* Native American author and poet, his works focus on his Kiowa background. p. 91

Morimoto, Minoru Japanese representative for International Whaling Commission. p. 637

Mother Teresa *1910–1997* A Catholic nun and winner of the Nobel Peace Prize in 1979 for her work with the sick and poor in Kolkata, India. p. 545

Mubarak, Hosni (mu•BAHR•uhk) *1928–* President of Egypt from 1981. p. 423

Mugabe, Robert *1924–* Prime minister of Zimbabwe from 1980 to 1987 and president from 1987. p. 497

Muhammad (muh•HA•muhd) *c. 570–632* Prophet who brought the message of Islam to the world. p. 375

Muhammad VI (moh•HA•muhd) *1963–* King of Morocco from 1999. p. 422

Mumtaz Mahal *?–1631* Wife of the Mogul emperor Shah Jahan of India. The Taj Mahal was built as a memorial to her in the seventeeth century. p. 539

Musharraf, Pervez *1943–* President of Pakistan from 1999. p. 543

N

Napoleon *1769–1821* French emperor. p. 578

Nasser, Gamal Abdel *1918–1970* Egyptian soldier, politician, and president of Egypt during the 1950s. p. 423

Nehru, Jawaharlal (NER•oo, juh•WAH•huhr•lahl) *1889–1964* Indian political leader and first prime minister of independent India. His work with Mohandas Gandhi helped bring about India's independence. p. 543

Nicholas II *1868–1918* Russian czar when the Russian Revolution began. p. 336

Nkrumah, Kwame (en•KROO•muh, KWAH•mee) *1909–1972* First president of the Ghana republic. He was the leader in liberating the Gold Coast in Africa from British rule. p. 456

Nyerere, Julius (nyuh•RAY•ray) *1922–1999* Led Tanganyikan nationalist movement in 1954 and later led a newly independent government in present-day Tanzania. p. 495

O

Obasanjo, Olusegun *1937–* President of Nigeria from 1999. Established the Human Rights Violations Investigation Commission. p. 458

O'Higgins, Bernardo *1778–1842* Chilean soldier and statesperson. Known as "Liberator of Chile." p. 241

P

Paz, Octavio *1914–* Mexican poet, writer, and diplomat. p. 171

Pedro *1798–1834* Portuguese prince and ruler of Brazil who peacefully granted independence for Brazil from Portugal in 1825. p. 241

Perkins, Charles *1936–2000* Aborigine leader and activist who fought for civil rights. p. 638

Peter I *1672–1725* Russian czar from 1682 to 1725. Also known as "Peter the Great," he helped place Russia among the great European powers. p. 335

Peter III *1728–1762* Grandson of Peter the Great and czar of Russia in 1762. p. 335

Piankhi (PYANG•kee) *c. 751 B.C.–716 B.C.* King of Kush and son of Kashta. He conquered Lower Egypt. p. 486

Pizarro, Francisco (pee•SAR•oh, fran•SIS•koh) *c. 1475–1541* Spanish conqueror of Peru. p. 235

Polo, Marco *1254–1324* Italian traveler who was among the first European traders to visit China and record his experiences. p. 563

BIOGRAPHICAL DICTIONARY

BIOGRAPHICAL DICTIONARY

Pope, Alexander *1688–1744* English poet and one of the most quotable of all English authors. p. 259

Ptolemy (TAHL•uh•mee) King of Egypt *(323–285 B.C.)* and founder of the Ptolemy dynasty. pp. 412

Putin, Vladimir *1952–* Elected president of Russia in 2000. p. 339

Q

Qaboos bin Said *1940–* Became sultan of Oman in 1970. p. 392

Qaddafi, Mu'ammar al- (kuh•DAH•fee, MOH•ah•mar el) *1942–* Led military takeover of Libya in 1969 and established himself as the new ruler of Libya. p. 424

R

Ramses (RAM•seez) Name of 11 kings of the nineteenth and twentieth dynasties of ancient Egypt. p. 408

Romero-Barcelo, Carlos *1932–* Puerto Rico's delegate to the United States Congress. p. 212

Ross, James Clark *1800–1862* A British explorer who discovered the Ross Sea and the Victoria Land region of Antarctica. p. 662

Roy, Arundhati *1961–* Author from India who won the Booker Prize in 1998. p. 539

Rurik *?– c. A.D. 879* Viking founder of the Rurik dynasty, which ruled Russia. p. 335

S

Sadat, Anwar as- (suh•DAH) *1918–1981* Egyptian soldier, statesperson, and president of Egypt after Nasser's death; a signer of the Camp David peace agreement. p. 423

San Martín, José de (san mar•TEEN) *1778–1850* Argentinian soldier and statesperson; led the fight for independence from Spanish rule in southern South America. p. 240

Sánchez, Óscar Arias *1941–* President of Costa Rica from 1986 to 1990 and creator of a Central American peace plan. Won Nobel Peace Prize in 1987. p. 209

Sankara, Thomas *1949–1987* President of Burkina Faso from 1983 to 1987. p. 473

Santayana, George *1863–1952* Spanish-born American author and philosopher. p. 1

Sargon (SAHR•gahn) *c. 2334 B.C.–2279 B.C.* Warrior who founded the Akkadian Empire and so became the first ruler of an empire in the Fertile Crescent. p. 373

Schroeder, Gerhard *1944–* Became German chancellor in 1998. p. 287

Shah Jahan (SHAH juh•HAHN) *1592–1666* During his reign Mogul power reached its highest point. He constructed the Taj Mahal, a beautiful tomb built in memory of his wife. p. 539

Shakespeare, William *1564–1616* British dramatist and poet. Considered among the greatest writers of all time. p. 280

Shanadakhete *?–160 B.C.* Queen of Meroë. p. 486

Shankar, Ravi *1920–* Sitar player from India. p. 539

Sharif, Nawaz (shah•REEF, nah•VAHZ) *1949–* Prime minister of Pakistan from 1990 to 1993 and again from 1997 to 1999. p. 540

Sharon, Ariel *1928–* Became prime minister of Israel in 2001. p. 389

Shi Huangdi (SHIR HWAHNG•DEE) *c. 259 B.C.–210 B.C.* Ruler of the Qin dynasty and unifier of China. p. 562

Smith, Adam *1723–1790* Scottish economist and author. p. 72

Sophie *1868–1914* Duchess of Hohenberg and wife of Archduke Francis Ferdinand; assassinated in 1914. p. 303

Stalin, Joseph (STAH•luhn) *1879–1953* Soviet dictator after Lenin's death. During his rule the Soviet Union became a totalitarian state and a world power. p. 304

Sundiata (sun•JAHT•ah) *?–1255* Founder and ruler of the ancient Mali Empire. p. 453

T

Tagore, Rabindranath *1861–1941* Indian Bengali poet, composer, and painter. Received Nobel Prize for literature in 1913. p. 539

Tennyson, Alfred (TEH•nuh•suhn) *1809–1892* English poet, commonly known as "Alfred, Lord Tennyson." His son Hallam was governor-general of Australia from 1902 to 1904. p. 251

Thutmose II (thoot•MOH•suh) *c. 1500s B.C.* Son of Thutmose I. He continued to expand Egypt's land. p. 409

Tito, Josip Broz (TEE•toh, YOH•sip BRAWZ) *1892–1980* First president of the republic of Yugoslavia. p. 305

Toledo, Alejandro *1946–* President of Peru. p. 242

Tolstoy, Leo *1828–1910* Russian novelist and moral philosopher. p. 343

Touré, Samori *c. 1830–1900* Led 30,000 soldiers in a 15-year campaign to keep the French from invading lands in Africa. He was finally defeated in 1898. p. 456

Toynbee, Arnold *1889–1975* English historian. p. 619

Tremonti, Giulio *1947–* Italian finance minister. p. 283

Tutankhamen (too•tahng•KAH•muhn) *c. 1370 B.C.–1352 B.C.* During his brief reign as pharaoh, his ministers restored the old religion of Egypt. He was buried in a solid-gold coffin. p. 408

U

Ulate, Otilio *1896–1973* President of Costa Rica from 1949–1952. p. 210

V

Vajpayee, Atal Behari *1924–* Prime minister of India, elected in 1998. p. 543

Van der Post, Laurens *1906–1996* A South African author. p. 477

Victoria *1819–1901* Queen of the United Kingdom and Ireland (1837–1901) and empress of India (1876–1901). p. 535

Walesa, Lech (vah•LEHN•suh) *1943–* Leader of a workers' group, called Solidarity, in Poland during the 1980s. He was elected president in Poland's first free election, in 1990. p. 308

Washington, George *1732–1799* Commander-in-chief of the Continental Army during the Revolutionary War and first President of the United States. p. 108

Wiesel, Elie (vee•ZEL, EH•lee) *1928–* Romanian author and winner of the Nobel Peace Prize in 1986. p. 315

Xerxes (ZERK•seez) *c. 519 B.C.–c. 465 B.C.* King of Persia and son of Darius I. p. 376

Yeltsin, Boris (YELT•suhn) *1931–* Russian political leader and first democratically elected president in Russia. p. 339

Yi Sĭng-gye General who overthrew Korea's Koryŭ dynasty and started the Yi dynasty, which lasted from 1392 to 1910. p. 565

Zoscales King of Axum during the first century A.D. p. 487

Zoser *c. 2600s B.C.* King of Egypt in the twenty-seventh century B.C. p. 408

Zweig, Stefan *1881–1942* German writer. p. 219

BIOGRAPHICAL DICTIONARY

Gazetteer

The Gazetteer is a geographical dictionary that will help you locate places discussed in this book. The page number tells where each place appears on a map.

A

Abu Dhabi The capital of the United Arab Emirates. (24°N, 54°E) p. 365

Abuja The capital of Nigeria. (9°N, 7°E) p. 436

Accra The capital of Ghana. (5°N, 0°W) p. 436

Aconcagua The highest peak of the Andes and of the Western Hemisphere; located in Argentina. p. A15

Addis Ababa The capital of Ethiopia. (9°N, 38°E) p. 479

Adriatic Sea An extension of the Mediterranean Sea; located east of Italy and west of the Balkan Peninsula. p. 261

Aegean Sea (ih•JEE•uhn) An arm of the Mediterranean Sea between Asia Minor and Greece. p. 261

Afghanistan A country in Southwest Asia; located between Pakistan and Iran. p. 357

Africa One of the world's seven continents. p. 12

Albania A country in Eastern Europe; located on the Balkan Peninsula, along the Adriatic Sea. p. 295

Alberta A province of Canada; located between British Columbia and Saskatchewan. p. 135

Aleutian Islands A chain of volcanic islands extending southwest from the Alaska Peninsula; they separate the Bering Sea from the Pacific Ocean. p. A6

Algeria A country in North Africa; located on the coast of the Mediterranean Sea. p. 401

Algiers The capital of Algeria; located in north-central Algeria on the Bay of Algiers. (37°N, 3°E) p. 401

Alps The largest group of mountains in Western Europe; located in France, Switzerland, Italy, Austria, Slovenia, Bosnia and Herzegovina, Yugoslavia, Albania, and Croatia. p. A12

Altai Mountains (al•TY) A mountain system in Asia where Russia, China, and Mongolia meet. p. 516

Amazon River The largest river in the world by amount of water; flows across northern Brazil in South America and into the Atlantic Ocean. p. 164

Amman The capital of Jordan. (32°N, 36°E) p. 365

Amsterdam The capital and the largest city of the Netherlands. (52°N, 5°E) p. 261

Amur River A river in northeastern Asia; forms part of the border between Russia and China. p. 327

Andaman Sea A body of water in South Asia; forms the eastern part of the Bay of Bengal. p. 516

Andes A mountain system in South America, extending along the western coast from Panama to Tierra del Fuego. p. 221

Andorra A country in Western Europe located in the Pyrenees mountains between Spain and France. p. 261

Angola A country in Southern Africa on the Atlantic coast. p. 436

Ankara The capital of Turkey. (40°N, 33°E) p. 365

Antananarivo The capital of Madagascar. (19°S, 47°E) p. 479

Antarctica One of the world's seven continents. p. 663

Antigua and Barbuda An independent nation in the Leeward Islands of the Caribbean Sea. p. 195

Apennines (A•puh•nynz) A mountain range; runs north and south through the center of Italy. p. 261

Apia The capital of Samoa. (13°S, 171°W) p. 655

Arabian Peninsula A peninsula bordered by the Red Sea, the Persian Gulf, and the Arabian Sea in Southwest Asia; occupied by the countries of Saudi Arabia, Yemen, Oman, the United Arab Emirates, Qatar, and Kuwait. p. 365

Arabian Sea The sea located west of India and east of the Arabian Peninsula; forms the southern border of southwestern Asia. p. 365

Aral Sea (AIR•uhl) A large inland body of water located in Kazakhstan and Uzbekistan in central Asia. p. 327

Arckhangel´sk A Russian port city in Europe. (65°N, 41°E) p. 327

Arctic Ocean One of the world's four oceans. p. 41

Argentina A country in South America, on the Atlantic coast. p. 221

Armenia A country in western Asia. p. 327

Ashgabat The capital of Turkmenistan. (40°N, 60°E) p. 327

Asia One of the world's seven continents. p. 12

Asmara The capital of Eritrea. (15°N, 39°E) p. 479

Astana The capital of Kazakhstan. (48°N, 68°E) p. 327

Asunción The capital of Paraguay. (25°S, 57°W) p. 221

Athens The capital of Greece; located near the southeastern coast of Greece. (38°N, 24°E) p. 261

Atlantic Ocean One of the world's four oceans. p. 12

Atlas Mountains A mountain system in northern Africa. p. 356

Australia One of the world's seven continents; a country filling the continent of Australia. p. 621

Austria A country in Western Europe. p. 261

Azerbaijan (a•zer•by•JAHN) A Western Eurasian republic; located west of the Caspian Sea. p. 327

B

Baghdad The capital of Iraq; located on both sides of the Tigris River in eastern Iraq. (33°N, 44°E) p. 365

Bahamas An archipelago of about 700 islands off the east coast of Florida. p. 195

Bahrain An archipelago in the Persian Gulf off the coast of Saudi Arabia. p. 365

Baku The capital of Azerbaijan; a port city on the Caspian Sea. (40°N, 50°E) p. 327

Balearic Islands (ba•lee•AIR•ik) An island group in the western Mediterranean Sea, off the eastern coast of Spain; forms the Spanish province of Baleares. p. A12

Baltic Sea The sea located on the southeastern side of the Scandinavian Peninsula. p. 261

Bamako The capital of Mali. (12°N, 8°W) p. 445

Bandar Seri Begawan The capital of Brunei . (5°N, 115°E) p. 516

Bangalore (bang•uh•LOHR) A city in southern India. (13°N, 78°E) p. 516

Bangkok The capital of Thailand; located on the southern end of the Chao Phraya River on the Gulf of Thailand. (14°N, 100°E) p. 585

Bangladesh (bahn•gluh•DESH) A country in South Asia on the coast of the Bay of Bengal. p. 525

Bangui The capital of the Central African Republic. (4°N, 18°E) p. 436

Banjul The capital of Gambia. (13°N, 16°W) p. 445

Barbados An island country in the Lesser Antilles, north of Venezuela. p. 195

Barcelona A province and city of Spain; located southeast of Madrid. (41°N, 2°E) p. 252

Barents Sea Part of the Arctic Ocean; located north of Norway and Russia, between Spitsbergen and Novaya Zemlya. p. 327

Basseterre The capital of St. Kitts and Nevis; located on St. Kitts. (17°N, 62°W) p. 195

Bay of Bengal An inlet of the Indian Ocean that runs alongside eastern India. p. 525

Beijing (bay•JING) The capital of China; located in northeastern China. (40°N, 116°E) p. 555

Beirut The capital of Lebanon. (34°N, 35°E) p. 365

Belarus (byeh•luh•ROOS) A Eurasion republic; located north of Ukraine, west of Russia, and east of Poland. p. 327

Belgium A country in Western Europe; located on the coast of the North Sea. p. 261

Belgrade The capital of Serbia; located at the junction of the Sava and Danube Rivers. (45°N, 21°E) p. 295

Belize (buh•LEEZ) A country in Central America, located on the Yucatá n Peninsula. p. 195

Belmopan The capital of Belize. (17°N, 88°W) p. 195

Benin (buh•NIN) A country in West Africa; located on the Gulf of Guinea. p. 445

Bering Sea Part of the North Pacific Ocean between northeastern Siberia and Alaska. p. 327

Berlin The capital of Germany; located in northeastern Germany. (53°N, 12°E) p. 261

Bern The capital of Switzerland. (47°N, 7°E) p. 261

Bhutan (boo•TAN) A country in South Asia; located south of China and north of India. p. 525

Bishkek The capital of Kyrgyzstan. (41°N, 75°E) p. 327

Bissau The capital of Guinea-Bissau. (12°N, 15°W) p. 445

Black Sea A sea between Europe and Asia; surrounded by Bulgaria, Romania, Moldova, Ukraine, Russia, Georgia, and Turkey. p. 327

Bogotá The capital of Colombia. (4°S, 74°W) p. 221

Bolivia A country in South America. p. 221

Bombay See **Mumbai.**

Borneo An island in the Malay Archipelago; third-largest island in the world. (1°N, 115°E) p. 585

Bosnia and Herzegovina (BAHZ•nee•uh and hert•suh•goh•VEE•nuh) A country in Eastern Europe. p. 295

Botswana A country in Southern Africa. p. 479

Brahmaputra River A river in South Asia; flows through China, India, and Bangladesh into the Bay of Bengal. p. 516

Brasília The capital of Brazil. (16°S, 48°W) p. 221

Bratislava The capital of Slovakia. (48°N, 17°E) p. 295

Brazil A country in eastern South America. p. 221

Brazzaville The capital of the Republic of the Congo. (4°S, 15°E) p. 445

Bridgetown The capital of Barbados. (13°S, 59°W) p. 195

Britain See **United Kingdom.**

Brunei A country in Southeast Asia. p. 585

Brussels The capital of Belgium. (51°N, 4°E) p. 261

Bucharest The capital of Romania. (44°N, 26°E) p. 295

Budapest The capital of Hungary. (47°N, 19°E) p. 295

Buenos Aires (bway•nohs EYE•rays) The capital and a port city of Argentina. (34°S, 58°W) p. 221

Bujumbura The capital of Burundi. (3°S, 29°E) p. 479

Bulgaria A country in southeastern Europe; located on the Balkan Peninsula. p. 295

Burkina Faso A country in West Africa. p. 445

Burma See **Myanmar.**

Burundi A country in East Africa. p. 479

C

Cairo The capital of Egypt; located in northeastern Egypt on the Nile River. (30°N, 31°E) p. 401

Calcutta See **Kolkata.**

Cambodia A country in Southeast Asia; located on the Indochina Peninsula. p. 516

Cameroon (ka•muh•ROON) A country in West Africa. p. 436

Canada A country in the northern part of North America. p. 135

Canberra The capital of Australia. (35°S, 149°E) p. 621

Cape Horn The southernmost point of South America. p. A6

Cape of Good Hope The southernmost point of Africa. p. A7

Cape Town A seaport city of Cape Province and the judicial capital of the country of South Africa. (34°S, 18°E) p. 436

Cape Verde An island country in the Atlantic Ocean; located off the coast of West Africa. p. 436

Caracas (kah•RAH•kahs) The capital of Venezuela; located near the coast of the Caribbean Sea. (11°N, 67°W) p. 221

Caribbean Sea The sea bordered by Central America, South America, and the Atlantic Ocean. p. 195

Caspian Sea A salt lake between Europe and Asia, east of the Black Sea. p. 327

Castries The capital of Saint Lucia. (14°N, 61°W) p. 195

Caucasus Mountains (KAW•kuh•suhs) A mountain range between the Black and Caspian Seas; borders Russia, Georgia, and Azerbaijan. p. 327

Central African Republic A country in Central Africa. p. 436

Ceylon See **Sri Lanka.**

GAZETTEER

Chad A country in Central Africa. p. 436

Chang Jiang (CHAHNG JYAHNG) A river in eastern China; flows from the Plateau of Tibet to the East China Sea. p. 516

Chennai (Madras) The capital of Tamil Nadu state in India. (13°N, 80°E) p. 516

Chile (CHEE•lay) A country on the southwestern coast of South America. p. 221

China A country in East Asia; currently the world's most heavily populated country. p. 516

Chisinau The capital of Moldova. (47°N, 28°E) p. 295

Colombia A country in northwestern South America. p. 221

Colombo The capital of Sri Lanka. (7°N, 80°E) p. 525

Comoros A country of three islands; located in the Mozambique Channel between Madagascar and southeastern Africa. p. 479

Conakry The capital of Guinea. (9°N, 13°W) p. 436

Congo, Democratic Republic of the A country in Central Africa. p. 436

Congo, Republic of the A country located in Central Africa. p. 436

Congo River A river in Central Africa; flows through the Democratic Republic of the Congo into the Atlantic Ocean. p. 436

Copenhagen The capital and a port city of Denmark. (56°N, 13°E) p. 261

Coral Sea The sea located north of Queensland, Australia, and south of Papua New Guinea. p. 655

Corsica A French island in the Mediterranean Sea; located west of Italy. (42°N, 9°E) p. 261

Costa Rica A country in Central America; located west of Panama; bordered by the Caribbean Sea and Pacific Ocean. p. 195

Côte d'Ivoire (koht dee•VWAHR) A country in western Africa; also known as the Ivory Coast. p. 436

Crete A large Greek island; located southeast of the Balkan Peninsula; separates the Mediterranean and Aegean Seas. p. 261

Croatia (kroh•AY•shuh) A country in Eastern Europe. p. 295

Cuba An island country; located south of the United States in the Greater Antilles in the Caribbean Sea. p. 195

Cuzco (KOOS•koh) A city in southern Peru. (14°S, 72°W) p. 221

Cyprus An island country in the eastern Mediterranean Sea. p. 357

Czech Republic (CHEK) A country in Eastern Europe. p. 295

D

Dakar The capital of Senegal. (14°N, 17°W) p. 436

Damascus (duh•MAS•kuhs) The capital of Syria, in Southwest Asia. (33°N, 36°E) p. 357

Danube River (DAN•yoob) A river in Eastern Europe; flows from southwestern Germany to the Black Sea. p. 295

Dar es Salaam The capital of Tanzania. (6°S, 39°E) p. 479

Dead Sea A salt lake in Israel and Jordan; the world's lowest place, at 1,312 feet (400 m) below sea level. p. 375

Deccan Plateau (DEH•kuhn) A triangle-shaped plateau in central India, between the Western and Eastern Ghats. p. 525

Denmark A country in Western Europe; occupies the northern part of the Jutland Peninsula. p. 261

Dhaka The capital of Bangladesh. (23°N, 90°E) p. 525

Djibouti (juh•BOO•tee) A country in East Africa; also the capital city of Djibouti. p. 479

Dnieper River (NEE•per) A river in Eastern Europe; flows from west of Moscow, Russia, to the Black Sea. p. 328

Doha The capital of Qatar. (25°N, 90°E) p. 357

Dominica (dah•muh•NEE•kuh) An island country in the eastern Caribbean. p. 195

Dominican Republic A country on the island of Hispaniola in the Caribbean. p. 195

Dublin The capital and a port city of the Republic of Ireland; located at the mouth of the Liffey River, on Dublin Bay. (53°N, 6°W) p. 261

Dushanbe The capital of Tajikistan. (38°N, 68°E) p. 327

E

East China Sea The part of the China Sea north of Taiwan. p. 516

East Timor A country in Southeast Asia; became an independent nation in 2002. p. 585

Easter Island An island off the western coast of South America, in the Pacific Ocean. p. 613

Eastern Ghats (GAWTS) A chain of mountains in southeastern India. p. 525

Ecuador (EH•kwah•dohr) A country in northwestern South America; located on the Pacific coast. p. 221

Egypt An ancient land and present-day country in northern Africa, on the coast of the Mediterranean and Red Seas. p. 357

El Aaiún The capital of Western Sahara. (27, 13°W) p. 401

El Salvador A country in Central America; located south of Guatemala, on the Pacific Ocean. p. 195

England One of the four divisions of the United Kingdom; occupies most of the southern part of Great Britain, the eastern island of the British Isles. p. 261

English Channel An extension and connection of the Atlantic Ocean and the North Sea; south of the British Isles and north of France. p. A12

Equatorial Guinea A country in West Africa. p. 436

Eritrea (air•ih•TREE•uh) A country on the Red Sea in East Africa; located north of Ethiopia. p. 479

Estonia A country in Eastern Europe. p. 295

Ethiopia A country in East Africa. p. 479

Euphrates River (yoo•FRAY•teez) A river that begins in Turkey, flows through Syria and Iraq, and empties into the Persian Gulf. p. 365

Europe One of the world's seven continents. pp. 252–253

F

Fiji An island country in Melanesia, in the southwestern Pacific Ocean. p. 612

Finland A country in Western Europe; located north of Estonia and east of the Gulf of Bothnia and Sweden. p. 261

Formosa See **Taiwan**.

France A country in western Europe. p. 261

Freetown The capital of Sierra Leone. (8°N, 13°W) p. 436

French Guiana An overseas department of France; located on the northern Atlantic coast of South America. p. 221

Funafuti The capital of Tuvalu. (8°S, 179°E) p. 612

G

Gabon A country in West Africa. p. 436

Gaborone The capital of Botswana. (24°S, 26°E) p. 479

Gambia A country on the Atlantic coast near the western tip of Africa. p. 436

Ganges River (GAN•jeez) A holy river in India; flows from the Himalayas into the Bay of Bengal. p. 525

Gdansk A port city in northern Poland; located on the Gulf of Gdansk, an inlet of the Baltic Sea. (54°N, 19°E) p. 295

Genoa A seaport on the coast of northwestern Italy; located on the Ligurian Sea. (44°N, 9°E) p. 407

Georgetown The capital of Guyana. (6°N, 58°W) p. 221

Georgia A Eurasian republic located on the Black Sea. p. 327

Germany A country in Western Europe. p. 261

Ghana (GAH•nuh) A country on the western coast of Africa. p. 436

Gibraltar, Rock of Mountain at the entrance of the Mediterranean Sea. p. A10

Glasgow A port city near the Atlantic coast of southwestern Scotland. (56°N, 4°W) p. A10

Gobi (Desert) A desert in eastern Asia; located in Mongolia and China. p. 555

Great Britain (Britain) See **United Kingdom**.

Greece A country in Europe; located on the southern end of the Balkan Peninsula. p. 261

Greenland The largest island in the world; located off northeastern North America; a territory of Denmark. p. 252

Grenada An island country; located in the Caribbean Sea north of Venezuela. p. 195

Guadalajara (gwah•duh•luh•HAR•uh) The capital of Jalisco state in central Mexico. (21°N, 103°W) p. 173

Guam An unincorporated United States territory; largest and southernmost of the Mariana Islands; located in the western Pacific Ocean. p. A5

Guangzhou (gwahng•JOH) A port city located on the Zhu River in southeastern China. (23°N, 113°E) p. 516

Guatemala A country in Central America. p. 195

Guatemala City The capital of Guatemala. (14°N, 90°W) p. 195

Guinea (GIH•nee) A country in West Africa. p. 436

Guinea-Bissau (GIH•nee bih•SOW) A country in West Africa. p. 436

Gulf of Mexico A gulf located south of the United States, east of Mexico, and west of Cuba. p. 195

Gulf of Thailand An inlet of the South China Sea; located between Malaysia and Thailand. p. 516

Guyana (gy•AH•nuh) A country in northern South America. p. 221

H

Hainan An island in the South China Sea; located in southeastern China. (19°N, 110°E) p. 555

Haiti A country on the island of Hispaniola in the Caribbean; located southeast of Cuba. p. 195

Hanoi (ha•NOY) The capital of Vietnam; located on the northern Red River. (21°N, 106°E) p. 516

Harare The capital of Zimbabwe. (17°S, 31°E) p. 479

Harbin The capital of Heilongjiang province; located in northeastern China. (45°N, 126°E) p. 516

Havana The capital of Cuba. (23°N, 82°W) p. 195

Hawaii A state of the United States; also the Hawaiian Islands, a chain of volcanic and coral islands in the north-central Pacific Ocean. p. 99

Helsinki The capital and a port city of Finland. (60°N, 25°E) p. 261

Himalayas (hih•muh•LAY•uhz) A mountain system on the northern edge of South Asia; runs through Nepal, Bhutan, southern Tibet, and northern India. p. 525

Hindu Kush A mountain system that extends southwest from the Pamirs in eastern Tajikistan, through northwestern Afghanistan. p. 525

Hiroshima (hir•uh•SHEE•muh) An industrial city located on the island of Honshu, Japan. (34°N, 133°E) p. 577

Hispaniola An island in the Greater Antilles in the Caribbean; occupied by the countries of Haiti and the Dominican Republic. p. 195

Ho Chi Minh City A city in Vietnam. (11°N, 107°E) p. 516

Honduras A country in Central America. p. 195

Hong Kong A large city in southeastern China. (22°N, 114°E) p. 516

Honiara The capital of the Solomon Islands; located on Guadalcanal. (9°S, 160°E) p. 612

Huang He (HWAHNG HUH) A river in China that flows east from the Plateau of Tibet. p. 516

Hungary A country in central Europe. p. 295

Hyderabad (HY•duh•ruh•bad) A city in central India. (17°N, 78°E) p. 516

I

Iberian Peninsula A peninsula forming southwestern Europe; extends into the Atlantic Ocean and the Mediterranean Sea; occupied by Portugal and Spain. p. A12

Iceland A European island country in the northern Atlantic Ocean; located southeast of Greenland. p. 261

India A country in southern Asia; occupies much of a large peninsula extending from central Asia into the Indian Ocean. p. 525

Indian Ocean One of the world's four oceans. p. 525

Indonesia A country of islands in Southeast Asia. p. 585

Indus River A river in South Asia; flows from Tibet, through northern India and Pakistan, and into the Arabian Sea. p. 516

Iran A country in Southwest Asia; located on the Persian Gulf. p. 365

Iraq A country in Southwest Asia. p. 365

GAZETTEER

Ireland A country in Western Europe, often called the Republic of Ireland; occupies most of the western island of the British Isles; also the name of the western island of the British Isles. p. 261

Irrawaddy River A river in south-central Myanmar. p. 516

Islamabad (is•LAH•muh•bahd) The capital of Pakistan. (34°N, 73°E) p. 525

Israel A country in Southwest Asia; located on the eastern coast of the Mediterranean Sea. p. 365

Istanbul The largest city in Turkey. (41°N, 28°E) p. 365

Italy A country in Western Europe; located on the Italian Peninsula. p. 261

Ivory Coast See **Côte d'Ivoire**.

Jakarta (Djakarta) The capital of Indonesia. (6°S, 106°E) p. 516

Jamaica An island country in the Greater Antilles in the Caribbean Sea. p. 195

Japan An island country in East Asia, off the Pacific coasts of China and Russia. p. 517

Java The most populated island of Indonesia; located in southern Indonesia. p. 585

Java Sea Part of the Pacific Ocean north of Java, south of Borneo, and east of Sumatra. p. 516

Jerusalem The capital of Israel. (31°N, 35°E) p. 365

Johannesburg A city in the country of South Africa. (26°S, 28°E) p. 479

Jordan A country in Southwest Asia. p. 365

K

Kabul The capital of Afghanistan. (34°N, 69°E) p. 365

Kalahari Desert A desert in southern Africa; located in Botswana, Namibia, and the country of South Africa. p. 436

Kamchatka Peninsula (kuhm•CHAHT•kuh) A peninsula in northeastern Russia; surrounded by the Sea of Okhotsk and the Bering Sea. p. 327

Kampala The capital of Uganda. (0°N, 32°E) p. 479

Kathmandu The capital of Nepal on the Indian subcontinent; located in a valley of the Himalayas. (27°N, 85°E) p. 516

Katowice A city in southern Poland. (50°N, 19°E) p. 295

Kazakhstan (ka•zak•STAN) A Eurasian republic. p. 327

Kenya A country in East Africa. p. 479

Khartoum The capital of Sudan. (15°N, 32°E) p. 479

Kiev (KEE•ef) The capital of Ukraine; located on the Dnieper River, in central Ukraine. (50°S, 31°E) p. 327

Kigali The capital of Rwanda. (2°S, 30°E) p. 436

Kingston The capital of Jamaica. (18°N, 76°W) p. 195

Kingstown The capital of St. Vincent and the Grenadines. (13°N, 61°W) p. 195

Kinshasa The capital of the Democratic Republic of the Congo. (4°S, 15°E) p. 436

Kiribati A country of 33 islands in the Pacific Ocean near the equator. p. 612

Kobe (KOH•bee) A seaport and commercial city in Japan; located on the southern coast of Honshu. (35°N, 137°E) p. 577

Kolkata (Calcutta) A large city and port in northeastern India; located on the Hugli River. (22°N, 88°E) p. 516

Koror The capital of Palau in the western Pacific Ocean. (7°N, 134°E) p. 612

Kuala Lumpur The capital of Malaysia. (3°N, 101°E) p. 585

Kunlun Shan (KOON•LOON SHAN) A mountain range in western China. p. 516

Kuwait (ku•WAYT) A country in Southwest Asia; located on the Persian Gulf between Iraq and Saudi Arabia; also the capital of Kuwait. p. 365

Kyoto (kee•OH•toh) A city in Japan; located in west-central Honshu. (35°N, 136°E) p. 577

Kyrgyzstan (kir•gih•STAN) A Eurasian republic. p. 327

L

La Paz The administrative capital and largest city in Bolivia. (16°S, 68°W) p. 221

Lagos A seaport in Nigeria. (6°N, 3°E) p. 436

Lake Chad A lake in northern Africa on the border of Chad, Cameroon, Nigeria, and Niger. p. 436

Lake Erie The fourth-largest of the Great Lakes; borders Canada and the United States. p. 92

Lake Huron The second-largest of the Great Lakes; borders Canada and the United States. p. 92

Lake Malawi A large lake along the eastern border of Malawi in southern Africa; also called Lake Nyasa. p. 480

Lake Michigan The third-largest of the Great Lakes, the only one entirely within the United States. p. 92

Lake Nyasa See **Lake Malawi**.

Lake Ontario The smallest of the Great Lakes; borders Canada and the United States. p. 92

Lake Superior The largest of the Great Lakes; borders Canada and the United States. p. 92

Lake Tanganyika (tan•guh•NYEE•kuh) A lake in Tanzania and the Democratic Republic of the Congo, in the Great Rift Valley of Southern Africa. p. 480

Lake Victoria A lake in Tanzania, Kenya, and Uganda in East Africa. p. 479

Laos A country located on the Indochina Peninsula in Southeast Asia. p. 585

Latvia A country in Eastern Europe. p. 295

Lebanon A country on the eastern shore of the Mediterranean Sea in Southwest Asia. p. 357

Lena River A river in Russia; flows into the Laptev Sea. p. 253

León A city in central Mexico; located northwest of Mexico City. (21°N, 102°W) p. 173

Lesotho An independent country located within the borders of the country of South Africa. (30°S, 28°E) p. 479

Liberia A country in West Africa; located on the Atlantic coast. p. 436

Libreville The capital of Gabon. (0°N, 9°E) p. 436

Libya A country in North Africa; located on the Mediterranean Sea. p. 401

GAZETTEER

Libyan Desert A desert in North Africa; located in Libya, Egypt, and Sudan. p. 401

Liechtenstein A country in West Europe; located between Switzerland and Austria. p. 261

Lilongwe The capital of Malawi. (14°S, 33°E) p. 436

Lima The capital of Peru. (12°S, 77°W) p. 221

Lisbon The capital of Portugal; located on the Atlantic coast. (39°N, 9°W) p. 261

Lithuania A country in Eastern Europe. p. 295

Ljubljana The capital of Slovenia. (46°N, 14°E) p. 295

Lodz A city in central Poland. (51°N, 19°E) p. 295

Lomé The capital of Togo. (6°N, 1°E) p. 436

London The capital of the United Kingdom; located on the Thames River, in southeastern England. (51°N, 0°) p. 261

Luanda The capital of Angola. (8°S, 13°E) p. 436

Lusaka The capital of Zambia. (15°S, 28°E) p. 436

Luxembourg A country in Western Europe; also the name of the capital of Luxembourg. (49°N, 6°E) p. 261

M

Macao (muh•KOW) A former Portuguese colony in southern China, on the South China Sea; today it is controlled by China. p. 516

Macedonia A country in Eastern Europe, near the Aegean Sea; located on lands that were once part of Greece and Turkey. p. 295

Mackenzie River A river in Canada; the second-largest river in North America; flows into Mackenzie Bay. p. 92

Madagascar An island country in the Indian Ocean; located off the eastern coast of Southern Africa. p. 479

Madras See **Chennai.**

Madrid The capital of Spain; located on the Manzanares River. (40°N, 4°W) p. 261

Majuro The capital of the Marshall Islands. (7°N, 171°E) p. 612

Malabo The capital of Equatorial Guinea. (3°N, 8°E) p. 436

Malawi (muh•LAH•wee) A country in Central Africa. p. 445

Malay Peninsula A peninsula in Southeast Asia, divided between Thailand and Malaysia. p. 585

Malaysia (muh•LAY•zhuh) An independent federation of states; located in southeastern Asia. p. 585

Maldives A group of atolls in the Indian Ocean. p. 525

Male The capital of Maldives. (4°N, 73°E) p. 525

Mali A country in West Africa. p. 436

Malta An island country in the Mediterranean Sea; located south of Sicily. p. 252

Managua The capital of Nicaragua. (12°N, 86°W) p. 195

Manama The capital of Bahrain. (26°N, 50°E) p. 357

Manila The capital of the Philippines. (14°N, 121°E) p. 585

Manitoba A province in central Canada. p. 135

Maputo The capital of Mozambique. (26°S, 32°E) p. 436

Marrakech A city near the Grand Atlas Mountains, in Morocco. (32°N, 8°W) p. 401

Marshall Islands A group of 32 islands and more than 867 reefs; located in the western Pacific Ocean. p. 655

Maseru The capital of Lesotho. (29°S, 27°E) p. 479

Mauritania (maw•ruh•TAY•nee•uh) A country in West Africa. p. 436

Mauritius (maw•RIH•shuhs) An island country in the Indian Ocean; located east of Madagascar. p. 479

Mbabane The capital of Swaziland. (26°S, 31°E) p. 479

Mecca (MEH•kuh) A city in Saudi Arabia near the Red Sea; a holy city for Muslims. (22°N, 40°E) p. 365

Medina A city in western Saudi Arabia. (25°N, 40°E) p. 365

Mediterranean Sea The sea south of Europe, north of Africa, and west of Asia; connects to the Atlantic Ocean, the Red Sea, and the Black Sea. p. 261

Mekong River A river in Southeast Asia; flows from the mountains of Tibet into the South China Sea. p. 516

Melanesia (meh•luh•NEE•zhuh) The group of southwestern Pacific Islands located northeast of Australia and south of the equator. p. A17

Mexico A country in southern North America; located between the United States and Central America. p. 173

Mexico City The capital of Mexico; located in central Mexico. (19°N, 99°W) p. 173

Micronesia (my•kruh•NEE•zhuh) The group of western Pacific Islands east of the Philippines and north of the equator. p. 655

Micronesia, Federated States of (my•kruh•NEE•zhuh) A country made up of a group of western Pacific Islands; located east of the Philippines and north of the equator. p. 612

Milan A city in northern Italy. (45°N, 9°E) p. A10

Minsk The capital of Belarus. (53°N, 24°E) p. 327

Mississippi River The largest river in the United States; flows from Lake Itasca in Minnesota to the Gulf of Mexico. p. 92

Missouri River A tributary of the Mississippi River; flows from Montana to St. Louis, Missouri. p. 92

Mogadishu (mah•guh•DIH•shoo) The capital of Somalia. (2°N, 45°E) p. 479

Moldova A country in Eastern Europe. p. 295

Mombasa An island port in southern Kenya; located on the coast of the Indian Ocean. (4°S, 40°E) p. 479

Monaco A country in Western Europe, on the northwestern Mediterranean coast; also the name of the capital of Monaco. p. 261

Mongolia A country in East Asia. p. 516

Monrovia The capital of Liberia. (6°N, 10°W) p. 436

Monterrey A city in northeastern Mexico. (26°N, 100°W) p. 164

Montevideo The capital of Uruguay. (35°S, 56°W) p. 164

Montreal Canada's largest city and chief port of entry. (46°N, 74°W) p. 92

Morocco (muh•RAH•koh) A country in North Africa; bordered by the Mediterranean Sea and the Atlantic Ocean. p. 401

Moroni The capital of Comoros; located on the island of Grande Comore. (11°S, 43°E) p. 479

Moscow The capital of Russia; located on the Moscow River. (56°N, 38°E) p. 327

Mount Everest The highest mountain in the world; located in the Himalayas between Nepal and Tibet. p. 516

Mount Kilimanjaro A mountain in East Africa; the highest point in Africa. p. 479

Mount McKinley The highest mountain in North America; located in Alaska. p. 161

Mozambique (moh•zuhm•BEEK) A country in Southern Africa. p. 479

Mumbai (Bombay) A city on the western coast of central India. (19°N, 73°E) p. 516

Muscat The capital of Oman. (23°N, 58°E) p. 365

Myanmar (Burma) A country on the Indochina Peninsula in Southeast Asia. p. 585

N

Nairobi The capital of Kenya. (1°S, 36°E) p. 437

Namibia A country in Southern Africa. p. 479

Naples (NAY•puhlz) A seaport in southern Italy; located on the western coast on the Tyrrhenian Sea. (41°N, 14°E) p. A10

Nassau The capital of the Bahamas. (25°N, 77°W) p. 195

N'Djamena (ehn•JAHM•uh•nuh) The capital of Chad. (12°N, 15°E) p. 436

Nepal (nay•PAWL) A country located in Southern Asia, north of India. p. 525

Netherlands A country in Western Europe; located on the North Sea. p. 261

New Delhi The capital of India; located in northern India. (29°N, 77°E) p. 525

New Guinea An island in the Malay Archipelago; located north of eastern Australia; occupied by Papua New Guinea and part of Indonesia. p. 655

New York City One of the world's largest cities; located in the northeastern United States. (40°N, 74°W) p. 92

New Zealand A country consisting of several islands in the southwestern Pacific Ocean; located southeast of Australia. p. 621

Newfoundland A province of Canada; an island in the Atlantic Ocean east of mainland Canada. p. 135

Niamey The capital of Niger. (13°N, 2°E) p. 436

Nicaragua A country in Central America. p. 195

Nicosia The capital of Cyprus. (35°N, 33°E) p. 357

Niger (NY•jer) A country in West Africa. p. 436

Niger River A river in West Africa; flows from Guinea through Mali, Niger, and Nigeria into the Gulf of Guinea. p. 436

Nigeria (ny•JIR•ee•uh) A country in West Africa; located on the Gulf of Guinea. p. 436

Nile River A river in northeastern Africa, the longest river in the world; flows from Lake Victoria through Uganda, Sudan, and Egypt and empties into the Mediterranean Sea. p. 409

North America One of the world's seven continents. p. 13

North Korea A country that lies north of the 38th parallel on the Korea Peninsula, off the coast of China. p. 555

North Sea The sea located east of Great Britain and west of Denmark. p. 261

Northern Ireland Part of the United Kingdom of Great Britain and Northern Ireland; occupies the northeastern section of the island of Ireland. p. 261

Northern Mariana Islands An island group in Micronesia; includes the unincorporated United States territory of Guam. p. 655

Norway A country in Western Europe; located on the Scandinavian Peninsula. p. 261

Nouakchott The capital of Mauritania, in West Africa. (18°N, 16°W) p. 436

Nova Scotia A province of Canada; located on the eastern coast of Canada. p. 135

Nubian Desert A desert region in Sudan; located east of the Nile River. p. A9

Nuku'alofa The capital of Tonga, in the southwestern Pacific Ocean. (21°S, 175°W) p. 612

O

Ohio River A tributary of the Mississippi River; begins in Pittsburgh, Pennsylvania, and ends in Cairo, Illinois. p. 92

Oman A country in Southwest Asia; located on the Arabian Peninsula. p. 365

Ontario A Canadian province; located between the provinces of Quebec and Manitoba. p. 135

Osaka (oh•SAH•kuh) A Japanese port city in southern Honshu; located where the Yodo River meets Osaka Bay. (35°N, 136°E) p. 577

Oslo The capital of Norway; located in southeastern Norway at the northern end of the Oslo Fjord. (60°N, 11°E) p. 261

Ottawa The capital of Canada; located in the province of Ontario. (45°N, 76°W) p. 92

Ouagadougou The capital of Burkina Faso, in West Africa. (12°N, 1°W) p. 436

P

Pacific Ocean The largest of the world's four oceans. p. 13

Pakistan A country in South Asia. p. 525

Palau An archipelago in the western Pacific Ocean near the Philippines. p. 612

Palikir The capital of Micronesia. (7°N, 158°E) p. 612

Panama A country in Central America. p. 164

Panama City The capital of Panama. (9°N, 79°W) p. 164

Papua New Guinea A country in Melanesia; occupies half the island of New Guinea and about 600 smaller islands. p. 612

Paraguay (PAH•rah•gwy) A country in central South America. p. 221

Paramaribo The capital of Suriname. (5°N, 55°W) p. 164

Paris The capital of France; located on the Seine River. (49°N, 2°E) p. 261

Persian Gulf A gulf in Southwest Asia; connected to the Gulf of Oman and the Arabian Sea. p. 365

Peru A country on the Pacific coast of South America. p. 221

Philippine Sea A part of the western Pacific Ocean east of the Philippines. p. 586

Philippines An archipelago and country in Southeast Asia; located east of the Indochina Peninsula. p. 586

Phnom Penh (NAHM PEN) The capital of Cambodia. (12°N, 105°E) p. 585

GAZETTEER

Poland A country in Eastern Europe, bordering on the Baltic Sea. p. 252

Polynesia (pah•luh•NEE•zhuh) The name of a group of central Pacific Islands; includes New Zealand, Samoa, Tahiti, and the Hawaiian Islands. p. A17

Port Louis The capital of Mauritius. (20°S, 57°E) p. 479

Port Moresby The capital of Papua New Guinea. (9°S, 147°E) p. 655

Port-au-Prince The capital of Haiti. (18°N, 72°W) p. 195

Port-of-Spain The capital of Trinidad and Tobago. (10°N, 61°W) p. 195

Porto-Novo The capital of Benin. (6°N, 2°E) p. 436

Portugal A country in Western Europe; located on the Iberian Peninsula. p. 261

Port-Vila The capital of Vanuatu. (17°S, 168°E) p. 612

Prague The capital of the Czech Republic; located on both sides of the Vltava River. (50°N, 14°E) p. 295

Praia The capital of Cape Verde. (15°N, 23°W) p. 436

Pretoria The administrative capital of the country of South Africa. (26°S, 28°E) p. 479

Prince Edward Island A Canadian province; located in the Gulf of St. Lawrence. p. 135

Puerto Rico An island and self-governing commonwealth of the United States; located in the Greater Antilles of the Caribbean Sea. p. 195

P´yongyang (pee•AWNG•yahng) The capital of North Korea; located on the Taedong River. (39°N, 126°E) p. 555

Pyrenees (PIR•uh•neez) The mountain range that separates the Iberian Peninsula from the rest of Europe; forms the border between Spain and France. p. 261

Q

Qatar A country in Southwest Asia; located on the west coast of the Persian Gulf. p. 365

Quebec A province in eastern Canada. p. 135

Quito The capital of Ecuador. (0°S, 78°W) p. 221

R

Rabat The capital of Morocco. (34°N, 7°W) p. 356

Rangoon See **Yangon**.

Red Sea The sea between northeastern Africa and the Arabian Peninsula; connected to the Mediterranean Sea by the Suez Canal and to the Arabian Sea by the Gulf of Aden. p. 365

Reykjavik The capital of Iceland. (64°N, 22°E) p. 261

Rhine River A river in Western Europe; flows across Switzerland, western Germany, and the Netherlands to the North Sea. p. A12

Riga The capital of Latvia in Eastern Europe. (57°N, 24°E) p. 295

Riyadh The capital of Saudi Arabia. (24°N, 46°E) p. 365

Romania A country in Eastern Europe, bordering the Black Sea. p. 295

Rome The capital of Italy; located on the Tiber River. (42°N, 13°E) p. 261

Roseau The capital of Dominica. (15°N, 61°W) p. 195

Russia A country in eastern Europe and northern Asia; borders the Black Sea, the Arctic Ocean, and the Pacific Ocean. p. 327

Rwanda A country in East Africa. p. 479

S

Sahara A desert covering the northern third of Africa. p. 401

Samoa A group of islands in Polynesia; located in the central Pacific Ocean. p. 612

San José The capital of Costa Rica. (10°N, 84°W) p. 195

San Marino A small country in Western Europe; located on Mount Titano within northern Italy; also the name of the capital. (46°N, 14°E) p. 261

San Salvador The capital of El Salvador. (13°N, 89°W) p. 195

Sanaa The capital of Yemen. (17°N, 51°E) p. 365

Santiago The capital of Chile. (33°S, 70°W) p. 221

Santo Domingo The capital of the Dominican Republic. (18°N, 70°W) p. 195

São Paulo The largest city in Brazil; located on the Tietê River. (23°S, 46°W) p. 221

São Tomé and Príncipe (sow tuh•MAY and PRIN•suh•puh) An island country off western Africa, in the Gulf of Guinea; São Tomé is the capital. (0°N, 6°E) p. 436

Sapporo A city in Japan; located on Hokkaido. (43°N, 141°E) p. 577

Sarajevo (sair•uh•YAY•voh) The capital of Bosnia and Herzegovina. (44°N, 18°E) p. 295

Sardinia An island in the Mediterranean Sea; located west of mainland Italy. p. 261

Saskatchewan A Canadian province; located in western Canada. p. 135

Saudi Arabia A country that occupies most of the Arabian Peninsula in Southwest Asia. p. 365

Sea of Japan The sea located west of Japan and east of Russia, North Korea, and South Korea. p. 555

Sea of Okhotsk (oh•KAHTSK) A sea off the eastern coast of Russia. p. 253

Senegal A country in West Africa. p. 436

Seoul The capital of South Korea. (38°N, 127°E) p. 516

Serbia A country in eastern Europe. p. 295

Seychelles An island group and country; located off the coast of Africa in the Indian Ocean. p. 479

Shanghai (shang•HY) A Chinese port city on the East China Sea; located near the mouth of the Chang Jiang. (31°N, 121°E) p. 555

Sicily An Italian island off the southwestern tip of the Italian Peninsula. p. 261

Sierra Leone A country on the Atlantic coast of West Africa. p. 436

Sierra Madre del Sur A mountain range in southern Mexico that runs along the Pacific coast. p. 173

Sierra Madre Occidental A mountain range in northwestern Mexico that runs along the Pacific coast. p. 173

Sierra Madre Oriental A mountain range in eastern Mexico that runs along the coast of the Gulf of Mexico. p. 173

Sinai Peninsula The peninsula between northeastern Africa and southwestern Asia; part of the country of Egypt. p. 401

Singapore A small island country off the southern tip of the Malay Peninsula, in Southeast Asia; also the name of the capital. (1°N, 103°E) p. 590

Skopje The capital of Macedonia. (42°N, 21°E) p. 295

Slovakia A country in Eastern Europe; located south of Poland. p. 295

Slovenia (sloh•VEE•nee•uh) A country in Eastern Europe. p. 295

Sofia The capital of Bulgaria. (43°N, 23°E) p. 295

Solomon Islands A country made up of a group of islands in Melanesia. p. 655

Somalia A country in East Africa. p. 479

South Africa A country located on the southern tip of Africa, between the Atlantic and Indian Oceans. p. 479

South America One of the world's seven continents. p. 13

South China Sea The part of the China Sea south of Taiwan. p. 555

South Korea A country that lies south of the 38th parallel on the Korea Peninsula, off the coast of China. p. 555

Spain A country in Western Europe; on the Iberian Peninsula. p. 261

Sri Lanka An island country in South Asia; located south of India in the Indian Ocean. p. 525

St. George's The capital of Grenada. (12°N, 61°W) p. 195

St. John's The capital of Antigua and Barbuda. (17°N, 61°W) p. 93

St. John's The capital of Newfoundland, Canada. (48°N, 53°W) p. 93

St. Kitts and Nevis An island country located in the eastern Caribbean Sea. p. 195

St. Lawrence River A river located in northeastern North America; forms part of the border between the United States and Canada. p. A14

St. Lucia An island country in the eastern Caribbean. p. 195

St. Petersburg A city in western Russia; located on the Neva River on the Gulf of Finland. (60°N, 30°E) p. 252

St. Vincent and the Grenadines An island country in the eastern Caribbean. p. 195

Stockholm The capital and largest city of Sweden; located on the Baltic Sea. (59°N, 18°E) p. 261

Strasbourg A city in northeastern France. (48°N, 8°E) p. 282

Sucre The capital of Bolivia. (19°S, 65°W) p. 221

Sudan A country on the east coast of northern Africa. p. 479

Suez Canal A canal linking the Mediterranean Sea and the Gulf of Suez; located in northeastern Egypt. p. 401

Sumatra (soo•MAH•truh) The westernmost island of Indonesia; located off the Malay Peninsula in southeastern Asia. p. 585

Suriname A country in South America. p. 221

Suva The capital of Fiji. (18°S, 178°E) p. 612

Swaziland A country in Southern Africa. p. 479

Sweden A country in Western Europe; located on the eastern part of the Scandinavian Peninsula. p. 261

Switzerland A country in Western Europe. p. 261

Syria A country located on the eastern end of the Mediterranean Sea. p. 357

Syrian Desert A desert in Southwest Asia; covers southeastern Syria, northeastern Jordan, western Iraq, and northern Saudi Arabia. p. 365

T

Tabriz (tuh•BREEZ) A city in northwestern Iran. (38°N, 46°E) p. 357

Taipei (TY•PAY) The capital of Taiwan. (25°N, 121°E) p. 516

Taiwan (TY•WAHN) An island country; located off the southeastern coast of China. p. 516

Tajikistan (tah•jihk•ih•STAN) A Eurasian republic. p. 327

Takla Makan A desert in northwestern China. p. 516

Tallinn The capital of Estonia. (59°N, 24°E) p. 295

Tanzania (tan•zuh•NEE•uh) A country in East Africa. p. 479

Tarawa The capital of Kiribati. (1°N, 173°E) p. 655

Tashkent The capital of Uzbekistan; located in western Asia. (41°N, 69°E) p. 252

Tegucigalpa The capital of Honduras. (14°N, 87°W) p. 195

Tehran The capital of Iran. (35°N, 51°E) p. 357

Thailand A country located in Southeast Asia on the Indochina and Malay Peninsulas. p. 585

Thar Desert Also called the Great Indian Desert; located in India and Pakistan. p. 525

Thimphu (thim•POO) The capital of Bhutan. (28°N, 90°E) p. 525

Tian Shan A mountain system in East Asia; extends northeast from the Pamirs into western China. p. 516

Tibet A region covering most of southwestern China. p. 555

Tigris River A river in Southwest Asia; begins in eastern Turkey and joins the Euphrates River in Iraq. p. 365

Tijuana (tee•WAH•nah) A town in Baja California in Mexico. (33°N, 117°W) p. 186

Timbuktu (tim•buhk•TOO) A city located in Mali in the Sahara, north of the Niger River. (17°N, 3°W) p. A8

Timor An island in eastern Indonesia. p. 585

Tiranë The capital of Albania. (41°N, 20°E) p. 295

Togo A country on the southern coast of West Africa. p. 436

Tokyo The capital of Japan. (36°N, 140°E) p. 555

Tonga A country comprised of about 150 small islands in the southwestern Pacific Ocean. p. 612

Toronto The capital of Ontario, Canada. (44°N, 79°W) p. 92

Transylvania A region in northwestern Romania. p. 295

Trinidad and Tobago A country comprised of two Caribbean islands; located off the east coast of Venezuela. p. 195

Tripoli The capital of Libya. (33°N, 13°E) p. 401

Tunis The capital of Tunisia. (37°N, 10°E) p. 357

Tunisia A country in North Africa. p. 357

Turkey A country in southeastern Europe and southwestern Asia. p. 357

Turkmenistan (terk•mehn•uh•STAN) A Eurasian republic. p. 252

GAZETTEER

Tuvalu A country comprised of nine islands in the western Pacific Ocean. p. 612

Tyrrhenian Sea (tuh•REE•nee•uhn) The sea located west of the Italian Peninsula, north of Sicily, and east of Sardinia and Corsica. p. A12

Uganda A country in East Africa. p. 479

Ukraine (yoo•KRAYN) A country in east-central Europe; formerly part of the Soviet Union. p. 327

Ulaanbaatar (Ulan Bator) The capital of Mongolia. (48°N, 107°E) p. 555

United Arab Emirates A country on the eastern Arabian Peninsula. p. 365

United Kingdom A European kingdom in the British Isles; made up of England, Scotland, Wales, and Northern Ireland. p. 252

United States A country in North America; a republic of 50 states. p. 99

Ural Mountains (YUR•uhl) A mountain range in Russia and Kazakhstan; extends south from the coast of the Arctic Ocean; boundary between Europe and Asia. p. 327

Uruguay (YUR•uh•gway) A country on the Atlantic coast of South America. p. 221

Uzbekistan (uz•behk•ih•STAN) A Eurasian republic. p. 252

Valletta The capital of Malta. (35°N, 14°E) p. 252

Vancouver A city in southwestern Canada; located in British Columbia. (49°N, 123°W) p. 92

Vanuatu An island country; located in the southwestern Pacific Ocean. p. 612

Vatican City One of the smallest countries in the world and headquarters of the Roman Catholic Church; located within the city of Rome, Italy. p. 261

Venezuela A country in northern South America. p. 221

Venice A city of 118 islands in northeastern Italy on the Adriatic Sea. (45°N, 12°E) p. 54

Veracruz A seaport in eastern Mexico, on the Gulf of Mexico. (19°N, 96°W) p. 173

Victoria Falls The Zambezi River waterfall; located between Zimbabwe and Zambia, in Southern Africa. (18°S, 26°E) p. 476

Vienna The capital of Austria; located on the Danube River. (48°N, 16°E) p. 261

Vientiane (vyen•TYAHN) The capital of Laos. (18°N, 103°E) p. 585

Vietnam A country in Southeast Asia; located on the Indochina Peninsula. p. 585

Volga River The longest river in Europe; runs from Russia to the Caspian Sea. p. 252

Volgograd A city in southern Russia; located on the Volga River. (49°N, 44°E) p. 252

Warsaw The capital of Poland. (52°N, 21°E) p. 295

Washington, D.C. The capital of the United States. (38°N, 77°W) p. 99

Wellington The capital of New Zealand. (41°S, 174°E) p. 612

Western Ghats (GAWTS) A chain of mountains in southwestern India. p. 525

Windhoek The capital of Namibia. (22°S, 17°E) p. 436

Xi'an (SHEE•AHN) A city in eastern China; also known as Sian. (34°N, 109°E) p. 516

Y

Yamoussoukro The capital of Côte d'Ivoire. (6°N, 5°W) p. 436

Yangon (Rangoon) The capital of Myanmar. (17°N, 96°E) p. 585

Yaoundé The capital of Cameroon. (4°N, 11°E) p. 436

Yaren The capital of Nauru. (0°S, 166°E) p. 655

Yellow Sea The sea west of the Korea Peninsula and east of China. p. 555

Yellowknife The capital of the Northwest Territories in Canada. (63°N, 114°W) p. 92

Yemen A country on the southern coast of the Arabian Peninsula. p. 365

Yerevan The capital of Armenia. (40°N, 44°E) p. 252

Yucatán Peninsula A peninsula extending from the eastern coast of Central America; occupied by the countries of Mexico, Belize, and Guatemala. p. 173

Yukon Territory A territory in northwestern Canada. p. 135

Z

Zagreb The capital of Croatia. (46°N, 16°E) p. 295

Zagros Mountains (ZAH•gruhs) A mountain range located in western and southern Iran. p. 357

Zambezi River A river in Southern Africa; flows from northwestern Zambia to the Indian Ocean. p. 436

Zambia A country in Southern Africa. p. 436

Zimbabwe (zim•BAH•bway) A country in Southern Africa. p. 479

GAZETTEER

Glossary

The Glossary contains important social studies words and their definitions. Each word is respelled as it would be in a dictionary. When you see this mark ´ after a syllable, pronounce that syllable with more force than the other syllables. The page number at the end of the definition tells where to find the word in your book.

add, āce, câre, pälm; end, ēqual; it, īce; odd, ōpen, ôrder; to͝ok, po͞ol; up, bûrn; yo͞o as *u* in *fuse*; oil; pout; ə as *a* in *above*, *e* in *sicken*, *i* in *possible*, *o* in *melon*, *u* in *circus*; check; ring; thin; this; zh as in *vision*

A

abdicate (ab´di•kāt) To give up control of a government. p. 336

abolish (ə•bol´ish) To end. p. 203

Aborigine (a•bə•ri´jə•nē) The name given to the original inhabitants of Australia. p. 625

absolute location (ab´sə•lo͞ot lō•kā´shən) Exact location on Earth. p. 2

absolute monarchy (ab´sə•lo͞ot mä´nər•kē) A system of government in which a monarch has complete control. p. 392

accent (ak´sənt) The special way of pronouncing words and phrases that is used by people from a certain area or country. p. 277

acculturation (a•kəl•chə•rā´shən) The exchange of culture traits that results from long-term contact with another society. p. 62

A.D. (ā´dē´) Stands for *anno Domini*, a Latin phrase meaning "in the year of the Lord." This abbreviation identifies approximately how many years have passed since the birth of Jesus Christ. p. 66

adapt (ə•dapt´) To change in order to make more useful. p. 2

adobe (ə•dō´bē) A mixture of sand and straw that is shaped into bricks and dried. p. 237

Afrikaans (a•fri•kä ns´) The language spoken by European settlers in South Africa. p. 491

alluvial soil (ə•lo͞o´vē•əl soil´) Soil created by sediment deposited when a river floods over its banks. p. 366

altitude (al´tə•to͞od) Elevation, or the distance above or below sea level. p. 36

amber (am´bər) Fossilized tree sap. p. 296

amendment (ə•mend´mənt) An addition or change to a document. p. 110

analyze (a´nə•līz) To break something down into its parts to see how those parts connect. p. 3

animism (a•nə•mi´zəm) A religious belief that natural objects or physical features have spirits. p. 462

annex (ə•neks´) To take over. p. 183

apartheid (ə•pä r´tāt) The former government policy of South Africa that stressed the separation, or "apartness," of races. p. 496

aquifer (a´kwə•fər) Underground layers of rock, sand, or gravel that hold water. p. 370

archipelago (ä r•kə•pe´lə•gō) A chain of islands. p. 194

arid (ar´əd) Very dry with little rainfall. p. 38

aristocracy (ar•ə•stä´krə•sē) A wealthy ruling class. p. 241

assimilation (ə•si•mə•lā´shən) The process in which the culture traits of newcomers to a country become similar to those of the people in the new country. p. 62

atoll (a´tôl) An island formed from a coral reef. p. 528

B

bauxite (bôk´sīt) The most important aluminum ore. p. 448

B.C. (bē´sē´) Stands for "before Christ." p. 66

B.C.E. (bē´sē´ē´) Stands for "before the Common Era" and refers to the same years as B.C. p. 67

bilingual (bī•ling´gwəl) Having the ability to speak two languages. p. 277

biodiversity (bī•ō•də•vûr´sə•tē) The number of different plants and animals that a region has. p. 589

biological resource (bī•ə•lä´ji•kəl rē´sôrs) A natural resource, such as an animal or a plant, that is or was living. p. 40

Boer (bōr) Afrikaner frontier farmers, white descendants of South Africa's original Dutch, German, or French colonists. p. 491

bog (bog) An area of marsh or swamp. p. 262

border (bôr´dər) The boundary or edge of a place, such as a country. p. 76

buffer zone (bə´fər zōn´) An area of land that serves as a barrier to separate two areas. p. 305

C

Cabinet (ka´bə•nit) The group of department heads who advise a nation's chief executive. p. 122

cacao (kə•kou´) A small tree on which beans used to make chocolate grow. p. 447

calligraphy (kə•li´grə•fē) The art of beautiful handwriting. p. 384

cardinal directions (kä r´də•nəl də•rek´shənz) The main directions—north, south, east, and west. p. A3

cartogram (kä r´tə•gram) A special map that gives information about places by the size shown for each place. p. 568

caste system (kast´ sis´təm) A system in which people's position in society is determined by their birth into a particular social class. p. 531

cataract (ka´tə•rakt) A waterfall or a spot where water runs fast over rocks. p. 403

cause (kôz) An event or action that makes something else happen. p. 2

cay (kē) A tiny, low-lying island or coral reef. p. 199

C.E. (sē´ ē´) Stands for "Common Era" and refers to the same years as A.D. p. 67

censor (sen´sər) To examine in order to hold back information. p. 576

chromium (krō´mē•əm) A hard metal that is strong and does not rust easily. p. 330

chronology (krə•nä´lə•jē) A record of events in the order in which they happened. p. 4

circle graph (sûr´kəl graf´) A graph that shows information by means of a circle divided into parts; also called a pie chart. p. 602

city-state (sit´ē•stāt) A city and its surrounding farmlands, with its own leaders and government. p. 269

civic participation (si´vik pä r•ti•sə•pā´shən) Concern with and involvement in the community, state, nation, or world. p. 9

civil war (siv´əl wôr´) A war in which groups of people from the same place or country fight one another. p. 209

civilization (siv•ə•lə•zā´shən) A culture with a complex economic, governing, and social system. p. 177

clan (klan) A group of families that are related to one another. p. 564

climate (klī´mət) The weather conditions in an area over a long period of time. p. 34

climograph (klī´mə•graf) A graph that shows both the average monthly temperature and the average monthly precipitation for a place. p. 332

coastal plain (kōs´təl plān´) Low land that lies along the coast. p. 100

cobalt (kō´bôlt) A mineral used to make metals harder. p. 449

code (kōd) A group of laws. p. 373

Cold War (kōld´ wär) A conflict of words and ideas between nations rather than armies. p. 338

collective (kə•lek´tiv) A large farm, sometimes owned by the government, on which people work together as a group. p. 304

colony (kol´ə•nē) An area of land ruled by a government in another land. p. 77

Columbian exchange (kə•lum´bē•ən iks•chānj´) The movement of people, animals, plants, diseases, and ideas between Europe and the Americas in the 1400s and 1500s. p. 204

column (kä´ləm) A section of words or numbers that goes up and down on a page, rather than across. p. 506

command economy (kə•mand´ i•kon´ə•mē) An economy in which the government owns almost all the land and natural resources and makes most of the decisions. p. 72

commercial farming (kə•mûr´shəl fä r´ming) A kind of agriculture in which crops are raised for sale. p. 201

common good (kä´mən good´) Helpful for all citizens as a group. p. 124

common market (kä´mən mä r´kit) A union formed to improve trade and encourage the economic growth of member nations. p. 282

commonwealth (kä´mən•welth) A self-governing territory associated with another country. p. 148

communism (kom´yə•niz´əm) A governing and economic system in which all property and all means of production belong to the people as a group. p. 211

compass rose (kum´pəs rōz´) A direction marker on a map. p. A3

compromise (kom´prə•mīz) To give up some of what you want in order to reach an agreement. p. 320

conformal projection (kən•fôr´məl prə•jek´shən) A map projection that shows directions correctly but distorts sizes, especially of places near the poles. p. 450

coniferous (kō•ni´fə•rəs) A kind of cone-bearing tree. p. 196

conservation (kon•sər•vā´shən) The protecting and wise use of natural resources. p. 43

constitution (kon•stə•tōō´shən) A document that describes a plan for governing. p. 109

constitutional democracy (kon•stə•tōō´shə•nəl di•mä´krə•sē) A kind of democracy in which the goals of the government and the ways it will work to achieve them are stated in a constitution. p. 122

constitutional monarchy (kon•stə•tōō´shə•nəl mä´nər•kē) A government with a written plan, or constitution, that includes a monarch as a ceremonial leader and a parliament or other legislature to make the laws. p. 286

contiguous (kən•tig´yōō•əs) Connected to or bordering another unit, such as a state. p. 98

Continental Divide (kon•ti•nen´təl də•vīd´) The crest of the Rocky Mountains that divides North America's river systems into those that flow east and those that flow west. p. 102

continental drift (kon•ti•nen´təl drift´) The movement of continental plates. p. 21

continental island (kon•ti•nen´təl ī´lənd) An island or island chain that was probably once part of a continent. p. 654

contour line (kon´tōor līn´) On an elevation map, a line that connects all points of equal elevation. p. 104

copper belt (kä´pər belt´) A major copper-mining region. p. 449

copra (kō´prə) Dried coconut meat. p. 657

coral (kôr´əl) The skeletal remains of tiny sea animals. p. 199

cordillera (kôr•dəl•yâr´ə) A mountain system made up of parallel ranges. p. 220

cosmonaut (koz´mə•nôt) The name given to a Russian space explorer. p. 346

Crusades (krōō•sādz´) A series of wars fought in the Middle Ages between Christians and Muslims over control of the Holy Land. p. 376

cultural borrowing (kul´chər•əl bär´ə•wing) The taking of culture traits from one culture for use in another. p. 61

cultural diffusion (kul´chər•əl di•fyōō´zhən) The spread of ideas from one place to others. p. 62

cultural diversity (kul´chər•əl di•vûr´sə•tē) The mixture of different ethnic groups within the same country. p. 64

cultural region (kul´chər•əl rē´jən) A region with the same culture traits. p. 78

culture (kul´chər) A unique way of life that sets a group of people apart from others. p. 8

culture trait (kul´chər trāt´) A characteristic of a culture. p. 61

cuneiform (kyōō•nē´ə•fôrm) A form of ancient writing in Southwest Asia. p. 372

current (kûr´ənt) A giant stream of ocean water. p. 30

czar (zär) A Russian title meaning "Caesar," or ruler. p. 335

D

debt service (det´ sûr´vəs) The repayment on a loan. p. 501

declaration (de•klə•rā´shən) An official statement. p. 108

deficit (de´fə•sət) A shortage. p. 127

delta (del´tə) A triangle-shaped piece of land built from soil deposited at the mouth of a river. p. 24

demand (di•mand´) The amount of a good or service that people want to buy at a given price. p. 73

demarcation line (dē•mär•kā´shən līn´) A line that marks a boundary. p. 234

democracy (di•mä´krə•sē) A governing system in which a country's people elect their leaders and rule by majority. p. 68

demographer (di•mä´grə•fer) A geographer who studies human populations. p. 57

dependency (di•pen´dən•sē) An area and its people dependent upon another country. p. 212

deposition (de•pə•zi´shən) The process of dropping, or depositing, sediment in a new location. p. 24

depression (di•pre´shən) A land area lower than the land around it. p. 405

desalinization (dē•sa•lə•nə•zā´shən) The process in which the salt is taken out of salt water. p. 370

descendant (di•sen´dənt) A person who is descended from a certain ancestor. p. 142

desertification (di•zər•tə•fə•kā´shən) The long-term process in which fertile land is changed into desert. p. 53

developed country (di•ve´ləpt kun´trē) A country with a well-established economy generally containing all four forms of industry. p. 71

developing country (di•ve´lə•ping kun´trē) A country whose economy is still being built. p. 71

dhow (dou) An Arab sailboat. p. 488

dialect (dī´ə•lekt) A variation of a language. p. 277

dictatorship (dik•tā´tər•ship) A governing system in which one person rules with absolute authority. Authority in a dictatorship is not inherited as in a monarchy. p. 70

Diet (dī´ət) Japan's elected legislature. p. 576

dike (dīk) A high bank of earth or concrete built to help reduce flooding. p. 372

diplomat (di´plə•mat) A person skilled in negotiations between nations. p. 542

discrimination (dis•kri•mə•nā´shən) Unfair treatment because of race or for other reasons. p. 116

displace (dis•plās´) To move from the usual or proper place; to move people against their will. p. 346

distortion (di•stôr´shən) An area that is not accurate on a map projection. p. 450

diversify (də•vûr´sə•fī) To make different or varied. p. 242

domesticate (də•mes´tə•kāt) To tame plants and animals for people's use. p. 371

dominion (də•min´yən) A self-governing nation. p. 146

domino effect (dä´mə•nō i•fekt´) The idea that if one country in a region were taken over by communists, the same might happen to other countries in the region. p. 595

double-bar graph (də´bəl•bär graf´) A bar graph that shows two sets of statistics, or facts shown with numbers. p. 238

draa (drä) A sand dune. p. 405

drainage basin (drā´nij bā´sən) The land drained by a river system. p. 27

dreamtime (drēm´tīm) An ancient time, Australian Aborigines believe, when spirits created that land and gave it to the people. p. 626

drought (drout) A period when little or no rain falls. p. 53

dynasty (dī´nəs•tē) A series of rulers from the same family. p. 408

E

economic indicator (ek•ə•nä´mik in´də•kā•tər) A measure of a country's economy and how well its people live. p. 141

economics (ek•ə•nä´miks) The study of the way that goods and wealth are produced, distributed, and used. p. 10

economy (i•kon´ə•mē) The way people use resources to meet their needs. p. 10

editorial cartoon (e•də•tôr´ē•əl kä r•tōōn´) A cartoon that presents the artist's point of view about people and current events. p. 288

effect (i•fekt´) The result of an event or action. p. 2

elevation (e•lə•vā´shən) The height of land in relation to sea level. p. 104

El Niño (el´ nēn´yō) An ocean and weather pattern in the Pacific Ocean in which ocean waters become warmer. p. 223

embargo (im•bä r´gō) A limit or ban on trade. p. 392

empire (em´pīr) A conquered land of many people and places governed by one ruler. p. 77

enculturation (en•kəl•chə•rā´shən) The process of learning culture. p. 60

environment (en•vī´rən•mənt) Surroundings. p. 52

equal-area projection (ē´kwəl•â r´ē•ə prə•jek´shən) A map projection that shows the sizes of regions in correct relation to one another but that distorts shapes. p. 450

equator (i•kwā´tər) An imaginary line that circles Earth halfway between the North Pole and the South Pole. The line divides Earth into the Northern Hemisphere and the Southern Hemisphere. p. 32

erg (ûrg) A great "sea" of sand. p. 405

erosion (i•rō´zhən) The natural process of moving sediment; shapes Earth's surface. p. 24

escarpment (es•kä rp´mənt) A steep slope between a high surface and a low surface. p. 221

estuary (es´chə•wâr•ē) A partially enclosed body of water in which salty seawater and fresh water mix. p. 225

ethnic cleansing (eth´nik klen´zing) The forcing out or killing of ethnic minorities. p. 309

ethnic group (eth´nik grōōp) A cultural group of people who share beliefs and practices learned from relatives and ancestors. p. 64

Eurasia (yōō•rā´zhə) The landmass made up of the continents of Europe and Asia. p. 260

euro (yōōr´ō) The currency of the European Union. p. 283

everglades (e´vər•glādz) A swampy grassland, such as in southern Florida. p. 100

exotic river (ig•zä´tik ri´vər) A river that begins in a wet region and then flows through a dry region. p. 369

export (eks´pôrt) Goods sent for sale to other places. p. 140

F

fact (fakt) A statement that can be proved true. p. 458

factors of production (fak´tərz əv prə•duk´shən) The human, capital, and natural resources needed for industry and business. p. 227

fault (fôlt) A crack in Earth's crust where a huge mass of rock, such as a plate, is in motion. p. 22

federal government (fed´ər•əl gə´vûrn•mənt) The central authority in a federation of states. p. 122

federal system (fed´ər•əl sis´təm) A governing system in which the states share authority with a national, or central, government. p. 151

federation (fe•də•rā´shən) A union of groups or states under a central authority. p. 208

fellahin (fel•ə•hēn´) Egyptian farmers. p. 426

fertile soil (fûr´təl soil´) Soil that is good for growing crops. p. 41

fiesta (fē•es´tə) A holiday or festival, especially in Mexico honoring a saint. p. 182

filial piety (fi´lē•əl pī´ə•tē) The respect and honor owed to one's parents. p. 572

finances (fī´nan•səz) Money matters. p. 184

firth (fərth) A funnel-shaped bay along Scotland's coast. p. 265

Five Pillars (fīv´pi´lərz) The five most important beliefs in Islam. p. 381

fjord (fē•ōrd´) A narrow, deep inlet of the sea, between high, rocky cliffs. p. 135

flax (flaks) A plant whose fibers are used for making linen thread and cloth and whose seeds are used for making linseed oil. p. 486

floodplain (flōōd´plān) A landform of level ground made up of sediment deposited by a river or stream. p. 24

flow chart (flō´chärt´) A group of pictures or boxed descriptions of the steps for making or doing something. p. 154

folktale (fōk´tāl) A traditional story that often teaches a lesson. p. 465

foreign debt (fôr´ən det´) Money that one country owes to another country. p. 500

fossil fuel (fä´səl fyōōl´) A nonrenewable resource formed from the remains of ancient plants and animals. p. 41

frame of reference (frām´ əv ref´ər•əns) A general viewpoint that can determine opinions and feelings about issues. p. 394

free election (frē´ i•lek´shən) An election in which all citizens can vote as long as they meet the requirements. p. 149

GLOSSARY

free enterprise (frē´ en´tər•prīz) An economic system in which people choose what to make, sell, or buy, without government control. p. 73

free trade (frē´ trād´) Trade without limits or protections. p. 140

free trade zone (frē´ trād´ zōn´) A region in which countries trade without barriers. p. 243

frost (frôst) A covering of tiny ice crystals that forms on a surface when dew or water vapor freezes. p. 175

G

GDP (jē´dē´pē´) Gross domestic product, or the total value of the goods and services produced in a country. p. 71

genocide (je´nə•sīd) The killing of an entire group of people. p. 272

geography (jē•äg´rə•fē) The study of Earth's physical and human features. p. 2

geothermal power (jē•ō•thûr´məl pou´ər) A renewable energy source produced from heat within Earth's surface. p. 635

glasnost (glaz´nōst) The "openness," or new freedom, that allowed Soviet citizens to speak out without fear of punishment. p. 338

Gospels (gos´pəlz) The first four books of the New Testament; they describe Jesus Christ's life and actions. p. 375

government (guv´ərn•mənt) An organized system that groups use to make laws and decisions. p. 9

green revolution (grēn´ re•və•loo´shən) A program in India that encouraged farmers to modernize their methods and so produce more food. p. 544

grid system (grid´ sis´təm) The north-south and east-west lines on a map that cross each other to form a rectangular pattern. p. A2

griot (grē´ō) A West African storyteller who passes on the oral history of a group of people. p. 465

guerrilla (gə•ri´lə) A member of a small group of soldiers who are not part of the regular army. p. 209

H

haiku (hī´koo) A 17-syllable Japanese poem that is often about nature. p. 574

hajj (haj) A Muslim pilgrimage, or special trip, to Mecca, a holy place. p. 382

Harambee (hä•räm•bāy´) A slogan that came from an old Swahili loggers' work chant meaning "Let's pull together!" p. 499

heavy industry (he´vē in´dəs•trē) Industry that usually involves manufacturing based on large commercial items. p. 345

heraldry (hâr´əl•drē) The system of colors, patterns, and picture symbols that knights used during the Middle Ages in Europe. p. 82

heritage (hâr´ə•tij) A set of ideas that have been passed down from one generation to another. p. 8

hieroglyphics (hī•rə•gli´fiks) A writing system in which pictures or symbols stand for sounds, whole words, or ideas. p. 411

high island (hī´ ī´lənd) A kind of island formed by a volcanic eruption. p. 654

historical empathy (hi•stôr´i•kəl em´pə•thē) Understanding the actions and feelings of people from other times and other places. p. 5

historical map (hi•stôr´i•kəl map´) A map that provides information about the past. Historical maps may show where events took place or what the world looked like at a certain time in the past. p. 378

history (his´tə•rē) The study of people and events of the past. p. 4

Holocaust (hō´lə•kôst) The mass killing of millions of Jews and other people during World War II. p. 272

homogeneous (hō•mə•jē´nē•əs) Having the same characteristics or traits. p. 319

human feature (hyoo´mən fē´chər) A building, bridge, farm, road, or people themselves. p. 2

human rights (hyoo´mən rīts´) Freedoms that most societies believe all people should have. p. 598

human society (hyoo´mən sə•sī´ə•tē) An organized group of people identified by its customs, traditions, and way of life. p. 60

humidity (hyoo•mid´ə•tē) The amount of water vapor in the air. p. 223

hurricane (hûr´ə•kān) A tropical storm that brings heavy rain, high seas, and winds 74 miles per hour or more. p. 101

hydroelectric (hī•drō•i•lek´trik) Describes electricity produced by moving water. p. 139

I

ice shelf (īs´ shelf´) A ledge of glacier ice over coastal water. p. 663

immigrant (i´mi•grənt) A person who comes to live in a country from another country. p. 114

import (im´pōrt) Goods brought in for sale from other places. p. 140

indentured servant (in•dent´shərd sûr´vənt) A person who agrees to work for a certain period of time, often in exchange for travel expenses. p. 203

independence (in•di•pen´dəns) Freedom to rule oneself. p. 108

indigenous (in•di´jə•nəs) Native to a place. p. 106

industry (in´dəs•trē) All the businesses that make one kind of product or provide one kind of service. p. 70

inflation (in•flā´shən) A continuing increase in the price of goods and services. p. 312

innovation (i•nə•vā´shən) A new way of doing something. p. 178

inset map (in´set map´) A small map within a larger map. p. A3

institution (in•stə•too´shən) An established organization, law, or custom. p. 279

insular (in´soo•lər) Related to islands. p. 585

intermediate direction (in•tər•mē´dē•ət də•rek´shən) The direction that is midway between two cardinal directions; northeast, northwest, southeast, and southwest. p. A3

invest (in•vest´) To spend or loan money in the hope of making a profit. p. 242

Iron Curtain (īr´ən kûr´tən) A term used during the Cold War to describe the countries controlled by the Soviet Union and closed off from contact and trade with other countries. p. 304

irrigation (ir•ə•gā´shən) The use of canals, ditches, or pipes to move water to dry areas. p. 53

irrigation canal (ir•ə•gā´shən kə•nal´) A human-made waterway for use in irrigation. p. 526

isthmus (is´məs) A small strip of land, with water on both sides, that connects two larger areas of land. p. 172

junta (hoon´tə) In Latin America, a governing council. p. 241

kastom (käs´təm) A system of behavior in the Pacific Islands, based on customs and traditional beliefs. p. 649

keiretsu (ká•ret´soo) A Japanese system in which a group of companies in an industry own parts of each other. p. 577

khan (kä n) The title given to strong Mongol leaders who sometimes brought rival clans together and created almost unstoppable fighting forces. p. 562

kinship (kin´ship) Relationship among people with the same ancestors. p. 464

krill (kril) Tiny shrimplike sea animals that are important food for larger wildlife. p. 664

L

land breeze (land´ brēz´) A night wind blowing from cool land to warmer water. p. 36

land use (land´ yoos´) How most of the land in a place is used. p. 266

landform (land´ fôrm) The shape of part of Earth's surface. Examples are plains, mountains, and hills. p. 20

landlocked (land´lokt) Completely surrounded by land, with no direct access to the sea. p. 241

lava (lä´və) Magma that has broken through Earth's crust and is on the surface. p. 23

legacy (le´gə•sē) Anything handed down from an ancestor. p. 204

life expectancy (līf´ ik•spek´tən•sē) A measure of the average number of years that people may expect to live. p. 141

light industry (līt´ in´dəs•trē) Industry that focuses on the production of consumer goods, such as appliances and clothing. p. 345

lignite (lig´nīt) A soft form of coal. p. 299

limited government (li´mə•tid guv´ərn•mənt) A government in which everyone, including those in authority, must obey the laws. p. 208

line graph (līn´ graf´) A graph that shows change over time by using one or more lines. The lines connect dots that stand for specific information. p. 640

lines of latitude (līnz´ əv la´tə•tood) East-west lines on a map or globe that are always the same distance apart. Also called parallels. p. 32

lines of longitude (līnz´ əv lon´jə•tood) North-south lines on a map or globe that run from pole to pole. Also called meridians. p. 32

literacy (lit´ə•rə•sē) The ability to read and write. p. 117

locator (lō´kā•tər) A small map or a picture of a globe. It shows where the area represented on a larger map is located in a state, in a country, on a continent, or in the world. p. A3

loch (lok) A kind of lake carved by glaciers and found in Scotland. p. 265

loess (les) Fine, windblown, fertile soil. p. 555

low island (lō´ ī´lənd) A kind of island formed by volcanic rocks or coral reefs. p. 654

Loyalist (loi´ə•list) An American who supported Britain during the American Revolution; in general, a person who supports the current government. p. 146

M

magma (mag´mə) Melted rock within Earth. p. 22

majority rule (mə•jôr´ə•tē rool´) A system in which the ideas and decisions supported by the most people are followed. p. 69

malnutrition (mal•noo•tri´shən) An unhealthy condition of the body that is caused by not getting enough food or enough of healthful foods. p. 501

mana (mä´nə) A kind of personal power said to be held by chiefs in the Pacific Islands. p. 651

Mandate of Heaven (man´dāt əv hev´ən) The right to rule; the Chinese believed heaven gave it to their emperors. When an emperor was weak or disasters occurred, the emperor was thought to have lost the Mandate of Heaven. p. 561

manorialism (mə•nôr´ē•ə•liz•əm) An economic system of exchanging land use and protection for goods and services; practiced during the Middle Ages in Western Europe. p. 270

mansa (mä n´sə) The title for a ruler in the Mali Empire of West Africa. p. 453

map key (map´ kē´) The part of a map that explains what the symbols on the map stand for; sometimes called a map legend. p. A2

map scale (map´ skāl´) The part of a map that compares distance on the map itself with distance in the real world. p. A3

map title (map´ tī´təl) The words on a map that describe the subject of the map. p. A2

maquiladora (mä•kē•lä•dôr´ä) A factory located along Mexico's northern border with the United States. p. 185

market economy (mä r´kit i•kon´ə•mē) An economy in which the people own and control businesses. p. 72

market price (mä r´kit prīs´) What people are willing to pay for a product or service. p. 125

marsupial (mä r•soo´pē•əl) An animal whose newly born young are carried by the female in a pouch on the front of her body. p. 623

masterpiece (mas´tər•pēs) Something that is made or done with great skill; a great work of art. p. 279

medina (mə•dē´nə) The old section of a North African city. p. 419

mercantilism (mûr´kən•tēl•i•zəm) An economic system based on the idea that a country's power was measured by its wealth. p. 271

mestizo (mes•tē´zō) A person of European and American Indian descent, living in the Spanish colonies. p. 182

metropolitan area (met•rə•pä´lə•tən â r´ē•ə) A city and all the suburbs and other population areas around it. p. 57

middle passage (mi´dəl pa´sij) The route along which enslaved people were shipped across the Atlantic from Africa to the Americas. p. 454

migrant worker (mī´grənt wûr´kər) Someone who has a job outside his or her home country. p. 499

migration (mī•grā´shən) Movement of groups of people from one place to another. p. 56

millet (mi´lət) A grain crop produced by a quick-growing grass. p. 473

minaret (mi•nə•ret´) A tower, on top of a mosque, from which the faithful are called to prayer. p. 416

mineral (min´rəl) A nonliving substance found in Earth's crust. p. 41

minority (mə•nôr´ə•tē) A small part of a group. p. 149

missionary (mi´shə•ner•ē) A person sent out to teach about a religion. p. 181

mixed economy (mikst´ i•kon´ə•mē) An economy with varying degrees of free enterprise and government control. p. 390

modify (mo´də•fī) To make a change in. p. 2

monarchy (mä´nər•kē) The system of government in which a king or a queen rules. p. 69

monsoon (mon•soon´) A strong seasonal wind in the Indian Ocean. p. 528

most-favored-nation status (mōst´ fā´vərd nā´shən stā´təs) A status that grants special trade advantages. p. 579

muezzin (moo•e´zən) A Muslim who calls the faithful to prayer. p. 416

mulatto (mə•lä´tō) A person of African and European background. p. 200

mummy (mu´mē) A preserved body. p. 410

mutual defense (myoo´chə•wəl di•fens´) A system in which a group of nations provides military defense for each other. p. 242

N

nationalism (nash´ə•nə•liz•əm) A strong feeling of loyalty to one's nation. p. 147

nation-state (nā´shən•stāt) A country having a strong central government and usually people with a common history and culture. p. 270

natural resource (na´chə•rəl rē´sôrs) Something found in nature that people can use. p. 40

nirvana (nir•vä´nə) In Buddhism, the escape from the cycle of rebirth. p. 536

nonrenewable resource (non•ri•noo´ə•bəl rē´sôrs) Resources, such as coal and oil, that cannot be replaced by Earth's natural processes or that are replaced very slowly. p. 42

O

oasis (ō•ā´səs) A place in the desert where a spring or well provides water. p. 367

oil shale (oil´ shāl´) Layered rock that yields oil when heated. p. 297

oligarchy (ä´lə•gä r•kē) A system in which a small group that is not elected controls the government. p. 70

opinion (ə•pin´yən) A statement of belief or judgment. p. 458

opportunity cost (ä•pər•tŏŏ´nə•tē kôst´) The cost of giving up something when choosing something else instead. p. 128

oral history (ôr´əl his´tə•rē) Accounts told by people who did not have a written language or who did not write down what happened. p. 4

outback (out´bak) Australia's inland region. p. 621

outrigger (out´ri•gər) A wooden frame placed on the side of a boat or canoe to keep the craft steady in rough seas. p. 648

overpopulation (ō•vər•pop•yə•lā´shən) Too many people living in one place. p. 419

P

pack ice (pak´ īs´) Sea ice that forms into a large mass. p. 664

paddy (pa´dē) A walled, flooded field in which rice is grown. p. 588

pagoda (pə•gō´də) A tower with many levels; a feature of East Asian architecture. p. 573

pan (pan) A shallow pond or lake that forms during rainy seasons. p. 481

Pan Africanism (pan´ a´fri•kə•ni•zəm) A movement that aimed to have all African nations united into one federation. p. 498

papyrus (pə•pī´rəs) A paperlike material that ancient Egyptians wrote on; made from reeds that grow in the Nile River. p. 411

parallel time line (par´ə•lel tīm´ līn´) A grouping of time lines that display different types of information for the same period of time. p. 66

parliamentary democracy (pär r•lə•men´trē di•mä´krə•sē) A governing system in which citizens elect members of a legislature called a parliament. p. 149

Patriot (pā´tre•ət) An American colonist who opposed British rule. p. 108

penal colony (pē´nəl kä´lə•nē) A settlement for criminals. p. 628

peninsula (pə•nin´sə•lə) A piece of land that is mostly surrounded by water. p. 172

per capita GDP (pûr´ ka´pə•tə jē´dē´pē´) The average income of a country's citizens. p. 141

perestroika (pâ r•ə•stroi´kə) A "restructuring," or rebuilding, of the Soviet political and economic systems. p. 338

permafrost (pûr´mə•frôst) The layer of soil that stays frozen all year in a polar climate. p. 328

perspective (pər•spek´tiv) A certain point of view. p. 5

petition (pə•ti´shən) A written request for action, signed by many people. p. 210

pharaoh (fer´ō) A ruler of ancient Egypt. p. 408

physical feature (fi´zi•kəl fē´chərz) A landform, a body of water, climate, soil, plant and animal life, or any natural resource. p. 2

plate tectonics (plāt´ tek•tä´niks) The theory that Earth's surface is divided into several major, slow-moving plates or pieces. p. 20

plateau (pla•tō´) A high, flat area of land. p. 173

pluralistic (plŏŏr•ə•lis´tik) Describes a society where people share common culture traits while also maintaining many of the traditional ways of their ancestors. p. 117

poacher (pō´chər) A person who kills wild animals illegally. p. 504

point of view (point´ əv vyŏŏ´) A person's set of beliefs that have been shaped by factors such as whether that person is old or young, male or female, rich or poor, or by the person's culture, religion, race, or nationality. p. 120

polder (pōl´dər) An area of low-lying land reclaimed from the sea. p. 264

politburo (pä´lət•byŏŏr•ō) A political bureau that sets policy for a government. p. 576

political party (pə•li´ti•kəl pär´tē) A group of people involved in government who try to get others to agree with their ideas and who choose leaders who share the group's point of view. p. 123

population cartogram (pop•yə•lā´shən kä r´tə•gram) A kind of map that shows population distribution and density. p. 568

population density (pop•yə•lā´shən den´sə•tē) The average number of people living on a square unit of land. p. 58

population distribution (pop•yə•lā´shən dis•trə•byŏŏ´shən) The way people are spread out in different places throughout the world. p. 52

population pyramid (pop•yə•lā´shən pir´ə•mid) A graph that shows how a country's population is divided by age and by gender. p. 548

postwar (pōst´wôr) After a war; a time reference used most often for the period following World War II. p. 283

prairie (prâr´ē) An area of flat or rolling land covered mostly by grasses and wildflowers. p. 135

presidential democracy (pre•zə•den´shəl di•mok´rə•sē) A governing system in which an elected president is the chief decision-maker. p. 184

primary industry (prī´mer•ē in´dəs•trē) An economic activity that directly involves natural resources or raw materials, such as farming and mining. p. 71

primary source (prī´mər•ē sôrs´) A record made by people who saw or took part in an event. p. 6

prime meridian (prīm´ mə•ri•dē•ən) The meridian marked 0° longitude. It runs north and south through Greenwich in England. p. 32

prime minister (prīm´ mi´nə•stər) The leader of a parliamentary government who heads both the executive and legislative branches. p. 149

privatize (prī´və•tīz) To change from government control to control by individuals. p. 312

projection (prə•jek´shən) On maps, one of many different views showing the round Earth on flat paper. p. 450

protectionism (prə•tek´shə•ni•zəm) A government policy that calls for some type of action, such as raising tariffs, to protect a market from imports. p. 140

protectorate (prə•tek´tə•rət) A country that maintains control of domestic policies but depends on another country to direct its foreign affairs. p. 594

province (prä´vəns) A self-governing region. p. 136

puppet ruler (pu´pət rōō´lər) A ruler without authority. p. 533

purchasing power (pûr´chə•sing pou´ər) The ability to spend money. p. 72

purdah (pûr´də) An Islamic custom in which some women cover their faces with veils. p. 538

purge (pûrj) To carry out a government order to kill or imprison citizens who oppose the government. p. 337

pyramid (pir´ə•mid) A burial place for the dead, often for a dead ruler. p. 411

Q

qanat (kä•nät´) An underground canal that brings water from mountain springs to dry areas. p. 370

quaternary industry (kwä´tûr•ner•ē in´dus•trē) Economic activities that involve specialized skills or knowledge. p. 71

Qur'an (kə•ran´ or kə•rän´) The holy book of Islam; the messages that Muhammed received from God. p. 375

R

rain forest (rān´ fôr´əst) A wet land with thick vegetation and tall trees that block the sunlight. p. 37

rain shadow (rān´ sha´dō) The dry area on the side of a mountain or mountain range. p. 36

raw material (rô mə•tir´ē•əl) Natural resources that can be made into useful products. p. 266

reclaim (ri•klām´) To take back, as the surrounding environment can do to human-made structures. p. 178

recycling (rē•sī´kling) The process of using materials again instead of throwing them away. p. 43

referendum (re•fə•ren´dum) An election in which citizens can vote to accept or reject a suggested law. p. 153

reform (ri•fôrm´) Changes meant to make things better. p. 334

refugee (re´fyōō•jē) A person who leaves his or her home or country to find shelter and safety elsewhere. p. 381

reg (reg) A broad, windswept gravel plain in the Sahara. p. 404

region (rē´jən) An area on Earth whose features make it different from other areas. p. 2

reincarnation (rē•in•kär•nā´shən) The belief that the soul lives on after death and returns to life in a new body. p. 536

relative location (re´lə•tiv lō•kā´shən) Where a place is in relation to other places. p. 2

relief (ri•lēf´) On a map, differences in elevation of an area of land. p. 104

Renaissance (re´nə•säns) The time from about 1400 to 1600 in which Europeans entered an age of thought, learning, art, and science; a French word meaning "rebirth." p. 270

renewable resource (ri•nōō´ə•bəl rē´sôrs) A resource, such as soil and trees, that can be replaced by nature or by people. p. 42

representation (re•pri•zen•tā´shən) Acting or speaking on behalf of someone or something. p. 107

representative democracy (re•pri•zen´tə•tiv di•mä´krə•sē) A governing system in which citizens elect people to make laws and decisions for them. p. 122

republic (ri•pu´blik) A form of government in which the citizens elect representatives to make and enforce the laws. p. 109

reservoir (re´zə•vwär) A human-made lake. p. 28

revolution (re•və•lōō´shən) A sudden, complete change in government. p. 108

rift (rift) A long, deep valley with mountains or plateaus on either side. p. 28

right (rīt) A freedom. p. 69

Ring of Fire (ring´ əv fīr´) The circle of volcanoes around the Pacific Ocean. p. 195

river system (ri´vər sis´təm) A network of a river and its tributaries. p. 26

Roma (rō´mä) A member of an ethnic group also known as Gypsies. p. 317

row (rō) In a chart or table, a section of words or numbers that goes across, rather than up and down. p. 506

S

samurai (sa´mə•rī) A Japanese warrior. p. 564

sanction (sang´shən) An economic or political penalty, such as an embargo, used by one or more countries to force another country to cease an act. p. 424

GLOSSARY

satellite nation (sa´təl•īt nā´shən) A country whose government and economy are controlled by another, more powerful country. p. 305

savanna (sə•va´nə) A grassy plain with scattered trees. p. 444

scale (skāl) The relationship between the distances on a map and the actual distances on Earth. p. 590

scarce (skârs) Limited. p. 43

scarcity (skâr´sə•tē) The condition of being limited, as goods and services can be; shortage. p. 128

sea breeze (sē´ brēz´) Wind blowing during daylight hours from cool water to warmer land. p. 36

secondary industry (se´kən•dâr•ē in´dus•trē) Economic activities that change raw materials created by primary industries into finished products. p. 71

secondary source (se´kən•dâr•ē sôrs´) A record of an event written by someone not there at the time. p. 6

self-government (self•guv´ûrn•mənt) A system of government in which people govern themselves. p. 212

separatist (se´prə•tist) A person who wants to become or remain separate from a government or group. p. 152

sharecropping (shār´kräp•ing) A system of working the land, in which the worker was paid with a "share" of the crop. p. 226

Shi`i (shē´ī) The second-largest branch of Islam. p. 382

shogun (shō´gən) In Japan, a "leading general" who held all the authority. p. 564

sierra (sē•âr´ə) A chain of mountains whose peaks look like the edge of a saw. p. 173

slash and burn (slash´ and bûrn´) To cut and burn forestlands to gain new farmland. p. 231

social class (sō´shəl klas´) A group that has a particular level of importance in a society. p. 235

society (sə•sī´ə•tē) An organized group of people living and working under a set of rules and traditions. p. 8

sorghum (sôr´gum) A kind of grain that grows in hot and dry areas. p. 473

Special Economic Zone (spe´shəl e•ko•nä´mik zōn´) A modern manufacturing area that uses democratic-style market economy practices. p. 578

specialize (spe´she•līz) To work at only one kind of job. p. 284

standard of living (stan´dûrd əv liv´ing) A measure of how well people in a country live. p. 72

standardization (stan•dər•də•zā´shən) The practice of making all things of a certain type alike. p. 562

staple (stā´pəl) Any article of food or other common item that is used regularly and is kept in a large amount. p. 473

states' rights (stāts´ rīts´) The idea that individual states have final authority over the national, or central, government. p. 208

station (stā´shən) The name for a sheep ranch or cattle ranch in Australia. p. 624

statistics (stə•tis´tiks) Facts shown with numbers. p. 238

steppe (step) An area of grassland and fertile soil that is south of the taiga in Russia. p. 328

strait (strāt) A narrow waterway that connects two larger bodies of water. p. 587

stupa (stoo´pə) A curved mound of brick that holds statues of Buddha. p. 533

subcontinent (sub•kon´tə•nənt) A large land area isolated from the rest of a continent. p. 524

subregion (sub´rē•jən) A small section of a region, such as a state. p. 77

subsistence farming (sub•sis´təns fär´ming) Farming in which people raise only enough food for their families. p. 72

sultan (sul´tən) A monarch in a Muslim country. p. 600

Sunni (soo´nē) The largest branch of Islam. p. 382

supply (su•plī´) The amount of a good or service offered for sale. p. 73

swamp (swämp) A low, wet area where trees and bushes grow; usually covered by shallow water at least part of the year. p. 100

T

table (tā´bəl) A chart that lists information in categories. p. 506

tabu (tə•boo´) Forbidden. p. 649

taiga (tī´gə) A forest of evergreen trees that is south of the tundra in Russia. p. 328

tandoor (tän•door´) A clay or brick oven. p. 538

technology (tek•no´lə•jē) The skills and knowledge to use science to make products or meet goals. p. 62

telescoping time line (te´lə•skōp•ing tīm´ līn´) On a main time line, a blown-up section that gives a closer view of one time period. p. 414

temperate (tem´pə•rət) Neither very hot nor very cold. p. 34

Ten Commandments (ten´ kə•mand´mənts) A set of laws for responsible behavior that, according to the Bible, were given to the Jewish people by God. p. 374

terrace (târ´əs) A flat area that was created on the slope of a steep mountainside to prevent soil loss and aid farming. p. 233

territory (târ´ə•tōr•ē) A large region that belongs to a country but does not have the same rights of self-government as the rest of the country. p. 136

terrorism (târ´ər•i•zəm) The deliberate use of violence to further a cause. p. 278

tertiary industry (tûr´shē•er•ē in´dus•trē) Economic activities that handle goods that are ready to be sold to consumers; also includes services, such as banking and health care. p. 71

thematic map (thi•ma´tik map´) A map with a specific theme or topic, such as population, culture, or history. p. 58

thermal spring (thûr´məl spring´) A source of warm water that bubbles from Earth. p. 296

tidal wave (tī´dəl wāv´) A giant ocean wave. p. 30

tide (tīd) The regular, rhythmic rise and fall of ocean waters. p. 30

tierra caliente (tē•âr´ə ka•lē•en´tā) A climate term used in Mexico meaning "hot land." p. 175

tierra fría (tē•âr´ə frē´ə) A climate term used in Mexico meaning "cold land." p. 175

tierra templada (tē•âr´ə tem•plä´dä) A climate term used in Mexico meaning "temperate land." p. 175

time zone (tīm´ zōn´) A division of Earth in which all places have the same time; the time is different from that in other zones. p. 340

Torah (tōr´ə) Jewish scriptures; the first five books of the Bible. p. 374

tornado (tôr•nā´dō) A funnel-shaped, spinning windstorm, sometimes called a cyclone or twister. p. 101

totalitarian (tō•ta•lə•târ´ē•ən) Having complete control over people's lives. p. 337

trade wind (trād´wind´) Wind blowing almost constantly from the northeast toward the equator. p. 198

trade-off (trād´ôf) Giving up of one thing in order to get another. p. 128

traditional economy (trə•dish´ə•nəl i•ko´nə•mē) An economy that does not change much over time, based mostly on farming. p. 72

transition zone (tran•zi´shən zōn´) A region or climate that shares characteristics of two or more areas that surround it, such as the Sahel in Africa. p. 446

transportation corridor (trans•pôr•tā´shən kôr´ə•dər) A route by which people and goods move from one place to another. p. 224

trench (trench) A deep ocean valley. p. 29

trend (trend) The way something changes over time. p. 640

tributary (tri´byə•târ•ē) A smaller river that feeds into a larger river. p. 26

tropic (trä´pik) An area on Earth at or near the equator. p. 35

trust territory (trust´ târ´ə•tôr•ē) An area placed under the temporary control of another country until it sets up its own government. p. 658

tsunami (sōō•nä´mē) A huge tidal wave created by undersea tectonic activity, such as an earthquake. p. 559

tundra (tun´drə) A cold, treeless plain where the ground is permanently frozen. p. 135

typhoon (tī•fōōn´) A tropical storm that brings violent winds, heavy rain, and high seas. p. 558

unlimited government (un•li´mə•təd guv´ûrn•mənt) A government in which no limits are imposed on the ruler's authority. p. 208

urban center (ûr´bən sen´tər) A city. p. 545

urban planning (ûr´bən plan´ing) A plan or strategy for the growth of a city. p. 531

urbanization (ûr´bə•nə•zā´shən) The movement of people from rural areas to cities, or urban areas. p. 56

Vedas (vā´dəz) The ancient books of sacred Hindu writings. p. 537

vegetation (ve•jə•tā´shən) Plant life. p. 37

veld (velt) Open grassland areas of South Africa. p. 482

viceroy (vīs´roi) The governor of a Spanish colony. p. 235

virtue (vûr´chōō) A good quality. p. 561

wadi (wä´dē) A dry riverbed in Southwest Asia. p. 369

water cycle (wô´tûr sī´kəl) The circulation of water from Earth's surface to the atmosphere and back. p. 31

weathering (we´thûr•ing) The process of breaking rocks into smaller pieces through heat, water, or other means. p. 23

western (wes´tûrn) The culture and customs of people descended from Europeans. p. 118

x-axis (eks´ ak´səs) The horizontal line at the bottom of a graph. p. 238

y-axis (wī´ ak´səs) The vertical line at the left of a graph. p. 238

ziggurat (zi´gə•rat) A huge mud-brick temple built by the ancient Sumerians. p. 372

Zionism (zī´ə•ni•zəm) The movement to establish a Jewish homeland. p. 389

GLOSSARY

Index

Page references for illustrations are set in italic type. An italic *m* indicates a map. Page references set in boldface type indicate the pages on which vocabulary terms are defined.

INDEX

INDEX

INDEX

INDEX

INDEX

T

INDEX

INDEX

for Man and Horse with Vols-Colonna Arms. North Italy, c, 1575. Steel. (c) The Cleveland Museum of Art, 2001,John L. Severance Fund, 1964.88; viii Louvre, Dpt. des Antiquites Orientales, Paris, France/Erich Lessing - Culture and Fine Arts Archives/Art Resource, NY; ix Founders Society Purchase, Clay Ford Fund for African Arts; Photograph (c)1989/The Detroit Institute of Arts; x Plate with Persimmon Branch Design: Old Kutani ware, Aode (green) Kutani Style. Japan, late 17th century, Edo Period. Porcelain with overglaze decoration, diameter 33.40 cm. (c) The Cleveland Museum of Art, 2001, Severance and Greta Millikin Collection, 1964.245; xi Harcourt, Courtesy Aboriginals: Art of the First Person, Sanibel, FL; 0-1 J. Messerschmidt/Bruce Coleman, Inc ; 1 Mittelrheinisches Landesmuseum, Mainz, Germany/The Bridgeman Art Library .; 3 (tl) Matthew Borkoski/Stock, Boston Inc./PictureQuest; 3 (tr) Jan Halaska/Photo Researchers; 3 (bl) Victor Englebert; 3 (br) David young-Wolff/PhotoEdit/ PictureQuest; 3 (cl) Peter Pearson/Stone/ Gettyimages; 3 (cr) Jeffery Muir Hamilton/stock, Boston Inc./PictureQuest; 4 (t), c), (b), The Granger Collection, New York, New York; 5 (t) Larry Williams/Corbis Stock Market; 5 (tc) Joe McDonald/Bruce Coleman, Inc.; 5 (c) Patricio Robles Gil/Bruce Coleman, Inc.; 5 (bc) Jeff Greenberg/Photo Researchers ; 5 (b) Julio Donoso/Woodfin Camp & Associates; 6 (l) DPA/The Image Works; 6 (r) Archive Photos/ Gettyimages/Gettyimages; 8 Lineair/Peter Arnold, Inc.; 9 (bg) Catherine Karnow/Woodfin Camp & Associates; 9 (inset) Pascal Quittemelle/ Stock, Boston; 10 (l) Chris Sharp/South American Pictures; 10 (tr) N. E. Newman/Woodfin Camp & Associates; 10 (cr) Norman Owen Tomalin/Bruce Coleman Inc. ; 10 (br) Jason Laure/Woodfin Camp & Associates.-

UNIT 1: Unit 1 Opener (object) The Metropolitan Museum of Art, Gift of J. Pierpoint Morgan, 1917, (17.190.636) Photograph (c) 1977 The Metropolitan Museum of Art; Unit 1Opener (bg) IFA-Bilderteam-Nature/Bruce Coleman, Inc. ; Unit 1 Opener (spread) Bruce Coleman, Inc.; 11 The Metropolitan Museum of Art, Gift of J. Pierpoint Morgan, 1917, (17.190.636) Photograph (c) 1977 The Metropolitan Museum of Art; 12 (l) Peter French/Bruce Coleman, Inc.; 12 (c) William Manning/Corbis Stock Market; 12 (r) Superstock; 13 (l) David Madison/Bruce Coleman, Inc.; 13 (c) Craig Duncan/D. Donne Bryant Stock; 13 (r) Superstock ; 14-17 (all globes): Photo Illustration by Steve Parady/NASA Map; 14 (r) The Image Bank; 15 (b) Wolfgang Kaehler Photography; 15 (tc) Courtesy, National Museum of the American Indian, Smithsonian Institution, Washington, D.C. (18.5783). Photo by Carmelo Guadagno; 16 (tc) Manu Sassoonian/Art Resource, NY ; 16 (b) Tim Acker/Auscape International; 17 (b) www.rainpalm.com.

CHAPTER ONE: 18-19 Art Wolfe/Danita Delimont, Agent; 22 (t) Russell D. Curtis/Photo Researchers; 22 (b) Reuters/Kamal Kishore/Hulton/Archive; 23 (l)(inset) Bill Bachman/Photo Researchers; 23 (r)(inset)Georg Gerster/Photo Researchers; 23 (bg) E. R.

Degginger/Bruce Coleman, Inc.; 24-25 Gordon Wiltbie/National Geographic Society; 25 (inset) Trip/Art Directors & TRIP Photo Library; 26 (bg) R. A. Mittermaier/Bruce Coleman, Inc.; 26 (inset) Loren McIntyre/Woodfin Camp & Associates; 28 Reza/National Geographic Image Collection; 30 National Geographic Society Image Collection; 31 David Falconer/David R. Frazier Photolibrary; 34 Tom & Pat Leeson/Photo Researchers; 36-37 (b) Bob Abraham/Corbis Stock Market; 37 (tc(inset) John Kaprielian/Photo Researchers; 37 (tr) Victor Englebert; 38 (t) Mark E. Gibson; 38 (b) Shaw McCutcheon/Bruce Coleman, Inc.; 39 (t) Art Wolfe/Photo Researchers; 39 (c) Charles Preitner/Visuals Unlimited; 39 (bl) Floyd Norgaard/Ric Ergenbright; 39 (br) Victor Englebert; 40 (t) David R. Frazier; 40 (b) Torleif Svensson/Corbis Stock Market; 42 (t) Paul Jensen/Fraser Photos; 42 (b) Jonathan T. Wright/Bruce Coleman, Inc.; 43 (t) Regis Bossu/Corbis Sygma; 43 (b) Argus Fotoarchiv/Peter Arnold, Inc.; 44 Dagmar Ehling/Photo Researchers; 45 (l) NASA/Science Photo Library/Photo Researchers; 45 (r) Corbis Sygma; 46 Dinodia Picture Agency; 47 (t) Madhusudan B. Tawde/Dinodia Picture Agency; 47 (b), (c) Dinodia Picture Agency.

CHAPTER TWO: 50-51 Katherine M. Feng/The Viesti Collection; 52 courtesy yourexpedition.com; 53 (t) Farrell Grehan/Photo Researchers.; 53 (b) C. Karnow/Woodfin Camp & Associates; 54 (t) Amanda Merullo/Stock, Boston; 54 (b) Corbis; 55 Sean Sprague/Stock, Boston; 56 (tl) Ken Cavanaugh/Photo Researchers; 56 (tr) Alain Evrard/Photo Researchers; 56 (bl) Group Atlantide/Bruce Coleman, Inc.; 56 (br) Stephanie Maze/Woodfin Camp & Associates; 57 Keith Gunnar/Bruce Coleman, Inc.; 60 (tl) Torleif Svensson/Corbis; 60 (tr) R. Belbin/The Viesti Collection; 60 (bl) F. Gohier/Photo Researchers; 60 (bc) M. Timothy O'Keefe/Bruce Coleman, Inc.; 60 (br) Joe McDonald/Bruce Coleman, Inc.; 61 Mike Yamashita/Woodfin Camp & Associates; 62 (l) Jacques Langevin/Corbis; 62 (r) AP/Wide World Photos; 63 Reza Deghatings Image Collection/National Geographic Society; 64 Beth A. Keiser/AP/Wide World Photos; 65 Travel Ink/Corbis; 66 (l) Bill Varie/Corbis; 66 (r) Stephanie Maze/Corbis; 68 Corbis; 70 (l) Lance Nelson/Corbis; 70 (r) S. Grant/Art Directors & TRIP Photo Library; 71 (l) & (r) Harcourt; 72 (l), (r) The Granger Collection, New York; 73 (l) Brad Rickerby/Bruce Coleman, Inc.; 73 (r) George Haling/Photo Researchers; 74 (t) Robert Fried/Stock, Boston; 74 (b) Smithsonian Institution National Numismatic Collection; 75 (all): Smithsonian Institution National Numismatic Collection; 76 Sal Dimarco/Black Star; 77 (t) The Granger Collection, New York, New York; 77 (b) Michael Dwyer/Stock, Boston; 79 (t) Lawrence Migdale/Stock, Boston; 79 (b) J. Witt/Sipa Press; 80 Katsuyoshi Tanaka/Woodfin Camp & Associates; 81 (l) Nathan Benn/Stock, Boston; 81 (r),(inset) Tom Tracy/Corbis Stock Market; 81 (r) Phil Degginger/Bruce Coleman, Inc.; 82 Institution of Civil Engineers/Mary Evans Picture Library; 86-87 (inset) Johann Schumacher Design; 86 (inset) Piero Guerrini/Woodfin Camp & Associates; 86-87 bg Tom Jelen/Panoramic Images; 87 (tl)(inset) IN/DPI Photo; 87 (tr)(inset) L. Zito/Fotoforem;

87 (bl)(inset) AP/Wide World Photos; 87 (tr)(inset) L. Zito/Fotoforem; 88 (l) Peter French/Bruce Coleman; 88 (c) William Manning/Corbis Stock Market; 88 (r) Superstock ; 89 (l) David Madison/Bruce Coleman, Inc.; 89 (c) Craig Duncan/D. Donne Bryant; 89 (r) Superstock ; 90 Harcourt.

UNIT 2: Unit 2 Opener (object) Werner Forman Archive, British Museum, London/Art Resource, NY; Unit 2 Opener (bg) Jay Dickman/National Geographic Society; Unit 2 Opener (spread) Jay Dickman/National Geographic Society; 91 Werner Forman Archive, British Museum, London/Art Resource, NY; 93 (t) Superstock; 93 (tc) Jamestown Settlement, Williamsburg, Virginia/Jamestown-Yorktown Foundation Photo; 93 (c) Scott Barrow, Inc.; 93 (bc) Sean O'Neill/Spectrum Stock93 (c) Scott Barrow, Inc.; 93 (b) Alan Schein/Corbis Stock Market; 94-95 (t) Tom Till Photogrpahy; 94 (tc) Mark Newman/ Bruce Coleman, Inc.; 94 (bc) Richard T. Nowitz; 95 (inset) Mark E. Gibson.

CHAPTER THREE: 96-97 David R. Frazier; 98-99 (b) James Randklev/Visions of America, LLC/PictureQuest; 99 (t) Renee Purse/Photo Researchers; 100 (tl) John Elk, III; 100 (tr) William Strode/Woodfin Camp & Associates; 100 (b) John Elk III ; 101 (t) Alan Schein/Corbis Stock Market; 101 (b) Harcourt; 102 Ric Ergenbright; 103 Mark E. Gibson Photography; 106 Ted Curtin/Plimoth Plantation; 108 (t) National Archives; 108 (b) Bettman Archive/Corbis; 109 Independence National Historic Park; 110 (t) The Granger Collection, New York; 110 (b) John Stobart Galleries/Maritime Heritage Prints; 111 (t) Culver Pictures; 111 (b) Peter Newark's Pictures; 112 (t) Independence National Historical Park; 112 (b) National Archives; 112 (b)(inset) Superstock ; 113 (t) National Archives; 113 (t),(inset) Stock Montage; 113 (b) Alex Wong/Liason/Gettyimages; 114 Culver Picture; 115 (t) John Elk III; 115 (bl) Patti McConville/International Stock; 115 (br) Churchill & Klehr; 116 (t) Archive Photos/Gettyimages; 116 (bl) Harcourt; 116 (bc) Smithsonian Institution; 116 (br) Harcourt; 117 (t) Lawrence Migdale/Stock, Boston; 117 (b) Michael Newman/PhotoEdit; 118 (tl) Archive Photos/Gettyimages/Gettyimages; 118 (tr) Rialto Archives/Eric Kohler; 118 (b) Sisse Brimberg/Woodfin Camp & Associates; 119 Daniel Hulshizer/AP./Wide World Photos; 120 Bettman/Corbis; 121 (bg) Flip Schulke/Corbis; 121 (inset) Bettmann/Corbis; 122 Tim Boyle/Gettyimages; 124 Harcourt; 125 (t) Brown Brothers; 125 (b) David R. Frazier; 126 (t) Jim Pickerell/Stock Connection/PictureQuest; 126-127 (b) John McGrail/Stock Connection/ PictureQuest; 128 Mark Richards/PhotoEdit; 129 Harcourt.

CHAPTER 4: 132-133 Dale Sanders/Masterfile; 134 Gloria H. Chomica/Masterfile; 136 (t) J.A. Kraulis; 136 (b) Norman Piluke/Spectrum Stock; 137 Frank Scott/Spectrum Stock; 138 Howie Garber/Wanderlust Images; 139 (inset) J. David Andrews/Masterfile; 139 (bg) J.A. Kraulis/ Masterfile; 140 (r) Bill Gallery/Stock, Boston; 140 (t) Peter Christopher/Masterfile; 140 (bl) John Elk III; 141 (l) & (r) Harcourt; 142 George

Catlin/Mary Evans Picture Library; 143 (tl)(inset) Erich Lessing/Museum of Mankind, London, Great Britain; 143 (t),(bg) John Foster/Masterfile; 143 (tr)(inset) John Elk III; 143 (bl) (inset) Haffenreffer Museum of Anthropology, Brown University, Rhode Island, USA/Werner Forman Archive/Art Resource; 144 Reunion des Musees Nationaux/Art Resource, NY; 145 (t) The Granger Collection, New York, New York; 145 (b) McCord/Museum of Canadian History, Montreal; 146 (t) Tony Mihok/Spectrum Stock; 146 (b) Denis Drever/Stectrum Stock; 147 (l) Winston Fraser; 147 (r) Ottmar Bierwagen/Spectrum Stock; 148 Derek Caron/Fraser Photos; 149 (t) Tom Hanson/Canadian Press CP; 149 (b) Reuters/Shaun Best/Archive Photos/Gettyimages; 151 (t) Fred Chartrand/Canadian Press CP; 151 (bl) Reproduced with the consent of the Library of Parliament/reproduit avec permission de la Bibliotheque du Parlement; 151 (br) Tom Hanson/Canadian Press CP; 152 (t) John Elk III; 152 (b) J. A. Wilkinson/Valan Photos; 153 J. A. Kraulis/Masterfile; 154 Fred Chartrand/CP Photo; 158-159 (inset) James Blank/Stock, Boston; 158 (inset) Neil Speers/A Perfect Exposure; 158-159 bg Winston Fraser/Fraser Photos; 159 (tl)(inset) Nancie Battaglia Photography; 159 (tc)(inset) Dave G. Houser/Corbis; 159 (tr)(inset) Nancie Battaglia Photography; 159 (b)(inset) William A. Allard/National Geographic Society ; 161 (t) Superstock; 161 (tc) Jamestown-Yorktown Foundation ; 161 (c) Scott Barrow, Inc.; 161 (bc) Sean O'Neill/Spectrum Stock ; 161 (b) Alan Schein/Corbis Stock Market; 162 Harcourt.

UNIT 3: Unit 3 Opener (object) Founders Society Purchase with funds from Richard A. Manoogian; Photograph (c)1992/The Detroit Institute of Arts ; Unit 3 Opener (bg) Robert Frerck/Odyssey/Chicago; Unit 3 Opener (spread) Robert Frerck/Odyssey/Chicago; ; 163 Founders Society Purchase with Funds from Richard A. Manoogin; Photograph (c)1992/The Detroit Institute of Arts; 165 (t) Eric Carle/Bruce Coleman, Inc.; 165 (tc) John Neubauer ; 165 (c) Heather R. Davidson; 165 (bc) Tony Morrison/South American Pictures ; 165 (b) Reuters Newmedia/Corbis; pages 166 through 169 (all) Christopher Knight.

CHAPTER FIVE: 170-171 Robert Frerck/Odyssey/Chicago; 172-173 Buddy Mays/Travel Stock Photography; 173 (inset) Robert Frerck/Odyssey/Chicago; 174 (t),(tc) & (bc) Albert Jaramillo Cepeda/Cenapred; 174 (r) Robert Frerck/Odyssey/Chicago; 175 (l) David Sanger Photography; 175 (r) Robert Frerck/Odyssey/Chicago; 176 Chris Sharp/South American Pictures; 177 (bg) & (inset) Kenneth Garrett Photography; 178 Buddy Mays/Travel Stock Photography; 179 Kenneth Garrett Photography; 181 John Neubauer; 182 (t) Robert Frerck/Odyssey/Chicago; 182 (b) Jimmy Dorantes/Latin Focus; 183 Chris Sharp/South American Pictures; 184 (t) Carlos S. Pereyra/DDB Stock Photo; 184 (b) Dirk Weisheit/DDB Stock Photo; 185 (t) Robert Frerck/Odyssey/Chicago; 185 (bl) Robert Frerck/Odyssey/Chicago; 185 (br) John Neubauer; 186 (tl) David Sanger Photography; 186 (tr) Kenneth Garrett; 186 (b)

Jimmy Dorantes/Latin Focus ; 187 Nik Wheeler; 188 D. Donne Bryant/DDB Stock Photo.

CHAPTER SIX: 192-193 Robert Fried Photography; 194-195 James D. Nations/DDB Stock Photo; 196 Robert Frerck/Odyssey/Chicago; 197 Robert Frerck/Odyssey/Chicago; 198 Greg Johnston/Danita Delimont, Agent; 199 Greg Johnston/Danita Delimont, Agent; 200-201 Mary Evans Picture Library/Explorer Archives; 201 Buddy Mays/Travel Stock Photography; 202 Wolfgang Kaehler Photography; 203 Robert Frerck/Woodfin Camp & Associates; 204 (l) Robert Francis/South American Pictures; 204 (r) Chris Sharp/South American Pictures; 205 (l) NASA/Sipa Press; 205 (r) Oswaldo Rivas/Reuters/Archive Photos/Gettyimages; 206 (t) & (bl) National Museum of American Art, Washington DC/Teodoro Vidal Collecton/Art Resource, NY; 206 (br) Smithsonian American Art Museum, Gift of the artist ; 207 (t) & (c) Smithsonian American Art Museum, Washington, DC/Art Resource, NY; 207 (b) 1980 Luis Jimenez/National Museum of American Art, Washington DC/Art Resource, NY; 208 AP/Wide World Photos; 209 AP/Wide World Photos; 210 (t) Sipa Press; 210 (b) Juan Carlos Ulate/Reuters/Archive Photos/Gettyimages/Gettyimages; 210 (inset) AP/Wide World Photos; 211 (l) AP/Wide World Photos; 211 (r) Louise Gubb/Corbis SABA; 212 Lee Foster; 213 Robert Fried; 214 (l) Hulton/Archive/Gettyimages; 214 (r) Rykoff Collection/Corbis.

CHAPTER SEVEN: 218-219 Yan Arthus-Bertrand/Photo Researchers; 220 (inset) David Ryan/DDB Stock Photo; 220-221 Robert Frerck/Odyssey/Chicago; 222 (bg) Nair Benedicto/N-Imagens/DDB Stock Photo; 222 (tc)(inset) Art Wolfe/Danita Delimont, Agent; 222 (tr)(inset) Wolfgang Kaehler ; 222 (bc)(inset) David Macias/Latin Focus; 222 (br)(inset) Gary Braasch; 222 (l)(inset) Art Wolfe/Danita Delimont, Agent; 223 (t) Francois Gohier/Photo Researchers; 223 (tc) Chris Sharp/DDB Stock Photo ; 223 (bc) John Curtis/DDB Stock Photo ; 223 (b) Peter Dixon/South American Pictures; 224 Tony Morrison/South American Pictures; 225 D. Donne Bryant; 226 (b) Paulo Fridman/Latin Focus; 226 No 1 Wolfgang Kaehler; 226 No 2 Wolfgang Kaehler; 226 No 3 Salomon Cytrynowicz/DDB Stock Photo; 228 Corbis Stock Market; 230 Robert Frerck/Odyssey/Chicago; 232 (t) The Granger Collection, New York; 232-233 (b) Robert Frerck/Odyssey/Chicago; 234 Archaeological Museum Lima/Dagli Orti/The Art Archive; 235 Robert Frerck/Odyssey/Chicago; 236 (t) AP/Wide World Photos; 236 (b) Robert Fried/DDB Stock Photo; 238 Michele Burgess/Stock, Boston; 240 (t) The Stapleton Collection/The Bridgeman Art Library; 240 (b) Museo Navale, Madrid, Spain/The Bridgeman Art Library; 241 Museo Historico Nacional Buenos Aires/Dagli Orti/The Art Archive; 242 (t) Pace Sansevier/Reuters/TimePix; 242-243 Alex O'Campo/Latin Focus; 243 (tl) & (tr) Guyana Space Center/South American Pictures; 246 (inset) Chris Sharp/D. Donne Bryant; 246-247 (bg) Ed Darack/D. Donne Bryant; 247 (tl)(inset) David Ryan/D. Donne Bryant; 247 (cl)(inset) Peter Francis/South American Pictures; 247 (bl)(inset) Michael Moody/D. Donne Bryant; 247

(r)(inset) Ed Darack/D. Donne Bryant ; 249 (t) Eric Carle/Bruce Coleman, Inc; 249 (tc) John Neubauer ; 249 (c) Heather R. Davidson; 249 (bc) Tony Morrison/South American Pictures ; 249 (b) Reuters Newmedia/Corbis; 250 (all)Harcourt.

UNIT 4: Unit 4 Opener (object) : Armor for Man and Horse with Vols-Colonna Arms. North Italy, c, 1575. Steel. (c) The Cleveland Museum of Art, 2001,John L. Severance Fund, 1964.88; Unit 4 Opener (bg) Walter Geiersperger/Stock, Boston; Unit 4 Opener (spread) Walter Geiersperger/Stock, Boston; 251 Armor for Man and Horse with Vols-Colonna Arms. North Italy, c, 1575. Steel. (c) The Cleveland Museum of Art, 2001,John L. Severance Fund, 1964.88; 252 (l) Dallas & John Heaton/Stock, Boston; 252 (c) R. Sheridan/Ancient Art and Architecture Collection ; 252 (r) Mark Wadlow/Russia and Eastern Images; 253 (l) Bettmann/Corbis; 253 (c) Superstock ; 253 (r) Rene Mattes/Explorer/Photo Researchers; 254 (l)(inset) Amanda Merullo/Stock, Boston; 254 (r)(inset) The Image Bank/Gettyimages; 254-255 (bg) David Toht/Greenleaf Publishing; 256 (t)(inset) David Toht/Greenleaf Publishing ; 256 (b)(inset) Wolfgang Kaehler Photography; 256-257 bg Bob Handleman/Stone/Gettyimages; 257 (inset) Dave G. Houser/Houserstock.

CHAPTER 8: 258-259 David Ball/Corbis Stock Market; 260-261 John Elk III/Bruce Coleman, Inc.; 261 Richard Nowitz; 262 Dallas & John Heaton/Stock, Boston; 263 (t) Dallas & John Heaton/Stock, Boston; 263 (b) C. Bowman/Robert Harding Picture Library; 264 (t) Robert Harding Picture Library; 264 (b) Ray Rainford/Robert Harding Picture Library; 265 (t) Richard Nowitz; 265 (b) Simon Fraser/Science Photo Library/Photo Researchers; 269 British Museum, London/Bridgeman Art Library Int'l, Ltd., London/New York; 270 Chantilly, Musee Conde/AKG Photo; 271 (t) Cabinet des Estampes Strasbourg/Dagli Orti/The Art Archive; 271 (b) Musee d'Orsay/AKG Photo; 272 Scott Swanson Collection/Archive Photos/Gettyimages; 273 Keystone/Archive Photos/Gettyimages/Gettyimages; 274 (t) David Simson/Stock, Boston; 274 (all others) National Postal Museum; 275 (all) National Postal Museum; 276 Dave Bartruff/Stock, Boston; 277 Robert Fried/Stock, Boston; 278 (t) Dave G. Houser/Houserstock; 278-279 (b) Peter Menzel/Stock, Boston; 279 (t) Ronald Sheridan/Ancient Art and Architecture Collection; 280 (b) Wolfgang Kaehler; 280 (tl) Tibor Bognar/Art Directors & TRIP Photo Library; 280 (tr) Fraser Hall/Robert Harding Picture Library; 281 Eric Carle/Bruce Coleman, Inc.; 282 Argus Fotoarchiv/Peter Arnold, Inc.; 283 (l) Photomorgana/Corbis Stock Market; 283 (r) Simon Harris/Robert Harding Picture Library; 284 (tl) Charles Kennard/Stock, Boston; 284 (tr) Nicolas Sapieha/The Art Archive; 284 (cl) Norman Owen Tomalin/Bruce Coleman, Inc.; 284 (cr) E. Simanor/Robert Harding Picture Library; 284 (b) Dagli Orti/Private Collection/The Art Archive ; 285 (t) Reuters/Pascal Rossignol/Hulton/Archive/Gettyimages; 285 (b) The Granger Collection, New York, New York; 286 John Elk III; 287 Arnd Wiegmann/Reuters/Archive Photos/Gettyimages; 288 (l) Delaware Art Museum, Howard Pile Collection; 288 (r)

Fine Arts Museum of San Fransisco/Achenbach Foundation for Graphic Arts/Bruno and Sadie Adriani Collection; 289 Cartoon Stock.

CHAPTER 9: 292-293 Simon Harris/Robert Harding Picture Library; 294 (t) MTI/Eastfoto; 294 (b) Courau/Explorer/Photo Researchers; 296 (t) Dennis Chamberlin/Black Star; 296 (b) Dave G. Houser; 297 (tl) Corbis; 297 (tr) Guido Cozzi/Group Atlantide/Bruce Coleman, Inc.; 297 (b) Torleif Svensson/Corbis Stock Market ; 298 Otis Imboden/National Geographic Society; 298 (cl) Sylvain Grandadam/Photo Researchers ; 298 (bl) Art Directors & TRIP Photo Library; 298 (bc) Christopher Rennie/Robert Harding Picture Library; 298 (br) Hans Reinhard/Bruce Coleman, Inc.; 300 Alon Reininger/Contact Press Images/PictureQuest; 301 MTI/Sovfoto/Eastfoto; 302 (t) Brown Brothers; 302 (b) The Art Archive/Miramare Palace Trieste/Dagli Orti ; 303 AP/Wide World Photos; 304 (t) Gettyimages; 304 (b) Owen/Black Star; 305 Sipa Press; 308 (t) AP LaserPhoto/Wide World Photos; 308 (b) Sipa Press; 309 (t) D-Novosti/Sovfoto/Eastfoto; 309 (b) Reuters/Nikola Solic/Hulton/Archive/ Gettyimages; 311 Dewitt/Sipa Press; 312 (t) CTK/Eastfoto; 312 (bl) Christopher Morris/Black Star Publishing/PictureQuest; 312 (br) Reuters Photo/Archive Photos/Gettyimages/ Gettyimages; 313 (l) Rompres/Eastfoto; 313 (r) Veronica Garustt/Panos Pictures; 314-315 (b) Barry Lewis/Corbis; 315 (tl) Harcourt; 315 (tr) Sovfoto/Eastfoto; 315 (br) CTK/Eastfoto; 316 (l) MTI/Eastfoto; 316 (r) Harcourt; 317 (t) Michele Burgess/Stock, Boston; 317 (b) John Eastcott/Yva Momatiuk/Stock, Boston; 318 CTK/Eastfoto; 319 Pawel Kopczynski/Reuters/Archive/ Gettyimages; 321 AP, CTK/Wide World Photos; 321(inset) Reuters/Gettyimages News Service.

CHAPTER 10: 324-325 Superstock; 326 Geoffrey .Clifford/Woodfin Camp & Associates; 327 Kevin Schafer/Peter Arnold, Inc.; 328 (t) TASS/Sovfoto/Eastfoto; 328 (b) Chuck Nacke/Woodfin Camp & Associates; 329 David D. Keaton/Corbis Stock Market; 330 (t) Hersch/Sovfoto/Eastfoto; 330-331 (b) Gerd Ludwig/National Geographic Image Sales; 331 (t) Dean Conger/National Geographic Society; 332 TASS/Sovfoto/Eastfoto; 334 Mark Wadlow/Russia and Eastern Images; 335 Hermitage, St. Petersburg, Russia/The Bridgeman Art Library; 336 (t) L.P.W./Woodfin Camp & Associates; 336 (b) Topham/The Image Works; 337 (tl) Lenin Library, Moscow, Russia/Eric Lessing/Art Resource, NY; 337 (tr) The Granger Collection, New York; 337 (b) Sovfoto; 338 (t) TASS/Sovfoto/Eastfoto; 338 (c) AP/Wide World Photos; 338 (b) Leo Erken/ Panos Pictures; 339 Porterfield/Chickering/ Photo Researchers; 340 TASS/Sovfoto/Eastfoto; 342 (l) Sovfoto/Eastfoto; 342 (c) H. Bradner/The Image Works; 342 (r) Juha Jormanainen/Woodfin Camp & Associates ; 343 (t) Harcourt; 343 (bc) Robert S. Semeniuk/Corbis Stock Market; 343 (bl)TASS/Sovfoto/Eastfoto; 343 (br) Joan Baron/Corbis Stock Market; 344 (t) Adam Tanner/The Image Works; 344 (tc) TASS/Sovfoto/Eastfoto ; 344 (bc) Sovfoto/Eastfoto; 344 (b) David Tumley/Corbis; 345 (t) TASS/Sovfoto/Eastfoto; 345 (b) Marc Garanger/Corbis; 346 (b)(inset) NASA Ames Research Center; 346 (bg) Mark Wadlow/Russia and Eastern Images; 346 (t)(inset) Neil Beer/Corbis; 347 Marcello Bertinetti/Photo Researchers; 350-351 A. Williams/Robert Harding Picture Library; 351 (tl)(inset)Richard T. Nowitz; 351 (tr)(inset) Richard T. Nowitz; 351 (b)(inset) Sheridan/Ancient Art and Architecture Collection ; 352 (l) Dallas & John Heaton/stock Boston; 352 (c) R. Sheridan/Ancient Art and Architecture Collection; 352 (r) Mark Wadlow/Russia and Eastern Images; 353 (l) Bettmann/Corbis; 353 (c) Superstock; 353 (r) Rene Mattes/ Photo Researchers; 354 Harcourt.

UNIT 5: Unit 5 Opener (object) Louvre, Dpt. des Antiquites Orientales, ; Paris, France/Erich Lessing - Culture and Fine Arts Archives/Art Resource; Unit 5 Opener (bg) Robert Frerck/Odyssey/Chicago; Unit 5 Opener (spread) Robert Frerck/Odyssey/Chicago; ; 355 Louvre, Dpt. des Antiquites Orientales, Paris, France/Erich Lessing - Culture and Fine Arts Archives/Art Resource, NY; 356 (l) Georg Gerster/Photo Researchers; 356 (c) Scala/Art Resource, NY ; 356 (r) R. Kord/H. Armstrong Roberts, Inc.; 357 (l) Superstock; 357 (c) Robert Leon ; 357 (r) Paul Rickenback/Photo Researchers; 358-359 (bg) Nik Wheeler; 359 (l)(inset) Nik Wheeler; 359 (r)(inset) Steven Allan; 360 (t)(inset) Annie Griffiths Belt/National Geographic Society; 360 (b)(inset) Steven Allan; 360-361 (bg) D. Wells/The Image Works; 361 (t)(inset) & (b)(inset) Steven Allan.

CHAPTER 11: 362-363 Charles and Mary Love/Image Source; 364-365 Group Atlantide/Bruce Coleman, Inc.; 366 (inset) Corbis; 366 Christopher Morris/Black Star/PictureQuest; 367 (t) Adam Woolfitt/ Woodfin Camp & Associates; 367 (b) Wolfgang Kaehler Photography; 368 (l) Robert Frerck/ Odyssey/Chicago; 368 (r) David Forman;Eye Ubiquitous/Corbis; 369 (t) Trip/H Rogers/Art Director & Trip Photo Library; 369 (b) Lior Rubin; 370 Trip/H Rogers/Art Directors & TRIP Photo Library; 371 Iraq Museum, Baghdad, Iraq/Scala/Art Resource; 372 Iraq Museum, Baghdad, Iraq/Erich Lessing/Art Resource; 374 (t) Haviv/Corbis SABA; 374 (b) Shai Ginott/Corbis; 375 Topham/The Image Works; 376 (l) Gerd Ludwig/Woodfin Camp & Associates; 376 (c) The Granger Collection, New York ; 376 (r) National Museum Damascus Syria/Dagli Orti/The Art Archive; 377 (bg) British Museum/Michael Holford Photographs; 377 (inset) Louvre, Dpt. des Antiquites Orientales, Paris, France/Erich Lessing/Art Resource NY; 378 Erich Lessing/Art Resource NY; 379 SEF/Art Resource NY; 380 (tl) A Ramey/Stock, Boston; 380 (tr) A. Ramey/Woodfin Camp & Associates; 380 (b) AP/Wide World Photos ; 381 (tl) Owen Franken/Stock, Boston; 381 (tc) Masao Endoh/Corbis SABA; 381 (tr) Trip/Eric Smith/Art Directors & Trip Photo Library; 381 (bl) Benjamin Rondel/Corbis Stock Market; 381 (bc) Tibor Bognar/Corbis Stock Market; 381 (br) Wolfgang Kaehler; 381 (cl) Diana Gleasner/The Viesti Collection; 382 (t) Harcourt; 382 (b) Peter Turnley/Black Star; 383 (l) Richard Nowitz; 383 (r) Robert Frerck/Odyssey/Chicago; 384 (t) The British Museum/Michael Holford Photographs; 384-385 (b) Trip/N & J Wiseman/The Viesti Collection; 386 (t) Harcourt; 386-387 (c) Harcourt; 386 (b) Peter Tumley/Corbis; 388 Robert Leon; 389 (t) Sion Touhig/Corbis Sygma; 389 (b) Ricki Rosen/Corbis SABA; 390 (t) Reuters/Archive/Gettyimages; 390-391 (b)(inset) Trip/The Viesti Collection; 390-391 (b)Trip/The Viesti Collection; 392 (l) Hodalic-Brecelj-Saola Oma/Liaison Agency; 392 (r) Maher Attar/ Corbis Sygma; 393 (l) David Rubinger/Corbis; 393 (r) Bassem Tellawi/AP/Wide World Photos; 394 Robert Maas/Corbis ; 395 (l) Francoise de Mulder/Corbis ; 395 (r) Sovfoto/Eastfoto.

CHAPTER 12: 398-399 Richard Steedman/Corbis Stock Market; 400 (l) Guy W. Midkiff/Danita Delimont; 400 (r) G. Buttner/Naturbild/Okapia/ Photo Researchers; 401 John and Lisa Merrill; 402 Dean Conger/National Geographic Society; 403 (t) Barry Durand/Odyssey/Chicago; 403 (b) John Elk III; 404-405 Susan Kaye/Houserstock; 406 Bettmann/Corbis; 408 The British Museum/Michael Holford Photographs; 409 The Metropolitan Museum of Art, Rogers Fund, 1931 (31.3.166)"copyright, 1995"; 410 Robert Frerck/Odyssey/Chicago; 411 Robert Hashimoto/The Art Institute of Chicago; 412 (t) British Museum, London/Werner Forman Archive/Art Resource, NY; 412 (b) British Museum, London, Great Britain/Art Resource, NY; 413 Brian Brake/Photo Researchers; 414 (l) Scala/Art Resource, NY; 414 (r) Erich Lessing Art Resource NY; 415 Giraudon/Art Resource, NY; 416-417 (b) Eye Ubiquitous/Corbis; 417 (t) B. Turner/Art Directors & TRIP Photo Library; 417 (bl) Christine Osborne/Corbis; 417 (bc) Dilip Mehtal/Contact Press Images/PictureQuest ; 417 (br) Alexander Nesbitt/Danita Delimont,Agent; 418 A.S.K./The Viesti Collection; 419 (l) & (r) Jesse Fueste Raga/Corbis Stock Market; 420 (t) John and Lisa Merrill/Danita Delimont,Agent; 420 (br) Wolfgang Kaehler; 420 (bl) Jon and Lisa Merrill/Danita Delimont, Agent; 421 Robert Frerck/Odyssey/Chicago; 422 Reuters NewMedia Inc./Corbis; 423 Alexander Nesbitt/Danita Delimont,Agent; 424 (t) Musee Conde, Chantilly, France/Giraudon/Art Resource, NY; 424 (b) Jim Holland/PictureQuest; 425 (l) Robert Frerck/Odyssey/Chicago; 425 (r) Richard T. Nowitz; 426 (l) Harcourt; 426 (r) Nicole Aquarone; 427 A.Tovy/Art Directors & TRIP Photo Library; 432 (l) Georg Gerster / Photo Researchers; 433 (l) Superstock; 432 (c) Scala/Art Resource; 432 (r) R. Kord/H. Armstrong Roberts, Inc.; 433 (c) Robert Leon; 430 (inset) Jeff Greenberg/Peter Arnold, Inc.; 430-431 (bg) Jose Fuste Raga/Corbis; 431 (t) John Henley/Corbis; 431 (bl)(inset) Christina Dameyer/Lonely Planet Images; 431 (inset),(br Mark A. Johnson/Corbis; 434 Harcourt.

UNIT 6: Unit 6 Opener (object) Founders Society Purchase, Clay Ford Fund for African Arts; Photograph (c)1989/The Detroit Institute of Arts; Unit 6 Opener (bg) Wolfgang Kaehler Photography; Unit 6 Opener (spread) Wolfgang Kaehler Photography; 435 Founders Society Purchase, Clay Ford Fund for African Arts; Photograph (c)1989/The Detroit Institute of Arts; 437(t) Mike Yamashita/Woodfin Camp & Associates; 437(c) Steve Thomas/Panos Pictures; 437(b) Reuters/Archive Photos/Gettyimages; 437

tc) AFP/Corbis; 437(bc) Mary Evans Picture Library/Photo Researchers.

CHAPTER 13: 442-443 Nik Wheeler; 446-447 (t) Fred Hoogervorst/Panos Pictures; 446 (b) Ulrike Welsch/Stock, Boston; 447 (b) Richard Nowitz, ; 448 (l)(inset) Kim Taylor/Bruce Coleman, Inc.; 448-449 (b) Corbis; 449 (tl) Charles D. Winters/Photo Researchers ; 449 (tlc) J & L Weber/Peter Arnold, Inc.; 449 (trc) Russ Lappa/Photo Researchers; 449 (tr) Ben Johnson/Photo Researchers; 452 Museum of Mankind (British Museum), Michael Holford Photographs; 453 (t) Collection Musee de 'Homme, Paris; 453 (b) Bibliotheque Nationale de France, Paris; 454 Werner Forman Archive/Art Resource, NY; 455 (inset) John Elk III; 455 Clive Shirley/Panos Pictures; 456 (t) Aldo Tutino/ National Museum of African Art, Smithsonian/ Art Resource NY; 456 (c) The British Museum/ J.R. Freeman/Robert Harding Picture Library; 456 (b) Owen Franken/Corbis; 457 (l) M & E Bernheim/Woodfin Camp & Associates; 457 (r) Betty Press/Panos Pictures; 458 Chris Hondros/Gettyimages ; 459 Victor Englebert ; 460 Zafer Kizilkaya/Atlas Geographic Magazine; 461 John Elk III; 462 Robert Burch; 463 (tl) Giacomo Pirozzi/Panos Pictures; 463 (tr) M & E Bernheim/Woodfin Camp & Associates; 463 (b) Trip/M. Barlow; 464 (t)& (bl) M. & E. Bernheim/Woodfin Camp & Associates; 464 (b)(inset) Nik Wheeler; 465 John Elk III; 466 (t) Owen Franken/Stock, Boston; 466 (bl) Purchase 1997 Mrs. Parker O. Griffith Bequest Fund 97.25.6. Collection of The Newark Museum/Art Resource, NY (detail); 466 (br) Owen Franken/ Stock, Boston; 467 (tl) Collection of The Newark Museum, Gift of Dr. Israel Samuelly and Michaela Samuelly, MD, 1993/Art Resource, NY (detail); 467 (tr) The Newark Museum/Art Resource, NY (detail) ; 467 (c) The Newark Museum/Art Resource, NY (detail); 467 (b) Collection of The Newark Museum, Gift of Mr. and Mrs. William U. Wright, 1985/Art Resource, NY (detail); 468-469 (b) Jane Dubraucik/Corbis; 470 Giacomo Pirozzi/Panos Pictures; 471 Robert Burch; 471 (inset) Bettmann/Corbis; 472 (t) Larry Lu; 472 (b) Benton W. Elliott, USMC; 473 Lineair(R. Giling)/Peter Arnold, Inc.

CHAPTER 14: 476-477 Gregory G. Dimijian/ Photo Researchers; 478-479 Lanz Von Horstein/ Images Of Africa Photobank; 480 David Keith Jones/Images of Africa Photobank; 481 Eric & David Hosking/Photo Researchers; 482 Hein Von Horstein/Images of Africa Photobank; 482-483 Gregory G. Dimijian/Photo Researchers; 484 M. Jelliffe/Art Directors & TRIP Photo Library; 485 Douglas Waugh/Peter Arnold, Inc.; 486 Museum Expedition, Nubian Gallery/Museum of Fine Arts, Boston; 487 (tr) Victor Englebert; 487 (c) Daniel Aubry/Corbis ; 487 (bl) Pietro Cenini/Panos Pictures; 489 A. Lambert/Art Directors & TRIP Photo Library; 490 South African Library/The Bridgeman Art Library International; 491 Wolfgang Kaehler Photography; 492 (inset) Carla Signorini Jones/Images of Africa Photobank; 492 David Keith Jones/Images of Africa Photobank; 494 David Keith Jones/Images of Africa Photobank; 495 Giacomo Pirozzi/Panos Pictures; 496 (t)Independent Electoral Commission, Pretoria,

South Africa; 496 (b) A. Ramsey/Woodfin Camp & Associates; 497 (t) AFP/Corbis; 497 (b) AP Photo/Andy Wong/Wide World Photos; 498 J. Laure/Woodfin Camp & Associates; 499 Orde Eliason/Link; 500 Orde Eliason/Link; 501 Y. Arthus-Bertrand/Peter Arnold, Inc.; 502 (t) Photo courtesy Dr. Dominique Corti, St. Mary's Lacor Hospital; 502 (b) Reuters/Juda Ngwenya/ Hulton/Archive/Gettyimages; 503 (t) & (b) Fred Hoogervorst/Panos Pictures; 504 (l) John Shaw/Bruce Coleman, Inc.; 504 (c) Wolfgang Kaehler Photography; 504 (r) David Keith Jones/Images of Africa Photobank; 505 Oldrich Karasek/Peter Arnold, Inc.; 510 (t) Mark Phillips/Photo Researchers; 510 (c) Adrian Bailey/Aurora & Quanta Productions; 510 (b) Roland Seitre/Peter Arnold, Inc.; 510-511 Wolfgang Kaehler Photography; 511 (tl) Martin W. Grosnick/Bruce Coleman, Inc.; 511 (tr) Peter Menzel/Stock, Boston ; 511 (bl)Les Bush/Link ; 511 (br) P. Chadwick/Art Directors & TRIP Photo Library; 513 (t) Mike Yamashita/Woodfin Camp & Associates; 513 (c) Steve Thomas/ Panos Pictures; 513 (b),(c) Mary Evans Picture Library/ Photo Researchers; 513 (b) Reuters/Archive Photos/Gettyimages/Gettyimages; 513 (tc) AFP/Corbis; 514 Harcourt.

UNIT 7: Unit 7 Opener (object) Plate with Persimmon Branch Design: Old Kutani ware, Aode (green) Kutani Style. Japan, late 17th century, Edo Period. Porcelain with overglaze decoration, diameter 33.40 cm. (c) The Cleveland Museum of Art, 2001, Severance and Greta Millikin Collection, 1964.245; Unit 7 Opener (bg) Photo Wood, Inc/Corbis Stock Market; Unit 7 Opener (spread) Corbis Stock Market; 515 Plate with Persimmon Branch Design: Old Kutani ware, Aode (green) Kutani Style. Japan, late 17th century, Edo Period. Porcelain with overglaze decoration, diameter 33.40 cm. (c) The Cleveland Museum of Art, 2001, Severance and Greta Millikin Collection, 1964.245; 516 (l) Roger Wood/Corbis; 516 (c) National Museum, Beijing, China/Erich Lessing/Art Resource, NY; 516 (r) Steve Kaufman/Peter Arnold, Inc.; 517 (l) Superstock; 517 (c) ERL/Sipa Press ; 517 (r) Joseph Sohm/Chromosohm/Corbis.

CHAPTER 15: 522-523 Ted Mahieu/Corbis Stock Market; 524-525 Porterfield/Chickering/Photo Researchers; 526-527Gordon Wiltsie/Peter Arnold, Inc.; 526 (inset) H. K. Poladia/Dinodia; 527 (inset) Suraj N. Sharma/Dinodia; 528 (t) Ashvin Mehta/Dinodia; 528 (b) Milind A. Ketkar/Dinodia; 529 Dinodia; 530 Jehangir Gazdar/Woodfin Camp & Associates; 532 (b) Dinodia; 532 (tl) Fitzwilliam Museum, University of Cambridge, UK/The Bridgeman Art Library International, Ltd.; 532 (tc) & (tr) Dinodia Picture Agency, Bombay, India/The Bridgeman Art Library International, Ltd.; 533 (t) Angelo Homak/Corbis; 533 (b) Ancient Art and Architecture Collection; 534 Underwood & Underwood/Corbis; 535 Tibor Bognar/Corbis Stock Market; 536 (inset) Mathias Oppersdorff/Photo Researchers; 536 Paolo Koch/Photo Researchers; 538 (b) Baldev/Sygma; 538 (tl) Andrew Holbrooke/Corbis Stock Market; 538 (tr) D. Sansoni/Panos Pictures; 539 (l) Rajesh H. Sharma/Dinodia; 539 (r) David Ball/Corbis Stock Market; 540 AFP/Corbis; 541 (t) & (b) The

Granger Collection, New York, New York; 542 Jayanta Shaw/Hulton Archive/Gettyimages; 543 AP/Wide World Photos; 544 Dinodia; 545 Jeffrey L. Rotman/Corbis; 545 (inset) Catherine Karnow/Woodfin Camp & Associates; 546 (t) Steven Rubin/The Image Works; 546 (b) Bill Wassman/Corbis Stock Market; 547 Ray Ellis/Photo Researchers.

CHAPTER 16: 552-553 Superstock; 554-555 Corbis; 556 Mike Yamashita/Woodfin Camp & Associates; 557 (t) Charles Preitner/Visuals Unlimited; 557 (b) Rita Ariyoshi/Pacific Stock; 558 (t) Katsumi Kasahara/APWide World Photos; 558 (b) Harry Hartman/Bruce Coleman, Inc.; 559 Tischler Fotografen/Peter Arnold, Inc.; 561 Maria Antoinette Evans Fund, Courtesy of Museum of Fine Arts, Boston, detail; 562 James Montgomery /Bruce Coleman, Inc.; 563 Corbis; 564 (t) Victoria and Albert Museum/Michael Holford Photographs; 564 (b) Superstock; 566 (l) John Elk III/Bruce Coleman, Inc.; 566-567 (c) The National Center for Korean Traditional Performing Arts; 567 (r) The National Center for Korean Traditional Performing Arts; 570-571 (b) Bohemian Nomad Picturemakers/Corbis; 571 (t) Catherine Karnow/Woodfin Camp & Associates; 572 (t) Archivo Iconografico, S.A./Corbis; 572 (b) John Paul Kay/Peter Arnold, Inc.; 573 (t) Superstock; 573 (b) Mike Yamashita/Woodfin Camp & Associates; 574 Harcourt; 575 Superstock; 576 (t) AFP/Corbis; 576 (b) Superstock; 577 Mike Yamashita/Woodfin Camp & Associates; 578 (t) Dallas & John Heaton/ Stock, Boston; 578 (b) AFP/Corbis; 579 AFP/Corbis.

CHAPTER 17: 582-583 Blair Seitz/Photo Researchers; 584 K. Muller/Woodfin Camp & Associates; 586 (tl) Auscape (J-P Ferrero)/Peter Arnold, Inc.; 586 (tr) BIOS (A. Compost)/Peter Arnold, Inc.; 586 (b) Jon Bertsch/Visuals Unlimited; 587 Mike Yamashita/Woodfin Camp & Associates; 588 Superstock; 589 BIOS (Klein and Hubert)/Peter Arnold, Inc.; 592 John Elk III/Bruce Coleman, Inc.; 594 Superstock; 595 (t) Bettman/Corbis; 595 (b) Keith Gunnar/Bruce Coleman, Inc.; 596 Superstock; 597 AFP/Corbis; 598 (t) AFP/Corbis; 598 (b) Nik Wheeler/Corbis; 599 AFP/Corbis; 600 (l) & (r)Superstock; 601 (t) AFP/Corbis; 601 (b) Superstock; 602 Russell Gordon, 606 (cr)(inset) Janis Burger/Bruce Coleman, Inc.; 606-607 bg Catherine Karnow/ Woodfin Camp & Associates; 607 (tl)(inset) Brian Vikander/Corbis; 607 (tr)(inset) Janis Burger/ Bruce Coleman, Inc.; 607 (cl)(inset) John Elk III/Bruce Coleman, Inc.; 607 (cr)(inset) Janis Burger/Bruce Coleman, Inc.; 607 (b)(inset) Steve Raymer/Corbis.; 608 (l) Roger Wood/Corbis; 608 (r) Steve Kaufman/ Peter Arnold, Inc. Inc.; 608 (c) National museum, Beijing, China/Erich Lessing/Art Resource, NY; 609 (l) Superstock; 609 (r) Joseph Sohm/Chromosohm/Corbis; 609 (c) ERL/Sipa Press; 610 Harcourt.

UNIT 8; Unit 8 Opener (object) Harcourt, Courtesy Aboriginals: Art of the First Person, Sanibel, FL; Unit 8 Opener (bg) Kevin Deacon/Auscape International; Unit 8 Opener (spread) Kevin Deacon/Auscape International; 611 Harcourt, Courtesy Aboriginals: Art of the